Lecture Notes in Computer Science   10243

Commenced Publication in 1973
Founding and Former Series Editors:
Gerhard Goos, Juris Hartmanis, and Jan van Leeuwen

Alexander Maedche · Jan vom Brocke
Alan Hevner (Eds.)

Designing the Digital Transformation

12th International Conference, DESRIST 2017
Karlsruhe, Germany, May 30 – June 1, 2017
Proceedings

Editors
Alexander Maedche
Karlsruhe Institute of Technologie (KIT)
Karlsruhe
Germany

Alan Hevner
University of South Florida
Tampa, FL
USA

Jan vom Brocke
University of Liechtenstein
Vaduz
Liechtenstein

ISSN 0302-9743   ISSN 1611-3349   (electronic)
Lecture Notes in Computer Science
ISBN 978-3-319-59143-8   ISBN 978-3-319-59144-5   (eBook)
DOI 10.1007/978-3-319-59144-5

Library of Congress Control Number: 2017941497

LNCS Sublibrary: SL3 – Information Systems and Applications, incl. Internet/Web, and HCI

Printed on acid-free paper

This Springer imprint is published by Springer Nature
The registered company is Springer International Publishing AG
The registered company address is: Gewerbestrasse 11, 6330 Cham, Switzerland

Preface

This volume contains selected research papers and descriptions of prototypes and products presented at DESRIST 2017 – the 12th International Conference on Design Science Research in Information Systems and Technology – held from May 30 to June 1, 2017, at Karlsruhe, Germany.

This year's DESRIST conference continues the tradition of advancing and broadening design research within the information systems discipline. DESRIST brings together researchers and practitioners engaged in all aspects of Design Science research (DSR), with a special emphasis on nurturing the symbiotic relationship between Design Science researchers and practitioners. As in previous years, scholars and design practitioners from various areas, such as information systems, business and operations research, computer science, and industrial design came together to discuss both challenges and opportunities of Design Science and to solve design problems through the innovative use of information technology and applications. The outputs of DESRIST, new and innovative constructs, models, methods, processes, and systems, provide the basis for novel solutions to design problems in many fields. The conference further built on the foundation of 11 prior highly successful international conferences held in Claremont, Pasadena, Atlanta, Philadelphia, St. Gallen, Milwaukee, Las Vegas, Helsinki, Miami, Dublin, and St. Johns.

The 12th DESRIST conference had the theme of "Designing the Digital Transformation" and emphasized the contemporary challenge of transforming businesses and society using information technologies. The rapid digital transformation of businesses and society creates new challenges and opportunities for information systems (IS) research with a strong focus on design, which relates to manifold application areas of IS research. This year's DESRIST, therefore, introduced selected themes in order to account for and further stimulate DSR in such areas. Specifically, DESRIST featured seven themes: DSR in business process management, DSR in human–computer interaction, DSR in data science and business analytics, DSR in service science, methodological contributions, domain-specific DSR applications, and emerging themes and new ideas. In total, we received 135 submissions (66 full research papers, 19 prototypes and products, and 50 research-in-progress papers) to the conference for review. Each research paper was reviewed by a minimum of two referees. This Springer volume contains 25 full research papers, with an acceptance rate of 38%, along with 11 short papers describing prototypes and products. Research-in-progress papers are published in separate proceedings.

We would like to thank all authors who submitted their papers to DESRIST 2017. We trust that the readers will find them as interesting and informative as we did. We would like to thank all members of the Program Committee as well as the many additional reviewers who took the time to provide detailed and constructive critiques for the authors. We are grateful for the support of many colleagues who took responsibility in chair positions – such as the doctoral consortium chairs, the industry track chairs, the product and prototype chairs, and the local arrangements chairs – as well as for the great dedication of the many volunteers, whose efforts were instrumental in bringing about another successful DESRIST conference. Our special thanks go to Dr. Stefan Morana, who managed the operational review and publication process in his role as proceedings chair. Furthermore, we thank the Karlsruhe Institute of Technology (KIT) and the sponsoring organizations, in particular SAP, Bosch, IBM, Senacor, as well as the Cyberforum/Digital Innovation Center, for their support. We believe the papers in these proceedings provide many interesting and valuable insights into the theory and practice of DSR. They open up new and exciting possibilities for future research in the discipline.

May 2017   Alexander Maedche
                                                        Jan vom Brocke
                                                          Alan Hevner

Organization

General Chairs

Jeffrey Parsons   Memorial University of Newfoundland, Canada
John Venable   Curtin University, Australia
Tuure Tuunanen   University of Jyväskylä, Finland

Program Chairs

Alexander Maedche   Karlsruhe Institute of Technology (KIT), Germany
Jan vom Brocke   University of Liechtenstein, Liechtenstein
Alan Hevner   University of South Florida, USA

Theme Chairs

DSR in Business Process Management

Wil van der Aalst   TU Eindhoven, The Netherlands
Jan Mendling   WU Vienna, Austria
Michael Rosemann   QUT Brisbane, Australia

DSR in Human–Computer Interaction

Marc Adam   The University of Newcastle, Australia
Rene Riedl   Johannes Kepler University Linz, Austria
Dov Te'eni   Tel Aviv University, Israel

DSR in Data Science and Business Analytics

Wolfgang Ketter   Erasmus University Rotterdam, The Netherlands
Sudha Ram   The University of Arizona, USA
Ahmed Abbasi   University of Virginia, USA

DSR in Service Science

Daniel Beverungen   University of Paderborn, Germany
Jan Marco Leimeister   University of St. Gallen, Switzerland
Jim Spohrer   IBM, USA

Methodological Contributions

Jan Pries-Heje   Roskilde Universitet, Denmark
Sandeep Purao   Bentley University, USA
Matti Rossi   Aalto University, Finland

Domain-Specific DSR Applications

Jörg Becker	University of Münster, Germany
Samir Chatterjee	Claremont Graduate University, USA
Brian Donnellan	Maynooth University, Ireland

Emerging Themes and New Ideas

Robert Winter	University of St. Gallen, Switzerland
John Venable	Curtin University, Australia
Monica Chiarini Tremblay	Florida International University, USA

Products and Prototypes

Peter Loos	Saarland University, Germany
Oliver Müller	IT University Copenhagen, Denmark
Jason Thatcher	Clemson University, USA

Doctoral Consortium Chairs

Shirley Gregor	Australian National University, Australia
Gerd Schwabe	University of Zürich, Switzerland
Stefan Seidel	University of Liechtenstein, Liechtenstein

Industry Chairs

Helmut Krcmar	Technical University of Munich, Germany
Norbert Koppenhagen	SAP SE, Germany
Gerhard Satzger	IBM and Karlsruhe Institute of Technology (KIT), Germany

Local Arrangements Chairs

Silvia Schacht	Karlsruhe Institute of Technology (KIT), Germany
Peter Hottum	Karlsruhe Institute of Technology (KIT), Germany

Proceedings Chair

Stefan Morana	Karlsruhe Institute of Technology (KIT), Germany

Program Committee and Reviewers

Adi Wolfson
Agnis Stibe
Aileen Cater-Steel
Akhilesh Bajaj
Akshay Bhagwatwar
Alex Winkelmann
Alexander Simons
Alivelu Mukkamala
Amir Haj-Bolouri
Amit Basu
Andreas Oberweis
Andreas Solti
Andrija Javor
Anindya Datta
Annika Lenz
Anthony Ross
Antonia Albani
Arin Brahma
Arturo Castellanos
Arun Sen
Atish P. Sinha
Axel Winkelmann
Balaji Padmanabhan
Barbara Dinter
Benedikt Morschheuser
Benedikt Notheisen
Bengisu Tulu
Benjamin Gaunitz
Benjamin Spottke
Björn Niehaves
Brian Cameron
Carson Woo
Carsten Felden
Cecilia Rossignoli
Celina Friemel
Charles Møller
Chen-Huei Chou
Chih-Ping Wei
Chris Zimmerman
Christian Bartelheimer
Christian Hrach
Christian Janiesch
Christine Legner

Christoph Müller-Bloch
Christoph Rosenkranz
Christoph Schneider
Christopher Jud
Christopher Yang
Chun Ouyang
Clare Thornley
Claudio Di Ciccio
Codrina Lauth
Cristina Cabanillas
Danny Poo
Dave Darcy
David Cornforth
David P. Darcy
Debashis Saha
Debra Vandermeer
Denis Dennehy
Derek Nazareth
Devi Bhattacharya
Dietmar Nedbal
Dimitris Karagiannis
Dominik Augenstein
Dominik Dellermann
Dominik Jung
Doo-Hwan Bae
Doug Vogel
Edward Curry
Eileen Doherty
Eric T.K. Lim
Erik Proper
Ewa Lux
Fabian Hunke
Florian Hawlitschek
Florian Müller
Frederik Ahlemann
Fu-Ren Lin
Gabriel Costello
Gabriela Beirão
George M. Wyner
George Widmeyer
Gerold Wagner
Gilbert Fridgen
Giovanni Maccani

Gondy Leroy
Guoqing Chen
Guy-Alain Amoussou
Hadar Ronen
Hajo A. Reijers
Hangjung Zo
Harry Jiannan Wang
Hedda Luettenberg
Hemant Jain
Henk Sol
Henrik Leopold
Herbert Jelinek
Hissu Hyvärinen
Hoang Nguyen
Inbal Yahav
Irit Hadar
Ishwar Murthy
Jae Choi
Jairo Gutierrez
James Rodger
Jan Hendrik Betzing
Jan Pawlowski
Jan Verelst
Jannis Beese
Jennifer Chandler
Jeremias Perez
Jerrel Leung
Jiexun Jason
Jim Kenneally
Jing Leon Zhao
Jinsoo Park
Joakim Lillieskold
Johannes Schneider
Johannes Starlinger
Jonas Sjöström
Joseph Walls
Juhani Iivari
Juho Lindman
Julie Kendall
Karl Werder
Karthikeyan Umapathy
Kaushik Dutta
Kazem Haki
Ken Peffers
Keng Siau
Keumseok Kang

Kevin Sullivan
Kevin Williams
Kittisak Sirisaengtaksin
Konstantina Valogianni
Kunihiko Higa
Lakshmi Iyer
Leona Chandra
Maedeh Yassaee
Mahei Li
Manjul Gupta
Marc Busch
Marco De Marco
Marcus Rothenberger
Mario Nadj
Mark Roxburgh
Markus Helfert
Markus Monhof
Markus Weinmann
Martin Matzner
Mathias Petsch
Maung Sein
Maximilian Brosius
Meira Levy
Michael Blaschke
Michael Schermann
Mikael Lind
Mike Goul
Mohammed Alsaqer
Monika Malinova
Munir Mandviwalla
Murali Raman
Narasimha Bolloju
Neelam Raigangar
Niall Connolly
Nick van Beest
Nils Bergmann
Novica Zarvic
Ohad Barzilay
Olayan Alharbi
Oliver Thomas
Onur Demirörs
Paidi O'Raghallaigh
Patrick Delfmann
Paul Ralph
Peter Fettke
Peter Sommerauer

Contents

Emerging Themes and New Ideas

Products and Prototypes

DSR in Business Process Management

Assessing Process Fit in ERP Implementation Projects: A Methodological Approach

Marcus Fischer[✉], David Heim, Christian Janiesch,
and Axel Winkelmann

Julius-Maximilians-Universität Würzburg, Würzburg, Germany
{marcus.fischer,david.heim,christian.janiesch,
axel.winkelmann}@uni-wuerzburg.de

Abstract. To remain competitive, SMEs rely on technologies that automate support for their operations. Although an increasing number of SMEs use ERP systems, one of the major challenges is the selection of a software that fully meets their business needs. ERP systems generally come as standardized software packages. They are designed to fit generic rather than enterprise-specific requirements. Thus, mutual alignments of business and IT are essential to ensure an implementation project's success. However, many organizational change efforts involving the introduction of new technologies fail due to the workforce's resistance towards changes in their workflows, business processes, and technology they use. These so-called technochange situations require appropriate solutions that are complete and implementable. Thus, changes to business and IT must be complementary and organization-enterprise system misfits must be minimized. Following the paradigm of design science research, this contribution addresses technochange in ERP projects by assessing the organization-enterprise system fit during ERP selection. Applying a process fit perspective, organizational process models can be compared to ERP reference models using measures of business process similarity. In an experiment, we illustrate how ERP systems can be distinguished and ranked by their process features, positively influencing organizational fit and the likelihood of an ERP project's success.

Keywords: Organization-enterprise system fit · Business process similarity · Enterprise resource planning system selection · Technochange

1 Introduction

To remain competitive in a rapidly changing environment, effective methods for processing, storing, and analyzing data are highly relevant for organizations. Due to the integration of business processes and information, enterprise resource planning (ERP) systems enable enterprises to organize their resources more effectively [1]. ERP systems generally come as standardized software packages and are designed to fit generic rather than enterprise-specific requirements, resulting in the necessity for mutual alignments of business and IT [2].

Although information systems positively affect the competitiveness of an enterprise, implementation projects often come with tremendous demands on time and

© Springer International Publishing AG 2017
A. Maedche et al. (Eds.): DESRIST 2017, LNCS 10243, pp. 3–20, 2017.
DOI: 10.1007/978-3-319-59144-5_1

financial resources. However, limited resources, such as a tight time schedule or a lack of process knowledge and IT skills, as well as the highly differentiated market, can turn the selection of an adequate ERP system into a highly complex task [3].

While business operations may increase in efficiency and effectiveness, the disruption of established workflows can result in users' resistance towards change, hampering the potential benefits of an ERP project [4]. Thus, ERP implementations are subject to major risks, including users avoiding or misusing the system, or adopting it in a way that fails to capture the project's potential benefits. In line with that, approximately 75% of organizational change efforts fail when they involve the introduction of a new technology [4]. High-risk situations that are characterized by IT triggering major organizational changes are referred to as *technochange,* simultaneously affecting an enterprise's organizational and technological structures. Thus, organizations face complex challenges that frequently place excessive demands on traditional approaches of IT project management and organizational change management causing organizational problems if not addressed appropriately. To tackle those challenges, adequate IT solutions are characterized by the properties of *completeness* and *implementability.* In terms of completeness, the alignment of business and IT must be performed on a mutual basis, applying complementary change efforts within both dimensions. Since the adaptability of an organization is limited, the property of implementability suggests the selection of an ERP system with minimal misfits to the existent organization [4]. However, the magnitude of organizational adaptations highly depends on the initial degree of organization-enterprise system fit. We argue that minimizing initial misfits can reduce technochange during ERP implementation and increase the likelihood of project success. Thus, the present paper uses methods and techniques of business process similarity (BPS) to manage process misfits during ERP selection. Consequently, we summarize our research question as follows:

"How can we improve traditional ERP selection methodologies to ensure an appropriate organization-enterprise system fit to reduce technochange during ERP implementation?"

To address this research question, Fig. 1 illustrates the applied design science research (DSR) approach to develop our contribution. First, we provide an overview of foundations on ERP selection and BPS methods and analyze the phenomenon of technochange during ERP implementation for problem identification. Subsequently, we derive objectives and recommendations for the artifact of our contribution. Initiating the design and development phase, we design and introduce a methodology for ERP

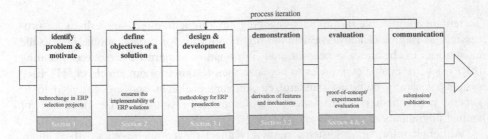

Fig. 1. Design science research approach [5]

selection, which incorporates the predefined objectives to address the overall problem. After its formalization and demonstration, we experimentally perform the artifact's evaluation in Sect. 4. We discuss the results and their limitations in Sect. 5, before Sect. 6 concludes with a summary of findings and an overview of future research potentials.

As our research progressed, we iteratively developed the configuration of the artifact [6]. Following Gregor and Hevner's [7] knowledge contribution framework, we consider our DSR contribution an exaptation of BPS to the design of software selection methods in the area of ERP research. It has explanatory power and provides design practice theory for the design and improvement of further methods that aim to improve the likelihood of success in ERP implementation projects.

2 Foundations

2.1 ERP Software Selection

Contributions regarding ERP implementation projects have been extensively discussed and can be divided into the four categories: methodologies, case studies, micro-sociological studies, and studies on critical success factors (CSF). Since we focus on the improvement of current methodologies for ERP selection, we center our investigation on existing methodologies and publications regarding CSF. So far however, there has been little discussion about the ERP selection phase and its requirements. Most studies solely reveal that organization-system fit is crucial for the success of an implementation project and that the potentials of business process re-engineering (BPR) should be considered, instead of making the best of non-competitive, i.e. sub-standard, processes [8–10].

A great share of methodological approaches understand ERP selection as a multi-stage process, generally including efforts in planning, requirements engineering, and system selection [8]. According to Stefanou [11], current and future business needs have to be balanced against various technological, work, and organizational constraints. Business processes are subject to radical adaptations when implementing an ERP system and the associated best practices from an industry [12]. Therefore, the organization's commitment to the project and its desire to change are critical to the success of the project. According to Verville and Halingten [13], external and internal information are important for the acquisition process. Aiming to avoid overlooking feasible systems, different information sources, such as the Internet, professional journals, or vendor exhibitions should be screened carefully [14]. However, due to a distinct information asymmetry, resulting from the complexity and number of available systems, Verville and Halingten [13] suggest to evaluate the gathered information in regard to its credibility and reliability. After the tasks of planning and requirements engineering, the selection stage is initiated, including the selection and evaluation of appropriate vendors, products, and supporting services. While each system provides broad standardized functionalities, Stefanou [11] emphasizes, that individual specifications, such as specializations for certain industries, result in different degrees of requirements fulfillment. Thus, Verville and Halingten [13] propose a three-staged approach to identify potential systems. To narrow down the diverse market for ERP software, a collection of general criteria is developed first. Eventually, evaluation criteria become more specific to generate an initial ranking. Potential aspects for a general evaluation include the availability of implementation assistance, the financial strength of the vendor, customer support, and the vendor's reputation. For an in-depth analysis, additional criteria such as estimated BPR efforts and system scalability are taken into account [13]. However, to gather adequate information during each of the evaluation stages, requests for proposals, information, and cost estimates are sent to potential vendors [13]. In order to structure the wide range of selection criteria, Wei et al. [14] suggest a classification into fundamental and mean objectives. After receiving the requested information, the selection decision is initiated using an analytic hierarchy process (AHP).

Although there is detailed methodological assistance, most approaches focus exclusively on high-level recommendations. While the task of gathering information appears to be important, most contributions focus on the conceptual *why* instead of providing guidance regarding the conceptual *how*. However, given a formalization of business needs, for example, in terms of an organizational process model, measures of BPS can enable enterprises to identify suitable ERP vendors while saving business resources. Thus, we propose that process misfits can be minimized and the magnitude of technochange during ERP implementation projects can be influenced positively.

2.2   Technochange in ERP Implementation Projects

While fit is only one criterion for selecting and implementing an ERP system, it is important because fixing misfits can be time-consuming and costly. When people's routines are shaken up by modifying organizational workflows and business processes, risks may be encountered, such as the avoidance or misuse of the system [15]. To tackle challenges associated with those so-called technochange situations, neither traditional IT project management nor organizational change management offer adequate solutions [4]. On the one hand, organizational change management puts a strong focus on the people affected by the introduction of an ERP system. Thus, their technological adoption decision is expected to be influenced by training offers, incentives, and redesigned jobs. However, little attention is paid to the way in which an ERP system alters organizational change [4]. On the other hand, most traditional IT projects aim to improve technical performance or to reduce costs of IT ownership or system maintenance.

While both ideas promise to be successful in their specific fields of application, technochange situations require a complementary approach that focuses on the fit between IT and organizational structures. To accomplish the promised improvements in organizational performance, tasks, jobs, and business processes need to change along with the IT [4]. When implementing an ERP system, having a well-defined and well-selected technological solution does not guarantee the overall success of the project. In fact, technology needs to be accompanied by a process of designing and implementing the solution into the organizational structure [4]. Thus, to manage technochange effectively, enterprises need to focus on the three conditions illustrated in Table 1.

Table 1. Conditions for managing technochange effectively

Completeness	Implementability	Appropriation of benefits
A workable solution	A working solution	A worked solution

First, the requirements for using an ERP system productively are summarized by the concept of completeness. In the process of implementing new IT solutions, an organization needs to reorganize itself to take advantage of new allocable capabilities. To do so, enterprises rely heavily on complementary change management, including adapting business processes and/or job designs, restructuring business units, and implementing new metrics and incentives [4].

Second, implementability describes an organization's ability to adopt and use a selected ERP system. Thus, solutions that are characterized by extensive discrepancies to the current or intended organizational structure, cultures, or procedures are more likely to produce resistance among the future users than systems with a sufficient initial fit [15]. Following Markus [4], multiple technochange solutions can accomplish organizational objectives if they are adopted and used, but not all are rejected by their users. However, the more features and characteristics of an ERP solution conflict with organizational structures, the higher the likelihood of resistance.

Third, turning the potential benefits of an ERP implementation into measurable results is defined as the appropriation of benefits. To achieve organizational goals such as an increase in performance, potential benefits in terms of efficiency or productivity need to be transformed into financial surpluses. While this does not happen automatically, key users need to be offered incentives in order to actively capture benefits [4].

Since each concept occurs within a different phase of implementing an ERP system, the introduced conditions are characterized by interdependencies, which are described in Table 2. Implementability depends heavily on features and characteristics of an ERP system and must be addressed by adequate decision-making before the actual implementation process is initiated. However, the degree to which a certain solution fits the organizational structure of an enterprise influences the feasibility of accomplishing completeness and the appropriation of benefits.

Table 2. Interdependencies in technochange solutions

	Completeness	Implementability	Appr. of benefits
Completeness	/	/	+
Implementability	+	/	+
Appr. of benefits	+	/	/

/ does not affect, + affects positively

Since completeness is achieved by implementing complementary change management, corresponding efforts occur during the implementation phase. Thus, completeness has a limited range as it only unfolds its full benefits during the rollout of an ERP solution and thus, does not influence implementability directly. However, effective change management can facilitate the realization of expected benefits.

As completeness describes the task of turning a working solution into a workable solution, it becomes less complex if the number of existing misfits is limited by a system that exhibits implementability. Furthermore, potential gains in productivity and efficiency can be captured faster, positively influencing an organization's performance and the generation of financial surpluses.

Finally, the appropriation of benefits occurs mostly during post-implementation. While implementability remains unaffected, offering the right incentives to the right people can increase the organization's willingness to adopt and use the ERP system, facilitating the definition of a complete solution.

2.3 Measures of Business Process Similarity

Existing concepts of BPS are primarily used within the application domains of business process management (BPM), inductive reference modeling, and business process collection management [16, 17].

As a conceptual foundation, Dijkman et al. [18] summarize the concepts of label matching, structural, and behavioral similarity and provide their practical evaluation. Li et al. [19] measure similarity as the sum of the high-level operations *insertion, elimination, substitution,* and *movement* to transform one business process model into another. Results guarantee the property of soundness, while transformation efforts are minimized. Additionally, Dijkman et al. [18] evaluate algorithms for the automatic computation of BPS metrics. Within the field of BPM, business process models are used as an analytical representation of an organization's structure [20–22]. While the popularity of using process models has increased significantly in recent years, ambiguity-induced issues between different models reduce their comparability and therefore hamper optimization potentials [23]. Hence, Ehrig et al. [24] introduce an ontology-based semantic modeling approach to support business process model interconnectivity and interoperability. However, the presented methods focus on establishing an exact matching of process models, resulting in high computation times and the need for a pairwise process comparison [16]. As we aim to provide a quick decision support when accessing the market for ERP software, exact (and computation intensive) measures of process similarity are not necessary.

In the stream of inductive reference modeling, the similarity of business processes can be used to derive a reference model from a variety of enterprise-specific process models [17]. Thus, genetic algorithms and statistical factor analysis are used to generate a process model with the minimum distance to the input models [17, 25]. Additionally, La Rosa et al. [26] adapt the measure of graph-edit distance to introduce a method for configurative reference modeling. However, the presented techniques are limited by a high computation time as well and focus on the generation of new models from a set of original process models. Thus, they are not suitable for the task of ERP selection.

In the field of *collection management*, techniques of BPM are used to identify similar process models within process repositories [27]. To improve the search process, Awad [28] defines the approach of BPMN-Q, which allows querying for a business process with a binary *match* or *no match* result. Yan et al. [16] abstract business process models to a set of constitutive features, which can be queried in a feature-repository. Thus, computation time can be reduced by the factor of 3.5 when identifying similar process models [16].

With more than 600 different ERP vendors in Germany, Austria, and Switzerland, companies face tremendous challenges when selecting an adequate system for their business operations. Thus, we argue, that metrics of BPS can provide an in-depth understanding on the organizational fit of an ERP system. Methods in the fields of BPM and inductive reference modeling aim at establishing an exact matching and exhibit a high computation time as well as the need for a pairwise comparison of the input process models. However, our approach aims to provide a quick decision support when accessing the complex ERP market. Thus, we focus our research on feature-based measures of BPS.

3 ERP Selection Based on Business Process Similarity

3.1 Feature-Based ERP Selection Process Overview

As illustrated in Fig. 2, the proposed process of ERP selection comprises four phases: objective definition, requirements engineering, market analysis and preselection, as well as final decision-making [29]. We used established methodologies, which we introduced in Sect. 2.1 to construct the procedure model.

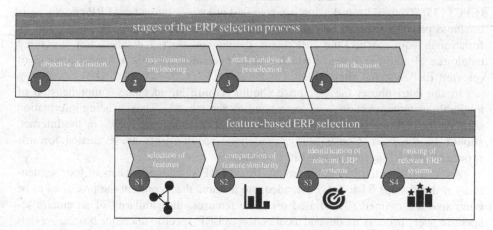

Fig. 2. ERP selection based on BPS [30]

In general, there are two major ways to use an ERP system advantageously. The first is aligning an enterprise's business processes to fit the software. The second is aligning the software to support the existent business processes [31, 32]. There have been numerous studies which discourage enterprises from extensive software customization [33, 34]. Following the first option, implementation errors can be avoided and software updates can be implemented smoothly, enabling enterprises to use the software's current releases without disruption. Consequently, highly specialized and successful processes must be modified, and therefore the enterprise might lose its competitive advantage. However, identifying the ERP system that best fits with an enterprise's targeted organizational structure can reduce efforts on BPR and software customization simultaneously while benefiting from industry best practices.

To achieve an adequate organization-system fit, ERP selection is initiated by objective definition (1), for which a cross-functional ERP team should be appointed. The team should consist of decision-makers, functional experts, and senior representatives of user departments. First, the ERP team should set the project's scope, building on the company's policy, business attributes, the industrial environment, and general strategic goals. Subsequently, objectives should be defined and classified into a fundamental-objective hierarchy and a mean-objective network. While fundamental objectives summarize a set of goals that are crucial for an enterprise to perform better, mean-objectives focus on ways to accomplish them. Appropriate methods for objectives classification can be found in [14].

Within the second phase, a careful assessment of business requirements must be performed (2). To gain a comprehensive understanding of existing business needs, this process should be performed top-down as well as bottom-up. Aiming to reduce the occurrence of technochange in subsequent phases of ERP implementation, requirements engineering should involve the existing organizational structure and its inherent characteristics. Since we aim to maximize the potential organization-enterprise system fit by reducing process misfits, business operations should be comprehensively documented using process modeling languages, such as the event-driven process chain (EPC) [35]. To avoid transferring sub-standard processes into a new ERP system, as-is business processes should be transformed into a to-be concept [36]. However, besides functional requirements, the ERP team should construct a detailed and structured catalogue of additional needs, which can be evaluated towards a smaller amount of relevant ERP systems afterwards.

In the third phase, the enterprise should acquire an adequate comprehension of available systems, vendors, and corresponding services (3). Thus, existing information sources for ERP software, such as magazines, exhibitions, yearbooks, or the Internet, should be screened. Consequently, predefined requirements are evaluated towards processes of ERP systems stored in a repository.

As also illustrated in Fig. 2, feature-based ERP selection consists of four sequentially ordered steps S1 to S4. First, adequate features that represent the processes to be compared are defined (S1). Based on those features, the similarity of an enterprise-specific query process model and a collection of ERP-specific reference process models is computed (S2). Third, relevant systems are identified according to their feature-similarity score (S3). Finally, identified systems are ranked, aiming to provide enterprises with a convenient decision support for ERP selection (S4).

Based on a reduced set of suitable ERP systems, traditional AHP decision methodologies can be applied more efficiently to reach a final decision (4). While basic implementability has been ensured, the objectives from the predefined categories can be evaluated subsequently. Thus, the ERP team must extract key qualitative and quantitative attributes derived from the predefined project objectives. Simultaneously, metrics should be defined to measure the effect of each attribute in terms of object achievement. AHP, as a multi-attribute evaluation method, involves three phases:

decomposition, comparative judgements and synthesis of priorities [14]. Eventually, results from each phase are evaluated and a final selection decision is made.

Applying the proposed methodology, the diversified ERP market can be narrowed down to a small number of ERP systems that fit best to the predominant process structure. Thus, the selection of a highly-ranked system ensures the solution's implementability, as misfits in workflows are reduced and the probability of resistance towards change is minimized. As described in Table 2, organizations manage technochange most effectively by satisfying the condition of implementability. On the one hand, working solutions require the management of a smaller number of initial misfits, increasing the completeness of an ERP solution. On the other hand, time and effort for a mutual alignment of the technological and organizational structure are reduced, facilitating the adoption of an ERP solution and accelerating the realization of benefits.

3.2 Business Process Model Features

According to S1 in Fig. 2, appropriate features must be defined first. In the domain of BPM, Yan et al. [16] investigate feature-based similarity by defining features as simple but representative abstractions of business process models. Using feature-based abstractions, relevant ERP systems can be identified by their major features, while computation time is kept to a minimum. Consequently, it enables enterprises to query large process repositories.

Business processes comprise activities executed in a certain order. Therefore, the constitutive features of a business process can be deduced from its labels, which represent the captured content, and its structure, uncovering interdependencies between activities and their order of execution [36, 37]. As label comparison is based on single process elements, using them as features is computationally insignificant [26, 38].

By contrast, structural characteristics must be extracted from a process's underlying process graph. To date, researchers have developed various methods for measuring structural graph equivalence [19, 37]. However, most approaches are limited by the fact that the problem of graph matching is NP-hard. To reduce computational complexity, the present paper focuses on using abstractions instead of full-scale graph structures. Thus, structural features are derived from an element's corresponding input and output context. Using the example of two functions of an EPC, their contextual information is determined by their preceding and succeeding events or nodes [38].

3.3 Feature Similarity and Feature Matching

As illustrated in Fig. 2, we compute feature-based similarity based on different techniques of BPS, which we introduce subsequently. Because similarity calculations should be processed automatically, a mechanism needs to be defined that guarantees the comparison of labels of the same type [16]. Definition 1 presents a formalism ensuring that functions are compared with functions and events with events. Subsequently, using *Type* as a precondition for further similarity calculations, a matching of different element types is avoided.

Definition 1 (Type-based Similarity). *Let EPC_1 and EPC_2 be two disjoint EPCs described by functions, events and connectors. Additionally, let $n \in EPC_1$ and $m \in EPC_2$ be two nodes from the EPCs' underlying process graph. Then 'type' is a binary function that returns 1, if and only if the types of the compared nodes are identical and 0 otherwise.*

$$type(n, m) = \begin{cases} 1 & Type(n) = Type(m) \\ 0 & Type(n) \neq Type(m) \end{cases}$$

Subsequently, label feature similarity can be computed based on syntactic and semantic metrics [18]. Syntactic equivalence is obtained by adding the number of the edit operations *insertion*, *deletion*, and *substitution* to transform one label into another. To measure syntactic similarity, we use the *Levenshtein* Algorithm [39]. However, a major weakness of syntactic similarity is that semantic information is not accounted for if no standardized ontology exists. This can cause inconsistencies, especially in the case of synonyms and homonyms [40]. We attempt to address these problems by incorporating semantic information using the lexical database GermaNet [41]. However, to reduce noise within the investigated labels, Dijkman et al. [18] suggest several preparatory steps. First, frequently occurring words such as 'a', 'an', and 'for' are eliminated. Second, inflectional and derivationally related words are reduced to their infinitive form by using the technique of word stemming [42]. Subsequently, the equivalence score is computed by assigning weighting factors to exact matches and synonyms. Dijkman et al. [18] have investigated the optimal value of these weights, proposing a weight factor of 1 for identical words and 0.75 for synonyms, which is set in our work accordingly.

Definition 2 (Label Similarity). *Let $l_1(n)$ and $l_2(m)$ be two strings representing the labels of two nodes from EPC_1 and EPC_2. Additionally, let $l_1(n)$ and $l_2(m)$ contain the sets of words $w_1 = l_1(n)$ and $w_2 = l_2(m)$. Label similarity can be computed based on the length of labels $|l_n(n_n)|$ and by the number of words $|w_n(l_n)|$ contained by those labels, where the binary function 'synonyms' defines if two words are synonyms or not and specifies the edit distance between two words.*

$$lsim\,(n, m) = type\,(n, m)$$
$$\cdot \frac{1.0 \cdot |w_1 \cap w_2| + 0.75 \cdot \sum synonyms(s, t) + \left(1.0 - \frac{ed(l_1(n), l_2(m))}{\max(|l_1(n)|, |l_2(m)|)} \right)}{\max(|w_1|, |w_2|)}$$

Although semantic information is considered, label-matching similarity can show interpretational weaknesses. To increase the reliability of results, we consider structural features by using the contextual information of process elements. Thus, an equivalence mapping between its surrounding elements is necessary. However, the mapping itself is based on the similarity of their corresponding nodes [38]. During this work, the equivalence mapping is derived by using the formalism presented in Definition 3.

Definition 3 (Equivalence Mapping). *Let EPC_1 and EPC_2 be two disjoint EPCs and let L_n be their corresponding labels. Additionally, let $l(syn + sem) : L_1 \times L_2 \rightarrow [0\ldots1]$*

be a similarity function that guarantees for all $l_1 \in L_1$ and $l_2 \in L_2$: $lsim(l_1, l_2) = lsim$ (l_2, l_1). An optimal equivalence mapping $M_{lsim}^{opt} : L_1 \nrightarrow L_2$ is an equivalence mapping such that for all other equivalence mappings M holds that:

$$\sum\nolimits_{(l_1, l_2) \in M_{lsim}^{opt}} lsim(l_1, l_2) \geq \sum\nolimits_{(l_1, l_2) \in M_{lsim}} lsim(l_1, l_2).$$

Given an optimal equivalence mapping, contextual similarity between two process elements can be computed. For example, to evaluate the input and output context of two functions, an equivalence mapping between their surrounding events is required.

Definition 4 (Contextual similarity). *Let EPC_1 and EPC_2 be two disjoint EPCs described by $EPC_n = (E_n, F_n, C_n, l_n, A_n)$ with $n_n \in F_n \cup E_n$ and let $l(syn + sem)$ be a similarity function. Additionally, let $M_{lsim}^{optin} : n_1^{in} \nrightarrow n_2^{in}$ and $M_{lsim}^{optout} : n_1^{out} \nrightarrow n_2^{out}$ be two optimal equivalence mappings between the preceding and succeeding nodes of n_1 and n_2.*

$$con(n, m) = type(n, m) \times \frac{\left| M_{l(syn + sem)}^{optin} \right|}{2 \cdot \sqrt{|n^{in}| \cdot |m^{in}|}} + \frac{\left| M_{l(syn + sem)}^{optout} \right|}{2 \cdot \sqrt{|n^{out}| \cdot |m^{out}|}}$$

Since similarity scores range from 0 to 1, an appropriate threshold for similarity declaration needs to be defined. In the case of label matching similarity, Dijkman et al. [18] demonstrate sound results using a threshold of 0.5.

Definition 5 (Node feature match, structural feature match). *Let EPC_1 and EPC_2 be two disjoint EPCs. Additionally, let $n \in EPC_1$ and $m \in EPC_2$ be two nodes from the EPC's underlying process graph. Two nodes features are matched if their similarity exceeds a certain similarity threshold.*

$$lsim(n, m) - con(n, m) \geq threshold$$

To illustrate an application of the methodology we rank two ERP systems. We compute the feature similarity score of two business processes based on the ratio of features matched to the total number of features within a mapping between their underlying process graphs.

4 Experimental Application and Evaluation

4.1 Use Case

As the methodological steps S2 to S4 comprise the approach's practical application, an evaluation use case is constructed that includes process data from two ERP systems. We provide further details on evaluating the methodology in the discussion section.

In general, business processes are scheduled and contain a logical sequence of activities, which is necessary to handle a relevant business object [36]. One class of business processes are end-to-end processes, which are characterized by their customer-sided initiation and termination. The drop-shipping process defines one of the main variants of the order-to-cash process, in which the retailer does not keep goods in stock but instead transfers customer orders to either the manufacturer or another wholesaler, who then ships the goods directly to the customer. Since it is integrated in most ERP systems, we use the drop-shipping process to evaluate the proposed methodology. For demonstration purposes, we have modeled a to-be drop-shipping process extracted from the *Handels-H* (engl., Retail-H) reference model [43].

Process modeling was performed in two steps. Since process data on ERP systems is hardly available, system processes were documented by a student research team. Experts in the field of BPM supervised the team. As the process data was conducted within a closed project, each modeler participated in the construction of a domain-specific ontology and performed the modeling tasks using standardized vocabulary. Thus, semantic ambiguities were eliminated before comparing the process models to increase the quality of results. Although the technique of semantic similarity remains unchallenged in this setup, it is of great importance when analyzing real-world process data that is neither pre-processed nor standardized. A comprehensive evaluation of semantic similarity measures can be found in [18, 24].

The second part, which included modelling the drop-shipping process extracted from the Handels-H reference model, was based on the same ontology. The resulting process model is illustrated in Fig. 3. After a customer order is received, potential contractors for a third-party order fulfillment are analyzed and contacted. The order is then transferred to a third party, which ships the ordered goods directly to the customer. Simultaneously, a customer invoice is generated and a contractor invoice is received. The process stops when incoming and outgoing payments are processed.

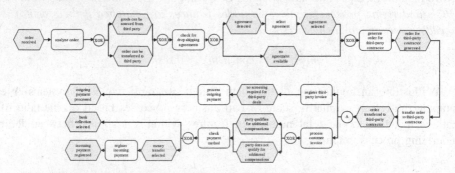

Fig. 3. Enterprise-specific sourcing process

4.2 Implementation Setup and Evaluation

Gregor and Hevner [7] argue that a proof-of-concept is a suitable first step when evaluating DSR. We aim at providing an additional experimental proof-of-concept, by evaluating the drop-shipping process from Fig. 3 towards the corresponding processes extracted from the ERP systems Microsoft Dynamics NAV 2016 and SAP Business

ByDesign.[1] These systems are each well-established, mature, all-sector solutions with a large user base and are regarded as particularly well suited for SMEs. The introduced similarity measures are used to establish an equivalence mapping between the enterprise-specific process and the reference process using a similarity threshold of 0.6. Although the threshold is rather high, it enables the generation of high-quality results that meet the process requirements of the enterprise. We understand labels contained by that mapping as label-matching features. A mapping based on contextual similarity is computed to account for the processes' structural characteristics using a threshold of 0.6 accordingly. Finally, we regard two features as matches if and only if they have been determined as similar in both mappings.

Table 3 illustrates the results and the computed feature-based similarity score. Matching features can be identified within both systems. Microsoft Dynamics NAV generated noticeably better results for matching label features and structural features. However, this could be due to more individual functionalities for the same business procedures. Although the number of matches is limited, it allows us to draw the conclusion that Microsoft Dynamics NAV better fits the targeted processes and therefore should be further scrutinized. The low number of matches can be explained by the high threshold of 0.6. The results entail that it is possible to reproduce the enterprise's third-party deal process precisely through the customizing of all systems, but with lower efforts in Microsoft Dynamics NAV, because fewer steps must be reconfigured. A final selection, however, can only be made after carefully reviewing the configuration and customization options in the ERP systems, as this decision cannot be made without considering situational implementation issues.

Table 3. Feature-based similarity of ERP systems

	Microsoft dynamics NAV	SAP business by design
Overall features	22	25
Matching label features	15	16
Matching structural features	14	13
Combined matches	**13**	**10**
Feature-based similarity	0.49	0.37
Rank	**1**	**2**

For a comprehensive evaluation, we suggest considering at least another 2–3 ERP systems and use multiple processes to avoid a single case bias. Also, to assess the relevance of the generated results, we suggest involving practitioners in the evaluation who can provide reference process models and assist in the qualitative analysis and interpretation of the results towards their processes.

---

[1] http://www.sap.com/germany/product/enterprise-management/business-bydesign.html, https://www.microsoft.com/de-de/dynamics365/nav-overview.

5 Discussion and Limitations

Although results from an experimental evaluation support the applicability of our approach when aiming to select an adequate ERP solution, various constraints limit the explanatory power of the implications drawn. The proposed methodology focuses on determining the organization-system fit by analyzing and comparing underlying process structures. From this process perspective, changes to intended workflows and job designs are limited and the likelihood of resistance towards the new system is reduced. However, this approach assumes that the degree of organization-system fit depends mainly on the equality of processes and functions. While process fit has been identified as a relevant aspect when selecting an information system, Strong and Volkoff [2] argue that potential sources of misfits between an ERP system and an organization can be divided into six categories that are summarized in Table 4.

Table 4. Categories of misfit between an ERP system and the organizational structure [2]

Misfit	Definition
Functionality	Occurs when executing business processes using an ERP system results in less efficiency and/or effectiveness compared to the situation before implementation
Data	Occurs when data stored in or needed by the ERP system result in poor quality in terms of inaccuracy, inconsistency, inaccessibility, lack of timeliness, or inappropriateness for users' contexts
Usability	Occurs when user interactions with the ERP system are obstructive and/or confusing
Role	Occurs when roles in the ERP system do not match the available skills; this creates imbalances in the workload or generates inconsistencies regarding responsibility and authority
Control	Occurs when control mechanisms in the ERP system are too strict and productivity is thereby reduced or minimized, so performance cannot be monitored appropriately
Culture	Occurs when operating the ERP systems conflicts with organizational or national norms

In line with that, Markus [4] refers to business processes, culture, and incentives as the most relevant types of organization-system misfits. While each misfit can cause ERP implementation projects to fail, the present paper argues that an insufficient process fit hampers system adoption significantly and facilitates the occurrence of other sources of misfits. Based on the re-engineering of business processes, user workflows and operations can be subject to severe adaptations, resulting in resistance and system avoidance. Thus, the probability of data misfits increases, since relevant data are not stored and processed appropriately when users work around the system. Furthermore, process misfits negatively affect the perceived usability of an ERP system and produce conflicts with the existing organizational structure and corresponding roles. As users avoid the system's functionalities, control mechanisms are ineffective, providing only limited insights into organizational performance measures. However, we do not argue that ensuring a sufficient degree of process fit offers a standalone solution to guarantee ERP implementation project success. In fact, each misfit must be addressed appropriately. Nevertheless, controlling for process fit within the system selection stage can limit project risks and increase the probability of a successful ERP implementation subsequently.

However, approaches of this kind have a variety of well-known limitations. The presented evaluation focuses exclusively on the comparison of single business processes instead of full-scale organizational structures. Thus, potential implications are limited since ERP selection should be based on the similarity of business process collections. Also, we did not yet perform an error analysis to determine why certain features did not match. We are, however, not aware of a significant feature that should have matched in our example.

Another major drawback results from the statistical noise produced by the similarity metrics used themselves. First, as we focused on methodological aspects, we did not control for the applicability of other configurations of the used similarity techniques and how they influence the quality of results and implications. An in-depth evaluation of different similarity computation methods should be performed to shed more light on their effects on ERP selection (e.g. [44]). Second, to generate an equivalence mapping between two business processes, a threshold needs to be defined that determines whether two business process elements are equal. As current literature does not provide comprehensive empirical validations, the mapping can be significantly biased by individual perceptions. Furthermore, changing the threshold can manipulate the results, negatively influencing validity and reliability. In line with that, the computation of semantic similarity is based on heuristically determined weighting factors. According to an experimental validation by Dijkman et al. [18], weight factors of 1 for equal words and 0.75 for synonyms produce the best results. Nevertheless, outcomes depend strongly on the experimental setup. Another major source of uncertainty lies in the use of GermaNet as a lexical-semantic database. Although GermaNet contains more than 100.000 synsets, it does not sufficiently cover the domain of BPM. Thus, the results' quality may suffer if no standardized ontology is available and processes are modeled in German language.

Additionally, label features and structural features equally influence the degree of feature-based similarity in the current setup. More evaluation of empirical data is necessary to determine whether specific weighting factors can improve the quality of results. Furthermore, the applicability of our approach depends highly on the availability of organizational process models, which especially for SMEs can be limited. In line with that, enterprises may not be able to define their organizational requirements with the accuracy necessary to use our methodology beneficially. In addition, process data from ERP systems must be available to ensure the practical applicability of our method. Thus, different procedures can be applied, including requesting reference process models from vendors, analyzing the process execution from a user perspective, or performing methods of process mining to extract and analyze data from change logs of ERP systems. However, endeavors of this kind can be complex and time consuming, hampering the potential benefits of our method. Finally, limitations result from the experimental evaluation of our work. Although the introduced hypotheses are experimentally validated, the number of evaluated business processes is too small to provide generalizable implications. Large randomized controlled trials could provide more definitive evidence.

6   Conclusion

Using a DSR procedure, we aimed to provide a novel methodology for managing the organization-enterprise system fit during the selection phase of an ERP implementation project. As the users' adoption is crucial for capturing the benefits expected from an ERP implementation, we investigated the phenomenon of technochange to gain valuable insights into the aspects that influence the process of technology adoption in an organizational environment. Findings and requirements were then transformed into an integrated methodology as the main artifact of this contribution. Future research will focus on the derivation of universal design principles to strengthen the theoretical soundness and instantiability of our findings.

Our results suggest that ERP solutions must cover a sufficient share of demanded functionalities and enable users to increase their efficiency and effectiveness. Furthermore, to reduce technochange, enterprises must ensure a mutual alignment of business and IT and they can increase the likelihood of a project's success by selecting a system that is implementable with the fewest number of conflicts to the existent organizational structure. Our contribution provides methodological guidance in the selection of an ERP system that fits the demanded business needs, thus requiring minimal efforts on BPR and less resistance towards change within the group of intended users. Applying our approach, enterprises are provided with a quick decision support for narrowing down the diversified market for ERP systems to a smaller number of suitable ERP solutions. Thus, inaccurate selection decisions can be avoided, users can adopt a system's functionalities at a faster pace, and the likelihood of an ERP project to be successful increases.

References

1. Hooshang, M.B., Bruce, K.B., Dale, A.H., James, G.L.: Selection and critical success factors in successful ERP implementation. Compet. Rev. **24**, 357–375 (2014)
2. Strong, D., Volkoff, O.: Understanding organization-enterprise system fit: a path to theorizing the information technology artifact. MIS Q. **34**, 731–756 (2010)
3. Ali, M., Cullinane, J.: A study to evaluate the effectiveness of simulation based decision support system in ERP implementation in SMEs. Procedia Technol. **16**, 542–552 (2014)
4. Markus, M.L.: Technochange management: using IT to drive organizational change. J. Inf. Technol. **19**, 4–20 (2004)
5. Peffers, K., Tuunanen, T., Rothenberger, M.A., Chatterjee, S.: A design science research methodology for information systems research. J. Manag. Inf. Syst. **24**, 45–78 (2007)
6. Baskerville, R., Pries-Heje, J., Venable, J.: Soft design science methodology. In: Proceedings of the 4th International Conference on Design Science Research in Information Systems and Technology - DESRIST 2009, p. 9 (2009)

7. Gregor, S., Hevner, A.R.: Positioning and presenting types of knowledge in design science research. MIS Q. **37**, 337–355 (2013)
8. Finney, S., Corbett, M.: ERP implementation: a compilation and analysis of critical success factors. Bus. Process Manag. J. **13**, 329–347 (2007)
9. Pérez-Salazar, M.D.R., Rivera, I., Cristóbal-Vázquez, I.M.A.: ERP selection: a literature review. Int. J. Ind. Syst. Eng. **13**, 309–324 (2013)
10. Scheer, A., Habermann, F.: Enterprise resource planning: making ERP a success. Commun. ACM **43**, 57–61 (2000)
11. Stefanou, C.: The selection process of enterprise resource planning (ERP) systems. In: AMCIS 2000 Proceedings, pp. 988–991 (2000)
12. Avison, D.E., Fitzgerald, G.: Information Systems Development: Methodologies. Techniques and Tools. McGraw Hill, London (1995)
13. Verville, J., Halingten, A.: A six-stage model of the buying process for ERP software. Ind. Mark. Manag. **32**, 585–594 (2003)
14. Wei, C.C., Chien, C.F., Wang, M.J.J.: An AHP-based approach to ERP system selection. Int. J. Prod. Econ. **96**, 47–62 (2005)
15. Venkatesh, V., Morris, M.G., Davis, G.B., Davis, F.D.: User acceptance of information technology: toward a unified view. MIS Q. **27**, 425–478 (2003)
16. Yan, Z., Dijkman, R., Grefen, P.: Fast business process similarity search with feature-based similarity estimation. In: Meersman, R., Dillon, T., Herrero, P. (eds.) OTM 2010. LNCS, vol. 6426, pp. 60–77. Springer, Heidelberg (2010). doi:10.1007/978-3-642-16934-2_8
17. Martens, A., Fettke, P., Loos, P.: A genetic algorithm for the inductive derivation of reference models using minimal graph-edit distance applied to real-world business process data. In: Tagungsband Multikonferenz Wirtschaftsinformatik, Paderborn (2014)
18. Dijkman, R., Dumas, M., Van Dongen, B., Krik, R., Mendling, J.: Similarity of business process models: metrics and evaluation. Inf. Syst. **36**, 498–516 (2011)
19. Li, C., Reichert, M., Wombacher, A.: On measuring process model similarity based on high-level change operations. In: Li, Q., Spaccapietra, S., Yu, E., Olivé, A. (eds.) ER 2008. LNCS, vol. 5231, pp. 248–264. Springer, Heidelberg (2008). doi:10.1007/978-3-540-87877-3_19
20. Dijkman, R., Dumas, M., García-Bañuelos, L.: Graph matching algorithms for business process model similarity search. In: Dayal, U., Eder, J., Koehler, J., Reijers, Hajo A. (eds.) BPM 2009. LNCS, vol. 5701, pp. 48–63. Springer, Heidelberg (2009). doi:10.1007/978-3-642-03848-8_5
21. Thomas, O., Fellmann, M.: Semantische ereignisgesteuerte prozessketten. In: Data Warehous, pp. 205–224 (2006)
22. Hoffmann, W., Kirsch, J., Scheer, A.-W.: Modellierung mit ereignisgesteuerten Prozeßketten (1993)
23. Gerth, C., Luckey, M., Küster, J.M., Engels, G.: Detection of semantically equivalent fragments for business process model change management. In: Proceedings - 2010 IEEE 7th International Conference on Services Computing, SCC 2010, pp. 57–64 (2010)
24. Ehrig, M., Koschmider, A., Oberweis, A.: Measuring similarity between semantic business process models. In: Proceeding APCCM 2007 Proceedings of the fourth Asia-Pacific Conference on Comceptual Modelling, vol. 67, pp. 71–80 (2007)
25. Martens, A., Fettke, P., Loos, P.: Inductive development of reference process models based on factor analysis. In: Proceedings of the 12th International Conference on Wirtschaftsinformatik, pp. 438–452, Osnabrück (2015)
26. La Rosa, M., Dumas, M., Uba, R., Dijkman, R.: Merging business process models. In: Meersman, R., Dillon, T., Herrero, P. (eds.) OTM 2010. LNCS, vol. 6426, pp. 96–113. Springer, Heidelberg (2010). doi:10.1007/978-3-642-16934-2_10

27. Eppler, M.J.: A process-based classification of knowledge maps and application examples. Knowl. Process Manag. **15**, 59–71 (2008)
28. Awad, A.: BPMN-Q: a language to query business processes. In: EMISA, vol. 119 (2007)
29. Weston, F.C.: ERP implementation and project management. Prod. Inventory Manag. J. **42**, 75–80 (2001)
30. Gronau, N.: Handbuch der ERP-Auswahl. GTO mbH Verlag, Berlin (2012)
31. Buonanno, G., Faverio, P., Pigni, F., Ravarini, A., Sciuto, D., Tagliavini, M.: Factors affecting ERP system adoption: a comparative analysis between SMEs and large companies. J. Enterp. Inf. Manag. **18**, 384–426 (2005)
32. Chen, I.J.: Planning for ERP systems: analysis and future trend. Bus. Process Manag. J. **7**, 374–386 (2001)
33. Light, B.: The maintenance implications of the customization of ERP software. J. Softw. Maint. Evol. Res. Pract. **13**, 415–429 (2001)
34. Sumner, M.: Critical success factors in enterprise wide information management systems projects. In: Proceedings of the 1999 ACM SIGCPR Conference on Computer Personnel Research, pp. 297–303. ACM Press, New York (1999)
35. Scheer, A.-W., Thomas, O., Adam, O.: Process modeling using event-driven process chains. In: Process-Aware Information Systems, pp. 119–145. Wiley, Hoboken (2005)
36. Becker, J., Kugeler, M., Rosemann, M.: Prozessmanagement. Springer, Heidelberg (2012)
37. Rosemann, M., van der Aalst, W.M.P.: A configurable reference modelling language. Inf. Syst. **32**, 1–23 (2007)
38. van Dongen, B., Dijkman, R., Mendling, J.: Measuring similarity between business process models. In: Bubenko, J., Krogstie, J., Pastor, O., Pernici, B., Rolland, C., Sølvberg, A. (eds.) Seminal Contributions to Information Systems Engineering, pp. 405–419. Springer, Heidelberg (2013)
39. Levenshtein, V.I.: Binary codes capable of correcting deletions, insertions, and reversals. Sov. Phys. Dokl. **10**, 707–710 (1966)
40. Ehrig, M.: Measuring similarity between semantic business process models (2007)
41. Hamp, B., Feldweg, H.: GermaNet - a lexical semantic net for German. In: Proceedings of ACL, pp. 9–15 (1997)
42. Porter, M.F.: An algorithm for suffix stripping. Progr. Electron. Libr. Inf. Syst. **14**, 130–137 (1980)
43. Becker, J., Schütte, R.: Handelsinformationssysteme. Redline Wirtschaft, Frankfurt am Main (2004)
44. Jung, J.J.: Semantic business process integration based on ontology alignment. Expert Syst. Appl. **36**, 11013–11020 (2009)

Extracting Business Objects and Activities from Labels of German Process Models

Philip Hake[1,2(✉)], Peter Fettke[1,2], Günter Neumann[2], and Peter Loos[1,2]

[1] Institute for Information Systems, Saarland University, Saarbrücken, Germany
{philip.hake,peter.fettke,peter.loos}@dfki.de
[2] German Research Center for Artificial Intelligence, Saarbrücken, Germany
neumann@dfki.de

Abstract. To automatically analyze and compare elements of process models, investigating the natural language contained in the labels of the process models is inevitable. Therefore, the adaption of well-established techniques from the field of natural language processing to Business Process Management has recently experienced a growth. Our work contributes to the field of natural language processing in business process models by providing a word dependency-based technique for the extraction of business objects and activities from German labeled process models. Furthermore, we evaluate our approach by implementing it in the RefMod-Miner toolset and measuring the quality of the information extraction in business process models. In three different evaluation scenarios, we show the strengths of the dependency-based approach and give an outlook on how further research could benefit from the approach.

Keywords: Business process modeling · Information extraction · Language processing · Business process management

1 Introduction

Beside the structure and process semantics contained in business process models, the language contained in the labels represents an important factor when it comes to describing the business activities. To automatically process these models in a way that the underlying process semantics is considered, i.e. analyzing, comparing, matching or even refactoring models, the contained natural language should be investigated. The automatic processing of natural language in shape of textual representations is dedicated to the field of computational linguistics. Over the past decade, a remarkable set of processing techniques for natural language texts have been successfully applied to various problems such as Optical Character Recognition (OCR), named entity recognition and sentiment analysis [1]. However, recent BPM (Business Process Management)-driven approaches have revealed shortcomings in the applicability of well-established natural language processing (NLP) techniques in the context of automatic language processing in business process models. These shortcomings are caused by the different languages that are used to describe processes in terms of process models and textual descriptions. While the latter contains what is known as natural language, the

© Springer International Publishing AG 2017
A. Maedche et al. (Eds.): DESRIST 2017, LNCS 10243, pp. 21–38, 2017.
DOI: 10.1007/978-3-319-59144-5_2

former can be considered a slightly controlled language, which is less complex regarding the sentence structure. Due to the mismatch of the two languages, the applicability of the techniques that are based on natural language models cannot be ensured. Therefore, a variety of approaches faces the challenge of processing the language contained in process model labels by successfully extending existing NLP techniques to process model-specific language characteristics. Among these are techniques dedicated to the detection of business objects and activities [2], which is fundamental regarding the comparison [3] and matching of process models [4]. While most of the BPM NLP approaches focus on processing the English language, [5] discusses characteristics of other natural languages. Since the language contained in the process models usually depends on a company's location, either a translation of the models or an adaption of existing techniques must be considered to automatically process these models.

Therefore, we aim at providing a German language-based approach for detecting business objects and activities in business process models. Our approach answers the following research question:

(RQ) How and to what extent can business objects and activities be extracted from German process models applying state of the art NLP techniques?

We address the research question by developing and evaluating a detection approach based on the insights from English extraction approaches and state-of-the-art NLP techniques. We contribute to the field of natural language processing in business process models by providing and assessing an approach for detecting business objects and activities of German process models. Our work follows a design science-oriented methodology. We aim at extending existing knowledge about the extraction of information from business process models. Furthermore, we propose a novel artifact, which will be beneficial for research fields relying on language processing in process models. We evaluate the artifact by providing an implementation and empirical evaluation using three different scenarios.

The remainder of the paper is structured as follows: In Sect. 2 we introduce BPM NLP foundations, the problem statement and our methodological approach. In Sect. 3 we present our approach for detecting business objects and activities. In Sect. 4 we present our evaluation, consisting of an implementation and an empirical investigation in three different scenarios. Section 5 analyzes and discusses the evaluation result. Finally, we conclude our work in Sect. 6 and outline impacts on future research.

2   Foundations

2.1   Natural Language Processing

To automatically detect business objects and activities in labels of process models, the language contained in the labels needs to be investigated. There exists a variety of modeling guidelines [6, 7] and artificial languages used for business process modeling, which significantly influence the natural language used in business process models. Moreover, there are fundamental methods and frameworks known to the field of NLP that are suitable for processing natural language contained in any process model. An extensive overview of approaches to processing language in business process management is provided in [8].

These approaches are based on manifold linguistic techniques and resources. Approaches investigating the language contained in labels of process models depend on filtering, parsing and chunking the labels, to segment the contained language. The segmentation [9] covers simple techniques, which obtain a list of words by splitting labels at whitespace characters, but also sophisticated machine learning-based approaches, which are trained on extensive linguistic datasets.

The segmentation of a label is crucial to automatically examine the semantic relation between labels. Approaches investigating the similarity of labels require information about semantic relations between single words. The synonym relation between two words is a widely-used relation type and enables approaches to identify similar labels, e.g. *create invoice* and *generate bill* [10]. However, looking up the relation in a database requires the words contained in the label to be available in its basic form known as *lemma*. Depending on the language and provided context, the automatic derivation of a lemma remains a challenging task.

Moreover, there are approaches investigating the syntactic structure of labels. Based on an identified word category, e.g. noun, verb, adjective, a category-based comparison of labels is conducted [9]. The derivation of these word categories reaches from simple techniques depending on dictionary lookups to complex heuristic techniques using pre-trained language models. Determining the syntactic word-category of the words contained in a sentence is called *part-of-speech (POS) tagging*.

In [11] the authors propose a framework for processing natural language in process models. This framework also covers the techniques presented in [8]. The components of this framework describe a toolchain of specific techniques and resources addressing several mostly high-level challenges, e.g. Named-Entity Recognition. However, this framework is not applicable to our approach since we use low-level NLP techniques, which are omitted in the framework. Given a corpus of process models in a machine-readable format, information extraction requires several chained NLP techniques including *parsing* and *tagging* the labels, as well as analyzing the contained words and their dependencies within the label. Each of the chained techniques influences the results of consecutive processing steps.

2.2 Information Extraction in Business Process Models

The goal of information extraction is to transform unstructured information contained in natural language texts into structured data. Information extraction refers to manifold linguistic problems such as named entity recognition, temporal analysis or relation detection and classification [1]. The approach proposed in this work is considered as classification and relation detection problem since we aim at extracting embedded objects and activities and reveal their relation. While [12] relies on a manual processing of labels to extract a business vocabulary, we focus on an automated information extraction approach. We denote a business object as a tangible or intangible artifact, which is described in a node label of a process model. An activity describes the manipulation, usage or generation of a business object within a label. An activity is always associated with a business object and vice versa.

Before we introduce our novel approach, we will revisit an approach for detecting process model labeling styles [8] since we rely on the same linguistic patterns identified in German business process models. The approach was recently used to detect labeling style violations in business process models and is also known for its applicability to extracting information from English business process models. The approach investigates the syntax of the labels. Based on the detected labeling style, segments of the label can be declared as objects and related activities. Since they aimed at measuring the style detection performance, the evaluation of the additionally provided techniques for extracting business objects and activities were neglected. The proposed labeling styles represent predefined syntactic patterns. Table 1 presents the patterns and the respective labeling styles for German and English labels. Based on the patterns, the authors propose a heuristic matching of labels to the proposed patterns. In case that a label starts with a verb in infinitive form, the label is assigned to the verb object style. The identification of the respective verb form is conducted via a lookup in a pre-tagged corpus. Since the syntactic function of a word might be ambiguous, the authors propose a disambiguation technique. Thus, the precision of the label style detection depends on the syntactic disambiguation and on whether a word can be looked up. After matching the label to a pattern, the business object and activities are determined. Given a label of verb object style, the identified verb can be denoted as the label's activity. The next object that follows the identified verb is denoted as business object.

Table 1. Activity labeling styles [8].

Style	Pattern	Language	Example
Verb object	verb (imperative) + noun	en, ger	Create invoice
			Erstelle Rechnung
Infinitive style	verb (infinitive) + noun	ger	Erstellen Rechnung
Objective-infinitive	noun + verb (infinitive)	ger	Rechnung erstellen
Action-noun (NP)	noun + noun	en	Invoice creation
Action-noun (of)	noun + 'of' + noun	en	Creation of invoice
Action-noun (gerund)	verb (gerund/nominalization) + [article] + noun	en, ger	Creating invoice
			Erstellung der Rechnung
Action-noun (irregular)	Anomalous	en, ger	–
			–
Descriptive	[noun] + verb (3P) + noun	en, ger	Mitarbeiter erstellt Rechnung
			Clerk creates invoice
No-action	Anomalous	en, ger	–

2.3   Problem Statement

The proposed derivation of business objects and activities in [13] is designed for the English language and covers action-noun and descriptive labels, as long as they do not contain a coordinate conjunction. We consider the evaluation of this derivation approach implicit, since the authors explicitly measure the label refactoring quality, which relies on the derivation results, but does not focus on the derivation results. In the following, we will examine German language characteristics that influence the adaption of the proposed conceptual considerations regarding an extraction of business objects and activities.

Contrary to the English language, the German language does not suffer as much from syntactic ambiguity. Capitalized nouns make it easier to determine the syntactic function of a word within a label. However, investigating the techniques and resources provided in [2, 8] reveals further challenges for the German language regarding the determination of the syntactic function, and consequently, for the extraction of business objects and activities:

(1) The resolution of verb forms to their respective infinitive form is based on pre-tagged English and German corpora. While they allow a resolution of English gerunds to their infinitive form (*creating* → *create*), this relation is not maintained for the German language (*Erstellung* → *erstellen*) regarding nominalizations.

(2) Furthermore, an investigation on the general applicability of lookup approaches revealed that the used corpora are likely to miss domain-specific knowledge. For instance, the widely-used TIGER corpus is based on texts published in the newspaper *Frankfurter Rundschau*. Considering the German language, a lookup approach highly depends on the maintained compound words within the corpus. Therefore, providing a domain independent technique is necessary to ensure an accurate detection of business objects and activities.

(3) Beside the German characteristics, the techniques introduced in [2] are not able to determine multiple objects and activities in more complex sentence structures such as conjunctive sentences. Furthermore, they rely on the part of speech information of each single word but do not investigate the dependencies of the words within the label.

Finally, the detection of business objects and activities has only been implicitly evaluated regarding the *action-noun* and the *descriptive* labeling styles. Hence, we aim at developing and evaluating an information extraction approach for German business process models to identify business objects and activities.

3   Business Object and Activity Extraction

Our approach is based on the insights concerning the different linguistic patterns used in German business process models [8]. The approach is subdivided into two processing steps. The first step consists of state of the art language processing techniques to investigate the syntactic structure of a label, i.e. the POS tags and the syntactic dependencies.

Based on the gathered syntactic information, we derive the business objects and activities in the second step. Since the language models and techniques are trained on natural language, the correct detection of the *POS tag* and the *dependencies* in short labels (less than three words) are difficult. Therefore, we also apply a rule-based detection for short labels using pre-tagged linguistic corpora.

3.1   Step 1: Language Processing Pipeline

Step 1 includes the extraction of POS information as well as the syntactic semantics between the words. Figure 1 shows the information we obtain by applying the POS tagger and dependency parser to the label *Es liegt eine digitale Rechnung vor (A digital invoice was received)*. We obtain a list of identified words called tokens, the respective part-of-speech tags and the dependencies between these words. Using the derived POS information, we know that the label contains a word tagged as noun (NN) *Rechnung* and a finite verb (VVFIN) *liegt*. The directed edges depicted in Fig. 1 describe the dependencies between the identified words. Additionally, we receive the type of dependency, e.g. direct object or genitive object. Hence, we know that the noun *Rechnung* is a direct object that depends on the finite verb *liegt*.

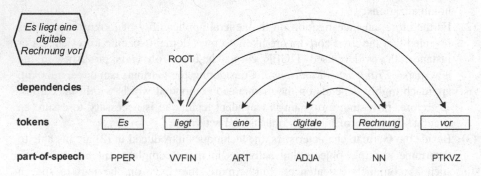

Fig. 1. Derived tokens, dependencies and part-of-speech information

In order to achieve the necessary degree of efficiency and robustness, our label analysis is based on DFKI's (German Research Center for Artificial Intelligence) multilingual statistical-based dependency analysis framework, called *MDParser* [14]. *MDParser* consists of a complete pipeline of tools for *text segmentation*, *tokenization*, *POS tagging*, morphological tagging, named entity (NE) recognition, and syntactic dependency analysis. There exist only a few other available similar complete NLP pipelines, notably, the Stanford dependency parser, which has also been applied to the detection of process model labeling styles [13]. In a recent comparison, *MDParser* was shown to be more than 5-times faster than the latest version of the Stanford dependency parser [15] and achieved a better performance on the tested universal dependency treebanks [16]. MDParser is a lightweight easy to train and applicable system, e.g., the POS tagger and parser component have been trained and tested on more than 52 languages (using the Universal Dependency treebanks v1.3.[1] Therefore, the conceptual considerations of our approach are transferable to an extensive number of languages.

The core of MDparser consists of a general name tagger (*GNT*) and the dependency parser *MDP*. Both are based on the same statistical-based Machine Learning engine (LIBLINEAR, [17]) and share a common data and annotation schema for training and application, i.e. the CONLL data format.[2] *GNT* is used for training and applying models for *POS tagging*. In contrast to comparable NLP applications in BPM, which also focus on an automated language processing, the applied parser is capable of handling information in brackets, punctuations and other special characters. Due to the observed difficulties using NLP parsers in [13], we employ the MDParser because of the performance measured in several benchmarks. The MDparser achieved 97.30% on the TIGER 2.2 test set (compared to 97.73% for the currently best result reported by [18]). Similarly, we achieve an F1 score of 73.91% on the GermEval 2014 dataset, which would have been the 3rd best result according to Metric3 [19].

The MDP dependency parser is currently one of the fastest statistical-based dependency parsers available - more than 5,000 sentences/second [16], which also enables a real-time application of our information extraction approach.

3.2   Step 2: Business Object and Activity Derivation

To derive the business objects and activities, we rely on the dependencies and the POS tags gathered in the previous step. At first, we investigate the label regarding the contained activity. Based on the activity, we determine the business object of a label. Based on the introduced German labeling styles (Sect. 2.2), we assume that the activity is contained as a verb *prüfen (examine)*, a simple nominalization *Prüfung (examination)* or a compound nominalization *Rechnungsprüfung (invoice verification)*. In case that a label contains different types of activities, we define an order based on which we apply the selection of the activity.

A verb dominates a simple nominalization and a simple nominalization dominates a compound nominalization. Our approach extracts *beenden (close)* as activitiy in the label *Rechnungsprüfung beenden (close invoice verification)*, since the compound nominalization *Rechnungsprüfung* is dominated by the verb *beenden*. If multiple activities of the same type occur and they are not dominated by another activity type, they are denoted as activities. In the label *Rechnungsprüfung und Qualitätskontrolle (invoice verification and quality check)* both compound nominalizations are identified as activities.

Since simple nominalizations and compound nominalizations are tagged as nouns, the distinction of nouns not describing an activity is difficult. A verb, however always describes an activity and only a few ambiguities considering the syntactical function exist, e.g. *Pflege (care)* as a noun and as an imperative form at the beginning of a sentence.

Therefore, we apply different dependency-based extraction approaches for both activity cases. At first, we obtain the tokens, POS tags, word dependencies and

---

[1] cf. http://universaldependencies.org/.

[2] cf. http://ufal.mff.cuni.cz/conll2009-st/task-description.html.

dependency types from the MDparser (Fig. 1). Then, we execute the dependency-based label analysis (DLA). If no activity could be determined, we apply an additional heuristic approach. Algorithm 1 describes the first dependency-based extraction. We determine the verbs contained in the description using the POS tag information. Our analysis not only covers the activity detection in verb object labels, but also the activities contained in infinitive style, objective infinitive style as well as the descriptive style and irregular labels. To identify a verb in the label, we use the function *getNextVerbPos*, which returns the position of the next verb in the list of tokens. If a verb is identified, the verb is added to the set of activities. Afterwards, we investigate the dependencies of the activity to nouns contained in the label to derive the business objects. If the identified verb and a noun are related regarding the derived dependencies, the noun is denoted as business object. Before adding the obtained business object to the result set, we call *getConj* to extract further related nouns based on a conjunction dependency.

```
Algorithm 1: DLA
Input: tokens, tags, depends, depTypes
Output: ({objects}, {activities})

activities:={};
objects:={};
while verbExists(tags)
  verbPos:=getNextVerbPos(tags);
  conjA:=getConj(verbPos,depends,depTypes);
  activities=activities U {tokens[verbPos]};
  while nounExists(tags)
    nounPos:=getNextNounPos(tags);
    object;
    if rootChildren(verbPos,nounPos,depends)
      object=tokens[nounPos];
    else if childParent(verbPos,nounPos,depends)
      object=tokens[nounPos];
    else if childParent(nounPos,verbPos,depends)
      object=tokens[nounPos];
    conjO:=getConj(nounPos,depends,depTypes,tokens,tags);
    objects= objects U conj U {object};
while nounExists(tags)
  nounPos:=getNextNounPos(tags);
  if genitive(depTypes[nounPos])
    depPos:=depends[nounPos];
    conjA:=getConj(depPos,depends,depTypes,tokens,tags);
    conjO:=getConj(nounPos,depends,depTypes,tokens,tags);
    activities=activities U {tokens[depPos]}U conjA;
    objects=objects U {tokens[nounPos]} U conjO;
return ({objects},{activities});
```

Hence, in the description *Rechnung und Qualität prüfen (check invoice and quality)* not only *Qualität* but also *Rechnung* is identified as business object, as both words exhibit a conjunction dependency. Our approach is also capable of identifying *Rechnung* and *Ware* in the label *Rechnung/Ware auf Vollständigkeit prüfen*.

Since German labels contain activities masked as nouns, we also examine the contained nouns if no verbs could be identified. Analogously, in [13] a label is assigned the action noun style if no verb could be identified. We then check the dependency of each noun contained in the label. The *genitive* function checks whether the noun holds a genitive relation to any other token in the label. If the genitive rule applies, the respective noun is denoted as business object. The related token of the noun is declared as business activity. Thus, in the label 'Erstellung der Rechnung' the activity 'Erstellung' and the object 'Rechnung' are identified. Furthermore, using *getConj*, we identify further objects and activities with a conjunction relation. If no activity is identified using Algorithm 1, we apply the heuristic label analysis (HLA). This algorithm covers the case that the linguistic processing does not identify a contained verb form. This mainly applies for short labels containing only two words. Thus, the identification of the business objects and activities requires lookups in a pre-tagged corpus. To minimize errors due to missing entries in the corpus, we apply multiple investigations of the label.

Given a label with two words, we assume that the second word either represents a noun referring to an activity or object, or a verb representing an activity. The first word is either an adverb, an adjective, an activity masked as verb or noun or an object represented by a noun. Identifying the position of the verb is the best way to also correctly identify the object. If the label contains two words, we look up the POS tags of the second token in a corpus. The function *isVerb* checks whether the token appears as a verb in the corpus. Using *isAd* we look up whether the first token is contained as adjective or adverb in the corpus. If the first word is an adverb or an adjective, the second token is denoted as activity. Otherwise, we additionally declare the first token an object. If the first token of the label is a verb according to the corpus look-up, the first word becomes the activity and the second word the object. If neither the first nor the second token could be identified as a verb, we declare the first token as an object if it is not contained as an adjective or adverb in the corpus and declare the second token the corresponding activity. If the label contains more than 2 words, we consider the first verb in the tokens as activity and the first noun as object. If still no verb is identified, we pick the first noun as activity and the second noun as object.

```
Algorithm 2: HLA
Input: tokens, tags, depends, depTypes
Output: ({objects}, {activities})

activities:={};
objects:={};
if length(tokens)==1
    activities=activities U {tokens[0]};
else if length(tokens)==2
  # check if second token is a verb
  if isVerb(tokens[1])&&!isAd(tokens[0])
    activities=activities U {tokens[1]};
    objects=objects U {tokens[0]};
  else if isVerb(tokens[0])
    activities=activities U {tokens[0]};
    objects=objects U {tokens[1]};
  else
    if isAd(tokens[0])
      activities=activities U {tokens[1]};
    else
      activities=activities U {tokens[0]};
      objects=objects U {tokens[1]};
  else
    if hasNextVerbCorpus(tokens)
      act:=getNextVerbCorpus(tokens);
      activities=activities U {activity};
      if hasNextNounCorpus(tokens)
        object:=getNextNounCorpus(tokens);
        objects=objects U {object};
    else if hasNextNoun(tokens)
      activity=getNextNounCorpus(tokens);
      object=getNextNounCorpus(tokens);
      activities=activities U {activity]};
      objects=objects U {object}
  return ({objects},{activities});
```

4   Evaluation

4.1   Evaluation Setup

We evaluate our information extraction approach for German business process models using three different evaluation scenarios with different sets of German process models and two different corpora containing natural language. To evaluate our approach, we implement the dependency-based and the heuristic extraction in the RefMod-Miner toolset.[3] We annotate each activity node of a process model, to provide a gold standard for information extraction approaches. Therefore, we tag each word describing a business object or business activity. The creation of the gold standard is an iterative procedure and involves two process modeling experts. At first, the experts are provided the definitions of business objects and activities as given in Sect. 2.2. Then, the experts are told to independently tag the process model nodes and indicate the words representing business objects and activities. Afterwards, the experts discuss all labeling decisions. If there is a consensus regarding the labeling decisions, the gold standard is achieved. Otherwise, the next iteration starts and the experts relabel all the nodes based on the insights acquired from the discussion.

We evaluate our approach, comparing the achieved results with the derived gold standard. To measure the performance of our approach, we use Precision, Recall and F-measure, which have already been applied in the field of process matching and label style detection. Hence, we denote an extracted information, i.e. object or activity, from a label as *true positive* if the respective information is contained in the gold standard of this label. An extracted information of a label is denoted a *false positive* extraction, if the respective gold standard does not contain the extracted information. In case the gold standard of a label contains an information, which is not identified by our approach, the neglected information is considered a *false negative* extraction.

Since we aim at measuring scenarios containing several models, we define *TP* the number of *true positive* extractions, *FP* the number of *false positive* extractions and *FN* the number of *false negative* extractions within a given set of process models. We define Precision, Recall and F-measure as follows:

$$Precision = TP/(TP + FP) \tag{1}$$

$$Recall = TP/(TP + FN) \tag{2}$$

$$F-measure = 2 * (Precision * Recall)/(Precision + Recall) \tag{3}$$

In our experimental evaluation, the processes are modeled as event-driven process chains containing functions, events and connectors. We extract the business objects and activities from the function nodes since events tend to describe states rather than activities. Each model set describes domain-specific business knowledge. The first scenario (S1) contains 56 models of the SAP R3 reference model [20]. The second scenario (S2) consists of 60 models of the Retail-H reference model [21]. While S1 and S2 represent real process models, the third set contains 25 artificial process models, each representing the same business process. These models were derived by graduate students in an exam.

Based on a provided textual description of the process, the students were told to model the information contained in the text using the event-driven process chain. Figure 2 shows the distribution of different label sizes. The label size is denoted as the number of words which are acquired by splitting up the label at each whitespace. Since

---

[3] http://refmod-miner.dfki.de.

Table 2. Evaluation of the scenarios S1, S2 and S3.

	S1 (SAP R3)	S2 (Handels H)	S3
Domain	Industry	Retail	Artificial
# models	56	60	25
# function labels	608	557	283
AVG words per label	2.79	3.87	2.77
SD words per label	1.45	1.85	1.25
# objects in gold standard	501	564	253
# max. objects per label	3	3	2
# activities in gold standard	619	643	289
# max. activities per label	2	3	3

the scenarios do not contain labels of size 11 and 13, we omitted the respective bars due to space constraints.

We give an overview of the label size distribution to analyze the influence of the different label sizes on the performance of our approach. Across the three scenarios, we observe a decreasing number of labels with four words and more. Moreover, in S1–S3 the number of labels of size two is higher than the number of labels of size one. While in S2 and S3 labels of size one represent 1% and 8% of all function labels, in scenario S3 16% of all function labels contain only one word. In S1 and S3 more than 50% of the labels (56% and 54%) are of size one or two, while S3 contains 32% of labels of the respective sizes. Table 2 shows the characteristics of the model sets as well as the derived gold standards. We chose three different scenarios to cover different maturity levels of process models as well as the specialization of the process.

We chose S1 and S2, since they represent reference models of two different domains, i.e. industry and retail. Furthermore, they hold a high maturity level, which also affects a consistent labeling style. The process of S3 describes the customer handling in a mileage bonus program and is chosen because of its narrow domain of application and low maturity level. Contrary to S1 and S2, the labeling does not follow a consistent style and the models contain a rather specific vocabulary and spelling errors. Therefore, we expect S3 to be the most challenging scenario, especially for our heuristic analysis. We use GermaNet 11.0 [22] and the TIGER corpus (v 2.2) [23] to derive POS information for the heuristic label analysis. Both have been successfully applied to the derivation of syntactic functions in labeling style detection and process matching.

GermaNet covers more than 140,000 lexical units. The TIGER corpus contains 50,000 distinct sentences consisting of approximately 900,000 tokens that are pre-tagged. Both corpora were created and verified by humans. In contrast, the correctness of the gathered POS tags and dependencies of our approach cannot be ensured. We evaluate the extraction of business objects and activities individually. Furthermore, we also investigate the impact of the applied algorithms in our approach. We compare the performance of the dependency-based label analysis (DLA) and the combination of DLA and the heuristic label analysis (HLA), which we denote as +HLA.

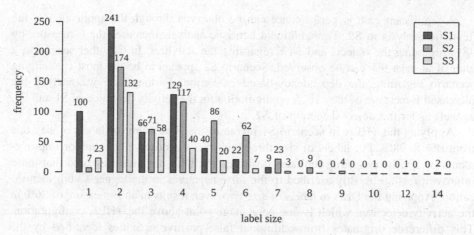

Fig. 2. Distribution of different label sizes across the scenarios.

4.2 Results Analysis

In the following, we report the results of our experimental evaluation. The evaluation of the extraction techniques of [13] applied to our scenario proves to be difficult, especially since they are not designed to handle *verb-object* style labels. By design, these algorithms are only capable of processing *action-noun* and *descriptive* labels. Moreover, the described dictionary-based concepts [8] to process the labels are only applicable for action-noun labels not containing nominalizations. This is not a conceptual problem of the approach per se, but rather the lack of German linguistic resources containing the relation between a nominalized verb and the verb itself. Only a small portion of action-noun labels could be processed correctly. Thus, a fair comparison of both approaches is not possible.

Table 3 summarizes the results of the business object and activity extraction step and shows the impact of our two configurations on the quality of the results. Across all scenarios, the +HLA configuration of the approach achieves the best results regarding the F-measure, ranging from 66% up to 92%. Table 3 also shows that DLA performs well in scenarios S1 and S3, while it only achieves moderate results in scenario S2.

Table 3. Results of the business object and activity extraction step.

		Objects			Activities		
	Algorithm	P	R	F	P	R	F
S1	DLA	0.91	0.90	0.91	0.91	0.74	0.82
	+HLA	0.90	0.91	0.91	0.92	0.91	0.91
S2	DLA	0.42	0.23	0.30	0.19	0.08	0.12
	+HLA	0.75	0.81	0.78	0.69	0.62	0.66
S3	DLA	0.94	0.89	0.91	0.88	0.84	0.86
	+HLA	0.93	0.90	0.91	0.85	0.88	0.87

P = Precision, R = Recall, F = F-measure

A significant gain in performance can be observed through the application of the heuristic analysis in S2. The additional heuristic analysis increases the F-measure by 48% regarding the objects and 54% regarding the activities. In the other scenarios, a gain of at most 9% can be observed. Scenario S2 appears to be the most challenging scenario regarding the dependency-based extraction. Furthermore, we analyze the increased F-measure of the +HLA configuration for the activity detection of S1 and S2, as well as for the object detection of S2.

Applying the +HLA in scenario S1 increases the F-measure for labels of size one from 0% to 98%. For labels of size three and five, we observe only minor improvements of 2%. Investigating the false positives and false negatives revealed that these improvements are mostly ascribed to the false negatives in the tagger's verb identification. Applying the DLA to labels of size two, even results in an F-measure of 96% in the activity detection, which is one percentage point above the +HLA configuration. This difference originates from additional false positive activities identified by the heuristic algorithm. The performance within the other label sizes remains unchanged. Therefore, the increased overall F-measure in the activity extraction of S1 is mainly attributed to the handling of labels of size one.

Scenario S2, however exhibits a stronger deviation between the performance of DLA and +HLA. Figure 3 describes the effect of +HLA on the activity detection in S2. Contrary to S1, the quality of the DLA is considerably low, especially for small labels. A further investigation of the false positives and false negatives revealed that our tagger is not capable of identifying imperative verb forms. While *prüfen* is recognized as a verb in the label *Rechnung prüfen*, *Prüfe* in *Prüfe Rechnung* is not classified as a verb. However, most of the labels of size two exhibit this imperative object style. Since we apply +HLA to avoid false negatives in the verb detection, the F-measure increases significantly. Nevertheless, Fig. 3 also shows that this effect diminishes with increasing label size. This is related to the characteristics of the labels contained in S2.

The usage of the German imperative might result in splitting up the verb into components; e.g. *durchführen* is split up in *führe* and *durch*. Even though the heuristic

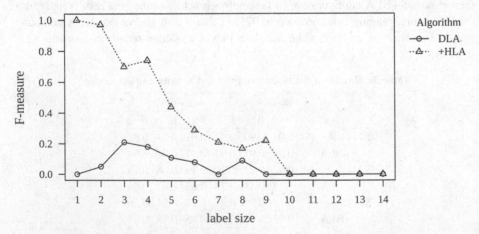

Fig. 3. Scenario S2: evaluation of the activity extraction using F-Measure.

analysis recognizes *führe* as a verb form, it is not capable of linking *durch* to the verb. The missing identification decreases the Recall and explains the drop of the F-measure regarding labels of size three. Moreover, with increasing label size the probability of a second verb occurring within the label grows. The tagger recognizes *prüfen (check)*, but not *Entscheide (decide)* in the label *Entscheide, ob Qualität zu prüfen ist (decide if the quality should be checked)*.

Figure 4 depicts the increase in performance by applying +HLA on the object extraction in scenario S2. Since the object detection relies on correct verb detection, the previously described label characteristics also affect the object extraction.

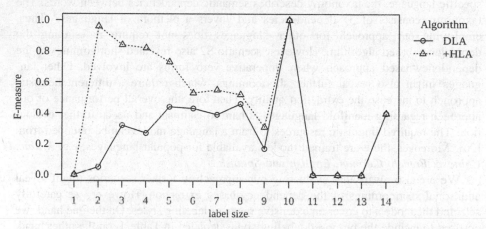

Fig. 4. Scenario S2: evaluation of the object extraction using F-Measure.

5 Discussion

The proposed dependency-based extraction achieves outstanding results in scenarios S1 and S3. The additional heuristic analysis did not yield a significant increase of quality in these scenarios. Moreover, the proposed technique does not rely on a linguistic corpus or a dictionary as the heuristic approach does. Thus, the correctness and completeness of a linguistic resource do not influence the quality of our approach. This is especially beneficial for German process models as the language exhibits a frequent usage of compounds, which often are not contained in dictionaries.

Furthermore, the dependency-based extraction can handle labels containing multiple activities and objects as well as conditional and conjunctive sentences. Up to a certain degree, we are also able to handle labels containing spelling errors, since the dependency parser not only relies on characteristics of the word itself but also on the context contained in the label.

Our approach requires either a trained language model or a tagged language corpus following the UD taxonomy, which enables us to automatically train a language model.

In contrast to scenarios S1 and S3, in scenario S2 DLA achieved only poor results for both, the object (30% F-measure) and activity (12% F-measure) detection. Here

+HLA led to a significant performance increase compared to DLA. The performance was good for the object extraction (78% F-measure), but only moderate concerning the activity extraction (66% F-Measure). Even though imperative verb forms rarely appear in linguistic corpora, due to morphological ambiguities to other verb forms, a corpus lookup could handle the imperative detection. Nonetheless, the missing dependency information about a potential direct object makes it hard to identify the related business object. Moreover, a lookup would not resolve the observed difficulties concerning split up imperative verbs.

Our dependency-based concept is also transferable to other natural languages, since we rely on the taxonomy of *universal dependencies* (UD) [24]. Independent from a specific language, the taxonomy describes semantic dependencies between words. The taxonomy consists of 37 dependencies and covers a plethora of languages.[4] Thus, employing our approach for other languages does not require redesigning the dependency-based algorithm. However, scenario S2 also revealed shortcomings of the dependency-based approach when imperative verb forms are involved. Other languages might also reveal further shortcomings, which require a different heuristic approach to increase the extraction quality. Therefore, the overall performance of our approach regarding manifold languages is hard to estimate and needs further evaluation. The required linguistic resources to train a language model can be obtained from [26]. Moreover, there are trained models available for popular languages, e.g. *Arabic, Chinese, French, German, English* and *Spanish*.[5]

We are also aware that evaluating our approach in further scenarios might reveal additional shortcomings of the dependency-based extraction. However, we carefully selected the models to cover an extensive range of labeling styles. On the one hand, we ensured to include the proposed labeling styles depicted in Table 1, on the other hand, we increased the diversity of natural language contained in labels by investigating models of high and low maturity levels.

6 Conclusion

We answered the research question by proposing, implementing and evaluating a novel artifact. We presented and evaluated an approach for deriving business objects and activities form node labels of business process models. Contrary to existing BPM approaches, which investigate the language contained in the labels, we focus on exploiting not only the POS tag of a word but also the syntactic dependencies between the words. Moreover, by relying on the derived word dependencies, we laid the foundations for the extraction of further information. Based on the dependencies, related adverbs, adjectives and participles could be derived. This additional information allows a precise disambiguation of business objects and activities. Therefore, our information extraction approach is beneficial to manifold research fields. Process model matching often relies on bag of word comparisons between two labels, which means

---

[4] The available languages are maintained at http://universaldependencies.org.

[5] cf. https://nlp.stanford.edu/software/lex-parser.shtml.

each word of the first label is compared to each word of the second label. Using our approach, a semantic and directed comparison of relevant information could be achieved. Consequently, comparisons based on the extracted business objects and activities would also support model comparisons [3]. Furthermore, an inductive mining of reference models [25] could benefit from our approach, since it provides techniques for extracting and relating essential linguistic components of business processes. Nevertheless, this implies a high accuracy concerning the applied dependency detection. Since the current configuration of our approach uses models trained on natural language texts, further research needs to investigate training language on process model data. Considering the recent flowering of neural networks and deep learning, the potential of these techniques should be investigated.

Acknowledgement. This research was funded in part by the German Federal Ministry of Education and Research under grant number 01IS12050 (project SemGo). The responsibility for this publication lies with the authors.

References

1. Jurafsky, D., Martin, J.H.: Speech and Language Processing: An Introduction to Natural Language Processing, Computational Linguistics, and Speech Recognition. Prentice Hall, Pearson Education International, Upper Saddle River (2009)
2. Leopold, H., Smirnov, S., Mendling, J.: Recognising activity labeling styles in business process models. Enterp. Model. Inf. Syst. Architect. (EMISA) **6**, 16–29 (2011)
3. Becker, M., Laue, R.: A comparative survey of business process similarity measures. Comput. Ind. **63**, 148–167 (2012)
4. Antunes, G., Bakhshandeh, M., Borbinha, J., Cardoso, J., Dadashnia, S., Di Francescomarino, C., Dragoni, M., Fettke, P., Gal, A., Ghidini, C., Hake, P., Khiat, A., Klinkmüller, C., Kuss, E., Leopold, H., Loos, P., Mcilicke, C., Niesen, T., Pesquita, C., Péus, T., Schoknecht, A., Sheetrit, E., Sonntag, A., Stuckenschmidt, H., Thaler, T., Weber, I., Weidlich, M.: The process model matching contest 2015. In: Kolb, J. (ed.) Enterprise Modelling and Information Systems Architectures, pp. 127–155. Gesellschaft für Informatik, Bonn (2015)
5. Leopold, H.: Natural Language in Business Process Models. Springer, Berlin (2013)
6. Mendling, J., Reijers, H.A., Recker, J.: Activity labeling in process modeling: empirical insights and recommendations. Inf. Syst. **35**, 467–482 (2010)
7. Mendling, J., Reijers, H.A., van der Aalst, W.M.P.: Seven process modeling guidelines (7PMG). Inf. Softw. Technol. **52**, 127–136 (2010)
8. Leopold, H., Eid-Sabbaghb, R.-H., Mendling, J., Guerreiro Azevedod, L., Araujo Baiãod, F.: Detection of naming convention violations in process models for different languages. Decis. Support Syst. **56**, 310–325 (2013)
9. Sonntag, A., Hake, P., Fettke, P., Loos, P.: An Approach For Semantic Business Process Model Matching Using Supervised Machine Learning. Association for Information Systems (AIS) (2016)
10. Dijkman, R., Dumas, M., van Dongen, B., Käärik, R., Mendling, J.: Similarity of business process models: metrics and evaluation. Inf. Syst. **36**, 498–516 (2011)

11. Bergner, M., Fill, H.-G., Johannsen, F.: Supporting business process improvement with natural language processing: a model-based approach. In: Mayr, H.C., Pinzger, M. (eds.) GI Informatik 2016, Klagenfurt, pp. 717–730 (2016)
12. Skersys, T., Butleris, R., Kapocius, K., Vileiniskis, T.: An approach for extracting business vocabularies from business process models. Inf. Technol. Control **42**, 150–158 (2013)
13. Leopold, H., Smirnov, S., Mendling, J.: On the refactoring of activity labels in business process models. Inf. Syst. **37**, 443–459 (2012)
14. Volokh, A., Neumann, G.: Dependency parsing with efficient feature extraction. In: Glimm, B., Krüger, A. (eds.) KI 2012. LNCS, vol. 7526, pp. 253–256. Springer, Heidelberg (2012). doi:10.1007/978-3-642-33347-7_26
15. Chen, D., Manning, C.D.: A fast and accurate dependency parser using neural networks. In: Empirical Methods in Natural Language Processing (EMNLP), pp. 740–750. Association for Computational Linguistics (2014)
16. Weichselbraun, A., Süsstrunk, N.: Optimizing dependency parsing throughput. In: 2015 7th International Joint Conference on Knowledge Discovery, Knowledge Engineering and Knowledge Management (IC3K), vol. 1, pp. 511–516 (2015)
17. Fan, R.-E., Chang, K.-W., Hsieh, C.-J., Wang, X.-R., Lin, C.-J.: LIBLINEAR: a library for large linear classification. J. Mach. Learn. Res. **9**, 1871–1874 (2008)
18. Müller, T., Schütze, H.: Robust morphological tagging with word representations. In: North American Chapter of the Association for Computational Linguistics: Human Language Technologies. Association for Computational Linguistics (2015)
19. Benikova, D., Biemann, C., Kisselew, M., Padó, S.: Germeval 2014 named entity recognition shared task: companion paper. In: GermEval 2014 Named Entity Recognition Shared Task, vol. 7, p. 10 (2014)
20. Keller, G., Teufel, T.: SAP R/3 prozeßorientiert anwenden – Iteratives Prozeß-Prototyping zur Bildung von Wertschöpfungsketten. Addison-Wesley, Bonn (1998)
21. Becker, J., Schütte, R.: Handelsinformationssysteme. MI Wirtschaftsbuch (2004)
22. Hamp, B., Feldweg, H.: GermaNet - a lexical-semantic net for German. In: Vossen, P., Adriaens, G., Calzolari, N., Sanfilippo, A., Wilks, Y. (eds.) ACL/EACL Workshop, pp. 9–15. Association for Computer Linguistics, Madrid (1997)
23. Brants, S., Dipper, S., Eisenberg, P., Hansen-Schirra, S., König, E., Lezius, W., Rohrer, C., Smith, G., Uszkoreit, H.: TIGER: linguistic interpretation of a German corpus. Res. Lang. Comput. **2**, 597–620 (2004)
24. De Marneffe, M.-C., Dozat, T., Silveira, N., Haverinen, K., Ginter, F., Nivre, J., Manning, C.D.: Universal stanford dependencies: a cross-linguistic typology, pp. 4585–4592 (2014)
25. Rehse, J.-R., Hake, P., Fettke, P., Loos, P.: Inductive reference model development: recent results and current challenges. In: Mayr, H.C., Pinzger, M. (eds.) INFORMATIK 2016. Jahrestagung der Gesellschaft für Informatik (INFORMATIK-2016), vol. P-259. GI, Bonn/Klagenfurt (2016)
26. Universal Dependencies. http://universaldependencies.org

Designing a Framework for the Development of Domain-Specific Process Modelling Languages

Sven Jannaber[1(✉)], Dennis M. Riehle[2], Patrick Delfmann[3],
Oliver Thomas[1], and Jörg Becker[2]

[1] Institute for Information Management and Information Systems,
University of Osnabrück, Osnabrück, Germany
{sven.jannaber, oliver.thomas}@uni-osnabrueck.de
[2] European Research Center for Information Systems,
University of Münster, Münster, Germany
{dennis.riehle, joerg.becker}@ercis.uni-muenster.de
[3] Institute for Information Systems Research,
University of Koblenz-Landau, Koblenz, Germany
delfmann@uni-koblenz.de

Abstract. Domain-specific process modelling has gained increased attention, since traditional modelling languages struggle to meet the demands of highly specialized businesses. However, methodological support on the development of such domain-specific languages is still scarce, which hampers the specification of adequate modelling support. To this end, the paper applies a design-oriented research approach to create an integrated framework that facilitates the development of domain-specific process modeling languages. The framework is a result of 23 consolidated requirements from relevant literature and contains essential building blocks that need to be considered during the development process. It is demonstrated that the framework satisfies the identified requirements by structuring and systematizing the development of domain-specific languages, which increases language adequacy and quality.

Keywords: Business process management · Domain-specific process modelling · Framework · Modelling language development

1 Introduction

Business Process Management (BPM) has become increasingly important in today's enterprise due to the high complexity of organizational operations. It is widely acknowledged in research and practice that sophisticated BPM effort in organizations is closely tied to increased operational performance [1]. Crucial prerequisite for any successful BPM endeavor is the identification and documentation of business processes, which represent one of the main success factors for companies [2]. For this purpose, business process modelling languages (BPMLs) have emerged that provide a variety of concepts and constructs to represent these organizational processes as semi-formal process models.

© Springer International Publishing AG 2017
A. Maedche et al. (Eds.): DESRIST 2017, LNCS 10243, pp. 39–54, 2017.
DOI: 10.1007/978-3-319-59144-5_3

However, traditional BPMLs suffer from severe shortcomings: Nowadays, common process modelling standards struggle to meet the requirements of highly diversified and specialized businesses. Studies indicate that especially niche domains grow more and more unsatisfied with generic languages, since they do not integrate domain knowledge [3, 4], Naturally, this issue translates to the end-users, who continue to rely on common visualization software (e.g. Microsoft PowerPoint) rather than on sophisticated modelling suites and traditional languages for process modelling [5]. Recently, domain-specific process modelling Languages (DSPMLs) have gained increased attention, which are designed to address the outlined shortcoming by capturing the needs of specific domains. By adapting, for instance, the level of abstraction, the terminology or the available subset of modelling elements to the needs of a specific application domain, DSPMLs significantly contribute a successful application of BPM. However, methodological support and guidance regarding the development of DSPMLs is still scarce. Although the creation domain-specific languages (DSL) are an already matured topic in computer science (e.g. [6]), insights have not yet been fully transferred to the BPM domain, which is a crucial gap considering the growing importance of DSPMLs with respect to the increasing specialization of business models and new emerging technology [7]. In BPM literature, DSPMLs have primarily been addressed from an application point of view, while neglecting conceptual design and development [8]. Hence, a structural view on DSPML building blocks and development can be seen as a first step to systematize modelling language development towards current and future demands.

To this end, the paper at hand aims at structuring and ultimately systematizing the development process of future-proof DSPMLs. For this purpose, a design-centered research methodology is applied in order to develop a DSPML framework as main IT artifact of this contribution. The framework consists of major building blocks deducted from insights of a literature review that need to be considered when designing or modifying process modelling languages towards specific business demands. Additionally, the building blocks are aligned in a way that highlights the interdependencies of the language constructs and concepts in order to shed light on the inner core of modelling languages. The DSPML framework supports language designers in research and practice by providing a comprehensive overview over a DSPMLs inner structure as a starting point for language development.

This paper is structured as follows: Succeeding the introduction, a brief outline on topic fundamentals is given in Sect. 2, followed by details on the applied research methodology in Sect. 3. The IS artifact design of this paper is presented in Sect. 4. First, the artifact's design requirements are deducted from the results of a structured literature review. Second, the DSPML framework is introduced as main outcome of this paper. Third, the artifact is being evaluated against the identified requirements. The paper concludes with a discussion and a summary of the findings in Sect. 5.

2   BPM and Domain-Specific Process Modelling

BPM is about "concepts, methods, and techniques to support the design, administration, configuration, enactment, and analysis of business processes" [9] (p. 5). One core concept of BPM is the representation of business processes in form of semi-formal process models. While traditionally process models have primarily been used for mere process documentation and knowledge sharing, models nowadays are being processed by sophisticated algorithms for process intelligence or process mining. Due to their semantic formalization, process models can also include several technical details and thus be directly translated into executable workflows. The way a process model is structurally created and visually notated is called business BPML. Due to the different objectives and purposes that process models can be created for, there exist a large variety of BPMLs. An overview can be found in [10] or [11]. In literature, BPMLs have been heavily featured, resulting in numerous application scenarios across different domains and multiple extensions to enrich their expressiveness towards new demands and domains [12, 13]. Some of the most popular BPMLs are the Business Process Model and Notation (BPMN), for which a full specification is available by [14], and the Event-driven Process Chains (EPC). Typically, BPMLs come alongside with modeling instructions, e.g. [15], modeling frameworks or reference architectures, such as SOM, MEMO or icebricks, for which a comparison can be found in [16].

While traditional standardized languages such as BPMN are widely-used, they provide rather generic constructs for process modelling, since those languages are intended to be generally applicable, i.e., they can be used to create process models for all kind of organizations independent of their domain. This purpose differs from DSPMLs, which focus on particular application domains and, by introducing domain-specific concepts, specifically integrate domain knowledge required to capture the highly specialized business processes of that domain. Therefore, DSPMLs directly contribute to model quality, model integrity and efficiency of process modelling [6, 17]. An example for a DSPML is PICTURE, which is used in BPM projects in the public administration domain and provides 24 pre-defined process bricks. Each brick describes an standard activity in public administration [18]. Hence, typical business processes of that domain can be captured more closely than with traditional languages. According to [18], PICTURE, on the one hand, is designed to represent complex administration processes that involve several different departments, while on the other hand, through its pre-defined process bricks, it is simple enough to be used by non-experts. As the level of abstraction and the used terminology are already defined with the available process bricks, models created with PICTURE are likely to be more standardized and comparable to each other, even if many different users were involved in creating the models. In contrast, modelling languages like BPMN or EPC are highly flexible and, therefore, put higher demands towards the process modeler.

DSPMLs are subject of ongoing discussion in BPM literature. Exemplarily, [8] provides guidelines for the conception of domain-specific modeling languages, while [17] specifies generic and meta model-based requirements. In addition, a macro process for designing a domain-specific language is provided. In [19], different guidelines are proposed within the categories language purpose, language realization, language content, concrete syntax and abstract syntax. A framework for deriving DSPML from a generic BPML is provided by [6], however a software development point of view is taken by providing model-to-model transformation rules. To the best of our knowledge, a framework that integrates existing knowledge in terms of DSPML development by highlighting required building blocks has not yet been proposed.

3 Research Design

For the conceptualization and design of a DSPML framework as primary outcome of this contribution, the paper at hand adheres closely to the design science (DS) research paradigm that has been predominantly introduced in the IS domain as a research framework by [20] and which is nowadays popularized and applied in the field of IS [21, 22]. Originated from the lack of legitimate Information Systems (IS) research methodologies that serve the need of IS as being an "'applied' research discipline" [22], the design science research approach addresses this issue by adapting design-oriented approaches taken from related disciplines such as natural sciences or engineering to the field of IS and thus closing the gap between IS research and practice [22, 23]. In his three cycle view on DS, [24] characterizes DS research as an interplay of relevance, design and rigor. The design cycle is the main cycle of DS research and iterates between the building artifacts and evaluating them against certain requirements [24]. These requirements are considered in the relevance cycle, which connects the artifact to the desired environment and thus determines the organizational problem to be addressed, the intended application domain and also defines the criteria for evaluation of the research result [24]. The rigor cycle relates the research activities with the knowledge base. This ensures that the artifact design is grounded established foundations and previous work, while also add new insights to the knowledge base [24]. Main outcome of design-centered research is an IS artifact, which may be a prototype, but also models, methods or instantiations [20].

In literature, multiple DS research conceptualizations have been proposed, for example the Design Science Research Cycle [25], which differentiates six phases of DS research in an iterative DS procedure model, or Wieringa's [26] DS framework, which is based on work by [20] and further specifies the relationship between environment, knowledge base and actual IS design. However, common DS approaches ultimately incorporate a standard build-evaluate pattern, which prescribes an ex post artifact evaluation, leading to delayed insight about the artifact's truth resp. validity. In their work, [27] propose a design science research approach that is applied as the research design of this paper. In particular, the proposed approach addresses the stated issues of the traditional build-evaluate pattern an instead introduces a more agile way of DS evaluation. Figure 1 visualizes the design science research cycle according to [27] and highlights the phases covered in this contribution. Essentially, the DSR cycle is divided into two main phases, namely ex ante evaluation and ex post evaluation. Besides the baseline DS research activities *problem identification*, *design*, *construct* and *use*, the novelty of this approach is a separate evaluation step after each activity. Subsequently, this allows for a meaningful evaluation even in early design stages of the artifact [27]. In addition, the proposed DS research procedure model comes with specific guidance on methods and criteria for each evaluation step, which we will adhere to in the following.

Adapting the framework in Fig. 1, we focus on the ex-ante phase in this paper. In doing so, we provide a problem statement, which is evaluated by conducting an extensive literature review, thus fulfilling evaluation step 1. As a result of both problem statement and design objectives deducted from the review, the DSPML framework is developed. Concluding the design step, the artifact is evaluated against the proposed

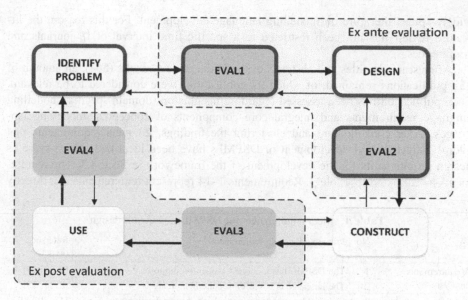

Fig. 1. Design science research cycle according to Sonnenberg and vom Brocke [27]

design objectives and requirements obtained through the literature review. Hereby, we focus on the criteria internal consistency, completeness and clarity, as mentioned by [27]. In accordance with [24], the contribution at hand makes heavy use of existing work included the IS knowledge base, since a consolidation of previous research effort is extracted via a systematic literature review. The review results do not only form the basis of the artifact's requirements, but are also integrated as building blocks into the final result. The presented work contributes a novel IS artifact to the knowledge base by providing a structured framework of essential DSPML building blocks, which may serve as a blueprint for future language design.

4   A Framework for Domain-Specific Modelling Languages

4.1   Literature Review and Design Requirements

To gather design requirements for the DSPML framework and thus query the IS knowledge base, a systematic literature review according to [28] has been conducted using the databases SpringerLink, Google Scholar, ScienceDirect and EbscoHost. The search terms "*model* *develop*", "*process* *model* *develop*", "*process* *language*" and "*model* *language*" have been used, as well as their German equivalents and brief abbreviations fit each search engine's modus operandi.

The choice of search terms has been generic on purpose, since literature specifically addressing crucial building blocks of process modelling language development is wide-spread across the BPM and conceptual modelling domain. Furthermore, the contribution at hand aims providing an overview over previous work existing in the IS knowledge base with the ultimate objective to obtain a holistic integration of the widely-spread literature on modelling language development. For this reason, the literature review has not been restricted to a specific time interval or IS journals and conferences.

After scanning titles and abstracts of the initial review results (564), an amount of 253 publications remained, of which 97 publications were considered to be relevant. Each publication has been assessed regarding insights on (domain specific) modelling language requirements and integral core components of conceptual modelling languages. After consolidating and clustering the findings, 23 meta requirements that address structure and development of DSPMLs have been identified, which serve as design requirements for the development of the framework in Sect. 4.2. The requirements are depicted in Table 1. Requirements 1–14 represent requirements that directly

Table 1. Meta requirements for DSPML framework design

	No.	Framework design requirement	Reference (ex.)
Requirements analysis	1	The DSPML has a defined scope and purpose	[8, 17, 29]
	2	The language is based on requirement analysis	[8, 17, 29]
	3	Stakeholder groups are considered during development	[17, 29, 30]
	4	Language building blocks integrate domain relevance	[8, 17, 19, 31]
Language specification	5	The modelling language is specified by a language meta model	[32, 33]
	6	The DSPML adheres to concrete syntax	[19, 32, 33]
	7	The DSPML adheres to abstract syntax	[19, 32–35]
	8	The language provides (formal) language semantics	[32, 33]
	9	The language considers modelling pragmatics	[17, 36]
Development process	10	The DSPML is a result of a systematic development approach	[19, 29, 37]
Concepts, constructs and elements	11	The language development is based on existing concepts	[8, 17, 19, 29]
	12	The DSPML language contains (domain-specific) modelling constructs to represent business processes:	[8, 17, 19, 31, 35, 38]
		Process elements	[34, 35, 39–41]
		Control flow pattern	[42–46]
		Resources	[34, 35, 40]
		Modularization	[35]
	13	The DSPML provides a graphical notation	[17, 47]
Evaluation	14	The language is assessable regarding its quality and correctness	[17, 48]
Language quality	15	*Uniqueness*	[37]
	16	*Consistency*	[37]
	17	*Scalability*	[37]
	18	*Supportability*	[17, 37]
	19	*Simplicity*	[37, 49–51]
	20	*Space economy*	[37]
	21	*Reversibility*	[37]
	22	*Reliability*	[37]
	23	*Seamlessness*	[37]

refer to modelling language core components that have been stated in the relevant literature and thus need to be considered for DSPML development. Requirements 15–23 concern the resulting language itself. However, since the framework aims at supporting the development of such languages, we argue that these result-centric requirements need to be reflected in the DSPML framework as well.

4.2 DSPML Framework Design

On the basis of the identified requirements, a framework for the development of domain specific process modelling languages is featured as the main IT artifact of this paper. Figure 2 shows the fully developed DSPML framework, which sheds light on crucial building blocks to a (domain-specific) process modelling language. Each of the building blocks is deducted from the framework design requirements presented in Table 1 and substantiated by corresponding literature. The DSPML framework consists of three succeeding main phases, which are aligned as iterating layers. The *requirements layer* lays ground for the subsequent language specification and evaluation. Initially, the development of domain specific languages requires the definition of scope and purpose of the language to be designed [17]. Essentially, this building block represents an initial planning phase, which on the one side details the indented value and long-term usage of the language, since any language component needs to be tailored towards a determined purpose [19]. On the other side, this building block also provides for first analyses regarding the feasibility and applicability. Succeeding scope and purpose, the identification of requirements is the core task in the requirements layer. The framework differentiates between two types of requirements: Generic requirements of any domain specific modelling language are closely tied to language pragmatics and encompass for instance abstraction level [17]. In the context of process modelling, such generic requirements also reflect necessity of a well-defined language specification. Hence, the specification of language syntax and semantics are treated as generic requirements that transits from the requirements layer into the language specification layer. Specific requirements however are set to shape the language towards the intended application domain. Exemplarily, studies demonstrate that the financial industry [4] has fundamental different demands regarding language concept and constructs to reflect their business domain than businesses in the chemical domain [3]. Accordingly, any modelling language needs to reflect the concepts and constructs relevant to their particular domain [8, 17, 19, 31]. In this paper, emphasis is also put on the technology involved in the intended modelling effort. Primarily, this building block refers to technical devices on which the language is applied. While literature on this matter is still scarce, it is undisputed that both mobile [52] and wearable [53] devices impose different requirements (e.g. limited screen size and interaction space) on process modelling languages than traditional modelling suites running on desktop computers. Each process domain is connected to a certain set of stakeholders involved. Gaining insight into stakeholder groups is considered a crucial task for language development [17, 29]. Potential stakeholders encompass persons involved in the language development process, hence domain experts or language designer [17, 29, 30]. Additionally, the target audience has to be kept in mind, since in practice process

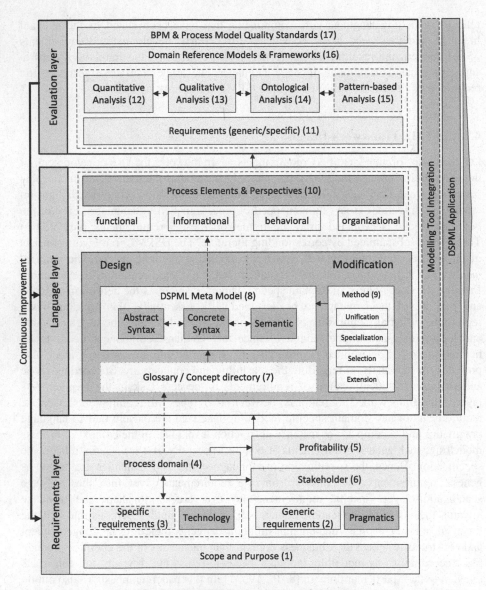

Fig. 2. The DSPML development framework

modelling is often conducted by employees who only possess limited modelling knowledge [54]. Influenced by both the intended application purpose and process domain, the profitability of the development process is embedded on the requirements layer. [29] states that every language development is associated with monetary investment, which is also reflected in the DSML development process of [17]. [8] also attached a profitability criterion at the evaluation layer of a modeling language.

Succeeding the requirements layer, the DSPML has to be designed and specified according to the elaborated requirements. The *language layer* consists of the two primary components language specification and design of process elements and perspectives. Core of the language specification is the meta-model of DSPML to be developed. In this case, the meta-model based specification of a modelling language subsumes the determination of the language's abstract and concrete syntax as well as its semantics [32]. The abstract syntax determines and details concepts, constructs and elements that are being used within the language [19]. The concepts, constructs and elements defined within the language specification are detailed using a glossary and concept directory, which is directly influenced by the process domain. Primary purpose of the directory is to ensure that the intended domain is correctly captured by applied terms and constructs [17].

For abstract syntax specification, language designers can draw from insight gained in [8, 17, 19, 31, 35, 38] to determine constructs essential to a modelling language, while maintaining a domain-driven point of view. Ultimately, decisions regarding potential language modularization, e.g. via sub processes, have to be made at this point in the development process [19], as well as a determination of relevant control structures to be provided by the language [43]. The concrete syntax specifies the grammar of the determined constructs, hence their interconnection and relationships. The concrete syntax can be represented by both textual syntax rules and the language meta-model. Lastly, (formal) semantics are essential to modelling languages in order to provide additional meaning to the language's elements and to prevent ambiguity in their definition. Most importantly, formal semantics are required for model automatization and execution, thus preventing deadlocks or livelocks in the resulting process model [55]. In accordance to [37], the language specification of this framework is divided into two development approaches: The first approach, Design, refers to a design from scratch approach in which a new DSPML is created bottom-up. As a second approach, Modification subsumes applicable methods to tackle language development on the basis of already existing languages. Unification refers to the integration of languages in order to benefit from their combined advantages. Specialization is achieved by restricting certain aspects of the language in order to specialize a given language towards a given purpose or domain [29]. Extension reflects the enhancement of a modelling language in order to obtain larger expressional capabilities (e.g. BPMN extensions provided in [13]). Lastly, Selection requires a partial usage of only a small subset of language constructs [29]. All aforementioned methods represent different design entry points which may also skip the requirements layer. However, all methods provide modifications on the language meta-model, hence the framework underlines their interconnection. Subsequent to the language specification, the definition of process elements and their graphical notation represents the last building block of the language layer. According to [38], relevant elements are associated with the four different perspectives functional, behavioral, informational and organizational when considering process modelling. Within these perspectives, concrete modelling elements need to be deducted from the abstract syntax [31]. Finally, each identified element needs to be assigned to a distinct graphical notation in order to enable the creation of semi-formal process models [17].

Following the language and element specification, the *Evaluation layer* aims at assessing the language against predefined criteria with the overall purpose to identify potential need for refinement and optimization. The initial building block of the evaluation layer refers to the requirements criterion. Here, the specified language needs to be checked against the generic and specific requirements that have been elaborated in the requirements layer. For DSPML analysis, we adhere to approaches proposed in [48]: On the one hand, qualitative and quantitative analyses are applied in order to gather intelligence about the language's applicability and feasibility as well as its profitability, for example via semi-structured interview or surveys [48]. For ontological analysis, the Bunge-Wand-Weber ontology, e.g. [56], can be used to investigate ontological deficits within a specified language grammar [48]. In [57], the capability of process pattern for language evaluation purposes is discussed. Henceforth, a pattern-based analysis, for example using the workflow patterns proposed in [58], is included. Reference and domain models are integrated into a separate building block in order to ensure adherence to domain-specific terms and constructs as well as best practices [59]. Lastly, although not particularly designed towards evaluating process modelling languages, common BPM standards, such as process·model quality frameworks and modelling guidelines, can be applied. Here, the core task is to determine whether a process model resulting from the developed DSPML framework is able to sufficiently fulfill these quality standards. Potential quality deficit in resulting models can thus be treated as hint for wrongly specified language building blocks. Exemplarily frameworks are, for example, the SEQUAL framework [60]. Modelling guidelines to take into consideration encompass for example the7PMG [61]. The results of the evaluation layer pass into the continuous improvement cycle, since all layers are interconnected iteratively. Depending on the detected faults and gaps, improvement can on the requirement as well as language layer.

As carried out in Sect. 2, the proposed DSPML framework is solely limited to the modelling language, hence it does not provide for implementation, application or algorithms. However, modelling tool integration and application are included as potential interfaces for further framework enhancement, directly attached to the deliverables of the language and evaluation layer, as their outputs are likely to be applied, whether the requirements only concern the language specification.

4.3   Evaluation and Discussion

For framework evaluation, we specifically address the criteria internal consistency, clarity and completeness as proposed in [27]. We argue that internal consistency is provided through the DSPML framework being deeply anchored in literature, as a structured literature review served as the foundation for the framework building blocks. Furthermore, additional consistency is given by the framework's alignment to related work in the field of language development, especially to the work of [17], whose development workflow is being closely reflected within the framework. In terms of clarity, we argue that the clear structure and visualization of the framework, thus the ordering of language building blocks and their interconnection, facilitates comprehensibility and understandability of the language development process. Therefore, clarity and transparency is provided. For completeness, we again refer to the extensive literature review that has been conducted, which, to the best of our knowledge, provides an overview over the main components that need to be considered when developing process modelling languages. To further strengthen the argument for completeness, the alignment of the identified requirements from literature with the buildings blocks of our DSPML framework follows.

Meta requirement 1 (Req. 1) is fulfilled by integrating building block Scope and Purpose (1) into the framework as preliminary planning phase. REquation 2 has been divided into multiple building blocks. Whereas building blocks (2) and (3) cover core requirements engineering, (4), (5) and (6) are tailored towards particular, domain-driven requirements. In terms of stakeholder (Req. 3), we decided to integrate a designated building block (6) to embrace the importance of stakeholders to the language development side as well as on the application side. Req. 4 is incorporated in multiple building blocks. First, domain specific relevance is ensured by conducting specific requirements (3) and taking characteristics of the process domain (4) into consideration. These characteristics are directly translated into a corresponding concept directory (7), which is the basis for meta-model development (Req. 5) and process element specification. Req. 6–8 are covered by the inner core of the DSPML meta-model, abstract syntax, concrete syntax and semantics. Req. 9 is considered in building block (2) in an early stage of language development, since pragmatics is closely tied to generic and stakeholder-related requirements. Req. 10 is primarily covered by building block (9), since the language designer can choose between different development approaches. However, the differentiation between Design and Modification also corresponds to this requirement. Regarding Req. 11, specifically building blocks (7) and (9) ensure that each developed languages is to a certain degree built on existing concepts. For once, these concepts can be referred to when determining the concept directory of the intended domain. Additionally, each method in (9) provides that at least one existing language is used as a basis for development. Req. 12 with its corresponding sub-requirements is particularly addressed within the concept directory (7), the meta-model specification (8) and determination of process elements (10). Designing the framework, we refrained from integrating element-specific building blocks ("Process elements", "Control flow Pattern") into the framework to maintain a coherent abstraction level. We argue that these requirements are covered nevertheless, because the abstract syntax specifically address constructs, concepts and elements relevant to the intended application purpose, which is domain-specific process modelling. For Req. 13, building block (10) defines both determinations of process elements as well as their visualization. Regarding Req. 14, the evaluation layer of the framework enables various forms of language assessment, for example via ontological analyses or alignment with domain reference models and process quality standards. While Req. 15–20, refer to actual modelling languages, we argue that the DSPML framework lays the foundation to develop languages that adhere to these requirements: Regarding Req. 15, domain-specific languages are unique per nature, since they are limited to concepts relevant to their particular domain. Additionally, sophisticated requirements analysis, existing work in the concept directory and syntactical and semantical formalizations ensure that there is no language overload and ambiguity. Consistency refers to "a purpose of the design of the language" in a way that this purpose translates through the whole development process [37]. The framework provides a consistent blueprint to language development, since its bottom-up approach ensures the permeation of scope and purpose throughout the development process. Req. 17 is covered by the frameworks abstraction level and domain focus. In terms of Req. 18, requirement analyses with a specific focus on pragmatics as well as the formalization of the language when specifying syntax and semantic ensures that the resulting language is both usable for humans and tools. Similar to Req. 15, Req. 19 is covered by strict adherence to requirements, pragmatics and existing constructs to be used. In addition, the domain-orientation ensures the usage constructs limited to the particular domain. While space economy (Req. 20) is hard to assess, we argue that the consideration of general requirements and pragmatics at an early development stage steer language designers to consider this requirement during their process. The framework is conceptualized iteratively, so that evaluation results and new insights can be integrated into language refinement, thus covering Req. 21. Req. 22 is fulfilled in two ways: First, the modular structure of the framework facilitates its implementation, for instance in a language meta-modelling tool. Second, the modeling language as a result of the framework can be implemented into common process modelling tools, since its meta-model is formalized and processable. For Req. 23, the argumentation of Req. 16 holds. Essentially, the strict usage of concept included in the concept directory as well as the suggested usage of already existing constructs for abstract syntax and element specification ensures a congruent usage of abstractions throughout the development process.

5   Discussion and Conclusion

The DSPML framework presented in this paper consolidates and integrates existing work in the field, and can be applied to systematize and structuring the development of modelling languages tailored towards specific domains or technology, which is an emerging issue in BPM. Hereby, the framework supports language designers in both research and practice, who can draw upon the identified building blocks when developing novel, domain and technology-specific modelling languages. However, limitations have to be considered: First, the framework represents a rather high-level overview over crucial components required for language development. For actual framework application, each building block needs to be detailed with respect to methods or tools (e.g. meta-modelling platform) and substantiated regarding its content. Second, at this point the framework is limited to the mere modelling language without addressing application, modelling software integration or algorithms. However, the stated areas pose additional challenges and requirements to the development of modelling languages that are not yet reflected in the model. Furthermore, only a descriptive evaluation is proposed. Applying the framework in practice may reveal different requirements that have not yet been considered. Subsequently, the artifact and its evaluation as well as the outlined limitations open up new possibilities for further research need: On the one hand, further work need to specify and substantiate each building block in detail regarding processed input and output as well as applied methodologies or tool support. On the other hand, the application of the framework in research and practice to develop domain-specific languages will reveal valuable insights to be incorporated into a subsequent DS iteration. An elaborate ex-post evaluation against DSPML quality or usability criteria as well as the degree of domain coverage may reveal the framework's applicability from both the language designer and resulting modelling language perspective. Furthermore, future work may enhance the framework by taking the structure and specific characteristics of existing modeling languages into account. Lastly, tool support that implements all layers of the framework with appropriate features and software components proves to be a fruitful expansion of the research presented.

Adhering to the applied DS methodology, this paper motivates the topic and provides a problem statement. Following a brief introduction of fundamentals, the results of an extensive literature review are condensed into 23 design requirements that lay ground for DSPML framework design. The evaluation demonstrates that the framework sufficiently addresses the needs expressed in relevant literature. Using the proposed artifact, the engineering of domain-specific process modelling languages can be methodologically grounded, which structures and systematizes the development process. Ultimately, this leads to an increased adequacy and quality of resulting languages, which need to be designed towards increasingly complex requirements driven by domain, technology and end-user.

References

1. Melenovsky, M.J.: Business process management's success hinges on business-led initiatives. Gart. Res. 1–6 (2005). https://www.gartner.com/doc/483847/business-process-managements-success-hinges
2. Becker, J., Mathas, C., Winkelmann, A.: Geschäftsprozessmanagement. Springer, Heidelberg (2009)
3. Eggersmann, M., Krobb, C., Marquardt, W.: A modeling language for design processes in chemical engineering. In: Laender, A.H.F., Liddle, S.W., Storey, V.C. (eds.) ER 2000. LNCS, vol. 1920, pp. 369–382. Springer, Heidelberg (2000). doi:10.1007/3-540-45393-8_27
4. Becker, J., Breuker, D., Weiß, B., Winkelmann, A.: Exploring the status quo of business process modelling languages in the banking sector – an empirical insight into the usage of methods in banks. In: ACIS 2010 Proceedings, Paper 8 (2010)
5. Harmon, P., Wolf, C.: The State of Business Process Management (2016)
6. Heitkötter, H.: A framework for creating domain-specific process modeling languages. In: 7th International Conference on Software Paradigm Trends (ICSOFT), Rome, Italy, pp. 127–136 (2012)
7. Houy, C., Fettke, P., Loos, P., Aalst, W.M.P., Krogstie, J.: Business process management in the large. Bus. Inf. Syst. Eng. **3**, 385–388 (2011)
8. Frank, U.: Some guidelines for the conception of domain-specific modelling languages. In: Proceedings of the 4th International Workshop on Enterprise Modelling and Information Systems Architectures, EMISA 2011, Hamburg, Germany, 22–23 September 2011, pp. 93–106 (2011)
9. Weske, M.: Business Process Management. Springer, Heidelberg (2012)
10. List, B., Korherr, B.: An evaluation of conceptual business process modelling languages. In: 2006 ACM Symposium on Applied Computing, pp. 1532–1539 (2006)

11. Lu, R., Sadiq, S.: A survey of comparative business process modeling approaches. In: Abramowicz, W. (ed.) BIS 2007. LNCS, vol. 4439, pp. 82–94. Springer, Heidelberg (2007). doi:10.1007/978-3-540-72035-5_7
12. Riehle, D.M., Jannaber, S., Karhof, A., Thomas, O., Delfmann, P., Becker, J.: On the de-facto standard of event-driven process chains: how EPC is defined in literature. In: Modellierung 2016, Karlsruhe, 2–4 März 2016, pp. 61–76. Köllen Druck+Verlag, Bonn (2016)
13. Braun, R., Esswein, W.: Classification of domain-specific BPMN extensions. In: Frank, U., Loucopoulos, P., Pastor, Ó., Petrounias, I. (eds.) PoEM 2014. LNBIP, vol. 197, pp. 42–57. Springer, Heidelberg (2014). doi:10.1007/978-3-662-45501-2_4
14. Object Management Group: Business Process Model and Notation (BPMN) Version 2.0 (2011). http://www.omg.org/spec/BPMN/2.0
15. Thomas, O.: Fuzzy Process Engineering. Gabler Verlag | GWV Fachverlage GmbH, Wiesbaden (2009)
16. Becker, J., Riehle, D.M., Clever, N.: Ansätze zur Unternehmensmodellierung – Eine Einordnung. In: Benker, T., Jürck, C., Wolf, M. (eds.) Geschäftsprozessorientierte Systementwicklung — Von der Unternehmensarchitektur zum IT-System, pp. 415–425. Springer, Wiesbaden (2016). doi:10.1007/978-3-658-14826-3_25
17. Frank, U.: Domain-specific modeling languages: requirements analysis and design guidelines. In: Reinhartz-Berger, I., Sturm, A., Clark, T., Cohen, S., Bettin, J. (eds.) Domain Engineering: Product Lines, Languages, and Conceptual Models, pp. 133–157. Springer, Heidelberg (2013)
18. Becker, J., Algermissen, L., Falk, T.: Prozessorientierte Verwaltungsmodernisierung: Prozessmanagement im Zeitalter von E-Government und New Public Management. Springer, Dordrecht (2009)
19. Karsai, G., Krahn, H., Pinkernell, C., Rumpe, B., Schindler, M., Völkel, S.: Design guidelines for domain specific languages. In: Proceedings of the 9th OOPSLA Workshop on Domain-Specific Modelling (2009)
20. Hevner, A.R., March, S.T., Park, J., Ram, S.: Design science in information research. MIS Q. **28**, 75–105 (2004)
21. March, S.T., Storey, V.C.: Design science in the information systems discipline: an introduction to the special issue on design science research. MIS Q. **32**, 725–730 (2008)
22. Peffers, K., Tuunanen, T., Gengler, C.E., Rossi, M., Hui, W., Virtanen, V., Bragge, J.: The design science research process: a model for producing and presenting information systems research. In: Proceedings of the First International Conference on Design Science Research in Information Systems and Technology, DESRIST 2006, vol. 24, pp. 83–106 (2006)
23. March, S.T., Smith, G.F.: Design and natural science research on information technology. Decis. Support Syst. **15**, 251–266 (1995)
24. Hevner, A.R.: A three cycle view of design science research. Scand. J. Inf. Syst. **19**, 87–92 (2007)
25. Peffers, K., Tuunanen, T., Rothenberger, M.A., Chatterjee, S.: A design science research methodology for information systems research. J. Manag. Inf. Syst. **24**, 45–77 (2008)
26. Wieringa, R.: DS as nested problem solving. In: Proceedings of the 4th International Conference on Design Science Research in Information Systems and Technology, DESRIST 2009, Philadelphia, Pennsylvania (2009)
27. Sonnenberg, C., vom Brocke, J.: Reconsidering the Build-Evaluate Pattern in Design Science Research. In: Proceedings of 7th Design Science Research in Information Systems and Technology, pp. 381–397 (2012)

28. vom Brocke, J.M., Simons, A., Niehaves, B., Riemer, K., Plattfaut, R., Cleven, A.: Reconstructing the giant: on the importance of rigour in documenting the literature search process. In: 17th European Conference on Information Systems, Verona, Italy, pp. 1–13 (2013)
29. Mernik, M., Heering, J., Sloane, A.M.: When and how to develop domain-specific languages. ACM Comput. Surv. **37**, 316–344 (2005)
30. Cho, H., Gray, J., Sun, Y., White, J.: Key challenges for modeling language creation by demonstration. In: ICSE 2011 Workshop on Flexible Modeling Tools, pp. 1–4 (2011)
31. Lin, F.-R., Yang, M.-C., Yu-Hua, P.: A generic structure for business process modeling. Bus. Process Manag. J. **8**, 19–41 (2002)
32. Clark, T., Sammut, P., Willans, J.: Applied Metamodelling. A Foundaton for Language Driven Development (2008)
33. Klör, B., Bräuer, S., Beverungen, D., Monhof, M.: A domain-specific modeling language for electric vehicle batteries. In: Wirtschaftsinformatik Proceedings 2015 (2015)
34. Casanova-Brito, V., Patig, S.: Requirements of process modeling languages – results from an empirical investigation. In: Wirtschaftsinformatik Proceedings 2011, pp. 756–765 (2011)
35. Zamli, K.Z., Ashidi, N., Isa, M.: A survey and analysis of process modeling languages. Malays. J. Comput. Sci. **17**, 68–89 (2004)
36. Seel, C.: Reverse Method Engineering: Methode und Softwareunterstützung zur Konstruktion und Adaption semiformaler Informationsmodellierungstechnikcn. Logos Verlag, Berlin (2010)
37. Paige, R.F., Ostroff, J.S., Brooke, P.J.: Principles for modeling language design. Inf. Softw. Technol. **42**, 665–675 (2000)
38. Curtis, B., Kellner, M.I., Over, J.: Process modeling. Commun. ACM **35**, 75–90 (1992)
39. de Cesare, S., Serrano, A.: Collaborative modeling using UML and business process simulation. In: Proceedings of the 39th Annual Hawaii International Conference on System Sciences (HICSS 2006), pp. 1–10 (2006)
40. Derniame, J.-C., Kaba, B.A., Wastell, D.: The software process: modelling and technology. In: Derniame, J.-C., Kaba, B.A., Wastell, D. (eds.) Software Process: Principles, Methodology, and Technology. LNCS, vol. 1500, pp. 1–13. Springer, Heidelberg (1999). doi:10.1007/3-540-49205-4_1
41. Chou, S.-C.: A process modeling language consisting of high level UML diagrams and low level process language. J. Object Technol. **1**, 137–163 (2002)
42. Figl, K., Mendling, J., Strembeck, M., Recker, J.: On the cognitive effectiveness of routing symbols in process modeling languages. In: Abramowicz, W., Tolksdorf, R. (eds.) BIS 2010. LNBIP, vol. 47, pp. 230–241. Springer, Heidelberg (2010). doi:10.1007/978-3-642-12814-1_20
43. Pichler, H., Eder, J.: Business process modeling and workflow design. In: Embley, D.W., Thalheim, B. (eds.) Handbook of Conceptual Modeling, pp. 259–286. Springer, Heidelberg (2011)
44. Wohed, P., van der Aalst, W.M.P., Dumas, M., ter Hofstede, A.H.M., Russell, N.: On the suitability of BPMN for business process modelling. In: Dustdar, S., Fiadeiro, J.L., Sheth, A.P. (eds.) BPM 2006. LNCS, vol. 4102, pp. 161–176. Springer, Heidelberg (2006). doi:10.1007/11841760_12
45. Schmidt, G., Braun, O.: Process language GPN. In: Bernus, P., Mertins, K., Schmidt, G. (eds.) Handbook on Architectures of Information Systems, pp. 197–214. Springer, Heidelberg (2006)

46. van Hee, K.M., Sidorova, N., van der Werf, J.M.: Business process modeling using petri nets. In: Jensen, K., Aalst, W.M.P., Balbo, G., Koutny, M., Wolf, K. (eds.) Transactions on Petri Nets and Other Models of Concurrency VII. LNCS, vol. 7480, pp. 116–161. Springer, Heidelberg (2013). doi:10.1007/978-3-642-38143-0_4
47. Schalles, C., Creagh, J., Rebstock, M.: A causal model for analyzing the impact of graphical modeling languages on usability. Int. J. Softw. Eng. Knowl. Eng. 24, 1337–1355 (2014)
48. Recker, J.: Evaluations of Process Modeling Grammars: Ontological, Qualitative and Quantitative Analyses Using the Example of BPMN. Springer, Heidelberg (2011)
49. Conradi, R., Liu, C.: Process modelling languages: one or many? In: Schäfer, W. (ed.) EWSPT 1995. LNCS, vol. 913, pp. 98–118. Springer, Heidelberg (1995). doi:10.1007/3-540-59205-9_47
50. Atkinson, D.C., Weeks, D.C., Noll, J.: The design of evolutionary process modeling languages. In: 11th Asia-Pacific Software Engineering Conference, pp. 73–82 (2004)
51. Luo, W., Tung, Y.A.: A framework for selecting business process modeling methods. Ind. Manag. Data Syst. 99, 312–319 (1999)
52. Kolb, J., Rudner, B., Reichert, M.: Towards gesture-based process modeling on multi-touch devices. In: Bajec, M., Eder, J. (eds.) CAiSE 2012. LNBIP, vol. 112, pp. 280–293. Springer, Heidelberg (2012). doi:10.1007/978-3-642-31069-0_24
53. Metzger, D., Niemöller, C., Berkemeier, L., Brenning, L., Thomas, O.: Vom Techniker zum Modellierer - Konzeption und Entwicklung eines Smart Glasses Systems zur Laufzeitmodellierung von Dienstleistungsprozessen. In: Thomas, O., Nüttgens, M., Fellmann, M. (eds.) Smart Service Engineering, pp. 193–213. Springer, Heidelberg (2017)
54. Recker, J.: Opportunities and constraints: the current struggle with BPMN. Bus. Process Manag. J. 16, 181–201 (2010)
55. Fellmann, M., Bittmann, S., Karhof, A., Stolze, C., Thomas, O.: Do we need a standard for EPC modelling? The state of syntactic, semantic and pragmatic quality. Lecture Notes Informatics (LNI), vol. P-222, pp. 103–117. Gesellschaft fur Inform (2013)
56. Wand, Y., Weber, R.: On the ontological expressiveness of information systems analysis and design grammars. Inf. Syst. J. 3, 217–237 (1993)
57. Recker, J., Rosemann, M., Krogstie, J.: Ontology- versus pattern-based evaluation of process modeling languages: a comparison. Commun. AIS. 20, 774–799 (2007)
58. van der Aalst, W.M.P., ter Hofstede, A.H.M., Kiepuszewski, B., Barros, A.P.: Workflow patterns. Distrib. Parallel Databases 14, 5–51 (2003)
59. La Rosa, M., Gottschalk, F., Dumas, M., Van Der Aalst, W.M.P.: Linking domain models and process models for reference model configuration. In: Hofstede, A., Benatallah, B., Paik, H.-Y. (eds.) BPM 2007. LNCS, vol. 4928, pp. 417–430. Springer, Heidelberg (2008). doi:10.1007/978-3-540-78238-4_43
60. Krogstie, J., Sindre, G., Jørgensen, H.: Process models representing knowledge for action: a revised quality framework. Eur. J. Inf. Syst. 15, 91–102 (2006)
61. Mendling, J., Reijers, H.A., van der Aalst, W.M.P.: Seven process modeling guidelines (7PMG). Inf. Softw. Technol. 52(2), 127–136 (2010)

DSR in Human Computer Interaction

Analysis and Design of an mHealth Intervention for Community-Based Health Education: An Empirical Evidence of Coronary Heart Disease Prevention Program Among Working Adults

Hoang D. Nguyen[1]([✉]), Danny Chiang Choon Poo[1], Hui Zhang[2], and Wenru Wang[2]

[1] Department of Information Systems, School of Computing, National University of Singapore, Singapore, Singapore
{hoangnguyen, dpoo}@comp.nus.edu.sg
[2] Alice Lee Centre for Nursing Studies, Yong Loo Lin School of Medicine, National University of Singapore, Singapore, Singapore
{nurzh, nurww}@nus.edu.sg

Abstract. The massive expansion of mobile technologies is leading to a digital revolution that is reshaping health education for improved population-level health outcomes. This study investigated the analysis and design of a mobile health (mHealth) intervention for community-wide education. Hence, we employed a design science approach capable of translating health and community activities into practical design guidelines for suitable interventions to improve knowledge and skills among working adults. An mHealth artifact was developed for a Coronary Heart Disease (CHD) prevention program on awareness, knowledge, stress and lifestyle management. The effectiveness of the artifact was demonstrated through a pilot randomized, controlled trial (RCT) with 80 participants as an imperative empirical evidence. The study, therefore, contributed to the cumulative theoretical development of HCI, mobile health, and public health education. Moreover, our findings provided a number of insights for academic bodies, health practitioners, and developers of mobile health in planning educational interventions for smartphone users.

Keywords: Mobile health (mHealth) · Community-based intervention · Health education · Coronary Heart Diseases (CHD) · Randomized controlled trial (RCT)

1 Introduction

The increasing ubiquity of mobile health (mHealth) technologies is transforming healthcare services for wider reach, improved health outcomes, and reduced financial burdens of health systems worldwide. By 2018, mHealth promises to extend its coverage to 1.7 billion people for mobile-based interventions [1]. Such interventions have been extensively studied as viable for chronic disease management [2–4], and health promotion [5–7].

© Springer International Publishing AG 2017
A. Maedche et al. (Eds.): DESRIST 2017, LNCS 10243, pp. 57–72, 2017.
DOI: 10.1007/978-3-319-59144-5_4

The current trends emphasize community-based interventions as the primary approach for achieving community-wide changes in health and risk behaviors. In spite of great efforts in community-based programs (e.g. Minnesota Heart Health Program, Stanford Five-City Projects…), modest population-level impacts were previously discussed [8, 9]. There was the lack of tools with customizations to penetrate every corner of the community for better outcomes [10]. Therefore, this research employed a design science approach to developing an mHealth intervention for community-based education to address such issue. By removing both geographical and temporal constraints, the use of mobile applications (apps) is the next suitable wave of health education support artifacts to extend social and technical boundaries towards personalized interventions. Furthermore, the study established theoretical foundations capable of translating health practices into practical design guidelines for community-based interventions.

As an empirical evidence, a pilot randomized, controlled trial (RCT) was conducted for a Coronary Heart Disease (CHD) Prevention Program. This community-based program successfully demonstrated the effectiveness of an mHealth intervention for improved CHD knowledge and stress levels among working adults.

Based on theoretical and practical groundwork, our study contributed to the cumulative theoretical development of mobile health and community-based health education. It provided a principled guideline to analysis and design of mHealth artifacts for academic bodies, health practitioners, and developers of mHealth.

The structure of the paper is as follows. Firstly, we described the literature background of our study in the next section. Secondly, the analysis of an mHealth intervention for community-based health education was discussed. And then, the paper illustrated the design concepts of our mHealth intervention. Fourthly, an RCT, in which 80 working adults were randomized to either the control group (n = 40) or the intervention group (n = 40), was presented with great details. Lastly, we concluded our paper with findings and contributions of the research in the final section.

2 Literature Background

2.1 Mobile Health (mHealth)

The rapid advancement of mobile technologies has paved the path for new health interventions, "mobile health" or "mHealth" [11]. It is broadly defined as "the use of mobile computing and communication technologies in healthcare and public health" [12] which is capable of delivering health services to a huge number of people as well as large communities. With the prevalence of over 6 billion smartphone users [13], mHealth has been introduced into a variety of activities such as disease management and prevention [14–16], care surveillance [17–19] and instructional interventions [16, 20] anytime and anywhere. In 2015, 44% of patients worldwide had witnessed the use of mobile devices by clinicians in healthcare processes [21].

With the significant advantages of usability and mobility [2, 22], mHealth apps are promising to penetrate broad communities to achieve public health impacts.

2.2   Community-Based Health Education

Community-based programs have been originally shaped in the 1980s when synergistic interaction effects were observed with the cost-effective mass media and communication channels [23]. Since then, the development of community-based health education has been gradually progressed beyond individual levels to provide population-wide strategies for targeting entire communities including large cohorts at different levels of risks [24]. Such programs were integrated and wide-ranging, not limited to geographic areas (e.g., worksites, medical care settings, schools, or organizations), and are targeted at diverse communities characterized by patterns of behavior (e.g., Internet chat rooms or smartphone users), experience (e.g., heart attack survivors), or norms and values (e.g., a culture of working population) [25]. Notably, the National Heart, Lung, and Blood Institute (NHLBI) has demonstrated three community-wide health education interventions: (i) the Minnesota Heart Health Program, (ii) the Stanford Five-City Project and, (iii) the Pawtucket Heart Health Program. These projects were rigorously designed to deliver community education sessions to promote healthy lifestyles and to reduce risks of cardiovascular diseases at a population level [26]. Nevertheless, Merzel and D'Afflitti [10] argued that the projects have several limiting factors such as insufficient tailoring capability to reach sub-segments of communities and inadequate community penetration to attain population-wide impacts. To bridge the gap between health educators and the population, this study proposed the analysis and design of an mHealth intervention for community-based health education.

Besides, using science-based materials, resources, and program structures of the NHLBI projects, a logic model for community education strategy was suggested by Hurtado et al. [27]. It described four main activities: (i) recruiting community members, (ii) identifying participants for health education, (iii) assessing participant knowledge and behaviors based on established instruments and measures, and (iv) conducting education sessions using educational materials and teaching tools. In this research, these activities are investigated to implement a community-wide intervention with customizable education programs.

3   Analysis of an mHealth Intervention for Community-Based Health Education

This study is a design science research (DSR) situated in the field of Human-Computer Interaction (HCI) in which the ways that people interact with mobile technologies are analyzed in order to design new artifacts [28]. It employed a theoretical framework as described by Nguyen and Poo [29] in Fig. 1 to comprehend mHealth interventions for community-based health education [27].

Grounded in Activity Theory [30] and Mobile Learning [31], such intervention is scrutinized as a collective activity system in which mobile devices are interactive agents capable of communicating with participants to deliver tailored health as well as behavioral knowledge and resources. The following components are constructed from the theoretical framework.

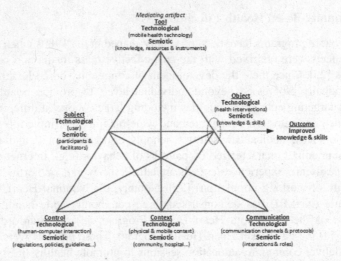

Fig. 1. Analysis and design framework for mHealth interventions [29]

(1) *Subject.* Two key roles are identified in community-based health education: participants who undertake interventions, and facilitators who enable interventions.

(2) *Object.* The primary objective is to provide educational interventions to improve knowledge and to develop behavior-change skills.

(3) *Tool.* It is a vital companion of community-based delivery via mobile devices. Mobile apps have excellent capabilities to facilitate health education activities [32, 33].

(4) *Control.* Full control over community-based program structures and information sharing are integrated into mHealth interventions.

(5) *Context.* Both locational and temporal constraints have been removed in the environment of mobile health. Communities can be virtually defined based on patterns of behavior or other factors.

(6) *Communication.* The use of mobile technologies empowers the participants with different forms of communication such as e-mail, short message service (SMS), and push notifications.

(7) *Outcome.* The outcome is a transformation of participants' knowledge and skills to modify behaviors and to reduce the individual risks at different levels.

Engagement between people and mobile technology develops meanings and objectives of these activity sub-systems; therefore, analyzing the complexity of community-based education entails operationalization of the dialectical relationship between people and technology as semiotic and technological aspects. Both perspectives are considered in details to improve participants' knowledge and skills as shown in Table 1.

Table 1. Analysis of mHealth interventions for community-based health education

Component	Semiotic perspective	Technological perspective
Subject	*Participants*: individuals, families, and social networks who undertake the mHealth interventions *Facilitators*: healthcare practitioners, community volunteers, and training agents who facilitate mHealth interventions	• Mobile devices (e.g., iPhone, iPad, Samsung Galaxy phones and tablets…) • Mobile applications for mHealth interventions
Object	*Participants*: • Knowledge and skills to be learned by health experts/facilitator • Achievements of program objectives • Applications and reinforcement of knowledge and skills *Facilitators*: • Ability to impart knowledge and skills to participants • Setup of program objectives • Assessment of participants' progress and achievements	• Mobile-enabled health education programs • Mobile-based subject-matter contents • High portability, availability and accessibility to knowledge and resources
Tool	• Knowledge and skill development resources • Multimedia for health education (e.g., videos, audios, and interactive formats) • Geographically agnostic program and content delivery environment • Alert and reminding mechanisms	• Device-independent capabilities on mobile devices • Mobile based health artifacts • Knowledge and skills assessment tools • Offline synchronization of programs and contents
Control	• Structured educational programs with objectives and guided steps • Enrolment and involvement in health education programs. • Control of intervention tools	• User-friendly and responsive design for multiple display resolutions • Individual and community-based access and privacy control • Longitudinal and activity tracking
Context	• Locational and temporal independent • Disease-specific communities • Multi-community participation	• Role-based management • Individual and community-based coordination • Geolocation services
Communication	• Locational and temporal independent • One-to-one communication between facilitators and participants • Community-based communications for health education • Information sharing and remote tracking	• Mobile communications (e.g., 4G, 3G, GPRS…) • Messaging via Short Message Service (SMS), email, and push notifications • Robust content and message delivery structure

4   Designing an mHealth Artifact for Community-Based Health Education

Based on the analysis of the mHealth intervention for health education, we proposed an mHealth platform as an IT artifact. It aims to bring community-based health education to the next level where programs and contents can be prepared for delivery via smartphones.

4.1   System Architecture

We designed our mHealth artifact with two major sub-systems: (i) a cloud-based service platform, (ii) mobile apps for health education. Figure 2 demonstrates the overall architecture of the mHealth platform.

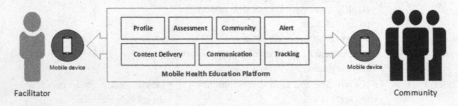

Fig. 2. Overall architecture of mHealth education platform

The cloud-based service platform leverages on an enterprise system architecture for developing and deploying modular and extensible modules and applications. It comprises of multiple services: profile and personalization, program and content delivery, assessment and tools, community management, communication and notifications, alerts and reminders, and tracking. These services expose RESTful interfaces to provide interoperability between cloud-based backbone framework and mobile apps.

4.2   Design Concepts of an mHealth Artifact for Community-Based Education

Leveraged on the proposed system architecture, the key design concepts of our mHealth artifact are highlighted as the following.

Profile Personalization. The mHealth intervention begins with facilitators inviting participants to join their health education program. Once invited, the participants are provided with the links in Apple AppStore and Google Play to download and to install the mHealth app. Upon completion of a self-enrolment process, the participant is automatically associated with a specific community and the health education program based on essential profile data. Furthermore, user preferences are captured for customization and tracking of program objectives and progress.

Program and Content Delivery. The mobile apps have capabilities of receiving dynamic community-specific programs and content packages during its loading process. A community-based education program is designed as a hierarchical collection of program objectives and sub-objectives; hence, participants' achievements are reflected in a detailed and structured manner during the intervention. Mobile-based subject-matter contents and media are presented with intuitive navigations in various display form factors and orientations. Offline synchronization features allow participants to view these always-at-hand knowledge and skill building resources. Figure 3 shows the screens of our mobile apps for the CHD prevention program with the multi-level program structure and learning resources.

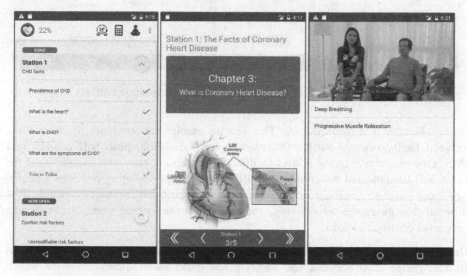

Fig. 3. Program and content delivery screens for CHD prevention program

Health and Assessment Tools. Tools play a critical role to facilitate the subjects to achieve objectives in mHealth interventions. The implementation of health and assessment tools in mobile apps, therefore, is necessary for educational activities. Community facilitators can employ such tool for knowledge assessment and disease-specific instruments. For instance, BMI, risk prediction of heart attack or coronary death, and calories consumption calculators are introduced in the CHD prevention program to raise awareness and modify lifestyle behaviors of the participants as illustrated in Fig. 4.

Activity Tracking. The mobile app is capable of tracking participants' activities, even in the absence of network connectivity. It employs view tracking technologies to capture movements and reading patterns in mobile screens, as well as uploads the de-identified data to the cloud-based service whenever the network is available. Such data are useful for facilitators to keep track of participants' progress and levels of involvement within the programs.

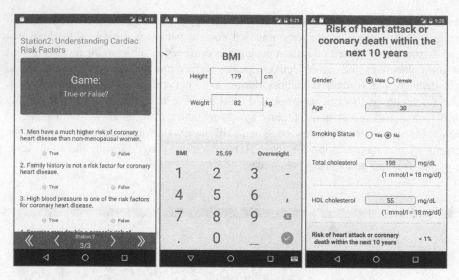

Fig. 4. Health and assessment tools for CHD prevention program

Communication and Notifications. This feature enables various types of interactions between facilitators and participants over in-app messaging, push notifications, and SMS. One-to-one messaging allows facilitators to keep in touch with an individual for direct and personalized intervention; while one-to-many messaging provides a necessary mechanism to reach out to a community, or specific sub-community groups. It is imperative to guarantee the delivery, and to monitor the reading status such message for useful communications.

Alerts and Reminders. The mHealth intervention offers alerts and reminders as tools for knowledge reinforcement and lifestyle modifications in community-wide health education. These tools aid facilitators to schedule multiple reminders tailoring to individuals and community members based on their profile data.

5   Coronary Heart Disease Prevention Program Among Working Adults

Coronary Heart Disease (CHD) is the most common type of Cardiovascular Disease (CVD), which has been long recognized as a major problem for public health [34]. It is predicted to be responsible for a total of 11.1 million deaths worldwide in 2020, and to remain as the top cause of death for next 20 years [35]. CHD is a result of lipid accumulation in coronary arteries which narrows blood flow and increase the risks of heart attacks and stroke [36]. Such risk causes detrimental impacts on the adult workforces leading to lower work performance, reduced income, and job insecure due to restricted work capacity [37]. With high rates of deaths and hospitalization found in many countries [27, 38, 39], CHD has become a bulky burden on the economies of working adults and existing healthcare systems.

Our empirical study was designed to evaluate the effectiveness of the proposed mHealth artifact for CHD prevention program in a community of working adults in Singapore. A comprehensive 4-week program was developed comprising a multi-level program structure, learning objectives, heart health assessment tools, and supporting materials [40]. There are four learning stations: (i) the facts about CHD, its prevalence in the community, and common signs and symptoms of CHD; (ii) the cardiac risks factors: non-modifiable and modifiable; (iii) the healthy lifestyle including balancing diet, physical exercise, regular health monitoring, and smoking cessation (for smokers); and (iv) the techniques for stress management. In addition, two educational videos for deep breathing exercise and progressive muscle relaxation were included in the mHealth intervention. Moreover, self-assessment calculators such as body mass index (BMI), daily calories, and CHD risk prediction for next 10 years were incorporated into the mobile apps. Figure 5 demonstrates the structure of the CHD prevention program and contents.

Facilitators of the CHD prevention program were cardio-trained practitioner nurses and research assistants who remotely coordinated the participants throughout the program. A 20-min briefing session was provided at the beginning of the mHealth intervention.

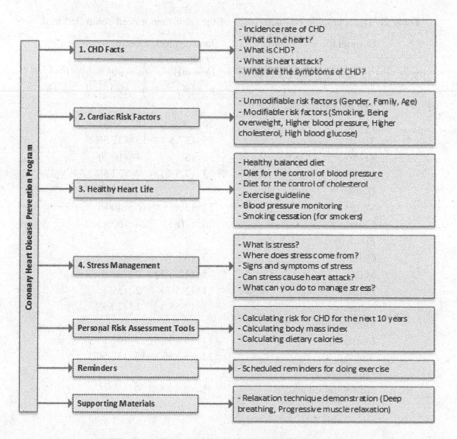

Fig. 5. CHD prevention program and contents

5.1   Empirical Settings

This study adopted a pilot randomized, controlled trial (RCT) in which participants were recruited from the working population via poster advertisements. They were full-time workers aged between 21 to 65 years old. As the mHealth artifact was developed in English, using smartphones in daily activities and understanding the language are compulsory criteria. The study excluded individuals who: (i) had a clinical history of heart-related diseases, (ii) worked in health-relevant institutions, (iii) had reading difficulties. The sample size of 80 was used in the RCT with 40 participants in a control group and 40 participants in an intervention group as suggested in previous work [41]. The mHealth intervention was offered to the participants of the intervention group; while, the control group was provided with web links to heart education materials for self-exploratory learning.

There were 60 participants (77.5%) aged between 21 and 40 years old, and 61 participants are Chinese (76.3%). Majority of the participants were female (n = 52, 65.0%), had less than 10 years of professional experience (n = 46, 57.6%), and married (n = 42, 52.5%). Table 2 reports the demographic characteristics of both the intervention group and the control group.

Table 2. Demographic characteristics of the pilot randomized controlled trial

Demographic variable	Intervention group (n = 40)		Control group (n = 40)	
	n	(%)	n	(%)
Age (years)				
21–30	20	(50%)	14	(35%)
31–40	15	(37.5%)	13	(32.5%)
41–50	2	(5%)	4	(10%)
51–65	3	(7.5%)	9	(22.5%)
Gender				
Male	12	(30%)	16	(40%)
Female	28	(70%)	24	(60%)
Ethnicity				
Chinese	33	(82.5%)	28	(70%)
Malay	5	(12.5%)	9	(22.5%)
Indian	1	(2.5%)	2	(5%)
Others	1	(2.5%)	1	(2.5%)
Marital status				
Married	17	(42.5%)	25	(62.5%)
Single	23	(57.5%)	15	(37.5%)
Education				
No formal education	1	(2.5%)	0	

(continued)

Table 2. (*continued*)

Demographic variable	Intervention group (n = 40)		Control group (n = 40)	
	n	(%)	n	(%)
Secondary School	7	(17.5%)	10	(25%)
ITE/Polytechnic/Junior College	16	(40%)	12	(30%)
University	16	(40%)	18	(45%)
Occupation				
Admin/Clerical	6	15%	6	(15%)
IT/Engineering	19	47.5%	16	(40%)
Teaching	1	2.5%	2	(5%)
Others	14	35%	16	(40%)
Years of working				
<5	17	(42.5%)	10	(25%)
5–10	9	(22.5%)	10	(25%)
11–20	11	(27.5%)	10	(25%)
21–30	1	(2.5%)	6	(15%)
31–50	2	(5.0%)	4	(10%)
Family history of CHD				
Yes	1	(2.5%)	4	(10%)
No	39	(97.5%)	36	(90%)

5.2 Instruments and Measures

Three questionnaires and outcome measures were employed in the study: (i) Social-demographic information questionnaire, (ii) Heart Disease Fact Questionnaire-2 (HDFQ-2), and (iii) Perceived Stress Scale-10 item (PSS-10).

Social-Demographic Information Questionnaire. The demographic characteristics of participants including gender, age group, marital status, ethnicity, occupation, and education were collected.

Heart Disease Fact Questionnaire-2 (HDFQ-2). A 25-item questionnaire of yes/no questions was utilized to assess the participants' knowledge of CHD risk factors (e.g., gender, age, family history, and heart-related lifestyles). A maximum of 25 points for each participant was calculated with 1-point for each correctly-answered question. The HDFQ-2 has adequate readability [42] and good internal reliability with Cronbach's alpha of 0.84 [43].

Perceived Stress Scale-10 Item (PSS-10). A 10-item instrument for measuring participants' stress level. It uses a 5-point Likert scale with higher score hinting greater stress level during the 4-week program. The PSS-10 score ranges between 10 to 50 self-reported by the participants. An acceptable internal consistency (Cronbach's alpha > 0.8) has been discussed in previous works [44, 45].

5.3   Evaluation and Discussion

The collected data of 80 working adults were analyzed using IBM Statistical Package for the Social Sciences (SPSS) 21.0.

The pilot RCT encompassed two factors: the within-subjects factor is time with two levels (baseline and 4-week intervention), and the between-subjects factor is an intervention (yes for the intervention group, and no for the control group). Mixed ANOVA models were employed to compare the mean differences of CHD knowledge between the two groups based on these factors. Figure 6 illustrates the effects of these factors on CHD knowledge and stress level.

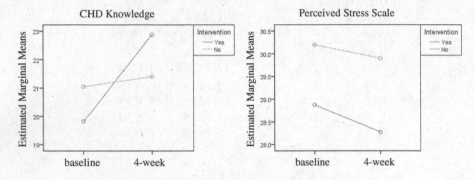

Fig. 6. Profile plots for HDFQ-2 score and PSS-10 scale

In terms of CHD knowledge, a significant difference across the two time points was identified where $F(1,78) = 27.37$, $p < 0.05$; but there was no significant differences between the groups with $F(1,78) = 0.94$, $p > 0.05$. Importantly, there was a significant interaction between time and intervention, $F(1,78) = 17.26$, $p < 0.05$ which was observable in Fig. 6. The follow-up examination of the interaction effect corrected with Bonferroni showed the following simple main effects: (i) for the intervention group, the 4-week mHealth intervention led to higher CHD knowledge than at the baseline ($F(1,78) = 44.04$, $p < 0,05$); while (ii) for the control group, the 4-week exploratory learning had no effect with $F(1,78) = 0.58$, $p > 0.05$.

For the PSS-10 score, the study utilized Chi-square tests to examine the effects of nonparametric distributions. There was no significant difference between the two groups at the baseline ($p = 0.218 > 0.05$); however, a significant difference between the two groups was identified after the 4-week intervention ($p = 0.038 < 0.05$). Figure 6 demonstrated the lower stress level in the intervention group after the intervention.

The study results provided empirical evidence on the effectiveness of the mHealth artifact for CHD prevention program. This education program is associated with significant improvements in CHD knowledge in the community of working adults for those who used the proposed mHealth mobile apps. Moreover, a lower level of stress was reported after the program which hints to the constructive effects of contents, tools and supporting materials on stress management.

6 Conclusion

The success of community-based health education greatly depends on educational program planning and design, as well as, the coordination between facilitators and participants which are being empowered by mHealth technologies. This study proposed a DSR approach to developing an effective artifact for such education program via mobile devices. A comprehensive set of design concepts for mHealth interventions was introduced to facilitate the community-wide process of knowledge and skills building. Moreover, the effectiveness of such mobile-based artifact was empirically demonstrated through a pilot randomized, controlled trial of a 4-week CHD prevention program. Improvements in CHD knowledge and stress management among working adults in Singapore have been found as the evidence for feasible community-based mobile health education.

This study contributed to the cumulative theoretical development of mobile health, and community-based health education in three folds. First, the relationship between mHealth innovations and health education was evidently highlighted to make clear the requirements for a theoretical discourse. Second, the proposed approach was capable of analyzing and designing health education programs for any types of communities in the direction of social learning. Last but not least, the study took one step further in advancing mHealth with an empirical evidence of effective mobile-enabled community-based health education.

There are multiple implications for developers of mobile-based health interventions. The study developed a holistic approach to system analysis and design of mHealth apps of community-based health education. Furthermore, its findings on semiotic and technological requirements are well-informed and practical for developing mobile-based education programs and contents.

This paper is not without limitations. It adopted the sampling method for pilot research which limits the external validity of the study. Besides, short-period effects were detected; however, long-term effects of such mobile-based interventions should be evaluated in future research. In this pilot RCT, monetary reimbursements were provided to prevent dropouts; nevertheless, changes in initiatives, incentive structures, regulations, and policies are required to establish effective community-based health education in the long-run.

Acknowledgement. This study is funded by a grant from Singapore Heart Foundation (grant number: RG2013/02).

References

1. Research2guidance: Global mobile health trends and figures market report 2013–2017. http://www.research2guidance.com/shop/index.php/mobile-health-trends-and-figures-2013-2017
2. Carroll, A.E., Marrero, D.G., Downs, S.M.: The HealthPia GlucoPack diabetes phone: a usability study. Diabet. Technol. Ther. **9**, 158–164 (2007)

3. Beratarrechea, A., Lee, A.G., Willner, J.M., Jahangir, E., Ciapponi, A., Rubinstein, A.: The impact of mobile health interventions on chronic disease outcomes in developing countries: a systematic review. Telemed. e-Health **20**, 75–82 (2014)
4. West, D., Branstetter, D.G., Nelson, S.D., Manivel, J.C., Blay, J.-Y., Chawla, S., Thomas, D. M., Jun, S., Jacobs, I.: How mobile devices are transforming healthcare **18**, 1–38 (2012). Brookings.Edu
5. Ybarra, M.L., Holtrop, J.S., Bosi, A.T.B., Emri, S.: Design considerations in developing a text messaging program aimed at smoking cessation. J. Med. Internet Res. **14**, e103 (2012)
6. Maddison, R., Pfaeffli, L., Whittaker, R., Stewart, R., Kerr, A., Jiang, Y., Kira, G., Leung, W., Dalleck, L., Carter, K., Rawstorn, J.: A mobile phone intervention increases physical activity in people with cardiovascular disease: results from the HEART randomized controlled trial. Eur. J. Prev. Cardiol. **22**, 701–709 (2015)
7. Steinberg, D.M., Levine, E.L., Askew, S., Foley, P., Bennett, G.G.: Daily text messaging for weight control among racial and ethnic minority women: randomized controlled pilot study. J. Med. Internet Res. **15**, e244 (2013)
8. Carlaw, R.W., Mittlemark, M.B., Bracht, N., Luepker, R.: Organization for a community cardiovascular health program: experiences from the Minnesota Heart Health Program. Health Educ. Q. **11**, 243–252 (1984)
9. Fortmann, S.P., Winkleby, M.A., Flora, J.A., Haskell, W.L., Taylor, C.B.: Effect of long-term community health education on blood pressure and hypertension control: the Stanford five-city project. Am. J. Epidemiol. **132**, 629–646 (1990)
10. Merzel, C., D'Afflitti, J.: Reconsidering community-based health promotion: promise, performance, and potential. Am. J. Public Health **93**, 557–574 (2003)
11. Kumar, S., Nilsen, W., Pavel, M., Srivastava, M.: Mobile health: revolutionizing healthcare through transdisciplinary research. Comput. (Long Beach Calif.) **46**, 28–35 (2013)
12. Fiordelli, M., Diviani, N., Schulz, P.J.: Mapping mHealth research: a decade of evolution. J. Med. Internet Res. **15**, e95 (2013)
13. World Bank: Information and Communications for Development 2012: Maximizing Mobile. World Bank Publications, Washington (2012)
14. Hervás, R., Fontecha, J., Ausín, D., Castanedo, F., Bravo, J., López-de-Ipiña, D.: Mobile monitoring and reasoning methods to prevent cardiovascular diseases. Sens. (Basel) **13**, 6524–6541 (2013)
15. Walton, R., DeRenzi, B.: Value-sensitive design and health care in Africa. IEEE Trans. Prof. Commun. **52**, 346–358 (2009)
16. Van Woensel, W., Roy, P.C., Abidi, S.S.: A mobile and intelligent patient diary for chronic disease self-management. In: MEDINFO 2015 eHealth-enabled Heal, pp. 118–122 (2015)
17. Prociow, P.A., Crowe, J.A.: Towards personalised ambient monitoring of mental health via mobile technologies. Technol. Health Care **18**, 275–284 (2010)
18. Magill, E., Blum, J.M.: Personalised ambient monitoring: supporting mental health at home. In: Advances in Home Care Technologies: Results of the Match Project, pp. 67–85 (2012)
19. Paoli, R., Fernández-Luque, F.J., Doménech, G., Martínez, F., Zapata, J., Ruiz, R.: A system for ubiquitous fall monitoring at home via a wireless sensor network and a wearable mote. Expert Syst. Appl. **39**, 5566–5575 (2012)
20. Junglas, I., Abraham, C., Ives, B.: Mobile technology at the frontlines of patient care: understanding fit and human drives in utilization decisions and performance. Decis. Support Syst. **46**, 634–647 (2009)
21. Mobile Ecosystem Forum: Global mHealth and wearables report 2015 (2015)
22. Istepanian, R.S.H., Zitouni, K., Harry, D., Moutosammy, N., Sungoor, A., Tang, B., Earle, K.A.: Evaluation of a mobile phone telemonitoring system for glycaemic control in patients with diabetes. J. Telemed. Telecare **15**, 125–128 (2009)

23. Farquhar, J.W., Fortmann, S.P.: Community-based health promotion. In: Ahrens, W., Pigeot, I. (eds.) Handbook of Epidemiology, pp. 419–438. Springer, New York (2014)
24. Pearson, T.A., Palaniappan, L.P., Artinian, N.T., Carnethon, M.R., Criqui, M.H., Daniels, S. R., Fonarow, G.C., Fortmann, S.P., Franklin, B.A., Galloway, J.M., Goff, D.C., Heath, G. W., Frank, A.T.H., Kris-Etherton, P.M., Labarthe, D.R., Murabito, J.M., Sacco, R.L., Sasson, C., Turner, M.B.: American heart association guide for improving cardiovascular health at the community level, 2013 update: a scientific statement for public health practitioners, healthcare providers, and health policy makers. Circulation **127**, 1730–1753 (2013)
25. Bruce, M.L., Smith, W., Miranda, J., Hoagwood, K., Wells, K.B.: Community-based interventions. Ment. Health Serv. Res. **4**, 205–214 (2002)
26. Winkleby, M.A., Feldman, H.A., Murray, D.M.: Joint analysis of three US community intervention trials for reduction of cardiovascular disease risk. J. Clin. Epidemiol. **50**, 645–658 (1997)
27. Hurtado, M., Spinner, J.R., Yang, M., Evensen, C., Windham, A., Ortiz, G., Tracy, R., Ivy, E.D.: Knowledge and behavioral effects in cardiovascular health: community health worker health disparities initiative, 2007–2010. Prev. Chronic Dis. **11**, 130250 (2014)
28. Carroll, J.M.: HCI Models, Theories, and Frameworks: Toward a Multidisciplinary Science. Morgan Kaufmann, San Francisco (2003)
29. Nguyen, H.D., Poo, D.C.C.: Analysis and design of mobile health interventions towards informed shared decision making: an activity theory-driven perspective. J. Decis. Syst. **25**, 397–409 (2016)
30. Mursu, A., Luukkonen, I.: Activity theory in information systems research and practice: theoretical underpinnings for an information systems development model. Inf. Res. **12**, 1–21 (2006)
31. Taylor, J., Sharples, M., O'Malley, C., Vavoula, G., Waycott, J.: Towards a task model for mobile learning: a dialectical approach. Int. J. Learn. Technol. **2**, 138 (2006)
32. Kollmann, A., Riedl, M., Kastner, P., Schreier, G., Ludvik, B.: Feasibility of a mobile phone-based data service for functional insulin treatment of type 1 diabetes mellitus patients. J. Med. Internet Res. **9**, e36 (2007)
33. Quinn, C.C., Shardell, M.D., Terrin, M.L., Barr, E.A., Ballew, S.H., Gruber-Baldini, A.L.: Cluster-randomized trial of a mobile phone personalized behavioral intervention for blood glucose control. Diabetes Care **34**, 1934–1942 (2011)
34. Gaziano, T.A., Bitton, A., Anand, S., Abrahams-Gessel, S., Murphy, A.: Growing epidemic of coronary heart disease in low-and middle-income countries. Curr. Probl. Cardiol. **35**, 72–115 (2010)
35. Mathers, C., Fat, D.M., Boerma, J.T.: The global burden of disease: 2004 update. World Health Organization, Geneva (2008)
36. Brunner, L.S., Smeltzer, S.C., Bare, B.G., Hinkle, J.L., Cheever, K.H.: Brunner and Suddarth's Textbook of Medical-Surgical Nursing. Lippincott Williams & Wilkins, London (2010)
37. National Academy on An Ageing Society: Heart Disease: A Disabling Yet Preventable Condition. National Academy on an Aging Society, Washington, DC (2000)
38. Awosan, K.J., Ibrahim, M.T.O., Sabir, A.A., Ejimodu, P.: Awareness and prevalence of risk factors of coronary heart disease among teachers and bankers in Sokoto. Nigeria. J. Med. Med. Sci. **4**, 335–342 (2013)
39. Mathers, C.D., Loncar, D.: Projections of global mortality and burden of disease from 2002 to 2030. PLoS Med. **3**, 2011–2030 (2006)

40. Wang, W., Zhang, H., Lopez, V., Wu, V.X., Poo, D.C.C., Kowitlawakul, Y.: Improving awareness, knowledge and heart-related lifestyle of coronary heart disease among working population through a mHealth programme: study protocol. J. Adv. Nurs. **71**, 2200–2207 (2015)

41. Billingham, S.A., Whitehead, A.L., Julious, S.A.: An audit of sample sizes for pilot and feasibility trials being undertaken in the United Kingdom registered in the United Kingdom Clinical Research Network database. BMC Med. Res. Methodol. **13**, 104 (2013)

42. Wagner, J., Lacey, K., Chyun, D., Abbott, G.: Development of a questionnaire to measure heart disease risk knowledge in people with diabetes: the Heart Disease Fact Questionnaire. Patient Educ. Couns. **58**, 82–87 (2005)

43. Chyun, D., Lacey, K.O., Katten, D.M., Talley, S., Price, W.J., Davey, J.A., Melkus, G.D.: Glucose and cardiac risk factor control in individuals with type 2 diabetes: implications for patients and providers. Diabetes Educ. **32**, 925–939 (2006)

44. Reis, R.S., Hino, A.A.F., Rodriguez Anez, C.R.: Perceived stress scale: reliability and validity study in Brazil. J. Health Psychol. **15**, 107–114 (2010)

45. Andreou, E., Alexopoulos, E.C., Lionis, C., Varvogli, L., Gnardellis, C., Chrousos, G.P., Darviri, C.: Perceived stress scale: reliability and validity study in Greece. Int. J. Environ. Res. Public Health **8**, 3287–3298 (2011)

Empathic Avatars in Stroke Rehabilitation: A Co-designed mHealth Artifact for Stroke Survivors

Hussain M. Aljaroodi[✉], Marc T.P. Adam, Raymond Chiong, David J. Cornforth, and Mario Minichiello

The University of Newcastle, Callaghan, NSW 2308, Australia
hussain.aljaroodi@uon.edu.au

Abstract. Stroke is the second highest cause of death and disability worldwide. While rehabilitation programs are intended to support stroke survivors, and promote recovery after they leave the hospital, current rehabilitation programs typically provide only static written instructions and lack the ability to keep them engaged with the program. In this design science research paper, we present an mHealth artifact that builds on behavior change theory to increase stroke survivors' engagement in rehabilitation programs. We employed a co-design methodology to identify design requirements for the stroke rehabilitation mHealth artifact, addressing stroke survivors' needs and incorporating expertise of healthcare providers. Guided by these requirements, we developed design principles for the artifact pertaining to visual assets that are essential in immersing users in the design. We carried out a two-stage development process by having workshops and interviews with experts. Following this, a prototype was developed and evaluated in a series of workshops with multiple stakeholders.

Keywords: Co-design · Empathic avatars · mHealth · Stroke rehabilitation

1 Introduction

Stroke is the second highest cause of death and disability worldwide [1], accounting for nearly six million deaths per year and another five million left in permanent disabilities. In a broader context, stroke is part of a global increase in non-communicable diseases (NCDs), linked, among other factors, to preventable lifestyle behaviors such as smoking, nutrition, alcohol over-consumption, and physical inactivity [2]. Stroke can be a devastating event in a person's life, leading to severe loss of mobility, cognitive impairment, inability to participate in daily living activities, associated loss of independence, curtailment of social life, isolation, and depression. A critical component for the mid- and long-term effects of stroke on a person's life is *rehabilitation*. Effective rehabilitation can aid stroke survivors to reduce physical impairment, recover movement, increase participation in everyday life, and improve the overall quality of life. However, rehabilitation is *often ineffective*, as it requires a high level of physical

© Springer International Publishing AG 2017
A. Maedche et al. (Eds.): DESRIST 2017, LNCS 10243, pp. 73–89, 2017.
DOI: 10.1007/978-3-319-59144-5_5

participation and emotional engagement from the stroke survivor, both of which are challenging for stroke patients to achieve [3].

In this paper, we follow a design science approach to explore how a mobile health (mHealth) solution can support stroke survivors in effective rehabilitation. Existing approaches for stroke rehabilitation are primarily about providing stroke survivors with *information* on exercise and medication regimes, usually conveyed by means of simple text documents with detailed instructions from their healthcare professional. In contrast, our study is rooted in *behavior change theory* [4, 5], and builds on the rationale that engaging stroke survivors in an empathic and meaningful way can increase compliance with exercise and medication regimes and improve overall health outcomes. In particular, we designed, implemented, and evaluated an mHealth artifact we refer to as *Regain*, which aims to support stroke survivors to stay engaged with their rehabilitation program. To ensure that our approach adequately considers the various perspectives in the complex landscape of stroke rehabilitation, we adopted a co-design approach that included workshops with multiple stakeholders such as carers, clinicians, health behavior psychologists, and actual stroke survivors.

The remainder of this paper is organized as follows. In Sect. 2, we identify the problem of effective stroke rehabilitation and requirements for a potential solution. In Sect. 3, we describe the employed co-design process and derive a set of design principles for maintaining users' motivation to use the device (e.g., animation, empathic self-avatars, familiar context). In Sect. 4, we outline the implementation and evaluation of the *Regain* app. In Sect. 5, the paper concludes with some general discussion of how *Regain* may assist stroke rehabilitation and directions for future research.

2 Problem Identification and Requirement Elicitation

Over the past decade, costs associated with NCDs have increased so rapidly that they threaten the healthcare systems of every developed nation [6]. As part of this development, there is growing pressure on healthcare professionals to discharge stroke survivors quickly from a hospital, creating a shift towards outpatient (i.e., out of hospital) rehabilitation in their home care environments. This shift, however, comes at the increased risk of non-compliance with medical advice in terms of exercise and medical regime [7], as the time and resources for clinician-patient interaction are scarce. In other words, current rehabilitation programs fail to effectively engage stroke survivors to comply with medical advice in a home care environment, leading to worse health outcomes because of non-compliance with medications and exercise programs and, ultimately, even higher costs for the healthcare system [8]. While mHealth technology offers important opportunities to increase patients' engagement in rehabilitation activities, the effectiveness of existing mHealth artifacts is low [9].

Stroke rehabilitation can only be effective if stroke survivors actively engage in targeted behaviors, and this almost always entails a change in behavior to align to the rehabilitation goals. The development of effective rehabilitation programs therefore has to take into account the psychology of behavior change. Current rehabilitation programs focus primarily on providing detailed verbal and written advice on exercise and medication regimes.[1] However, there is a large body of psychological literature showing that providing accurate information alone is necessary, but *not sufficient* for achieving sustainable behavior change. Based on a systematic review of behavior change literature, Michie et al. developed a comprehensive framework that integrates the interacting components that make up and define human behavior, namely opportunity, capability, and motivation [4]. Engaging individuals in targeted behaviors requires one to adequately address each of these components in the given context. Building on behavior change theory, we derive the following set of requirements for effective stroke rehabilitation.

The first requirement (R1) refers to the stroke survivors' *psychological capability*, that is, "the necessary knowledge and skills" (p. 4, [4]) to engage in rehabilitation activities. Due to their medical condition, which usually involves some level of cognitive impairment, stroke survivors often find it difficult to understand the verbal and written instructions provided to them, limiting their psychological capacity to engage in rehabilitation activities [10], as well as understanding their personal health benefits from following the rehabilitation plan. However, without the psychological capacity to engage in targeted behavior, it is impossible for stroke survivors to perform the activities that are necessary for effective rehabilitation. Hence, recent research suggests to focus on technological and methodological innovations to assist compliance by exploring new ways of communicating medical advice [11].

R1: *The design artifact has to communicate medical advice in a way that increases stroke survivors' psychologically capability to engage in rehabilitation activities, addressing their understanding of how to perform the activities as well as the benefits of these activities in terms of health outcomes.*

The second requirement (R2) refers to the stroke survivors' *physical capability*, that is, the physical ability to perform the activities required by the rehabilitation plan. In other words, stroke survivors should only be recommended activities that they are physically able to perform. Ideally, these activities should be challenging to the patients, yet not too challenging, as this can lead to increased stress, despair, or even injury [12]. As the negative impacts of a stroke on the survivors' mobility and the improvements from rehabilitation vary strongly from person to person, the activities have to reflect individual physical capabilities of the stroke survivors.

R2: *The design artifact has to select rehabilitation activities that individual stroke survivors are physically capable to perform, ensuring that the activities are sufficiently challenging while at the same time avoiding activities that are too challenging.*

The third requirement (R3) refers to the stroke survivors' opportunity to engage in rehabilitation activities, that is, "the factors that lie outside the individual that make the behavior possible or prompt it" (p. 4, [4]), which may include restriction, environmental

---

[1] It is important to highlight that recent research has successfully explored the application of virtual reality for stroke rehabilitation (e.g., see [53, 54]). Yet, these approaches are used to a lesser extent compared to traditional rehabilitation techniques.

restructuring, and enablement. At present, limited Information Technology (IT)-mediated approaches for directly changing the home care environments of stroke survivors exist. However, there are several elements in the context of environmental restructuring that can be addressed by IT (e.g., enabling to perceive their home care environment in a different way by showing them how to engage in rehabilitation activities within that given environment).

R3: *The design artifact has to create opportunities for stroke rehabilitation by nudging stroke survivors to engage in rehabilitation activities and showing them how these activities can be performed in their home care environments.*

The fourth requirement (R4) refers to increasing stroke survivors' motivation for sustained behavior change, that is, "all those brain processes that energize and direct behavior" (p. 4, [4]). Even when individuals have the physical and psychological capacity as well as the opportunity to engage in targeted behavior, behavior change will not occur unless there is a sufficient level of motivation. Motivation can be directly driven by increased levels of capability and opportunity [4], e.g., by understanding how rehabilitation activities will lead to benefits in terms of better health outcomes. However, if the benefits have no meaning to an individual, particularly if they do not translate into achievable, short-term milestones, behavior change will not occur. Hence, addressing motivation needs to go beyond the mechanisms associated with capability and opportunity, e.g., by leveraging the potential of social cues and short-term feedback.

R4: *The design artifact has to include elements that motivate stroke survivors to engage in rehabilitation activities.*

The fifth requirement (R5) refers to providing accessibility for healthcare professionals to monitor the progress of stroke survivors, and making adjustment to the rehabilitation program based on the progress. In order to achieve this, it is necessary for a healthcare professional to select a set of adequate rehabilitation activities (R2), then measure progress against those goals. For instance, feedback from users, consisting of physiological measures such as heart rate and skin conductance, has been shown to permit the adjustment of difficulty in real-time during stroke rehabilitation in a study by Cornforth et al. [12]. Such measures can be used to assess the mood of the user (see p. xiv, [13] for some detailed discussion on content validity and construct validity in the context of physiological measurements), and then adjust the difficulty of a video game used in the context of stroke rehabilitation. IT systems can support R5 by providing data that can be sent back to the healthcare professional, in order to assist in assessment and to provide opportunities for intervention in the form of modification of exercise programs and other aspects of a rehabilitation program.[2]

---

[2] Although the technology for such interventions exists, it seems that this opportunity has been overlooked: out of 29,000 medical apps in the US iTunes® store, 130 (16%) could be used in rehabilitation, but less than 1% specifically assist the caregiver to better face the challenges of stroke survivors [55]. Our artifact differs from these apps by building on the theory of behavior change, a co-design process with multiple stakeholders, and empirical validation using clinical trials.

R5: *The design artifact has to enable healthcare professionals to have access to the stroke survivors' data remotely and in a secure way in order to assess the progress, and make adjustment to the rehabilitation program.*

3 Design

Recent reviews indicate that research into patient-centric mHealth IT systems is still at an early stage, and a wide range of existing mHealth approaches have shown to yield little or no effectiveness [9, 14]. Samhan et al. identified specific gaps in the literature, including limited knowledge of the effects of mHealth IT systems on health outcomes, and how these systems can be designed for patients with a particular disease [14]. Co-design, sometimes also referred to as participatory design, is a methodology in which multiple stakeholders contribute to ensure that the design solution aligns with users' needs and experiences [15]. Typical elements of co-design include idea generation, problem understanding, prototyping, and storytelling. Empirical evidence has shown that the best health outcomes are derived via models co-designed with users and healthcare professionals' inputs [16]. Co-design therefore goes beyond designing for a given audience but directly involves the audience in the design.

In this study, we build on the co-design methodology, using workshops involving stakeholders, to explore issues of communication, accessibility and motivation. These issues were approached through storytelling and prototyping, in order to achieve problem understanding, and to collaboratively design an artifact for stroke rehabilitation. After this, the multidisciplinary research team iteratively built interactive visual assets into compelling user interface elements, using empathic patient-centered scenarios and characters. The underlying paradigm of this approach is that the resulting solutions will be more patient-centric and will meet the needs of stroke survivors, rather than being designed by researchers and health practitioners who have not experienced this illness themselves. Figure 1 illustrates the design process of the work described here. It commences with informal workshops held with researchers from design, health, and IT, to facilitate problem understanding through storytelling and explore the boundaries of what is possible through idea generation from the viewpoints of users and capabilities of the relevant technology. These workshops led to the production of an early prototype that enabled the research team to co-design a full prototype with the key stakeholders of stroke survivors and healthcare professionals.

Fig. 1. Illustration of the co-design process used in developing the artifact.

3.1 Empathic Self-Avatars

An important design aspect in addressing requirements R1 and R4 is to build inter-active visual assets into the *Regain* app, using empathic patient-centered scenarios and characters. Instead of simply communicating *information* on healthcare advice to stroke survivors, such empathic elements can be used to convey medical advice in a way that they translate into the life of the user, increasing their psychological capacity (R1) and motivation (R4) to engage in targeted rehabilitation behaviors. Recent research has shown that the so-called *self-avatars*, i.e., avatars that "resemble users' physical appearances" [17], can be an effective way to convey social cues and encourage targeted behaviors. From the theoretical perspective, instigating behavior change via self-avatars can be achieved through the *Proteus Effect* [18]. This effect describes a phenomenon in which the behavior of an individual is changed by the visual charac-teristics of their avatar [18]. Wrzesien et al. argued that the appearance of self-avatars can influence behavior, and this change in behavior can be utilized to encourage desirable behaviors [19]. Importantly, *empathic* self-avatars may motivate users to adopt new behaviors (desirable or undesirable) associated with digital representations [20] (R4). Here, *empathy* is defined as the process of placing oneself in the place of someone else, seeing matters from the other's point of view, perceiving the other's emotion and thoughts, and conveying this awareness to that specific individual [21].[3] Moreover, the expression of feeling from avatars will increase the likelihood of behavioral change in the real world [22].

The use of empathic avatars in co-design requires the artifact to incorporate sce-narios based on a user's experience, in order to help make the avatar 'real' [23]. This can be achieved through systematic action research, reviews, observations, and inter-views [24]. In the context of technology-enhance learning, it has been shown that empathic avatars can encourage learners to stay engaged with a learning program [25]. In addition, empathic avatars can demonstrate the usefulness of engaging in desirable behaviors (R1), e.g., showing that the movement of the avatar gets better every time the avatar finishes an exercise, to ensure that stroke survivors follow the instructions from their rehabilitation program. Taken as a whole, the more empathic an avatar is, the more likely it will influence user behavior towards targeted behaviors, and this emo-tional link can be strengthened by making the avatar customizable [26]. In the context of the *Regain* app, these behaviors refer to engaging in the rehabilitation program, where self-avatars are able to respond to stroke survivors and address their mood [27].

Design Principle 1 (P1). *Use empathic, customizable self-avatars to convey social cues, increase stroke survivors' psychological capabilities, and ensure that they have a compelling experience to stay engaged with the rehabilitation program.*

---

[3] It appears that the notion of empathy is of particular importance in healthcare settings, as individuals are experiencing a life-changing event with potentially devastating consequences on their everyday lives. For instance, Javor et al. found that Parkinson's disease patients exhibit significantly lower trust levels towards other humans than healthy subjects do [56]. In a follow-up study, Javor et al. showed that trust levels can be increased by using avatars [57].

3.2 Animations in a Familiar Environment

The animation principle refers to illustrating the typical exercise that has to be performed by stroke survivors, enabling them to better understand the activities that they need to engage in (R1) and reshaping their perception of their home care environment to create opportunities to engage in this behavior (R3). Animation allows a more immersive illustration of exercise than textual descriptions or even line drawings, as the user can see how the avatar completes the entire exercise, in contrast to a static image. Including animation with an avatar conveys more compelling and enhanced communication [28, 29], which can provide an entertaining and hence motivating experience (R4), and ensure that the user follows and stays engaged with a program. Dodds et al. found that avatar animation can be used to simulate certain behavior, and to enable users to move and perform better [30]. Therefore, animation can be useful in stroke rehabilitation as a means to increasing the psychological capability of stroke survivors, and to provide the necessary knowledge and motivation for them to stay engaged with the program (R1). Such animation shows stroke survivors how to do a certain exercise, which in turn can increase their understanding of its benefits. Avatars can provide stroke survivors an animated, personal, and engaging interaction, which in turn can influence patients' behavior [31].

Importantly, the animation should be situated in a familiar context for stroke survivors, in a way that they feel more comfortable and relaxed [32]. Previous research has shown that being in a familiar physical environment will help to motivate targeted behaviors in patients and, overall, patients prefer home care (i.e., a familiar environment) over clinical-based therapy [33]. Hence, situating the animation in a familiar environment, e.g., a home garden or a living room, would make stroke survivors feel more relaxed and comfortable while performing the rehabilitation activities [34]. In other words, illustrating the empathic self-avatar in a familiar environment for stroke survivors will provide an opportunity to reduce their feeling of anxiety, and increase their confidence because they will perform activities in their familiar context [32, 35]. In addition to the positive influence on stroke survivors' emotional states, the approach of using a familiar environment creates an opportunity for stroke survivors to engage in rehabilitation activities (R3), as it reshapes users' perceptions of their home care environment, demonstrating how this environment can be used to engage in behaviors while at the same time taking advantage of the relaxing influence of their home.

Design Principle 2 (P2). *Use animations with the empathic self-avatar in a familiar environment to convey information on how to perform the rehabilitation activities to the stroke survivors in an effective and motivating way, creating an opportunity to engage in such activities in their home care environment.*

3.3 Shape and Color Aesthetics

The shape and color principles refer to the use of shapes and colors that can positively influence stroke survivors' perceptions and behaviors. As for shape aesthetics, the artifact makes use of *gestalt* (i.e., shapes or forms) for shapes used in the self-avatar design and animation. It has been shown that a more round face-like shape appears more friendly to users [36], hence designing self-avatars with a round face-like feature would indicate friendliness of the character to stroke survivors. A study shows that round shapes with face-like features can enforce positive emotion on learners [37]. Such shapes can be used in designing the empathic self-avatar to induce positive emotion upon stroke survivors, which can keep them motivated (R4) and engaged (R4) with the rehabilitation program. Therefore, the empathic self-avatar will be designed using a round face-like characteristic to enforce friendliness in engaging animations. Gestalt should have similar characteristics to humans' features, but not too realistic to avoid affecting stroke survivors with the *uncanny valley effect*. This uncanny valley effect describes a phenomenon that arises when designing visual artifacts that are intended to resemble human features (e.g., an avatar) in an overly realistic way, and it can cause an aversive response in humans and make them feel uncomfortable [38, 39], which in turn may disengage stroke survivors from the rehabilitation program.

Design Principle 3 (P3). *Use gestalt (round face-like shapes) with an empathic self-avatar to indicate friendliness of the self-avatar while avoiding photorealistic features.*

The visual design of the user interface does not only have to consider the shape aesthetics but also the colors used in combination with those shapes. Um et al. stated that saturated warm colors and round face-like shapes can induce positive emotion in users, and increase their learning capability [36]. Hence, warm colors and round face-like shapes can be used to induce positive emotion, and increase users' psychological capability and motivation (R1, R4). Color theory is the study of the effect colors exert on the cognitive and affective processes of individuals [40]. According to this theory, a color can be used to trigger a broad range of emotional responses, e.g., to increase attention and deliver information (R1) [41]. More importantly, colors can have beneficial but also detrimental effects on human behavior [42]. Particularly high hue colors, that is, pure colors with high levels of brightness and saturation such as red, blue, green and yellow, exhibit a strong influence on user perception, physiology and behavior (R4) [43]. For example, Greene et al. found that warm colors (e.g., yellow, red, and orange) can prevent boredom and maintain activities [44]. Such colors may motivate stroke survivors (R4) and increase their psychological capability (R1). Moreover, using the green color has the ability to reduce stress and make users more calm and relax [42]. Applying high hue colors and rounded shapes to the empathic self-avatars and background environment therefore is expected to provide a positive impression and emotional appeal that will encourage use of the artifact.

Design Principle 4 (P4). *Use high hue colors (e.g., yellow, red, blue, and green) with the empathic self-avatar and the animations in order to draw stroke survivors' attention to the empathic self-avatar and create an engaging user experience.*

4   Implementation and Evaluation

4.1   Implementation

The design artifact presented in this paper was developed in a two-stage implementation process (see Fig. 1). In a pilot study that was undertaken in late 2014, a multi-disciplinary team of researchers with convergent interests, which include clinicians, health informatics specialists, programmers and designers, was assembled. The output was an early prototype that demonstrates how empathic avatars can be created for stroke rehabilitation using design of visual assets and animation. First, visual assets were created by the multidisciplinary team using a co-design process. The result of this stage was an early prototype as shown in Fig. 2.[4] The left part shows an example of an empathic avatar (P1) in the early prototype that was developed in order to provide animated scenes illustrating typical rehabilitation exercises. The animation allows a more immersive illustration of exercise than line drawings, as the avatar completes the entire exercise, in contrast to a static image (P2). A male version and a female version of the avatar were designed in consultation with experts in user experience design. The color scheme was designed to avoid the dreary nature of illustrations commonly used in written healthcare advice, making use of compelling gestalt features (P3) and bright colors (P4). Once the appearance was designed, pivot points were created, as indicated in the avatar on the left of Fig. 2 using circles.

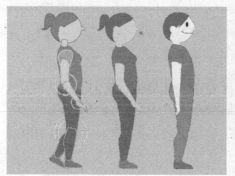

Fig. 2. Left: empathic avatars developed for animation from the *early prototype*. Right: a screenshot of the *early prototype* with the avatar animated into a sequence. (Color figure online)

The right part of Fig. 2 shows an animation created using the designed avatars. In this case, the exercise is "lift and carry" and it encourages the stroke survivor to improve balance and manipulation skills by grasping a small object and carrying it for a few steps. The animated avatar is situated in a familiar environment (P2), i.e., a home garden scene. This illustrates the possibilities for this technology, but also the implied message, which in this case is one of escape and self-empowerment through increased mobility in recovery following these exercises. Once the preliminary design was realized, as can be seen in the left part of Fig. 2, it was shown to healthcare professionals and health behavior psychologists with an interest in stroke rehabilitation – these people are important stakeholders for embedding the future product into a rehabilitation program in practice. This early prototype was designed to explore the

---

[4] The process is summarized in a short video: http://youtu.be/MV23MdmlfAg.

characteristics of an avatar in the context of a mobile app on a tablet device. After informal and formal workshops and interviews, design goals were developed to assist in the production of an improved prototype. The full prototype was developed in collaboration with professional user experience designers and software developers.

Figure 3 shows two screenshots from the full prototype. Based on comments received from stakeholders in the co-design workshops, the amount of textual material has been reduced to the minimum required for explanation. This can be seen in the brief instructions for an individual exercise, coupled with an image representing the exercise, shown in the left part of Fig. 3, and the small amount of text used in the exercise description, shown in the right part of Fig. 3. Furthermore, following the advice of professional designers and health behavior psychologists, the menu has been implemented using images that represent the type of exercise (left part of Fig. 3).

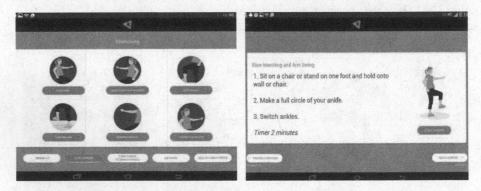

Fig. 3. Left: selection of exercises in the *full prototype*. Right: instructions provided for a typical rehabilitation exercise in the *full prototype*.

4.2   Future Development

Building on the existing prototypes, the *Regain* app will be iteratively evaluated and improved with users (stroke survivors) and carers. The future implementation will follow the process shown in Fig. 4. The first step is to have focus groups with stroke survivors and carers to introduce the full prototype of *Regain*, providing these important stakeholders a platform to share their stories and have in-depth discussions about the opportunities of mobile technology and the design of *Regain*, ensuring their current and emerging requirements are documented and addressed. Through supervised interaction with the designed visual assets based on mobile platforms, stroke survivors will be invited into the design process to work in focus groups to explore their experiences, collect feedback, and to continuously involve users in the design process.

Fig. 4. Illustration of the implementation process of the commercial app.

Participants will be invited to take a tablet computer home, loaded with the full prototype app, for an extended period of time. Then, data collection and analysis will take place after the full prototype of the *Regain* app has been used in clinical trials or home environments by users, to check their interactions with the app and gather their feedback. The *Regain* app will be refined based on the results from the data analysis and user feedback, and that will assist in developing the (final) commercial app.

4.3 Evaluation

At this stage, evaluation of functionality was achieved by face to face interviews with domain experts in the fields of user interface design, clinical care, health informatics, software development, health behavior psychology, health insurance and health policy, as well as with stroke survivors. The mHealth literature supports such a sample and an interdisciplinary approach [45]. In addition, the co-design approach requires the involvement of application-oriented practitioners who work in these mHealth contexts, encompassing industry, government and technology viewpoints [46]. Existing networks within the University of Newcastle and Hunter New England Local Health District were used to identify and recruit participants, who were invited via email. Semi-structured interviews were used, of approximately one hour in duration. Questions revolved around details of the prototype design, as well as more general questions about what elements or features were considered appropriate. Interviews were transcribed and coded according to thematic recurring elements. The thematic elements identified are: (1) provide user-created and customizable empathic avatars, as these can assist user capability and motivation; (2) make avatar appearance similar enough to the user so that a connection can be made; (3) make sure the avatar is not too similar in appearance to make the user uneasy (as reflected in design principles P1–4).

These identified themes were taken into account in the iterative development of the above stated design principles and the co-design process. In relation to the design requirements, we note that requirement R1 was met by the ability of the prototype to communicate medical advice. This directly addresses the psychological capability of stroke survivors [4]. R3 was met by the technological innovation of presenting medical advice in this new format. The prototype was able to demonstrate the possibility to nudge stroke survivors to engage in rehabilitation activities and how these activities can be performed in their home care environment. R4 was met by the manner of the avatar based training, which can increase stroke survivors' motivation for sustained behavior change. On the other requirements, we note that at present the prototype does not meet R2 by allowing medical practitioners to select the exercises. However, this is a trivial addition to the *Regain* app and is planned to be included in the clinical trials. The current prototype also does not address R5, that is, to provide feedback to a medical practitioner. This is more of a challenge but is planned for the clinical trial. As for the specific design principles, feedback from the face-to-face interviews showed a high degree of convergence between the design principles and the operation of the prototype.

5 Discussion and Conclusion

5.1 Discussion of Results

Stroke has such a high prevalence in the modern society that if this phenomenon was caused by an infection, it would be regarded as a pandemic [47]. Rehabilitation programs are employed to assist stroke survivors and promote recovery after leaving the hospital. In order to harness the whole benefits of rehabilitation programs, it is important that stroke survivors are informed not only with written texts, but also in a way that is entertaining and engaging. This is particularly challenging as the general trend of increases in NCDs will ultimately lead to a shift in responsibility from the collective to the individual, as treatment costs are rising in an unsustainable manner [6]. In addition, there is pressure on clinical personnel to discharge stroke survivors quickly from the hospital, increasing the risk of non-compliance with medical advice [7]. As a consequence, there are issues with communicating information to stroke survivors as well as issues with depression and social impairment [27]. In this paper, we used a co-design approach to pursue the development of an mHealth artifact to support stroke rehabilitation by increasing stroke survivors' psychological and physiological capability, motivation, and opportunity based on behavior change theory [4, 5]. The overall goal of this approach is that stroke survivors will receive improved communication of health advice, become engaged with the rehabilitation program, and be motivated to follow that advice leading to better health outcomes.

First, based on workshops with design, health and IT professionals, we identified five specific design requirements for a solution artifact (R1–5). The artifact has to provide and communicate the necessary skills and knowledge that will aid in increasing the psychological capabilities of stroke survivors in order to enable them to understand how rehabilitation activities should be performed and what their benefits are (R1). In addition, the artifact has to suggest rehabilitation activities that are not too challenging for stroke survivors, which in turn aids in increasing the physical capabilities of stroke survivors (R2). The artifact has to create opportunities for stroke survivors to engage in the rehabilitation activities by changing their perception of their home care environment (R3). Also, the artifact has to increase motivation (1) indirectly through increased capability and opportunity and (2) directly through compelling user interface elements (R4). Importantly, healthcare professionals should have access to the stroke survivors' data to enable progress assessment and adjustment in the rehabilitation program (R5).

Second, we developed a set of specific design principles (P1–4) for the mHealth artifact in order to meet the identified requirements related to the interaction of the stroke survivor with the user interface (R1, R3, R4). We proposed a new approach to the self-management of stroke rehabilitation, using a mobile device to assist with carrying out a rehabilitation program in a home care environment. This approach, which follows the co-design methodology, features frequent consultation with stakeholders, including stroke survivors, carers, clinicians and IT specialists, to provide an end result product that meets the needs of its intended audience. An empathic self-avatar has been identified as a concept that will assist in creating a sense of emotional connection (i.e., attachment) with stroke survivors as well as a powerful medium to enable behavior change (P1). Animations in a familiar environment are used in combination with the empathic self-avatar to increase the psychological capabilities of stroke survivors as well as provide entertaining experience in such an environment (P2). One way to make the avatar more empathic in a future extension of the artifact might be to capture the user's facial expression with a camera and change the appearance of the avatar accordingly [48]. Shape and color aesthetics are used to deliver information to stroke survivors in friendly and engaging ways, designed to reduce anxiety and increase attention to keep stroke survivors engaged with their rehabilitation program (P3, P4). This proceeds not with static factual information, but through the medium of some moving guide to the exercise, which the user can identify with by use of an avatar.

Third, we evaluated the effectiveness of the design artifact in workshops with multiple stakeholders such as carers, clinicians, health behavior psychologists, and actual stroke survivors. To this end, a prototype has been developed based on feedback from design, health and IT professionals. Building on the early prototype and the full prototype, the future development and evaluation will include focus groups with stroke survivors and their carers, as well as clinical studies. The former will provide feedback on usability that will be used to improve the prototype to the point of a commercially ready artifact, while the latter will provide clinical evidence of the efficacy of an intervention using the employed design principles, when compared to the control group that will receive only the conventionally used written instructions and line drawings. This approach will provide a positive experience for stroke survivors that validates their importance and gives them a voice in the design of the next wave of rehabilitation assistance. In addition, this will provide knowledge to inform further research, including how avatars can help to convey various health messages, what kind of impact such technologies might have, and how the needs of stroke patients can be met.

5.2 Limitations and Future Research

Our study must be seen in view of several limitations. First, some functionality has not been implemented yet, because the design process focused primarily on the user interface for the stroke survivors rather than on data sharing, which requires consultation with additional stakeholders. This functionality relates to enabling healthcare professionals to select specific exercises and individually adjust the rehabilitation program (R2), and to assess and monitor the progress of stroke survivors (R5). However, these two functionalities are not crucial to the assessment of the empathic avatars, and are planned for inclusion in the commercial app. Second, the current design does not include serious games and gamification elements, which may offer additional advantages to address user capability, opportunity and motivation to engage in rehabilitation activities [5, 49]. Using game elements in the *Regain* app may add entertainment aspects for stroke survivors, which in turn may motivate them to follow the rehabilitation program and promote recovery. A five minute gaming experience with certain avatars is sufficient to reverse behavioral patterns [50]. One likely explanation is that immersion [51], derived from the gaming experience imbues people with agency. Third, cultural aspects have not been included in the design of the visual assets in the *Regain* app. For instance, previous research has shown that culture may affect the meaning of colors and their influence on user perception and behavior [52]. Hence, future research may explore how the color schemes in apps for stroke survivors may need to be adapted for different cultures. The advantages and disadvantages of including these elements will be explored in the focus groups with stroke survivors and their carers. Finally, the overall effectiveness of the artifact in improving the health outcomes of stroke survivors will have to be empirically established in clinical trials. Participants in the clinical trials will be invited to take a tablet computer loaded with the *Regain* app home for an extended period of time, after which the focus groups will be held to gather feedback to be used for refining the software.

5.3   Concluding Remarks

This study explored how mobile technology may support stroke survivors in their rehabilitation program, by providing an engaging experience for stroke survivors and communicating information in an entertaining way rather than just written instructions. Using a co-design methodology to include inputs from different disciplines has ensured that stroke survivors have a say on the design of the *Regain* app, and their requirements are addressed. Importantly, the use of animated empathic self-avatars in a familiar environment with warm colors and round face-like shapes will help stroke survivors to increase their psychological and physical capabilities, as defined by the model of Michie et al. [4], thereby making sustained participation more likely. In addition, the *Regain* app can help to create an opportunity to facilitate recovery in a home care environment. Using mobile technology can provide the required information for healthcare professionals about the stroke survivors and enable them to assess their progress and make adjustments. Using such design principles will ensure that stroke survivors are motivated and engaged with their rehabilitation program.

Acknowledgments. The first author would like to acknowledge the full scholarship from the Institute of Public Administration (IPA) in the Kingdom of Saudi Arabia to study a PhD degree in Information Systems at the University of Newcastle, Australia. We thank John Attia and Mark Roxburgh for their valuable advice in the design of the Regain app. We would also like to thank the two anonymous reviewers for their insightful feedback and suggestions, which assisted in improving the paper.

References

1. WHF: Stroke. World Heart Federation (2017)
2. RACGP: Smoking, Nutrition, Alcohol and Physical Activity (SNAP): A Population Health Guide to Behavioural Risk Factors in General Practice. Royal Australian College of General Practitioners (RACGP), Melbourne (2015)
3. Jelinek, H.F., August, K., Khandoker, A., Issam, H.M., Koenig, A., Riener, R.: Heart rate asymmetry and emotional response to robot-assist task challenges in post-stroke. In: Proceedings of Computing in Cardiology Conference, pp. 521–524 (2011)

4. Michie, S., van Stralen, M.M., West, R.: The behaviour change wheel: a new method for characterising and designing behaviour change interventions. Implement. Sci. **6**, 1–11 (2011)
5. Noorbergen, T., Adam, M.T.P., Attia, J.R., Cornforth, D.J., Minichiello, M.: Using mobile heart rate measurements for health promotion: an integrative theoretical framework. In: Chiong, R., Cornforth, D., Bao, Y. (eds.) Applied Informatics and Technology Innovation, pp. 1–22. Springer (in press)
6. Mladovsky, P., Srivastava, D., Cylus, J., Karanikolos, M., Evetovits, T., Thomson, S., McKee, M.: Health policy responses to the financial crisis in Europe. World Health Organization (2012)
7. Linder, S.M., Rosenfeldt, A.B., Reiss, A., Buchanan, S., Sahu, K., Bay, C.R., Wolf, S.L., Alberts, J.L.: The home stroke rehabilitation and monitoring system trial: a randomized controlled trial. Int. J. Stroke **8**, 46–53 (2013)
8. Iuga, A.O., McGuire, M.J.: Adherence and health care costs. Risk Manag. Healthc. Policy **7**, 35–44 (2014)
9. Free, C., Phillips, G., Galli, L., Watson, L., Felix, L., Edwards, P., Patel, V., Haines, A.: The effectiveness of mobile-health technology-based health behaviour change or disease management interventions for health care consumers: a systematic review. PLoS ONE **10**, 1–45 (2013)
10. NIH: Post-Stroke Rehabilitation. National Institutes of Health (2014)
11. de Jongh, T., Gurol-Urganci, I., Vodopivec-Jamsek, V., Car, J., Atun, R.: Mobile phone messaging for facilitating self-management of long-term illnesses (review). Cochrane Database Syst. Rev. **12**, 1–50 (2012)
12. Cornforth, D.J., Koenig, A., Riener, R., August, K., Khandoker, A.H., Karmakar, C., Palaniswami, M., Jelinek, H.F.: The role of serious games in robot exoskeleton-assisted rehabilitation of stroke patients. In: Loh, C.S., Sheng, Y., Ifenthaler, D. (eds.) Serious Games Analytics. AGL, pp. 233–254. Springer, Cham (2015). doi:10.1007/978-3-319-05834-4_10
13. Riedl, R., Davis, F.D., Hevner, A.R.: Towards a NeuroIS research methodology: intensifying the discussion on methods, tools, and measurement. J. Assoc. Inf. Syst. **15**, i–xxxv (2014)
14. Samhan, B., Dadgar, M., Joshi, K.D.: Mobile health information technology and patient care: methods, themes, and research gaps. In: Transactions of the International Conference on Health Information Technology Advancement, pp. 18–29 (2013)
15. Sanders, E.B.N., Stappers, P.J.: Co-creation and the new landscapes of design. CoDesign **4**, 5–18 (2008)
16. Donetto, S., Tsianakas, V., Robert, G.: Using Experience-Based Co-design to Improve the Quality of Healthcare: Mapping Where We are Now and Establishing Future Directions. King's College London, London (2014)
17. Suh, K., Kim, H., Suh, E.K.: What if your avatar looks like you? Dual-congruity perspectives for avatar use. MIS Q. **35**, 711–729 (2011)
18. Yee, N., Bailenson, J.N.: The Proteus effect: the effect of transformed self-representation on behavior. Hum. Commun. Res. **33**, 271–290 (2007)
19. Wrzesien, M., Rodríguez, A., Rey, B., Alcañiz, M., Baños, R.M., Vara, M.D.: How the physical similarity of avatars can influence the learning of emotion regulation strategies in teenagers. Comput. Hum. Behav. **43**, 101–111 (2015)
20. Luppicini, R.: Handbook of Research on Technoself: Identity in a Technological Society. IGI Global, Hershey (2012)
21. Davis, M.: Empathy: A Social Psychological Approach. Westview Press, Boulder (1996)
22. Parks, P., Cruz, R., Ahn, S.J.G.: Don't hurt my avatar: the use and potential of digital self-representation in risk communication. Int. J. Robots Educ. Art **4**, 10–20 (2014)
23. Laurel, B.: Design Research: Methods and Perspectives. The MIT Press, London (2003)

24. Minichiello, M.A., Anelli, L., Kelly, D.: Drawing to aid recovery and survival. In: Tracey Special Issue, STEAM, pp. 1–15 (2014)
25. Chen, G.D., Lee, J.H., Wang, C.Y., Chao, P.Y., Li, L.Y., Lee, T.Y.: An empathic avatar in a computer-aided learning program to encourage and persuade learners. J. Educ. Technol. Soc. 15, 62–72 (2012)
26. Kim, H.-K., Kim, S.-H.: Understanding emotional bond between the creator and the avatar: change in behavioral intentions to engage in alcohol-related traffic risk behaviors. Comput. Hum. Behav. 62, 186–200 (2016)
27. Eslinger, P.J., Parkinson, K., Shamay, S.G.: Empathy and social-emotional factors in recovery from stroke. Curr. Opin. Neurol. 15, 91–97 (2002)
28. Merz, B., Tuch, A.N., Opwis, K.: Perceived user experience of animated transitions in mobile user interfaces. In: Proceedings of the 2016 CHI Conference Extended Abstracts on Human Factors in Computing Systems, Santa Clara, California, USA, pp. 3152–3158 (2016)
29. Horain, P., Soares, J.M., Rai, P.K., Bideau, A.: Virtually enhancing the perception of user actions. In: Proceedings of the 2005 International Conference on Augmented Tele-existence, Christchurch, NZ, pp. 245–246 (2005)
30. Dodds, T.J., Mohler, B.J., Bülthoff, H.H.: Talk to the virtual hands: self-animated avatars improve communication in head-mounted display virtual environments. PLoS ONE 6, 1–12 (2011)
31. Cruz-Cunha, M.M.: Encyclopedia of e-Health and Telemedicine. IGI Global, Hershey (2016)
32. Stephenson, S., Wiles, R.: Advantages and disadvantages of the home setting for therapy: views of patients and therapists. Br. J. Occup. Ther. 63, 59–64 (2000)
33. Hong, G.R.S., Song, J.A.: Relationship between familiar environment and wandering behaviour among Korean elders with dementia. J. Clin. Nurs. 18, 1365–1373 (2009)
34. Nordin, Å., Sunnerhagen, K.S., Axelsson, Å.B.: Patients' expectations of coming home with very early supported discharge and home rehabilitation after stroke - an interview study. BMC Neurol. 15, 1–9 (2015)
35. Wottrich, A.W., Von Koch, L., Tham, K.: The meaning of rehabilitation in the home environment after acute stroke from the perspective of a multiprofessional team. Phys. Ther. 87, 778–788 (2007)
36. Um, E., Plass, J.L., Hayward, E.O., Homer, B.D.: Emotional design in multimedia learning. J. Educ. Psychol. 104, 485–498 (2012)
37. Plass, J.L., Heidig, S., Hayward, E.O., Homer, B.D., Um, E.: Emotional design in multi-media learning: effects of shape and color on affect and learning. Learn. Instr. 29, 128–140 (2014)
38. Mori, M., MacDorman, K.F., Kageki, N.: The uncanny valley. IEEE Robot. Autom. Mag. 19, 98–100 (2012)
39. Riedl, R., Mohr, P.N.C., Kenning, P.H., Davis, F.D., Heekeren, H.R.: Trusting humans and avatars: a brain imaging study based on evolution theory. J. Manag. Inf. Syst. 30, 83–114 (2014)
40. Birren, F.: Color Psychology and Color Therapy: A Factual Study of the Influence of Color on Human Life. Pickle Partners Publishing, Chicago (2016)
41. MacKay, D.G., Ahmetzanov, M.V.: Emotion, memory, and attention in the taboo stroop paradigm an experimental analogue of flashbulb memories. Psychol. Sci. 16, 25–32 (2005)
42. Jalil, N.A., Yunus, R.M., Said, N.S.: Environmental colour impact upon human behaviour: a review. Procedia Soc. Behav. Sci. 35, 1–21 (2012)
43. Valdez, P., Mehrabian, A.: Effects of color on emotions. J. Exp. Psychol. 123, 394–409 (1994)

44. Greene, T.C., Bell, P.A., Boyer, W.N.: Coloring the environment: hue, arousal, and boredom. Bull. Psychon. Soc. **21**, 253–254 (1983)
45. Burke, L.E., Ma, J., Azar, K.M., Bennett, G.G., Peterson, E.D., Zheng, Y., Riley, W., Stephens, J., Shah, S.H., Suffoletto, B., Turan, T.N.: Current science on consumer use of mobile health for cardiovascular disease prevention. Circulation **132**, 1157–1213 (2015)
46. Hevner, A.R., March, S.T., Park, J., Ram, S.: Design science in information systems research. MIS Q. **28**, 75–105 (2004)
47. Marrero, S.L., Bloom, D.E., Adashi, E.Y.: Noncommunicable diseases: a global health crisis in a new world order. JAMA **307**, 2037–2038 (2012)
48. Wei, X., Zhu, Z., Yin, L., Ji, Q.: A real time face tracking and animation system. In: IEEE Computer Society Conference on Computer Vision and Pattern Recognition Workshop, pp. 1–8 (2004)
49. Staiano, A.E., Calvert, S.L.: The promise of exergames as tools to measure physical health. Entertain. Comput. **2**, 17–21 (2011)
50. Yoon, G., Vargas, P.T.: Know thy avatar: the unintended effect of virtual-self representation on behavior. Psychol. Sci. **25**, 1043–1045 (2014)
51. Weinstein, N., Przybylski, A.K., Ryan, R.M.: Can nature make us more caring? Effects of immersion in nature on intrinsic aspirations and generosity. Pers. Soc. Psychol. Bull. **35**, 1315–1329 (2009)
52. Cyr, D.: Modeling web site design across cultures: relationships to trust, satisfaction, and e-loyalty. J. Manag. Inf. Syst. **24**, 47–72 (2008)
53. Laver, K.E., George, S., Thomas, S., Deutsch, J.E., Crotty, M.: Virtual reality for stroke rehabilitation. Cochrane Database Syst. Rev. **2015**, 1–107 (2015)
54. Silver, B.: Virtual reality versus reality in post-stroke rehabilitation. Lancet Neurol. **15**, 996–997 (2016)
55. Piran, P., Thomas, J., Kunnakkat, S., Pandey, A., Tanner, T.G., Burton, D., Balucani, C., Jensen, A., Levine, S.R.: A systematic review of commercially available medical mobile applications for stroke survivors and caregivers. In: Proceedings of International Stroke Conference (2015)
56. Javor, A., Riedl, R., Kirchmayr, M., Reichenberger, M., Ransmayr, G.: Trust behavior in Parkinson's disease: results of a trust game experiment. BMC Neurol. **15**, 126 (2015)
57. Javor, A., Ransmayr, G., Struhal, W., Riedl, R.: Parkinson patients' initial trust in avatars: theory and evidence. PLoS ONE **11**, 1–21 (2016)

Designing Anonymous Collaboration in Computer-Supported Organizational Participation

Thomas Wagenknecht[1]([⊠]), Olga Levina[1], and Christof Weinhardt[2]

[1] FZI Research Center for Information Technology,
Friedrichstraße 60, 10117 Berlin, Germany
{Wagenknecht,levina}@fzi.de
[2] Karlsruhe Institute of Technology,
Institute of Information Systems and Marketing,
Fritz-Erler-Straße 23, 76133 Karlsruhe, Germany
weinhardt@kit.edu

Abstract. Voicing one's opinion, especially when it is not in conjunction with the opinion of the senior management, can be difficult in organizational contexts. Thus, platform facilitators in organizational participation processes might want to grant their users a way to communicate anonymously. However, this might have adverse effects, such as hoax and foul language. In this study, we describe the rigorous design process, evaluation and instantiation of an artifact that allows the postings of opinions and issues concerning the strategic and operational decisions in a public organization without revealing the identity of the author. Building on a thorough literature review and the involvement of key stakeholder groups allowed us to design and realize an artifact that mitigates the negative effects, while supporting reticent employees and those in fear of their superiors to speak their mind. We discuss both theoretical and practical implications.

Keywords: Design instantiation · Organizational participation · Anonymity · Crowdsourcing

1 Introduction

Firms are restructuring their organizations to find new ways in building a more meaningful and productive workplace [1]. Computer-supported collaborative work (CSCW) becomes more important [2] – especially with the ascent of the social networking technology [3]. For instance, a recent survey by McKinsey & Company, a management consultancy, found that almost 60% of corporations are currently using enterprise social networks [4]. Besides enterprise social networks [2], employers also use open innovation and internal crowdfunding platforms [5–7] as well as other forms of computer-supported organizational participation [8] to engage their employees in the decision-making processes at their organizations.

On these platforms, employees often demand means for anonymous communication. Research suggests that, by protecting the user's privacy, anonymity might encourage reticent as well as lower-level employees to voice their opinion, even if it is

© Springer International Publishing AG 2017
A. Maedche et al. (Eds.): DESRIST 2017, LNCS 10243, pp. 90–103, 2017.
DOI: 10.1007/978-3-319-59144-5_6

against their superior managers' views [9–13]. Furthermore, anonymity reduces conformity as well as ownership biases [14, 15], which could lead to increased group performance [13] and potentially more creative solutions in open innovation engagements [7, 16, 17]. Yet, user anonymity might have both positive as well as negative effects. For instance, a recent report by CareerBuilder argues that 18% of US companies have already dismissed employees over inappropriate comments in social networks [18]. Anonymity in online discussions has repeatedly been shown to have detrimental effects on discourse quality due to polarization, hate speech and foul language [10, 13, 15, 19–21]. For instance, anonymous users might use swear words to describe their colleagues or even senior management. In effect, participation and satisfaction with the discussion might decrease [10, 22, 23]. In general, how anonymous communication enfolds depends on a variety of factors, including group size, proximity and group history [24]. For instance, anonymous posts might take other forms on broad social networks (e.g., Facebook, Twitter, etc.) than in an enterprise social network of a small firm with few offices. Nonetheless, when designing information systems for organizational participation, developers have to leverage the potential benefits while mitigating the downsides of user anonymity in discussions. The challenge is to include and engage as many employees of an organization as possible, while simultaneously keeping the discussion at a well-behaved, comfortable level [25].

In this study, we apply a design science research (DSR) approach [26–28] to explore "Opt in anonymity", a feature of an information technology (IT) artifact that aims to significantly improve current state-of-the-art information systems designed for participation in organizational contexts by reaping the positive effects of user anonymity. We design and evaluate a participation platform that enables employees to contribute various proposals for the strategic planning of their organization. Therefore, the scope of our study is anonymous participation in an organizational context, using CSCW. In an effort to provide new opportunities for all staff members to participate in the decision-making processes of the organization, we designed a digital platform where all employees can propose, develop and vote on ideas, which the senior management takes as a basis to discuss in their regular board meeting. The studied artifact is an instantiation and part of a comprehensive socio-technical system for computer-supported organizational participation [8, 29, 30]. We evaluated it during a five-month prototype test at a public organization. A survey among the users was conducted at the end of the testing period to evaluate whether our artifact fulfills its requirements.

This study makes two main contributions to the DSR and wider Information Systems (IS) literature. First, it presents a rigorous approach to design a feature that mitigates the negative effects of user anonymity in discussions while leveraging the positive sides. Second, we demonstrate that our solution entails a number of theoretical as well as practical implications to the ongoing debate on organizational participation.

In terms of structuring this paper, we follow Gregor and Hevner's proposition for presenting DSR research [31]. Thus, the remainder of this study is organized as follows. In Sect. 2, we illustrate our theoretical background by briefly reviewing the research on the topics at hand. Section 3 outlines our research method, while Sect. 4 describes our artifact. We present results of our evaluation in Sect. 5 and discuss both theoretical as well as managerial implications in Sect. 6. Finally, we draw a conclusion in Sect. 7.

2   Literature Review

Research in Information Systems (IS), Communication Science and other disciplines has extensively investigated the effects of anonymity in human interactions. In this section, we briefly review some studies on anonymous communication in the context of organizational participation and, more specifically, crowdsourcing. Following a DSR approach, our study represents an exaptation [31]. Thus, our literature review focuses on the known solutions to similar problems in the related fields.

2.1   Organizational Participation

Employees increasingly seek to be involved in the decision-making processes of their employer in order to shape its strategy, processes and culture [32]. Initiatives that foster employee participation are able to meet these demands [33]. The positive effects on job satisfaction, employee motivation and productivity of organizational participation is well recognized in work and organizational psychology [33, 34]. For instance, research in this field found that organizational participation can increase employees' commitment, intrinsic motivation as well as feelings of self-efficacy [35, 36].

As companies often work in spatially and timely dispersed teams, computer-supported organizational participation becomes all the more relevant as group decision support systems (GDSS) are able to expand the benefits of organizational participation across boundaries of the entire organization [8]. This is especially relevant because GDSS are, if designed appropriately, able to improve key outcomes of collaborative tasks [37]. In practice, organizations of different sizes implement various forms of social software to facilitate participation and collaboration, including enterprise social networks (ESNs), open innovation, prediction markets and crowdsourcing platforms [5, 6, 38–40].

2.2   Crowdsourcing

Pedersen et al. [41] define crowdsourcing as a collaboration model that uses human-centric information systems to address organizational, individual and societal problems by engaging on a crowd of interested people. Thus, crowdsourcing leverages the expertise, skills and creativity of the general public or a specific target group [42]. While target groups might also be customers, several corporations have launched crowdsourcing platforms only for their employees [5, 6, 43]. Instead of limiting research and development to a dedicated unit, companies can tap into the wisdom of their entire staff base via crowdsourcing. In effect, they are able to gain more knowledge, make better informed decisions and generate more diverse and higher quality ideas and solutions [8, 17, 41, 42, 44, 45].

Crowdsourcing engagements usually include phases of idea generation, collaboration and evaluation [46], all of which have been analyzed extensively in IS research in the past decade [7]. So by its nature, crowdsourcing regularly produces large amounts of ideas and proposals [47–49]. Facilitators often ask users to collectively evaluate and develop the suggestions of their peers further.

One important finding is that, for a crowdsourcing engagement to be successful, that the information systems needs to convey a motivational and trusted environment [50]. However, it is difficult to create trust when (some) users are unidentifiable [51].

2.3   Anonymity in GDSS

Anonymity, as the inability of a user to identify another user [52], has been studied in detail in Human Computer Interaction (HCI), computer-mediated communication (CMC), other areas of IS and beyond. It has been shown to have various effects on human perceptions and, eventually, decision-making processes [13]. While this can be very beneficial in some areas – particularly related in the work environment, anonymity has more recently been identified as a major deterrent in online discussions as it provides a veil of protection for those using foul language, polarizing arguments and hate speech [10, 19, 20]. However, anonymity and its effect are highly context specific. Valacich et al. [24] propose a conceptual framework for anonymity in group support systems that suggests that the size, proximity as well as the history and composition of a group significantly influence anonymity. They also distinguish between process (i.e., "Who is contributing?") and content (i.e., "What is contributed?") anonymity. Accordingly, group factors determine whether content or users can be de-anonymized due to social and contextual clues [24].

In GDSS, user anonymity is usually achieved by omitting a profile name and picture or using some form of placeholder (e.g., a grey avatar, pseudonyms, etc.). Yet, anonymous users are often perceived as less trustworthy and having lower expertise [53–55]. Research suggests that this effect may occur because profile pictures signif-icantly contribute to establishing trust in human interactions, which is closely related to the perception of social presence [51]. Social presence can be described as a feeling of a personal, sociable, and sensitive human contact when using a communication med-ium [56]. It depends on intimacy, established through physical proximity, shared interests or conversation [57] and immediacy, which is invoked through verbal and nonverbal cues [58, 59]. While it is arguably difficult to establish social presence in CMC, IS research has repeatedly demonstrated that it can indeed be induced using socially rich descriptions and images [15, 60–64]. However, the absence of personal and social cues makes it more challenging for people to develop feelings of social warmth [13, 65]. This might be one explanation for using hate speech and similar language as concerns of hurting anyone are too abstract, which would be in line with the deindividuation effect [58].

Considering the many negative outcomes that user anonymity produces, one could ask why facilitators should not simply force every user to disclose her or his identity. Especially in the work context, though, anonymity has considerable benefits. As people often experience discrimination based on their age, gender, ethnicity and other observable factors, anonymity was found to increase the subjective quality of debates for some users [9, 10, 66].

Moreover, lower-level employees or staff new to the organization might be reluctant to share their opinion. For instance, some hold their opinion back in order to avoid any form of repression from senior management when opinions diverge. Without an option for anonymous communication, discussions might result in fewer expressed arguments and, in turn, might lead to less informed decisions and lower employee satisfaction [10, 14, 67]. For instance, Feldmann et al. [6] demonstrated in an evaluation of an internal crowdfunding process at IBM that lower-level employees took significantly longer to decide for a project to fund than senior managers. Even more interestingly, projects suggested by lower-level employees were not as quickly funded as those proposed by their more senior colleagues. While this might well be due to a better understanding of the organization of the senior staff's side, the researchers suggest that "social pressure might urge users to back ideas by superiors instantaneously" (p. 7) [6]. Moreover, due to a long-standing group history and composition (e.g., shared values, work processes, etc.), anonymity might have less detrimental effects in organizational settings as colleagues operate in a trusted environment, knowing each other [24]. Nonetheless, there is still a risk that anonymous users could target senior management or regular colleagues with their hate speech.

To our best knowledge, there is no study investigating the effect of anonymity in the context of enterprise social software. Thus, we claim that an extension of the body of knowledge is required as research on anonymous communication in the context of organizational participation is still scarce and suggested mixed effects.

3 Method

Based on the seminal work by Hevner et al. [26] and Peffers et al. [27], design science research (DSR) can be understood as a means to address fundamental problems in the productive application of information technology (IT). DSR aims to capture both the practical side of relevant business environmental conditions (i.e., people, organizations and technology) as well as the theoretical foundations and rigorous IS research methodologies in order to develop artifacts and theories that can then be evaluated in practice [26]. As a result, design theories are able to provide prescriptions for the architecture of information systems by investigating the technological and social systems as well as the outcome of the interaction of both systems [28].

The present study has the purpose to design a crowdsourcing platform that can be used for idea generation, development and evaluation [7, 46] as well as to allow for anonymous communication in an organization. In our case, we designed the platform for a public organization with three offices in rural Germany that serves a constituency of more than 200,000 people and has more than 110 staff members, who are tasked with placing and training people of various backgrounds for new jobs. Based on the prior research on anonymous communication in CSCW, design principles of this artifact employ the notion of usability, privacy protection and integration into the given IT architecture. Thus, the phase of problem identification included an extensive literature review on the relevance of the subject at hand as well as on the prior research results in the related fields with the focus on functionality requirements.

We designed the artifact under strong collaboration with external experts and project partners as well as the future users. This research is part of a Government-funded joint project with Liquid Democracy and partou, two software developers, and HRpepper, a management consultancy. While the software developers were responsible for programming and implementation, both the authors as well as HRpepper were involved in the design and development of the IT artifact. The public organization agreed to serve as an associated partner for the implementation and evaluation of our software development. Note that none of the entities involved received any funding from this public organization, ensuring an impartial evaluation. We built on the prior developments of our project partner Liquid Democracy, which developed a software based on an open source project called "Adhocracy". We collected user requirements starting with general requirements for crowdsourcing platforms found in the literature, enriched them based on our expert interviews, and consolidated them with the current software architecture.

In the setting of this study, two groups of actors were identified as future users. First, the managerial group, which initiated and supported active participation of the employees in the decision and strategic processes on one hand. We view this group as the recipient of the possible performance effects of the designed software. Second, the employees are the user group, which uses the designed software for the input and voting. To assess the managerial requirements and pre-evaluate the problem relevance, we conducted interviews with members of both groups and subsequently shared a first deduction of system requirements with them during a series of workshops on premise of the public organization. We began with a workshop that involved the managerial group, which we asked for various participatory processes at the organization and in which we gathered information on the organization's organizational structure. Thereafter, we created user stories that described the information system's functions. In a second workshop that addressed members of both user groups, we collaboratively developed the artifact further using these easy-to-understand user stories.

During the workshops, it became clear that both the management as well as the employees of the public organization considered anonymous posting an essential feature for active participation. It is interesting to note, that the two stakeholder groups had a different understanding of the posting options. While the senior management exclusively wanted to use the anonymous posting option, the employees insisted on the possibility of posting proposals and comments under their real names.

In the evaluation phase, we tested the entire system for its validity and usability. A small group of employees began with a pre-test during a one- month-period. Being young and tech-savvy, this small group can be considered a set of friendly users. After incorporating some minor changes (e.g., changing some style sheets to better fit Internet Explorer), we started a five-month test run (from August 2016 to January 2017) open to all employees of the public organization. Both regular employees as well as senior managers were invited to register for the system. Thereafter, the users were asked to complete a survey on the usability and utility of the designed system (within two weeks in mid-January 2017). While, as system designers and IS researchers, we were interested in asking questions on the specific usage of anonymous communication, the management and worker's council of the public organization asked us to exclude such items in order to strictly preserve every employee's privacy. Therefore, we included a control questions, checking whether users noticed that proposals and comments could be submitted anonymously. Moreover, we assessed whether users are reluctant to speak against the opinion of their superiors in general. Furthermore, we analyzed user-generated data to enhance our evaluation.

4　Artifact Description

We designed an artifact that closely interacts with its sociotechnical environment [31, 68]. At the public organization, a management board meets each month to discuss and decide on important issues for the entire organization. From the beginning, all employees were free to join these board meetings as listeners and contributors (although decision-making was limited to three board members). However, attendance by the staff was very low. Thus, in order to increase employee participation, senior management decided to implement a software for computer-supported organizational participation. Therefore, the expected main users of the constructed artifact were the employees (i.e., non-board members) of the public organization.

The overall system is based on the Adhocracy platform, which is mainly coded in Python. It allows users to propose ideas, comment on them, like or dislike them and, after a previously set period of time, collectively vote on which proposal is selected as the winner and should be discussed in the management meeting. The senior management committed itself to include this winning proposal on its board meeting agenda and to provide feedback about the discussion and potential actions shortly afterwards. Thus, the software functions are largely in line with other information systems for crowd-sourcing processes [7, 41, 46], along with a fixed commitment by the organization's leadership [8].

Our main contribution and key feature of the designed system is "opt-in anonymity," which is a feature that comprehensively addresses the use case by leveraging user anonymity's positive effects whilst mitigating the negative sides. The feature functions as follows. In order to post a proposal, the user opens a dialog and types the suggestion in a text field. In the current version, there are no special formatting or attachment options, since only the brief description of the suggestion is expected. Users simply have to tick a box next to the "Submit" button. Thereafter, the systems presents the post without a profile picture and the name "Anonymous User." The database stores no link to the user profile, so that users are unable to edit their texts later on. However, neither other users nor administrators are able to identify anonymous postings. Nonetheless, administrators are still able to delete both proposals and comments in case (anonymous) users make use of foul language.

Per default, the text field is designed for posting under the users' real names. After submission, the proposal becomes a visible item in the "proposal list" on the software login page. Other users can discuss each of the suggestions in the discussion forum. In order to do so, they open a proposal and contribute a comment, a "like" or a "dislike" either by using their real name or posting anonymously in the same way as mentioned above. Thus, users can contribute without switching the systems, making it very easy to stay anonymous [69]. Furthermore, users can either up- or down-vote each proposal. However, due to design considerations, voting is completely anonymous, but limited to one vote per user. The proposal with the most positive votes after a previously fixed period is labeled as a "winner" and is forwarded to the management board for discussion in their upcoming strategy meeting. Employees are still invited to join these meetings in person in order to discuss the proposals (and comments) further. Figure 1 illustrates the posting process and highlights the "opt-in anonymity" feature.

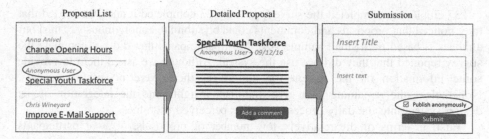

Fig. 1. System illustration (feature functions highlighted in ovals)

5   Evaluation

A public organization identified the need to and the desire from the employees to be a part of the strategic decision processes. The project was initiated by the management level of a public organization, who sought to increase employees' participation in the strategic decision process. Given the distributed working environment and the difficulties to align the multiple time schedules involved, a digital solution for participation was an obvious solution. Therefore, the development of the artifact was motivated and promoted from the management but also by the employees (in the form of the worker's council). The evaluation of the artifact was aimed at the fulfilment of the functional as well as discussion-related requirements.

During the problem identification and relevance evaluation phases of the DSR process in Fig. 1, the requirements mentioned above were identified, converted into software functions and implemented into the software solution.

We conducted the first phase of the validity testing after the requirements workshops. Here, the basic features of the framework for democratic decision making were implemented and opened for tests with friendly users. Since idea management and discussion possibilities were seen as the basic features of the instantiation, users were enabled to include them in their daily processes providing (positive) feedback.

After the implementation phase, all employees (including non-users) were invited to a survey asking for their early experience with the utility and usability of the artifact and especially the anonymity feature.

User take-up of the system as a whole was moderate. Of the 110 employees at the public organizations, 81 registered for the platform, using their real full names as usernames. They contributed a total of 13 proposals and 20 comments as well as 77 likes. During the testing phase, we analyzed the users' proposals and comments in order to evaluate the application of the anonymity feature as well as the quality of the content posted. During the entire phase, users did not post any form of post with offensive or disinhibited content. It was also evident that the number of proposals and comments posted under the username and the number of posts posted anonymously were almost equal. However, we did not find a similar quantitative composition among the suggestions marked as winners, where there was only one anonymous winner, while the other six winners were posted by identified users.

37 employees completed the survey, yet only 23 completed it and 20 reported that they noticed that proposals and comments could be submitted anonymously. Thus, our analysis is based on a small sample size. Most participants that did not complete the survey reported that they did not use the system. Although we asked them to provide some information on the reason for non-usage, there were no useful answers. Nonetheless, the remaining data give important insights into the integration of the design system into the daily processes and its perceived usefulness.

First, in terms of the relatively low number of proposals, 50% of participants self-critically report that they did not think participation was at sufficient levels. However, a majority still said that they liked the quality of the submissions (45% vs. 40%).

Second, we establish the relevance of the "Opt-in anonymity" feature. We find that while 60% of participants report that they are not afraid to post something, which is not in conjunction with what senior management thinks, a significant subset (30%) is indeed worried or very worried. Thus, an option for anonymous communication might meaningfully support them. Third, we evaluated the feature's usability by asking for whether users believe that the identity of users contributing proposals or comments anonymously was completely untraceable. We find that the vast majority of users (78%) thinks this is the case, while only few (9%) do or rather do not agree (see Fig. 2).

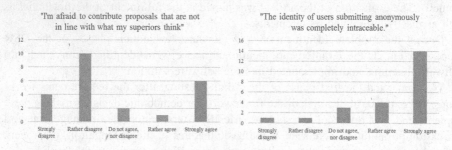

Fig. 2. Users' rate of agreement (n = 23)

6   Discussion

We followed a rigorous research process that allowed us to detect the specific requirements for the different stakeholder groups early in the system design. The assessed requirements were implemented and their fit was evaluated in a survey.

The evaluation results show that the IT artifact feature at hand – "opt-in anonymity" – was willingly included into the daily workflow by the employees. We were able to address the concerns of reticent employees, who would otherwise not dare to speak against their superiors. Moreover, as there was no disinhibited behavior in the discussions, we were able to mitigate some of the negative effects of user anonymity during our five-month test phase. This differs markedly from prior research as it would have suggested polarizing arguments and hate speech [10, 19, 20]. However, considering that employees of the public organization know each other fairly well (i.e., having a long history together), these social norms might have contributed to the prevention of foul language as well as the salience of individuals and social norms decreases the influence of the deindividuation effect [58]. However, it is noteworthy that the number of anonymous suggestions among the winner suggestions is not equal to the number of suggestions made using a real username. This fact implies that there might still exist a trust bias against anonymous posts. Note that this trust bias may have occurred although users were not even represented with a profile picture, which could have only increased the problem, making the difference between anonymous and identified users even more salient [51]. Moreover, we experienced a relatively moderate up-take by employees of the overall platform. Thus, we cannot fully dismiss the possibility that user anonymity could have contributed to a decreasing participation. Moreover, this might be a negative indication for the future adoption of the overall system.

One of the important factors for the success of the IT-artifact going forward is the continuation of its usage by the management group. The discussion in, and more importantly, the implementation of the suggestions made by the employees by the management group is essential for the future acceptance of the tool [70]. If senior management fails to communicate and implement proposals proposed on the platform, employees will eventually lose interest [8]. Already now, employees' opinion is divided over the overall system's usefulness for the organization. However, acknowledging that the platform is embedded within a sociotechnical environment with many activities happening offline, it is not clear whether the moderate rate of participation and perceived usefulness is entirely due to the IT artifact.

We suggest that this setting as well as the open source foundation of the software at hand grant a great generalizability to our study as both practitioners as well as researchers are able to transfer our findings easily to other applications and the designed artifact into other contexts.

7 Conclusion

In this study, we followed a rigorous DSR approach to investigate how an IT artifact can be designed that aims to enable employee participation at a public organization, granting users a possibility to submit proposals and comments anonymously. In this context, we aimed to mitigate anonymity's negative effects (e.g., hoax, foul language, etc.) in order to profit from the positive sides (e.g., activating reticent employees, reducing conformity biases). We developed "opt-in anonymity" as a key feature, which allowed seamless switching between identified and anonymous posting. We were able to show that users perceived the feature to be effective. Moreover, during the entire testing phase, users did not submit any content with foul language or hoax. Users were also satisfied with the quality of submissions and the overall system's ease of use, though its usefulness is up for debate. Nonetheless, a majority reported that they intend to use the system in the near future.

Going forward, the functionality features and their fit to the requirements will be additionally evaluated in a more in-depth analysis by way of a series of interviews with heavy users and senior management in order to better understand under which circumstances users made use of "opt-in anonymity" and how this contributed to the organization. Moreover, it might be interesting to learn about how the board members and other senior staff perceived the system's usefulness. Future research could also further investigate the effects of anonymity on participation, content and quality of participatory processes with regard to the intention and background of the users. For instance, their personal goals for promotion or recognition might have an influence.

This study needs to be considered against its limitations. First, despite our best efforts, only 81 users registered for the test and only 37 participants filled out the evaluation survey. Moreover, due to German privacy protection laws at the workplace, senior management and worker's council of the organization asked us to exclude questions on the specific use of our "opt-in anonymity" feature. Thus, our results can only be considered an approximation with further research to come.

Acknowledgements. This study was part of the joint research project "Participation as a Service" (PaaS), funded by the German Federal Ministry of Education and Research (under grant no. 01IS150120). We would like to thank our project partners at Liquid Democracy e.V., partou eG and HRpepper GmbH & Co. KGaA and the public organization as well as the two anonymous reviewers of this paper.

References

1. Bock, L.: Work Rules!: Insights from Inside Google That Will Transform How You Live and Lead. Hodder and Stoughton, London (2016)
2. Behrendt, S., Richter, A., Trier, M.: Mixed methods analysis of enterprise social networks. Comput. Netw. **75**, 560–577 (2014)
3. Cook, N.: Enterprise 2.0: How Social Software Will Change the Future of Work. Gower Publishing, Ltd., Farnham (2008)
4. Bughin, J., Chui, M., Pollak, L.: Organizing for change through social technologies. McKinsey Global survey results (2013)
5. Muller, M., Geyer, W., Soule, T., Daniels, S., Cheng, L.-T.: Crowdfunding inside the enterprise: employee-initiatives for innovation and collaboration. In: Proceedings of the SIGCHI Conference on Human Factors in Computing Systems, pp. 503–512 (2013)
6. Feldmann, N., Gimpel, H., Muller, M., Geyer, W.: Idea assessment via enterprise crowdfunding: an empirical analysis of decision-making styles. In: Proceedings of the Twenty Second European Conference on Information Systems, Tel Aviv, pp. 1–10 (2014)
7. Wagenknecht, T., Crommelinck, J., Teubner, T., Weinhardt, C.: Ideate. Collaborate. Repeat. A research agenda for idea generation, collaboration and evaluation in open innovation. In: 13th International Conference on Wirtschaftsinformatik (2017)
8. Wagenknecht, T., Filpe, R., Weinhardt, C.: Towards a design theory of computer-supported organizational participation. J. Enterp. Inf. Manag. **30**, 188–202 (2017)
9. Connolly, T., Jessup, L.M., Valacich, J.S.: Effects of anonymity and evaluative tone on idea generation in computer-mediated groups. Manag. Sci. **36**, 689–703 (1990)
10. Haines, R., Hough, J., Cao, L., Haines, D.: Anonymity in computer-mediated communication: more contrarian ideas with less influence. Group Decis. Negot. **23**, 765–786 (2014)
11. Weisband, S., Kiesler, S.: Self disclosure on computer forms: meta-analysis and implications. In: Proceedings of the CHI 96 Conference on Human Factors in Computing Systems, pp. 3–10. ACM (1996)

12. Acquisti, A., Brandimarte, L., Loewenstein, G.: Privacy and human behaviour in the age of information. Science **347**, 509–514 (2015)
13. Postmes, T., Lea, M.: Social processes and group decision making: anonymity in group decision support systems. Ergonomics **43**, 1252–1274 (2000)
14. Valacich, J.S., Dennis, A.R., Nunamaker, J.F.: Group size and anonymity effects on computer-mediated idea generation. Small Group Res. **23**, 49–73 (1992)
15. Sia, C.-L., Tan, B.C.Y., Wei, K.-K.: Group polarization and computer-mediated communication: effects of communication cues, social presence, and anonymity. Inf. Syst. Res. **13**, 70–90 (2002)
16. Blohm, I., Riedl, C., Leimeister, J.M., Krcmar, H.: Idea evaluation mechanisms for collective intelligence in open innovation communities: do traders outperform raters? In: Proceedings of the International Conference on Information Systems, pp. 1–24 (2011)
17. Leimeister, J.M.: Collective intelligence. Bus. Inf. Syst. Eng. **4**, 245–248 (2010)
18. Rapacon, S.: How using social media can get you fired (2016). http://www.cnbc.com/2016/02/05/how-using-social-media-can-get-you-fired.html
19. Siegel, J., Dubrovsky, V., Kiesler, S., McGuire, T.: Group processes in computer-mediated communication. Organ. Behav. Hum. Decis. Process. **37**, 157–187 (1986)
20. Cho, D., Kim, S., Acquisti, A.: Empirical analysis of online anonymity and user behaviors: the impact of real name policy. In: Proceedings of the 45th Hawaii International Conference on System Science, pp. 3041–3050 (2012)
21. Charness, G., Gneezy, U.: What's in a name? Anonymity and social distance in dictator and ultimatum games. J. Econ. Behav. Organ. **68**, 29–35 (2008)
22. Omernick, E., Sood, S.O.: The impact of anonymity in online communities. In: International Conference on Social Computing, pp. 526–535 (2013)
23. Kilner, P.G., Hoadley, C.M.: Anonymity options and professional participation in an online community of practice. In: Proceedings of the 2005 Conference on Computer Support for Collaborative Learning, pp. 272–280. International Society of the Learning Sciences (2005)
24. Valacich, J.S., Jessup, L.M., Dennis, A.R., Nunamaker, J.F.: A conceptual framework of anonymity in group support systems. Group Decis. Negot. **1**, 219–241 (1992)
25. Postmes, T., Spears, R., Sakhel, K., de Groot, D.: Social influence in computer-mediated communication: the effects of anonymity on group behavior. Pers. Soc. Psychol. Bull. **27**, 1243–1254 (2001)
26. Hevner, A.R., March, S.T., Park, J., Ram, S.: Design science in information systems research. MIS Q. **28**, 75–105 (2004)
27. Peffers, K., Tuunanen, T., Rothenberger, M., Chatterjee, S.: A design science research methodology for information systems research. J. Manag. Inf. Syst. **24**, 45–78 (2007)
28. Gregor, S., Jones, D.: The anatomy of a design theory. J. Assoc. Inf. Syst. **8**, 312–335 (2007)
29. Ulbrich, F.: Adopting shared services in a public-sector organization. Transform. Gov. People Process Policy **4**, 249–265 (2010)
30. Mumford, E.: The story of socio-technical design: reflections on its successes, failures and potential. Inf. Syst. J. **16**, 317–342 (2006)
31. Gregor, S., Hevner, A.R.: Positioning and presenting design science research for maximum impact. MIS Q. **37**, 337–355 (2013)
32. Tumasjan, A., Strobel, M., Welpe, I.: Employer brand building for start-ups: which job attributes do employees value most. J. Bus. Econ. **81**, 111–136 (2011)
33. Wilkinson, A., Gollan, P., Marchington, M., Lewin, D. (eds.): The Oxford Handbook of Participation in Organizations. Oxford University Press, Oxford (2010)
34. Wegge, J., Jeppesen, H.J., Weber, W.G., Pearce, C.L., Silva, S.A., Pundt, A., Jonsson, T., Wolf, S., Wassenaar, C.L., Unterrainer, C., Piecha, A.: Promoting work motivation in organizations. J. Pers. Psychol. **9**, 154–171 (2010)

35. Spreitzer, G.M.: Psychological empowerment in the workplace - dimensions, measurement, and validation. Acad. Manag. J. **38**, 1442–1465 (1995)
36. Humborstad, S.I.W.: When industrial democracy and empowerment go hand-in-hand. A co-power approach. Econ. Ind. Democr. **35**, 391–411 (2014)
37. Briggs, R.O., Albrecht, C.C., Dean, D.R., Kolfschoten, G., de Vreede, G.-J., Lukosch, S.: A seven-layer model of collaboration: separation of concerns for designers of collaboration systems. In: Proceedings of the International Conference on Information Systems 2009, pp. 1–14 (2009)
38. Urbach, N., Smolnik, S., Riempp, G.: Determining the improvement potentials of employee portals using a performance-based analysis. Bus. Process Manag. J. **17**, 829–845 (2011)
39. Leonardi, P.M., Huysman, M., Steinfeld, C.: Enterprise social media: definition, history, and prospects for the study of social technologies in organizations. J. Comput. Commun. **19**, 1–19 (2013)
40. Leimeister, J.M., et al.: Leveraging crowdsourcing: activation-supporting components for IT-based ideas competition. J. Manag. Inf. Syst. **26**, 197–224 (2009)
41. Pedersen, J., Kocsis, D., Tripathi, A., Tarrell, A., Weerakoon, A., Tahmasbi, N., Xiong, J., Deng, W., Oh, O., De Vreede, G.J.: Conceptual foundations of crowdsourcing: a review of IS research. In: Proceedings of the Annual Hawaii International Conference on System Sciences (2013)
42. Adamczyk, S., Bullinger, A.C., Möslein, K.M.: Innovation contests: a review, classification and outlook. Creat. Innov. Manag. **21**, 335–360 (2012)
43. Feldmann, N., Gimpel, H., Kohler, M., Weinhardt, C.: Using crowd funding for idea assessment inside organizations: lessons learned from a market engineering perspective. In: Proceedings of the 3rd International Conference on Social Computing and its Applications, pp. 525–530 (2013)
44. Lakhani, K.R., Jeppesen, L.B.: Getting unusual suspects to solve R&D puzzles. Harv. Bus. Rev. **85**, 30–32 (2007)
45. Poetz, M.K., Schreier, M.: The value of crowdsourcing: can users really compete with professionals in generating new product ideas? J. Prod. Innov. Manag. **29**, 1–31 (2012)
46. Hrastinski, S., Kviselius, N.Z., Ozan, H., Edenius, M.: A review of technologies for open innovation: characteristics and future trends. In: Proceedings of the Annual Hawaii International Conference on System Sciences (2010)
47. Riedl, C., Blohm, I., Leimeister, J.M., Krcmar, H.: The effect of rating scales on decision quality and user attitudes in online innovation communities. Int. J. Electron. Commer. **17**, 7–36 (2013)
48. Klein, M.: Enabling large-scale deliberation using attention-mediation metrics. Comput. Support. Coop. Work **21**, 449–473 (2012)
49. Klein, M., Garcia, A.C.B.: High-speed idea filtering with the bag of lemons. Decis. Support Syst. **78**, 39–50 (2015)
50. Ebner, W., Leimeister, J.M., Krcmar, H.: Community engineering for innovations: the ideas competition as a method to nurture a virtual community for innovations. R&D Manag. **39**, 342–356 (2009)
51. Teubner, T., Adam, M.T.P., Camacho, S., Hassanein, K.: Understanding resource sharing in C2C platforms: the role of picture humanization. In: Proceedings of the Twentyfifth Australasian Conference on Information Systems, pp. 1–10 (2014)
52. Marx, G.T.: What's in a name? Some reflections on the sociology of anonymity. Inf. Soc. **15**, 99–112 (1999)
53. Fogg, B.J., Tseng, H.: The elements of computer credibility. In: Proceedings of the SIGCHI Conference on Human Factors in Computing Systems, pp. 80–87 (1999)

54. Weber, C., Dunaway, J., Johnson, T.: It's all in the name: source cue ambiguity and the persuasive appeal of campaign ads. J. Polit. Behav. **34**, 561–584 (2012)
55. Jiang, Z.J., Choi, B.C.F.: Privacy concerns and privacy-protective behavior in synchronous online social interactions. Inf. Syst. Res. **24**, 579–595 (2013)
56. Short, J., Williams, E., Christie, B.: The Social Psychology of Telecommunications. Wiley, New York (1976)
57. Argyle, M., Dean, J.: Eye-contact, distance and affiliation. Sociometry **28**, 289–304 (1965)
58. Jessup, L.M., Connolly, T., Galegher, J.: The effects of anonymity on GDSS group process with an idea-generating task. MIS Q. **14**, 313–321 (1990)
59. Tu, C.-H., McIsaac, M.: The relationship of social presence and interaction in online classes. Am. J. Distance Educ. **16**, 131–150 (2002)
60. Gefen, D., Straub, D.W.: Consumer trust in B2C e-commerce and the importance of social presence: experiments in e-products and e-services. Omega **32**, 407–424 (2004)
61. Hassanein, K., Head, M.: Manipulating perceived social presence through the web interface and its impact on attitude towards online shopping. Int. J. Hum. Comput. Stud. **65**, 689–708 (2007)
62. Cyr, D., Head, M., Larios, H., Pan, B.: Exploring human images in website design: a multi-method approach. MIS Q. **33**, 539–566 (2009)
63. Qiu, L., Benbasat, I.: A study of demographic embodiments of product recommendation agents in electronic commerce. Int. J. Hum. Comput. Stud. **68**, 669–688 (2010)
64. Walther, J., Slovacek, C., Tidwell, L.: Is a picture worth a thousand words? Photographic images in long-term and short-term computer-mediated communication. Commun. Res. **28**, 105–134 (2001)
65. Di Blasio, P., Milani, L.: Computer-mediated communication and persuasion: peripheral vs. central route to opinion shift. Comput. Hum. Behav. **24**, 798–815 (2008)
66. Koch, S., Mueller, B., Kruse, L., Zumbach, J.: Constructing gender in chat groups. Sex Roles **53**, 29–41 (2005)
67. Nunamaker, J.F., Dennis, A.R., Valacich, J.S., Vogel, D., George, J.: Electronic meeting systems. Commun. ACM **34**, 40–61 (1991)
68. Niederman, F., March, S.T.: Design science and the accumulation of knowledge in the information systems discipline. ACM Trans. Manag. Inf. Syst. **3**, 1:1–1:15 (2012)
69. Koufaris, M.: Applying the technology acceptance model and flow theory to online consumer behavior. Inf. Syst. Res. **13**, 205–223 (2002)
70. Goldenson, D.R., Herbsleb, J.D.: After the appraisal: a systematic survey of process improvement, its benefits, and factors that influence success (1995)

User Evaluation of Hand Gestures for Designing an Intelligent In-Vehicle Interface

Hessam Jahani[1(✉)], Hasan J. Alyamani[1], Manolya Kavakli[1],
Arindam Dey[2], and Mark Billinghurst[2]

[1] VISOR Research Group, VR Lab, Department of Computing,
Macquarie University, Sydney 2109, Australia
Hessam.jahani-fariman@hdr.mq.edu.au
[2] Empathic Computing Lab, University of South Australia,
Adelaide 5095, Australia

Abstract. Driving a car is a high cognitive-load task requiring full attention behind the wheel. Intelligent navigation, transportation, and in-vehicle interfaces have introduced a safer and less demanding driving experience. However, there is still a gap for the existing interaction systems to satisfy the requirements of actual user experience. Hand gesture as an interaction medium, is natural and less visually demanding while driving. This paper aims to conduct a user-study with 79 participants to validate mid-air gestures for 18 major in-vehicle secondary tasks. We have demonstrated a detailed analysis on 900 mid-air gestures investigating preferences of gestures for in-vehicle tasks, their physical affordance, and driving errors. The outcomes demonstrate that employment of mid-air gestures reduces driving errors by up to 50% compared to traditional air-conditioning control. Results can be used for the development of vision-based in-vehicle gestural interfaces.

Keywords: Human computer interaction · Gesture recognition · In-vehicle interface · Human-centred design · User evaluation

1 Introduction

Development of autonomous and intelligent vehicles has gained massive popularity among the researchers and technologists recently [1]. Driving is considered as the primary major task in a vehicle, which requires full attention, while performing a group of concurrent tasks to safely reach the target destination. The required skills are influenced by the drivers' cognitive load that usually comes from the complexity of the driving task. To automate those tasks properly, drivers' behavior such as perceptual, cognitive and physical skills need to be considered. Modern vehicles consists of advanced technological tools and interfaces for phone calls, navigation, and controlling the radio [2] that increase cognitive load of the driver. This is especially important, since researchers have identified that high cognitive load could lead to more accidents while driving [3].

© Springer International Publishing AG 2017
A. Maedche et al. (Eds.): DESRIST 2017, LNCS 10243, pp. 104–121, 2017.
DOI: 10.1007/978-3-319-59144-5_7

One way to decrease the occurrence of cognitive load is to develop an intelligent in-vehicle User Interface (UI), to support the performance of a secondary task. Mid-air gestures have been proven to be capable of providing a less cumbersome in-vehicle interface for a safer driving experience [8]. Despite the recent developments in gesture-driven technologies facilitating the multi-touch and mid-air gesture recognition [4], in-vehicle interface systems have yet to provide a more efficient gesture vocabulary for performing secondary tasks. User-defined gesture sets in interaction design require analysis of characteristics and functions of the tasks, as well as user preferences to outline user requirements. Task analysis is necessary to provide an efficient in-vehicle gestural interface for specific secondary tasks.

The goal of this paper is to evaluate the appropriateness of a previously developed gesture vocabulary [5] for in-vehicle secondary tasks. [5] conducted experiments with 22 participants in a driving simulator using two different driving scenarios (involving high and low cognitive load situations). In their experiments, the participants were required to perform mid-air hand gestures for six specific air-conditioning (A/C) control tasks. In this paper, we conducted a survey for user-evaluation with 79 new participants to validate the gesture vocabulary proposed in [5]. In our experiments, the participants ranked gestures for 18 major in-vehicle secondary tasks. We conducted a detailed analysis on the physical affordance of mid-air gestures and the relationships between cognitive load and driving errors. Building upon this analysis, we propose a more detailed gesture vocabulary (GestDrive) for in-vehicle gestural interface than the one proposed by [5]. The main contribution of this paper can be highlighted as follows:

- User studies with 79 participants to define and validate mid-air gestures for 18 major in-vehicle tasks.
- Demonstration of a detailed analysis on in-vehicle mid-air gestures: Preferences of gesture sets, driving errors, and the physical affordance of gestures.

2   Related Works

In this section, we review cognitive load, driving errors and driving safety, physical affordance of gestures, and neuro-physiological performance in UI design.

2.1   Cognitive Load, Driving Errors and Driving Safety

Over-speeding, drunk driving, and driver's distraction are three main reasons for major car accidents [6]. Employment of intelligent vehicle systems (IVS) helps the driver in handling hazardous situations [7]. A collaborative driving system [8] may serve as an auxiliary instructor for the driver by providing information not only for navigation but also an in-vehicle control system. An advanced driving assistance system (ADAS) [9] may handle potential risky situations while driving. Using information provided by ADAS in a collaborative driving system, it is possible to build a mutual understanding for driver-vehicle communication which would guarantee a safer driving experience.

Driver's distraction is mainly originate from cognitive load which is usually caused by moving the attention from the primary task to performing a secondary task in the vehicle [10]. Most modern in-vehicle interface [2] systems such as media control systems, phone calling and navigation engage user perception and increase cognitive loading interaction. Normark et al. [10] determined that performing any in-vehicle secondary tasks would take from the same perceptual and cognitive resources as the driving task itself. A recent study by Metz et al. [11] found that performing secondary tasks would cause 25% (without a passenger) to 40% (with a passenger) more visual distraction that are more likely to occur in traffic standstills than during high-speed driving. [12] suggests that continuous tracking of pupil diameter as well as blink rate is an efficient technique to measure cognitive load. In terms of driving errors, a hypothesis to investigate is that high cognitive load will cause high number of driving errors.

2.2   Physical Affordance in UI Design

Physical affordance has been defined as one of four main affordance categories by Hartson [13] for the interaction design purpose. It is basically known as the potential action derives from the physical shape of the object or the way of interface utilization. Kaptelinin and Nardi [14] also suggests the instrumental affordances as a subclass for physical affordances which arguably has the potential to describe different aspects of interface design. Considering mid-air gestures for interaction, lack of adequate physical affordance has been considered as a challenge to employ them for free-hand interface design [15]. While, the visual affordance can easily be embedded into UIs, inability in recognizing physical affordances by the users, may lead to false affordances and performing the incorrect gestural action [16]. Moreover, when it comes to interface design, gestures with similar physical affordances may cause difficulties such as confusion in classification. Therefore, another hypothesis to investigate is that tasks with similar physical affordance should employ same set of hand gestures.

2.3   Neuro-Physiological Performance in UI Design

Understanding the application of neuro-science theories as the way human brain works, is an added value for designing any human-computer interaction platform [17]. Neuro-physiological measures such as EMG [18] and EEG [19] help improving the process of user-centered interface design by monitoring the brain activity and cognitive load. Boyali and Hashimoto [20] proposed a hybrid wheelchair empowered by using both hand gestures and EMG signals from the amputees. Another study by Rodgers [21], introduced monitoring cortisol levels as an efficient method to measure errors and elapse time for training tasks, decreasing the errors by controlling the cortisol levels, and as a result improving the overall acceptance of the developed health-care application. In addition in [22], an adaptive interface design for rehabilitation has been developed by employing users' physical abilities from hand gestures (data gloves), eye tracker, and brain activity signals from EEG.

2.4   Mid-Air Gestures for In-Vehicle Interfaces

Evolution of car technology demands a more efficient in-vehicle UI than the traditional one. Considering UI design, a very first alternative is the touch-based UI system which has been widely employed in modern vehicles [23]. However, Jaeger et al. [24] determined that the touch-based UIs cause distraction for the driver behind the wheel. Another study by Doring et al. [4] found that multi-touch UI system increases the visual demands for the driver. Beside touch-based UI, speech is another obvious alternative for in-vehicle UI design. However, it can increase the cognitive load for the driving task, distract the driver and as a result reduce safety [25]. Jamson et al. [25] proved that using speech for in-vehicle UI design can delay the driver's reaction by 30%. Other research also suggested that using speech for in-vehicle secondary tasks would make it hard for drivers to manage and prioritize different tasks [26].

Regarding in-vehicle gestural interface, Riener [23] suggest that mid-air gestures can be an efficient alternative for touch-based interfaces which require permanent observation and feedback. Riener et al. [27] asked 67 participants to list their performed tasks, following by ranking the major secondary tasks extraction. The result was a list of the most frequent control and media tasks that could be performed with gesture. The previous research used specific pre-defined gesture codes and simple implementations rather than natural user gestures. There is still a gap to explore users' need, user evaluation, and preference for designing a user-defined gestural interface for in-vehicle purpose.

2.5   User-Elicitation for Interface Design

When it comes to gesture-based interface design, a common mistake is to prioritize ease of implementation to the actual user requirements, preferences and also neglecting interaction affordance [14]. User elicited-based approaches makes it possible to understand users behaviour and preference to design a more efficient UI [28]. It has been successfully applied for various gesture recognition applications, e.g., table-tops [28], mobile phones [29], humanoid robots [30], gameplay [31] and 3D remote object manipulation [32]. Gesture interfaces are often designed without fully consulting end-users, or sacrifice usability for ease of implementation and practical reasons. As defined by user elicitation studies, UI designers often do not share the same conceptual models as the end-users that should be catered to [33]. User elicitation studies ideally result in a common set of suitable gestures which were determined by the highest number of agreed gestures among participants. User elicitation approach not only makes it possible to understand users behaviour and preference to design a more efficient UI, but also it is practically more desired as comes from a natural under-standing [28].

Within this context, this paper aims at evaluating a user-elicited vocabulary [5] for in-vehicle gestural interface using major secondary tasks from [27]. The major sec-ondary task in [5] was controlling A/C system which comprised of 6 different sub-tasks. Whole elicitation phase was performed using a driving simulator environ-ment as due to their characteristics, such as safety and flexibility of designing driving scenarios [2], they are considered as a useful tool to study issues related to driving. Following this, 79 new participants are asked to validate the appropriateness of the gesture vocabulary. More analysis on gestures' physical affordance, driving errors, and cognitive loads while driving would be maintained. Also, we hypothesize that a user-elicited vocabulary will provide a more efficient in-vehicle gestural A/C interface compared to the traditional A/C interface.

3 Methods

The methodology in this paper consists of a comparative analysis and a user evaluation study on the previously developed user-elicited gesture vocabulary (GestDrive) [5]. In the previous work [5], we conducted experiments in a driving simulation to define an initial gesture vocabulary called GestDrive for 6 A/C control tasks and 12 mid-air gestures. In this study, we have conducted further experiments to validate the efficiency of the gesture-based interface over the traditional in-vehicle interface (physical knobs and panels), and evaluated the appropriateness of GestDrive for additional major secondary tasks from [27]. In this section, we describe the entire methodology in detail.

3.1 Data Collection and Experimental Design

In this section, we present details of data collection, experimental illustration, and manual classification of gestures. The overall procedure can be summarized in the following temporal order:

- A user study in the driving simulation with 22 participants: comparison of gestural A/C and Traditional A/C.
- To manually classify and modify GestDrive using the same method as [5].
- To perform an evaluation study for 12 gestures from GestDrive with 79 new participants: examining the appropriateness of GestDrive for 18 major secondary tasks (see Table 1).

Gestural Interface vs. Traditional Interface Experiment
In the previous study [5], the experiments were designed to develop a gesture taxonomy for an in-vehicle driver interface. The study population was comprised of 22 participants, 5 females and 17 males, aged 19–38 (average 25, SD: 2.5). All participants carried a driver's license and 15 of them were right-handed. The setup was composed of a driving simulator [28] running in a three-monitor configuration (see Fig. 1). Each participant was asked to perform mid-air gestures for controlling the air-conditioning system while driving in the simulated environment. They were encouraged to use as many gestures as possible. The focus was on extracting natural gestures for the designated tasks, to propose an efficient in-vehicle gestural interface.

Following from the previous user study, here we re-performed the same driving setup but this time, asked the participants to use the traditional A/C panel and knobs. The purpose of this stage was to examine how well mid-air gestures can be performed in control tasks in comparison with the traditional A/C control system. We randomly

Table 1. Major driving secondary tasks modified from [8].

Category	Secondary tasks
A/C control tasks	(1) Turn on/off A/C
	(2) Adjust the temperature level
	(3) Adjusting A/C middle panel: horizontally
	(4) Adjust A/C middle panel: vertically
	(5) Adjust A/C driver-side panel: horizontally
	(6) Adjusting A/C driver-side panel: vertically
Car-control tasks	(7) Turn on/off engine
	(8) Indicate left/right
	(9) Open/Close window
	(10) Adjust high/low beam light
	(11) Wipe windshield
	(12) Turn on/off flasher
Media-control tasks	(13) Turn on/off radio
	(14) Accept a call
	(15) Increase/decrease volume
	(16) Change song title
	(17) Switch radio source
	(18) Mute radio

Fig. 1. Driving simulator (Forum 8) setup, camera views for recording middle/driver side gestures.

assigned participants to perform gestures in a given time (15 s for each gesture) for either (1) a high-load-simulated driving task or (2) a low-load-simulated driving task. Participants were recorded with two cameras (see Fig. 1). Two 5 min scenarios with different levels of driving load (i.e. traffic, intersections and roundabouts). All instructions regarding navigation and timing for each control task, were indicated on the driver's screen. Also, for the familiarization phase, all the participants were asked to drive about 10 min in a simulated environment. Potential participants with the risk of motion sickness, were recognized and excluded from the study. Finally, we asked participants to repeat both scenarios—after a 10-min break to avoid fatigue—and perform 6 A/C control tasks by actually using the traditional A/C panel and knobs. Forum 8 (Fig. 1) provides a log file of the driving history which allowed to extract the driving errors. A final analysis of driving errors would be performed for a gesture-based A/C control system versus a traditional A/C system.

Manual Classification Approach for Defining GestDrive Vocabulary

The goal in the previous research [5] was to contribute to the domain with a more detailed gesture vocabulary (GestDrive) based on the Wobbrock et al.'s [28] form-based dimension taxonomy. The proposed GestDrive vocabulary provides a better understanding of the whole interface design process using gestures only (Table 2) as a communication medium. Wobbrock's gesture codes showed potential to be used in practical applications by Microsoft, as well as Kühnel et al. [34]. The idea is to build upon Wobbrock's gesture codes and through manual classification of in-vehicle gestures. With a close look at the GestDrive vocabulary developed in [5], we have found that with some slight modifications, the vocabulary can be easier to apply. For instance, vertical and horizontal movement with the same gesture (such as FH3), can be separated into two different gesture codes. Table 2 shows the modified GestDrive gesture vocabulary comprised of 12 gesture codes and their definitions.

User-Evaluation Survey

To validate the user-elicited gesture vocabulary from the actual in-vehicle experiments, a user evaluation study was performed. The evaluation surveys were designed based on gestures from the user elicitation experiments. We demonstrated three online surveys with 79 new participants, 24 females and 55 males, aged 18–68 (average: 28, SD: 3.5) to examine the usability of user-elicited gestures. each participant was asked to rank the appropriateness of gestures for a specific secondary task from Table 1. Survey 1 was about A/C control tasks, Survey 2 about major car control tasks, and Survey 3 about evaluating six media control tasks (As in Table 1). In each survey, the participant goes through a short unlabeled video instruction for each gesture followed by a five-level Likert test to rank the usefulness of the shown gesture for each secondary task. In fact, the participants were asked to guess which gestures can perform which secondary tasks (on the contrary to the user-elicitation study [5]). The results of this evaluation determine how applicable the user-defined gestures are for new sets of participants and new set of secondary tasks.

Table 2. Gesture codes and functions for proposed vocabulary (GestDrive).

	Gesture Code	Gesture Function	
Full-hand	**FH1** Static Pose	Hand pose is held in one location	
	FH2 Dynamic pose with full hand	Hand pose changes in one location	
	FH3 Full hand static pose & move left/right	Hand pose is held as hand moves to let/right	
	FH4 Full hand static pose & move up/down	Hand pose is held as hand moves to up/down	
	FH5 Full hand static pose & path	Hand pose is held as hand turn around	
Two-finger	**TF6** Dynamic pose with 2 fingers	Two fingers' pose changes as hand turns around	
	TF7 Static pose & move left/right with 2 fingers	Two fingers' pose is held as moves to left/right	
	TF8 Static pose & move up/down with 2 fingers	Two fingers' pose is held as moves up/down	
	TF9 Two-fingers hold	Static pose with two fingers	
One-finger	**OF10** One-finger hold	Static pose with one finger	
	OF11 One-finger move left/right	Static pose & move left/right with one finger	
	OF12 One-finger move up/down	Static pose & move up/down with one finger	

3.2   Analysis

Gesture Evaluation Approach for In-Vehicle Secondary Tasks

To validate the appropriateness of the gesture vocabulary, we designed three online surveys. Each survey included unlabelled short videos of 12 gestures from GestDrive. For each gesture, participants were asked to rank the gesture usability for a list of tasks using a five-level Likert test from 1 (Very useful) to 5 (Not useful at all). Then, we ranked gesture appropriateness for each task based on the mean score (1 to 5), presented the result of gesture evaluation, and preformed further affordance analysis.

Cognitive Load and Driving Error Analysis

Using a log file that was provided by Forum 8, we also considered the types and the number of driving errors for each user-study scenario, to draw a comparison to see whether there are any significant differences and in the preferences for high/low cognitive load environments. Comparisons were drawn based on 3 different error types and for both driving scenarios (high and low cognitive load). High and low cognitive load driving scenarios have been designed technically inside the driving software considering parameters such as traffic loads, speed limits, and complex or simple road scenarios. Take an example, for high-cognitive load driving scenario the participants have been asked to perform driving in a high traffic full of roundabouts and intersections where they need to perform secondary tasks. Error types comprise duration of over-speeding, number of lane-changing, and number of wrong enter/exit to/from roundabout and intersections. In regards to cognitive load and driving errors, the hypothesis for this paper is that driving task with higher cognitive loads would cause more driving errors.

Affordance Analysis

Following the user evaluation survey for gestures from GestDrive, we perform the physical affordance analysis for 2 new sets of in-vehicle tasks from Reiner et al. [27] as well as 6 A/C control tasks from the user-study. The main hypothesis for physical affordance analysis is that in-vehicle secondary tasks with the similar physical affordances, can be performed employing same sets of hand gesture. These new in-vehicle tasks simply consist of: **Set 1:** 6 car-control tasks such as turn on/off the engine; and **Set 2:** 6 media-control tasks such as turn on/off the radio (Table 1). First, we identify the secondary tasks with similar physical affordance. We classified in-vehicle secondary tasks based on their potential demands into 4 main types of physical affordance: **(a)** Turning on/off, **(b)** Level/Degree adjustment, **(c)** Horizontal adjustment, and **(d)** Vertical adjustment (See Table 3). Take an example, task (6): Adjusting the A/C panel vertically and task (9): Opening/Closing the window, both demand employment of similar gestures, for vertical interaction. Then, we explore user preferred gestures, from GestDrive vocabulary, for each of these tasks and compare them to the results of evaluation surveys to check the validity of our initial hypothesis. A detailed comparison will be discussed further in results, affordance analysis, and discussion sections.

Table 3. Secondary tasks with the hypothetically similar gesture employment.

Type of physical affordance	Tasks with hypothetically similar gesture employment
Turning on/off	(1), (7), (12), (13), (14), (18)
Level/degree adjustment	(2), (10), (15), (16), (17)
Horizontal adjustment	(3), (5), (8), (11)
Vertical adjustment	(4), (6), (9)

4   Results

In this section, further analysis on the complexity of gesture vocabulary, physical affordances, and driving errors are discussed.

4.1   GestDrive: Analysis of Evaluation Surveys

In total 900 gestures have been acquired, classified into 12 gesture types from GestDrive, and rated from 1 (Very useful) to 5 (Not useful at all) for each of 18 secondary tasks in the evaluation surveys. Figure 2 depicts the rating for each survey separately. Also, Table 4 shows a list of 3 most preferred (Mean score closer to 1) gestures for each task. In survey 1, we have investigated subjective preferences of using 12 different gesture types for six different secondary tasks related to in-vehicle A/C control. We have asked participants to rate each gesture type for their usability in all tasks. There were 26 participants. Accordingly, we have a total of $26 \times 6 \times 12 = 1872$ data points. We ran a repeated measure ANOVA to analyze this data and recorded significance level at $p < .01$. We found significant main effects of both Gesture type F $(11, 275) = 13.96$, $p < .001$, partial $\eta^2 = .36$ and Task F$(5, 125) = 22.42$, $p < .001$, partial $\eta^2 = .47$. Expectedly, we have also noticed an interaction effect of Task $\times$ Gesture F$(55, 1375) = 19.31$, $p < .001$, partial $\eta^2 = .44$, which indicates some gestures were more suitable to a task than other gestures (see Fig. 2). Namely per Fig. 2 and Table 4, for Turning on/off the A/C, FH5 (Full-hand static pose & path) has the highest mean score (≈ 1.5) and thus is the most preferred gesture for the task. TF6 (Two-finger dynamic pose) and FH1 (Full-hand static pose) are next most preferred gestures for Turn on/off A/C task.

Considering Survey 2, we have investigated subjective preferences of using 12 different gesture types for six different secondary tasks related to general in-vehicle controls such as turning the engine on or off. There were 28 participants. Accordingly, we have a total of $28 \times 6 \times 12 = 2016$ data points. We ran a repeated measure ANOVA to analyze this data and recorded significance level at $p < .01$. We found significant main effects of both Gesture type F$(11, 297) = 5.6$, $p < .001$, partial $\eta^2 = .17$ and Task F$(5, 135) = 5.31$, $p < .001$, partial $\eta^2 = .16$. Expectedly, we have also noticed an interaction effect of Task $\times$ Gesture F$(55, 1485) = 12.27$, $p < .001$, partial $\eta^2 = .31$, which indicates some gestures were more suitable to a task than other gestures (see Fig. 2). Namely per Fig. 2 and Table 4, for Wiping the windshield, FH3 (Full hand static pose & move left/right) has the highest mean score (≈ 2.3) and thus is

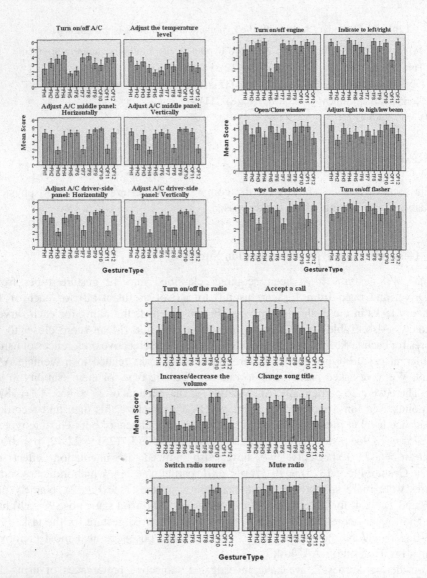

Fig. 2. Result of evaluation survey 1, ranking of 12 gestures for 6 A/C control tasks (from 1: very useful to 5: not useful at all).

the most preferred gesture for the task. TF7 (two-finger Static pose & move left/right) and OF11 (One-finger move left/right) are next most preferred gestures for Wipe the windshield task.

In Survey 3, there were 25 participants. Accordingly, we have a total of $25 \times 6 \times 12 = 1800$ data points. We ran a repeated measure ANOVA to analyze this data and recorded significance level at $p < .01$. We found significant main effects of both Gesture type $F(11, 264) = 8.19$, $p < .001$, partial $\eta^2 = .25$ and Task $F(5, 120) = 14.77$, $p < .001$, partial $\eta^2 = .38$. Expectedly, we have also noticed an interaction effect of

Table 4. Most preferred gestures (mean score closer to 1) for major in-vehicle secondary tasks. Colors indicate tasks which employ similar gestures.).

Secondary tasks	Gesture preferences (*based on ranking from surveys*)
(1) Turn on/off A/C	FH5-TF6-FH1
(2) Adjust the temperature level	FH5-TF6-FH4
(3) Adjusting A/C middle panel: Horizontally	FH3-TF7-OF11
(4) Adjust A/C middle panel: Vertically	FH4-OF12-TF8
(5) Adjust A/C driver-side panel: Horizontally	FH3-TF7-OF11
(6) Adjusting A/C driver-side panel: Vertically	FH4-OF12-TF8
(7) Turn on/off engine	FH5-TF6-FH1
(8) Indicate left/right	OF11-TF7-FH3
(9) Open/Close window	TF8-OF12-FH4
(10) Adjust high/low beam light	FH2-TF6-TF9
(11) Wipe windshield	FH3-TF7-OF11
(12) Turn on/off flasher	FH2-TF6-TF9
(13) Turn on/off radio	TF6-FH1-FH5
(14) Accept a call	TF7-OF11-FH3
(15) Increase/Decrease volume	FH5-TF6-FH4
(16) Change song title	OF11-TF7-FH3
(17) Switch radio source	TF7-FH3-OF11
(18) Mute radio	FH1-OF10-TF9

Task × Gesture $F(55, 1320) = 20.34$, $p < .001$, partial $\eta^2 = .46$, which indicates some gestures were more suitable to a task than other gestures (see Fig. 2). Namely per Fig. 2 and Table 4, for switching radio sources, TF7 (Two-finger Static pose & move left/right) has the highest mean score (≈ 1.6) and thus is the most preferred gesture for the task. FH3 (Full hand static pose & move left/right) and OF11 (One-finger move left/right) are next most preferred gestures for Switch radio source task. More detailed analysis will be presented in affordance analysis as well as discussion section.

4.2 Affordance Analysis

As it has been discussed in the methodology section (See Analysis description), for physical affordance analysis our hypothesis was that in-vehicle secondary tasks with the similar physical affordances, can be performed employing the same sets of hand gesture. We initially grouped in-vehicle secondary tasks into 4 types of affordance (See Table 3). Following analysis of evaluation surveys, tasks with similar gesture employments are grouped using colors. Besides 4 main types of physical affordance hypothesized for secondary tasks, we identified 2 new sets of tasks with similar gesture employments:

- New physical affordance from survey 2 (general car control tasks): which consists of task (10) adjusting high/low beam light and task (12) turning on/off the flasher. Both tasks were performed using Full-hand dynamic pose (FH2), Two-finger dynamic pose (TF6), and Two-finger hold (TF9) respectively.
- New physical affordance from survey 3 (media control tasks): which includes task (14) accepting a call, (16) changing song titles, and (17) switching radio sources. The most preferred gestures were Two-finger static pose and move left/right (TF7), One-finger move left/right (OF11), and Full-hand static pose and move left/right (FH3).

According to Table 4, task (18), muting the radio was the only secondary task that does not fit in any group of gesture preferences. It demands its own set of most preferred gestures namely, Full-hand static pose (FH1), One-finger hold (OF10), and Two-finger hold (TF9). We will describe a more detailed interpretation of results as well as implication for future interface design in the discussion.

4.3   Analysis of Driving Errors: Gesture-Based vs. Traditional A/C Control System

In the last stage of the experiments, we asked participants to repeat both scenarios by actually using the traditional A/C panel. After the analysis of recorded driving videos, we compared driving errors between mid-air gestures and traditional A/C control panel. Tables 5 and 6 depict driving errors of 22 participants, for traditional and gesture-based A/C control systems, respectively. Comparisons were drawn based on 3 different error types and for both driving scenarios (high load). Error types comprise duration of over-speeding, number of lane-changing, and number of wrong enter/exit to/from roundabout and intersection. Considering the differences of driving errors' in driving scenarios, for traditional A/C system (Table 5), the results show that driving errors have slightly decreased in scenario 2 (which associated with low cognitive load). This slight drop was predictable considering the cognitive load differences between the two scenarios. Conducting a two-sample t-test for over-speeding errors showed no significant differences between two scenarios ($\alpha = 0.05$, $t(30) = 3.54$, $p = 0.25$).

Table 5. Comparison of driving errors participants has made using standard A/C panel/knobs to perform A/C control tasks.

Traditional A/C control system	Error type		
	Over-speeding (*seconds*) (#total) **percentage**	Lane-changing (*to left/middle curb*)	Wrong enter/exit (*to/from roundabout & intersection*)
Driving scenario 1	681 (3504) **19.43%**	110	50
Driving scenario 2	513 (4256) **12.05%**	97	43

Likewise, for gesture-based A/C control system (Table 6), drop in over-speeding was not significant in the 2nd low cognitive load scenario ($\alpha = 0.05$, $t(30) = 3.88$, $p = 0.15$). Comparing traditional A/C control system (Table 5) with mid-air gesture-based A/C control system (Table 6), the error rates dropped dramatically in gesture-based system. Over-speeding for scenario 1 in traditional A/C system ($M = 0.88$, $SD = 0.51$), dropped down to less than half (from 19.43% to 8.31%) for scenario 1 in gesture-based A/C system ($M = 0.37$, $SD = 0.24$). The result of two-pair t-test showed significant different from traditional to gesture-based A/C system ($\alpha = 0.05$, $t(30) = 4.19$, $p = 0.0001$). Likewise, for scenario 2, there was a significant difference for over-speeding errors in two A/C systems ($\alpha = 0.05$, $t(30) = 4.74$, $p = 0.0002$). Regarding lane-changing error rate, it has been decreased by 30% when the driver employed mid-air gestures. In addition, participants performed approximately 50% less errors when it comes to enter/exit roundabout and intersection in both scenarios. T-test comparisons (on only scenario 1) for both Lane-changing ($\alpha = 0.05$, $t(40) = 5.21$, $p = 0.0029$) and enter/exit roundabout/intersection ($\alpha = 0.05$, $t(38) = 4.78$, $p = 0.0001$), depicted significantly less errors for gesture-based A/C control system.

Table 6. Comparison of driving errors participants has made using mid-air gestures to perform A/C control tasks.

Gesture-based A/C control system	Error type		
	Over-speeding (*seconds*) (#total) **Percentage**	Lane-changing (*to left/middle curb*)	Wrong enter/exit (*to/from roundabout & intersection*)
Driving scenario 1	289 (3475) **8.31%**	76	23
Driving scenario 2	207 (4213) **4.91%**	65	17

5   Discussion

In this section, we discuss interpretation of gesture analysis as well as the implications of our findings for in-vehicle gestural interface and limitations. Considering gesture taxonomy break-down and analysis, findings can be summarized as follows.

5.1   The Effect of Cognitive Load on In-Vehicle Gesture Employments and Driving Errors

According to GestDrive taxonomy breakdown and further statistical t-test analysis, even though driving scenario 2 was designed with a lower cognitive load, but there are no significant differences in the types of gesture employment between two scenarios ($\alpha = 0.05$, $t(16) = 0.15$, $p = 0.44$). Moreover, in regards to driving errors analysis (See Tables 5 and 6) for both gesture-based and traditional A/C control system, increase in cognitive load has no significant effect on while-driving errors. Thus, driving cognitive load has no significant effects on driver's gesture employment and while-driving error performance in the simulated environment.

5.2   Effectiveness of Mid-Air Gestures for In-Vehicle Gestural A/C Interfaces

As the last step to the analysis of the gesture vocabulary, we designed a study on controlling A/C system to test the efficiency of mid-air gestures in comparison to the traditional A/C control panel. In terms of error decrement for the nominated secondary task (A/C control), statistical analysis of the results showed that employment of mid-air gestures caused significantly less driving errors (See Table 6). It should be considered that higher error rates for the traditional A/C system, occurred in situations which participants were already familiar with driving scenarios (as gesture-based experiments have been performed prior to the traditional experiments and to avoid fatigue they had a 10-min rest time). Thus, in terms of error decrement for the nominated secondary task (such as A/C control), employment of mid-air gestures was significantly efficient. In other words, if we interpret less driving errors as a sign of safety, mid-air hand gestures for an A/C control system improve the safety in driving regardless of cognitive load (both high and low cognitive load).

5.3   Physical Affordance Analysis

Comparing the results of evaluation surveys in regards to gesture employments in Table 7, with secondary tasks initial physical affordance in Table 4, indicates that for 12 out of 18 tasks the affordance was as hypothesized. In other words, 12 tasks (66%) were classified in the same group as the initial hypothesis (See Table 4), 5 tasks into new types of physical affordances, and one task, muting the radio, which demanded its own set of gestures. In total, for major in-vehicle secondary tasks and in regards to 900 mid-air gestures, we identified 6 main physical affordances, each one demands performing a specific set of gestures. In total for in-vehicle secondary tasks, we identified 7

Table 7. Classification of in-vehicle secondary tasks based on types of physical affordances and major corresponding gesture preferences.

Tasks with similar physical affordance	Gesture preferences (3 highest-ranked gestures from surveys)
(1), (7), (13)	TF6 – FH1 – FH5
(2), (15)	FH5 – TF6 – FH4
(3), (5), (8), (11)	FH3 - TF7 – OF11
(4), (6), (9)	FH4 – OF12 – TF8
(10), (12)	FH2 – TF6 – TF9
(14), (16), (17)	TF7 – OF11 – FH3
(18)	FH1 – OF10 – TF9

major gesture preferences (including gesture preferences for misfit task 18). These 7 major gesture patterns can be applied as patterns to develop an efficient gesture recognizer in the next step.

5.4 Implications for In-Vehicle Gestural Interface

Considering results of evaluation surveys with 79 participants, we derived several factors in regards to an in-vehicle gestural interface design:

- In the evaluation study, we explored using 12 gestures from GestDrive to examine wider range of in-vehicle secondary tasks, namely 18 major tasks from [27]. 900 gestures were ranked through 5 level Likert usability surveys. Again, here GestDrive showed significant results in capability to describe all 18 major secondary tasks. Moreover, physical affordance and gesture preference analysis constructed a more detailed taxonomy of GestDrive including identification of 6 types of physical affordances and 7 major gesture preferences.
- As part of evaluation surveys, participants were asked to suggest any potential gestures they would think of, beside 12 gestures from GestDrive. Comments from 79 online surveyors showed that 65 of them (82%) thought the proposed GestDrive can describe major in-vehicle secondary tasks.

5.5 Limitations and Next Steps

The user evaluation study approach proposed mainly disregard the user's feedback and second chance to employ an alternative gesture for each task. As a drawback to this approach, legacy bias [35] may have a significant effect on the user study as there is no optimal way to determine the most proper gesture for each task. Also, the context of secondary tasks as well as type of in-vehicle console (traditional or modern) may have impact on users' choice of employed gestures. One possible next step would be to explore feasibility of GestDrive vocabulary for further user study with the real vehicle environment rather than driving simulation. These issues are worth to investigate, but are beyond the scope of the current study.

6 Conclusion and Future Work

Employing hand gestures for interface design has been shown promising results lately. With the development of modern vehicle systems, there is a demand for an easy to use and safe in-vehicle interface that decreases the driver distraction. In this paper, a methodology to develop a user-defined gesture vocabulary for 18 major in-vehicle tasks has been presented, after the evaluation study performed by 79 participants. We analyzed 900 mid-air gestures, their physical affordances, preferences for each task, driving errors, and their association with cognitive load. The analysis for each of 18 control tasks helped us modify and extend GestDrive that consists of 12 gesture patterns, and 7 gesture preferences. Analysis of driving errors demonstrated superiority of mid-air gestures for in-vehicle A/C control where it caused error reduction from 30% to 50%, compared to a traditional A/C system. A potential extension to our study is to use the developed user-defined GestDrive vocabulary, and 7 major gesture preferences to implement a vision-based gesture recognizer for an in-vehicle interface and perform the system efficiency analysis and measure the real-time recognition rates. Also, there is a potential to conduct a separate research study on developing a mid-air gesture recognition system with the optimal physical affordance regarding in-vehicle applications.

References

1. Victor, T., Rothoff, M., Coelingh, E., Ödblom, A., Burgdorf, K.: When autonomous vehicles are introduced on a larger scale in the road transport system: the Drive Me project. In: Watzenig, D., Horn, M. (eds.) Automated Driving, pp. 541–546. Springer, Cham (2017). doi:10.1007/978-3-319-31895-0_24
2. Drews, F.A., Yazdani, H., Godfrey, C.N., Cooper, J.M., Strayer, D.L.: Text messaging during simulated driving. Hum. Factors: J. Hum. Factors Ergon. Soc. **51**, 762–770 (2009)
3. Gregoriades, A., Sutcliffe, A., Papageorgiou, G., Louvieris, P.: Human-centered safety analysis of prospective road designs. IEEE Trans. Syst. Man Cybern.-Part A: Syst. Hum. **40**(2), 236–250 (2010)
4. Döring, T., Kern, D., Marshall, P., Pfeiffer, M., Schöning, J., Gruhn, V., Schmidt, A.: Gestural interaction on the steering wheel: reducing the visual demand. ACM (2011)
5. Fariman, H.J., Alyamani, H.J., Kavakli, M., Hamey, L.: Designing a user-defined gesture vocabulary for an in-vehicle climate control system. In: Proceedings of 28th Australian Conference on Computer-Human Interaction, Launceston, Tasmania, Australia. ACM (2016)
6. Ruikar, M.: National statistics of road traffic accidents in India. J. Orthop. Traumatol. Rehabil. **6**(1), 1 (2013)
7. Bonin-Font, F., Ortiz, A., Oliver, G.: Visual navigation for mobile robots: a survey. J. Intell. Rob. Syst. **53**(3), 263 (2008)
8. Lin, S.-P., Maxemchuk, N.F.: The fail-safe operation of collaborative driving systems. J. Intell. Transp. Syst. **20**(1), 88–101 (2016)
9. Velez, G., Otaegui, O.: Embedding vision-based advanced driver assistance systems: a survey. IET Intell. Transp. Syst. **11**(3), 103–112 (2016)
10. Normark, C.J., Tretten, P., Gärling, A.: Do redundant head-up and head-down display configurations cause distractions. (2009)
11. Metz, B., Landau, A., Just, M.: Frequency of secondary tasks in driving–results from naturalistic driving data. Saf. Sci. **68**, 195–203 (2014)
12. Chen, S., Epps, J.: Using task-induced pupil diameter and blink rate to infer cognitive load. Hum.-Comput. Interact. **29**(4), 390–413 (2014)
13. Hartson, R.: Cognitive, physical, sensory, and functional affordances in interaction design. Behav. Inf. Technol. **22**(5), 315–338 (2003)
14. Kaptelinin, V., Nardi, B.: Affordances in HCI: toward a mediated action perspective. ACM (2012)
15. Merrill, D.J.: FlexiGesture: a sensor-rich real-time adaptive gesture and affordance learning platform for electronic music control. Massachusetts Institute of Technology (2004)
16. Norman, D.A.: Affordance, conventions, and design. Interactions **6**(3), 38–43 (1999)

17. Riedl, R., Davis, F.D., Banker, R., Kenning, P.H.: Neuroscience in Information Systems Research: Applying Knowledge of Brain Functionality Without Neuroscience Tools. Springer, Heidelberg (2017)
18. Jahani Fariman, H., Ahmad, S.A., Hamiruce Marhaban, M., Ali Jan Ghasab, M., Chappell, P.H.: Simple and computationally efficient movement classification approach for EMG-controlled prosthetic hand: ANFIS vs. artificial neural network. Intell. Autom. Soft Comput. **21**, 1–15 (2015). Taylor and Francis
19. Kucukyildiz, G., Ocak, H., Karakaya, S., Sayli, O.: Design and implementation of a multi sensor based brain computer interface for a robotic wheelchair. J. Intell. Rob. Syst. 1–17 (2017)
20. Boyali, A., Hashimoto, N.: Spectral collaborative representation based classification for hand gestures recognition on electromyography signals. Biomed. Signal Process. Control **24**, 11–18 (2016)
21. Rodger, J.A.: Reinforcing inspiration for technology acceptance: improving memory and software training results through neuro-physiological performance. Comput. Hum. Behav. **38**, 174–184 (2014)
22. Lin, Y., Breugelmans, J., Iversen, M., Schmidt, D.: An adaptive interface design (AID) for enhanced computer accessibility and rehabilitation. Int. J. Hum Comput Stud. **98**, 14–23 (2017)
23. Riener, A.: Gestural interaction in vehicular applications. Computer **4**, 42–47 (2012)
24. Jæger, M.G., Skov, M.B. Thomassen, N.G. You can touch, but you can't look: interacting with in-vehicle systems. ACM (2008)
25. Jamson, A.H., Westerman, S.J., Hockey, G.R.J., Carsten, O.M.: Speech-based e-mail and driver behavior: effects of an in-vehicle message system interface. Hum. Factors: J. Hum. Factors Ergon. Soc. **16**(4), 625 639 (2004)
26. Akl, A., Valaee, S.: Accelerometer-based gesture recognition via dynamic-time warping, affinity propagation, & compressive sensing. IEEE (2010)
27. Riener, A., Ferscha, A., Bachmair, F., Hagmüller, P., Lemme, A., Muttenthaler, D., Pühringer, D., Rogner, H., Tappe, A., Weger, F.: Standardization of the in-car gesture interaction space. ACM (2013)
28. Wobbrock, J.O., Morris, M.R., Wilson, A.D.: User-defined gestures for surface computing. ACM (2009)
29. Ruiz, J., Li, Y., Lank, E.: User-defined motion gestures for mobile interaction. ACM (2011)
30. Obaid, M., Häring, M., Kistler, F., Bühling, R., André, E.: User-defined body gestures for navigational control of a humanoid robot. In: Ge, S.S., Khatib, O., Cabibihan, J.-J., Simmons, R., Williams, M.-A. (eds.) ICSR 2012. LNCS, vol. 7621, pp. 367–377. Springer, Heidelberg (2012). doi:10.1007/978-3-642-34103-8_37
31. Silpasuwanchai, C., Ren, X.: Designing concurrent full-body gestures for intense gameplay. Int. J. Hum. Comput. Stud. **80**, 1–13 (2015)
32. Ha, T., Billinghurst, M., Woo, W.: An interactive 3D movement path manipulation method in an augmented reality environment. Interact. Comput. **24**(1), 10–24 (2012)
33. Nielsen, M., Störring, M., Moeslund, T.B., Granum, E.: A procedure for developing intuitive and ergonomic gesture interfaces for HCI. In: Camurri, A., Volpe, G. (eds.) GW 2003. LNCS, vol. 2915, pp. 409–420. Springer, Heidelberg (2004). doi:10.1007/978-3-540-24598-8_38
34. Kühnel, C., Westermann, T., Hemmert, F., Kratz, S., Müller, A., Möller, S.: I'm home: defining and evaluating a gesture set for smart-home control. Int. J. Hum. Comput. Stud. **69**(11), 693–704 (2011)
35. Seyed, T., Burns, C., Costa Sousa, M., Maurer, F., Tang, A.: Eliciting usable gestures for multi-display environments. ACM (2012)

DSR in Data Science and Business Analytics

Design and Evaluation of a System Dynamics Based Business Model Evaluation Method

Thomas Moellers[1(✉)], Bastian Bansemir[2(✉)], Max Pretzl[2(✉)],
and Oliver Gassmann[1]

[1] Institute of Technology Management, University of St. Gallen,
Dufourstrasse 40a, 9000 St. Gallen, Switzerland
thomas.moellers@unisg.ch
[2] Business Analytics & Insights, BMW Group,
Heidemannstrasse 164, 80939 Munich, Germany
{bastian.bansemir,max.pretzl}@bmw.de

Abstract. The business model has become an increasingly important concept to facilitate competitive advantages. However, due to its complexity managers face difficulties to evaluate how changes in the business model affect its performance. Existing approaches fall short to facilitate sufficient understanding of the influencing factors that drive the business models behavior. Drawing from System Dynamics, we propose a multi-step evaluation method to effectively support decision making in the context of complexity. Thereby we focus on the integration of available knowledge and data to explicate and quantify the essential cause-effect relationships inside the business model. The artifact is evaluated through multiple use cases inside the BMW Group. It reveals that System Dynamics enhances business model understanding not only for the decision maker but also for the stakeholders which enhances subsequent implementation of business model changes.

Keywords: Business model · System Dynamics · Evaluation

1 Introduction

Over the last decade and a half the business model concept has increasingly attracted attention from both practitioners and academics alike [1]. As a management tool the business model aims to facilitate higher profitability [2] and eventually competitive advantage [3]. Their potential has been revealed in particular by a number of companies that have transformed whole industries based on a holistic business model design. Uber exemplifies this through its current valuation of 68 bn US$ that is higher than the one of BMW, a long-established industry leader for premium cars. However, for such established companies the innovation of a business model is an often lengthy, risky and costly enterprise that implies significant organizational changes. That is due to the complexity inherent to the business model [4]. Behind the success stories such as Uber often told [5] the business model is a set of choices and consequences [6] that is far from trivial. As a chain of factors that span across company boundaries the mechanics at work create feedback loops and dynamics that the human mind is incapable of grasping holistically

A. Maedche et al. (Eds.): DESRIST 2017, LNCS 10243, pp. 125–144, 2017.
DOI: 10.1007/978-3-319-59144-5_8

[7, 8]. External complexity manifested through increasing intensity and speed of competition as well as rapid technological advancements further exacerbates decision making for managers and the outcome of their choices typically contradict the intended consequences [9]. This context holds particularly true for business model choices in the automotive industry in which digitization, autonomous driving, electrification and changing customer needs constitute a highly complex interplay of diverse developments.

Understanding the business model behind the stories by understanding the set of choices and consequences is a manager's dream because it allows for the evaluation of business model decisions before implementation [10]. Up to now evaluation approaches typically undervalue the effect of dynamics for business model choices or lack of oversimplification. Personal experience and further alternative substitutes typically replace evidence in the light of complexity [11].

This paper presents the design and evaluation of a System Dynamics based method for business model evaluation mutually developed between BMW and the Institute of Technology Management at the University of St. Gallen.

In contrast to existing evaluation alternatives the method builds on System Dynamics to make use of system thinking and computational processing power to deal with the complexity inherent to business models. The method enables managers to advance their understanding for decision making in the context of business model change. It does so by facilitating the holistic modelling of business models as complex systems that contain non-linear cause-effect relationships. This allows for simulation and scenario building to better anticipate the outcome of external effects and alternatives for action. While the method has been evaluated through a number of mostly isolated models with varying contexts each model required significant modelling resources. Therefore we aim to further optimize the method by modelling connections between these models that would allow for increasing reusability in future business models.

The paper is structured as follows: After the introduction, the applied research approach is outlined. Section three specifies the problem of business model evaluation and deduces requirements for a solution. Section four presents the knowledge base our artifact is based on. Subsequently the artifact is presented (section five) and evaluated (section six). Section seven concludes with limitations and implications for future research.

2   Research Design

2.1   Research Methodology

The generated System Dynamic Models for the evaluation of choices each related to a specific business model are materialized representations, instantiations, resulting out of the developed method. Therefore the design artifact enables to extend boundaries of human cognition to facilitate better understanding of the mechanics encompassing the business model. The application of SD to the domain of business models is novel but its innovativeness is revealed in respect to the advancing digitization that allows for unparalleled possibilities of data integration [12]. Hence, the research qualifies well for a design science research approach [13, 14]. We therefore follow the design science research process as described by Pfeffers et al. [15].

Table 1 provides an overview of how we applied the DSRM process model to develop our artifact. The first column refers to the activities outlined in literature that are - despite their sequential listing – of iterative nature. In the second column we

Table 1. Application of DSR for developing the business model evaluation artifact [15]

Activity and key events	Method	Outcome
Identify problem & motivate E_1	• Observation of evaluation of alternative business model choices • Discussion with managers responsible for decision making on the business model level in several firms • Literature review	• Analysis of key problems related to business model evaluation: justified problem statement • Identification of problem significance to advance the knowledge base for decision making
Define objectives of solution E_2, E_3, E_4	• Discussion with IS and management scholars • Literature review • Initial prototype	• Definition of knowledge base & requirements
Design & development E_3, E_4, E_5	• Prototyping to test the applicability for: 1. hypothetical business model and 2. long-established business model for which a lot of experience was available	• Validated artifact in artificial and semi-natural settings
Demonstration E_6, E_7	• Demonstrating the usefulness for: 3. existing business model that required a concrete business decision 4. hypothetical variation of existing business model	• Validated artifact in natural settings
Evaluation E_7	• Interviews on varying management levels (stakeholders affected by business model decisions, managers responsible for evaluation of BM choice alternatives, higher level management) • Analysis of concrete choices related to BM on which method had been applied	• Field tested artifact, ready to systematic use
Communication E_5, E_7	• Presentation at internal research conference in front of several potential internal customers and executive board members • Academic conference/journal contribution	• Structured rollout of method for BM evaluation • Peer-reviewed publication

describe the corresponding activities we conducted in our specific context. The third column describes the result of these activities and the current state of progress. In particular the design and evaluation of the artifact has been highly iterative and has driven a continuous learning process.

2.2   Research Timeline

The design of the artifact took place as a collaborative research endeavor between May 2014 and December 2016. A number of selected key events, visualized in the timeline below (Fig. 1) represents how each phase of the applied DSR approach (Table 1) was carried out. An in-depth description of all events from E1 to E7 can be found in part 6. It also reveals the iterative nature of the DSR process [15] in this specific case.

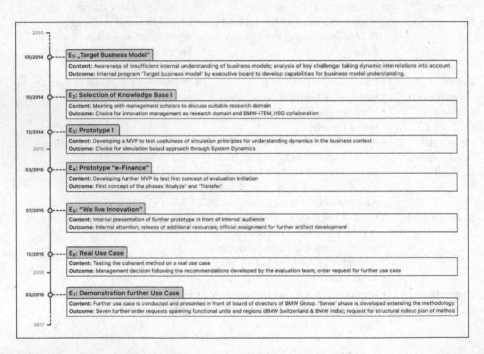

Fig. 1. Key events in the design of the artifact

3   Problem Specification

The analysis of existing practices revealed a number of shortcomings that impede informed decision making in the business model context. This was based on BMW internal observations, interviews with internal decision makers as well as those from various other organizations and a literature review on evaluation methods for business models. The analyzed evaluation approaches ranged from mainly qualitative descriptions such as the business model canvas [16] or the business model triangle [17] to quantitative business case calculations and combinations of both.

The origins of the artifact development lie in the BMW top management awareness of a discrepancy between increasing importance of new ways to do business and insufficient understanding on how to describe those. This resulted in E_1 "Target Business Models" an official research program to advance the knowledge base for decision making in the business model context. Inquiring into the problem one of the researchers identified the existing focus on static descriptions for a phenomenon he noticed at that time to be significantly driven by dynamic developments as the root cause behind it.

KP1: Insufficient Understanding

Policy design for business models commonly lacks in understanding about essential details of the business model among decision makers (cfr. [1]). Qualitative approaches tend to undervalue the importance of quantitative figures required for decision making in a corporate environment and provide little help to secure holistic considerations of the relationship (cfr. [18, 19]) among the different business model components. Instead we observed a tendency to look into a small selection of isolated figures. The short-coming of qualitative approaches has also been highlighted in management research. Euchner and Ganguly (2014) state: *"Strong business models cannot be generated by brainstorming the elements of a business model using a tool like the Business Model Canvas. The canvas may be useful in representing a business model, but it misses the key dynamic elements of working business models—it does not represent coherence (or the relationship among elements); it does not represent the competitive position (which is off the canvas); and it does not quantify the economic"* [20]. Quantitative approaches in contrast typically appear to consider only a small set of business model components and focus on operational data. All approaches share significant deficits regarding the dynamics of the business model. We either found static evaluations for a specific moment in time (cfr. [10]) or consideration of dynamics for a limited number of selected variables such as market share, price, and investment sums each forecasted in isolation. That is also because typical evaluation approaches, e.g. those utilizing Excel do not allow for integration cyclical references and delays (cfr. [21, 22]).

RQ 1:   Integrate (isolated) expert knowledge into a holistic business model logic
RQ 2:   Consider all relevant dynamic cause-effect relations of a business model
RQ 3:   Specify options for decisions and their impact on the business model

KP2: Opacity of Hypotheses and Data Validity

The situation often constitutes a risk because the majority of underlying hypotheses behind the evaluations remain implicit. This is due to the nature of the applied approaches that require little rigidness for the causal structure and its consistency (cfr. [7]) and instead focus on isolated information and figures. Consequently, discussions on the evaluation of choices reveal conflicting mental models that lead to distrust of certain assumptions. The nature of the existing approaches provide little help to challenge the respective underlying hypotheses in order to build common understanding. Therefore, discussions tend to favor substitutes of evidence to base decisions on.

RQ 4:   Support data-driven decision making
RQ 5:   Support the explication of hypotheses

RQ 6:   Enhance cognitive limitations
RQ 7:   Foster joint efforts to facilitate rational decision making

4   Knowledge Base

The construction of the artifact draws from work of two domains, the business model concept and System Dynamics. The business model concept defines distinct components that are required to take into consideration for the context of evaluation. System Dynamics provides the methodological foundation to leverage the existing knowledge about those components for evaluation purposes

The knowledge base was selected through discussions with academic scholars (E_2: Selection of Knowledge Base I) and a subsequent literature review. The former supported the assumption to choose the business model as a central concept to build the artifact on. The literature review and the background of one of the researchers in simulation directed us to System Dynamics as the second central concept the artifact is built on.

Business Models

The business model concept has only found partially common understanding among scholars [5, 23]. However, most definitions share a number of themes which help us for subsequent artifact development, namely the existence of distinct business model components and their interplay, the dynamic evolution of business models over time, a system's perspective, the usefulness of material artifacts and computational processing.

Business model research has acknowledged the existence of components that jointly considered constitute the business model [24]. Most prominent are the notions of value proposition, value creation and value capture, which is captured in the definition by Teece (2010, p. 173): *"In short, it's about the benefit the enterprise will deliver to customers, how it will organize to do so, and how it will capture a portion of the value that it delivers"* [25].

Over time dynamics emerge inside and between these components and drive the development of the business model [26, 27]. The RCOV framework is an approach that responds to this insight and depicts distinct interrelations between the components of a business model: The RCOV framework falls into line with the emerging theme to conceptualize the business model as a system that consists of different elements that interrelate with each other whereas interrelations also exist to factors outside the business model [28–30]. Instead of interrelated elements some scholars specify these as sets of choices and consequences [6] or activity systems [31].

Specifically for the context business model design in established firms the role of artifacts is considered as a necessity [32]. Physical representations of business models allow for the collective construction of shared understanding and represent important sensemaking resources [33, 34]. Hence, the value of artifacts is not limited to the evaluation of business models but enhances the subsequent implementation into operativional reality [32]. In this context the anticipated enhancement of simulation to support management decision making has been emphasized [10].

System Dynamics

System Dynamics is a computer-aided tool to enhance analysis and decision making for dynamic systems in a variety of contexts [35]. 'Dynamic system' here refers to systems that are characterized by interdependencies and mutual interaction of elements, feedback and circular causality [8]. Developed by J.W. Forrester in the 1960s system dynamic relies on a system's approach, i.e. considering all interacting elements influencing the behavior of the system [36]. It in particular aims to overcome bounded rationality and mental models [8]. This is achieved through modelling and simulation [37] and the ability to integrate various data sources [12]. System Dynamics has been applied to various contexts, in particular also in the management domain and for strategic decision making [38–40]. In contrast to many alternative tools, system dynamics allows for the integration of feedback, delays and accumulation. Feedbacks cause cyclical consequences inside a system: any intervention on a certain element triggers effects that eventually refer back to and influence the original element. Two types of feedback are distinguished: self-reinforcing loops that dominate the system over time if not hampered and balancing loops that constitute this effect. Delay means that such effects or more generally a consequence of a certain intervention may require

Table 2. *Distinctive features of SD (adapted from* [41]).

Focus on feedback-driven, mainly internally generated dynamics:
The model systems are networks of closed loops of information. However, they are not limited to the representation of 'closed systems', in that (a) flows can originate from outside the system's boundaries, (b) exogenous factors or systems can be incorporated into any model as parameters or special modules and (c) new information can be accommodated via changes to a model. Neither are they deterministic; stochastic variables and relationships have been a standard modelling feature since Forrester's Industrial Dynamics (1961) was published

High degree of operationality:
SD relies on formal modelling. This fosters disciplined thinking; assumptions underlying equations and quantifications must be clarified. Feedback loops and delays are visualized and formalized; there- with the causal logic inherent in a model is made more transparent and better discussable than in most other methodologies. Also, the achievable level of realism is higher than, for example, in econometric models. Far-reaching possibilities for the combination of qualitative and quantitative aspects of modelling and simulation: The focus is not on point-precise prediction, but on the generation of insights into the patterns of behavior generated by the systems under study

High level of generality and scale robustness:
The representation of dynamical systems in terms of stocks and flows is a generic form, which is adequate for an enormous spectrum of potential applications. This spectrum is both broad as to the potential subjects under study, and deep as to the possible degrees of resolution and detail

Availability of powerful application software:
The packages (Stella/Ithink, PowerSim, VENSIM and MyStrategy) are easy to handle and give access to a high variety of mathematical functions. Part of this applications array offers optimization procedures and validation tools. Also, some support for collaborative modelling and the communication with databases is provided

Potential synergies: Combination with many other tools and methodologies is possible, both conceptually and technically

some time to arise. Accumulation implies that a state of any element can be a function of its previous state. If feedback, delays and accumulation overlap intuition on system behavior fails. For that reason system dynamics applies computational processing power to overcome these cognitive limitations [8, 35].

System Dynamics features a number of distinctive features that cumulatively contribute to its value for decision making in complex systems (Table 2).

5   Design and Features of the Artefact

In the following we describe our artifact, a method for business model evaluation. In this regard a key feature of conducting the method is the construction of an artifact itself an instantiation in form of a System Dynamics model. The method is divided into six phases each featuring a number of sub-phases or 'steps' as we call them that will be described separately. Table 3 provides an overview of the different phases from various dimensions. However, it remains to consider that the phases and in particular the sub-phases have an iterative character. In practice they are not followed strictly sequentially. Hence, the proposed phases represent an ideal setting to enhance understanding of the underlying conceptualization. The table also briefly depicts how each requirement is addressed across the phases of the methodology.

Across the various phases we differentiate between three parties, the *decision maker*, the *(key) stakeholders* and the *evaluation team*. The decision maker is the person or small group of people responsible for strategic changes of the business model. Typically they approach the evaluation team to ask for support. The decision maker has a well-developed understanding of the main factors and mechanics that influence the business model. She/he/they may be part of the (key) stakeholders but may also be distinct from this group. The (key) stakeholders are the cross-department group of people directly and significantly affected in their operative activities by strategic changes in the business model. In contrast to the decision maker their expertise is of high detail in their operative domain. The evaluation team is no primary stakeholder of the business model to be evaluated. It is responsible for the preparation of the decision template, however, acts mainly as a facilitator during the process to access and structure the available knowledge. Therefore their expertise comprises the following evaluation method, the business model and system dynamics domain.

Sense

Purpose: The first phase of the evaluation aims to assess the expected usefulness of the method for a specific business model decision.

Key Steps: This assessment is contains one step that considers the formal suitability and a further step directly related to the problem content. The *Formal check* is a formal discussion between the key stakeholder of the business model and the evaluation team that inquires into four distinct criteria related to the stakeholder and the problem. For the key stakeholder it is critical to identify his or her motivation to advance the understanding about the business model. Analyzing the decision maker's motivation is qualitative and largely subjective, however it aims to reveal three aspects that are

Table 3. Six phase business model evaluation method including the respective format, sub steps and reference to RQs

SENSE	ANALYZE	TRANSFER	AGGREGATE	SIMULATE	DECIDE
Assessing usefulness of method for context	Understanding the fundamental mechanics of the business model	Build an initial causal loop representation	Develop a sophisticated model that allows for simulation	Run simulations to develop scenarios for decision making	Extract the central insights from the simulation to develop a lean decision template
Discussion between decision maker and evaluation team	Workshop with evaluation team and key stakeholders	Evaluation team driven modelling process with selected points of interaction with stakeholders to discuss and include all information required		Discussion and workshop setting between selected key stakeholders and the evaluation team	
1. Formal check 2. Initial problem specification	-	1. Holistic model development, 2. Lean model 3. Ad-hoc quantification 4. Hypotheses formulation I	1. Stock-and-Flow model (qualitative) 2. Embedding pre-existing patterns. 3. Pre-quantification 4. Quantification by experts 5. Sensitivity analysis I 6. Validation	1. Hypotheses formulation II 2. Simulation	1. Selection of viable alternatives 2. Development of action sets 3. Preparation of decision template

RQ 1					RQ 3
	RQ 2			RQ 6	
		RQ 4			
		RQ 5			
		RQ 7			

essential preconditions for a successful application of the method: (a) is the decision maker truly interested in external support by the evaluation team, (b) is he/she open to the application of new tools and approaches, (c) is the decision maker interested in rational decision making? Further the evaluation team checks for budgets the stakeholder has gathered or approved for the evaluation. Available resources are considered as additional indicators for the stakeholder's motivation but serve as well to verify the financial feasibility to apply the evaluation method. Finally, the key stakeholder is required to be confronted with a distinct business model decision to make. Only a precisely articulated evaluation problem facilitates the usefulness of the method. Without it the approach most certainly produces unsatisfying results because the lack of focus in the modelling process leads to a loose collection of cause effect relationships that are in some way related to the business model. Regarding the business model at hand it is required that the evaluation problem exists due to dynamics encompassing the business model. In case the problem appears to be of static nature the approach is still be suitable but also too sophisticated and evaluation based on static approaches and tools (such as the business model canvas or Excel) is recommended for reasons of resource efficiency.

In case the formal check is passed the subsequent *initial problem specification* targets on the understanding of the problem roots. Based on the exchange with the decision maker the evaluation team decomposes the problem into its main elements and their relationships in order to reconstruct it applying a system's perspective. In this step, only the causal or logic relationships of elements is defined. During the simulation step, all relationships between elements have to be quantified and therefore their impact on the overall system is weighted. In the follow up meeting the decision maker is supposed to find his train of thoughts represented in the basic model presented. Ideally this draft may already enable him/her to see the main mechanisms more clearly.

Outcome: A rough description based on cause-effect relationships of the root causes that provide a challenge for decision making in order to mutually confirm sufficient understanding of the evaluation problem. Subsequently, an agreement for or against the application of the evaluation method is reached.

Analyze

Purpose: The analyze phase targets to establish a common understanding between parties involved, the evaluation team and the key stakeholders. This requires (a) the evaluation team to understand the relevant mechanisms inside the business model and (b) the stakeholders to gain a basic understanding of the knowledge base, business models and system dynamics, applied.

Key Steps: This phase takes place in form of a workshop setting. The key insights conveyed to the stakeholders are the main components any business model comprises and a system's perspective for complex constructs that is the description of phenomenon as a network of elements that are linked by cause-effect relationships. The evaluation team however needs to understand the main elements and interrelation inside the business model. That often takes place by clarifying specific terms and abbreviations used in the discussion with the stakeholders. Such a discussion is led by the evaluation team and starts with the focus on the customer's value proposition because it is the aspect most stakeholders can sufficiently relate to.

Outcome: A detailed and differentiated semantic description of the business model at hand.

Transfer

Purpose: In the transfer phase the semantic description of the business model is advanced into a model of cause-effect relationships.

Key Steps: Following the initial workshop the subsequent transfer phase is an interplay between the evaluation team and selected stakeholder that provide additional infor- mation. The *holistic model development* starts with a first model draft by the evaluation team that results out of the knowledge gained in the Analyze phase. For this purpose PowerSim, a simulation software, is used. Since the model focus lies on the value proposition the business model stakeholders quickly can follow the idea of the eval- uation approach. Interviews with individual stakeholders improve and complement the initial draft into other business model components that can be derived. Over time the different viewpoints create a holistic viewpoint of the relevant causal structure. A subsequent workshop, with the participants of the first workshop confronts them with the understanding derived from the interviews. It serves to demonstrate how the different perspectives relate to each other and to put emphasis on elements some might have not be aware of initially. However, eventually it initiates the process to mutually eliminate the elements of little importance for the underlying decision. This *lean model* is enriched by *ad-hoc quantification* integrating data and knowledge the stakeholder have immediate access to. During *hypotheses formulation I* the model behavior is tested against a number of hypothetical scenarios. This facilitates sensitivity for nec- essary model improvement but also to derive a set of hypotheses which courses of action may be promising for the business model decision at hand.

Outcome: A semi-quantified causal-loop model that has facilitated a refined formu- lation of the decision problem and the derivation of a number of hypotheses how a solution may look like.

Aggregate

Purpose: The purpose of the aggregate phase is to increase the quality of the model until it is trusted by the stakeholders and allows to derive the hypotheses for subsequent scenario testing.

Key Steps: The aggregate phase is conducted mainly by the evaluation team. Exchange only follows in later stages when data validity is optimized and the final hypotheses are developed. Those hypotheses represent a reformulation of the initial need for decision support and the conditions that should be analyzed by the simulation. An imaginative hypothesis for analysis would be formulated as follows: 'Due to higher sales volumes, profits will remain at 7 bn € even if selling prices are cut by 10%'. Building on the causal loop model the step *Stock-and-Flow model (qualitative)* begins by dividing the existing elements into stocks and flows. Translating a causal loop into a stock-and-flow model is not trivial because these additional element features require to add further ones to keep the model consistent. Rather often this step is considered to be 'more art than science', involving iteration and a trial-and-error approach. Thereby the most suitable approach has proven to develop the model by sequentially transforming the main causal loops. The step is followed by *embedding pre-existing patterns*. Such patterns are modules of recurring causal structures that have proven to exist across different system dynamic models. Word-of-mouth, network effects and price elasticity are some of the most common effects we detected. These patterns were identified based on the actual problems that needed solution within the given business context. Embedding these patterns typically enhances efficiency of the modelling process through the reuse of complete sets of elements as well as model quality because the patterns have been already validated in different models. Once the qualitative Stock-and-Flow model has been developed the *Pre-quantification* by the evaluation team enriches the model through the integration of publicly or internally available data. The subsequent *Quantification by experts* adjusts or extends the data with particular focus on the specific context. Thereby the necessary data validity depends on the expected influence on the model behavior; the higher the influence is the higher is the required quality level. We differentiate between three main levels 'educated guess', 'expert knowledge' and 'data driven'. Educated guess refers to knowledge gathered by publicly available sources. Expert knowledge is information provided by stakeholders based on knowledge and experience in closely related domains. Data driven is the highest validity level and refers to primary information typically taken from data bases containing exactly the information required. In this step the evaluation team keeps track of all necessary data and assigns tasks to different stakeholders to collect specific information. For this purpose the evaluation team uses a MS Excel sheet tracking data such as the list of data required, the used data source – which commonly is one of the stakeholders, and data validity level. Following the quantification of the model *sensitivity analysis I* reveals those elements that require higher levels of data validity based on their real influence on the model. As such an upgrade sometimes is not directly possible instead the element is further fragmented into its underlying sub-components for which sufficient data can be gathered. Eventually the *validation* is a workshop to present the final model and receive approval by all stakeholders.

Outcome: Quantified Stock-and-Flow model including sufficient data validity that allows to refine the set of hypotheses.

Simulate

Purpose: The simulate phase serves to gain a precise and holistic understanding of all relevant cause-effect relationships affecting the business model. Eventually, this understanding facilitates the confirmation or rejection of the hypotheses on the actions to be taken regarding the business model decision.

Key Steps: Once the model is approved the *hypotheses formulation II* refines or extends the hypotheses ultimately tested. The refinement in particular concerns the definition of variables/elements to be optimized, the so called 'Key Business Metrics' (KBMs) and desirable output values (Fig. 2). Further, the evaluation team and the stakeholders define the possible parameter changes of predefined input or throughput elements, however, those choices may also imply structural changes concerning the

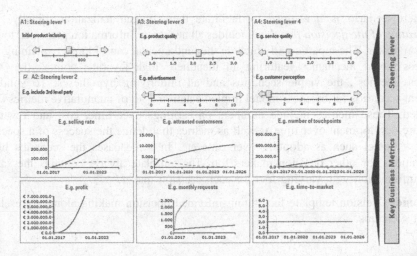

Fig. 2. Decision cockpit including 'steering levers' and 'key business metrics (KBMs)'

relationships between a number of elements (see [30]). In this stage, all relationships between elements are quantified based on the input data and their maturity level. Given the imaginative hypothesis presented in the aggregate step, the hypothesis would be disproved or proved. This would imply that including all optimizations and possible changes on the business model a profit level of 7 bn € would either be impossible (disprove) to achieve or possible (prove). The subsequent *simulation* step generates multiple scenarios thereby optimizing in respect to the KBMs. An important insights for these scenarios are 'high leverage elements', those model entities that have decisive influence on the system behavior. These elements mostly extend the causal loop initially identified and allow for more precise understanding based on the quantified scenarios.

Outcome: A set of scenarios optimized to the defined KBMs

Decide

Purpose: The decide phase is aims to transform the deep understanding gained about the business model into simple and precise decision recommendations in respect to the specific context of each relevant stakeholder addressed.

Key Steps: Typically the previous simulation generates multiple scenarios that achieve either some or all of the predefined values for the KBMs. The decide phase is initiated by the *selection of viable alternatives*. This refers to the three to five scenarios that are presented to the decision maker. The viability of a scenario refers to aspects such as political or ethical correctness which are also correlated to the radicality of the change implications in terms of assets, structures or processes. Assessing the viability of a scenario requires close collaboration between the business model stakeholders and the evaluation team because organizational inertia and business potential need to be balanced against each other. Once the alternatives are selected the essential *set of action* for each scenario is *developed* to facilitate their operationalization. Finally, the *preparation of the decision template* includes all necessary information presented to the decision maker. These particularly include the fundamental causal loops explaining the business model mechanics featuring all identified 'high leverage points', the 'key business metrics', the viable scenarios and all underlying hypotheses. To validate different scenarios for business model implementation a set of quantitative metrics was included. These metrics include numbers on earnings over time, cost and revenue structure development over time as well as metrics that define the success of a specific business model such as adoption over time etc. In some cases the scenarios hold implications for other decision makers too. The template always contains the same basic information with varying foci for each decision maker.

Outcome: Decision template facilitating informed decision making along a preselection of scenarios.

6   Artifact Evaluation

To evaluate the artifact we tested the usability in varying settings thereby moving from purely artificial ones for early prototypes of the different phases to natural settings that represented exactly the intended use context for the artifact. By now the artifact has been field tested through a number of cases exposing it to varying evaluation and business model contexts. We assessed the usefulness of the artifact based on three main criteria. We consider the artefact to be useful if

- it receives extensive internal attention, i.e. from higher & top management as well as across different divisions and regions. Usefulness is considered particularly high if attention is converted into concrete evaluation requests
- the method is stated to be useful by the key stakeholders after the completed evaluation
- one of the suggested decision alternatives is picked up by the decision maker and leads to subsequent changes in the business model.

6.1   Artificial and Semi-natural Setting

E_3, E_4, E_5: The evaluation of the artifact in an artificial and semi-natural setting took part over the course of three distinct cases. Each of the cases helped to evaluate isolated steps of the method. The cases either represented a hypothetical or existing business model but no business model decision was pending. One of the use cases represented a business model scenario for e-mobility. In particular in this context themes related to 'sharing economy' and 'on-demand services' played a major role. Regarding the methodological development, in one case a creative approach using post-its on a big whiteboard concerning the four fields value proposition, value creation, costs and revenues was conducted to test for building common understanding and to determine requirements for the subsequent transfer and aggregate steps. The tests helped to adjust each phase. One of the most notable changes concerned the

usage of an additional software besides PowerSim for visualizing the causal structure of the business models as it was hard to digitize the post-its whiteboard results. This software was also applied to enhance the discussion with key stakeholders but it turned out that the additional value of better visualization was quite marginal and did not justify the work for the manual transfer into PowerSim. We further noticed that the stakeholders had trouble to grasp the business model concept and thus to identify the necessary cause-effect relationships. For that reason the value proposition was identified as the central component to start the discussions out of which the other elements and relationships are derived. Finally, the three distinct data validity levels were introduced to weight resource efficiency in the modelling process against model accuracy. This principle is in line with research on system dynamics [8].

6.2 Natural Setting and Field Test

E_6, E_7: For the evaluation of the usefulness or the artifact in a natural setting we applied it to two different use cases. In the first case we specifically asked upper management for a case in which a business model required a decision for adjustments and for which existing evaluation approaches had failed to provide necessary insights. The method quickly revealed inconsistencies in the mental models of the involved stakeholder that resulted in conflicting positions. For example, division A had the idea to offer a new service. However, the new service would only be profitable if division B would subsidies their own offer for the sake of the new service. Taken division A's and division B's profits together it was assumed that profits would increase even though division B would earn less. At the end, it turned out that profits of the new service would never compensate division B's reduced profits from subsidies. The inconsistency in mental models (new service is profitable vs. new service is not profitable) could be resolved. Through the discussion with the stakeholders and subsequent the model generation the views could be integrated and suggestions for business model changes were challenged. This process clarified a number of wrong assumptions and achieved to dissolve the conflicting views. The final suggestions for adjustments in the business model were followed by the decision maker. Interviews with all involved parties further confirmed the satisfaction with the applied method. Following the presentation of the results the request for a further use case was raised. This time the evaluation concerned the decision for or against the introduction of a not yet existing business model. The business model can be characterized as an already existing industry scheme and with little distance to other implemented ones of BMW. The presentation of the evaluation results raised internal attention reaching beyond BMW Financial Services lead to a further presentation of the method and this use case in front of the business unit directors of BMW Group. Essentially this lead to further evaluation requests from different regions (Switzerland & India) as well as different business units were raised of which seven were accepted. The highly heterogeneous nature of the seven cases following the presentation in front of the business unit directors served as a field test assessing the application potential of our artifact. Eventually the board of BU directors ordered a plan for a structured internal rollout of the method. The rising interest in the evaluation method lead to refinements of the decision criteria in the sense phase.

7 Conclusion

In this paper we proposed a novel design for a business model evaluation method. In respect to the increasing complexity of interrelations influencing the outcomes of business model decisions our artifact supports decision makers to understand (a) the essential mechanics of the business model and (b) how to make use of them to achieve the desired results. Specifically our artifact meets all identified requirements. Thereby the artifact intends to prevent managers from poor decision making due to limitations in their cognitive models. We did so by incorporating System Dynamics into our artifact, which has demonstrated its usefulness for policy making in complex systems of other contexts. Highlighted by scholars as a promising endeavor [42, 43] our artifact represents the first evaluated method to apply System Dynamics for the evaluation of business model decisions. The evaluation of our artifact passed through different stages from pilots for artificial settings to the application in a wide range of natural settings.

Despite demonstrating the usefulness of our artifact in the course of its evaluation, we identify limitations regarding the nature of the natural settings. So far the artifact has only been applied to BMW internal cases. However, BMW operates already across various industries, ranging from financial services (BMW leasing and financing operations) to mobility services (from DriveNow, to ChargeNow or ParkNow). The conducted use cases were conducted in this 'multi-industry' environment. Use cases typically crossed the domain of a purely automotive focus. Hence, it is assumed that the artefact will also be beneficial in other industry contexts. Additionally, since the business model is an industry independent concept [5, 17] such as is System Dynamics we expect general usefulness also outside the automotive sector. However, its usefulness may be particularly strong in the context of a multinational corporation operating in a long-established industry. Even greater attention requires the fact that the applied use cases represent business models that are essentially aligned with the business logic of this industry. The radicality of the suggested scenarios for business model decisions can be considered as moderate. Our artifact has demonstrated its usefulness to counteract limited rationality by cognitive limitations thereby serving the calculative purposes of the business model [44]. It may however, be limited in its usefulness to evaluate highly radical business model changes that imply competition among dissimilar business models (see [45]). In such cases the possibilities to detect and understand all essential cause-effects and to reach sufficient data quality may decrease and thereby the insights extracted from the artifact (cfr. [8]). Still, the explication of cause-effect relationship considerations and consecutive simulation have revealed high value when decision systems at place have failed to support decisions adequately. Hence, simulating more disruptive business models are nevertheless a prime settings to unfold great potential of the method. Consequently we will extend our field test for the evaluation of more radical change options of the business model. This allows us to more precisely adjust the evaluation requirements in the sense phase.

As briefly noted earlier we consider this artifact as a distinctive evolutionary stage. It allows to be transferred into different organizational contexts. However, each use case we conducted to evaluate and further adjust our artifact revealed connections to certain aspects of System Dynamics models that had been mutually developed earlier.

Those for example could be certain databases or influencing factors that were integrated into multiple models. We intend to further inquire into the implications of this insight for our artifact. Potentially we may be able to increase efficiency and effectiveness of our artifact through future adjustments that in turn may provide difficulties for the transfer into different contexts.

Our research also contributes to recent inquiries on the role artifacts for business model change. Changes of business model originate in cognitive operations. However, they require changes in organizational constituents (structures, resources, etc.) to become reality [32, 46]. Artifacts fundamentally contribute to this transformation. They extend the verbal exchange as well as cognitive process capacity of individuals and groups and facilitate the transition of understanding among individuals through the externalization of cognitive work [47, 48]. Thereby new shared knowledge structures are created together [33, 49]. Our research highlights two important aspects that influence the quality of prospective sensemaking in this context, the 'artifact type' and the 'externalization process'. In our context, sensemaking specifically refers to the process of understanding the mechanics of a particular business model and the subsequent evaluation decision alternatives that eventually initiate organizational change (cfr. [33, 47]). We found that our context required a sophisticated physical representation such as the System Dynamics model to achieve new understanding on the individual and group level. Specifically the first use case applied for the evaluation of the designed method in a natural setting revealed that 'giving sense to one another' and 'making sense together' [33] depend on the type of the artifact. We find that the complexity of the situation therefore needs to be considered for the choice of the artifact. In order to achieve the mutual construction of shared understanding an artifact is required to explicate the fundamental logic that leads to a certain 'sense'. But also the externalization process itself requires management. The System Dynamics model, a materialized output of our artifact, allows to 'explicate the fundamental logic' behind the evaluation of business model choices. However, the design process revealed the importance to focus the integration of the available knowledge. This ultimately leads to the definition of distinctive phases of our method. In this regards future research may inquire more deeply into these two aspects.

The design process of the artifact can itself be characterized as complex and resource-intensive. From a time perspective it spanned so far over a period of 2.5 years since the initialization of the design process. Thereby it required the involvement and interaction of multiple internal as well as external stakeholders. Finally, it required an extensive amount of human resources and capital. This required us to purposely pass through the design science process only doing the minimum during the design & development of the artifact as well as its demonstration in order to achieve early communication. Communication in our case was mainly addressed to upper management levels that hold the authority over resources but also to business model decision makers to attract them for the evaluation of our artifact. Once these gates were passed we iterated through the design & develop and demonstration phase to design the real artifact. We consider this as a major idiosyncrasy of our research process, since we would have otherwise not been able to reach this stage of the design. However, we theorize that this kind of iteration can be observed in any design science research process that relates to such 'big' artifacts in a similar way. Existing literature on the design science research process so far has barely inquired more deeply into this phenomenon. For example Hevner et al. touch on the size and complexity of possible design solutions for any problem and advocate for a satisfactory solution, artifacts, that 'work' well [13]. However, also here the authors do not directly refer to the stated challenge. In regards to the real contexts in which artifact design takes place we anticipate valuable insights from research analyzing different context idiosyncrasies. Thereby research may build on insights from other fields such as entrepreneurship literature (e.g. [50]).

References

1. Johnson, M.W., Christensen, C.M., Kagermann, H.: Reinventing your business model. Harv. Bus. Rev. **86**(12), 50–60 (2008)
2. Chesbrough, H.: Business model innovation: opportunities and barriers. Long Range Plan. **43**(2–3), 354–363 (2010)
3. Casadesus-Masanell, R., Zhu, F.: Business model innovation and competitive imitation: the case of sponsor-based business models. Strateg. Manag. J. **34**, 464–482 (2013)
4. Rumble, R., Mangematin, V.: Business model implementation: the antecedents of multi-sidedness. Bus. Model. Model **33**, 97–131 (2015)
5. Magretta, J.: Why business models matter. Harv. Bus. Rev. **80**, 86–92 (2002)
6. Casadesus-Masanell, R., Ricart, J.E.: From strategy to business models and onto tactics. Long Range Plan. **43**, 195–215 (2010)
7. Massa, L., Tucci, C.L.: Business model innovation. In: Dodgson, M., Gann, D.M., Phillips, N. (eds.) The Oxford Handbook of Innovation Management, vol. 20, no. December, p. 18. Oxford University Press, Oxford (2014)
8. Sterman, J.D.: Systems Thinking and Modeling for a Complex World, vol. 6, no. 1 (2000)
9. Galanakis, K.: Innovation process. Make sense using systems thinking. Technovation **26** (11), 1222–1232 (2006)
10. Osterwalder, A., Pigneur, Y., Tucci, C.L.: Clarifying business models: origins, present, and future of the concept clarifying business models: origins, present, and future of the concept. Commun. Assoc. Inf. Syst. **15**(May), 1–125 (2005)
11. Jeffrey, P., Sutton, R.I.: Evidence-based management. Harv. Bus. Rev. **84**(January), 62–72 (2006)
12. Barabba, V., Huber, C., Cooke, F., Pudar, N., Smith, J., Paich, M., Barabba, V., Huber, C., Cooke, F.: A multimethod approach for creating new business models: the general motors OnStar project. Interfaces (Providence) **31**(1), 20–34 (2002)
13. Hevner, A.R., March, S.T., Park, J., Ram, S.: Design science in information systems research. MIS Q. **28**(1), 75–105 (2004)
14. Markus, M.L., Majchrzak, A., Gasser, L.: A design theory for systems that support emergent knowledge proccesses. MIS Q. **26**(3), 179–212 (2002)
15. Pfeffers, K., Tuunanen, T., Rothenberger, M.A., Chatterjee, S.: A design science research methodology for information systems research. Source J. Manag. Inf. Syst. **24**(3), 45–77 (2007)
16. Osterwalder, A., Pigneur, Y.: Business Model Generation: A Handbook for Visionaries, Game Changers, and Challengers. Wiley, Hoboken (2010)
17. Gassmann, O., Frankenberger, K., Csik, M.: The Business Model Navigator. Pearson, Harlow (2014)

18. Furnari, S.: A cognitive mapping approach to business models: representing causal structures and mechanisms. Adv. Strateg. Manag. **33**, 1–40 (2015). Special Issue on Business Models
19. Groesser, S.N., Jovy, N.: Business model analysis using computational modeling: a strategy tool for exploration and decision-making. J. Manag. Control **27**(1), 61–88 (2016)
20. Euchner, J., Ganguly, A.: Business model innovation in practice. Res. Manag. **57** (November-December), 33–39 (2014)
21. Sterman, J.D.: System dynamics modeling: tools for learning in a complex world. Calif. Manag. Rev. **43**(4), 8–25 (2001)
22. Köpp, S., Schwaninger, M.: Scrutinizing the Sustainability of Business Models: System Dynamics for Robust Strategies, no. 60 (2014)
23. Afuah, A., Massa, L., Tucci, C.L.: a critical assessment of the business model and the business model innovation literature. Working paper (2016)
24. Wirtz, B.W., Pistoia, A., Ullrich, S., Göttel, V.: Business models: origin, development and future research perspectives. Long Range Plan. **49**(1), 36–54 (2016)
25. Teece, D.J.: Business models, business strategy and innovation. Long Range Plan. **43**(2–3), 172–194 (2010)
26. Demil, B., Lecocq, X.: Business model evolution: In search of dynamic consistency. Long Range Plann. **43**(2–3), 227–246 (2010)
27. Tikkanen, H., Lamberg, J.-A., Parvinen, P., Kallunki, J.-P.: Managerial cognition, action and the business model of the firm. Manag. Decis. **43**(6), 789–809 (2005)
28. Frankenberger, K., Weiblen, T., Csik, M., Gassmann, O.: The 4I-framework of business model innovation: a structured view on process phases and challenges. Int. J. Prod. Dev. **18** (January), 249 (2013)
29. Baden-Fuller, C., Haefliger, S.: Business models and technological innovation. Long Range Plan. **46**(6), 419–426 (2013)
30. Aversa, P., Haefliger, S., Rossi, A., Baden-Fuller, C.: From business model to business modelling: modularity and manipulation. Adv. Strateg. Manag. **33**, 151–185 (2015)
31. Zott, C., Amit, R.: Business model design: an activity system perspective. Long Range Plan. **43**(2–3), 216–226 (2010)
32. Demil, B., Lecocq, X.: Crafting an innovative business model in an established company: the role of artifacts. Adv. Strateg. Manag. **33**, 31–58 (2015)
33. Stigliani, I., Ravasi, D.: Organizing thoughts and connecting brains: material practices and the transition from individual to group-level prospective sensemaking. Acad. Manag. J. **55** (5), 1232–1259 (2012)
34. Gephart, R.P.: The textual approach: risk and blame in disaster sensemaking. Acad. Manag. J. **36**(6), 1465–1514 (1993)
35. Forrester, J.W.: System dynamics—the next fifty years. Syst. Dyn. Rev. **23**(2/3), 359–370 (2007)
36. Bala, B.K., Arshad, F.M., Noh, K.M.: Systems thinking: system dynamics. In: Bala, B.K., Arshad, F.M., Noh, K.M. (eds.) System Dynamics: Modelling and Simulation. STBE, pp. 15–35. Springer, Singapore (2017). doi:10.1007/978-981-10-2045-2_2
37. Forrester, J.W.: Industrial dynamics - after the first decade. Manag. Sci. **14**(7), 398–415 (1968)
38. Graham, A.K., Morecroft, J.D.W., Senge, P.M., Sterman, J.D.: Model-supported case studies for management education. Eur. J. Oper. Res. **59**(1), 151–166 (1992)
39. Gary, M.S., Kunc, M., Morecroft, D.W., Gary, M.S.: System dynamics and strategy. Syst. Dyn. Rev. **24**(4), 407–429 (2009)
40. Lyneis, J.M.: System dynamics for business strategy: a phased approach. Syst. Dyn. Rev. **15** (1), 37–71 (1999)

41. Schwaninger, M.: System dynamics and the evolution of the systems movement. Syst. Res. Behav. Sci. **23**, 583–594 (2006)
42. de Reuver, M., Bouwman, H., Haaker, T.: Business model roadmapping: a practical approach to come from an existing to a desired business model. Int. J. Innov. Manag **17**(1), 1340006 (2013)
43. Weil, H.B.: Application of system dynamics to corporate strategy: an evolution of issues and frameworks. Syst. Dyn. Rev. **23**(2/3), 137–156 (2007)
44. Doganova, L., Eyquem-Renault, M.: What do business models do? Innovation devices in technology entrepreneurship. Res. Policy **38**(10), 1559–1570 (2009)
45. Casadesus-Masanell, R., Ricart, J.E.: How to design a winning business model. Harv. Bus. Rev. **89**(1–2), 100–107 (2011)
46. Orlikowski, W.J., Scott, S.V.: Challenging the separation of technology, work and organization. Acad. Manag. Ann. **2**(1), 433–474 (2008)
47. Weick, K.E.: Sensemaking in Organizations. Sage Publications, Thousand Oaks (1995)
48. Clark, A., Chalmers, D.: The extended mind. Analysis **58**(1), 7–19 (1998)
49. Rouleau, L., Balogun, J.: Middle managers, strategic sensemaking, and discursive competence. J. Manag. Stud. **48**(5), 953–983 (2011)
50. Blank, S.: Why the lean start-up changes everything. Harv. Bus. Rev. **91**(5), 63–72 (2013)

Towards Distributed Cognitive Expert Systems

Schahin Tofangchi$^{(\boxtimes)}$, Andre Hanelt, and Lutz M. Kolbe

University of Goettingen, Goettingen, Germany
{schahin.tofangchi,andre.hanelt,lkolbe}@uni-goettingen.de

Abstract. The process of *Datafication* gives rise to ubiquitousness of data. Data-driven approaches may create meaningful insights from the vast volumes of data available to businesses. However, coping with the great volume and variety of data requires improved data analysis methods. Many such methods are dependent on a user's subjective domain knowledge. This dependency leads to a barrier for the use of sophisticated statistical methods, because a user would have to invest a significant amount of labor into the customization of such methods in order to incorporate domain knowledge into them. We argue that machines may efficiently support researchers and analysts even with non-quantitative data once they are equipped with the ability to develop their own subjective domain knowledge in a way that the amount of manual customization is reduced. Our contribution is a design theory – called the *Division-of-Labor* Framework – for generating and using *Experts* that can develop domain knowledge.

Keywords: Machine learning · Domain knowledge · Distributed computing · Real-time analytics · Deep learning

1 Introduction

Due to the growing ubiquitousness of data as a result of technological advances in areas like mobile computing, social networking, and smart vehicles, businesses have the opportunity to gain previously unobtainable information about their customers and market position [4]. However, in order to gain business value from these data, businesses require better data analytics architectures that can extract relevant information from data [4]. With the growing attention paid to big data analytics in information systems (IS) research, Abbasi et al. [1] outline a research agenda and identify great opportunities for design science research for big data and real-time analytics artifacts. Goes [12] describes how the knowledge of the IS community and its research methods can positively impact big data research. He argues that big data constitutes an interesting field of research for a community traditionally engaged in interdisciplinary research. Similarly, Agarwal and Dhar [2] state that the IS community possesses knowledge of data management as well as value creation through data. They suggest that the IS community, therefore, holds a comparative advantage for conducting research on big data.

© Springer International Publishing AG 2017
A. Maedche et al. (Eds.): DESRIST 2017, LNCS 10243, pp. 145–159, 2017.
DOI: 10.1007/978-3-319-59144-5_9

Abbasi et al. [1] call for new design theories aimed at gaining not only information but insights through data analyses. Although methods for automated data analyses exist, the process of gaining insights from data is often accompanied with great amounts of human labor [7]. Despite these amounts of human labor, the results obtained are, especially with unstructured data, not always satisfactory, due to shallow learning algorithms [7]. In an attempt to get more informative results from the analyses of unstructured data, researchers and practitioners often incorporate more prior knowledge into algorithms, essentially relocating human labor from the postprocessing step to the preprocessing step. While this approach may indeed improve the results of the analysis step, a decrease in human effort will not be observed, because the incorporation of prior knowledge is usually not a trivial task, but has to be performed individually for each given problem.

We suggest that an efficient solution to complex data analysis problems lies in a modular design of the analysis process – that is, a design comprising independent and possibly reusable data analysis modules. Our contribution is, thus, a design theory for distributed expert systems. Our design theory, named "the Division-of-Labor (DoL) Framework", addresses the issue of solving complex information extraction tasks from any combination of numerical, categorical and unstructured data. The DoL Framework handles complex tasks by treating them as compositions of less complex sub-tasks, which are distributed among several processing units. Aside from reducing the complexity of tasks, task distribution also enables horizontal scalability of learning and data analysis algorithms, making the framework suitable for analyses of big data [15].

2   Related Work

The presented design theory is a framework that employs multiple consecutive layers of feature learning and information extraction to solve data analysis problems. As such, it can be considered a "deep learning" framework. As an emerging field of research, deep learning does not have a clear, established definition [11]. However, deep learning methods are said to learn "feature hierarchies with features from higher levels of the hierarchy formed by the composition of lower level features" [5, p. 5]. Deng and Yu [11, p. 201] name two commonly identified aspects of deep learning: "(1) models consisting of multiple layers or stages of nonlinear information processing; and (2) methods for supervised or unsupervised learning of feature representation at successively higher, more abstract layers". We proceed by giving a short overview of contributions made to this field.

Many deep learning methods have been developed in the recent past such as Deep Feedforward Neural Networks and Deep Recurrent Neural Networks [13], Convolutional Neural Networks [20], Deep Boltzmann Machines [26], and Deep Belief Networks [17]. In addition to these methods, other machine learning (ML) methods have been developed, which do not themselves constitute deep learning methods, but serve as important building blocks of deep learning architectures. Examples for such methods are Autoencoders and representation learning methods [6], which extract important features from data that can be used in subsequent processing steps to perform more meaningful analyses. Bengio [5] describes principles for the implementation of deep learning algorithms.

In addition to deep learning, the DoL Framework draws on concepts of "ensemble learning". We describe these concepts in Sect. 2.1 and relate them to our framework.

2.1 Relationship to Ensemble Learning

Ensemble learning describes a class of ML methods that combine a set of weak, supervised learning models to obtain a single, ideally more accurate, model [27]. One generally distinguishes ensemble methods in "bootstrap aggregating" (bagging) [9] and "boosting" [27] methods. Bagging methods combine weak models by averaging or taking a majority vote of their individual predictions [9]. Random Forests are a prominent example of bagging learning systems, making use of Decision Trees as a base set of weak classifiers [9]. Boosting methods, in turn, not only specify a way of combining the output of models, but also affect the training procedure of these models. They train different models with emphases on different subsets of the data such that individual models perform particularly well on different subsets [31]. The output combination may be performed through (weighted) averaging/voting [31].

Our DoL Framework builds on concepts used by ensemble learning and distributes data among multiple learning models. However, it applies less strict conditions on the individual models and the way data are distributed. That is, it not only allows a developer to employ bagging and boosting methods, but also allows for the application of different kinds of ensemble methods. The principles of data/task distribution in the DoL Framework are described in Sect. 3.4.

3   A Design Theory for Distributed Expert Systems

In response to the call for IS research in the context of data analytics by Abbasi et al. [1], we propose a design theory – the Division-of-Labor Framework – following the steps developed by Gregor and Jones [14]. We adopt these steps to develop our design theory, because they encourage and enable formalization of knowledge of the artifact's shape and configuration, rather than incorporation of implicit knowledge in the artifact.

The goal of our design is a product, namely a distributed cognitive expert system. We label this product as "cognitive", because of its increased employment of self-governance and interaction with its environment (see Sect. 3.2). We describe the purpose and scope of our framework in Sect. 3.1, our justificatory knowledge – underlying knowledge giving an explanation for our design – in Sect. 3.2, constructs of our theory in Sect. 3.3, principles of form and function – the framework's architecture – in Sect. 3.4, principles of implementation in Sect. 3.5, artifact mutability – anticipated changes of the artifact in future research – in Sect. 3.6, and testable propositions – predictions about the outcome of artifact implementations – in Sect. 3.7. We omit the optional step of presenting an expository instantiation for space reasons.

3.1   Purpose and Scope

The purpose of the proposed design theory is to provide guidelines for the development of systems that deal with complex data analysis tasks – that is, analysis tasks that aim to model non-shallow relationships between some attributes. In contrast to traditional ML algorithms that are often equipped with rather high amounts of prior knowledge and deep neural network architectures that require relatively little prior knowledge but in turn much computational power [20], our design deals with computational scalability by distributing the workload on multiple processing units and requires a moderate amount of prior knowledge. This prior knowledge typically assumes the form of specifications on how to distribute incoming data analysis tasks. For example, in the context of customer churn prediction, a developer may incorporate prior knowledge into a system developed according to the DoL Framework by specifying that customers are to be segmented based on their age, income, and location.

Our design theory is applicable to supervised and unsupervised ML problems based on structured and unstructured data. However, the design theory is particularly interesting in the context of unstructured data such as texts and images. Analyses of such data often aim to unveil deep patterns, whereas quantitative data are often analyzed using shallow methods, and, unlike quantitative data analyses, typically leave room for interpretation. Unstructured data analyses are, therefore, often enhanced through the incorporation of domain knowledge [29] – a process that is automated in the DoL Framework.

3.2   Justificatory Knowledge

We provide justificatory knowledge for our design theory by motivating the need for the DoL Framework from three different viewpoints, namely the viewpoints of (mathematical) optimization theory, economics, and artificial intelligence.

The DoL Framework is based on the assumption that complex tasks can be solved more efficiently by subdividing them into less complex sub-tasks solved by Experts. We justify this assumption – from the viewpoint of optimization theory – by using the fact that splitting an optimization problem (i.e., a task) into a set of smaller optimization problems (i.e., sub-tasks) generally reduces the search space of that problem. Although not necessarily the case for all optimization scenarios, in practice, most of them are solved faster once the search space is reduced [5]. For an illustration of search space reduction by splitting a problem into sub-problems, consider the following formalization.

Formalization: Search space reduction through task division

Let $\mathcal{H}$ be an optimization problem comprising N optimization problems $\forall_{i=1}^{N} : \mathcal{H}^{(i)}$, all of which, for reasons of simplicity, have a search space of size $\forall_{i=1}^{N} : s\left(\mathcal{H}^{(i)}\right) = d$. Solving these optimization problems individually yields a total search space of size

$$s_{individual} = \sum_{i=1}^{N} s\left(\mathcal{H}^{(i)}\right) = N \cdot d. \tag{1}$$

On the other hand, solving the whole optimization problem $\mathcal{H}$ corresponds to jointly – rather than individually – solving the sub-problems and yields a search space of size

$$s_{joint} = \prod_{i=1}^{N} s\left(\mathcal{H}^{(i)}\right) = d^{N}. \tag{2}$$

One may notice that $s_{individual} < s_{joint}$ for $\forall N > 2, d > 1$. That is, the search space of the overall optimization problem is in virtually all cases larger than the sum of search spaces of the sub-problems.

From an economist's viewpoint, the concept of "division of labor"[1] states that splitting a task into smaller, yet semantically coherent, sub-tasks allows for a specialization of agents in their respective tasks [28]. Division of labor, as proposed by Smith and Krueger [28], assumes an economy involving humans and requires agents to be adaptive – that is, being capable of learning through observations. The authors argue that specialization of individuals in different tasks, enabled by the adaptability of these individuals, leads to a faster and more effective processing of these task.

While adaptability has also been of interest in the data analysis and ML community, as evidenced by methods developed by Bengio et al., Bifet and Gavalda, and Vaughan and Bohac [6,8,30], the majority of research is concerned with static data analysis rather than dynamic, time-varying models [3,18,24]. Common exceptions are embedding methods such as Word2Vec models [21], which map data into different spaces and can be used in further building blocks of different tasks, and deep learning methods that hierarchically process an input through a number of processing layers [6].

Finally, we motivate our framework from the viewpoint of artificial intelligence. Research in this area has been moving away from symbolic problem representation as part of the so-called "good old-fashioned artificial intelligence" [22]. Harnard [16, p. 1] defines the Symbol Grounding Problem as the problem of making "semantic interpretation of a formal symbol system...*intrinsic* to the system, rather than just parasitic on the meanings in our heads" (emphasis in original). That is, symbolic representations are high-level and human-readable,

---

[1] Not to be confused with our Division-of-Labor Framework.

but they do not allow a system to attribute meaning to those representations on their own. They are mainly used for problems that suffer from a low degree of uncertainty. Non-symbolic computation allows an agent to self-govern and interpret information, but at the same time makes it infeasible for outsiders to interpret the computation steps [16]. Nowadays, parts of the ML community move towards non-symbolic approaches, but the dependence on symbolic computation still largely remains. The DoL Framework encourages researchers to make use of non-symbolic problem representations while maintaining a fair share of symbolic computation steps to allow for domain knowledge incorporation.

3.3   Constructs

In this section, we name and describe the constructs, that is, the entities of interest [14], of our theory (see Table 1). We use these constructs to structure our framework's form and function in Sect. 3.4.

3.4   Principles of Form and Function

The DoL Framework comprises two component types – the Expert and the Central Executive (CE). Each class of tasks is processed by one CE and one or more Experts. Experts are specialized in a certain class of sub-tasks, whereas CEs are required to possess general knowledge of the task and be capable of consulting the right Expert(s) for an incoming task and handling their responses accordingly. The features of an Expert and a CE are described in the following paragraphs.

Expert. An Expert is an agent that is specialized in a certain kind of tasks, for which it possesses domain knowledge. It receives tasks from the CE, processes them and transmits solutions back to the CE. An Expert can also simultaneously play the role of the CE of a sub-task (see Fig. 1).

Specialization. An Expert is specialized in a certain domain and class of tasks. Thus, the specialization area of an Expert is classified by these two properties. With A and B each denoting an area of specialization consisting of k sets each corresponding to the range of a dimension, we obtain the following implication for the degree of specialization (dos):

$$dos(B) > dos(A) \iff (\exists_{1 \leq i \leq k} : |A_i \setminus B_i| > 0) \land (\forall_{1 \leq i \leq k} : A \supseteq B). \quad (3)$$

That is, one dos is higher than another dos, only if the area of specialization covers a narrower range in at least one dimension of inputs and goals and an equally as broad range in the rest of the dimensions.

An Expert's degree of specialization is always at least as high as that of its superordinate CE.

Table 1. Constructs of the Division-of-Labor Framework

Category	Construct	Description
Problem specification	Task	A task is an instance of a class of data analysis problems. It is concerned with the application of learned models to unseen data
	Sub-task	A sub-task is a separable unit of one task. A sub-task's solution can be used to facilitate finding a solution to its super-task
Input	Data	Data enter the system as part of a task or for the purpose of achieving specialization. Data contain relevant information regarding a given or future task(s)
	Data type	Different kinds of data require different kinds of analysis techniques. We distinguish between structured (numerical and categorical) and unstructured data
	Domain	Data are associated with domains. A domain refers to a data set describing the same class or related classes of objects
Cognitive system	Intelligent agent	An agent is any entity that perceives its environment through sensors and acts upon it through actuators [25]. "Intelligent agents are characterized on the one hand by the fact that they comply with and exploit their ecological niche, and on the other that they exhibit diverse behavior" [22, p. 67]
Specialization	Specialization	Specialization, as a concept of division of labor [28], refers to an increased knowledge of a certain area. An agent's area of specialization is its domain and task of interest
	Degree of specialization	An agent's degree of specialization is the narrowness of its area of specialization. A degree of specialization can be quantified only in a manner relative to another specialization, provided that one of the areas of specialization is narrower or equal to the other area in all of its dimensions
	Expert	The Expert is an agent and an intrinsic component of the DoL Framework. One Expert is specialized on one or more domains and processes one class of sub-tasks and data sets
Task distribution	General knowledge	General knowledge is knowledge of a variety of domains and/or tasks. As the opposite of specialization, generality is a relative property
	Task distribution	Tasks can be divided into sub-tasks and distributed among Experts. Task distribution comprises dividing tasks into sub-tasks and assigning them to the right Experts
	Semantic coherence	Semantic coherence is the connectedness of a set of entities on the semantic level. That is, a semantically coherent set of entities contains entities that are semantically similar
	Combination of partial solutions	Tasks can be divided into sub-tasks that are treated individually. The solutions to sub-tasks are partial solutions that have to be combined to obtain a solution to the super-task
	Central executive	The Central Executive is an agent and an intrinsic component of the DoL Framework. It possesses general knowledge, distributes tasks, and combines partial solutions into an overall solution
Performance	Feedback	After a task is processed, outside feedback may be given to the system to evaluate its performance
	Adaptation	Given some outside feedback, the system re-evaluates and improves its analysis steps
	Sustainability	Sustainability refers to the ability of a system to theoretically sustain itself indefinitely. That is, it is able to continuously learn from new data without suffering a significant increase in computation time
Interpretation	Explanation	For reasons of interpretability by outsiders, the system's components may provide explanations as to why a task was solved in a particular way

Adaptation. Experts receive new data and feedback from their CEs and use them to improve their performance. An Expert updates its statistics and learning

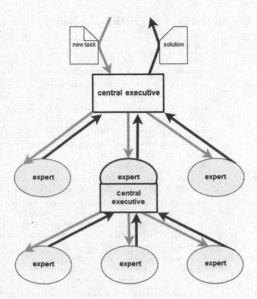

Fig. 1. The Division-of-Labor Framework. Gray and black arrows indicate the transmission of (sub-)tasks and their solutions, respectively. Hierarchical re-distribution of tasks is enabled through agents that serve as both experts and central executives.

models as well as possible data repositories when new input is received. Effective adaptation is achieved through a model-specific definition. That is, adaptation should be specified not as a general-purpose process, but with regard to the base models used in the data analysis system.

Sustainability (Optional). An Expert's models have to be adapted when new data are seen. For reasons of scalability, it is necessary for an Expert to update, rather than recompute, its models. That is, with $\mathcal{M}_t$ being an Expert's model at time t and x_t being the data point received at time t, the Expert has to apply a function $u(\cdot)$ with a finite output size (i.e., independent of the number of data points) to update its model according to (4).

$$\mathcal{M}_{t+1} = u(\mathcal{M}_t, x_t) \tag{4}$$

However, for some models such as many non-parametric models and data indexes, it is not possible to apply a function of finite output size, because those models require storing all data points. For such models, it is necessary to prune the data set when before the storage capacity or computational limit is exceeded.

We label sustainability an optional function, because, while scalability problems related to big data are becoming increasingly relevant, there are still many practical scenarios, in which data sets are sufficiently small to neglect scalability problems.

Explanation (Optional). Data analysts are faced with the prediction-explanation trade-off [1]. That is, sophisticated data analysis methods such as neural networks may perform well on data analysis tasks, but their solutions are hard to interpret. An Expert processes tasks in depth and should communicate the rationale behind its solutions (i.e., which particular circumstances led to these particular solutions). The modular structure of the DoL framework facilitates interpretability of results, because a researcher may examine solutions to subtasks of a lower complexity rather than solutions to complex super-tasks.

We label explanation an optional function, because it does not directly contribute to the performance of the system, but rather provides researchers with insights that may be used to further improve the system or the design theory.

Central Executive. The Central Executive is an agent that processes an incoming task by splitting it into semantically coherent and independent subtasks. Semantic coherence and independence are important criteria for the individual sub-tasks, because they will be processed independently by subordinate Experts. From a set of available Experts, the CE then selects the best-suited Expert for each sub-task. CEs possess fairly general knowledge regarding their respective tasks such that they can categorize sub-tasks and assign them to the right Expert units. After receiving the results for the sub-tasks from the Experts, the CE combines them to obtain the result for its main task. A CE, in turn, can be an Expert of a super-task, allowing for hierarchies of arbitrary heights. The hierarchy may be either provided by a developer who specifies the number of hierarchy levels and which tasks are solved on each level or automatically inferred by the system by employing an algorithm with each Expert that decides whether a task is to be further divided into sub-tasks. This decision may be based on the heterogeneity of a given sub-set of the data.

General Knowledge. The CE possesses general knowledge of domains and/or tasks. Each sub-task processed by an Expert is also known to its superordinate CE. However, the CE processes tasks at a lower level of depth. That is, it models the overall domain associated to a task using a single model, whereas Experts use one model per sub-task, which are typically associated with much smaller domains.

Task Distribution and Combination of Partial Solutions. A CE distributes an incoming task according to either of the principles of "division of labor" and "wisdom of the crowds". Distribution according to the division of labor principle occurs by splitting a task or a class of tasks into sub-tasks or classes of sub-tasks that whose domains are disjoint or only partially overlapping. Individual Experts then each process a class of sub-tasks and the results are combined by the CE in an adequate manner. Distribution according to the wisdom of the crowds principle occurs by forwarding each task without performing any splitting. The Experts then solve that task using their respective models. A combination of individual solutions in this case can often be achieved by computing a (weighted) average or majority vote.

Feedback. CEs may gather feedback from outside of the system. This feedback may assume the shape of "the correct solution" to a task or a quality statement for a solution developed by the system. Let x be a given data point and $\hat{y}$ a solution computed by the system. The feedback may then be the correct solution y – typically available in supervised learning settings – or a real-valued rating $r(\hat{y})$ associated with the solution – observed in unsupervised learning settings or supervised settings, in which the outcomes are not directly observable.

Adaptation. In addition to the principles stated for Experts, the CE updates its own models and redirects the feedback and the corresponding data to Experts involved in the task. In addition to further models used, the CE updates its task distribution and re-combination mechanisms.

Sustainability. The principles described for the sustainability of Experts also hold for CEs.

3.5   Principles of Implementation

Having described the constructs of our design theory and their respective functions in Sects. 3.3 and 3.4, we now proceed to formulate the principles of implementation. For this purpose, we refer to data analysis systems developed according to the DoL Framework as "DoL systems". Given a certain class of data analysis tasks, described by the data specification and the desired information to be extracted from the data, a DoL system is implemented by implementing the CEs and according Experts. We describe the implementation steps for Experts and CEs in the following paragraphs.

Training of Experts. An Expert is provided with data (i.e., training examples) over its life cycle. It autonomously processes and learns from these data in accordance with the task(s) that it will solve. The specialization of an Expert in a certain task and domain is achieved by the CE's task distribution and does not require additional effort by the Expert, other than learning to solve its task based on the provided data. Nevertheless, there are issues that need to be considered.

As previously stated, tasks arrive in a one-at-a-time manner. Consequently, in order to enable adaptability, an Expert's learning models have to specify an algorithm for incremental updates, as, for instance, provided by incremental linear regression [19] and incremental neural networks [10].

Further constraints arise for an Expert, due to the DoL Framework's aim for sustainability. While incremental learning models address storage capacity and computational limits, methods like clustering and indexing, which, in their standard forms, require access to all previously seen data points, are not in line with sustainability. In order to make these methods sustainable, the number of stored data points has to be restricted and data points are to be removed from the system once the storage capacity is reached. The order of removal is determined by an importance measure, that is, the least important data points are removed first. The importance of a data point may be measured by the recency of its last access.

Finally, an Expert may provide explanations for its solutions. Explanations show which features in the data influenced the outcome the most. For models like linear regression, these features can, for instance, be identified looking at the largest products of pairs of weights and features. For multi-layered models such as neural networks, deriving explanations is less straightforward and requires iterative explanations, with explanations of higher-level layers building on explanations of preceding layers.

Identification and Assignment of Tasks. As Pfeifer and Bongard [22] stated in the context of physical agents, it is important that all components of a system are developed in accordance with each other to enable a high synergy. For this reason, we propose that the CE is in charge of managing the training of Experts and, thereby, enables their specialization. That is, it selects the data that are used to train each of the Experts. For this purpose, the CE has to decide how many Experts to create and how to distribute the data among these Experts. In order to decide on this matter, the CE has to associate tasks with domains (i.e., perform a categorization of tasks). In the following paragraph, we describe how this decision process can be implemented.

A CE starts without any knowledge of the kind of tasks it will solve. Therefore, each task is initially processed by a single Expert. As the number of processed tasks increases, the CE may introduce further Experts to cope with the complexity of the data distribution. We consider three kinds of task distribution problems (from most simple to hardest case): (1) Tasks are pre-categorized before entering the system. In this case, the CE simply forwards the task according to its category. (2) Task categories are revealed after the task has been solved. In this case, the CE is faced with a classification problem. A classifier is trained to associate inputs with categories. (3) Task categories are never revealed. In this case, there is no objective notion of categories and the CE has to decide on a categorization without receiving any feedback. We elaborate on this case in more detail: Unsupervised categorization, that is, the problem of dividing the task space into sub-spaces that are each processed by a certain Expert, can be treated as a clustering problem. So we refer to these sub-spaces as "clusters". Because tasks are processed one at a time, the CE has to employ an incremental clustering algorithm without a fixed number of clusters. In order for the CE to decide if further Experts and, therefore, clusters are needed, it maintains a model of the expected performance of individual Experts. The performance can be estimated either in terms of within-cluster homogeneity or, if labeled data are available in the case of classification and regressions tasks, by directly measuring the average accuracy of solutions for past tasks. Once the performance of an Expert does not meet a certain requirement, the corresponding cluster is split into two new clusters. This requirement may, for instance, be defined as a function of the performance of the CE or a function of the performance of other Experts. More formally, let k be the number of Experts and $p(\mathcal{M})$ denote the performance of some model $\mathcal{M}$. Then, cluster i, associated to Expert E_i, is split, if the following condition is satisfied:

$$p(E_i) < f(\{\forall_{j \neq i} p(E_j)\}), \tag{5}$$

where $f(\cdot)$ is a user-defined function such as the average function. Clusters are merged, if storage limits are reached or if (6) is satisfied, with τ being a certain threshold.

$$p(E_i) > f(\{\forall_{j \neq i} p(E_j)\}) + \tau \tag{6}$$

The sustainability of CEs is achieved through the same principles as used for Experts.

3.6   Artifact Mutability

The DoL Framework offers some room for modifications. Due to the steady development of novel methods in the ML community, the principles of implementations may be considered highly mutable. As new learning algorithms are developed, the implementation steps may be incrementally refined. Moreover, researchers may further develop the principles of form and function of our design, consisting of two components – the CE and the Expert –, through minor and major adaptations.

Minor adaptations are additions, removals, and modifications of component properties. They will be required, if certain functions are deemed incomplete or unnecessary or new functions are introduced that can be related to an existing component in a meaningful way. The modification of the CE's function "task distribution and combination of partial solutions" by adding a third task distribution principle is an example of a minor adaptation.

Major adaptations are additions and removals of entire components. Major adaptations should be performed to improve the structure of the framework by attributing related functions to the same component and separating independent functions. An example for a major adaptation is the introduction of an intermediate component between the CE and the Expert, which neither plays a role in the task distribution part nor in the specialization part, but deals with input/output transformations between the CE and Expert instead. Leveraging the DoL Framework's modularity, such a component may be particularly interesting in the context of transfer learning [23].

3.7   Testable Propositions

In this section, we propose truth statements (i.e., hypotheses) about products designed according to our theory. These statements may be verified or falsified in future research.

The aim of data analysis algorithms is to automatically extract information from a given data set with respect to a certain task. Algorithms are typically evaluated based on the quality of their solutions to a task and the rapidness of their execution. Based on the property of specialization inherent to Experts and the task distribution employed by CEs, we propose a higher accuracy of DoL systems compared to a mere use of shallow ML algorithms. Further, we propose that the adaptation property of Experts allows for processing tasks in real time.

(i) Data analysis systems developed according to the DoL Framework under the use of shallow ML base models produce more accurate solutions than using the same shallow ML models in a stand-alone manner.

(ii) Data analysis systems developed according to the DoL Framework process tasks in real time.

Furthermore, solutions obtained through data analysis algorithms are preferred to be interpretable [1]. This interpretability is enabled by the optional Expert property of explanation emerging from the modularity of the framework and leads us to the following proposition:

(iii) Data analysis systems developed according to the DoL Framework are positioned at a high level of interpretability, compared to other deep learning architectures, especially in comparison to deep neural networks.

Our final proposition is based on the optional property "sustainability" of Experts and relates to scalability issues. We consider an algorithm scalable to big data, if it is able to cope with more data by adding more computing units and the number of required computing units to process the data in a certain time is in linear proportion to the number of data points. We formulate proposition (iv) as follows:

(iv) Data analysis systems developed according to the DoL Framework scale to big data.

4   Conclusion

We developed a design theory – the Division-of-Labor Framework – for distributed data analysis. Based on a modular design, the theory leverages specialization of individual components to gain in-depth insights from data. It addresses the need for both new design theories for sophisticated data analysis methods and scalable solutions for the increasingly relevant phenomenon of big data.

Having described the design theory's components in detail and presented principles of its implementation, we made four propositions that can be tested by implementing products according to our theory.

References

1. Abbasi, A., Sarker, S., Chiang, R.H.: Big data research in information systems: toward an inclusive research agenda. J. Assoc. Inf. Syst. **17**(2), 1–32 (2016)
2. Agarwal, R., Dhar, V.: Editorialbig data, data science, and analytics: the opportunity and challenge for is research. Inf. Syst. Res. **25**(3), 443–448 (2014)
3. Alippi, C., Roveri, M.: Just-in-time adaptive classifiers in non-stationary conditions. In: 2007 International Joint Conference on Neural Networks, pp. 1014–1019. IEEE (2007)
4. Baesens, B., Bapna, R., Marsden, J.R., Vanthienen, J., Zhao, J.L.: Transformational issues of big data and analytics in networked business. MIS Q. **40**(4), 807–818 (2016)
5. Bengio, Y.: Learning deep architectures for AI. Found. Trends® Mach. Learn. **2**(1), 1–127 (2009)
6. Bengio, Y., Courville, A., Vincent, P.: Representation learning: a review and new perspectives. IEEE Trans. Pattern Anal. Mach. Intell. **35**(8), 1798–1828 (2013)
7. Bengio, Y., Lecun, Y.: Scaling Learning Algorithms Towards AI. MIT Press, Cambridge (2007)
8. Bifet, A., Gavalda, R.: Learning from time-changing data with adaptive windowing. In: SDM, vol. 7, pp. 443–448. SIAM (2007)
9. Breiman, L.: Random forests. Mach. Learn. **45**(1), 5–32 (2001)
10. Bruzzone, L., Prieto, D.F.: An incremental-learning neural network for the classification of remote-sensing images. Pattern Recogn. Lett. **20**(11), 1241–1248 (1999)
11. Deng, L., Yu, D.: Deep learning: methods and applications. Technical report (2014)
12. Goes, P.B.: Editor's comments: big data and is research. MIS Q. **38**(3), iii–viii (2014)
13. Goodfellow, I., Bengio, Y., Courville, A.: Deep Learning. MIT Press, Cambridge (2016)
14. Gregor, S., Jones, D.: The anatomy of a design theory. J. Assoc. Inf. Syst. **8**(5), 312–335 (2007)
15. Grolinger, K., Hayes, M., Higashino, W. A., L'Heureux, A., Allison, D. S., Capretz, M.A.: Challenges for MapReduce in big data. In: 2014 IEEE World Congress on Services (SERVICES), pp. 182–189. IEEE (2014)
16. Harnad, S.: The symbol grounding problem. Physica D: Nonlinear Phenom. **42**(1–3), 335–346 (1990)
17. Hinton, G.E., Osindero, S., Teh, Y.-W.: A fast learning algorithm for deep belief nets. Neural Comput. **18**(7), 1527–1554 (2006)
18. Huang, G.-B., Wang, D.H., Lan, Y.: Extreme learning machines: a survey. Int. J. Mach. Learn. Cybernet. **2**(2), 107–122 (2011)
19. Huiwen, W., Yuan, W., Lele, H.: Incremental algorithm of multiple linear regression model. J. Beijing Univ. Aeronaut. Astronaut. **11**, 1487–1491 (2014)
20. LeCun, Y., Bengio, Y., et al.: Convolutional networks for images, speech, and time series. In: The Handbook of Brain Theory and Neural Networks, vol. 3361, no. 10 (1995)
21. Mikolov, T., Chen, K., Corrado, G., Dean, J.: Efficient estimation of word representations in vector space. CoRR, abs/1301.3781 (2013)
22. Pfeifer, R., Bongard, J.C.: How the Body Shapes the Way We Think: A New View of Intelligence. The MIT Press, Cambridge (2006)
23. Pratt, L.Y., Hanson, S., Giles, C., Cowan, J.: Discriminability-based transfer between neural networks. In: Advances in Neural Information Processing Systems, p. 204 (1993)

24. Quionero-Candela, J., Sugiyama, M., Schwaighofer, A., Lawrence, N.D.: Dataset Shift in Machine Learning. The MIT Press, Cambridge (2009)
25. Russel, S., Norvig, P.: Artificial Intelligence - A Modern Approach, 3rd edn. Pearson Education Inc., Upper Saddle River (2010)
26. Salakhutdinov, R., Hinton, G.E.: Deep Boltzmann machines. In: Proceedings of the International Conference on Artificial Intelligence and Statistics, vol. 12, pp. 448–455 (2009)
27. Schapire, R.E.: The strength of weak learnability. Mach. Learn. **5**(2), 197–227 (1990)
28. Smith, A., Krueger, A.B.: The Wealth of Nations. Bantam Classics, New York City (2003)
29. Tan, A.-H., Lai, F.-L.: Text categorization, supervised learning, and domain knowledge integration. In: Proceedings, KDD-2000 International Workshop on Text Mining, Boston, vol. 20 (2000, to appear)
30. Vaughan, A., Bohac, S.V.: Real-time, adaptive machine learning for non-stationary, near chaotic gasoline engine combustion time series. Neural Netw. **70**, 18–26 (2015)
31. Zhou, Z.-H.: Ensemble Methods: Foundations and Algorithms. CRC Press, Boca Raton (2012)

DSR in Service Science

Developing Design Principles
for a Crowd-Based Business Model
Validation System

Dominik Dellermann[(✉)], Nikolaus Lipusch, and Philipp Ebel

ITeG, University of Kassel, Kassel, Germany
{dellermann, nikolaus.lipusch, ph.ebel}@uni-kassel.de

Abstract. The high uncertainty of creating business models demands entrepreneurs to re-evaluate and continuously adapt them. Therefore, incubators offer validation services. However, systematic, and scalable information systems to enable interaction with a crowd of potential customers, investors, or other stakeholders and entrepreneurs do not exist. Our aim is thus to develop tentative design principles for crowd-based business model validation (CBMV) systems. Such systems should support entrepreneurs to reduce the uncertainty about the validity of their business model. Thus, we apply a theory-driven design approach based on knowledge drawn from literature and complemented by empirical insights. For developing such information systems, we combine the concept of crowdsourcing with findings from research on decision support systems to propose theory-grounded design principles for a CBMV system. The identified design principles describe a potential solution to a problem that previous research proved as viable.

Keywords: Service · Decision support · Crowdsourcing · Business model · Entrepreneurship

1 Introduction

The rapid digital transformation of businesses and society creates tremendous possibilities for novel business models to create and capture value. Many Internet startups such as Hybris, Snapchat, and Facebook are achieving major successes and quickly disrupting whole industries. Yet, many digital ventures fail. One reason for this is that entrepreneurs face high uncertainties when creating their business models. Consequently, entrepreneurs must constantly re-evaluate and continuously adapt their business models to succeed [1].

One way to deal with uncertainty during the development of business models is the validation of the entrepreneur's assumptions by testing them in the market or with other stakeholders such as suppliers or complementors [2]. Such a validation allows the entrepreneur to gather feedback to test the viability of the current perception of a business model and adapt it, if necessary, before potentially wasting money. For this purpose crowdsourcing has proven to be a valuable mechanism [3] in other contexts.

© Springer International Publishing AG 2017
A. Maedche et al. (Eds.): DESRIST 2017, LNCS 10243, pp. 163–178, 2017.
DOI: 10.1007/978-3-319-59144-5_10

Literature on business models provides a rich body of knowledge about different components or the initial design [4, 5], however, they do not provide any information systems that support such processes and enable the integration of the diverse voices of stakeholders [6]. Thus, service institutions that create a supportive environment for startups, so-called incubators, function as intermediaries that connect different actors such as consultants, business angels, or venture capitalists with entrepreneurs for the exchange of services. Although business model validation services are a repetitive activity of incubators, systematic and scalable solutions to enable interaction to validate business models do not exist. In this context, IT creates opportunities to design systems that support the entrepreneur in business model validation.

Therefore, the aim of this paper is to develop tentative design principles for crowd-based business model validation (CBMV) systems. Such information systems support entrepreneurs in learning and reducing the uncertainty about the validity of their assumptions. With this aim in view, we develop design principles that guide the design of prototypes for CBMV systems. We refer to design principles as the tentative properties of a generic solution drawn from literature that address the potential solution space of such artifacts. The purpose of this paper is thus to develop design principles for information systems that feature crowd-based business model validation.

To derive our design principles, we follow a design science approach [7, 8] guided by the process of Vaishnavi and Kuechler [9]. This paper follows a theory-driven design approach based on knowledge drawn from literature and complemented by empirical insights. For developing CBMV systems, we combine the concept of crowdsourcing with findings from research on decision support systems to propose tentative design principles. The identified design principles describe the core of a solution to a problem that previous research proved as viable. We therefore ensure theoretical rigor while developing a system to solve a real-world business problem.

Following a design science approach, this paper proceeds as follows: In Sect. 2, we introduce related work. Section 3 provides a brief overview of our research methodology. We then give insights into the problem awareness and our identified design requirements derived from our kernel theory and interviews in Sects. 4 and 5. Section 6 then reviews design-relevant knowledge to guide the development of design principles that address these requirements. Concluding in Sect. 7, we close with a discussion of our findings and contribution.

2   Related Work

2.1   Business Model Validation in Early-Stage Startups

To formulate the problem for our design research approach, we reviewed current literature on business model development. The concept of business models has gathered substantial attention from both academics and practitioners in recent years [6]. In general, it describes the logic of a firm to create and capture value [4, 10]. Although there is no commonly accepted definition of the term, this concept provides a comprehensive approach toward describing how value is created for all engaged stakeholders, the allocation of activities among them, and the role of information technology

[11, 12]. Following Teece [13], a business model reflects the assumptions of an entrepreneur and can therefore be considered as a set of "hypotheses about what customers want, and how an enterprise can best meet those needs, and get paid for doing so".

In the context of early-stage startups, business models become particularly relevant as entrepreneurs define their ideas more precisely in terms of how market needs might be served. In addition to that, it helps the entrepreneur to examine which kind of resources have to be deployed to create value and how that value might be distributed among the stakeholders [14]. Such early conceptualizations of a startup's business model represent an entrepreneur's assumptions about what might be viable and feasible but are mostly myopic in terms of the outcome as entrepreneurs are acting under high levels of uncertainty [15]. Since entrepreneurs are operating under high levels of uncertainty, they start a sense-making process in which they test their initial beliefs about the market through iterative experimentations and learning from successful or failed actions [16]. When the entrepreneurs' assumptions contradict with the reaction of the market, this might lead to a rejection of erroneous hypotheses. This will require a reassessment of the business model to test the market perceptions again. Thus, the business model evolves toward the needs of the market and changes the assumptions of entrepreneurs [15, 17]. The success of startups thus heavily depends on the entrepreneurs' ability to develop and continuously adapt their business models to the reactions of the environment.

2.2 Previous Work on Crowd-Based Validation

Practitioner literature recognizes that many business models fail due to wasting resources before validation [2]. Consequently, entrepreneurs should test the assumptions about their business model with customers, partners, complementors, and suppliers to gather feedback and validate the current version before continuing and possibly wasting money. The feedback from external actors enables entrepreneurs to reflect on the current version. Thus, entrepreneurs may start thinking about the drawbacks of their hypothesized business model and exert effort on resolving these by reassessing, pivoting, or even abandoning elements [18, 19].

One mechanism that has proven to be valuable to gain access to such feedback is crowdsourcing [18–21]. Research on crowdsourcing shows the value of integrating customers and other stakeholders into the evaluation process to support decision making during the development of new products. For instance, crowd voting provides extensive evidence for the suitability of a crowd in evaluation tasks as it is equally capable of identifying viable ideas [22–24]. Therefore, many companies have started to use the collective intelligence of a heterogeneous crowd to evaluate ideas [19]. Thereby, a heterogeneous crowd, most commonly end users of a certain product, rates certain product ideas. Crowd-based online validation of innovation is particular beneficial compared to industry expert evaluation due to time and cost efficiency reasons [21], the reduction of individual biases through averaging the results [18], and the possibility to focus on the demand side perspective of innovation [23] including a much higher number of raters compared to offline approaches. This assessment constitutes a proxy to distinguish between high- and low-quality ideas and the feedback of the crowd is then used as decision support on how to proceed [25–27]. The appropriateness for using a crowd has also been shown for business models [3, 28]. We thus argue that crowd-based validation is also suitable for the highly uncertain context of startup business models and provides a superior approach compared to consultancy feedback or offline approaches such as design thinking, which might force the entrepreneur to follow biased individual feedback or to draw conclusions from small samples.

3   Methodology

For developing design principles for a CBMV system, we conducted a design science research project [7, 29] in the broader context of a research project that attempts to provide crowd-based services for incubators to design a new and innovative artifact grounded in theoretical rigor that helps to solve a real-world problem. Therefore, we followed the design research cycle methodology as introduced by Vaishnavi and Kuechler [9] (Fig. 1).

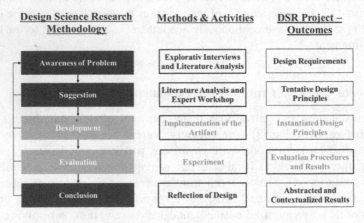

Fig. 1. Research approach

First, we conducted a literature analysis as well as exploratory qualitative interviews. We contacted executives of German business incubators (n = 17) that provide business model validation services and decision makers in startups (n = 28) to analyze the status quo of business model validation, the limitation of those, and requirements for a solution. For this procedure, we used a semi-structured interview guideline, which followed the theoretical concepts of opportunity creation theory. This theory-guided approach provides two benefits. First, we could justify the design requirements derived from theory. Second, we obtained a deeper understanding of the requirements from the practical problem domain. The requirements identified through the interviews were aggregated and coded. Thus, we could derive four additional design requirements. The interviews lasted between 30 and 45 min and were coded by two of the authors. A cross case analysis was conducted to identify common themes. To develop suggestions for a solution, we applied a theory-driven design approach and opportunity creation theory [15–17], which explains how business models are co-created, as general scientific knowledge base that provides theoretical abstraction of the cause and effect of the problem space and informs our design [30, 31]. From this kernel theory, we derived design requirements that were validated and complemented with findings from the interviews. We then used previous work on crowdsourcing evaluation as well as decision support systems as relevant knowledge base that provides us with guidance in the development of the design principles for the CBMV system. Such design principles drawn from literature are tentative properties that may inform the design of a first prototype. Through an expert workshop (n = 7) we evaluated the validity of our conceptual tentative design principles. These design principles will then be instantiated into an IT artifact and finally evaluated in an experimental setting of a business model competition. Applying this approach allows us to use theoretical rigorous knowledge for developing an innovative IT artifact, which helps to solve a real-world problem, thus ensuring practical relevance.

4 Awareness of the Problem

The design science research project is motivated by both a gap in IS research on systems that support business model validation services and practical problems of entrepreneurs and incubators. Therefore, we conducted exploratory interviews with incubators (n = 17) as well as entrepreneurs (n = 28) to include a two-sided perspective on the problem and to create awareness. The interviews were guided by the central question of how incubators as service providers typically conduct the validation of entrepreneurs' business models and the perceived limitations of these approaches. By analyzing the interviews, we gained a deeper understanding of practical business model validation for startups and discovered four key problems:

- **Problem 1:** Incubators do not use structured processes to conduct business model validation services, which represent a repetitive task.
- **Problem 2:** Both incubators and entrepreneurs have only limited access to expertise. Access to demand-side knowledge is especially scarce.
- **Problem 3:** The feedback of consultancy services is frequently perceived as subjective, industry bound, and thus misleading.
- **Problem 4:** Resource constraints make scalable and iterative validations of business models impossible.

Although the validation of business models is one of the most pivotal parts of business model creation [21], to the best of our knowledge, there are no systems that support this service.

5 Theory-Driven Design for CBMV Systems

To define the objectives of the solution for our design science approach, we zoomed in on the entrepreneurial process and identified opportunity creation theory (OCT) [15–17] as a kernel theory [31] that informs us about the requirements of a CBMV. OCT is a theoretical lens to examine business co-creation under uncertainty [32]. This perspective implies that opportunities emerge from the iterative actions undertaken with the social environment [16, 17]. Entrepreneurs create business models based on their individual beliefs and perceptions, imagination, and social interaction with the environment [15, 33]. Entrepreneurial actors then wait for responses from testing their models in the market to understand the perceptions of customers and other stakeholders and then adjust their beliefs accordingly to adapt their business models [34, 35]. During the validation of the entrepreneur's assumptions, a mismatch between the entrepreneurial idea and the opinion of the social environment may become evident [15]. The entrepreneur will therefore need to reassess his assumptions and adapt the business model to the feedback of the market [35]. This integration of customers, suppliers, and other stakeholders into the evolvement of a business model enables the entrepreneur to learn and further develop the initial version of the business model; it also reduces uncertainty about the validity of his assumptions [34].

5.1 Design Requirements from Opportunity Creation Theory

This entrepreneurship theory perfectly fits the context of our research as it explains how entrepreneurs create their businesses under uncertainty and helps to understand the problem domain of business model validation [34]. Using this kernel theory, we developed the design requirements for our artifact.

During the process of business model creation, entrepreneurs should validate their assumptions [35] to validate the initial form of the business model and reassess parts of it if needed [34, 36]. To support this validation process, the CBMV system should consequently be able to support the entrepreneur in engaging in social interaction with potential customers or other stakeholders to validate the assumptions about the business model with the broader environment and make sense of it.

DR1: *Business model validation should be supported by systems that enable social interaction with potential customers or other stakeholders to test an entrepreneur's assumptions and support the sense-making process.*

To capitalize from social interaction, entrepreneurs gather external feedback on the viability of their business model hypothesis to make sense of their assumptions [15]. Therefore, the feedback providers require suitable mechanisms to provide adequate responses [18]. Following this argumentation, CBMV systems should support the entrepreneur in gathering feedback through social interaction and, on the other hand, enable the crowd to provide such.

DR2: *Business model validation should be supported by systems that enable providing and receiving feedback to test an entrepreneur's assumptions and support the sense-making process.*

The creation of an initial version of the business model represents an entrepreneur's individual assumptions and beliefs [37]. To start a sense-making process by interacting with external actors who provide feedback, entrepreneurs must translate their mental model of what is viable into a transferable format to communicate the imagined business model to others [35]. Thus, entrepreneurs need to turn their assumptions regarding their business model into a transferable format to create a shared understanding between themselves and the external environment, which should provide feedback.

DR3: *Business model validation should be supported by systems that enable the entrepreneur to transfer their mental representation of a business model to the external environment for creating a shared understanding.*

Such mental representations of business models are not static but rather emergent assumptions that evolve through the process of social interaction and feedback [15, 38]. Thus, the creation process of a business model is highly iterative as entrepreneurs should start a sense-making process again when their assumptions about a desired business model change [34, 39]. To reduce incongruities in the assumptions of the business model, entrepreneurs incorporate the feedback from external actors [33]. Validating a business model might therefore need multiple iterations. Thus, systems that support business model validation should provide two affordances to enhance the iterative development of an entrepreneur's business model. First, such systems should easily allow for the adaption of the business model representation (see DR3); and second, they should enable the entrepreneur to iterate the process of gathering feedback and adapting the business model.

DR4: *Business model validation should be supported by systems that enable the iterative development and adaption of the business model representation during the sense-making process.*

Finally, entrepreneurs need to learn from the feedback and integrate the learning into the reassessment of their business model [35]. The feedback that actors provide will include specific knowledge or expertise [40] and thus change the information that is available for the entrepreneur during this emergent process [16]. Such feedback serves as a form of formative assessment that alters an entrepreneur's assumptions and accelerates learning [33, 36]. Thus, feedback-based learning might create a mental shift that orients the entrepreneur toward a specific direction. However, to facilitate the process of learning from the supply of extra knowledge through feedback from the social environment, entrepreneurs need guidance on what to do and how to derive actions based on this [41]. Systems for business model validation should therefore support entrepreneurial learning through guidance on how to leverage feedback for the interpretation and update of an entrepreneur's assumptions and finally improve future versions of the business model [34, 38].

DR5: *Business model validation should be supported by systems that enable the entrepreneur to learn from the results of the sense-making process through guidance that instructs future entrepreneurial actions.*

5.2 Practical Requirements

To complement the theoretical design requirements, we gathered practical requirements from the problem domain to balance the artifact's grounding in both theoretical rigor as well as practical relevance. We therefore derived additional design requirements from the qualitative interviews with executives of incubators (n = 17) and entrepreneurs (N = 28) following the data collection approach stated in Sect. 3.

As resource constraints are one of the major problems for early-stage startups, the interviewees agreed on the theme of time and money as the crucial requirements for the usefulness of a CBMV systems. The dynamic and fast-changing environment as well as the limited time that entrepreneurs typically spend within incubators require the collection of feedback as fast as possible. Such rapid feedback was identified as particularly important to reduce the amount of time for each validation iteration.

DR6: *Business model validation should be supported by systems that enable the entrepreneur to obtain rapid feedback.*

Furthermore, limited financial resources are a main reason that hinders entrepreneurs to validate their assumptions as they are typically not able to afford multiple rounds of consultancy, conducting workshops with potential customers, or building a community around their business idea.

DR7: *Business model validation should be supported by systems that enable the entrepreneur to obtain cost-efficient feedback.*

Apart from resource constraints, entrepreneurs are concerned about the competency of their feedback providers. They demand to obtain feedback from multiple sources (e.g., customers, investors, consultants) rather than from a single person who might be biased due to subjective perceptions of the entrepreneur's business model.

DR8: *Business model validation should be supported by systems that enable access to multiple feedback sources to enhance objectivity.*

Finally, one additional requirement derived from the interviews is the heterogeneity of knowledge among the feedback providers. The interviewees agreed that the convergence of traditionally separated industries (e.g., manufacturing and IT) requires novel types of business models that might blur traditional industry standards. CBMV systems should therefore provide access to heterogeneous knowledge to obtain adequate feedback.

DR9: *Business model validation should be supported by systems that enable access to heterogeneous knowledge to enhance the feedback quality* (Fig. 2).

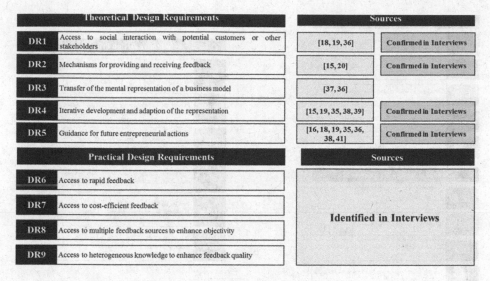

Theoretical Design Requirements		Sources	
DR1	Access to social interaction with potential customers or other stakeholders	[18, 19, 36]	Confirmed in Interviews
DR2	Mechanisms for providing and receiving feedback	[15, 20]	Confirmed in Interviews
DR3	Transfer of the mental representation of a business model	[37, 36]	
DR4	Iterative development and adaption of the representation	[15, 19, 35, 38, 39]	Confirmed in Interviews
DR5	Guidance for future entrepreneurial actions	[16, 18, 19, 35, 36, 38, 41]	Confirmed in Interviews
Practical Design Requirements		Sources	
DR6	Access to rapid feedback	Identified in Interviews	
DR7	Access to cost-efficient feedback		
DR8	Access to multiple feedback sources to enhance objectivity		
DR9	Access to heterogeneous knowledge to enhance feedback quality		

Fig. 2. Deriving design requirements

6 Translating Design Requirements into Tentative Design Principles

Based on the nine design requirements derived from opportunity creation theory and the qualitative interviews, we continued our research by identifying tentative design principles for a CBMV system (e.g., [42]). First, we identified design principles by analyzing literature to identify design-relevant knowledge from previous work, which helped us to address the identified design requirements. Second, to ground our artifact in practical relevance, we conducted an expert workshop (n = 7) to justify the tentative design principles derived from the literature. The participants in the workshop had both expertise in software engineering to evaluate the usability of the design principles (DPs) to be implemented in an IT artifact as well as knowledge of the problem domain (i.e., business model validation) to assess the efficiency of the derived principles to solve the practical problem (see Fig. 3).

To gain access to social resources that might be used to validate the entrepreneur's assumptions quickly and iteratively, using a crowdsourcing platform constitutes a suitable approach [43]. This approach is based on the findings of previous studies, which showed that a heterogeneous crowd can assess the value of creative solutions, such as an entrepreneur's business model, at a level comparable to that of experts, but at substantially lower costs [19, 23]. As neither incubators nor entrepreneurs have so far been able to build a community around their efforts, using existing crowd platforms can be leveraged through APIs (e.g., Amazon Mechanical Turk) to gain access to hundreds of thousands of problem solvers [43]. Thus, CBMV systems allow access to huge crowds to validate an entrepreneur's business model. This design principle is suitable due to various reasons. First, it provides a scalable and cost-efficient way for tapping social resources to obtain feedback. Second, it enables the entrepreneur to provide

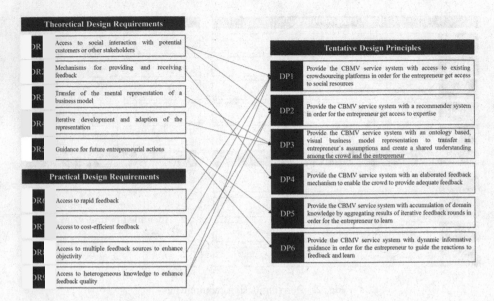

Fig. 3. Design requirements and design principles for a CBMV system

monetary incentives to ensure participation [22]. Third, creating tasks and retrieving validation results from individual participators, whose previous ratings by other users cannot be seen, avoids information cascades [18, 27]. Thus, we suggest:

DP1: *Provide the CBMV systems with access to existing crowdsourcing platforms to provide the entrepreneur access to social resources.*

This procedure continues at least until the crowd has the necessary knowledge of the context in which they validate a business model. Past literature shows that a judge who is qualified for validating a business model is also an expert in the respective context [44, 45]. Such appropriateness then results in a higher ability to provide valuable feedback. This enables the prediction of the potential future success of a business model even in highly dynamic contexts [46]. Therefore, a participant in the crowd should have two types of expertise to be suitable as a judge and provide more accurate predictions [45]: demand- and supply-side knowledge. While the first type is necessary to understand users' needs and wants explaining the desirability of a business model, the latter one consists of knowledge on feasibility [47, 48]. Both are necessary for the crowd to accurately validate an entrepreneur's business model, which represents the problem-solution fit. For this purpose, recommender systems that ensure to find a fit between the expertise requirements for being suitable as a judge and the validation task have proven to be a suitable approach in crowdsourcing [49]. In particular, expertise retrieval, which suggests people with relevant expertise for the topic of interest, can be leveraged to find suitable judges on existing crowd platforms [50].

DP2: *Provide the CBMV systems with a recommender system in order that the entrepreneur obtains access to expertise.*

To apply crowd-based business model validation, entrepreneurs must transfer their implicit assumptions to the crowd participants for creating a shared understanding. Business models are mental representations of an entrepreneur's individual beliefs that should be made explicit by transferring them into a digital object [51, 52]. In particular, approaches to transfer such knowledge into a common syntax are required [53]. Therefore, ontologies can be used to leverage knowledge sharing through a system of vocabularies, which is the gold standard in the context of business models [5]. Previous work on human cognition showed that the representation of knowledge in such an object (i.e., digital representation of the business model) should fit the corresponding task (i.e., judging the business model) to enhance the quality of the crowd's feedback [54, 55]. Due to the fact that judging a business model is a complex task, a visual representation is most suitable as it facilitates cognitive procedures to maximize the decision quality [56].

DP3: *Provide the CBMV systems with an ontology-based, visual business model representation to transfer an entrepreneur's assumptions and create a shared understanding among the crowd and the entrepreneur.*

To validate an entrepreneur's business model, the crowd needs adequate feedback mechanisms to evaluate the assumptions [18]. From the perspective of behavioral decision-making, this feedback can be categorized as a judgment task in which a finite set of alternatives (i.e., business models) is evaluated by applying a defined set of criteria by which each alternative is individually assessed by using rating scales [57, 58]. In the context of crowd validation, individual ratings can be aggregated to group decisions [59]. Using rating scales for judging and thus validating an entrepreneur's business model is therefore most suitable for improving the quality of crowd evaluations [18, 26]. In particular, elaborated rating scales with multiple response criteria lead to more consistent results of crowd-based validations [27]. These multi-criteria rating scales should thus cover the viability and probability of success of a business model by assessing dimensions, which are strong predictors for the future success, such as the market, the business opportunity, the entrepreneurial team, and the resources [60].

DP4: *Provide the CBMV systems with an elaborated feedback mechanism to enable the crowd to provide adequate feedback.*

As business model validation is an iterative process of adapting the current version of the business model and validating it again, CBMV systems should aggregate the results of each validation round to transient domain knowledge to show how the crowd feedback changes an entrepreneur's assumptions and how such changes are again evaluated by the crowd [43]. The accumulation of such knowledge can trigger cognitive processes that restructure the entrepreneur's understanding of the domain [61]. Learning can occur when entrepreneurs add new information from the feedback to their existing knowledge and cognitive schemas [62].

DP5: *Provide the CBMV systems with an accumulation of domain knowledge by aggregating the results of the iterative feedback rounds so that the entrepreneur can learn.*

The feedback from the crowd provides extra knowledge about the validity of an entrepreneur's assumptions. To support entrepreneurs in reducing uncertainty and executing their task of adapting and further developing their business model, the CBMV systems should provide guidance to facilitate learning from the system [63]. Such decisional guidance, often studied in the context of decision support systems [64], is a design principle that intends to reduce an entrepreneur's uncertainty and directs an entrepreneur's future actions by structuring decision-making processes under uncertainty [66]. Decisional guidance can either be suggestive (i.e., explicitly recommending what to do) or informative, "providing pertinent information that enlightens the user's choice without suggesting or implying how to act" [64]. This type of guidance provides information that supports the entrepreneur in reaching a conclusion of what to do. As the aim of the guidance of a CBMV system is fostering entrepreneurial learning, informative guidance is most suitable, especially for complex tasks such as adapting business models [59, 67]. Informative guidance outputs are the result of the crowd's judgment and support the entrepreneurs in learning from this additional information by enlightening the understanding of the social environment's reaction to their assumptions, especially when this feedback adds new perspectives, and lead to more reflective and deliberate thinking. Such learning may therefore increase the confidence of the entrepreneurs and develop a greater understanding of the problem domain. The mode of guidance is dynamic as the system should "learn" from the input of the judgment by the crowd and provide the guidance on demand when the entrepreneur decides to iterate the validation process. This mode is particularly effective for improving the decision quality, the entrepreneurial learning, and the decision performance [68].

DP6: *Provide the CBMV systems with dynamic informative guidance so that the entrepreneur can guide the reactions to the provided feedback and learn.*

7   Discussion and Conclusion

In this paper, we investigated tentative design principles for a CBMV systems that supports business model validation services to provide concrete principles that may guide the development of an IT artifact to solve a real-world problem. Therefore, we identified OCT as kernel theory to explain business model creation under uncertainty and derive five design requirements from this theory. These are complemented by four additional requirements identified during interviews. Based on findings from literature, we develop six design principles that match our derived requirements for a CBMV systems and were validated within an expert workshop (see Fig. 4).

The tentative design principles drawn from literature manifest a potential solution space of tentative properties that may inform the design of a first prototype.

Our findings provide several contributions. First, we contribute to the body of knowledge on crowdsourcing and crowd evaluation [e.g. 18–27] by extending these mechanisms from the evaluation of creative ideas to the uncertain and complex context of startups business models, where we intend to show that the crowd is also able to assess the desirability and feasibility of entrepreneurial opportunities. Second, we provide a design for decision support systems based on collective intelligence. We

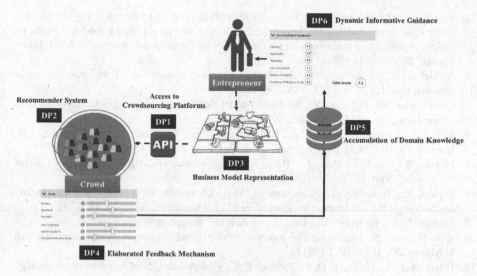

Fig. 4. Visualization of core results

show that using this approach enables academia and practice to extend decision support services to the context of entrepreneurship and innovation. Finally, our tentative design principles provide practical guidance for providers of business model validation services, such as incubators, to develop information systems as well as a novel, crowd-based approach to conduct such services.

Although our research approach of iteratively integrating theoretical insights from literature and empirical evidence from interviews into the problem domain aims at enhancing both theoretical rigor and practical relevance, our study has several limitations. While each of our principles has proven in prior research to be valuable in addressing the requirements, the instantiation into an IT artifact will reveal how the configuration of these tentative design principles solves a real-world problem. Thus, the selection of relevant theories for deriving our design principles is not conclusive. While we believe that focusing on theories of crowd judgment and evaluation for decision support is most suitable for developing design principles for a CBMV systems, the consideration of other theoretical knowledge may have led to a different collection of design principles. With further research, we will therefore leverage the outlined design principles for instantiating them into an IT artifact. These design principles will then be evaluated in a real-life setting of a business model competition in which we will focus on quasi experimentally evaluating the validity of the crowds' feedback, time and cost efficiency as well as entrepreneurs' perceived learning effects.

References

1. Andries, P., Debackere, K.: Adaptation and performance in new businesses: understanding the moderating effects of independence and industry. Small Bus. Econ. **29**, 81–99 (2007)

2. Blank, S.: Why the lean start-up changes everything. Harv. Bus.Rev. **91**, 63–72 (2013)
3. Ebel, P.A., Bretschneider, U., Leimeister, J.M.: Can the crowd do the job? Exploring the effects of integrating customers into a company's business model innovation. Int. J. Innov. Manag. **20**, 1650071 (2016)
4. Al-Debei, M.M., Avison, D.: Developing a unified framework of the business model concept. Eur. J. Inf. Syst. **19**, 359–376 (2010)
5. Osterwalder, A., Pigneur, Y.: Business Model Generation: A Handbook for Visionaries, Game Changers, and Challengers. Wiley, Hoboken (2010)
6. Veit, D., Clemons, E., Benlian, A., Buxmann, P., Hess, T., Kundisch, D., Leimeister, J.M., Loos, P., Spann, M.: Business models. Bus. Inf. Syst. Eng. **6**, 45–53 (2014)
7. Hevner, S., March, P., Park, J.J., Ram, S.: Design science research in information systems. Manag. Inf. Syst. Q. **28**, 75–105 (2004)
8. Peffers, K., Tuunanen, T., Rothenberger, M.A., Chatterjee, S.: A design science research methodology for information systems research. J. Manag. Inf. Syst. **24**, 45–77 (2007)
9. Vaishnavi, V., Kuechler, W.: Design research in information systems (2004)
10. Zott, C., Amit, R., Massa, L.: The business model: recent developments and future research. J. Manag. **37**, 1019–1042 (2011)
11. Bharadwaj, A., El Sawy, O.A., Pavlou, P.A., Venkatraman, N.: Digital business strategy: toward a next generation of insights. MIS Q. **37**, 471–482 (2013)
12. Morris, M., Schindehutte, M., Allen, J.: The entrepreneur's business model: toward a unified perspective. J. Bus. Res. **58**, 726–735 (2005)
13. Teece, D.J.: Explicating dynamic capabilities: the nature and microfoundations of (sustainable) enterprise performance. Strateg. Manag. J. **28**, 1319–1350 (2007)
14. Demil, B., Lecocq, X., Ricart, J.E., Zott, C.: Introduction to the SEJ special issue on business models: business models within the domain of strategic entrepreneurship. Strateg. Entrep. J. **9**, 1–11 (2015)
15. Alvarez, S.A., Barney, J.B., Anderson, P.: Forming and exploiting opportunities: the implications of discovery and creation processes for entrepreneurial and organizational research. Org. Sci. **24**, 301–317 (2013)
16. Alvarez, S.A., Barney, J.B.: Discovery and creation: alternative theories of entrepreneurial action. Strateg. Entrep. J. **1**, 11–26 (2007)
17. Alvarez, S.A., Barney, J.B.: Entrepreneurship and epistemology: the philosophical underpinnings of the study of entrepreneurial opportunities. Acad. Manag. Ann. **4**, 557–583 (2010)
18. Blohm, I., Riedl, C., Füller, J., Leimeister, J.M.: Rate or trade? Identifying winning ideas in open idea sourcing. Inf. Syst. Res. **27**, 27–48 (2016)
19. Kornish, L.J., Ulrich, K.T.: The importance of the raw idea in innovation: Testing the sow's ear hypothesis. J. Mark. Res. **51**, 14–26 (2014)
20. Leimeister, J.M., Huber, M., Bretschneider, U., Krcmar, H.: Leveraging crowdsourcing: activation-supporting components for IT-based ideas competition. J. Manag. Inf. Syst. **26**, 197–224 (2009)
21. Toubia, O., Florès, L.: Adaptive idea screening using consumers. Mark. Sci. **26**, 342–360 (2007)
22. Klein, M., Garcia, A.C.B.: High-speed idea filtering with the bag of lemons. Decis. Support Syst. **78**, 39–50 (2015)
23. Magnusson, P.R., Wästlund, E., Netz, J.: Exploring users' appropriateness as a proxy for experts when screening new product/service ideas. J. Prod. Innov. Manag. **33**, 4–18 (2016)
24. Soukhoroukova, A., Spann, M., Skiera, B.: Sourcing, filtering, and evaluating new product ideas: an empirical exploration of the performance of idea markets. J. Prod. Innov. Manag. **29**, 100–112 (2012)

25. Di Gangi, P.M., Wasko, M.: Steal my idea! Organizational adoption of user innovations from a user innovation community: a case study of Dell IdeaStorm. Decis. Support Syst. **48**, 303–312 (2009)
26. Di Gangi, P.M., Wasko, M.M., Hooker, R.E.: Getting customers' ideas work for you: learning from Dell how to succeed with online user innovation communities. MIS Q. Exec. **9** (2010)
27. Riedl, C., Blohm, I., Leimeister, J.M., Krcmar, H.: The effect of rating scales on decision quality and user attitudes in online innovation communities. Int. J. Electr. Commer. **17**, 7–36 (2013)
28. Goerzen, T., Kundisch, D.: Can the Crowd Substitute Experts in Evaluation of Creative Ideas? An Experimental Study Using Business Models (2016)
29. March, S.T., Smith, G.F.: Design and natural science research on information technology. Decis. Support Syst. **15**, 251–266 (1995)
30. Briggs, R.O.: On theory-driven design and deployment of collaboration systems. Int. J. Hum.-Comput. Stud. **64**, 573–582 (2006)
31. Gregor, S., Jones, D.: The anatomy of a design theory. J. Assoc. Inf. Syst. **8**, 312 (2007)
32. Sarasvathy, S.D.: Causation and effectuation: toward a theoretical shift from economic inevitability to entrepreneurial contingency. Acad. Manag. Rev. **26**, 243–263 (2001)
33. Tocher, N., Oswald, S.L., Hall, D.J.: Proposing social resources as the fundamental catalyst toward opportunity creation. Strateg. Entrep. J. **9**, 119–135 (2015)
34. Ojala, A.: Business models and opportunity creation: how IT entrepreneurs create and develop business models under uncertainty. Inf. Syst. J. **26**, 451–476 (2016)
35. Wood, M.S., McKinley, W.: The production of entrepreneurial opportunity: a constructivist perspective. Strateg. Entrep. J. **4**, 66–84 (2010)
36. Nambisan, S., Zahra, S.A.: The role of demand-side narratives in opportunity formation and enactment. J. Bus. Ventur. Insights **5**, 70–75 (2016)
37. Gioia, D.A., Chittipeddi, K.: Sensemaking and sensegiving in strategic change initiation. Strateg. Manag. J. **12**, 433–448 (1991)
38. Eggers, J.P., Kaplan, S.: Cognition and capabilities: a multi-level perspective. Acad. Manag. Ann. **7**, 295–340 (2013)
39. Dimov, D.: Grappling with the unbearable elusiveness of entrepreneurial opportunities. Entrep. Theory Pract. **35**, 57–81 (2011)
40. Zott, C., Huy, Q.N.: How entrepreneurs use symbolic management to acquire resources. Adm. Sci. Q. **52**, 70–105 (2007)
41. Huy, Q.N.: Time, temporal capability, and planned change. Acad. Manag. Rev. **26**, 601–623 (2001)
42. Arazy, O., Kumar, N., Shapira, B.: A theory-driven design framework for social recommender systems. J. Assoc. Inf. Syst. **11**, 455 (2010)
43. John, T.: Supporting Business Model Idea Generation Through Machine-generated Ideas: A Design Theory (2016)
44. Amabile, T.: Creativity in Context. Westview Press, Boulder (1996)
45. Ozer, M.: The roles of product lead-users and product experts in new product evaluation. Res. Policy **38**, 1340–1349 (2009)
46. Terwiesch, C., Xu, Y.: Innovation contests, open innovation, and multiagent problem solving. Manag. Sci. **54**, 1529–1543 (2008)
47. Magnusson, P.R.: Exploring the contributions of involving ordinary users in ideation of technology-based services. J. Prod. Innov. Manag. **26**, 578–593 (2009)
48. Lüthje, C.: Characteristics of innovating users in a consumer goods field: an empirical study of sport-related product consumers. Technovation **24**, 683–695 (2004)

49. Geiger, D., Schader, M.: Personalized task recommendation in crowdsourcing information systems—current state of the art. Decis. Support Syst. **65**, 3–16 (2014)
50. Deng, H., King, I., Lyu, M.R.: Enhanced models for expertise retrieval using community-aware strategies. IEEE Trans. Syst. Man Cybern. Part B (Cybern.) **42**, 93–106 (2012)
51. Bailey, D.E., Leonardi, P.M., Barley, S.R.: The lure of the virtual. Org. Sci. **23**, 1485–1504 (2012)
52. Carlile, P.R.: A pragmatic view of knowledge and boundaries: boundary objects in new product development. Org. Sci. **13**, 442–455 (2002)
53. Nonaka, I., von Krogh, G.: Perspective—tacit knowledge and knowledge conversion: controversy and advancement in organizational knowledge creation theory. Org. Sci. **20**, 635–652 (2009)
54. John, T., Kundisch, D.: Creativity Through Cognitive Fit: Theory and Preliminary Evidence in a Business Model Idea Generation Context (2015)
55. Khatri, V., Vessey, I., Ramesh, V., Clay, P., Park, S.-J.: Understanding conceptual schemas: exploring the role of application and IS domain knowledge. Inf. Syst. Res. **17**, 81–99 (2006)
56. Speier, C., Morris, M.G.: The influence of query interface design on decision-making performance. MIS Q. 397–423 (2003)
57. Dean, D.L., Hender, J.M., Rodgers, T.L., Santanen, E.L.: Identifying quality, novel, and creative ideas: constructs and scales for idea evaluation. J. Assoc. Inf. Syst. **7** (2006)
58. Zhao, Y., Zhu, Q.: Evaluation on crowdsourcing research: current status and future direction. Inf. Syst. Front. **16**, 417–434 (2014)
59. Todd, P., Benbasat, I.: Evaluating the impact of DSS, cognitive effort, and incentives on strategy selection. Inf. Syst. Res. **10**, 356–374 (1999)
60. Song, M., Podoynitsyna, K., van der Bij, H., Im Halman, J.: Success factors in new ventures: a meta-analysis. J. Prod. Innov. Manag. **25**, 7–27 (2008)
61. Sengupta, K., Abdel-Hamid, T.K.: Alternative conceptions of feedback in dynamic decision environments: an experimental investigation. Manag. Sci. **39**, 411–428 (1993)
62. Wooten, J.O., Ulrich, K.T.: Idea generation and the role of feedback: evidence from field experiments with innovation tournaments. Product. Oper. Manag. (2016)
63. Gönül, M.S., Önkal, D., Lawrence, M.: The effects of structural characteristics of explanations on use of a DSS. Decis. Support Syst. **42**, 1481–1493 (2006)
64. Silver, M.S.: Decisional guidance for computer-based decision support. MIS Q. 105–122 (1991)
65. Silver, M.S.: Decisional guidance. Broadening the scope. Adv. Manag. Inf. Syst. **6**, 90–119 (2006)
66. Mahoney, L.S., Roush, P.B., Bandy, D.: An investigation of the effects of decisional guidance and cognitive ability on decision-making involving uncertainty data. Inf. Org. **13**, 85–110 (2003)
67. Montazemi, A.R., Wang, F., Nainar, S.K., Bart, C.K.: On the effectiveness of decisional guidance. Decis. Support Syst. **18**, 181–198 (1996)
68. Parikh, M., Fazlollahi, B., Verma, S.: The effectiveness of decisional guidance: an empirical evaluation. Decis. Sci. **32**, 303–332 (2001)

Design Principles for Business-Model-based Management Methods—A Service-Dominant Logic Perspective

Michael Blaschke[1,2(✉)], M. Kazem Haki[1], Uwe Riss[2],
and Stephan Aier[1]

[1] Institute of Information Management,
University of St. Gallen, St. Gallen, Switzerland
{michael.blaschke,kazem.haki,stephan.aier}@unisg.ch
[2] SAP Research and Innovation Hub,
SAP Switzerland Inc., St. Gallen, Switzerland
{uwe.riss,michael.blaschke}@sap.com

Abstract. Extant research gives rise to the notion of business-model-based management that stresses the pivotal role of the business model concept in organizational management. This role entails a shift in research from predominantly examining business model representation to the use of the business model concept in the design of management methods. In designing respective management methods, managers need to not only account for the business model concept, but also consider the characteristics of the emerging business environments in which business models are devised. To this, our study guides the design of *business-model-based management methods* through exploiting service-dominant logic, a theoretical lens that conceptualizes the emerging business environment. By means of design science research, this study develops four design principles for business-model-based management methods namely, ecosystem-, technology-, mobilization-, and co-creation-oriented management. This study also articulates the principles' rationale and implications and discusses their contribution in achieving business-model-based management.

Keywords: Design principles · Business model (BM) · Business-model-based management (BMBM) · Service-dominant (S-D) logic · Design science research (DSR)

1 Introduction

"The rise of globe-spanning service-based business models has transformed the way the world works" [1, p. 665].

Seminal marketing studies [2–4] highlight a paradigmatic shift in economic exchange from a goods-dominant (G-D) to a service-dominant (S-D) logic. S-D logic moves the spotlight of economic exchange and value creation from a single organization to a broader actor-to-actor network—comprising competitors, suppliers, partners, regulators, and customers—in which an organization operates (*network-centric focus*). Moreover, S-D logic stresses that tangible goods (products and services) are no longer

© Springer International Publishing AG 2017
A. Maedche et al. (Eds.): DESRIST 2017, LNCS 10243, pp. 179–198, 2017.
DOI: 10.1007/978-3-319-59144-5_11

the sole object of exchange, but also associated or stand-alone intangible offerings in which the extent of information content is high (*information-centric focus*). In addition, S-D logic emphasizes a shift in the outcome of economic exchange, from features and attributes of goods to the value that is *co-created* (*experience-centric focus*) [5]. Pivotal to S-D logic is that value is determined by the quality of a *value-in-use* experience and not by the quality of goods' *value-in-exchange* [6, 7]. For instance, Hilti, a global market leader for professional drilling and mounting technologies, has initiated its shift to S-D logic with a first step of selling *drilling equipment utilization* (value-in-use, S-D logic) instead of selling *drilling equipment* (value-in-exchange, G-D logic).

The shift from G-D to S-D logic requires re-thinking the way economic exchange is executed and eventually the way value for customers is co-created. Therefore, while realizing such a shift, the most immediate and fundamental effect in organizational practice is on an organization's *business model* (BM). BMs conceptualize the core business logic of an organization describing the rationale of how an organization creates, proposes, delivers, and captures value [8]. For instance, Swiss Federal Railways has started re-arranging its BM to become a mobility service integrator instead of a mere mobility service provider. As such, instead of providing station-to-station service, it offers a door-to-door mobility service through orchestrating the mobility ecosystem in a network of various mobility providers. This endeavour requires understanding, designing, and managing actor-to-actor and *service*-based BMs, which has become a strategic imperative and focal subject for managing organizations [1, 9–11].

The study at hand investigates the design of *business-model-based management* (BMBM) [12, 13] *methods* to achieve the above-discussed shift. These methods use the BM concept to structure organizational units and actors, employ the boundary-spanning aspects of the BM concept (i.e., provider and customer interfaces), and align operations within and across organizations [12, 13]. Our study is in fact motivated by the lack of guidance on designing BMBM methods. Our research hence seeks to answer the following question: *What are design principles guiding the design of BMBM methods to eventually account for and realize an S-D logic?*

Even though prevalent BM research lays emphasis on uncovering the *BM concept/terminology* [14], *BM structure* [15], and *BM management process* [16], guidance on the design of BMBM methods is lacking [17]. To this end and owing to S-D logic's distinctive conceptualization on value co-creation, we employ S-D logic as a kernel theory [2–4] and derive a set of design principles for BMBM methods.

The remainder of this paper is structured as follows. Section 2 presents the state-of-the-art of BM research and the theoretical background of S-D logic. Section 3 explicates the employed research methodology and its instantiated activities. Section 4 reports the four design principles offered to guide the design of BMBM methods. Section 5 discusses the developed principles and provides concluding remarks.

2   Research Background

In seeking for drawing on and integrating in the extant business model (BM) and service-dominant (S-D) logic research, in this section we briefly synthesize existing knowledge and position our study.

2.1   State-of-the-Art: The Business Model Concept

Management research and practice has witnessed an ever-growing interest in the BM concept and perspective whose unique properties and effects are becoming fundamental in understanding and guiding organizational management [17]. Even though definitions still vary, extant research has adopted the notion of BM as a way of grasping the core business logic of an organization and describing its rationale in creating, proposing, delivering, and capturing value [8]. As such, management research theorizes the BM concept as an emerging unit of analysis that emphasizes a system-level, holistic approach to explain how organizations "do business" [14]. Prevalent BM research mainly lays emphasis on the *BM concept/terminology* (i.e., definitions and scope) [14], *BM structure* (i.e., forms, components, value system, actors and interaction, and innovation) [15], and *BM management process* (i.e., design, implementation, operation, change and evolution, performance and controlling) [16].

The *BM concept/terminology* has been predominantly investigated in IS research so that IS scholars discuss the concept's broad diversity as well as ambiguity of its understandings, uses, and positions in the organization [18, 19]. More recently, IS research has shed light on the BM concept in various IS phenomena such as BMs in IT industries and IT-enabled or digital BMs [20]. Regarding *BM structure*, IS research engages in the ongoing discourse on the BM's ontological constituents [19, 21]. A prominent example is Osterwalder et al.'s [19] proposition for an ontology to describe a BM. Peters et al. [21] also propose a morphological box for the analysis, description, and classification of IT-enabled service BMs. Regarding *BM management process*, IS research is particularly interested in frameworks for BM management [13], IT support for BM design and management [22], and the design of IT platform BMs [23].

Recently, management research has started underscoring the pivotal role of BM in the management of organizations [14, 17, 24–26]. Such a role—underserved in extant research [27]—goes beyond understanding, designing, or managing a single or multiple BMs, which is predominant in the existing research discourses. Instead, it emphasizes the BM concept as a crucial perspective and a means to manage the entire organization. This novel role has been recently reflected on the notion of *business-model-based management* (BMBM) [12] as a way of developing *management methods that draw on the BM concept to holistically plan, organize, direct, and control the structure and dynamics of an organization* [13]. While organizations mainly leverage BMs in an innovation context to ensure the economic viability of new products and services [1, 22], the BM concept's potential to manage organizations over their entire life cycle [28] is widely ignored. As such, BMBM aims to adopt the *BM concept in management methods* to eventually guide practitioners in constructing and maintaining their organizations' business logic [12, 13].

We underscore the distinction between BM management and BMBM methods. While the former refers to designing and managing one or multiple BMs, the latter employs the BM concept as a means to manage an organization and to increase organizational performance. As such, BMBM methods are different from BM management in that BMBM methods (i) facilitate strategy implementation; (ii) employ the BM concept as a holistic, boundary-spanning management framework; (iii) structure organizations and their units guided by a BM representation; (iv) facilitate a common ground for communication; and (v) align different BMs *vertically* within organizations and *horizontally* across cooperating organizations to increase business success [12, 27]. Notwithstanding the relevance of BMBM methods, practitioners still struggle with designing such methods due to their novelty and ambiguity [12]. Therefore, the main outcome of this study is a set of design principles guiding the design of BMBM methods.

2.2 Theoretical Background: A Service-Dominant Logic Perspective

The notion of service is researched in both service science and S-D logic, both of which developed in parallel but independent from each other [29, 30]. They have in common the premise that value occurs when heterogeneous actors work together for mutual benefit, the key being orchestration of these actors for effective service provision [1, 30]. However, while service science seeks to understand and design innovative services under abstract philosophical assumptions [31, 32], S-D logic seeks to establish a unified theoretical foundation as a potential perspective on service science [30]. Owing to their relevance, both service science and S-D logic are present in IS research. While service science has long been discussed and used in IS research [31, 33], IS scholars have recently started to introduce and employ S-D logic in investigating IS phenomena [5, 34]. We opt for S-D logic over service science since (i) it offers a penetrative conceptualization of the emerging business environments in which BMBM methods are devised; and (ii) it provides a well-defined and unified theoretical basis through which the design of BMBM methods can be informed and guided.

S-D logic is rooted in marketing research, where it gained momentum since its inception by the landmark study of Vargo and Lusch [2], followed by further amendments [3, 4]. We synthesis knowledge on S-D logic on four levels, which reflect its descriptive and prescriptive nature (see Fig. 1).

S-D logic has been introduced through descriptive theoretical assumptions, which are formulated as *meta-theoretical foundations* of S-D logic (**Level I**) [5, 35]. Subsequently, scholars captured these foundations in a set of S-D logic's *foundational premises* to explicate S-D logic's worldview (**Level II**) [2–4]. Later, scholars captured managerial implications of S-D logic's theoretical foundations in real-world practices. This endeavour resulted in a set of *derivative propositions* that inform practitioners on how to compete in an S-D logic orientation (**Level III**) [36]. Levels I to III are offered by seminal S-D logic literature. They provide descriptive knowledge to explicate S-D logic with an increasing degree of applicability in practice. Drawing on these three

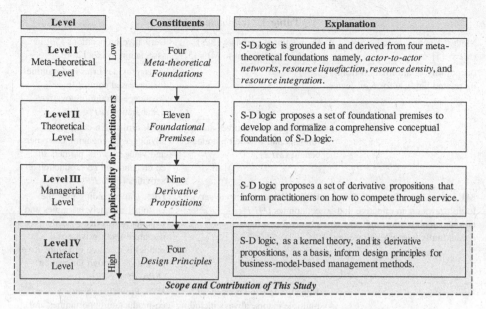

Fig. 1. Service-dominant logic: from descriptive to prescriptive knowledge

levels, we position our study as one step further in translating S-D logic's descriptive basis into prescriptive means in our phenomenon of interest. The central outcome of this design science research (DSR) is thus prescriptive knowledge in the form of design principles for BMBM methods (**Level IV**). Emphasizing the move from descriptive to prescriptive knowledge, Fig. 1 summarizes these levels; each of which is briefly explained below. Further, building on the seminal S-D logic studies, Table 1 shows the relation between constituents of Level I, II, and III.

Table 1. Service-dominant logic: the relations between meta-theoretical foundations, foundational premises, and derivative propositions *(with relations in brackets)*

Meta-theoretical foundations (MFs) [5]	Foundational premises (FPs) [2–4] in association to MFs [5]	Derivative propositions [36] in association to FPs [2–4]
MF1 (Actor-to-Actor-Networks). S-D logic draws on a network-centric actor-to-actor generalization	**FP1.** Service is the fundamental basis of exchange *(MF1)*	**DP1.** Competitive advantage is a function of how one firm applies its operant resources to meet the needs of the customer relative to how another firm applies its operant resources *(FP1, FP4)*
	FP2. Indirect exchange masks the fundamental basis of exchange *(MF1, MF3)*	**DP2.** Collaborative competence is a primary determinant of a firm's acquiring the knowledge for competitive advantage *(FP4, FP9)*
MF2 (Resource Liquefaction). S-D logic draws on the	**FP3.** Goods are distribution mechanisms for service provision *(MF3)*	**DP3.** The continued ascendance of IT with associated decrease in communication and computation

(continued)

Table 1. (*continued*)

Meta-theoretical foundations (MFs) [5]	Foundational premises (FPs) [2–4] in association to MFs [5]	Derivative propositions [36] in association to FPs [2–4]
decoupling of information from its related physical form or device		costs, provides firms opportunities for increased competitive advantage through innovative collaboration (*FP6, FP8*)
	FP4. Operant resources are the fundamental source of strategic benefit (*MF2*)	**DP4.** Firms gain competitive advantage by engaging customers and value network partners in co-creation and co-production activities (*FP6, FP9*)
MF3 (Resource Density). S-D logic draws on an effective and efficient mobilization of contextually relevant knowledge	**FP5.** All economies are service economies (*MF1*)	**DP5.** Understanding how the customer uniquely integrates and experiences service-related resources (both private and public) is a source of competitive advantage through innovation (*FP6, FP8, FP9*)
	FP6. Value is co-created by multiple actors, always including the beneficiary (*MF1, MF4*)	**DP6.** Providing service co-production opportunities and resources consistent with the customer's desired level of involvement leads to improved competitive advantage through enhanced customer experience (*FP6, FP8, FP9*)
MF4 (Resource Integration). S-D logic draws on the view that all social and economic actors as resource integrators	**FP7.** Actors cannot deliver value but can participate in the creation and offering of value propositions (*MF1*)	**DP7.** Firms can compete more effectively through the adoption of collaboratively developed, risk-based pricing value propositions (*FP6, FP7*)
	FP8. A service-centered view is inherently beneficiary oriented and relational (*MF4*)	**DP8.** The value network member that is the prime integrator is in a stronger competitive position. The retailer is generally in the best position to become the prime integrator (*FP1, FP4, FP9*)
	FP9. All social and economic actors are resource integrators (*MF1, MF4*)	**DP9.** Firms that treat their employees as operant resources will be able to develop more innovative knowledge and skills and thus gain competitive advantage (*FP4*)
	FP10. Value is always uniquely and phenomenologically determined by the beneficiary (*MF4*)	
	FP11. Value co-creation is coordinated through actor-generated institutions and institutional arrangements (*MF1, MF4*)	

Meta-theoretical Foundations (Level I). On a meta-theoretical level, S-D logic is grounded in four meta-theoretical foundations namely, *actor-to-actor networks*, *resource liquefaction*, *resource density*, and *resource integration* [5]. *Actor-to-actor-networks* emphasizes a shift from one-way process of value exchange in traditional supply chains (i.e., neoclassical industrial perspective) to a collaborative process of value co-creation in service ecosystems (i.e., network-centric perspective). *Resource liquefaction* describes the shift from information coupled to physical matter to digitized, decoupled, and more useful information. *Resource density* emphasizes a shift from ineffective /-efficient mobilization of resources for integration at a given time and place to mobilization of an ideal combination of relevant resources in the most effective/efficient way for a particular situation. *Resource integration* underscores a shift from the production of fixed asset goods to the integration of specialized resources into complex services.

Foundational Premises (Level II). On a theoretical level, Vargo and Lusch proposed [2]—and further made amendments on [3, 4]—a set of foundational premises (FPs) for S-D logic to distinguish it from G-D logic. This effort has culminated in eleven FPs [4], which explicate the ontological basis of S-D logic and which are related to S-D logic's meta-theoretical foundations (see Table 1). Overall, in promoting foundational premises, S-D logic re-conceptualizes *service* (the process of applying specialized competencies for the benefit of and in conjunction with another actor), *exchange* (not the exchange of outputs but the exchange of the performance of specialized activities), *value* (occurs when the offering is useful to service beneficiary), and *resource* (anything an actor can draw on for support) [5].

Regarding *resource*, S-D logic distinguishes operan*d* and operan*t* resources. Operan*d* resources refer to tangible, static, and passive components of goods that actors employ to obtain support [2]. In S-D logic, they are seen as "vehicles for service provision, rather than primary to exchange and value creation" [37, p. 374]. Conversely, operan*t* resources refer to intangible, dynamic, and active resources (e.g., human knowledge, skill, and experience) that act on other resources [2]. In S-D logic, operant resources have a pivotal role since they are seen as "the fundamental source of competitive advantage" [3, p. 7]. S-D logic perceives information technology (IT) artefacts as both operand and operant resources as they not only facilitate service exchange among actors, but also trigger value co-creation activities and processes [5].

Regarding *value*, recent literature [29, 38] extracts *co-production* and *value-in-use* as the primary theoretical constructs of value. In *co-production*, value accrues through mutually integrating the organization's, partners', and targeted customers' resources *before* the service usage time [39]. Conversely, in *value-in-use*, value accrues through a process of consumption *during* the actual usage time by the customer [38].

Derivative Propositions (Level III). On a managerial level, building on foundational premises (FPs) of S-D logic [4], Lusch et al. [36] derive nine propositions as the practical implications of the FPs to inform practitioners on how to compete in the real world with an S-D logic orientation (see Table 1). As a practical approach, the derivative propositions' overall theme is to more successfully innovate and compete through service thinking. The derivative propositions start from the premise that in order to "survive and prosper in a networked economy, the organization must learn how to be a vital and sustaining part of the value network" [35, p. 21].

Artefact (Level IV). As a new level proposed by the study at hand, this level concerns the development of artefacts that help practitioners exercising the promoted service thinking by S-D logic. As one step in this level, we draw on Lusch et al.'s [36] derivative propositions to derive design principles for our phenomenon of interest i.e., business-model-based management methods.

Extant research has already started incorporating network- and customer-oriented views in BM research [17]. While some studies introduce networks and partnerships in BM representation [40] or emphasize the importance of customers in BM design [6, 41], others lay emphasis on management tool to control the value distribution in joint value creation [40, 42]. These endeavours demonstrate the ever-increasing importance of S-D logic's theoretical constituents in BM research. Nevertheless, the focus of our study is on the design of management methods, which are informed by the BM concept and can be applied to realize the shift to S-D logic.

3 Research Methodology

To systematically develop design principles, we opt for Sonnenberg and vom Brocke's [43, p. 392] *cyclic DSR process,* which is extended by Abraham et al. [44]. It represents a step-by-step and well-structured DSR process to cyclically build and evaluate DSR artefacts from scratch and independent of the domain of interest. The *cyclic DSR process* (i) incorporates a design-evaluate-construct-evaluate pattern; and (ii) includes the DSR activities namely, *problem identification*, *design*, *construction*, and *use* followed by four distinct corresponding *evaluation* activities referred to as Eval1 to Eval4. We employ the *cyclic DSR process* due to its continuous assessment of the progress achieved in the DSR process [43, p. 390, 44]. That is, the employed methodology ensures multiple evaluation episodes throughout a single iteration of a DSR process. Table 2 summarizes the DSR activities that we conduct to develop our targeted principles. In this section, we sequentially explicate how the instantiation of the four stages has led to *design principles for BMBM methods from the perspective of S-D logic*.

I. Problem Identification and Eval1. This research has been conducted in adjacency to an R&D project at SAP, a world leading business software provider [12]. This project follows a co-innovation format with 20 senior executives of European multi-national enterprises. It aims at iteratively designing consultancy services and software products for BM design and innovation. Its application in consulting projects, workshops, and trainings revealed that although managers are provided with the means to innovate and develop BMs, they severely struggle in efficiently and effectively designing management methods based on the BM concept (*PROBLEM IDENTIFICATION*). Consequently, we reviewed extant BM literature, which uncovered a lack of understanding and guiding the design of BMBM methods. To ensure that the stated problem is not only academically relevant, but also meaningful for practitioners, we conducted a one-hour focus group with BM experts and the senior executives. The semi-structured focus group discussion

Table 2. The applied build and evaluation activities of the *cyclic DSR process* in our design principles development [adapted from 43, 44]

Activity	Purpose of Activity	Applied Method	Output
1.1. PROBLEM IDENTIFICATION	Selecting and formulating a problem	Review of a Practitioner Initiative	*Justified Problem Statement*: Practitioners lack guidance to efficiently and effectively design business-model-based management methods.
1.2. EVAL1	Ensuring that the stated problem is meaningful	Literature Review, Focus Group	
2.1. DESIGN	Constructing an artefact design for the stated problem	Literature Review, Logical Reasoning	*Validated Design Specification*: Employing S-D logic and drawing on its nine derivative propositions to derive design principles for business-model-based management methods.
2.2. EVAL2	Showing that an artefact design progresses to a solution of the stated problem	Logical Reasoning, Demonstration	
3.1. CONSTRUCTION	Constructing a prototypical artefact instance	Expert Workshop, Logical Reasoning	*Validated Artefact Instance in an Artificial Setting*: Validating the prototypically constructed design principles against practitioners' requirements as well as the BM concept.
3.2. EVAL3	Demonstrating if and how well the artefact is designed	BM Expert Interview	
4.1. USE	Constructing a complete artefact instance	Literature Review, Logical Reasoning	*Validated Artefact Instance in a Partially Naturalistic Setting*: Validating the fully-constructed design principles with real users.
4.2. EVAL4	Showing that the artefact is both applicable and useful in practice	Focus Group	

revealed that practitioners acknowledge the lack of design guidance for BMBM methods in dealing with the contemporary business environment (*EVAL1*).

II. Design and Eval2. After *EVAL1* we opted for S-D logic as a kernel theory. We reviewed prevalent S-D logic literature[1] to inform two major design decisions. *First*, drawing on seminal S-D logic studies [2–5], we logically reason that S-D logic is an appropriate perspective on BMBM methods because S-D logic explicates how an organization ought to "do business" and compete [1]. *Second*, S-D logic has been formulated on a meta-theoretical [5], theoretical [4], and managerial [36] level (see Sect. 2). However, extant research underserves a prescriptive guidance in applying S-D logic, in general, and in designing BMBM methods from an S-D logic perspective in particular. Therefore, we opted for deriving design principles, as an appropriate DSR artefact [47, 48], for BMBM methods from S-D logic's nine derivative propositions [36] (*DESIGN*). These two design decisions, the derivative propositions (as kernel theory) and design principles (as DSR artefacts), were evaluated in a 90-min demonstration with BM experts and five executives of major European multi-national enterprises (*EVAL2*). *EVAL2* revealed that linking S-D logic and the BM concept is timely, relevant, and useful. This

---

[1] We include relevant studies on S-D logic that are published in world leading marketing journals. Precisely, we include eleven marketing journals that are ranked *(world) leading* (tagged with *) by at least one of the ratings included in the 57th Harzing Journal Quality List (2016). We search in the Business Source Premier database employing the EBSCOhost search engine since S-D logic's inaugural year 2004 [2]. The 30 selected papers have the phrases *"service-dominant"*, *"service logic"*, or *"dominant logic"* in title, abstract, or keywords. In addition, we include studies on and/or using S-D logic that are published in the AIS basket-of-eight journals. This adds another 15 papers, most of which are part of the MISQ special issues on "Service Innovation in the Digital Age" [45] and on "Co-creating IT Value" [46].

is because, *first*, the BM concept—alike S-D logic—is inherently focused beyond the organization and concerns its network comprising suppliers, strategic partners, customers, competitors, and regulators [14, 15]. *Second*, in designing and implementing service-based business, the BM concept has been adopted as an immediate reflection and realization of S-D logic in real-world organizational practices [1, 49, 50].

III. Construction and Eval3. The design principles were then prototypically constructed. This process was kicked-off by an expert workshop comprising three of the software provider's BM experts, two of which are co-authors of the study at hand. The expert workshop participants discussed in-depth why, whether, and how design principles can be derived from S-D logic's nine derivative propositions [36] (CONSTRUCTION). To validate and improve the initial design principle instances in an artificial setting, another 60 min semi-structured expert interview was conducted with BM experts *unfamiliar* with S-D logic. It revealed that the prototypical formulation of the four initial design principles was immature for the following reasons: (1) too abstract and non-applicable by managers due to overemphasizing theoretical and abstract S-D logic language; (2) insufficiently linked with and integrated into the BM concept, and (3) too unstructured in their presentation. Shortcomings (1) and (2) were addressed by specifically employing language that practitioners use in reasoning about service and BMs, and tightly integrating this language to S-D logic and BM thinking. Shortcoming (3) was addressed by employing a threefold structure for the systematic presentation of design principles [51, 52] comprising the design principle's *statement*, *rationale*, and *implications* (EVAL3).

IV. Use and Eval4. The fourth step of fully constructing and using the final design principles to evaluate their usefulness and applicability in a *naturalistic* setting is still in the process of iterative refinement. To this, we accounted for the three realities (real tasks, real systems, and real users) [43, p. 396] and conducted a one-hour semi-structured focus group to discuss and evaluate the use of design principles in the early stage of designing a BMBM method with potential real users. This discussion comprised two BM experts and four executives of major multi-national European enterprises. The first iteration of this phase revealed that the initially proposed four design principles are basically useful, but require further reduction of abstractness and more fine-granular explication of their implications. This shortcoming was addressed by explicitly employing vocabulary that the focus group's attendees deem useful for the design principles' purpose (EVAL4).

4   Design Principles for Business-Model-based Management

This section describes the derived design principles for BM-based management (BMBM) methods, which are informed by the BM concept and can be applied to realize the shift to S-D logic. Our intent here is not only to capture the general design guidance for BMBM methods, but also to illustrate their implications in organizations. Table 3 summarizes the four design principles. Each principle is discussed in detail following a tripartite structure comprising the design principle's *statement*, *rationale*, and *implications* [51, 52]. We use the notion *Pn* to refer to the nth derivative proposition of S-D logic [36, p. 8] and present the respective proposition in *italics*.

Table 3. Design principles for business-model-based management methods

Principle	Description	Association to S-D logic's derivative propositions [36]
Principle 1: Ecosystem-oriented management	BMBM methods should account (i) for orchestration of specific actor roles in a service ecosystem; (ii) for positioning of an organization's role as focal orchestrator in a service ecosystem; as well as (iii) for sharing of economic risks, costs, and revenues among a multitude of various actor roles in a service ecosystem	P2, P7, P8
Principle 2: Technology-oriented management	BMBM methods should account (i) for the application of digital infrastructures; (ii) for decoupling informational assets from products and facilitate their commercialization; as well as (iii) for driving value creation through digital channels and digitally enhanced customer relationships	P3
Principle 3: Mobilization-oriented management	BMBM methods should account (i) for the mobilization of operant resources; (ii) for uncovering and utilizing internal knowledge for new fields of business; as well as (iii) for identifying and activating operant resources of partners and customers in the service ecosystem	P1, P4, P9
Principle 4: Co-creation-oriented management	BMBM methods should account (i) for customer involvement, enhancing value-in-use and sustaining their engagement; (ii) for reflecting on value co-creation through customer journeys as dynamic interaction; as well as (iii) for recalibrating service bundles to optimize customer experience	P4, P5, P6

4.1 Principle #1: Ecosystem-oriented Management

Statement. BMBM methods leverage the BM concept to facilitate an efficient and effective orchestration of mostly loosely coupled social and economic actors in service ecosystems regarding their specific actor roles.

Rationale. Per S-D logic, *collaborative competence is a primary determinant of a firm's acquiring the knowledge for competitive advantage (P2)*. As a part of the BM concept, an organization's network model (i.e., suppliers, partners, customers, and competitors) [17] helps understand the specific actor roles in a service ecosystem.

Moreover, *P7* tells us that *firms can compete more effectively through the adoption of collaboratively developed, risk-based pricing value propositions*. An organization's revenue model (i.e., revenue streams and pricing mechanisms) and financial model (i.e., financing model, capital model, and cost structure model) [17] are essential component of the BM concept. BMBM methods leverage these to ensure that economic risks, costs, and revenues are fairly shared among the multitude of actor roles. This is a precondition for a service ecosystem to run and evolve in a stable manner.

Finally, we learn from *P8* that the *value network member that is the prime integrator is in a stronger competitive position*. This proposition first and foremost points to the leading role of the prime integrator in the service ecosystem. Beyond, it concerns the roles of all its members as a function of the prime integrator's BM. Consequently, BMBM methods consider the distribution of power within a service ecosystem in the organization's BM to strengthen its position or become a prime integrator.

Generally, S-D logic underscores that economic exchange always takes place in actor-to-actor networks [5]. Dynamic and co-evolving communities of diverse actors jointly determine the BM to create and capture new value through both collaboration and competition. While in G-D logic value creation is mainly understood as taking place in the single organization, the very locus of value (co-)creation becomes increasingly diverse and complex in S-D logic's actor-to-actor network orientation. G-D logic considers partners only as resource suppliers, while the central role of customers as value co-creators is ignored. Zott and Amit [24] already pointed to the fundamental role of the BM concept for orchestrating service ecosystems, and, more recently, Leminen et al. [53] have emphasized the role of BMs as a unique means for materializing the opportunities of digital service ecosystems. Prominent BM representations consider service ecosystems implicitly so that the network character only becomes apparent in the interfaces of the focal organization to its immediate partners and customers. However, multi-sided BMs evident in the service economy require more complex network representations. Such network-based BM representations are to guide an ecosystem-oriented management to reflect S-D logic's actor-to-actor network orientation.

Implications. (1) Management methods make use of BM concept to extend their management focus from processes, activities, resources, and practices *within* their own organization to the coordination and governance of entire service ecosystems; (2) BMs are employed to enable planning and facilitating value co-creation by establishing a variety of roles associated to different actors in the network (e.g., service offeror, service beneficiary, ideator, designer, and intermediary).

4.2   Principle #2: Technology-oriented Management

Statement. BMBM methods leverage IT to increase the efficiency and effectiveness of BMs' function by decoupling physical matter and informational assets, by capturing and sharing data, and by facilitating economic and social interaction.

Rationale. S-D logic advises that the effective application of operan*t* resources is "the fundamental source of competitive advantage" [3, p. 7]. This is particularly true for digital resources. S-D logic emphasizes that the *continued ascendance of information technology with associated decrease in communication and computation costs, provides firms opportunities for increased competitive advantage through innovative collaboration (P3)*. This proposition reflects the growing importance of IT due to its prominent role in digital innovation [54]. Through the ascendance of IT, information is no longer embedded in physical matter or devices. Conversely, it can be decoupled and shared independent of the cost and time of physical transport. The BM concept is a means for materializing such opportunities of digitalization [8] through comprising IT in the design, commercialization, and monetarization of service [45]. Management methods should assume such a growing entwinement of business and technology. This is reflected in overhauled BMs, with technology-enabled value propositions at their core, based on the opportunities of digital infrastructures [55–57]. The design principle of technology-oriented management is consistent with service science, emphasizing the fundamentally changed role of IT [5] that enables a multitude of novel and complex service-based BMs [1] to utilize the opportunities of the networked service economy.

Implication. (1) Management methods incorporate IT and digital resources to design innovative value propositions comprising operant resources (e.g., data, information, knowledge, experience, skills); (2) they particularly focus on the decoupling of information and matter, the de-linking of ownership and value creation, and the systematic use of IT as means to achieve collaborative competence; (3) they consider digital infrastructure as means to co-create value in service ecosystems.

4.3   Principle #3: Mobilization-oriented Management

Statement. BMBM methods facilitate the access to relevant internal (e.g., employees) and external (e.g., partner) resources and constantly question and renew the existing BM. BMBM methods facilitate resources' mobilization, and consider their combination in the most effective and efficient way for the particular service context.

Rationale. S-D logic states that *competitive advantage is a function of how one firm applies its operant resources to meet the needs of the customer relative to how another firm applies its operant resources (P1)*. The access to particular operant resources enables organizations to differentiate from competitors. Resources are an essential component of the BM, which relates them to the organization's core activities and considers their contribution to the value proposition.

Moreover, *P4* explains that *firms gain competitive advantage by engaging customers and value network partners in co-creation and co-production activities*. Such co-creation and co-production is mainly facilitated by the resources that partners and customers contribute. The BM concept reflects the availability of resources and thus enables the reflection on how they can be mobilized from and to pivotal actors. We refer to resource mobilization as "extending the access to and the use of resources" [31, p. 4]. There is also a relation to previous design principle because digital technologies help mobilize slack resources of partners and customers' resources.

Turning to internal resources, S-D logic asserts: *Firms that treat their employees as operant resources will be able to develop more innovative knowledge and skills and thus gain competitive advantage (P9)*. BMs consider these internal resources but mostly those that are actively used. Latent resources are often neglected despite their potential for future business and provide a main target of internal resource mobilization. In this vein, BMBM methods constantly revisit the existing BM in that they employ partners' and customers' (external) as well as employees' (internal) operant resources to create new business. Another major reservoir for new business lies in the mobilization of operan*t* resources that could not be used due to high transaction or coordination costs in the past. S-D logic motivates to see operant resources as enabler for new business. For instance, Airbnb and Uber make use of the partners' unused apartments, vehicles, and workforce. However, the potential is much larger than these examples.

Implication. (1) Management methods aim at the identification of available but so far mostly unused internal and external resources; (2) they reflect on the utilization of digital technologies to make these resources accessible to be utilized for value co-creation purposes; (3) they use this overview of available resources to analyse the organization's respective advantage in comparison to competitors.

4.4   Principle #4: Co-creation-oriented Management

Statement. BMBM methods leverage the BM concept to establish, extend, and manage the partner and customer interactions rather than to produce goods which are exchanged in a singular transaction. BMBM methods aim at encouraging co-creation interactions by reconciling value propositions, customer relationships, and interaction channels.

Rationale. This principle refers to the core insight of S-D logic that *firms gain competitive advantage by engaging customers and value network partners in co-creation [...] activities (P4)*. Such value co-creation allows for longer and more intensive interaction between actors (*value-in-use*) than via the traditional production and delivery of goods (*value-in-exchange*). The idea of servitization, that is, the replacement of offering of products by related but often more effective services, is the perfect paragon in this respect. BMs consider the respective elements for interaction and can therefore be used to systematize the interaction.

Turning particularly to the customer side, *understanding how the customer uniquely integrates and experiences service-related resources (both private and public) is a source of competitive advantage through innovation (P5)*. BMs use value proposition and customer journeys [58] to understand the way customers use services in an integrated way, which helps better design combined services and better address the particular customer context.

A final aspect in this respect is that *providing service co-production opportunities and resources consistent with the customer's desired level of involvement leads to improved competitive advantage through enhanced customer experience (P6)*. In addition to the previous two propositions, *P6* points to the motivation of customers to take part in value co-creation processes and activities. BMs consider such motivations in customer journeys, in which they analyse the specific interaction with customers, reflecting on their thoughts and motivations to engage in such interactions.

Whilst economic actors have always integrated their resources, most of this integration took place inside organizations. Recently pervasive digitalization of organizational life has led to massive integration of resources beyond organizational boundaries, which expands the integration over the organizational boundaries [5, 34, 45]. One of the central advantages of such value co-creation is that it allows companies to address customer needs in the most efficient way. For example, car sharing does not only entail making a car available, but also requires to place the most suitable car at the right time at the right place at the optimal disposal of customers. Services that provide such information do not necessarily belong to the car provider. Management methods that use the BM concept to improve the value-in-use can take advantage of the opportunity of today's service economy.

Implication. (1) Management methods analyse the customers' objectives and their available resources to facilitate the interaction in the business ecosystem with the goal to enhance customers' value-in-use; (2) to this end and in arranging the tripartite of value propositions, customer relationships, and channels of interaction, management methods aim at the optimal interaction with customers and partners to obtain the most desirable combination of resources for a contextually required service; (3) based on BM tools such as customer journeys, BMs move away from static value propositions to dynamic interaction designs to elaborate how customers can be engaged in value co-creation and what their motivation is to do so.

5 Discussion and Conclusion

The central outcome of this design science research is prescriptive knowledge in the form of four design principles namely, *ecosystem-*, *technology-*, *mobilization-*, and *co-creation-oriented management*. The offered design principles guide the design of business-model-based management (BMBM) methods. The principles are built upon service-dominant (S-D) logic's derivative propositions [36]—representing managerial implications of S-D logic—and grounded in the business model (BM) concept. As such, the offered principles account for S-D logic and the BM concept to reflect the most foundational aspects that contemporary organizations have to consider in their management methods to compete and prosper in a networked, digital service economy [59]. The underlying assumption is that organizations that abide by the offered principles in designing their BMBM methods would effectively compete through service BMs [36].

Contribution. The study's theoretical contribution is twofold. *First*, it contributes to *BM research* in using the BM concept to advance management methods. While extant BM research predominantly lays emphasis on the BM's concept [15], terminology [14], structure [15], representation [60], and management process [16], we use the concept of BM in designing management methods. Such BM-based management methods— particularly those designed following the offered principles—spotlight (1) the logic of business ecosystems beyond traditional supply and value chains; (2) the pivotal role of information technology as facilitator of novel business logics; (3) operan*t* resources as the fundamental source of competitive BMs; and (4) the processes and activities underpinning value co-creation among actors in the business ecosystem. *Second*, the extant S-D logic research is dominated by theoretical discourses and lacks factual implications in the real-world organizational practices [61–63]. This research contributes to *S-D logic literature* in going one step further in expanding S-D logic beyond the realm of philosophy and theory (see Fig. 1). Thus, we employ S-D logic's descriptive knowledge base to derive principles as applicable knowledge to guide the design of BMBM methods (i.e., prescriptive knowledge).

Implications. *Researchers*, through the proposed principles, are offered four key themes to more precisely understand antecedents, manifestations, and consequences of novel socio-technical phenomena, such as service-based BMs [1], digital infrastructure [56], or service ecosystems [59, 64]. These novel phenomena emerge in the course of a networked and digital service economy [59] and cause major business and technology shifts. This research also provides guidance for *managers* in the design of a particular class of management methods. Adapting to emergent service and networked economies in current business environments is both relevant and complex for managers. Through applying the offered principles, managers can thus more clearly analyse requirements and design specifications of management methods that adhere to BM and service thinking. This may be especially useful for organizations during early planning and implementation phases of BMBM. Using the principles, managers might anticipate areas of concerns and take appropriate measures in the instantiation of BMBM.

Limitations and Future Research. Interpreting and applying the design principles should be done cautiously due to this research's limitations. *First*, given the socio-technical nature and the scope of BMBM methods, a naturalistic evaluation comprising real tasks, real systems, and real users [43, p. 396] is resource consuming. While a first iteration of such an evaluation has been conducted (see Sect. 3), the principles' usefulness can be further enhanced through applying the principles to a concrete instantiation of a BMBM method in a naturalistic setting [43]. *Second*, since the principles remain purposefully abstract for context-independent instantiations of BMBM methods, they provide limited *actionable* advice. That is, we propose one step further in translating S-D logic's descriptive knowledge base into prescriptive means for a novel class of management methods (i.e., BM-based). However, we do not provide detailed guidance on how to exactly design BMBM methods or extend extant management methods. Consequently, we encourage future research to shed further light on (i) how to realize the principles' implications (see Sect. 4) and (ii) the dynamics and the process of a reorientation in extant management methods toward BMBM methods. A first actionable step in BMBM can be representing to what extend a customer co-determines the cost structure, revenue model, and revenue sharing [49, 50]. Moreover, BMBM methods need to represent how an organization's resources and processes are integrated into a customer's resources and processes [49, 50]. *Third*, the offered principles are not exhaustive. Given the highly aggregated problem class of how to methodologically manage an organization, there are complementary theoretical lenses that help advancing the principles. Drawing on S-D logic's resource orientation, resource-based view (RBV) and resource dependence theory (RDT) can be considered as complementary theoretical bases. Therefore, in advancing the offered principles, we encourage future research to employ RBV in, for instance, identifying and exploiting valuable, rare, inimitable, and non-substitutable operant resources inside and outside the organization [65]. Similarly, prospective research can employ RDT to shed light on, for instance, how BMBM methods can help organizations in reducing environmental interdependence and uncertainty with appropriate BMs [66].

Conclusion. The rise of digital and ecosystemic business leads to new demands in business management. BMs play an increasingly pivotal role in such business contexts, which suggests that they are to be placed at the centre of new management methods. The latter requires a concise set of design principles for designing such methods. Relying on the descriptive insights by S-D logic on the requirements of a service business, these design principles deal with the core area of future organizational management such as orchestrating ecosystems, employing operant resources, novel logics of mobilizing resources between actors, and re-bundling of resources for novel value propositions through value co-creation.

Acknowledgements. This work has been supported by the Swiss National Science Foundation (SNSF).

References

1. Maglio, P.P., Spohrer, J.: A service science perspective on business model innovation. Ind. Mark. Manag. **42**, 665–670 (2013)
2. Vargo, S.L., Lusch, R.F.: Evolving to a new dominant logic for marketing. J. Mark. **68**, 1–17 (2004)
3. Vargo, S.L., Lusch, R.F.: Service-dominant logic: continuing the evolution. J. Acad. Mark. Sci. **36**, 1–10 (2008)
4. Vargo, S.L., Lusch, R.F.: Institutions and axioms: an extension and update of service-dominant logic. J. Acad. Mark. Sci. **44**, 5–23 (2016)
5. Lusch, R.F., Nambisan, S.: Service innovation: a service-dominant logic perspective. MIS Q. **39**, 155–175 (2015)
6. Prahalad, C.K., Ramaswamy, V.: Co-creating unique value with customers. Strategy Leadersh. **32**, 4–9 (2004)
7. Macdonald, E.K., Kleinaltenkamp, M., Wilson, H.N.: How business customers judge solutions: solution quality and value in use. J. Mark. **80**, 96–120 (2016)
8. Loebbecke, C., Picot, A.: Reflections on societal and business model transformation arising from digitization and big data analytics: a research agenda. J. Strateg. Inf. Syst. **24**, 149–157 (2015)
9. Bharadwaj, A., El Sawy, O.A., Pavlou, P.A., Venkatraman, N.: Digital business strategy: toward a next generation of insights. MIS Q. **37**, 471–482 (2013)
10. Bharadwaj, A., El Sawy, O.A., Pavlou, P.A., Venkatraman, N.: Visions and voices on emerging challenges in digital business strategy. MIS Q. **37**, 633–661 (2013)
11. Tallon, P.P.: A service science perspective on strategic choice, IT, and performance in U.S. banking. J. Manag. Inf. Syst. **26**, 219–252 (2010)
12. Eisert, U., Doll, J.: Business model based management: bridging the gap between strategy and daily business. 360° – Bus. Transform. J. **15**, 15–28 (2015)
13. Terrenghi, N., Schwarz, J., Legner, C., Eisert, U.: Business model management: current practices, required activities and IT support. In: Proceedings of the 13th Internationale Tagung Wirtschaftsinformatik (WI 2017), pp. 972–986, St. Gallen (2017)

14. Zott, C., Amit, R., Massa, L.: The business model: recent developments and future research. J. Manag. **37**, 1019–1042 (2011)
15. Hedman, J., Kalling, T.: The business model concept: theoretical underpinnings and empirical illustrations. Eur. J. Inf. Syst. **12**, 49–59 (2003)
16. Hienerth, C., Keinz, P., Lettl, C.: Exploring the nature and implementation process of user-centric business models. Long Range Plann. **44**, 344–374 (2011)
17. Wirtz, B.W., Pistoia, A., Ullrich, S., Göttel, V.: Business models: origin, development and future research perspectives. Long Range Plann. **49**, 36–54 (2016)
18. Tsalgatidou, A., Pitoura, E.: Business models and transactions in mobile electronic commerce: requirements and properties. Comput. Netw. **37**, 221–236 (2001)
19. Osterwalder, A., Pigneur, Y., Tucci, C.L.: Clarifying business models: origins, present, and future of the concept. Commun. Assoc. Inf. Syst. **16**, 1 (2005)
20. Veit, D., Clemons, E., Benlian, A., Buxmann, P., Hess, T., Kundisch, D., Leimeister, J.M., Loos, P., Spann, M.: Business models. Bus. Inf. Syst. Eng. **6**, 45–53 (2014)
21. Peters, C., Blohm, I., Leimeister, J.M.: Anatomy of successful business models for complex services: insights from the telemedicine field. J. Manag. Inf. Syst. **32**, 75–104 (2015)
22. Ebel, P., Bretschneider, U., Leimeister, J.M.: Leveraging virtual business model innovation: a framework for designing business model development tools. Inf. Syst. J. **26**, 519–550 (2016)
23. Giessmann, A., Legner, C.: Designing business models for cloud platforms. Inf. Syst. J. **26**, 551–579 (2016)
24. Zott, C., Amit, R.: The fit between product market strategy and business model: implications for firm performance. Strateg. Manag. J. **29**, 1–26 (2008)
25. Teece, D.J.: Business models, business strategy and innovation. Long Range Plann. **43**, 172–194 (2010)
26. Richardson, J.: The business model: an integrative framework for strategy execution. Strateg. Change **17**, 133–144 (2008)
27. Massa, L., Tucci, C., Afuah, A.: A critical assessment of business model research. Acad. Manag. Ann. **11**(1), 73–104 (2017). doi:https://doi.org/10.5465/annals.2014.0072
28. Afuah, A., Allan, A.: Business Models: A Strategic Management Approach. Mcgraw Hill Book Co, New York (2003)
29. Galvagno, M., Dalli, D.: Theory of value co-creation: a systematic literature review. Manag. Serv. Qual. Int. J. **24**, 643–683 (2014)
30. Vargo, S.L., Lusch, R.F., Akaka, M.A.: Advancing service science with service-dominant logic. In: Maglio, P.P., Kieliszewski, C.A., Spohrer, J.C. (eds.) Handbook of Service Science, pp. 133–156. Springer, New York (2010)
31. Böhmann, T., Leimeister, J.M., Möslein, K.: Service-systems-engineering. Wirtschaftsinformatik **56**, 83–90 (2014)
32. Maglio, P.P., Vargo, S.L., Caswell, N., Spohrer, J.: The service system is the basic abstraction of service science. Inf. Syst. E-Bus. Manag. **7**, 395–406 (2009)
33. Alter, S.: Challenges for service science. J. Inf. Technol. Theory Appl. **13**, 22 (2012)
34. Srivastava, S.C., Shainesh, G.: Bridging the service divide through digitally enabled service innovations: evidence from indian healthcare service providers. MIS Q. **39**, 245–267 (2015)
35. Lusch, R.F., Vargo, S.L., Tanniru, M.: Service, value networks and learning. J. Acad. Mark. Sci. **38**, 19–31 (2010)
36. Lusch, R.F., Vargo, S.L., O'Brien, M.: Competing through service: Insights from service-dominant logic. J. Retail. **83**, 5–18 (2007)
37. Pels, J., Vargo, S.L.: Toward a transcending conceptualization of relationship: a service-dominant logic perspective. J. Bus. Ind. Mark. **24**, 373–379 (2009)

38. Ranjan, K., Read, S.: Value co-creation: concept and measurement. J. Acad. Mark. Sci. **44**, 290–315 (2016)
39. Etgar, M.: A descriptive model of the consumer co-production process. J. Acad. Mark. Sci. **36**, 97–108 (2008)
40. Nenonen, S., Storbacka, K.: Business model design: conceptualizing networked value co-creation. Int. J. Qual. Serv. Sci. **2**, 43–59 (2010)
41. Yip, G.S.: Using strategy to change your business model. Bus. Strategy Rev. **15**, 17–24 (2004)
42. Smedlund, A.: Value cocreation in service platform business models. Serv. Sci. **4**, 79–88 (2012)
43. Sonnenberg, C., vom Brocke, J.: Evaluations in the science of the artificial – reconsidering the build-evaluate pattern in design science research. In: Peffers, K., Rothenberger, M., Kuechler, B. (eds.) DESRIST 2012. LNCS, vol. 7286, pp. 381–397. Springer, Heidelberg (2012). doi:10.1007/978-3-642-29863-9_28
44. Abraham, R., Aier, S., Winter, R.: Fail early, fail often: towards coherent feedback loops in design science research evaluation. In: Proceedings of the International Conference on Information Systems - Building a Better World through Information Systems, pp. 2417–2428. Association for Information Sytems, Auckland (2014)
45. Barrett, M., Davidson, E., Prabhu, J., Vargo, S.L.: Service innovation in the digital age: key contributions and future directions. MIS Q. **39**, 135–154 (2015)
46. Grover, V., Kohli, R.: Cocreating IT value: new capabilities and metrics for multifirm environments. MIS Q. **36**, 225–232 (2012)
47. Chaturvedi, A.R., Dolk, D.R., Drnevich, P.L.: Design principles for virtual worlds. MIS Q. **35**, 673–684 (2011)
48. Yang, L., Su, G., Yuan, H.: Design principles of integrated information platform for emergency responses: the case of 2008 Beijing Olympic Games. Inf. Syst. Res. **23**, 761–786 (2012)
49. Zolnowski, A., Böhmann, T.: Customer integration in service business models. In: Proceedings of the 46th Hawaii International Conference on System Sciences, pp. 1103–1112 (2013)
50. Zolnowski, A., Semmann, M., Böhmann, T.: Introducing a co-creation perspective to service business models. In: Proceedings of Enterprise Modelling and Information Systems Architectures (EMISA) 2011, pp. 243–248 (2011)
51. Richardson, G.L., Jackson, B.M., Dickson, G.W.: A principles-based enterprise architecture: lessons from texaco and star enterprise. MIS Q. **14**, 385–403 (1990)
52. Aier, S., Fischer, C., Winter, R.: Construction and evaluation of a meta-model for enterprise architecture design principles. In: Bernstein, A., Schwabe, G. (eds.) Proceedings of the 10th International Conference on Wirtschaftsinformatik (WI 2011), Zurich, pp. 637–644 (2011)
53. Leminen, S., Westerlund, M., Rajahonka, M., Siuruainen, R.: Towards IOT ecosystems and business models. In: Andreev, S., Balandin, S., Koucheryavy, Y. (eds.) NEW2AN/ruSMART -2012. LNCS, vol. 7469, pp. 15–26. Springer, Heidelberg (2012). doi:10.1007/978-3-642-32686-8_2
54. Ross, J., Sebastian, I., Beath, C., Mocker, M., Moloney, K., Fonstad, N.: Designing and executing digital strategies. In: ICIS 2016 Proceedings (2016)
55. Hanseth, O., Lyytinen, K.: Design theory for dynamic complexity in information infrastructures: the case of building internet. J. Inf. Technol. **25**, 1–19 (2010)
56. Henfridsson, O., Bygstad, B.: The generative mechanisms of digital infrastructure evolution. MIS Q. **37**, 907–931 (2013)
57. Tilson, D., Lyytinen, K., Sørensen, C.: Digital infrastructures: the missing IS research agenda. Inf. Syst. Res. **21**, 748–759 (2010)

58. Stickdorn, M., Schwarzenberger, K.: Service design in tourism. Entrep. Tour. Unternehmerisches Denk. Erfolgskonzepte Aus Prax. 2261 (2016)
59. El Sawy, O.A., Malhotra, A., Park, Y., Pavlou, P.A.: Seeking the configurations of digital ecodynamics: it takes three to tango. Inf. Syst. Res. **21**, 835–848 (2010)
60. Baden-Fuller, C., Morgan, M.S.: Business models as models. Long Range Plann. **43**, 156–171 (2010)
61. Day, G.S.: Achieving advantage with a new dominant logic in "invited commentaries on 'evolving to a new dominant logic for marketing'". J. Mark. **68**, 18–27 (2004)
62. Levy, S.J.: How new, how dominant? In: Lusch, R.F., Vargo, S.L. (eds.) The Service-Dominant Logic of Marketing: Dialog, Debate, and Directions, pp. 57–64. M.E. Sharpe, New York (2006)
63. Jain, H., Tanniru, M., Spohrer, J., Hsu, C., Zhao, L., Zhao, L.: ICIS 2007 panel report: bridging service computing and service management: how MIS contributes to service orientation? Commun. Assoc. Inf. Syst. **22**, 145 (2007)
64. Akaka, M.A., Vargo, S.L., Lusch, R.F.: An exploration of networks in value cocreation: a service-ecosystems view. Rev. Mark. Res. **9**, 13–50 (2012)
65. Wade, M., Hulland, J.: The resource-based view and information systems research: review, extension, and suggestions for future research. MIS Q. **28**, 107–142 (2004)
66. Drees, J.M., Heugens, P.P.: Synthesizing and extending resource dependence theory a meta-analysis. J. Manag. **39**, 1–33 (2013)

Methodological Contributions

Evaluating Knowledge Types in Design Science Research: An Integrated Framework

Jacky Akoka[1], Isabelle Comyn-Wattiau[2(✉)], Nicolas Prat[2],
and Veda C. Storey[3]

[1] CEDRIC-CNAM, Paris, France
jacky.akoka@cnam.fr
[2] ESSEC Business School, Cergy-Pontoise, France
{wattiau,prat}@essec.edu
[3] Department of Computer Information Systems, Georgia State University,
Atlanta, GA, USA
vstorey@gsu.edu

Abstract. As the design science research (DSR) paradigm has evolved, several frameworks and taxonomies have been proposed to aid researchers in understanding and applying DSR principles and practices to evaluate the knowledge produced. This paper attempts to integrate two such efforts, the evaluation methods taxonomy and the genres of inquiry framework, in an attempt to derive a more complete evaluation standard. The integration is based on various knowledge types, using mapping and merging techniques. Doing so results in three artifacts. The first is the integrated framework which refines the genres of inquiry framework with six recognized knowledge types (definitional, descriptive, prescriptive, explanatory, predictive, and explanatory and predictive). Evaluation criteria for each knowledge type emerge from the integration. The second contribution is a guidance scheme that helps in determining relevant evaluation criteria, based upon the type of DSR contribution and the role of the evaluator (DSR researcher, author, reader, or reviewer). Finally, the approach to the integration, including the integration algorithm, is adaptable to other contexts where criteria to evaluate different knowledge types need to be integrated.

Keywords: Design science research · Nomothetic design · Nomothetic science · Evaluation criteria · Evaluation methods taxonomy · Genres of inquiry framework · Knowledge types · Mappings · Artifacts · Integrated evaluation framework

1 Introduction

Many efforts in design science research have focused on analyzing this research approach to propose ways to effectively carry out meaningful research and to guide research initiatives. An important aspect of design science research is the evaluation of the results (e.g., [1]), although there is no generally-accepted, systematic way to do so. Prat et al. [2], for example, develop a detailed Evaluation Methods Taxonomy for information systems artifacts, including a hierarchy of criteria, derived from analysis of existing studies on design science research. The Genres of Inquiry Framework [3] is

© Springer International Publishing AG 2017
A. Maedche et al. (Eds.): DESRIST 2017, LNCS 10243, pp. 201–217, 2017.
DOI: 10.1007/978-3-319-59144-5_12

comprised of two dimensions: knowledge goal (design or science), and knowledge scope (idiographic or nomothetic), from which general evaluation criteria are derived (based upon general scientific research) for each of the resulting four quadrants. These two approaches share the common goal of providing specific criteria for evaluation in design science research. The Genres of Inquiry Framework has a broad scope, proposing general evaluation criteria for the four combinations of knowledge goal and knowledge scope. The Evaluation Methods Taxonomy has a more specific scope as it focuses on the evaluation of artifacts contributed by design science researchers. In other words, the focus of the Evaluation Methods Taxonomy is on nomothetic design. The criteria proposed in this taxonomy are at a finer level of granularity than those of the Genres of Inquiry Framework and are only one among the six dimensions of evaluation methods for information systems artifacts. Thus, the two approaches are complementary in the sense that both attempt to provide specific criteria for artifact or knowledge evaluation in design science research, but differ in terms of scope and level of detail.

Since there is no generally accepted way to carry out the evaluation process in design science research, integrating these two complementary approaches might lead to insights on how a more general approach might be developed. The objective of this research, then, is to explore and integrate these two approaches in an attempt to develop a more complete set of evaluation criteria from which a set of actionable evaluation guidelines in design science research could be proposed.

To conduct the research, the integration is carried out by first considering the set of six types of design science research knowledge proposed by Johannesson and Perjons [4], to which the criteria can be associated. Then, mapping and merging rules are developed and applied to integrate the Evaluation Methods Taxonomy with the Genres of Inquiry Framework. The results highlight missing criteria, which are needed to develop a more complete set of evaluation criteria.

The mapping and merging results in an integrated evaluation framework, where the criteria depend on the knowledge type. Some criteria are organized hierarchically and decomposed into sub-criteria. This paper focuses on the results from the integration of criteria for nomothetic knowledge. Criteria for evaluating idiographic knowledge could be integrated following the same principles. Application of the integrated evaluation framework is facilitated by a guiding scheme that helps to identify relevant evaluation criteria, based on the type of design science research contribution and the role of the evaluator. To illustrate, the guidance scheme is then applied to four types of DSR contributions from articles published in journals from the AIS Senior Scholars' basket (www.aisnet.org).

The primary contribution of this research is the integrated evaluation framework. In addition, the guidance scheme for the identification of relevant criteria is detailed as well as the integration approach, which includes an integration algorithm.

The next section reviews work in design science research evaluation, the Evaluation Methods Taxonomy, and the Genres of Inquiry Framework. The integration approach is described in the following section, followed by the results of carrying out the integration. Then, the insights gained are presented as a new guidance scheme that considers the knowledge type and actor's role. This is illustrated by four examples where the role is that of a researcher. The conclusion summarizes the research and suggests avenues for future work.

2 Related Research

We briefly review previous work on evaluation in DSR, focusing specifically on evaluation criteria. Then, the essence of the Evaluation Methods Taxonomy and the Genres of Inquiry Framework are presented to identify their complementarities, which provides the basis for performing the integration.

2.1 Evaluation in DSR

Evaluation is a critical part of design science research [2, 5]. According to Goes [6, pp. v–vi], a major concern of design science research is to "*create knowledge through meaningful solutions that survive rigorous validations through proof of concept, proof of use, and proof of value.*" As a result, design science researchers need to understand and apply acceptable criteria to evaluate the outcomes of their research [3].

Traditionally, DSR is decomposed into two activities: build and evaluate [7, 8]. However, artifact building and evaluation are intertwined, with several micro-evaluations [9] carried out during design. Evaluation is central to the DSR process presented by Hevner [10]. This process comprises three inter-related cycles: relevance, design (build and evaluate), and rigor. The DSR methodology of Peffers et al. [11] comprises an activity dedicated to evaluation. Sonnenberg and vom Brocke [12] distinguish four different evaluation activities. Each of these four activities has specific goals, evaluation criteria, and evaluation methods. Some evaluations are carried out early in the DSR process. The benefit of these early evaluation activities should be outweighed by their cost [13]. Moreover, coherence should be ensured between the evaluation activities [14]. In addition to evaluations carried out as part of the DSR process, retrospective evaluation has been suggested to gain knowledge from both successful and unsuccessful DSR projects [15].

A Framework for Evaluation in Design Science (FEDS) [1] has been proposed that encompasses many aspects of evaluation in DSR. It comprises two dimensions: the purpose of the evaluation (formative or summative) and the paradigm of the evaluation (artificial or naturalistic). From this framework, evaluation strategies may be defined. An evaluation strategy is a planned trajectory along the two dimensions of the framework. There are also steps identified for the evaluation process, including the choice of the evaluation strategy. However, FEDS is a high-level framework. March and Smith [7] list some evaluation criteria for the four types of artifacts that they define: constructs, models, methods, and instantiations. This list does not necessarily aim at completeness, similarly for that proposed by Hevner et al. [5] and Sonnenberg and vom Brocke [12]. The criteria by Aier and Fischer [16] draw on those defined by Kuhn [17] for traditional science, but are specific to design theories. Thus, the literature lacks a complete list of evaluation criteria for DSR, covering the different types of knowledge and artifacts. Two systematic approaches to developing criteria for DSR have been proposed [2, 3] and are reviewed below. These approaches are complementary, in that one is based on the analysis of existing work on artifact development in design science research and the other started from the general literature on scientific research. Combining these approaches leads to the derivation of an integrated evaluation framework that systematically specifies applicable evaluation criteria for the different types of DSR knowledge.

2.2 Evaluation Methods Taxonomy

The development of the Evaluation Methods Taxonomy [2] was motivated by the need to investigate the "what" and the "how" of information systems artifact evaluation. That is, what the artifacts are, and what the criteria of evaluation are, as well as the relationship between the "what" and the "how." By doing so, the research identifies important relationships between different dimensions of design science research artifact evaluation. The taxonomy of evaluation methods comprises six dimensions, including criterion and evaluation technique. The dimension "criterion" proposes a complete hierarchy of evaluation criteria for information systems artifacts. Based on a systems view of artifacts, the first level of the hierarchy is formed by the five aspects constituting the canonical form of systems: goal, environment, structure, activity, and evolution, each of which has criteria, sub-criteria, and sub-sub-criteria.

2.3 Genres of Inquiry Framework

The Genres of Inquiry Framework for design science research [3], recognizes four modes of reasoning that can exist in design science research as derived from analyzing the knowledge goals (design versus science) and knowledge scope (idiographic and nomothetic) in knowledge production. The result is the four genres of idiographic design (ID), idiographic science (IS), nomothetic design (ND), and nomothetic science (NS), each of which has its own evaluation criteria.

3 Integration of Evaluation Approaches

The Evaluation Methods Taxonomy is intended to express evaluation methods, including evaluation criteria, in a systematic way. The focus is on evaluating artifacts contributed by design science researchers, primarily constructs, models or methods. This corresponds to the quadrant of nomothetic design in the Genres of Inquiry Framework. The latter framework has coarse categories. Thus, the Genres of Inquiry Framework has a broader scope, in that it considers all types of DSR knowledge and proposes general criteria to evaluate the four types of knowledge (ND, NS, ID and IS). The Evaluation Methods Taxonomy has a more specific scope, presenting detailed criteria, and more generally, evaluation methods, for artifacts that are typically constructs, models, or methods (ND). Given these complementarities, integrating the Evaluation Methods Taxonomy with the Genres of Inquiry Framework should result in a more complete approach to evaluation in DSR, at a finer level of granularity. The process for integrating these two approaches involves mapping from one approach to the other. This process requires the following steps: mapping between genres of inquiry and knowledge types, artifact positioning, criteria mapping, and criteria integration.

These four steps are detailed and applied below, resulting in an integrated framework of evaluation criteria organized by knowledge type.

3.1 Step 1. Mapping Between Genres of Inquiry and Knowledge Types

The Evaluation Methods Taxonomy deals mainly with artifact evaluation. The Genres of Inquiry Framework focuses on knowledge evaluation and characterizes knowledge by its scope and goal. In order to integrate both evaluation mechanisms, we rely on a pivot concept based on the knowledge types proposed by Johannesson and Perjons [4]. The authors distinguish six knowledge types: definitional, descriptive, prescriptive, explanatory, predictive, and explanatory and predictive. These knowledge types are closely related to the types of theories defined by Gregor [18]. We should note the distinction between definitional and descriptive knowledge, refining Gregor's notion of "theories for analyzing." For example, the terminological box in an ontology is definitional knowledge, and the assertion box is descriptive knowledge.

We position the six knowledge types into the four quadrants of the Genres of Inquiry Framework. We justify this matching by the fact that both structures (quadrants and Johannesson and Perjons' [4] categories) represent different knowledge. The resulting knowledge types are shown in bold characters in Fig. 1 (the rest of the figure

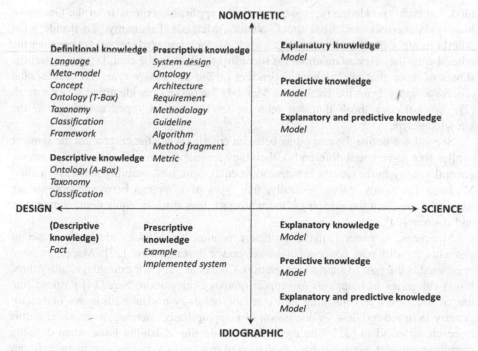

Fig. 1. Towards an integrated evaluation framework: mapping knowledge types and artifact types to genres

is explained in Sect. 3.2). Explanatory, predictive, and explanatory and predictive knowledge pertain to the "science" dimension. The other types of knowledge are related to design. Each knowledge type is defined at the nomothetic and idiographic level. There is no definitional knowledge at the idiographic level. Descriptive knowledge at the idiographic level may be considered outside the scope of research. Thus, this integration results in ten knowledge types.

3.2   Step 2. Artifact Positioning

From the results of step 1, we identify the types of artifacts associated with each knowledge type. Employing the typology of artifacts proposed by Sangupamba Mwilu et al. [19], we enrich it to include models generated by quantitative or qualitative research. We also extend the typology of artifacts by adding classification [20], as distinguished from the concept of taxonomy. The result of this step is presented in Fig. 1. The mapping and integration, described below, focuses on the integration of criteria for knowledge types in the nomothetic quadrants, because the latter deal with general theories or concepts that cover a set of classes.

3.3   Step 3. Criteria Mapping

First, for each knowledge type, we specify the applicable criteria from the Genres of Inquiry Framework and from the Evaluation Methods Taxonomy. To decide what criteria to apply from the Genres Framework, for each knowledge type, we consider the criteria from the relevant quadrant (as identified by Baskerville et al. [3]) and select the subset of those that are relevant depending on the knowledge type. To decide what criteria to apply from the Evaluation Methods Taxonomy (as identified by Prat et al. [2]), we consider those that are relevant for the artifact types associated to the knowledge type.

Second, we define the mappings between criteria. When the criteria are the same or similar (but represented differently), then they are mapped to each other. For example, generalizability in the Genres Framework is equivalent to adaptability in the Evaluation Methods Taxonomy. More generally, five types of mappings between concepts are adopted to perform the mappings: more abstract, less abstract, equivalent, compatible, and disjoint [21].

Mappings, in general, make explicit a relationship between elements, or set of elements, of different conceptualizations and/or instantiations [22]. Mappings have been used in the past to support integration. Choi et al. [23], for example, identify three broad categories of mappings to support ontology integration. Noy [24] proposes the use of ontologies and mapping to a common ontology to deal with issues of heterogeneity in structured data. A discussion of mapping-based merging, as required in this research, is found in [25]. The methods focus on the scalability issue when defining mappings requires a combinatory explosion of two-by-two concept comparison. In our context, scalability is not an issue. Thus, we manually completed the mapping matrices (one per knowledge type). The mapping matrix for predictive knowledge in the nomothetic science quadrant is shown in Table 1. The applicable criteria from the Genres Framework are shown in the columns. Those from the Evaluation Methods Taxonomy appear in the rows.

Table 1. Mapping matrix for NS predictive knowledge

NS predictive	validity	utility	generality	completeness	simplicity	understandability	consistency	fidelity to modeled phenomena	accuracy	adaptability
applicability	⊥	⊥	*	⊥	⊥	⊥	⊥	⊥	⊥	≡
generalizability	⊥	⊥	*	⊥	⊥	⊥	⊥	⊥	⊥	≡
external validity	⊆	⊥	⊥	⊥	⊥	⊥	⊥	⊆	⊥	⊥
consistency	⊥	⊥	⊥	⊥	⊥	⊥	≡	⊥	⊥	⊥
reliability	⊥	⊥	⊥	⊥	⊥	⊥	⊆	⊥	⊥	⊥
internal validity	⊆	⊥	⊥	⊥	⊥	⊥	⊥	⊆	⊥	⊥
objectivity	⊥	⊥	⊥	⊥	⊥	⊥	⊥	⊥	⊥	⊥

Legend: ⊇ more abstract than   ≡ equivalent to   ⊥ disjoint from
⊆ less abstract than   * compatible with

3.4 Step 4. Criteria Integration

This step is dedicated to the integration of criteria based upon mapping matrices. Based upon these mappings, the criteria are integrated using the algorithm shown in Fig. 2. This algorithm enables the integration of the criteria for each mapping matrix in a systematic and replicable way, defined specifically for this research. The main principles underlying the algorithm are: (i) order the five mapping types as follows: equivalent, more abstract, less abstract, compatible, disjoint; (ii) examine, step by step, all the mapping types; (iii) merge the equivalent criteria; (iv) transform more abstract or less abstract mappings into generalization links between criteria; (v) create a common criterion for compatible criteria; and (vi) remove disjoint links and potential multiple inheritance cases. Thus, we obtain a unique hierarchy of criteria for each knowledge type.

INTEGRATION ALGORITHM
{This algorithm builds a list of criteria which may contain
ISA links}
*** *Step 0 - Initialization - Graph construction*
Each criterion is a node, each "equivalent" (resp. "less
abstract" or "compatible") link is an edge labeled with
"equivalent" (resp. "less abstract" or "compatible"). Only
"less abstract" labeled edges are directed. "More abstract"
links lead to inverse edges labeled "less abstract".

*** *Step 1 - Transformation of "equivalent" edges*
For each "equivalent" edge
Do Merge all the nodes belonging to the corresponding
equivalence class
        Call routine 1 for naming the resulting node
        Call routine 2 for transferring edges from initial
nodes to the resulting merged node
        Delete the "equivalent" edge
End For {notice that, at the end of this step, there is no
remaining "equivalent" edges}

*** *Step 2 - Transformation of "less abstract" edges*
For each "less abstract" edge
Do Create an ISA link between corresponding nodes
        If it generates a multiple inheritance
        Then call routine 3 for deleting the multiple inher-
itance
        End If
        Delete the "less abstract" edge
End For {notice that, at the end of this step, there is
neither remaining "equivalent" nor "less abstract" edges}

*** *Step 3 - Transformation of "compatible" edges*
For each "compatible" edge
If   the two corresponding nodes and possibly others also
        linked to them by "compatible" edges have no common ge-
        neric node
Then   Create a generic node
        Call routine 1 for naming this new node
        If it generates a multiple inheritance
        Then call routine 3 for deleting the multiple inher-
itance
        End If
End If
Delete the "compatible" edge
End For

*** *Step 4 - end of process*
The remaining criteria are added to the resulting graph.
The expert can improve this result, especially by examining
in detail the hierarchies notably those where the specific
criteria do not completely cover the generic criterion.

Fig. 2. Integration algorithm

```
  Routine 1 {naming a node resulting from the mapping pro-
cess}
  If   the initial nodes share the same name
       Then   the new node will also share the same name
       Else   concatenate the names of initial nodes
  End If       {An expert may also suggest a better naming}
  End routine 1


  Routine 2 {in case of node merging, the routine transfers
the edges connected to the initial nodes}
  For  each edge connecting the merged node to another node N
  Do   Transfer this edge such that it now links the new node
resulting from the merging to node N
  End For
  If   at the end of the step, two edges share the same label
between two nodes
       Then   merge these edges
  End If
If       at the end of the step, two edges exist between two
         nodes with one label "less abstract" and the other la-
         bel "compatible"
       Then   merge these edges and assign the label "less ab-
stract"
  End If
  If   at the end of the step, two inverse edges with label
"less abstract" link two same nodes
       Then   merge the two nodes
       Call routine 1 for naming the new node
  End If
  End routine 2


  Routine 3 {deletion of multiple inheritance}
  If   there exists a multiple inheritance (i.e. two ISA links
start from the same node)
       Then   the expert must check the definitions of crite-
              ria associated to the target nodes in order to
              decide whether they have to merge
       If     he/she decides to merge them
              Then   merge the two nodes
                     Call routine 1 for naming the new node
              Else   the expert must check the definitions of
                     criteria associated to the source node and
                     to all cousin nodes in the ISA hierarchy
                     in order to decide which link is more rel-
                     evant
                     Delete the less relevant ISA link
       End If
  End If
  End routine 3
```

Fig. 2. (continued)

To further enrich the hierarchies of criteria, we used two other sets of criteria, complementing those of the Evaluation Methods Taxonomy and the Genres of Inquiry Framework: the criteria proposed by Weber [26] for evaluating theories in information systems, and those proposed by Kuhn for general scientific research [17]. Thus, for each knowledge type, we applied steps 3 and 4 in three successive iterations:

- *Iteration 1*: map and integrate the applicable criteria from the Genres Framework and the Evaluation Methods Taxonomy.
- *Iteration 2*: map and integrate the criteria resulting from iteration 1 and the applicable criteria from Weber [26].
- *Iteration 3*: map and integrate the criteria resulting from iteration 2 and the applicable criteria from Kuhn [17].

The six resulting hierarchies for the nomothetic quadrants are depicted in Figs. 3 and 4.

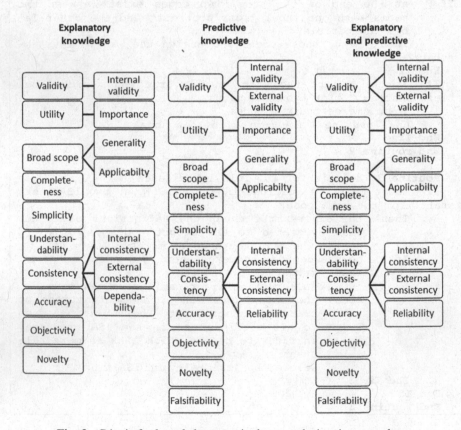

Fig. 3. Criteria for knowledge types in the nomothetic science quadrant

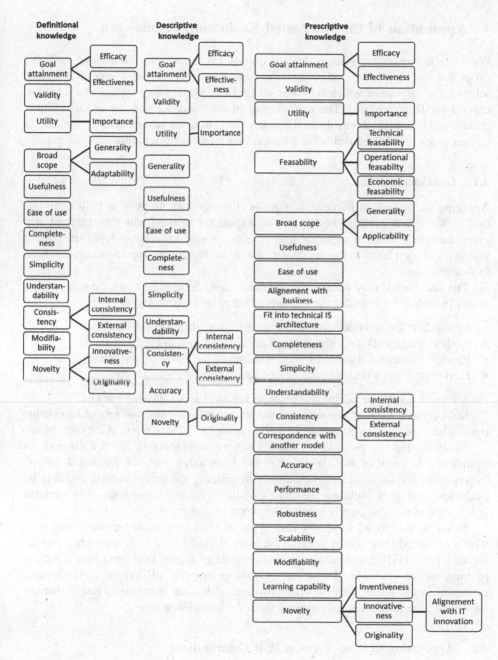

Fig. 4. Criteria for knowledge types in the nomothetic design quadrant

4   Application of the Integrated Evaluation Framework

We have defined integrated evaluation criteria for nomothetic knowledge in DSR. From the results of integrating the two approaches, we derive a criteria selection scheme, the purpose of which is to provide guidance for selecting applicable evaluation criteria for DSR projects. The overall goal of the guidance scheme is to facilitate, enrich, and transform the evaluation process. The guidance scheme and its application to four types of DSR contribution are each illustrated using a published DSR paper.

4.1   Guidance Scheme

Applying the integrated framework requires characterizing the type of DSR contribution which means placing the research in a quadrant of the framework (at least at a given moment). Since a quadrant may contain several knowledge types, placement within a quadrant leads to the selection of a specific knowledge type from among those in that quadrant.

The framework may be used in different ways, depending upon the roles of the actors in DSR. We consider the following four roles (stakeholders):

- Researcher: framework helps define a research path for evaluation.
- Author: framework provides a set of criteria to apply in the evaluation.
- Reader: framework facilitates understanding of the research activities.
- Reviewer: framework suggests appropriate criteria for evaluation.

An author is a subtype of researcher and a reviewer is a subtype of reader.

DSR contributions can now be defined as chronological ordered sets of knowledge types where the evaluation should focus on certain knowledge types in the ordered set.

Summarizing, we provide a guidance scheme for aiding in the definition of an evaluation. It consists of: (i) defining the knowledge path as illustrated below; (ii) choosing the focus of the evaluation; (iii) deriving the sets of criteria that may be evaluated; and (iv) building the corresponding evaluation methods. The detailed description of the last step is beyond the scope of this paper.

In the next section, we derive four types of DSR contributions, illustrating each with a published DSR paper. We take the point of view of the DSR researcher. For the fourth type of DSR contribution, we also illustrate examples of criteria from the point of view of the reviewer. The proof of concept consists of comparing the criteria evaluated in the paper with the criteria suggested by our framework. Recall that the suggested criteria are deduced directly from the knowledge type.

4.2   Application to Four Types of DSR Contributions

Type 1: ND definitional → *ND prescriptive* → ID prescriptive, where the focus of evaluation is on ND prescriptive.

This path occurs when the researcher: (i) proposes an artifact among (language, concept, meta-model, ontology, taxonomy, framework, classification), belonging to definitional knowledge, (ii) proposes an artifact among (methodology, algorithm, method fragment, guideline, etc.) based on this artifact, generating prescriptive knowledge, (iii) applies the artifact, generating idiographic prescriptive knowledge. Moreover, this type is related to the case where the focus of evaluation is on the second artifact (ND prescriptive).

Arnott [27] perfectly exemplifies this type. He proposes a taxonomy of cognitive biases (ND definitional) with an evolutionary DSS development methodology that uses cognitive bias theory as a focusing construct (ND prescriptive). The methodology is applied to a strategic DSS project (ID prescriptive). The focus of the contribution and evaluation is the DSS development methodology that uses the taxonomy of cognitive biases. Arnott [27] evaluated the effectiveness (degree to which the artifact achieves its goal in a real situation) and the operational feasibility (integration of the artifact in the daily practice of users) of the methodology. He could also have evaluated the simplicity and the understandability of the methodology by conducting another case study in which the analyst would have been different.

Type 2: *ND definitional* → **ND prescriptive** → **ID prescriptive, where the focus of evaluation is on ND definitional.**

Adomavicius et al. [28] develop the REQUEST query language and associated RA algebra (ND definitional), a mapping algorithm from REQUEST to RA (ND prescriptive), with an application to examples (ID prescriptive). The focus of the research is on the evaluation of the query language and associated algebra. The researchers evaluate the efficacy of REQUEST by applying it to example queries. They also evaluate the expressive power (completeness) of REQUEST and RA. They could also have applied other criteria relevant for ND definitional knowledge, as suggested in Fig. 4. For example, they could also have evaluated the simplicity of REQUEST and RA, or the understandability of REQUEST by conducting a laboratory experiment. Note that in this type of DSR contribution, the ordered set of knowledge types is the same as that for Type 1. However, for Type 2, the evaluation focuses on ND definitional, as opposed to ND prescriptive for Type 1.

Type 3: *ND prescriptive* → **ID prescriptive** → *ND definitional*, **where the focus of evaluation is on ND prescriptive and ND definitional.**

Nickerson et al. [29] present a methodology for taxonomy development (ND prescriptive) and application of the methodology (ID prescriptive). The application of the methodology results in a taxonomy of mobile applications (ND definitional). The authors evaluate the usefulness of the taxonomy using a laboratory experiment. They could also have applied other criteria, such as completeness or modifiability, as well as the other ND definitional criteria. By building this taxonomy, they validated operational feasibility of the methodology (evaluation of the ND prescriptive knowledge). The authors listed a set of desirable properties for such methodologies that they evaluated using an informed argument. These properties correspond to performance, simplicity, and utility in our ND prescriptive quadrant. Note that the authors mention two properties very specific to taxonomy building, namely the possibility of taking into consideration alternative approaches and the reduction of arbitrariness.

Type 4: *NS explanatory and predictive* → *ND prescriptive* → **NS predictive** → **IS prescriptive, where the focus of evaluation is on NS explanatory and predictive and ND prescriptive.**

Arazy et al. [30] propose elements for a design theory of social recommender systems, based on the components of information system design theories [31]. The researchers introduce the concept of "applied behavioral theory," making the link between Walls et al.'s [31] kernel theories and meta requirements. In their case, the applied behavioral theory is a theory that explains and predicts willingness to accept advice. The applied behavioral theory (NS explanatory and predictive) leads to the meta requirements and meta design of social recommender systems (ND prescriptive), followed by testable product hypotheses (NS predictive), and then, a system implementation (IS prescriptive). The applied behavioral theory is carefully tested for reliability and validity (e.g., discriminant validity). It is also judged too complex (simplicity) for practical use, and is simplified from a PLS model (explanatory and predictive) into a regression model (essentially predictive). Our criteria for NS explanatory and predictive knowledge suggest other possible criteria for evaluating the applied behavioral theory, e.g. importance (this criterion may be evaluated ex-post, e.g. based on use of the applied behavioral theory in other DSR projects). With respect to the evaluation of the meta design, the authors focus on technical feasibility (through the implementation of a system) and accuracy. Our criteria for ND prescriptive knowledge suggest other possible criteria, e.g., utility or innovativeness.

Other paths, highlighting DSR contributions, can be defined. However, whatever the path, the integrated evaluation framework can potentially help in the evaluation process for all stakeholders. The framework offers the possibility of providing the researcher with a more complete set of relevant criteria, including three parameters: the scope of knowledge (nomothetic or idiographic), the goal of knowledge (science or design), and the type of knowledge (definitional, prescriptive, etc.). For each triple of parameter values, a hierarchy of criteria is derived.

5   Conclusion and Future Research

Despite the fact that design science research evaluation of artifacts has been addressed from different aspects (e.g., tactical and operational [2] versus strategic [1]), there is still a need for a comprehensive approach to artifact and knowledge evaluation. This research has attempted to integrate two complementary approaches, the Evaluation Methods Taxonomy and the Genres of Inquiry Framework, to derive a more complete set of integrated evaluation criteria. The result is an integrated evaluation framework. This framework:

1. refines the Genre of Inquiry Framework with the six types of design science research knowledge proposed by Johannesson and Perjons [4], as illustrated in Fig. 1; and
2. proposes a hierarchy of criteria for each knowledge type in the nomothetic quadrants, by mapping and integrating the criteria from the Genres of Inquiry Framework and the Evaluation Methods Taxonomy (Figs. 3 and 4).

To guide the choice of applicable evaluation criteria in the integrated evaluation framework, a guidance scheme is proposed. This scheme considers: (1) the type of DSR contribution, defined as a chronological ordered set of knowledge types where the evaluation should focus on certain knowledge types in an ordered set; and (2) the role of the actor (researcher, author, reader, or reviewer). To evaluate the efficacy and utility of the integrated evaluation framework and associated guidance scheme, they are applied to four studies (DSR papers published in the AIS basket of journals).

The benefit of the approach can be realized by a researcher, author, reader or reviewer. If they can identify where a DSR project or paper fits in terms of knowledge types, then they can use the identified criteria, depending on their role. One limitation of the approach is that different research paradigms (e.g., positivist versus interpretivist) have different views on criteria for evaluating knowledge, and on whether it is possible to objectively evaluate scientific knowledge. Consequently, the epistemological challenges of combining different criteria in a single evaluation framework deserve further consideration. Moreover, even if we contend that DSR should benefit from comprehensive hierarchies of evaluation criteria, some criteria may not be defined a priori and are specific to particular research endeavors.

Future research can proceed in several directions. The guidance scheme can be extended by identifying other types of DSR contributions, in addition to the four types illustrated. Our approach needs to be evaluated more extensively and expanded to deal with the idiographic quadrants [3]. Although the guidance scheme supports the identification of relevant evaluation criteria, it does not suggest when these criteria should be evaluated (e.g., formative versus summative evaluation). To assist in the definition of an overall evaluation agenda, we may combine our approach with evaluation strategies [1]. Another possibility is to adapt and extend the evaluation methods identified by Prat et al. [2].

Acknowledgement. Veda Storey's research was supported by the J. Mack Robinson College of Business, Georgia State University.

References

1. Venable, J., Pries-Heje, J., Baskerville, R.: FEDS: a framework for evaluation in design science research. Eur. J. Inf. Syst. **25**, 77–89 (2016)
2. Prat, N., Comyn-Wattiau, I., Akoka, J.: A taxonomy of evaluation methods for information systems artifacts. J. Manag. Inf. Syst. **32**, 229–267 (2015)
3. Baskerville, R.L., Kaul, M., Storey, V.C.: Genres of inquiry in design-science research: justification and evaluation of knowledge production. MIS Q. **39**, 541–564 (2015)
4. Johannesson, P., Perjons, E.: Knowledge types and forms. In: Johannesson, P., Perjons, E. (eds.) An Introduction to Design Science, pp. 21–38. Springer, Cham (2014)
5. Hevner, A.R., March, S.T., Park, J., Ram, S.: Design science in information systems research. MIS Q. **28**, 75–105 (2004)
6. Goes, P.B.: Design science research in top information systems journals. MIS Q. **38**, iii–viii (2014)

7. March, S.T., Smith, G.F.: Design and natural science research on information technology. Decis. Support Syst. **15**, 251–266 (1995)
8. Winter, R.: Design science research in Europe. Eur. J. Inf. Syst. **17**, 470–475 (2008)
9. Vaishnavi, V., Kuechler, B.: Design science research in information systems, pp. 1–45 (2004). http://desrist.org/design-research-in-information-systems
10. Hevner, A.R.: A three cycle view of design science research. Scand. J. Inf. Syst. **19**, 87–92 (2007)
11. Peffers, K., Tuunanen, T., Rothenberger, M.A., Chatterjee, S.: A design science research methodology for information systems research. J. Manag. Inf. Syst. **24**, 45–77 (2007)
12. Sonnenberg, C., vom Brocke, J.: Evaluations in the science of the artificial – reconsidering the build-evaluate pattern in design science research. In: Peffers, K., Rothenberger, M., Kuechler, B. (eds.) DESRIST 2012. LNCS, vol. 7286, pp. 381–397. Springer, Heidelberg (2012). doi:10.1007/978-3-642-29863-9_28
13. Braunnagel, D., Leist, S.: Applying evaluations while building the artifact - experiences from the development of process model complexity metrics. In: 49th Hawaii International Conference on System Sciences (HICSS), pp. 4424–4433. IEEE (2016)
14. Abraham, R., Aier, S., Winter, R.: Fail early, fail often: towards coherent feedback loops in design science research evaluation. In: 2014 International Conference on Information Systems (ICIS), pp. 1–12. Association for Information Systems (2014)
15. Uppström, E.: Re-visiting IS design science artifacts: making a case for critical realism. In: 50th Hawaii International Conference on System Sciences (HICSS), pp. 4675–4684. IEEE (2017)
16. Aier, S., Fischer, C.: Criteria of progress for information systems design theories. Inf. Syst. e-Bus. Manag. **9**, 133–172 (2011)
17. Kuhn, T.S.: The Essential Tension: Selected Studies in Scientific Tradition and Change. University of Chicago Press, Chicago (1977)
18. Gregor, S.: The nature of theory in information systems. MIS Q. **30**, 611–642 (2006)
19. Sangupamba Mwilu, O., Comyn-Wattiau, I., Prat, N.: Design science research contribution to business intelligence in the cloud—a systematic literature review. Future Gener. Comput. Syst. **63**, 108–122 (2016)
20. Parsons, J., Wand, Y.: Emancipating instances from the tyranny of classes in information modeling. ACM Trans. Database Syst. **25**, 228–268 (2000)
21. Bouquet, P., Giunchiglia, F., van Harmelen, F., Serafini, L., Stuckenschmidt, H.: C-OWL: Contextualizing Ontologies. In: Fensel, D., Sycara, K., Mylopoulos, J. (eds.) ISWC 2003. LNCS, vol. 2870, pp. 164–179. Springer, Heidelberg (2003). doi:10.1007/978-3-540-39718-2_11
22. Pérez, A.G., Gargantilla, J.Á.R.: Semantic mappings: out of ontology world limits. In: International Conference on Complex, Intelligent and Software Intensive Systems (CISIS), pp. 907–912. IEEE (2008)
23. Choi, N., Song, I.-Y., Han, H.: A survey on ontology mapping. SIGMOD Rec. **35**, 34–41 (2006)
24. Noy, N.F.: Semantic integration: a survey of ontology-based approaches. SIGMOD Rec. **33**, 65–70 (2004)
25. Pottinger, R.: Mapping-based merging of schemas. In: Bellahsene, Z., Bonifati, A., Rahm, E. (eds.) Schema Matching and Mapping, pp. 223–249. Springer, Berlin (2011)
26. Weber, R.: Theory building in the information systems discipline: some critical reflections. In: Gregor, S.D., Hart, D.N. (eds.) Information Systems Foundations: Theory Building in Information Systems, pp. 1–20. Australian National University, Canberra (2012)
27. Arnott, D.: Cognitive biases and decision support systems development: a design science approach. Inf. Syst. J. **16**, 55–78 (2006)

28. Adomavicius, G., Tuzhilin, A., Zheng, R.: REQUEST: a query language for customizing recommendations. Inf. Syst. Res. **22**, 99–117 (2011)
29. Nickerson, R.C., Varshney, U., Muntermann, J.: A method for taxonomy development and its application in information systems. Eur. J. Inf. Syst. **22**, 336–359 (2013)
30. Arazy, O., Kumar, N., Shapira, B.: A theory-driven design framework for social recommender systems. J. Assoc. Inf. Syst. **11**, 455–490 (2010)
31. Walls, J.G., Widmeyer, G.R., El Sawy, O.A.: Building an information system design theory for vigilant EIS. Inf. Syst. Res. **3**, 36–59 (1992)

A Framework for Identifying Design Science Research Objectives for Building and Evaluating IT Artifacts

Sarah Alismail$^{(\boxtimes)}$, Hengwei Zhang, and Samir Chatterjee

Claremont Graduate University, Claremont, CA 91711, USA
{Sarah.alismail,hengwei.zhang,
samir.chatterjee}@cgu.edu

Abstract. Even though many types of Design Science Research (DSR) frameworks and methods exist, little effort has been made to examine and little attention has been paid to investigate objectives identification in DSR. We believe that it is worthwhile to draw attention to the role that DSR objectives play in building and evaluating designed artifacts. Thus, this study developed a framework to answer two research questions: (1) What kinds of objective dimensions can be identified and used for different information technology (IT) artifacts? (2) How can these objectives be linked to the process of building and evaluating IT artifacts? The framework was demonstrated and evaluated by a case study and expert interviews. Our aim was to assist current and future Design Science researchers in the information systems (IS) discipline in identifying research/project objectives.

Keywords: Design science · Framework · IT artifacts · Objectives

1 Introduction

The intention of Design Science Research (DSR) in information systems (IS) is to build/design artifacts to solve real, and practical problems. Since DSR was introduced to the IS community in the early 1990s, great effort has been invested in validating and legitimizing Design Science (DS) as an IS research paradigm. Several researchers have proposed valuable frameworks and methods for DSR.

Many methods for DSR exist [1, 2]; however, the authors in [3], have explicitly emphasized the "objectives" as one element in the DSR process. In addition, based on our knowledge only [4–6] have explicitly included transforming problems into system objectives (meta-requirements/requirements), which is similar to Peffers et al.'s [3] notion of objectives. However, little effort has been made to examine and little attention has been paid to investigate the role of objectives in DSR. Thus, we believe that it is worthwhile to study the role of objectives in building and evaluating designed information technology (IT) artifacts. It is important to note that objectives are different from goals. Even though both terms are purpose-oriented and ideally consist of clearly-defined terminologies, [7] stated that a "Project goal provides the rationale

© Springer International Publishing AG 2017
A. Maedche et al. (Eds.): DESRIST 2017, LNCS 10243, pp. 218–230, 2017.
DOI: 10.1007/978-3-319-59144-5_13

behind the project and describes its long-term objective" (p. 26), so a set of objectives are specific statements within a general goal [8].

This paper aims to present a new framework for DSR objectives that embodies our insights and understanding of how to clearly identify the objectives for a DS research/ project. Therefore, this research seeks to answer the following questions: What kinds of objective dimensions can be identified and used for different IT artifacts? How can these objectives be linked to the process of building and evaluating IT artifacts?

The paper is structured as follows. The first section describes the problem. In the next section, the objectives of a solution to satisfy the research question and, ultimately, solve the identified problem are defined. Then, the design and descriptions of the proposed artifact are provided. A use case is, then, presented to demonstrate the application of the proposed framework. Finally, we conclude by providing a summary of the findings and a discussion of the work, including the limitation of the current work and recommendations for future work.

2   Problem Identification

It is commonly accepted that artifacts should be at the core of IS research, and the core of DSR is building and evaluating novel artifacts to solve an interesting real-world problem. A problem can be expressed as the outcome of the differences between "a goal state" and the actual system state [1]. Moreover, [4] pointed out that goal orientation is a core element of a design theory.

Simon [9] defined an objective of design activity as providing the description of an artifact, taking into consideration both the artifact's organization and its functions. The purpose and the scope of the designed/developed artifact should be specified in the problem definition and research objectives. Peffers et al. [3] defined the activity of defining the objectives for a solution as inferring "the objectives of a solution from the problem definition and knowledge of what is possible and feasible…the objectives should be inferred rationally from the problem specification" (p. 55). In this paper, we use the word "objectives" to refer to the specification of what should be accomplished in terms of the requirements or properties of an artifact that are needed to ultimately satisfy the problem.

Researchers need to define and identify suitable and relevant objectives in terms of a problem's characteristics and its context. According to [10], the definitions of the problem and the objectives are used to indicate the goal and scope of the developed/ designed artifact in DSR [10]. According to [11], this activity assists in the process of outlining the IT artifact in order to address the "explicated problem and to elicit requirements on that artefact" (p. 103) [11]. It seeks to identify what type of artifact can be selected for solving a real-world problem. As noted in the methodology proposed in [3], the designed IT artifacts are built and evaluated based on the identified objectives. More specifically, at the minimum, part of the evaluation activity helps determine whether or not the IT artifacts meet the objectives, which is a process that has been neglected by some researchers.

Although several attempts have been made to provide guidelines and frameworks for DSR activities, there is no comprehensive guideline for identifying DSR objectives to assist DS researchers in building and evaluating IT artifacts. In DSR, the objectives are presented in a fragmented, ambiguous and/or incomplete manner, which might be the reason why the evaluation of IT artifacts is inefficient and insufficient.

3 Defining the Objectives of the Solution

This paper aims to design a framework for identifying research/project objectives in DSR. Therefore, the proposed framework seeks to meet the following objectives: (1) be consistent with the findings reported in previous DS literature; (2) determine the key dimensions for identifying DSR objectives; and (3) provide general guidelines that DSR researchers/practitioners can use to build and evaluate IT artifacts.

3.1 Consistent with Existing Research

In essence, the method for developing a framework for objectives that is presented in this paper is, itself, a DSR approach. Our proposed framework should be consistent with the existing literature.

3.2 Key Dimensions for Identifying the DSR Objectives

The second objective of the proposed framework is to describe and identify which dimensions should be considered in order to identify DSR objectives for the purpose of solving a real-world problem. Moreover, identifying the key dimensions might assist researchers/practitioners in prioritizing and elaborating upon their DSR objectives.

3.3 General Guidelines for DSR Researchers for the Two Most Important DSR Activities

The last objective is to provide a tool to assist DSR researchers/practitioners in the process of designing, building, and evaluating proposed artifacts to solve a real-practical problem in terms of identifying the objectives. This may allow us to understand how to bridge the gap that exists in current studies regarding identifying objectives in DS research/projects.

4 Design: Development of the Framework

Setting and identifying objectives could be seen as a way to create a bridge between defining problem statements and designing and evaluating artifacts. Identifying the objectives for solutions has the ability to transform a problem into requirements for the proposed artifact in order to guide researchers/practitioners in addressing and examining the problem. More specifically, after a problem has been defined, the goal and purpose can be set, and then the objectives can be defined to assist researchers/ practitioners in the process of building, designing, and evaluating an artifact that satisfies the requirements (objectives). In other words, satisfying the objectives will lead to accomplishing the desired goal, and, ultimately, to solving the identified problem.

Figure 1 describes where the objectives fit within the scope of two major DSR activities. It is important to note that there is a debate regarding the structure of the problem, in which [12] noted that Simon indicated that certain problems "may be ill-structured and not immediately solvable" (p. 35). Therefore, the scope of our study is limited to cases in which the problem is well-structured. In addition, in any DS research/project, the problem should be important and relevant [13].

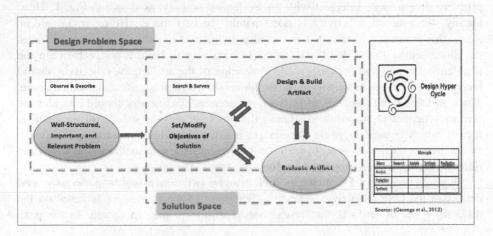

Fig. 1. Link between the objectives and two major DSR activities

We believe that the problem is the consequence of what we observe from the real-world that we inhabit, and due to the limitation of the scope, it is possible to describe the problem. Afterwards, the process of searching and surveying can occur, and this assists in uncovering the requirements. It also indicates that a DSR research/ project is always conducted using an iterative approach, moving back and forth between several DSR activities. Thus, the objectives could be changeable since the design and evaluation process could be iterative.

In addition, the design and evaluation activities involve the hyper-cycle and micro-cycle proposed by [14]. According to [14], a combination of the "macro model (analysis, projection, synthesis)" and "the learning phases in the micro model (research, analysis, synthesis, realization)" (p. 94) is used to design the hyper-cycle. Moreover, [14] stated that "for each phase of the macro cycle (analysis, projection, and synthesis), four steps are undertaken in the micro-cycle (research, analysis, synthesis, and realization)" (p. 96).

We can view the design process as a series functioning steps within two overlapping spaces (design problem space and solution space) as shown in Fig. 1. It is important to highlight that the objectives of the solutions play a significant role in both spaces. For the purpose of the present article, we define the two spaces as follows:

- *Design Problem Space*: The collection of the problem representations, rules, associated solution requirements, and mapping between the attributes and the artifacts. In this paper, we adopt the approach recommended by [6] of combining problem space and design space.
- *Solution Space*: The design artifact moves from the solution requirements to real-world applications.

One remarkable aspect of Fig. 1 is the artifact evaluation, which, ideally, would be conducted not only within the problem design space, but also after the artifact has been deployed in the real-world (solution space). For that reason, the boundaries of the problem design space intersect with the evaluation activity, as shown in Fig. 1. Thus, ideally, the evaluation activity is done within the two spaces. However, in seldom cases, this evaluation cannot be conducted as in the case of radical innovation artifacts.

Since setting the DSR objectives could be a way to build a bridge between the problem statement and the design and evaluation of the artifact, the objectives should have some properties to transform the problem into a design specification and outcome. Thus, in identifying the DSR objectives, researchers/practitioners should consider the artifact type that is proposed to address the problem, and the success of the requirements, which is used to guide the design, build, and evaluate the artifact. Also, the researchers/practitioners need to identify the logical reasoning method(s) in which the rational and systematic steps are applied throughout the process.

Figure 2 presents a 5 * 3 table, which includes two dimensions, and the associated details of the DSR objectives. The first dimension of the framework is based on the different types of artifacts that researchers/practitioners plan to design. In the past,

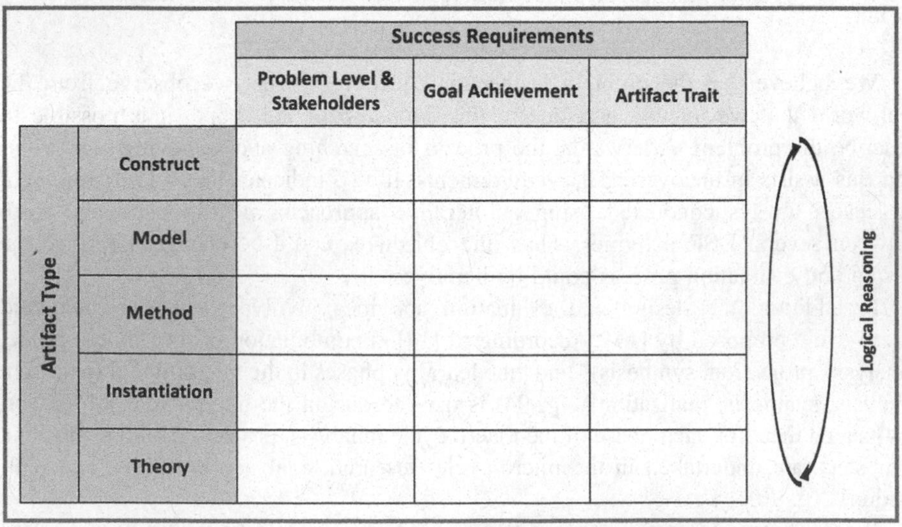

		Success Requirements		
		Problem Level & Stakeholders	Goal Achievement	Artifact Trait
Artifact Type	Construct			
	Model			
	Method			
	Instantiation			
	Theory			

Logical Reasoning

Fig. 2. Dimensions of the DSR objectives

numerous DSR artifact classifications have been proposed. This paper follows the widely-recognized classification contributed by [13, 15], including constructs/concepts, models, methods, and instantiations. Afterwards, [10] added design theories as a fifth "upper-level" form of an artifact.

These dimensions are defined as follows:

- *Construct*: provides a conceptual vocabulary and syntax for a domain to describe the problem and/or solution (e.g., classification systems, language standards, or ontologies).
- *Model*: a set of propositions or statements that can be explicated and that can describe the relationships between the constructs (e.g., mental model or reference model).
- *Method*: a set of steps or a process used to solve a specific problem or classes of problems (e.g., DSR method for conducting DS research, algorithms).
- *Instantiation*: the concrete realizations and operationalization of the constructs, models, or methods.
- *Theories*: there is no universal agreed upon definition of theory. However, [16] defined theories as a set of "statements of relationships among constructs… that aims to describe, explain, enhance understanding of the world and, in some cases, to provide predictions" regarding the future (pp. 613, 616).

The success of the requirement dimension includes three sub-dimensions, which present the different perspectives needed to generate desirable outcomes:

- Problem Level and Stakeholders: DSR aims to solve a real-world problem; as such, it may focus on the technical, organizational, and/or strategic level [17]. In addition, DSR also aims to improve human well-being. Researchers also need to identify the potential stakeholders of the designed solution. Habermas [18] indicated that the failure of considering and including potential stakeholders in design science research/project leads to a mismatch between the artifact under development and the potential stakeholders' perceptions. The perceptions, to some extent, encompass a research direction's viability of the design problem space. In this paper, we ignore potential disagreement in the perceptions of multiple stakeholders. This sub-dimension can influence a researcher's selection of different criteria, and this can have a direct impact on the evaluation activity.
- Goal Achievement: this indicates the degree to which the artifact accomplishes its goal, including, but not limited to, efficiency, effectiveness, and validity.
    - Efficiency: the degree to which an artifact effectively generates the desired effect without wasting resources (e.g., achieving the goal) [11].
    - Effectiveness: the degree to which an artifact generates the desired effect in practice [11].
    - Validity: the artifact works or functions as it is supposed to [10].
- Artifact trait: the artifact needs to have utility, be novel, and be feasible in order to contribute to the problem environment and knowledge base.
    - Utility: under the usefulness model, this indicates the degree to which the artifact is useful in measuring the quality of its application in practice [19]. On the other

hand, [6] defined utility as "the choice mechanisms guiding artifact design" (p. 18) in the fitness-utility model (more information will be presented later in the paper).

– Novelty: describes the degree to which the artifact is novel, i.e., whether it is an improvement or if it is totally brand new.
– Feasibility: describes whether an artifact will work in a consistent manner.

Logical reasoning method refers to the different types of logic that researchers/practitioners plan to deploy to guide the design and development of the artifact. The objectives represent their vision on how addressing the problem from one or more perspectives in an existing situation could lead to the realization of the desired, satisfied outcome. Thus, for each outlined artifact, researchers/practitioners need to identify one form of logical reasoning, or a combination of forms, to solve the problem. However, some situations require one form of reasoning more than another (further explanations provided below). Three approaches are discussed by [20–22]:

• Deductive: This scientific method is more appropriate in situations where certain aspects of an artifact are needed to be evaluated by logical reasoning in which prior knowledge is used to build/design and evaluate the artifact. The main function here is *to state what should be* [22].
• Inductive: A researcher proposes a specific solution to solve a real-world problem, and then generalizes it into a general solution. The main function here is *to states from what is* [20, 22].
• Abductive: Through the abductive process, creativity plays a significant role in the building and, perhaps, in the evaluation process in which suggestions for a solution to a real-world problem are drawn from the previous knowledge/theory "to propose robust solutions that can be used to improve the current situation by solving the problem under study" (p. 121) [22, 23]. "It is the only scientific method that enables the introduction of a new idea" (p. 61). It is the process of generating explanatory hypotheses for a certain phenomenon in which the main function is *to states from what is*. It is important to note that if abduction method is used this does not mean that other scientific methods are not used. Yet, this method is more suitable and appropriate in situations where activities and creative reasoning is needed [22].

As seen in Fig. 3, attention needs to be drawn to the artifact trait sub-dimension in the Success Requirement dimension. There are two evaluation models: usefulness model and fitness-utility model in which the word "utility" has different meaning. Figure 3 presents how the "utility" varies within the two approaches.

The two evaluation models are complementary [6]. Therefore, the assessment of the elements in the artifact trait varies in the two models. To illustrate the differences, the elements are demonstrated individually in the usefulness model. On the other hand, a broader scope of elements will be considered as a set of variables involved in the fitness-utility model. The usefulness model emphasizes the usefulness of the artifact, in which "utility" typically refers to usefulness, while the fitness-utility model focuses on improving the estimate of the artifact fitness. In the fitness-utility model, "utility" has a broader scope, and, according to [6], it is used as a utility function in which "it serves

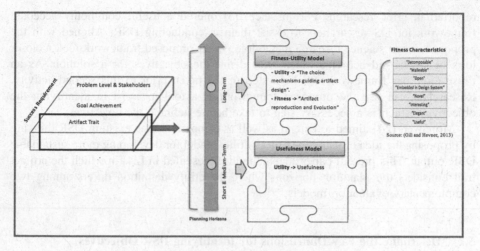

Fig. 3. Utility function in two complementary DSR evaluation models

as the basis of ranking decision alternatives" (p. 2). The characteristics are not limited to feasibility, utility, and novelty; rather, they can also include other artifact characteristics that impact the goal achievement.

Gill and Hevner [24] summarized the differences between the two models in "A Fitness-Utility Model for Design Science Research." The planning horizons is one distinct characteristic that we would like to highlight. That is, if the researchers/ practitioners are focusing on short-term and medium-term planning horizons, then they will be employing the usefulness evaluation model. On the other hand, the fitness-utility model is more compatible if they are focusing on a long-term planning horizons. The eight exploratory characteristics of fitness proposed by [6] contribute to aiding the sustainable development of designs over time. For instance, if the problem to be addressed has a several interrelated attributes that leads "to a larger possible solution space with many local peaks" (p. 2) [25], researchers and practitioners should consider adopting the "utility" meaning under the fitness-utility evaluation model.

5 Evaluation

We demonstrate and evaluate the proposed framework by a case study and expert interviews. The socio-technical evaluation was used to determine the designed framework's value with evidence of its utility to estimate the fitness.

Following the authors in [3], the proposed framework will be evaluated against the pre-identified objectives as follows:

5.1 Consistent with Prior DS Research

First, based on the existing literature, the developed framework for identifying DSR objectives for building and evaluating IT artifacts is consistent with the findings reported in prior research. For instance, [3] offered a useful commonly accepted framework for DS researchers to assist them in conducting DSR. Aligned with the proposed design science research methodology, our proposed framework took a closer look at the second activity, which is to define the objectives for a solution. As an illustration, our framework can be a step that is taken prior to this second activity. Researchers can use the proposed framework as a tool to assist in identifying the objectives, which is a necessary step to take before defining the objectives.

Moreover, [24] aimed to extend as well as complement the existing DSR thinking by proposing the idea of using the fitness-utility model for developing more sustainable DSR output. This present paper adapts the idea presented in [24] in which the artifact trait considers the planning horizons where the utility definition differs among two complementary evaluation models.

5.2   Determine the Key Dimensions for Identifying DSR Objectives

The proposed framework satisfies the second objective, which is to determine the key dimensions used to identify the DSR objectives. These dimensions, the artifact type, and successful requirements including three sub-dimensions (problem level, goal achievement, and artifact trait), were evaluated through expert interviews.

We obtained DSR experts' opinions about our framework in terms of its value and utility. We used the experts' feedback to generate ideas for improving and enhancing the proposed framework, and to suggest ideas for future work. We used purposeful sampling to select five recognized DSR experts. Moreover, as a data collection technique, we conducted 20-to-30-min qualitative semi-structured interviews, either via telephone or face-to-face. Follow-up emails were also used as a secondary data source. Appendix A contains a list of the pre-formulated questions used in the interviews.

In an iterative manner, we sought to improve the framework based on the experts' opinions and feedback. In the initial version of the framework, Hevner [26] indicated that the representation of the framework dimensions was confusing. Hence, we transformed the dimensions' representation into a 5 * 3 table, as shown in Fig. 2. Afterwards, we incorporated the fitness-utility model with the usefulness model to define "utility" based on the planning horizons. In a personal communication, Gregor [27] expressed her approval and mentioned "that is a good idea having both the long-term and short-term" planning horizons. Hevner [26] agreed with the update, and indicated that we are on "the right track to an interesting research contribution."

The definitions of the terms in the framework underwent several revisions. For instance, we renamed "Logical Reasoning" based on Gregor's [27] inquires. Moreover, in a personal communication, Vaishnavi [28] indicated that our definitions for deductive, inductive, and abductive were too narrow. Thus, we provided a broader definition of each form of reasoning.

Overall, the result of the evaluation indicated that we addressed an interesting gap, consistent with Henver's [26] vision of the problem space. As Henver [26] noted, there is a "need to understand what you are solving, how are you measuring it, and evaluating these ideas of goodness." Moreover, Vaishnavi [28] recommend that the nature of the problem and the contribution are linked to the state-of-the-art in the problem area.

5.3   General Guidelines for DSR Researchers in the Two DSR Major Activities

In order to meet the third objective, providing general guidelines for DSR researchers/ practitioners in the building and evaluating IT artifacts, a use case was employed to demonstrate how to use the proposed framework. We applied the framework retroactively to a published IS DS research/project. We showed the process of how the case identifies its solution objectives, and the relationship between the solution objectives and other DSR major activities.

Use Case: Extending the Enterprise Evolution Contextualization Model.

Problem Identification and Motivation. de Vries et al. [29] say that a number of studies have evaluated different kinds of approaches, such as incorporating various subsystems and aspects of the enterprise and aligning the enterprise system and the environment system, but the predominant research limit is that this fragmentation only aligns enterprise design within the business-IT scope. Thus, there is a need for a comprehensive view of the enterprise from different approaches.

Objective of the Solution. In this case, the authors present a clear statement regarding the DSR objectives:

1. To provide the setting in terms of a descriptive model to serve as a common reference model to fully understand and encapsulate the Enterprise Engineering (EE) knowledge base;
2. To contextualize a broader set of enterprise design/alignment/governance approaches; and
3. To enable an EE/ Enterprise Architect (EA) practitioner to describe, understand, and compare different enterprise design/alignment/governance approaches used to evolve/change the enterprise.

The objectives presented above can be mapped into our framework as shown below (Table 1):

Table 1. Dimensions of objectives

Artifact Type	Success Requirements			
	Problem Level/ Stakeholders	Goal Achievement	Artifact Trait	
Model (reference model)	Organizational / practitioners	Extend existing scope; Help describe, understand, and compare different approaches	Improvement solutions; Utility	Inductive Reasoning

Demonstration and Discussion. The problem presented and addressed in this case was the lack of a comprehensive view from different approach to understand enterprise design. Despite the fact that enterprise engineering is an emerging discipline, some good models already exist but with some drawbacks and limitations. By digging into the problem, the authors outline the solution. The possible approaches included solving this problem by extending the existing scope and aligning the enterprise with a subsystem other than the business-IT scope, which indicated that it was necessary to establish a relationship between different views. In addition, to assess their project's success it was necessary to evaluate the design product to determine if it could help practitioners better understand, describe, and compare the different views. In other words, the design artifact emphasized the "long-term usefulness". Since the model represented the "sets of propositions or statements expressing relationships between constructs" [22], it was assumed to be a good candidate. Meanwhile, the problem and project goals were reached as a consensus, which meant that we started from the local problem.

Following this idea, the researchers launched their design and development journey. They started developing the artifact inductively by extending an existing business-IT alignment model (BIAM). The result of the design effort was a model that can be used to contextualize existing enterprise design/alignment/governance approaches, called EECM version 1.

Once the EECM version 1 was developed, the researchers started a thorough evaluation process. The EECM version 1 was evaluated against its objectives by using a participative approach, where 38 mentored research participants were interviewed to contextualize the existing seven approaches with the proposed model. The result of the evaluation indicated that the proposed design model (EECM version 1) did not satisfy the objectives. Thus, the researchers refined the problem scope, re-identified the objectives by limiting scope to "developing guiding indicators/prerequisites", redesigned their artifacts, and developed EECM version 2. Demonstration and elaboration were adopted as the evaluation method, which was built on the basis of previous results and by focusing, especially, on the parts that were modified. The evaluation result showed that EECM version 2 was as useful to the practitioner as the proposed design model was expected to be. It is important to note that the EECM was proposed to fit into a long-term timeframe and its evaluation should be aimed at improving the model's ability to estimate artifact fitness, which refers to the fitness-utility model.

From this case, our proposed model (DSR Objectives framework) could identify the objectives dimensions in a design science research/project, which successfully facilitates the process of building and evaluating artifacts.

6 Discussion and Conclusion

This paper presents a novel artifact framework, since there is no pre-existing framework for identifying objectives in DSR. Although [3] explicitly highlighted the need to define the objectives for a solution as an activity in the DSRM, there are no comprehensive guidelines for identifying DS research/project objectives. Therefore, we believe that taking a closer look at the role of objectives and proposing a framework to identify DSR objectives in the process of building and evaluating designed artifacts will assist DS researchers/practitioners. This paper identified two essential dimensions for identifying DSR objectives, including artifact type, and success requirements, with three sub-dimensions (problem level and stakeholders, goal achievement, and artifact trait), which should be considered in the process of identifying the objectives. Yet, for each outlined artifact, researchers/practitioners need to identify one form of logical reasoning, or a combination of forms, to guide the design and development of the artifact. Additionally, the "utility" definition in the artifact trait differs based on the planning horizons.

Several of the interviewed experts indicated the need to apply the proposed framework to a couple of real-life examples to see if they fit. As a utility demonstration, we applied one study to our framework as discussed above. We believe that there is still space for improvements in coming up with criteria that assist and enable design science researcher/practitioners in differentiating between short/medium planning horizons and the long-term ones.

The proposed framework was tested against one use case, and the experts' evaluations were obtained. However, to overcome this limitation, future research is needed to extend the number of cases with the assistance of empirical studies that use the proposed framework to identify objectives and to assist in further evaluating the utility and effectiveness of the framework.

Acknowledgments. We wish to thank all the experts who participated in the evaluation process. We would like to express our gratitude to Alan Hevner, Shirley Gregor, Vijay K. Vaishnavi, and Mia Plachkinova for the time and effort they spent on evaluating the proposed framework.

Appendix A: Semi-structured Interview Questions

- Is the proposed framework clear and easy to understand?
- Is the proposed framework unnecessarily complex?
- What changes to the proposed artifact would you recommend?
  - How can we improve the proposed framework?
- Did we miss any dimensions or are there some dimensions that we did not take into consideration?
- Based on your experience and knowledge, what fallacies, consistencies, and inconsistencies appear?

References

1. Hevner, A., Chatterjee, S.: Design Research in Information Systems: Theory and Practice, vol. 22. Springer Science & Business Media, Berlin (2010)
2. Vaishnavi, V., Kuechler, W.: Design Science Research Methods and Patterns: Innovating Information and Communication Technology. Auerbach, New York (2008)
3. Peffers, K., Tuunanen, T., Rothenberger, M.A., Chatterjee, S.: A design science research methodology for information systems research. J. Manag. Inf. Syst. 24(3), 45–77 (2007)
4. Walls, J., Widmeyer, G., El Sawy, O.: Building an information system design theory for vigilant EIS. Inf. Syst. Res. 3(1), 36–59 (1992)
5. Eekels, J., Roozenburg, N.F.M.: A methodological comparison of the structures of scientific research and engineering design: their similarities and differences. Des. Stud. 12(4), 197–203 (1991)

6. Gill, T.G., Hevner, A.R.: A fitness-utility model for design science research. ACM Trans. Manag. Inf. Syst. **4**(2), 1–24 (2013). doi:10.1145/2499962.2499963
7. Baccarini, D.: The logical framework method for defining project success. Proj. Manag. J. **30** (4), 25–32 (1999)
8. Rouillard, L.: Goals and Goal Setting: Achieving Measured Objectives. Cengage Learning, Boston (2003)
9. Simon, H.A.: The Sciences of the Artificial, 3rd edn. MIT Press, Cambridge (1996)
10. Gregor, S., Hevner, A.R.: Positioning and presenting design science research for maximum impact. MIS Q. **37**(2), 337–355 (2013)
11. Johannesson, P., Perjons, E.: An Introduction to Design Science. Springer, Berlin (2014)
12. Huppatz, D.J.: Revisiting Herbert Simon's "science of design". Des. Issues **31**(2), 29–40 (2015)
13. Hevner, A.R., March, S.T., Park, J., Ram, S.: Design science in information systems research. MIS Q. **28**(1), 75–105 (2004)
14. Gacenga, F., Cater-Steel, A., Toleman, M., Tan, W.G.: A proposal and evaluation of a design method in design science research. Electron. J. Bus. Res. Methods **10**(2), 89–100 (2012)
15. March, S.T., Smith, G.F.: Design and natural science research on information technology. Decis. Support Syst. **15**(4), 251–266 (1995)
16. Gregor, S.: The nature of theory in information systems. MIS Q. **30**(3), 611–642 (2006)
17. Österle, H., Winter, R.: Business Engineering. In: Österle, H., Winter, R. (eds.) Business Engineering - Auf dem Weg zum Unternehmen des Informationszeitalters, pp. 4–20. Springer, Berlin (2003)
18. Habermas, J.: Moral Consciousness and Communicative Action. MIT Press, Cambridge (1990)
19. Prat, N., Comyn-Wattiau, I., Akoka, J.: Artifact evaluation in information systems design-science research-a holistic view. In: PACIS, p. 23, June 2014
20. Fischer, C., Gregor, S.: Forms of reasoning in the design science research process. In: Jain, H., Sinha, A.P., Vitharana, P. (eds.) DESRIST 2011. LNCS, vol. 6629, pp. 17–31. Springer, Heidelberg (2011). doi:10.1007/978-3-642-20633-7_2
21. Iivari, J.: Distinguishing and contrasting two strategies for design science research. Eur. J. Inf. Syst. **24**(1), 107–115 (2015)
22. Dresch, A., Lacerda, D.P., Antunes Jr., J.A.V.: Proposal for the conduct of design science research. In: Dresch, A., Lacerda, D.P., Antunes Jr., J.A.V. (eds.) Design Science Research, pp. 117–127. Springer, Cham (2015)
23. Vaishnavi, V., Kuechler, W.: Design Science Research in Information Systems, 20 January 2004. http://www.desrist.org/design-research-in-information-systems/. Accessed 15 Nov 2015
24. Gill, T.G., Hevner, A.R.: A fitness-utility model for design science research. In: Jain, H., Sinha, A.P., Vitharana, P. (eds.) DESRIST 2011. LNCS, vol. 6629, pp. 237–252. Springer, Heidelberg (2011). doi:10.1007/978-3-642-20633-7_17
25. Gill, T.G., Murphy, W.: Task complexity and design science. In: 9th International Conference on Education and Information Systems, Technologies and Applications (2011)
26. Hevner, A.: Personal Interview, 18 November 2016
27. Gregor, S.: Personal Interview, 30 November 2016
28. Vaishnavi, V.: Personal Interview, 8 December 2016
29. de Vries, M., van der Merwe, A., Gerber, A.: Extending the enterprise evolution contextualisation model. Enterp. Inf. Syst. 1–41 (2015)

Strategic Reading in Design Science: Let Root-Cause Analysis Guide Your Readings

Oscar Díaz[1], Jeremías P. Contell[1(✉)], and John R. Venable[2]

[1] ONEKIN Web Engineering Group,
University of the Basque Country (UPV/EHU), San Sebastián, Spain
{oscar.diaz,jeremias.perez}@ehu.eus
[2] School of Information Systems, Curtin University,
Perth, Western Australia, Australia
j.venable@curtin.edu.au

Abstract. Reading literature is important, but problematic. In Quora and other PhD forums, students moan about their frustrating reading and literature review experiences. Strategic reading might help. This term is coined to conceive of reading as a process of constructing meaning by interacting with text in a targeted way. The fact that strategic reading is purpose-driven suggests that the purpose might qualify the reading. If this purpose is Design Science Research (DSR), what would be the strategy for reading? Traditionally, students are encouraged to annotate while reading. Digital annotations are expected to be useful for supporting comprehension and interpretation. Our belief is that strategic reading can be more effective if annotation is conducted in direct relationship to a main DS activity: root-cause analysis (RCA). RCA can provide the questions whose answers should be sought in the literature. Unfortunately, this process is not supported by current tools. When reading papers, researchers might not be all aware of the issues being raised during RCA. And the other way around, when it comes to RCA, evidences found in the literature might not be promptly accessible. This paper reports on research to develop a technical solution to this problem: a plug-in for Google Chrome that provides seamless integration between the RCA platform (i.e. MindMeister) and the reading platforms (i.e. Mendeley). The aim: improving RCA awareness while reading so that annotations can be traced back to the RCA issues. First evaluations are positive as for improving reading focus and facilitating reference recoverability.

Keywords: Strategic reading · Root cause analysis · Mind mapping

1 Introduction

"Strategic reading" is a term coined to conceive reading as a process of constructing meaning by interacting with text [1]. While reading, individuals use their prior knowledge along with clues from the text to construct meaning, and place the new knowledge within this frame. Research indicates that effective or expert readers are strategic [2]. This means that they have purposes for their reading and adjust their reading to each purpose and for each reading task. The fact that strategic reading is purpose-driven suggests that the purpose might qualify the reading. If this purpose is

© Springer International Publishing AG 2017
A. Maedche et al. (Eds.): DESRIST 2017, LNCS 10243, pp. 231–246, 2017.
DOI: 10.1007/978-3-319-59144-5_14

Design Science Research (DSR), different questions arise: is there a DSR way of reading, are DSR researchers following it, how could DSR researchers be assisted to excel at strategic reading?

DSR has been defined as "research that invents a new purposeful artefact to address a generalised type of problem and evaluates its utility for solving problems of that type" [3]. Being problem-driven, DSR endows a preponderant role to root-cause analysis (RCA). DSR requires a profound understanding of the problem to be solved, the consequences to be alleviated, and the causes to be prevented. This in turn usually implies extracting evidence from the literature that warrants the project's RCA. We can then rephrase a key part of *strategic reading (in DSR) as the process of extracting evidence from the literature that sustains the project's RCA*. If a pivotal skill for researchers is that of asking the right questions then, we can conjecture that RCA could be the means to find these questions. We then conceive of RCA and reading as two inter-related processes which re-adjust and feed off each other: RCA progresses as new insights are obtained from the literature while the literature is scrutinised along the concerns that arise during RCA. This is not very far from linguistic theory, where writing and reading are regarded as partners in constructing meaning [4]. Here, we do not address writing but RCA can be regarded as the prelude to writing.

Unfortunately, this interdependency lacks appropriate support in current reading tools (e.g. Acrobat Reader) or reference managers (e.g. Mendeley, NVivo, or End-Note). What is needed is a way to bridge the gap between conceptualizing tools – where ideas are shaped and framed–, and reading tools –where ideas are sustained and opposed. We believe the challenge is not on leveraging existing tools, but on coupling tools with minimal interference with existing practices. What is needed is for tools to keep their autonomy, but interact with a double aim: (1) to guide reading (where reading purposes are to be sought in RCA), and (2), to draw on and document supporting evidence for RCA issues (where evidences are obtained from reading but used during RCA). These two flows are in overlapping motion: RCA concerns guide the reading while the reading comes up with new insights that confirm or refute the RCA issues. This work then addresses the following problem-based research question.

How can we provide seamless integration between RCA tools and reading tools to improve strategic reading for novice DSR researchers?

If DSR is defined as "research that invents a new purposeful artefact" [3], this work resorts to a Chrome plug-in, DScaffolding, which bridges the gap between MindMeister (as the RCA tool) and Mendeley (as the reference manager). During reading, DScaffolding makes practitioners aware of the evidences being looked for ("the purpose pipe"). During RCA, DScaffolding makes researchers aware of the evidences that sustain/refute the causes/consequences in the RCA ("the annotation pipe"). DScaffolding is available for download at the Chrome Web Store (see later). Evaluation is being conducted with five PhD students.

2 Literature Review

2.1 Problem: Causes and Consequences

One of the most important skills for researchers to acquire is that of asking the right questions when accessing the literature [5]. The answers you get much depend on the questions you ask. This skill is especially important for PhD students, who struggle with an increasing number of papers and stringent PhD deadlines. Based on Mendeley data from 2008, PhD students were the main readers of articles [6]. This puts PhD students at the forefront of scientific literature consumption, even ahead of their supervisors! However, in Quora and other PhD forums, it is not rare to come across students moaning about their frustrating reading experiences (refer to [7] and its 54 comments). Causes can be multi-fold: lack of time (with increasing reading loads), lack of motivation (no prompt feedback from supervisors), reading considered to be an ancillary activity (as opposed to actually conducting the research), or lack of knowledge (not clear what to look for). If we focus on the latter, forums give some advice:

- "Before you start reading, have a clear idea of what information you are looking for in these papers. This by itself is about 60% of psyching yourself up for reading papers" [8].
- "Make notes of how the research in the paper you're reading connects with your own" [9].
- "Reading a scientific paper should not be done in a linear way (from beginning to end); instead, it should be done strategically and with a critical mindset, questioning your understanding and the findings" [10].
- "As you read, look for the author's main points. Generate questions before, during, and after reading. Draw inferences based on your own experiences and knowledge. And to really improve understanding and recall, take notes as you read" [11].
- "If you want to make it a productive exercise, you need to have a clear idea of which kind of information you need to get in the first place, and then focus on that aspect" [12].
- "When reading papers, it helps me to have a writing task so that I am being an active reader instead of letting my eyes glaze over mountains of text only to forget everything I just read. So for example, when I read for background information, I will save informative sentences from each article about a specific topic in a Word document" [12].
- "At the beginning, new academic readers find it slow because they have no frame of reference for what they are reading. But there are ways to use reading as a system of creating a mental library, and after a few years, it becomes easy to slot papers onto your mental shelves. Then you can quickly skim a paper to know its contribution" [12].

The underpinning assumption seems to be the existence of a "frame of reference". This frame serves to guide the reading, helping to provide "a clear idea of which kind of information you need to get in the first place". Strategic reading is then a distinctive feature of scientific reading, as opposed to let's say, playful reading, where the aim is not to know the outcome, but instead to enjoy the poetic narrative and thrilling plot. To get the best of scientific reading, a frame of reference needs to be present.

This work addresses the case for Design Science Research (DSR). The first question is then how will a *"DSR's frame of reference"* look like. This paper's main assumption is that most of the readings during DS projects have (at least) five main foci, namely, (1) finding evidence for the importance of the problem, (2) ascertaining causal relationships in the problem, (3) becoming acquainted with works addressing similar problems, (4) becoming acquainted with work that can serve as a kernel theory or other inspiration, or (5) becoming acquainted with work relevant to research (method) design for the DSR project. RCA relates to the first two of these. We can then state **the problem** as:

PhD students not bearing "the RCA frame" in mind when reading
This might have a manyfold impact:

- Important facts might be overlooked when reading. This in turn, might involve a loss of opportunity for DSR projects. If not properly documented in the RCA, reading insights might be forgotten by the time they could impact the project's design, leading to overconfident problem analysis.
- Unfocused reading might result in boredom, lack of engagement and research effort discontinuity among PhD students.
- Literature references might not be traced back to their RCA rationales. This might cause poor reference recoverability when it comes to writing the paper, and hence, forcing re-reads.

So far, we can only hypothesise those consequences. Some studies exist on the impact of reading comprehension [13–15] but this is for settings other that scientific reading. We are unaware of any study that looks into those symptoms for PhD students. That said, the frequent recurrence of this issue in the so-called grey literature (e.g. Q&A forums), provides substantial evidence of the existence of this problem. As a case in point, refer to this Quora entry [9] with 774 followers. Causes include:

- No RCA frame available (yet). The importance of RCA in DSR projects cannot be stressed enough. This paper underlines its role as a reading guideline.
- A RCA frame is available but not easy accessible. Reading and RCA are conducted through different tools. So far, the coupling falls on the shoulders of the students through the use of book-notes and copying & pasting between the tools.

This work tackles the second cause. It is not uncommon for researchers to struggle with switching back and forth between e.g. Endnote and Word, to add notes. These approaches tend to be highly manual and error prone, even if conducted through state-of-the-art reference managers. In the end, keeping track of readings represents a considerable burden for students. We then refine the research question as follows:

How can we bridge reading tools and RCA tools to ensure the presence of both RCA concerns when reading, and of reading evidences when conducting RCA?

2.2   Meta-Requirements

Meta-requirements are generalised requirements for solving a general problem, in this case, bridging between reading tools and RCA tools (generally, regardless of which reading and RCA tools we're talking about). This section draws six meta-requirements for this bridging. For our purposes, "tool bridging" is not limited to piping data among the platforms but also includes extending participant platforms to collect/access this data.

MR1: Provide support for setting reading purposes based on RCA issues

For our aims, a "reading purpose" (hereafter, just "purpose") is an issue that has arisen during RCA (or other research concern, as described above) that needs to be tracked down during reading. This includes: finding evidence of the problem's consequences, ascertaining the causes (used to identify potential ways to solve the problem), looking into someone else's work to avoid re-inventing the wheel, and better assessing the distinctive contributions of the DSR project at hand. However, not all issues arising during RCA become a "purpose". RCA is a moving target. RCA is a gradual endeavour that builds up as better problem comprehension develops. RCA issues come up, disappear and receive different attention as the research progresses. Hence, not all issues should be addressed right away. Prioritisation is needed so that the most important problems are addressed first. Those issues that are not going to be the subject of the current investigation are left outside the reading radar and postponed to a later occasion. Researchers should be able to tick off which RCA issues become the current "purposes".

MR2: Provide support for annotating literature resources as relevant to RCA issues ("the purpose pipe")

The previous paragraph defines what a "purpose" is. Now, we tackle "resource" and "annotation". First, resources. The main resources are papers coming from the traditional research literature, particularly those available through reference managers. In addition, interesting insights might also be gained through the so-called "grey literature": blogs, product reviews, stakeholder comments, or Q&A forums might also sustain RCA. Most software practitioners do not publish in academic forums, which means that their voice is limited. Hence, the notion of "resource" refers not only to traditional papers but also extends to other Web resources.

As for annotations, they are typically used to convey information about a resource. Examples include a comment or a tag on a single web page, or a highlight upon a passage in a document. Traditionally, students are encouraged to annotate while reading. Digital annotations are expected to be useful for supporting comprehension and interpretation [16, 17]. But, how is annotation conducted? Our belief is that comprehension and meaning construction can be more effective if RCA reading purposes somehow "pop up" when annotating.

MR3: Provide support for framing and incorporating annotations during RCA ("the annotation pipe")

With current technology, annotations tend to be locked within a resource (e.g., a paper) itself or, at best, managed by a proprietary annotation repository (e.g. Mendeley). This hampers tracing annotations back to the purpose that triggered the annotation, which hinders researchers from having a global view, not only of what they read, but also about the purpose of these readings. Meta-requirement MR3 mandates integrating annotations into RCA. Doing so should assist identifying which RCA issues have been overlooked (i.e. no annotations for these issues) and (thus far) lack appropriate literature evidence. Linking annotations to issues turns RCA diagrams into a kind of index to literature references.

MR4: Interoperability: The exchange of annotations between reference managers and RCA tools should be facilitated
The previous requirements introduce two pipes, i.e. **"the purpose pipe"** (from RCA tools to reading tools) and **"the annotation pipe"** (from reading tools to RCA tools). This moves interoperability to the forefront. The ability of the artefact to work together with distinct platforms for exchanging data, requires embracing standards, intensive usage of APIs, and open architectures.

MR5: GUI Seamlessness: GUIs of the coupled tools should be preserved as much as possible
We should capitalise on whatever aspect the target audience is familiar with so that users can re-apply what they already know (transfer of learning). Basically, this involves sticking with the tools' GUI gestures. Existing mechanisms might be revised and repurposed, but the addition of new buttons or other kind of widgets should be avoided.

MR6: Process Seamlessness: Interference with either the reading flow or the RCA should be minimized
Coupling between annotation repositories and RCA tools should not be achieved at the cost of losing flexibility during either RCA or reading. The reading flow should not suffer as the result of the coupling. Likewise, new causes can arise during the RCA while others might need to be rephrased or re-arranged along the causal net as researchers delve into the literature. The coupling should not hinder this dynamicity.

So far, we have presented a nascent Design Theory whereby an artefact design that fulfils the aforementioned meta-requirements would have utility to reduce some of the causes of poor strategic reading, through providing coupling between annotation repositories and RCA tools. The next two sections describe the general features of a meta-design fleshing out this Design Theory, and an example instantiation: DScaffolding. DScaffolding is implemented as a Chrome plug-in that bridges MindMeister (as the RCA tool) and Mendeley (as the reference manager).

2.3   The Tools Coupled in DScaffolding

The RCA Tool: MindMeister
MindMeister is a web-based collaborative mind mapping application, which allows its users to visualise their thoughts in terms of mind maps [18]. A mind map is a diagram used to visually organise information. This can be pre-set in terms of a map template, i.e. a set of labelled nodes which can be later expanded by the user by adding new child

nodes. This provides a guide to gather information, especially interesting when this information is abundant and multi-sourced. This ductility together with the popularity mind maps enjoy, make mind mapping an interesting approach when it comes to explicate the problem, i.e. "to formulate the initial problem precisely, justify its importance, investigate its underlying causes, provide evidences and acknowledge related work" [19].

Figure 1 depicts the *ExplicateProblem* template at the onset. The template provides a head-start as for the information to be collected. Specifically, we resort to Coloured Cognitive Maps (CCM) [20]. The template supports the two types of CCM introduced in [20]:

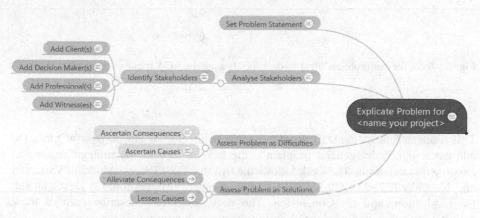

Fig. 1. Conducting RCA through MindMeister: the *ExplicateProblem* template.

– the "Problem as Difficulties" node, which focuses on the problem, what is undesirable about it (i.e. consequences), and what causes the problem and allows it to persist, and,
– the "Problem as Solutions" node, which focuses on the solution of the problem, what benefits would accrue from solving the problem or what causes of the problem might be reduced or eliminated to solve the problem.

Figure 2 instantiates the RCA template for the problem *"PhD students not bearing the RCA frame in mind when reading"*, i.e. our very problem!

The Reading Tool: Mendeley

Mendeley is an Elsevier-owned desktop and web program helping to manage and share research papers [21]. Papers can be arranged into folders, and tagged for easy retrieval. It includes a PDF viewer with sticky notes, text highlighting and full-screen reading. Quote annotation is achieved through highlighting where different colours are available.

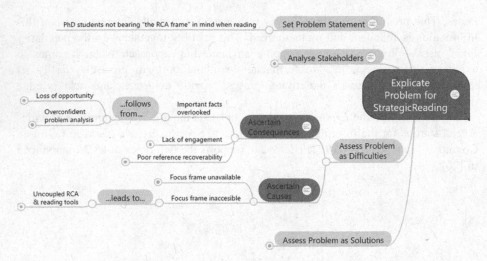

Fig. 2. RCA for our problem "PhD students not bearing the RCA frame in mind when reading".

3 Method

This research follows the DSR paradigm, in that it develops a new purposeful artefact to address a significant general problem – the lack of support for strategic reading in existing research tools. The work follows the five-step DSR Process Model of Vaishnavi and Kuechler [22, 23]: (1) Awareness of Problem, (2) Suggestion, (3) Development, (4) Evaluation, and (5) Conclusion. The next subsections describe each of these activities as conducted or planned during the research reported in this paper.

Awareness of Problem came from supervision of PhD students by the authors together with awareness of literature on recommended practices of strategic reading. Analysis of the problem identified causes of the problem as described earlier in this paper.

Suggestion came from awareness and availability of potential tools, interest by the first two co-authors in integrating different web-based tools, and researching the application programming interfaces (APIs) of available web-based tools. Suggestion was also drawn from understanding of different DSR methods and techniques what might be supported by a new artefact. The suggestion phase also involved development of functional requirements and non-functional requirements, as described above. Suggestion was also accomplished multiple times as different prototypes were tried out and new features were needed to make further improvements.

Development was undertaken in an iterative approach of prototyping different aspects of DScaffolding. Multiple versions were developed and reviewed and experimented with by the authors. Different versions of user interfaces were developed, tried out, and features deleted, modified, and added. Early versions focussed on integrating MindMeister and Mendeley. Prototypes were also evaluated by PhD students and DSR researchers at four different universities and formal and informal feedback gathered each time.

Evaluation thus far has been formative in nature. The research has undergone multiple cycles of suggestion, development, and formative evaluations. While version 1 of the purposeful artefact (the DScaffolding plug-in) has been released at the Chrome Web Store, DScaffolding is still under revision and we plan to make some more improvements (and also develop more documentation and learning materials) before conducting a formal evaluation of DScaffolding.

4   Artefact Description: Strategic Reading with DScaffolding

This section describes the features that make up the purposeful artefact developed to address the meta-requirements for a solution to the problem of "Strategic Reading in DSR". The outcome is a Chrome plug-in that realizes "the purpose pipe" and "the annotation pipe" for the specific case of MindMeister and Mendeley: DScaffolding. This plug-in is available at the Chrome's Web Store: https://chrome.google.com/webstore/detail/hkgmnnjalpmapogadekngkgbbgdjlnne.

Videos are provided for:

- Installation: https://youtu.be/hl6pnJGbVXY
- The Strategic Reading Process: https://youtu.be/jHP1MiqjVBM

Strategic reading is about targeted constructing of meaning by interacting with text [1]. By qualifying strategic reading as "RCA-driven", we stress that "the meaning" to be constructed is that of a (or should serve) RCA. This in turn requires a seamless integration between RCA tools and reading tools. The requirements with which this integration should comply were identified in Sect. 3, including three functional (MR1, MR2, MR3) and three non-functional (MR4, MR5, MR6) requirements. Table 1 highlights the functional requirements and the features within DScaffolding that realise those requirements.

Table 1. Features addressing functional meta-requirement in DScaffolding.

Functional meta-requirements	DScaffolding features
MR1: Identify RCA concerns	*"Supporting Evidences?"* node
	"Who else addresses it?" node
*MR2: Annotate resources according to current RCA concerns (**the purpose pipe**)*	Concern cheat sheet
	Right mouse context menu for concerns
*MR3: Incorporate annotations as part of RCA (**the annotation pipe**)*	*"Annotation"* node
	Background colour & icons used to capture "the quality of the annotation"
	Tracking of annotation repositories

This section elaborates on a Design Theory for this scenario. A Design Theory includes "a relationship between requirements and design that prescribes instantiating the design to achieve the requirements or simply indicates that there is utility to be had in instantiating the design for achieving the requirements" [20]. DScaffolding instantiates this theory for MindMeister and Mendeley. Next, we elaborate on DScaffolding's support for each functional requirement.

4.1   MR1: Provide Support for Setting Reading Purposes Based on RCA Issues

MindMeister supports RCA through mind mapping. MR1, i.e. identifying RCA issues, is then re-phrased as pinpointing those map nodes that will play the role of "reading purposes". In line with the non-functional requirements, this is realized as follows:

- GUI seamlessness. RCA nodes are turned into "Purpose nodes" through adding two possible children: the "Supporting Evidences?" node and the "Who else addresses it?" node. Introducing such nodes turns the father into a Purpose node. DScaffolding decorates Purpose nodes with one of up to eight different background colours (see Fig. 3).
- Process seamlessness. "Supporting Evidences?" and "Who else addresses it?" are created as any other node. However, DScaffolding constraints these nodes to hang from the appropriate fathers, i.e. cause/consequence nodes and means nodes, respectively (see Fig. 3).

The example in Fig. 3 shows three current RCA reading concerns: the problem statement (in green), "Poor reference recoverability" (in pink), and "Uncoupled RCA and reading tools" (in purple). Some evidence has already been collected for these concerns drawn from the literature. Note that the automatically generated background colours will later be mapped to Mendeley annotation background colours.

In accordance with the dynamic nature of RCA, researchers can alter which nodes play the role of "purpose" throughout the DS project. This is achieved by using the standard mechanism for node creation and deletion, i.e. by removing or adding "Supporting Evidences?" and "Who else addresses it?" nodes. No new interaction to be learnt by MindMeister users.

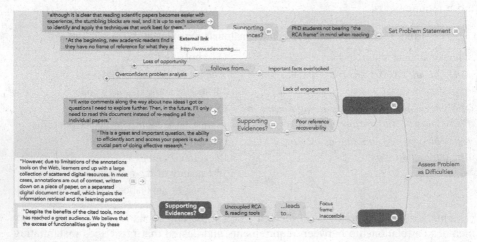

Fig. 3. DScaffolding RCA map with three purpose nodes. Available at https://www. mindmeister.com/830267652. (Color figure online)

4.2   MR2: Provide Support for Annotating Literature Resources as Relevant to RCA Issues ("the Purpose Pipe")

Annotating is the act of creating associations between a reading resource (e.g. a PDF document or a Web page) and metadata in terms of a comment, ranking stars, or a highlight that qualifies the resource. Here, we are constrained to the annotating mechanism provided by the reading platform, specifically, those for annotating excerpt rather than the whole resource. For Mendeley, this is restricted to highlighting since tags are used to characterize the whole resource.

No matter the approach, the important point is that now annotating is not conducted in a vacuum, but framed by the current concerns within RCA. RCA issues provide researchers with the questions to be answered when reading. Annotation mechanisms (tags & highlighting colours) now convey RCA meaning. DScaffolding captures these issues through Purpose nodes. As discussed earlier, Purpose nodes are those that have "Supporting Evidences?" and "Who else addresses it?" as a child. Purpose nodes hold a label and a background colour. Labels become tags while background colours equate to those used for highlighting in Mendeley. This sets the mapping between RCA concerns (in MindMeister) and annotations (in Mendeley). But this is not enough.

Even if a mapping is set, it is very unlikely that researchers will remember it (i.e. what colour matches which purpose). We need to make Mendeley "purpose-aware". However, annotation mechanisms (e.g. highlighting) are wired-in, only accessible to tool owners. Hence, we have to resort to external means: a cheat sheet to be placed by the Mendeley desktop (see Fig. 4).

Mendeley provides eight different colours for annotation highlighting. Yellow is left for "structural" highlighting (i.e. attributing different levels of importance). The remaining seven are mapped to RCA issues' background colours. A cheat sheet about what these colours stand for can be obtained from MindMeister. Researchers can then place this cheat sheet by their Mendeley desktop application (see Fig. 4).

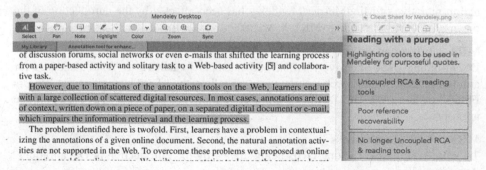

Fig. 4. Cheat sheet used for RCA awareness in Mendeley (left side). The CheatSheet is obtained as a screenshot from MindMeister. In the screenshot, the velvet highlight colour corresponds to the "RCA & reading tool coupling" issue whose rationales should be found in the RCA. (Color figure online)

4.3   MR3: Provide Support for Framing and Incorporating Annotations as Part of RCA ("the Annotation Pipe")

In our vision, annotations do not exist in a vacuum, but are contextualised by RCA. DScaffolding fleshes this out by naming Mendeley folders and MindMeister maps alike. Once this link is set, DScaffolding tracks annotations made in resources held in these folders, to later enrich the namesake MindMeister map. In so doing, DScaffolding realizes the annotation pipe. But what is meant by "enrich"? Enrich refers to DScaffolding automatically creating Annotation nodes out of annotations coming from Mendeley repositories.

An Annotation node addresses an RCA issue, and as such, it hangs from the corresponding RCA node (see Fig. 3). Node properties include: a label, an attached comment and a background colour. For Annotation nodes:

- the label holds the text being highlighted in the annotated resource,
- the comment keeps a link to the resource URL (if available). Researchers can click on the link icon to move straight to the manuscript in Mendeley,
- the background colour reflects the nature of the source: "white" for annotations coming from journals and conferences, and "grey" if coming from the grey literature (not discussed here).

In addition, annotations inherit the reputation of their sources. Annotations coming for reputable sources add a "star" icon to their labels. So far, the reputation is set by users. For instance, Mendeley allows users to tick a "star" to mark sources as favourites. Although "favourite" is quite an elusive notion (no clear rationale for ticking this off), DScaffolding interprets the star as a sign of the source's reputation and soundness. This reputation travels together with the reference.

4.4   Features Implementing the Non-functional Meta-Requirements

This section addresses the impact on interoperability (MR4), and whether the interaction narrative of MindMeister/Mendeley has been affected by the introduction of the means for strategic reading (MR5 & MR6).

MR4 – Interoperability
DScaffolding uses intensively APIs, and attempts to adhere to W3C standards for annotation description. Architecture wise, we follow the "Tool Integration via Process Flows" pattern [24]. This facilitates bringing in new "reading tools" by developing the appropriate components.

MR5 – GUI seamlessness
To what extent have existing GUIs being altered by the introduction of DScaffolding? Answers follow:

- MindMeister. Its GUI is being extended with a "CheatSheet" button that permits to obtain a screenshot of the current "reading purposes".
- Mendeley. No change in its GUI.

MR6 – Process seamlessness

To what extent have traditional practices being altered by the introduction of DScaffolding? Answers follow:

- practice: node creation. We stick to MindMeister practices. For traditional MindMeister users, the only difference stems from some nodes (e.g. Annotation nodes) being automatically generated. Once created, Annotation nodes are handle as any other node: they can be reshaped or moving around at users' wish
- practice: annotation. Mendeley users need now to look at the CheatSheet to select the appropriate background highlighting colour (see Fig. 4).

5 Evaluation

Evaluation followed a naturalistic approach: 5 PhD students were free to use DScaffolding for three months, and next enquired about their experience. This sample size is certainly not enough, but might be sufficient for understanding initial reactions. Figure 5 displays the questionnaire along the results. Next, results are commented along the two aims of the evaluation: assessing usability and effectiveness.

Usability has to do with seamlessly integrating DScaffolding with existing processes (MR5 & MR6) so that the existing flows are minimally disturbed. Questions 1 and 2 check the eventual disturbance brought about by DScaffolding. For MindMeister, this involves the need to create "Supporting nodes?". For Mendeley, this involves the use of a CheatSheet. Except subject S2, DScaffolding did not seem to involve a main disruption from previous habits. Specifically, the requirement of having the CheatSheet by the Mendeley desktop does not seem to imply a main hassle.

Effectiveness has to do with RCA issues serving as appropriate focal points during reading (question 3). As a by-product, we also assessed the interest of including annotations as part of RCA diagrams (question 4, 5 & 6). Questions 7 and 8 provide a general sentiment about the tool. In general, subjects were "mild" about the effectiveness of DScaffolding to keep them focus. However, an unexpected outcome was the help that indexing annotations along RCA concerns brings to reference recoverability (the highest ranked assertion). This seems to suggest that using RCA issues for strategic reading, might not only facilitate focus but also help root-cause analysis. The question is whether this impact on RCA can be regarded as an evidence of strategic reading?

If we go back to the definition of strategic reading, i.e. conceiving reading as a process of constructing meaning by interacting with text [1], the notion of "constructing meaning" can certainly be equated to developing the RCA map. By framing Mendeley annotations into the RCA map, researchers are seamlessly "constructing meaning": making sense of their cause analysis.

One main thread to validity is that of subjects belonging to the same research group that the DScaffolding authors. Though this risk was explicitly warned about, existing relationships could have biased the outcome.

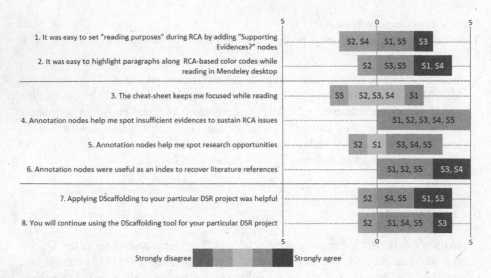

Fig. 5. Diverging stacked bar chart for the satisfaction questionnaire using likert scales. The "5" on the left means the five subjects, i.e. S1, S2, etc., *Strongly Disagree,* while "5" on the right corresponds to all *Strongly Agree.* Gradients in colour indicate the strength of their (dis) agreement. (Color figure online)

6   Conclusions

Strategic reading is a main skill for researchers. Our Design Theory is that RCA may provide main drivers of attention when reading. The theory states that this can be achieved by sustaining both "RCA awareness" while reading (i.e. the purpose pipe that channels RCA issues to reading platforms) and "literature awareness" while conducting RCA (i.e. the annotation pipe that channels literature evidences towards RCA platforms). DScaffolding is used to assess the extent to which this theory holds. First evaluations indicate that not only reading but also RCA might benefit from a tight coupling between these two processes.

The insights for this theory can be of interest to:

- RCA tool developers, as for the importance of evidence gathering within the tool itself to spot analysis weaknesses and improving reference recoverability,
- reading tool developers, as for the use of RCA issues to anchor focus, and hence, enabling strategic reading,
- the DSR community, as for stressing even further the importance of RCA, now as a strategic reading enabler.

Acknowledgments. First author is in debt with Antoni Olivé for introducing him to DSR. This work is co-supported by the Spanish Ministry of Education, and the European Social Fund under contract TIN2014-58131-R. Contell has a doctoral grant from the University of the Basque Country.

References

1. McEwan, E.: The power of strategic reading instruction. In: Seven Strategies of Highly Effective Readers: Using Cognitive Research to Boost K-8 Achievement. Corwin Press, Thousand Oaks (2004)
2. Renear, A.H., Palmer, C.L.: Strategic reading, ontologies, and the future of scientific publishing. Science 325(5942), 828–832 (2009)
3. Venable, J.R., Baskerville, R.: Eating our own cooking: Toward a more rigorous design science of research methods. Electron. J. Bus. Res. Methods 10(2), 141–153 (2012)
4. Raphael, T.E., Englert, C.S.: Writing and reading: partners in constructing meaning. Read. Teach. 43(6), 388–400 (1990)
5. Wallace, M., Wray, A.: Critical Reading and Writing for Postgraduates, 3rd edn. SAGE Publications Ltd., Thousand Oaks (2016)
6. Mohammadi, E., Thelwall, M., Haustein, S., Larivière, V.: Who reads research articles? An altmetrics analysis of Mendeley user categories. J. Assoc. Inf. Sci. Technol. 66(9), 1832–1846 (2015)
7. Ruben, A.: How to read a scientific paper. http://www.sciencemag.org/careers/2016/01/how-read-scientific-paper. Accessed 6 Feb 2017
8. Quora: I am a robotics PhD student and I have a hard time reading research papers. I am very slow at it and find the task kind of boring. Is there any way I can make paper reading fun and become faster at it? https://www.quora.com/Iam-a-robotics-PhD-student-and-I-have-a-hard-time-reading-research-papers-Iam-very-slow-at-it-and-find-the-task-kind-of-boring-Is-there-any-way-I-can-makepaper-reading-fun-and-become-faster-at-it. Accessed 6 Feb 2017
9. Quora: PhD students: how do you keep your notes while reading scientific papers? https://www.quora.com/PhD-students-How-do-you-keep-your-notes-while-reading-scientific-papers. Accessed 6 Feb 2017
10. Rodriguez, N.: Infographic: how to read a scientific paper. https://www.elsevier.com/connect/infographic-how-to-read-a-scientific-paper. Accessed 6 Feb 2017
11. Purugganan, M., Hewitt, J.: How to read a scientific article. http://www.owlnet.rice.edu/~cainproj/courses/HowToReadSciArticle.pdf. Accessed 6 Feb 2017
12. Pain, E.: How to (seriously) read a scientific paper. http://www.sciencemag.org/careers/2016/03/how-seriously-read-scientific-paper. Accessed 6 Feb 2017
13. Israel, S.E., Duffy, G.G.: Handbook of Research on Reading Comprehension. Routledge, Abingdon (2014)
14. Margolin, S.J., Driscoll, C., Toland, M.J., Kegler, J.L.: E-readers, computer screens, or paper: does reading comprehension change across media platforms? Appl. Cogn. Psychol. 27(4), 512–519 (2013)
15. Stern, P., Shalev, L.: The role of sustained attention and display medium in reading comprehension among adolescents with ADHD and without it. Res. Dev. Disabil. 34(1), 431–439 (2013)
16. Marshall, C.C.: Toward an ecology of hypertext annotation. In: 9th ACM Conference on Hypertext and Hypermedia: Links, Objects, Time and Space, pp. 40–49, ACM, New York (1998)
17. O'hara, K., Sellen, A.: A comparison of reading paper and on-line documents. In: ACM SIGCHI Conference on Human Factors in Computing Systems, pp. 335–342. ACM, New York (1997)
18. Wikipedia: Mindmeister. https://en.wikipedia.org/wiki/MindMeister. Accessed 6 Feb 2017
19. Johannesson, P., Perjons, E.: An Introduction to Design Science. Springer, Heidelberg (2014)

20. Venable, J.R.: Using Coloured Cognitive Mapping (CCM) for design science research. In: Tremblay, M.C., VanderMeer, D., Rothenberger, M., Gupta, A., Yoon, V. (eds.) DESRIST 2014. LNCS, vol. 8463, pp. 345–359. Springer, Cham (2014). doi:10.1007/978-3-319-06701-8_25
21. Wikipedia: Mendeley. https://en.wikipedia.org/wiki/Mendeley. Accessed 6 Feb 2017
22. Vaishnavi, V., Kuechler, W.: Design Research in Information Systems. AISWorld (2004). http://desrist.org/design-research-in-information-systems/. Accessed 6 Feb 2017
23. Vaishnavi, V., Kuechler, W.: Design Science Research Methods and Patterns: Innovating Information and Communication Technology, 2nd edn. CRC Press, Boca Raton (2015)
24. Karsai, G., Lang, A., Neema, S.: Design patterns for open tool integration. Softw. Syst. Model. 4(2), 157–170 (2005)

Extending CCM4DSR for Collaborative Diagnosis of Socio-Technical Problems

Raphael D. Schilling[(⊠)], Stephan Aier, Maximilian Brosius,
M. Kazem Haki, and Robert Winter

Institute of Information Management, University of St.Gallen, St. Gallen,
Switzerland
{raphael.schilling,stephan.aier,maximilian.brosius,
kazem.haki,robert.winter}@unisg.ch

Abstract. The identification of a problem, its causes and its consequences are integral parts of designing useful solutions in Design Science Research (DSR). Many problems addressed in DSR are of a socio-technical nature, and they are collaboratively solved in multidisciplinary teams. Accordingly, analysis techniques are needed which integrate diverse perspectives of problem analysis. Colored Cognitive Mapping for DSR (CCM4DSR) is such a technique. By applying CCM4DSR to an exemplary socio-technical problem, this paper reports on observed challenges and offers four extensions to CCM4DSR. These extensions provide guidance in adequately stating the problem, considering path dependencies, explicating different stakeholder perspectives, and integrating different perspectives through a comprehensive process.

Keywords: Colored Cognitive Mapping for Design Science Research (CCM4DSR) · Collaborative problem analysis · Enterprise Architecture (EA)

1 Introduction

Design Science Research (DSR) in Information Systems (IS) aims to find "technology-based solutions to important and relevant business problems" [1, p. 83]. Therefore, most authors recommend to start DSR projects with the systematic "identification of the important and relevant problem that is going to be addressed" [2, p. 97]. Beyond the identification of the problem, actually understanding the problem and its inherent causes and consequences is considered to be a major step in the process of designing useful solutions [3].

The multi-stakeholder engagement in problem solving for artefact-oriented IS research implies that a close collaboration among diverse stakeholder groups such as users, software developers, or software architects is required [4]. However, it is particularly challenging to reach a shared understanding of the problem since each of the stakeholders may perceive the problem, its causes, and its consequences differently due to an individual information filtering process (i.e., cognition). Consequently, a technique to *collaboratively* explicate and integrate the potentially deviating perspectives, and to eventually obtain a comprehensive understanding of the problem is desirable. In

A. Maedche et al. (Eds.): DESRIST 2017, LNCS 10243, pp. 247–263, 2017.
DOI: 10.1007/978-3-319-59144-5_15

tackling these challenges, cognitive mapping has recently gained attention within the field of DSR [5].

Cognitive mapping techniques aim to transfer hidden structures, which we shape in our brains about the relationships among different concepts, into a graphical depiction, i.e., a cognitive map [6]. Such a visualization is supportive for gaining a comprehensive problem understanding. Venable [5, 7, 8] has further developed cognitive mapping and introduced *colored cognitive mapping for DSR* (CCM4DSR), a technique "for analyzing problems to understand their causes and consequences and for identifying potential ways to solve the problem(s)" [5, p. 345].

Despite its initial evaluation by the technique's propagator the CCM4DSR technique has not yet been further evaluated and its application has only been demonstrated in a limited number of cases [e.g., 9]. We have evaluated the first phase of CCM4DSR—problem diagnosis—through applying it for understanding a *socio-technical problem* in our own DSR project. In fact, problems to be addressed in DSR are often socio-technical in nature and wicked, i.e., they are "poorly formulated, confusing, and permeated with conflicting values of many decisions makers or other stakeholders" [10, p. 731].

In the paper at hand, we thus seek to (1) evaluate the applicability of CCM4DSR for collaborative problem diagnosis of socio-technical problems and to (2) identify potential extensions that improve the applicability of the technique. This endeavor contributes to the existing body of knowledge on CCM4DSR by proposing conceptual as well as procedural extensions.

In Sect. 2, we discuss the particularities of problem formulation in DSR and provide a theoretical introduction to cognitive mapping techniques. In Sect. 3, the research approach, in general, and the problem definition and the solution objectives, in particular, are explained. In the subsequent section, four extensions of the *problem diagnosis* phase of CCM4DSR are proposed. Finally, we discuss the resulted insights and outline further research opportunities.

2   Related Work

An important discourse in DSR deals with the question of how to capture, formulate, and communicate design solutions. According to Gregor [11], what distinguishes DSR is the focus on "how to do something". Nevertheless, any formulation of a solution starts with understanding the problem [2].

Extant DSR literature has long been propagating the necessity to understand and represent problems for designing prospective solutions. For instance, Hevner et al. [1] stress the means of simplification and decomposition of a problem into its sub-problems. They suggest that a problem representation, through for instance constructs and models, contributes to a shared understanding and allows to further communicate the given problem. In this vein, Peffers et al. [12] suggest to atomize a problem into a subset of means and ends. The inherent contribution of such an entanglement is to gain mutual understandability and to systematically develop solution components for specific problem aspects.

The four traditionally distinguished artefacts types in DSR (i.e., constructs, models, methods, and instantiations) are used to form the abstract foundation to understand, represent, and connect the problem space and the solution space [13]. Where prior research propagates abductive or inductive strategies with rather rigid structures to derive solutions [14], recent research in DSR has urged on a coevolution of the problem and the solution space. It is argued that every solution also contributes to better understanding the respective problem [15]. While acknowledging that proper techniques are required to define the two spaces, most publications focus on the presentation of the solution space due to the solution-oriented paradigm of DSR. However, in order to build artefacts that build a bridge between the problem space and the solution space, techniques which allow us to understand complex socio-technical problems, are highly relevant. Soft systems methodology (SSM), a system development methodology which emerged from action research and system science, for example provides guidance in understanding and solving a particular socio-technical problem of a particular client [16]. While SSM is an established system development method and thus rather practice-oriented [16], cognitive mapping has been proposed to understand complex socio-technical problems of general validity.

2.1   Cognitive Mapping

The term *cognitive map* originates from psychology where it was first introduced by Tolman [17]. Contrary to former research, Tolman showed that rats do not follow a simple stimulus-response pattern. Instead, based on selected stimuli they build cognitive-like maps of the environment, offering alternative responses to certain stimuli (i.e., indicating routes towards the hidden food in a maze) [17]. Cognition is thereby described as an individual's filtering of information through clusters of acquired concepts and beliefs. Cognitive research has proven that people use map-like structures to make sense of information available in their environment and derive corresponding actions [18, 19]. In essence, cognitive maps are "internally represented schemas or mental models for particular problem-solving domains that are learned and encoded as a result of an individual's interaction with their environment" [20, p. 188]. Cognitive maps particularly comprise information about the relationships (e.g., proximity, similarity, cause-effect, category, contiguity) among concepts (or constructs) that support a faster decision making process in complex environments [20].

Whereas cognitive maps in psychology refer to information processing within an individual's brain, the term *cognitive mapping* is used for creating graphical representations of such cognitive maps [6]. Research on cognitive mapping aims to make the taken-for-granted assumptions, connections, and interdependencies visible to both the individual as well as the outside world. In this way they describe how individuals view a particular domain (i.e., what is known and believed) and may explain the reasoning behind certain actions or problems [21]. Due to the complexity and interrelatedness of an individual's view, graphical representations (e.g., maps, networks) often appear to be more suitable than verbal descriptions. Going further, we use the term cognitive map to refer to such kind of graphical representations.

In order to create cognitive maps (i.e., transferring the hidden structures into a graphical representation), several *cognitive mapping techniques* have been proposed [21]. Generally, they all strive to first extract the individual concepts and their relations and then build graphical representations of the same [20]. It is beyond the scope of this paper to provide an exhaustive overview on the proposed techniques. Following, we provide two examples of such techniques, a more detailed description of proposed cognitive mapping techniques in the context of business management can be found in [22]. A frequently used technique is *causal mapping*, where the directional (cause and effect) relationships between constructs of a problem space are graphically represented in a network view [23]. If the problem space was for example to understand why people do extra hours, a possible relationship could be: "additional working hours" lead to "more work done" and eventually lead to "appraisal for good work performance". A second cognitive mapping technique is *semantic mapping* or *mind mapping*. In this technique, a central problem statement is extended by clusters of arguments. The problem statement "people do extra hours" could for example be extended by the clusters "motivation", "reasons", and "consequences". These clusters would then be further extended.

Cognitive mapping techniques have been applied in various disciplines such as political science [24, 25], management science [20, 22, 26–28], and—more recently— IS research [3, 21]. The motivation for creating cognitive maps in these disciplines is often the same: To make diverse ideas accessible, sorted, transferrable, and to initiate debates among the involved individuals [6]. This detailed depiction of an individual's— or group of individuals'—view on a given problem space is said to improve the problem definition and decision making. This is also why Venable [5] has proposed CCM4DSR as a cognitive mapping technique for DSR.

2.2   Colored Cognitive Mapping in DSR

According to Venable [5], earlier methodological contributions in DSR provide very limited guidance on how a problem can be defined and represented. Furthermore, the processes for breaking down a problem and derive design requirements to ultimately derive creative ideas for potential solutions are—despite their widely-discussed importance—ill-defined in existing literature and mostly left out to the individual researcher. Venable [5, 7, 8] designed the CCM4DSR technique to not only overcome the above-mentioned challenges but also to improve the way of collaboration and communication within research teams.

CCM4DSR is an extension of earlier cognitive mapping techniques (i.e., causal mapping) that is purposefully designed to be applied in DSR projects. Compared to traditional causal mapping techniques, CCM4DSR is more explicit about the desirability of causes and consequences (in CCM4DSR reflected as colored nodes) and follows a detailed procedure in designing a cognitive map. The creation of a CCM4DSR is proposed to be conducted as a group activity. CCM4DSR can be considered to be more than combining cognitive models of different stakeholders in a unified graphical representation. It further aims to integrate stakeholders' potentially deviating world views. It also aims to be a creativity technique to derive potential solutions, which extends the original scope of cognitive maps.

A CCM4DSR is created in three steps (see Fig. 1). Step 1 *Problem Diagnosis* explores the consequences and causes of a problem statement. In this step, we put the problem statement in the middle and note down negative and positive consequences (and consequences of consequences) above the problem statement and, in turn, note down causes (and causes of causes) below the problem statement. The result is a graphical representation of a cognitive map in its traditional design (e.g., causal mapping). In step 2 *CCM Conversion* the so-called problem-space is converted into a solution-space. Therefore, all consequences and causes identified in step 1 are transferred from a negative connotation into a positive one (and vice versa). By doing so, a positive view on how things should be is derived. Earlier negative causes and consequences become positive and thus desirable. In step 3 *Solution Derivation*, ideas on how this desirable state may be achieved are derived by having a close look at the causes of positive consequences.

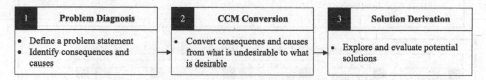

Fig. 1. Process steps of CCM4DSR [7]

3 Research Approach

The reported insights in the paper at hand resulted from applying CCM4DSR in the *problem identification* phase [29], the very first phase, of a larger project. In that project, we aim to investigate the means affecting the consideration of Enterprise Architecture (EA) goals and principles in IS design decisions by local decision makers in organizations (see Fig. 2). Extant EA research often proposes centralized, governance-based approaches to EA management (EAM) in order to align local business needs with enterprise-wide and global perspectives on IS [30]. However, the sustained growth of IS complexity of many organizations raise questions about the effectiveness of such centralized and governance-based approaches. In this EA project, we are therefore interested in understanding why decision makers do not sufficiently consider EA goals and principles in their IS design decisions. The ultimate goal is to develop new or improved artefacts, e.g., management methods, in achieving the promised objectives of EA. The EA project is a suitable context to apply CCM4DSR as it requires engagement of diverse perspectives (i.e., IT and business perspectives) and it also comprises both technical (e.g., application integration) and social (e.g., decision making) aspects of a typical socio-technical phenomenon. Nevertheless, during the process of applying CCM4DSR, several methodological challenges occurred. With the aim to provide solutions to these challenges, we initiated a separate research project for extending CCM4DSR so that the paper at hand reports the results of this CCM4DSR extension project. To ensure a systematic solution identification, we decided to follow a DSR process as proposed by Peffers et al. [29]. Figure 2 illustrates the relation between the larger EA project and the CCM4DSR extension project.

A total of six researchers participated in the research process. The participants had an average of 10 years of experience in the field of EA research. They have been introduced to CCM4DSR by John Venable, the technique's propagator.[1] Afterwards, all team members felt comfortable to apply, evaluate, and potentially further develop the technique. The procedure of applying CCM4DSR in problem identification was prepared and led by one of the team members.

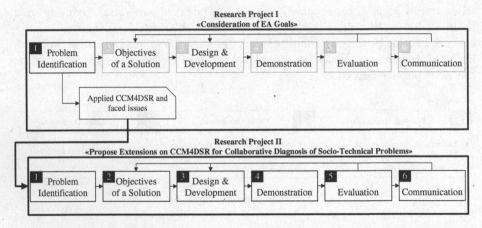

Fig. 2. Overview of the research approach (referring to the proposal of Peffers et al. [29])

In the following section, we briefly introduce the identified problems in applying CCM4DSR, and provide information on the defined solution objectives and how we developed and evaluated solutions for the identified problems.

Problem Identification. After developing a CCM4DSR for our EA problem, a retrospective session was held to evaluate this technique. We focused on the problem diagnosis step of CCM4DSR (see Fig. 1) due to the challenges we faced in this step. We identified a total of four issues, which will be described in more detail as part of the results section (Detailed Problem Identification). They all emerged out of our endeavor to collaboratively create a CCM4DSR for our EA problem:

- We struggled to define a common problem statement;
- We realized that path dependencies heavily influence the relation of the concepts in the CCM4DSR;
- We missed guidance on how to consider different stakeholder perspectives;
- We perceived it challenging to integrate these different perspectives into a common CCM4DSR.

---

[1] The introduction to CCM4DSR was an essential part of a DSR course hold by John Venable at the University of St.Gallen, Switzerland, between September and October 2016. The corresponding PowerPoint slides are not published but shared on request (j.venable@curtin.edu.au).

Since these issues are not problem specific (i.e., relate to the consideration of EA goals problem), we consider them to be of general relevance.

Objectives of a Solution. Our initial goal was to find solutions to the above-mentioned issues for our own purpose. We looked for extensions of the technique that are of practical use, i.e., effective and easy to implement. Since we opted to communicate our research result within the community, the extensions needed to be of general validity, described in detail, and suitable to be integrated into the existing CCM4DSR process flow.

Design and Development. Our extensions are based on earlier publications in related research fields such as collaborative cognitive mapping [e.g., 23] or problem formulation in strategic management [e.g., 31]. It is this *justificatory knowledge* [32] that informed our design. In an iterative process, we discussed ideas from the team members to extend CCM4DSR.

Demonstration. We have applied the proposed extensions in the context of research project I, "consideration of EA goals". In particular, we created a new CCM4DSR following our newly proposed extensions. In addition to that, the written descriptions of the extensions were provided to two colleagues who were interested in creating a CCM4DSR for their own research project but were not part of the team designing the extensions.

Evaluation. Our extensions were evaluated through a qualitative approach. In order to ensure effectiveness and ease of implementation, each of the authors had to evaluate the proposed extensions individually. The criterion for evaluation were not aligned beforehand but defined by each individual. Applied criteria were, besides others, the personal perception whether the extension would be supportive to overcome the problem(s) identified, be applicable in other contexts, and understandable for persons who were not part of the creation process. The results of these individual evaluations were then discussed and the extensions were only accepted if all team members agreed that they improved the CCM4DSR creation process.

Communication. Assuming our extensions would be of general interest, we decided to present our findings to the DSR community. Given that our evaluation is based on a rather limited scope in terms of persons involved and research topics covered, we also aim to trigger a further evaluation and improvement cycle.

4   Results

In the following section, we present four extensions to CCM4DSR for collaborative problem diagnosis of socio-technical problems. The four extensions provide guidance in (I) adequately stating the problem, (II) understanding path dependencies, (III) considering different stakeholder perspectives, and (IV) integrating different perspectives through a comprehensive process. These extensions target the first process step in CCM4DSR (i.e., problem diagnosis, see Fig. 1), and support the collaborative creation process of a CCM4DSR. It is noteworthy that, while extensions I, II, and III should be applied in an iterative fashion, extension IV is a procedural guideline. We introduce each extension by first describing the faced challenge (*Detailed Problem Identification*). We then present the actual extension with regard to existing research (*Design & Development*). The presentation of the extension is followed by giving an example of how supportive it was in our EA project (*Demonstration & Evaluation*).

4.1   Extension I: Problem Statement Definition

Detailed Problem Identification. Even though defining a proper problem statement is the primary step and at the core of CCM4DSR, existing literature does not offer any guidance on how it should be carried out. When applying CCM4DSR, we struggled to achieve an agreement on the problem statement because we came up with a number of different statements, some including cause-effect relations, some providing different descriptions of the same situation, or some providing evaluations of their own observations. According to the literature on building conventional cognitive maps, a precise understanding of the purpose of the cognitive map is key: "If the purpose is not well defined, the search for relevant variables (factors) is likely to lack direction and the model can easily grow to an unmanageable size" [3, p. 47]. Given the fact that, in conventional cognitive maps, the purpose of the map is not even part of the graphical representation, the central problem statement based on which the CCM4DSR is built has a high impact on the result. By stating that the "Problem Diagnosis begins with one or more statement(s) of the problem (or problems if there are several)" [5, p. 351], it is assumed that all participants have already agreed on the boundaries of the topic of discussion. This is, to our experience, not always the case in larger and/or diverse teams. Thus, guidance on how the problem statement should be defined is beneficial in order to save time and to give the initial discussions a clear direction.

Design and Development. Our proposal is based on strategic management research, where the differentiation between the activities of problem definition and problem solving has a long tradition. Despite the acknowledged importance of the problem definition, research has been vague about this process and did not offer precise guidance on how a problem should be stated [31]. Baer et al. [31] have recently proposed a process for comprehensive problem definition, which we find to be relevant for CCM4DSR. This process aims to compensate for situations where teams are "comprising individuals with different information sets and cognitive structures" [31, p. 201] and incentive mechanisms do not hinder objective problem definition (e.g., actors could be negatively affected through loss of decision power by potential solutions). According to Baer et al. [31], any problem definition needs to start with the identification of symptoms and only in a second phase consider causes. Since the derivation of causes is already an integral part of CCM4DSR, we conclude that the problem statement should only reflect the main symptoms of the problem and leave out any indication of potential causes. In order to provide a clear direction to the solution derivation in the later steps, we learned that it is beneficial to express the symptoms of the problem through an action performed by a particular actor. This gives a clear indication on who would behave differently once the solution has been implemented. We therefore propose to structure the problem statement in the following way: [ACTOR] + [ATTRIBUTE] + [ACTION], e.g., "Management Information Systems are slow in predicting changing customer needs" or "Data shared by our partners are often not meeting the agreed data quality level". The *actor* represents the person or object of main concern—they might be negatively affected by the problem or not acting as desired. The *attribute* describes the way in which a certain action is performed by the actor. In the problem statement, the attribute has most likely a negative connotation, while in the solution space, this attribute is likely to turn into a positive connotation. By describing the *action* in the problem space, a certain behavior is described. Depending on the attribute, the solution will target to either enforce or reduce such behavior.

Demonstration and Evaluation. We defined our problem statement according to the first extension:

> *"Decision makers within organizations do not sufficiently take EA goals into account for their daily IS design decisions."*

The proposed structure along actor, attribute, and action was helpful to define the perspective from which the CCM4DSR should be designed. We opted to take decision makers such as project managers as actors. By using the attribute "not sufficiently", we could express that decision makers consider EA goals in certain cases, indicating the fact that there is also a desirable behavior which is observable. The inclusion of a particular action enables us to focus on a certain behavior (i.e., daily IS design decisions). Our discussions would have gone in a different direction if we stated "EA guidelines are ignored".

4.2 Extension II: Consideration of Path Dependencies

Detailed Problem Identification. The available solutions to a problem (or a problem statement) are dependent on certain decisions/actions taken in the past and will thus impact the available options for prospective solutions. For example, organizations react differently to changes in their environment due to organizational rigidities and structural inertia, which are associated with the existence of patterns such as "awkward routines, groupthink or fixed cognitive maps" [33, p. 689]. Such patterns are a product of the taken actions in the past (e.g., definition of processes, selection criteria for new employees, design of IS landscape). They lead to situations where the number of options for solutions gets limited: organizations are path dependent. Another often used example of path dependency is the QWRTY keyboard. Even though it has been proven that other keyboard designs could increase typing efficiency, a design decision taken in the past makes it nearly impossible to change the design today due to the typing routines of most people.

Assumption surfacing techniques, of which cognitive mapping is one instantiation, have been proposed to "make hidden patterns in organizational settings accessible, to open them up for critical reflection, and to put them on the organizational discourse agenda" [33, p. 702]. This implies that a CCM4DSR will look differently depending on the organization it is created in. Path dependencies, as shown in Fig. 3 for our EA project, need to be considered. Even though the same problem has been analyzed, both the consequence as well as the potential causes differ depending on actions/decisions taken in the past.

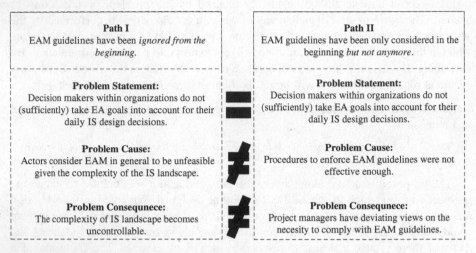

Fig. 3. Impact of past actions/decisions (path dependency) on CCM4DSR (Example)

Path dependencies are not visible within a single CCM4DSR, but may become identifiable when multiple CCM4DSR are created. If participants involved in the creation process of the CCM4DSR do not have a common understanding on the historic context (i.e., relevant decisions/actions taken in the past), they may struggle to define a common solution. Further, if the participants have a common understanding of the historic context and on the possible solutions, then the derived solution would most likely not be of general applicability (i.e., not being valid for different historic contexts).

Design and Development. Information about relevant decisions/actions taken in the past needs to be made explicit in CCM4DSR. This should be conducted right after the initial problem definition and continuously extended during the process of CCM4DSR creation. Depending on the targeted generalizability level of the derived solution, several CCM4DSR should be created (one for each possible alternative of relevant actions/decisions taken in the past). If the goal of applying CCM4DSR is to derive solutions that are applicable independent of the path dependency, only those solutions that have been derived from all created CCM4DSR should be considered. Alternatively, organizations could be clustered along their path dependencies and situational design methods derived [34].

Demonstration and Evaluation. As shown in Fig. 3, the derived consequences and causes of the problem are dependent on the organization's past decisions concerning EA. In our EA project we therefore had to clarify if we were interested in finding solutions for situations, where EA guidelines had always been ignored (path I) or where they had been considered at the beginning but not anymore (path II). We opted to work on path I and wrote the corresponding decision next to the problem statement. After having clarified these path dependencies, we felt much more comfortable in identifying both causes and consequences to the problem statement.

4.3   Extension III: Explication of Different Stakeholder Perspectives

Detailed Problem Identification. Cognitive maps were originally developed to derive and to make explicit the hidden relationships among concepts that are inherent in the individual's mind. By their nature, these cognitive maps differ from one individual to the other. The challenge of creating a cognitive map as a group activity is therefore twofold: On the one hand, team members themselves need to explicate their own cognitive maps. On the other hand, these possibly deviating maps need to be understood within the group [23].

The deviation in individuals' cognitive maps might be caused by two different factors. First, it can be due to the perspective from which the problem is perceived (e.g., different job roles). When applying CCM4DSR, we experienced that what might be desirable from one perspective might be undesirable from another perspective. For instance, a project manager might argue, that the ignorance of EAM guidelines has a positive impact on the project's success because multiple functionalities can be implemented within one single application. At the same time, having multiple functionalities within one application is not desirable from an enterprise architects' perspective since this role is more in favor of a modular structure of the IS landscape.

Second, this deviation can be due to differences among the individual's values and beliefs. When applying CCM4DSR, we observed participants' distinctive assumptions on the expected behavior of the actors. While some believed that extensive documentation would lead to a better understanding (as more information is accessible), others argued that this would decrease the shared understanding because the documentation would become too time consuming to read.

Design and Development. We suggest to explicitly indicate the perspective from which the problem is perceived. To do so, we suggest to include actors' roles in the problem statement (see extension I). This could ultimately mean that several cognitive maps need to be created, each representing a particular perspective (e.g., one from the enterprise architect perspective and one from the project manager's perspective). Nevertheless, next to actors' roles, different values and beliefs is another factor in the resulting cognitive maps (as discussed earlier). Langfield-Smith [23] have thoroughly analyzed the process of creating cognitive maps in groups and conclude that collective cognitions are a "product of negotiation, argument and interaction" [23, p. 361]. Within the creation process of CCM4DSR, such a discussion should be encouraged and the result should be graphically depicted. In order to support this process, Langfield-Smith propose to make commonly shared values and beliefs more explicit. Transferred to the context of CCM4DSR, this means that the consequences and causes should be categorized based on actors' roles.

Demonstration and Evaluation. We have extended the graphical result of phase 1 of our EA project (i.e., problem diagnosis) with information about team members who supported a certain argument (see Fig. 4 for a shortened version of the same). By doing so, we were able to better identify the commonalities, which allow us to find arguments that are supported by all team members. However, this extension makes it complicated to design a CCM4DSR, if the team size was very large. In this case, we propose to only mark arguments that are not supported by all team members.

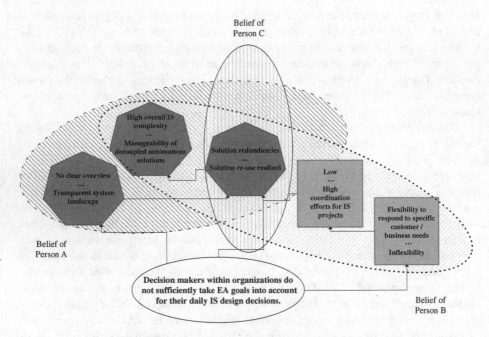

Fig. 4. CCM4DSR extended with information about personal beliefs

4.4   Extension IV: Procedure to Integrate Different Stakeholder Perspectives

Detailed Problem Identification. By making heterogeneous perspectives explicit (extension III), the goal to create one single CCM4DSR has not yet been reached. The main challenge in creating collective cognitive maps is to overcome the integration problem as well as the time required for this process [35]. Therefore, clear procedural guidance is required to integrate individual cognitive maps without favoring the view of certain actors. Tegarden and Sheetz [35] have analyzed earlier proposed approaches to create collective cognitive maps [23, 28, 36] and proposed a software supported approach. While the use of such a software supported approach may lead to better results, in the paper at hand we aim to understand the foundational mechanism and translate this into a respective CCM4DSR extension. Nonetheless, the procedure implemented by the software can be used to derive our targeted procedural guidelines.

Tegarden and Sheetz [35] suggest to define the problem statement prior to the session during which the collective cognitive map will be created. The session then starts with an individual creation of concepts related to the problem statement. These concepts are anonymously shared with the other participants. During a next round, but in the same manner as for concepts, categories of the proposed concepts are created. During the following discussion round, the participants agree on categories and assign the available concepts to the categories. Each participant then identifies causal relationships between the categories. The software finally creates a map depicting the relationships identified by all participants. Different views allow the individuals to compare their conceptualization and agree on a common version.

Design and Development. Based on the procedure described by Tegarden and Sheetz [35], we propose a more detailed guidance on the problem diagnosis phase of CCM4DSR with a clear differentiation between tasks performed by the team lead, the individual team members, and the team as a whole (see Table 1).

Table 1. Procedure for integrating different perspectives

Task		Phase in venable [7]	Relevant extension	Task performed by		
				Team lead	Individual	Team (meeting)
1	Propose initial problem statement	1 Problem diagnosis	I	X		optional
2	Provide written feedback		I		X	
3	Review feedbacks & agree on the problem statement		I			X
4	Identify path dependencies		II			X
5	Identify consequences				X	
6	Group consequences					X
7	Build relationships between consequences				X	
8	Build CCM showing personal beliefs		III	X		
9	Agree on a shared map					X
10	Repeat tasks 5–9 for causes					

The process should be initiated by the team lead, proposing an initial version of the problem statement to the team (task 1). Depending on the familiarity of the team members with the problem to be solved and the degree of deviating views regarding the relevance of the problem, the initial problem statement should be presented during a team meeting. Each team member then has time to provide a written feedback (task 2). It can thus be ensured that all concerns are treated equally during the following discussion in the first team meeting (task 3). During the same meeting, relevant path dependencies are identified and clarified (task 4). Each team member then individually creates consequences (and consequences of consequences etc.) (task 5). The team then meets again to group the identified consequences (task 6). During a next step, everyone builds a relationship model between the consequences and shares the same with the team lead (task 7), who prepares an integrated view (task 8). Based on this integrated view, the team agrees on a common map (task 9). Tasks 5–9 are then repeated for causes (and causes of causes, etc.) (task 10). This also marks the end of the problem diagnosis phase as described by Venable [7].

Demonstration and Evaluation. We applied and evaluated the proposed guideline in our EA project. One team member offered to guide through the process and proposed a problem statement to the team. After having discussed the problem statement via email, the team gathered to identify consequences of this problem statement. During this discussion, we realized that we need to be more explicit on path dependencies and made the same explicit. We agreed on certain assumptions about the past. Each individual wrote down consequences, which then were grouped by the team. We then built relations among these groups. Since the discussion of the consequences took much more time than initially planned, we scheduled a second meeting in order to identify causes. According to the feedback of the team members, the efficiency of the CCM4DSR creation was increased by differentiating between process steps where team members worked individually and other steps where collaboration was in place.

5   Discussion and Conclusion

In DSR projects, researchers target problem classes that are mainly of socio-technical nature and need to be collaboratively dealt with in order to eventually produce plausible and generalizable solutions. Relying on practical promises of cognitive mapping techniques in problem identification and since CCM4DSR is purposefully developed for cognitive mapping in DSR projects, we applied CCM4DSR in an enterprise architecture project (as a socio-technical IS phenomenon). By applying CCM4DSR, we tried to collaboratively achieve a common understanding of the problem of interest (i.e., why decision makers do not sufficiently consider enterprise architecture goals in their IS design decisions).

With the aim of improving the CCM4DSR technique in collaboratively dealing with socio-technical problems, the paper at hands reports the faced challenges in the first step of applying CCM4DSR (i.e., problem diagnosis) and proposes four extensions to the technique. These extensions provide guidance in (I) defining the problem statement, (II) dealing with path dependencies, and (III) considering different stakeholder perspectives. Furthermore, we proposed (IV) a procedure to consolidate different stakeholder perspectives. We further applied the proposed extensions in the context of our EA project to demonstrate their practical use and to validate their impact on achieving improved results. Therefore, our study contributes to the limited collection of techniques in DSR that allow us better understand the problem and align distinctive perceptions of the same problem. It goes beyond the extant use of cognitive mapping techniques, which have mostly been used to support decision making processes. It also provides additional guidelines and insights into how CCM4DSR can successfully be applied in better understanding socio-technical problems.

Persons interested in applying the extended CCM4DSR technique, should familiarize themselves with the CCM4DSR creation process. The articles of Venable [5, 7, 8] provide a detailed guidance and further examples on how to create a CCM4DSR.

Our proposed extensions are limited to the "problem diagnosis" step of the CCM4DSR technique. These extensions are informed by extant research (e.g., collective cognitive mapping and problem definition in strategic management) and helped us overcome certain challenges.

The evaluation of the proposed extensions is currently limited to the team of authors. This implies, that it could not yet be verified in how far the proposed extensions would also be valuable in a different context. We thus encourage other researchers and practitioners to apply CCM4DSR and the proposed extensions to facilitate a further evolution of the technique. Going further, the proposed extensions could be evaluated in a more rigid, quantitative manner. We propose to take the six evaluation criteria of progress for design theories by Aier and Fischer [37] as a reference for such an endeavor. The assessment of *utility* (1) would first require a verification of the relevance of the problems addressed. This could be done by asking individuals who have applied CCM4DSR in its original form to list down the challenges they faced. If the extensions address relevant problems, the challenges listed by the individuals will be at least similar to the problems solved by the extensions. Individuals who have been introduced to the extensions, could rate the likelihood of applying them in the future, which may serve as an indicator of their efficiency. If relevance and efficiency are given, a proposed extension is util. The evaluation of the *internal consistency* (2) should verify whether the single extensions do not contradict each other and whether terms are used consistently. One could do so by drawing relations between extensions (e.g., the formulation of the problem statement in extension I influences the identification of path dependencies in extension II) and creating a list of expressions applied. Given that the proposed extensions are based on justificatory knowledge, *external consistency* (3) could be evaluated by positioning the corresponding articles: Have they been criticized by other authors? How established are they in their domain? Further, the extensions should to be evaluated regarding their *purpose and scope* (4). Proposed artefacts such as the extensions need to be of general validity and applicable in different contexts for different purposes [37]. A possible approach could be to take the problem definitions of a larger number of (DSR) publications and creating CCM4DSRs in order to evaluate the general validity of the proposed extensions. Reviews of individuals applying our extensions will also be an indicator for *simplicity* (5). If they manage to describe the relevant content in a simpler way, the original extensions should be adjusted. Lastly, the *fruitfulness of new research findings* (6)—in particular of our extensions—should be discussed. Given that we have extended an existing technique, one could analyze the impact on the use of the CCM4DSR approach (e.g., novelty of the results, satisfaction of the team members, number of research projects where CCM4DSR is applied).

In addition, future research could also consider additional extensions in the *CCM Conversion* and *Solution Derivation* steps of CCM4DSR. For example, the impact of including additional creativity techniques to facilitate solution derivation could be analyzed. As the problem identification is an underserved topic in the existing DSR literature, we encourage prospective research to investigate or propose other techniques and methods.

Acknowledgements. This work has been supported by the Swiss National Science Foundation (SNSF).

References

1. Hevner, A.R., March, S.T., Park, J., Ram, S.: Design science in information systems research. MIS Q. **28**, 75–105 (2004)
2. Winter, R.: Problem analysis for situational artefact construction in information systems. In: Carugati, A., Rossignoli, C. (eds.) Emerging Themes in Information Systems and Organization Studies, pp. 97–113. Physica, Heidelberg (2011)
3. Montazemi, A.R., Conrath, D.W.: The use of cognitive mapping for information requirements analysis. MIS Q. **10**, 45–56 (1986)
4. Cronholm, S., Göbel, H., Lind, M., Rudmark, D.: The need for systems development capability in design science research: enabling researcher-systems developer collaboration. Inf. Syst. e-Bus. Manag. **11**, 335–355 (2013)
5. Venable, J.R.: Using Coloured Cognitive Mapping (CCM) for design science research. In: Tremblay, M.C., VanderMeer, D., Rothenberger, M., Gupta, A., Yoon, V. (eds.) DESRIST 2014. LNCS, vol. 8463, pp. 345–359. Springer, Cham (2014). doi:10.1007/978-3-319-06701-8_25
6. Fiol, C.M., Huff, A.S.: Maps For managers: where are we? Where do we go from here? J. Manag. Stud. **29**, 267–285 (1992)
7. Venable, J.R.: Coloured cognitive maps for modelling decision contexts. In: Bui, T., Gachet, A. (eds.) Proceedings of the First International Workshop on Context Modeling and Decision Support, Paris, France, pp. 1613–0073 (2005)
8. Venable, J.R.: Supporting problem formulation in is development with coloured cognitive maps. In: Proceedings of AIS SIGSAND European Symposium on Systems Analysis and Design: Practice and Research, Galway, Ireland, p. 105 (2006)
9. Haj-Bolouri, A., Svensson, L.: Designing for heterogeneous groups of end-users: towards a nascent design theory. In: Proceedings of World Conference on E-Learning in Corporate, Government, Healthcare, and Higher Education, pp. 765–776 (2014)
10. Pries-Heje, J., Baskerville, R.L.: The design theory nexus. MIS Q. **32**, 731–755 (2008)
11. Gregor, S.: The Nature of Theory in Information Systems. MIS Q. **30**, 611–642 (2006)
12. Peffers, K., Tuunanen, T., Rothenberger, M., Chatterjee, S.: A design science research methodology for information systems research. J. Manag. Inf. Syst. **24**, 45–77 (2007)
13. Mettler, T., Eurich, M., Winter, R.: On the use of experiments in design science research: a proposition of an evaluation framework. Commun. Assoc. Inf. Syst. **34**, 223–240 (2014)
14. Fischer, C., Gregor, S., Aier, S.: Forms of discovery for design knowledge. In: The 20th European Conference on Information Systems, Barcelona (2012)
15. Conboy, K., Gleasure, R., Cullina, E.: Agile design science research. In: Donnellan, B., Helfert, M., Kenneally, J., VanderMeer, D., Rothenberger, M., Winter, R. (eds.) DESRIST 2015. LNCS, vol. 9073, pp. 168–180. Springer, Cham (2015). doi:10.1007/978-3-319-18714-3_11

16. Baskerville, R.L., Pries-Heje, J., Venable, J.R.: Soft design science methodology. In: Fourth International Conference on Design Science Research in Information Systems and Technology (DESRIST 2009), pp. 1–11. ACM, Philadelphia (2009)
17. Tolman, E.C.U.: Cognitive maps in rats and men. Psychol. Rev. **55**, 189–208 (1948)
18. Neisser, U.: Introduction: The ecological and intellectual bases of categorization. In: Neisser, U. (ed.) Concepts and conceptual development: Ecological and intellectual factors in categorization, pp. 1–11. Cambridge University Press, Cambridge (1987)
19. Lakoff, G.: Cognitive models and prototype theory. In: Margolis, E., Laurence, S. (eds.) Concepts: Core Readings. The MIT Press, Cambridge (1999)
20. Swan, J.: Using cognitive mapping in management research: decisions about technical innovation. Br. J. Manag. **8**, 183–198 (1997)
21. Siau, K., Tan, X.: Use of cognitive mapping techniques in information systems development. J. Comput. Inf. Syst. **48**, 49–57 (2008)
22. Huff, A.S.: Mapping Strategic Thought. Wiley, Chichester (1990)
23. Langfield-Smith, K.: Exploring the need for a shared cognitive map. J. Manag. Stud. **29**, 349–368 (1992)
24. Hart, J.A.: Cognitive maps of three Latin American policy makers. World Polit. **30**, 115–140 (1977)
25. Axelrod, R.: Structure of decision: The cognitive maps of political elites. Princeton University Press, Princeton (1976)
26. Eden, C., Jones, S.: Publish or perish? - a case study. J. Oper. Res. Soc. **31**, 131–139 (1980)
27. Klein, J.H., Cooper, D.F.: Cognitive maps of decision-makers in a complex game. J. Oper. Res. Soc. **33**, 63–71 (1982)
28. Bougon, M.G.: Congregate cognitive maps: a unified dynamic theory of organization and strategy. J. Manag. Stud. **29**, 369–387 (1992)
29. Peffers, K., Tuunanen, T., Gengler, C.E., Rossi, M., Hui, W., Virtanen, V., Bragge, J.: The design science research process: a model for producing and presenting information systems research. In: Chatterjee, S., Hevner, A.R. (eds.) 1st International Conference on Design Science in Information Systems and Technology, Claremont, CA, pp. 83–106 (2006)
30. Boh, W.F., Yellin, D.: Using enterprise architecture standards in managing information technology. J. Manag. Inf. Syst. **23**, 163–207 (2007)
31. Baer, M., Dirks, K.T., Nickerson, J.A.: Microfoundations of strategic problem formulation microfoundations of strategic problem formulation. Strateg. Manag. J. **34**, 197–214 (2013)
32. Gregor, S., Jones, D.: The anatomy of a design theory. J. Assoc. Inf. Syst. **8**, 312–335 (2007)
33. Sydow, J., Schreyögg, G., Koch, J.: Organizational path dependence: opening the black box. Acad. Manag. Rev. **34**, 689–709 (2009)
34. Winter, R.: Design solution analysis for the construction of situational design methods. In: Ralyté, J., Mirbel, I., Deneckère, R. (eds.) ME 2011. IAICT, vol. 351, pp. 19–33. Springer, Heidelberg (2011). doi:10.1007/978-3-642-19997-4_4
35. Tegarden, D.P., Sheetz, S.D.: Group cognitive mapping: a methodology and system for capturing and evaluating managerial and organizational cognition. Omega **31**, 113–125 (2003)
36. Eden, C., Ackermann, F.: Making Strategy: The Journey of Strategic Management. Sage Publications, London (1998)
37. Aier, S., Fischer, C.: Criteria of progress for information systems design theories. Inf. Syst. E-Bus. Manag. **9**, 133–172 (2011)

Domain-Specific DSR Applications

Predictive Procurement Insights: B2B Business Network Contribution to Predictive Insights in the Procurement Process Following a Design Science Research Approach

Jan Gruenen[1], Christoph Bode[1(✉)], and Hartmut Hoehle[2]

[1] Business School, University of Mannheim, 68131 Mannheim, Germany
{gruenen,bode}@bwl.uni-mannheim.de
[2] Sam M. Walton College of Business,
University of Arkansas, Fayetteville, AR 72701, USA

Abstract. Significant recent developments in the domain of big data analytics provide the basis for leveraging predictive procurement insights in the procurement process. Following the path of other business domains, B2B business networks now have the potential to fill the gap of providing sufficient data for predictive technologies to be applied to the procurement domain, opening the door for significant efficiency gains. Based on the conceptual framework of the procurement process the methodology of design science research is applied to analyze prototype dashboards that leverage available data from B2B business networks.

Keywords: Predictive analytics · E-procurement · Electronic marketplace · Design science research

1 Introduction

Recent developments in the domain of big data predictive analytics have not yet arrived in the domain of procurement, presumably due to the lack of relevant and sufficient data. The focus of this paper is to analyze how predictive analytics could be applied in procurement and supply chain management by leveraging data from B2B business networks. In accordance with existing research, we define B2B business networks as electronic commerce business networking systems connecting multiple corporate customers and suppliers in order to facilitate purchasing activities across various spend categories [17]. In the context of this study, the B2B business network acts as a neutral and public collaboration platform, a setup in which an electronic intermediary is established as a digital trading platform facilitating the procurement process between companies [1, 27]. The main goal of B2B business networks is to streamline business processes and foster collaboration beyond the four walls of an individual firm. They serve to better discover, connect, understand and collaborate between customers, suppliers, banks, transportation providers, and other trading partners along the main three phases of a transaction: information, agreement and settlement [5].

© Springer International Publishing AG 2017
A. Maedche et al. (Eds.): DESRIST 2017, LNCS 10243, pp. 267–281, 2017.
DOI: 10.1007/978-3-319-59144-5_16

In contrast to existing research, this study analyses potential areas where B2B business networks can extend and build on their core function towards providing market information transparency and future prognosis capabilities. In an environment in which new digitalization technologies enable greater visibility, it becomes a competitive necessity for firms to better understand the demand signals coming through the supply chain. The hypothesis is that B2B business networks can help market participants anticipating, understanding, and acting on the signals in a collaborative network. Therefore, the paper describes the functions that provide predictive market insights to the participants based on the data collected in the network. Predictive analytic examples from neighboring fields show the potential these technologies provide: For example, in the domain of healthcare Google is able to predict influenza trends by analyzing online search data [32]. Examples from marketing show how companies leverage predictive insights to sell high-tech products [14], how machine learning is applied at a cable company [26], or how predictive analytics is used for measuring marketing performance [23]. Examples from the area of predictive maintenance suggest that predictive models can be used to determine the optimal replacement period for a rail track [20] or describe how predictive insights from machines running at clients sites are used at Heidelberger Druckmachinen [2]. Finally, there seem predictive analytics potentials in farming, where data from humidity sensors is combined with weather forecasts to optimize irrigation equipment and reduce water use [29].

2 Conceptual Background

In order to analyze the potential of B2B business networks to provide predictive insights, we start by revisiting the body of literature in the area of predictive analytics. Predictive analytics is not new, especially when abstracting the concept to the question if formal rules could be used to draw valid conclusions. Already Aristotle (384–322 B.C.) formulated a precise set of laws governing the rational part of the mind and for example Thomas Hobbes (1588–1679) built on that paradigm by arguing that reasoning was like numerical computation [21]. A core requirement of data science in this context is its predictive power, not just its ability to explain the past [6]. Predictive learning and descriptive learning needs to be separated: In the concept of predictive learning, training data is provided to learn the mapping of inputs and outputs from a set of data to create a formula which can then be applied to the entire data set to identify similar patterns. In contrast, descriptive learning is a process to find interesting patterns in the data as such, without the goal to formulate predictive statements [22]. Predictive business analytics is the technique to conduct future prognosis as compared to descriptive business analytics as the mean to visualize and package up historic data for consumption [18]. The concept of predictive learning includes setting a predictive framework in a process where data is analyzed for certain patterns, leveraging machine learning technologies, in order to formulate predictive statements, concluding in predictive models. These models and statements can then be applied to a specific set of data to make predictions along the identified patterns. Probabilities of predictive statements can be included in order to produce the most probable outcome based on the given data set [22]. Figure 1 shows how predictive statements are first tested to create a predictive model that can then be applied to further data sets in order to provide predictions [32].

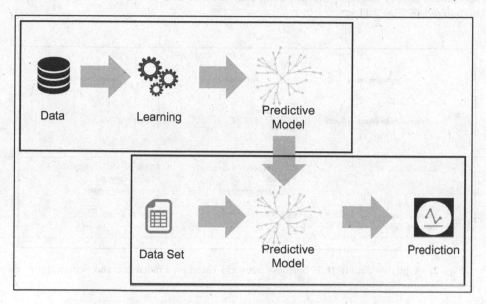

Fig. 1. Predictive learning and application based on Siegel [32].

Looking at the input data used for the analysis or prediction, big data promises actionable knowledge creation and superior predictive models [6]. Big data is characterized by the volume of data as well as by the variety in terms of unstructured information and the velocity (speed and dynamics) in which the data occurs [31]. This research follows the concept of predictive as forward looking analytics and calls the application to the procurement process as predictive procurement insights.

3 Predictive Procurement Insights in the Domain of B2B Business Networks

3.1 General Considerations on Predictive Procurement Insights from B2B Business Networks

The application of predictive analytics to the field of procurement and B2B business networks requires separation of information gathered from B2B business networks as compared to general available market research information. Williamson [36] outlines in his transaction cost framework that a reduction in transaction costs will facilitate trading and create an economic benefit. In contrast to aggregated bucket analysis, B2B business networks allow real-time dynamic data analytics directly from the network, providing real-time insights into actual commerce activities. To improve data integration of the data elements from various B2B business networks into the transactional client systems standards are emerging [8]. A B2B business network gathers significant data along the procurement process from information phase, agreement phase and settlement phase, including master data, transactional data as well as external data as visualized in Fig. 2 [16].

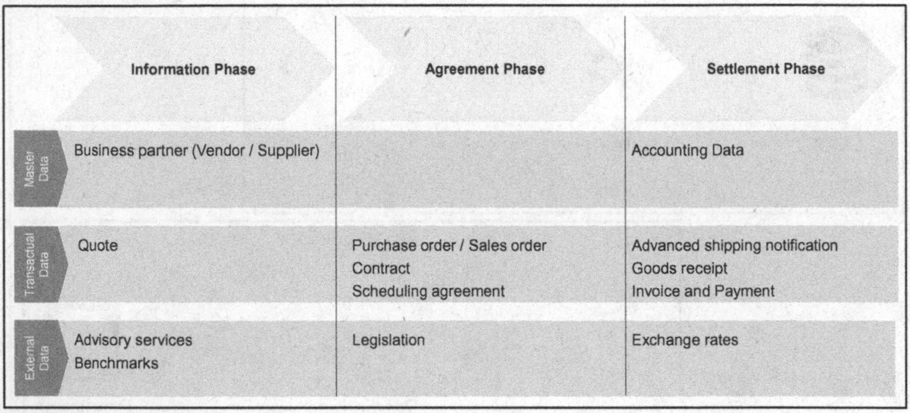

	Information Phase	Agreement Phase	Settlement Phase
Master Data	Business partner (Vendor / Supplier)		Accounting Data
Transactual Data	Quote	Purchase order / Sales order Contract Scheduling agreement	Advanced shipping notification Goods receipt Invoice and Payment
External Data	Advisory services Benchmarks	Legislation	Exchange rates

Fig. 2. Available data in B2B business networks based on Lindemann and Schmid [16].

"Master data" captured in a B2B business network covers the following aspects: Business partner master data of vendors as well as suppliers along with the necessary details for completing the transactions such as name of business partner, address and bank account. Accounting data includes company codes and account categories in the general ledger, such as projects or assets. The master data of the participants allows analysis of the company size, industry and geography, of which elements such as financial health, payment information and other compliance aspects could be derived by passing risk parameters down from region and industry. Data privacy compliance requires that all participants agree to share their master data with the participants of the network for the dedicated usage, including predictive procurement insights [25]. Furthermore, customers always have to have a clear opt-in into the usage of their data [3].

Transactional data could be made anonymous and then aggregated in order to be leveraged to provide insights in macro-level information on commercial activities in industries, geographies, and markets. The dynamic predictive models could then be applied to the dedicated information derived from the individual participant in order to provide predictions, following the predictive modeling approach from supervised learning. Further usage of the general transactional data, including prices, volumes, and timing of purchase units, is strictly limited and subject to aggregation and anonymization, since it is not owned by the B2B business network itself but belongs to the participants. Research elaborating on this crucial area of data privacy and commercial usage – outlining the problems of privacy issues with a focus on private persons which can possibly be applied to B2B environments – already exists [9, 34]. To conclude, the assumption is that transactional data could anonymously be derived from the underlying transactions such as quotes, sales respectively purchase orders, contracts, shipping documents including goods receipts, and invoice as well as payment documents with the following attributes: buyer, vendor, item, price, volume, and time stamp. This information could be leveraged to dynamically build predictive models which could then be applied on demand by the client on its' own individual data set as part of the prediction process as outlined in the conceptual background section. Table 1 illustrates the main documents and their attributes part of the procurement process.

Table 1. Transactional data documents and attributes.

Document	Description
Quote	Document describing the requested product/material or service from vendor and buyer side in conjunction with a request for price proposals
Sales order	Offer by a supplier to the customer to deliver a quantity of materials or perform a specified service within a specified time
Purchase order (including PO change revisions)	Request from a buyer to an external supplier to deliver a quantity of materials or perform a specified service within a specified time
Contract	Document outlining the scope of the traded object as well as the terms of usage
Scheduling agreement	Document informing the vendor which quantities of a product are to be delivered on which date/time
Advanced shipping notification	Document containing all data necessary for triggering and monitoring the delivery process
Goods receipts	Statement of physical acceptance of goods or materials into stock at customer side
Invoice	Document that states the invoice recipient's obligations to the company that sold the products
Payment (including payment proposals, payment schedules, remittance advice, etc.)	Notification that a payment is triggered in the payment run at client side

Finally, external data is captured during the procurement process and covers the following areas: market studies and other advisory services including benchmarks and legislative advisories, mostly occurring during the information and agreement phase of the procurement process. During the settlement phase, exchange rates become relevant and can be derived from external sources for international payments.

3.2 Application of Predictive Procurement Insights in B2B Business Networks

As discussed above, predictive analytics in sales and marketing is a well-researched domain. Although sellers and buyers play an evenly important role on two-sided B2B business networks [7], the further analysis of potential predictive procurement insights will focus on the buyer and procurement perspective. The concept assumes that business data is derivable from B2B business networks, as a facilitator of procurement transactions and provider of the relevant data. The goal is to get more clarity on the potential application of predictive procurement insights, as this topic is not well covered in existing research. This subsection therefore elaborates on specific examples how predictive procurement insights could be operationalized and provide a basis for B2B business networks to enter that space.

Description of Methodological Approach. In order to visualize and illustrate the potentials of predictive analytics in the procurement domain the design science approach is chosen for this research. This approach seems ideal because according to Hevner et al. [11] the design-science paradigm seeks to extend the boundaries of human and organizational capabilities by creating new and innovative artifacts. In addition, according to March and Storey [19], the problem-focused approach to bridge the challenges between research and practitioners is ideal to describe desired organizational information processing capabilities and their relationship with present and desired organizational situations, and develop actions that enable the implementation of information processing capabilities that move the organization toward desired situations. Gregor and Hevner [10] further elaborate that the design science methodology is well suited to outline and design process elements as conducted below. In order to illustrate the potentials of predictive procurement insights, we selected the design science research process suggested by Peffers et al. [28]. Each prototype comprises a design illustrated in prototypes of a schematic management dashboard, which consumes the predictive procurement insights from a user perspective. The business motivation of each prototype is set before the actual artifact and evaluation metrics are given directly after each dashboard, with the goal to "observe and measure how well the artifact supports a solution to the problem." [28, p. 56]. This analysis is done in line with the argumentation from Vaishnavi and Keuchler [35], who point out that design and evaluation of an artifact typically require different skills and are therefore often conducted separately. They elaborate that although the initial presentation of a research model provides some evaluation of the artifacts, the primary evaluation is usually completed as other researchers analyze the artifacts and put them into other settings. Thus, a complete design and evaluation is rarely completed in the same paper [35]. Therefore the business value segment discusses potential benefits arising from the processes outlined, each highlighting a number of economic means to measure the benefits. This approach is applying what Hevner et al. [28] referred to as the "informed argument" method. Therefore, those metrics provide a measurement framework for further research evaluating the assumptions in real world scenarios or in lab environments that will then as well provide the basis to isolate training data records and approaches to concrete predictive models. This is a future research topic on the researchers' agenda and not part of the present study.

Problem Identification and Objectives of the Solution. In order to identify specific applications how predictive procurement insights can be provided based on the information available on B2B business networks, a simplified view of the procurement process is required. Figure 3 below shows strategic as well as operational procurement

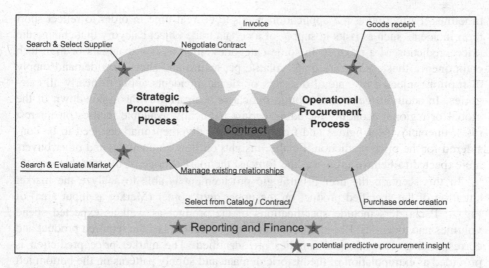

Fig. 3. Simplified view on procurement processes highlighting potential predictive procurement insight areas based on Johnson and Flynn [12].

activities and supporting overarching functions from finance and reporting, high-lighting areas where predictive procurement insights could be leveraged [12].

In the strategic procurement process the areas of "market research and evaluation" and "supplier search and selection" are candidates for prototyping predictive pro-curement insight potentials. Predictive procurement insight 1 is located in the infor-mation phase of the procurement process whereas predictive procurement insight 2 is embedded in the supplier selection process part of the agreement phase. In the context of operational procurement, that deals with the procurement execution inside frame contracts and selective spot-buy activities of non-catalog items, predictive procurement insight 3 can be envisioned in the activity of purchasing and goods receive as part of the settlement phase. Finally supporting functions to the end-to-end procurement process from finance and reporting provide a good opportunity for predictive pro-curement insights 4 and 5. All predictive insights as described here represent an early warning system, helping the various procurement functions to control the risks of their tasks and to enable them to act based on the best available real-time knowledge [16].

Prototypes. The following prototypes highlight potential areas where predictive pro-curement insights can be injected into existing processes and applications. The sce-narios are simplified for the purpose of visualizing the potential applications and benefits for the different stages in the procurement process. They are not meant as a specification of how a solution could look like. The ultimate design depends on how these functions are realized in the individual existing procurement solution.

Predictive Procurement Prototype 1. Uncertainty and missing transparency on price trends, globally, regionally, or category related, is one of the main challenges in pro-curement and this application tries to predict the future prices of selected procurement objects. An ideal solution includes simulation capabilities along quantities and timelines. Furthermore, the application needs to be real time in order to reflect short term incidents such as risks in supply of a certain trade object category that change the price prediction of a product. In some categories, such as raw materials or high tech components, these prices are quite volatile per nature and short term demand/supply disruptions injected by natural disasters or similar incidents apply to nearly all categories. In addition, general economic indicators such as growth or slowdown of the global or regional economy including certain publically available metrics on interest rates, unemployment figures and from related and divergent markets need to be considered for the price prediction. Finally, insights on how competitors and other buyers are expected to behave influence the forecast the market price of the tradable object.

In this scenario the user in strategic procurement is able to analyze the market situation of the specified product on the upper right corner (Market as input area) of Fig. 4. Parameters include specifications of the product as well as expected spend volumes and locations. Based on this, information vendors of the required product and corresponding demands and supplies are identified. The market price prediction is provided as extrapolation of the historic demand and supply patterns on the bottom left (marked as prediction area), here presented on a yearly time scale, but potentially a monthly, weekly or daily time horizon could be as valid, depending on the price volatility in the market.

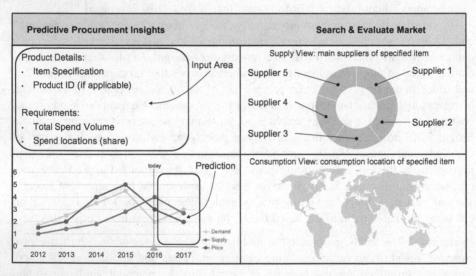

Fig. 4. Predictive procurement insight 1: price prediction in search and evaluate market phase.

Valid predictions of future prices are undoubtedly very beneficial for procurement functions. Simulation capabilities along existing inventories and future requirements can provide guidance on the ideal time to buy, relevant especially in volatile markets with strong price fluctuations. The potentials derive from a now possible strategy where predictive insights are leveraged to decide on the right time to buy a certain product as compared to a periodic or purely demand driven procurement plan, benchmarking own purchase conditions to general trends and enabling the procurement function to leverage price predictions to trigger procurement at times of relative low prices. Sellers on the network that offer more attractive prices and conditions are made transparent. Interesting for the participants will be the impact on the price of a certain trading object from global or regional trends as well as from related and divergent markets. For the predictive model this means that not only historic purchasing patterns from within one company are relevant for training the predictive model, but the data is enriched with purchasing behavior of competitors as well. As a side note, for sellers it will be interesting to analyze the industry usage patterns of their trading object and identify changing trends of usage of their products in order to identify new markets, as outlined by Kim and Mauborgne [13]. For increasing the sellers' performance additional analytics such as providing insights into their respective customer base as elaborated by Lee et al. [15] might be of interest.

Predictive Procurement Prototype 2. Transparency of risk patterns of the trading partners are essential for procurement and most beneficial if these are not only based on historic figures but include a risk prediction component. This application is designed to predict the risk of the selected suppliers and provide transparency of the risk-price ratio. Parameters defining the risk score are inventory and production locations of the supplier in comparison with the specified item required location. The risk score is then a result of the existing network of vendor relationships of the selected supplier and a combination of the risk of the suppliers of the supplier. The actual risk patterns are derived from historic figures on the individual suppliers along delivery accuracy, product quality and inventories as well as transportation distances and times and financial aspects of the supplier. These insights are most valuable if they include regulatory and market risks of the trading partner due to the specific political, economic or geographical market environment. Finally sustainability and environmental aspects can be included in the risk patterns, helping purchasing organizations to understand the sustainability aspects of their suppliers and leverage these in the supplier selection phase.

In this scenario, visualized in Fig. 5, the user in strategic procurement is drilling down into a specific supplier from the list (marked as input area) to learn more on the environment of the vendor, resulting in the predicted risk patterns (as shown in the prediction area).

Based on this, predictive information suppliers are evaluated by risk price ratio. More comprehensive scenarios could even allow for drill down into 2nd and 3rd tier suppliers of the supplier along the product bill of material and produce a combined risk score including these elements. This enables the procurement organization to evaluate suppliers of the required item from a risk point of view, to ultimately identify the supplier offering at the best price with the lowest possible risk. An example shows how such functionality could be leveraged to automatically and systematically detect fraud in ecommerce [4], despite the focus on private individuals as market participants allows only a partial application to B2B environments. Finally, predictive procurement insights that allow drilling-down into components and ingredients along product pedigrees and bill of materials, create additional value along quicker and more sophisticated product compliance and risks analysis, proactively as well as exception based.

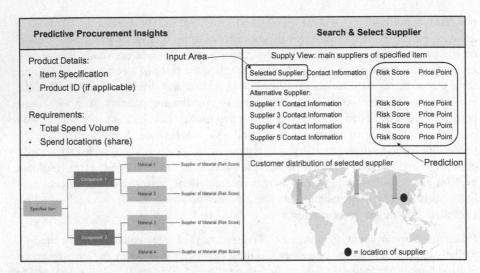

Fig. 5. Predictive procurement insight 2: risk prediction in supplier search and select phase.

Predictive Procurement Prototype 3. Operational procurement functions lack predictive procurement insights in lead times and expected arrival dates outside of the agreed terms and conditions with the supplier. This application should predict the estimated arrival time from the supplier and add a risk premium to the lead times. The risk predictions can be derived from historical lead times from own purchase orders as well as delivery performance information from other deliveries from the same supplier, as available on the network [30]. This predictive information can further be enriched with information from weather forecasts or bottlenecks for example resulting from natural disasters, which could impact the delivery performance of suppliers from certain geographies.

In the scenario displayed in Fig. 6 the user in operational procurement is selecting a specific supplier from the list of certified suppliers for a specific purchase item based on the required delivery time and standard lead times as well as potential expedition charges (input areas). The output of agreed timelines is enhanced with predicted delivery forecasts on standard and express delivery options (prediction area).

Predictive procurement insight 3 covers a prediction of the logistics performance of the supplier, improving the on-time delivery ratios. Based on this prognosis buyers can leverage the data for operational procurement planning and logistics activities, reducing inventory levels via reduced re-order points made possible by the insights from lead times estimations as part of the goods receipt forecast process. Ultimately this leads to reduced tied-up capital in working assets.

Predictive Procurement Prototype 4. Transparency on contract spending, including prediction and forecast, often is a challenge and requires a lot of effort, especially when looking at the predicted usage of agreed volume discounts in contracts, and providing guidance for operational procurement behavior. Therefor this application predicts the spend behavior within a given frame contract. This information can be derived from

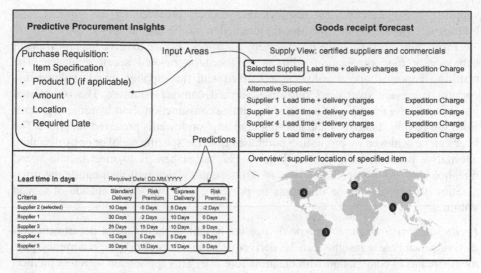

Fig. 6. Predictive procurement insight 3: risk premium prediction on delivery lead times.

multiple sources, such as forecasts on planned spending from inside the organization as well as historical own spend patterns with the supplier as well as supplier spend patterns from other buyers on the network, as well as general economic trends.

Figure 7 visualizes the reporting scenario on contract spend predictions, where the user in the procurement reporting function selects a specific contract from the list of suppliers (input area). The table shows the timelines of the contracts and the actual spend volumes year to date as well as potentially agreed thresholds for spend volumes. From here the user can drill into contractual details and departments leveraging the

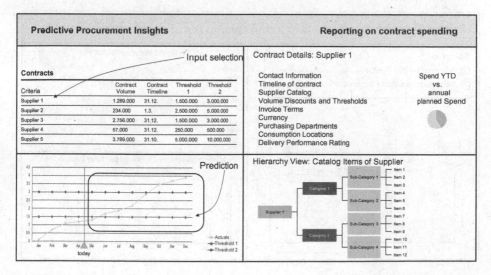

Fig. 7. Predictive procurement insight 4: contract spending predictions for reporting.

supplier. The hierarchy view displays the products provided by the supplier. The bottom left (prediction area) shows the prediction on the annual spend.

From this information the procurement department is able to drive the procurement behavior of the organization with an enhanced operational spend guidance. The resulting improved spend volumes, as agreed with the supplier, enable volume discounts or prevent overspend outside of agreed contract volumes. The operational guidance can for example be executed by cutting consumption short by removing items from the buying catalogues and steering consumption towards preferred suppliers. The later can be achieved by promoting purchases from the specific supplier or by disabling alternative products from the catalogues. This target here is to meet certain spend thresholds or at least enable early plan adjustments, which will then entitle the organization to agreed volume discounts or prevent costly overspend outside of agreed volumes.

Predictive Procurement Prototype 5. For the benefit of the financial department predictive procurement insights can be derived from invoices and foreign currency payment streams in conjunction with business forecasts. This application therefore predicts the liquidity requirements from a procurement perspective. This prediction will allow for insights required to plan for cash flow liquidity in order to optimize on early payment discounts and currency hedging preventing risks from currency fluctuations incurred by cross border multi-currency transactions.

In this context, as shown in Fig. 8, the finance department has the option to choose either minimum total spend, optimizing on early payment discounts, or minimum liquidity requirements, paying the bills as late as possible (input area). The selection depends on multiple aspects, including the liquidity situation of the company but as well general interest rates and conditions on the financial markets. The predictions on cash and foreign currency requirements can in addition be based on internal

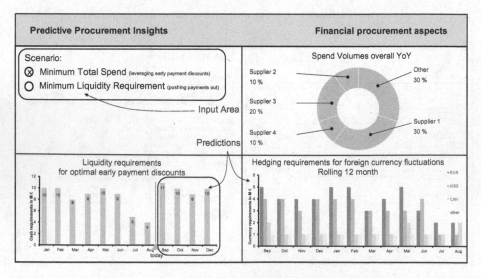

Fig. 8. Predictive procurement insight 5: financial spend prediction on liquidity requirements.

information on planned spending volumes from the reporting scenario above, enhanced with external information on general market and financial market predictions which have the potential to strongly influence interest rates as well as foreign currency exchange rates.

From a financial aspect this predictive procurement insight enables the finance department to optimize the payment runs based on the terms of payment without incurring default charges with minimum liquidity requirements. Currency hedging requirements from cross border multi-currency transactions are another aspect that can be optimized with this function. Ultimately this enables the finance department to lower the cash liquidity reserves while optimizing the usage of liquidity to benefit from early payment discounts.

4 Discussion

The results of this study suggest there are numerous areas where predictive procurement insights, potentially harvested from B2B business networks, are interesting and relevant for managers. However, several prerequisites and environmental aspects have to be carefully analyzed and addressed in order for these examples to become reality. For valuable and significant predictive procurement insights, the data basis of the B2B business network must be sufficiently large in order to provide meaningful insights, not only on a global level but also when drilling down into certain aspects of the business along dedicated categories and geographies. Thus, predictive procurement insights require an extensive usage of the trading platform for operational procurement activities, a prerequisite which most probably can only be attained by a few operators in that field and only from operators covering a broad spectrum of spend categories across a broad customer community. Alternatively, the procurement organization could build their own predictive application to harvest the data from multiple sources and conduct their own predictive procurement insights – an undertaking which takes significant effort and still depends on accurate data provisioning from the outside. Furthermore, the topic of privacy is a crucial one for the data providers to solve. While Solove [33], in his taxonomy of privacy, limits the scope to outline possible problem areas of privacy, Ohm [25] differentiates collection, use, and disclosure of data and highlights the "Fair Information Practice Principles" as well as the OECD guidelines on the protection of privacy and trans-border flows of personal data. These standards will need to be obeyed strictly by any B2B business network provider of predictive procurement insights. In addition, these operators will need to make sure that the terms of condition are known by their customers and do actually allow them to use the data in those manners outlined above.

5 Conclusion

Can B2B business networks contribute to the procurement process by providing predictive procurement insights? As suggested by the results of this paper, this is the case, if certain parameters are fulfilled: Firstly, the data collected in the network must be large and sufficiently rich in order to provide meaningful insights on micro-levels of the business; secondly, the legal and ethical aspects of data privacy must be addressed appropriately, including updated and agreed terms of usage of the network by the participants, in order for the B2B business network operator to use the data obtained in the process. These two issues are not easy to tackle and it might take more years of consolidation and experience in the field, until the potential of B2B business networks as sources for predictive procurement insights can be fully exploited. It might be a sensible approach to leverage the data in a step-wise manner and to introduce the concept incrementally. In a first step, the data could be analyzed in internal pilot projects in research collaboration with firms experienced in the field of data analytics and predictions, without monetization and only with a limited focus. Experience from those pilots could then be used to convince participants from the benefits and be shared jointly with the updated usage term contracts, convincing participants to opt-in. The field of predictive analytics is broad and there is much to learn along the journey. Further research should therefore select a promising field of predictive procurement insights of B2B business networks and develop an example based on data available to showcase the potentials in a real world or lab environment. Privacy concerns will be there along the way and it will be crucial to address them in every pilot and with every iterative approach in this domain.

References

1. Agrawal, A., De Meyer, A., Van Wassenhove, L.: Managing value in supply chains: case studies on the sourcing hub concept. Calif. Manag. Rev. **56**(2), 23–54 (2014)
2. Allmendinger, G., Lombreglia, R.: Four strategies for the age of smart services. Harvard Bus. Rev. **83**(10), 131–138 (2005)
3. Bell, J.: Machine Learning: Hands-On for Developers and Technical Professionals. Wiley, Indianapolis (2015)
4. Chiu, C., Ku, Y., Lie, T., Chen, Y.: Internet auction fraud detection using social network analysis and classification tree approaches. Int. J. Electron. Commer. **15**(3), 123–147 (2011)
5. Cross, R., Gray, P.: Where has the time gone? Addressing collaboration overload in a networked economy. Calif. Manag. Rev. **56**(1), 50–66 (2013)
6. Dhar, V.: Data science and prediction. Commun. ACM **56**(12), 64–73 (2013)
7. Eisenmann, T., Parker, G., Van Alstyne, M.: Strategies for two-sided markets. Harvard Bus. Rev. **84**(10), 92–101 (2006)
8. Folmer, E., Luttighuis, O.P., van Hillegersberg, J.: Do semantic standards lack quality? A survey among 34 semantic standards. Electron. Markets **21**(2), 99–111 (2011)
9. Galanxh, H., Nah, F.: Privacy issues in the era of ubiquitous commerce. Electron. Markets **16**(3), 222–232 (2006)
10. Gregor, S., Hevner, A.: Positioning design science research for maximum impact. MIS Q. **37**(2), 337–355 (2013)
11. Hevner, A., March, S., Park, J., Ram, S.: Design science in information systems research. MIS Q. **28**(1), 75–105 (2004)
12. Johnson, P., Flynn, A.: Purchasing and Supply Management. McGraw-Hill, New York (2015)

13. Kim, W., Mauborgne, R.: Blue Ocean Strategy: How to Create Uncontested Market Space and Make the Competition Irrelevant. Harvard Business School Press, Boston (2007)
14. Kumar, V., Venkatesan, R., Reinartz, W.: Knowing what to sell, when, and to whom. Harvard Bus. Rev. **84**(3), 131–150 (2006)
15. Lee, J., Son, J., Suh, K.: Can market knowledge from intermediaries increase sellers' performance in on-line marketplaces? Int. J. Electron. Commer. **14**(4), 69–102 (2010)
16. Lindemann, M., Schmid, B.: Framework for specifying, building, and operating electronic markets. Int. J. Electron. Commer. **3**(2), 7–21 (1998)
17. Mahadevan, B.: Making sense of emerging market structures in B2B E-Commerce. Calif. Manag. Rev. **46**(1), 86–100 (2003)
18. Maisel, L., Cokins, G.: Predictive Business Analytics: Forward Looking Capabilities to Improve Business Performance. Wiley, Hoboken (2014)
19. March, S., Storey, V.: Design science in the information systems. MIS Q. **32**(4), 725–730 (2008)
20. Merrick, J., Soyer, R., Mazzuchi, T.: Are maintenance practices for railroad tracks effective? J. Am. Stat. Assoc. **100**(469), 17–25 (2005)
21. Minelli, M., Chambers, M., Dhiraj, A.: Big Data, Big Analytics: Emerging Business Intelligence and Analytic Trends for Today's Businesses. Wiley, Hoboken (2013)
22. Murphy, K.: Machine Learning: A Probabilistic Perspective. MIT Press, Cambridge (2013)
23. Nichols, W.: Advertising analytics 2.0. Harvard Bus. Rev. **91**(3), 60–68 (2013)
24. OECD Guidelines on the Protection of Privacy and Transborder Flows of Personal Data (2013). http://oe.cd/privacy. Accessed 04 Jan 2016
25. Ohm, P.: Changing the rules: general principles for data use and analysis. In: Lane, J. (ed.) Privacy, Big Data, and the Public Good: Frameworks for Engagement. Cambridge University Press, New York (2014)
26. Olson, R.: How machines learn (and you win). Harvard Bus. Rev. **93**(11), 36–40 (2015)
27. Ordanini, A.: The effects of participation on B2B exchanges: a resource based view. Calif. Manag. Rev. **47**(2), 97–113 (2005)
28. Peffers, K., Tuunanen, T., Rothenberger, M., Chatterjee, S.: A design science research methodology for information systems research. J. Manag. Inf. Syst. **24**(3), 45–77 (2007)
29. Porter, M., Heppelmann, J.: How smart, connected products are transforming companies. Harvard Bus. Rev. **93**(10), 96–114 (2015)
30. Rabinovich, E., Knemeyer, M.: Logistic service providers in internet supply chains. Calif. Manag. Rev. **48**(4), 84–108 (2006)
31. Sharda, R.: Business Intelligence and Analytics: Systems for Decision Support. Pearson, Boston (2015)
32. Siegel, E.: Predictive Analytics: The Power to Predict Who Will Click, Buy, Lie, or Die. Wiley, Hoboken (2013)
33. Solove, D.: A taxonomy of privacy. Univ. Pennsylvania Law Rev. **154**(3), 477–564 (2006)
34. Spiekermann, S., Acquisti, A., Böhme, R., Hui, K.: The challenges of personal data markets and privacy. Electron. Markets **25**(2), 161–167 (2015)
35. Vaishnavi, V., Kuechler, W.: Design Science Research Methods and Patterns: Innovating Information and Communication Technology. Auerbach, New York (2007)
36. Williamson, O.: The Economic Institutions of Capitalism. Free Press, New York (1985)

Budget Transparency for Monitoring Public Policies: Limits of Technology and Context

Erico Przeybilovicz[1(✉)], Maria Alexandra Cunha[1],
and Angela Póvoa[2]

[1] Fundação Getulio Vargas – Escola de Administração de Empresas de São Paulo,
São Paulo, SP, Brazil
{erico.prz, alexandra.cunha}@fgv.br
[2] Pontifícia Universidade Católica do Paraná, Curitiba, PR, Brazil
angelapovoa@gmail.com

Abstract. The purpose of this study was to develop a method to seek information for organization of civilian society to monitor public budgeting. To this end, a methodological approach based on Design Science Research through the building of artifacts was used, making theoretical and practical contributions to the field. The research question that guided the study was: how can a civil society organization monitor the achievement of public policy goals using information available on transparency websites? The objects of the study were the National Education Plan (NEP), which sets the goals for the development of education in Brazil, and the public budget of the federal government. By constructing the method, it was possible to deduce some aspects regarding the implications of transparency for the monitoring and projection of public policies. In the context in question, budget transparency was scarce on the websites. When monitoring is possible, society is interested in using budget transparency to project the enactment of a public policy rather than only monitor the past. A generalized method was proposed for monitoring public policies that enables this projection in the Brazilian context.

Keywords: Transparency · Design Science Research · Public budget · Public policy

1 Introduction

Transparency is the process of making state actions public. Governments can promote transparency to improve the acceptance and legitimacy of political processes. Citizens, non-governmental organizations and other groups can demand transparency to promote their own interests and monitor state actions. In this context, there is an element which, according to Grönlund [1] and Macintosh [2], is a tool for transparency, Information and Communications Technology (ICT), especially the websites. Websites can enable citizens to interact with their representatives, stating their needs, voicing their opinions on public policies and monitoring the actions of the state.

In this study, a method was developed to seek information on government budget execution, for the purpose of monitoring and control of the goals of federal public

© Springer International Publishing AG 2017
A. Maedche et al. (Eds.): DESRIST 2017, LNCS 10243, pp. 282–295, 2017.
DOI: 10.1007/978-3-319-59144-5_17

policy for basic education as expressed in the National Education Plan (NEP). The method was drawn up at the request of an organization in civilian society, the Marista Solidariedade Foundation, which promotes programs, projects and actions to support and help children and young people. In Brazil, it operates through 21 education and social centers, one of which is the Marista Center for the Aid and Support of Children (CEDIN), where the present study was conducted.

In Brazil, the public budget is controlled by a set of laws and regulations that oblige the state to plan and account for expenditure and investments. The budget is connected to public policies for the development of the nation, such as education, for which there are long-term plans. In the case of education, the NEP is a public policy with directives, strategies and goals to promote schooling in the country. However, the budgeting and financial tools of the government are cumbersome. As a result, it is difficult for society to monitor public policies.

To research this theme, the Design Science Research is used in this study. Design science seeks solutions through the production of artifacts, transforming the existing situation into a desired one [3]. The study was guided by the following question: how can a civil society organization monitor the achievement of public policy goals using information available on transparency websites? The construction of the method enabled a response to the question and reach conclusions regarding the implications of budget transparency to monitor and project public policies in the Brazilian context.

From a theoretical viewpoint, this study seeks to complement studies on the implications of the social use of ICT, especially the websites, in developing countries such as Brazil. These studies have resulted in innovative reflections due to the fact that they take social and cultural aspects into account, which has been a scarce feature in the literature [4]. It also helps to identify elements regarding the different views pessimist, optimist and pragmatic of the use of websites in transparency actions. From a practical viewpoint, the study aids the search for a solution to a specific problem of an organization: the need for a method for monitoring public policies.

In this Sect. 1, we present the theme of our work. In the Sect. 2, we detail public budget, public policy for education in Brazil and some transparency concepts and the website role for transparency. Section 3 give a short presentation about Design Science Research and our research argument. The methodological procedures used for data collection and analysis is presented in Sects. 4 and 5 presents the discussion of the results. In Sect. 6 we conclude this work with our considerations.

2 Public Budget, Public Policy for Education in Brazil and Transparency

There are two views on the concept of public budget: the traditional and the modern. In the traditional view, the main function of a budget is political control, a disciplinary instrument of public finance. In the modern view, a budget has the added function of being an instrument of administration, helping the executive branch in the administrative process of programing, executing and monitoring finances and government work [5]. More recently, the public budget has had another added characteristic, as a document for divulging government actions to the public, returning to its function as an instrument for the social monitoring and control of public money [6].

In Brazil, the public budget is formed using three instruments: the annual budget, also known as the Annual Budget Law (LOA), which is the budget per se, lasting for one year. The Law of Budgetary Directives (LDO) is an instrument that operationalizes programs for sectors and regions in the medium term, also lasting for one year. The Law for the Multi-year Plan (PPA) is the framework for national plans in which large objectives and goals are set, together with strategic projects and basic policies, lasting for four years.

The budget contains the financial information on revenue and expenditure. Expenditure is listed in different ways in the budget. One way is the functional classification, made up of functions and sub-functions. A function is the highest level of expenditure. A sub-function is immediately below the function and explains the nature of a government action. Combining functions and sub-functions basically means asking 'in which areas of expenditure will government action be taken'.

Responsibility for public education in Brazil is shared by the federal, state and municipal governments. Education is divided into basic and higher learning. Basic education includes elementary school, junior high and high school. Part of the resources earmarked for basic education comes from the federal government budget and the remainder is divided between the states and municipalities.

The federal government, together with the states and municipalities, has a specific law for public education policies, the National Education Plan (NEP). The law in force from 2014 to 2024 contains ten objective directives and twenty goals and specific strategies for their implementation. Social movements and organized groups have worked to establish a dialogue with the government to discuss the current problem of insufficient funds for education and monitoring it. These groups propose bolder goals, and for this there is a need to analyze their technical and budgetary feasibility. This is one of the more controversial points [7], as is monitoring budget execution to achieve these goals. ICTs resources like websites are one of the tools that can be used for this purpose. ICT can help to gain access to certain information and present it more clearly. This would affect people's ability to share and understand decision making [1]. Access to ICT could also enable people to work as partners and promote social benefits, such as transparency [8]. On the one hand, technology can become an instrument of rhetoric in the hands of politicians, and on the other a tool for democratic explanations and an opportunity for citizens to influence decision making processes [1].

When it comes to transparency there is a paradox. If on the one hand there are authors who believe that ICT will empower citizens in the democratic process [9–12], there are others that believe that governments will use ICT to increase their control over people and those in power will only publicize the information that they deem to be convenient [13–15]. There are also those with a more pragmatic view, recognizing in ICT a potential for a more participative form of democracy [16–18], enabling citizens to participate more directly in government decision making.

Public information is a social right, explicitly guaranteed in the legislation of most democratic countries. In the case of Brazil, it is included in the Federal Constitution of 1988 and in Law 12.527/2011, known as the Freedom of Information Act [10]. It can also be found in Complementary Law 131/2009 and Complementary Law 101/2000.

These laws regulate access to information and compel all branches of governments to publish their data [18]. In many countries, the effectiveness of these laws is directly linked to the implementation of initiatives based on ICT [19], especially on the website [18], which offers a new approach to the creation of transparency and the promotion of social control [8].

From an optimistic viewpoint, access to government information, accounts and publications as means for the public to obtain data [1] would facilitate the monitoring [20] and vigilance of representatives and institutions [11, 12]. By having access to these data, the public can be better informed regarding the political process, which would lead citizens to make informed choices and communicate their representatives and government agencies [21]. Although it is too early to measure the impact of initiatives based on websites concerning transparency and social monitoring, there are some signs that websites can promote transparency and fight corruption [22]. It can provide information on government rules and citizen's rights, information on government decisions and actions, enable monitoring of government actions and expenditure and the divulging of information on government performance.

The discussion on the transparency of government actions has become particularly relevant given the rapid growth and evolution of website. Around the world and in Brazil tools have been created to make information available from many government spheres. People can access this information on the websites. The websites by allowing access to information made available by public agencies from anywhere in the world, 24 h a day [23], may be one instrument for building a more effective democracy.

Other studies do not have such optimistic results. Initiatives founded on websites as a tool for transparency and social control of public policies are not guaranteed success in every country that implements them and they do not always lead to advances in transparency [8]. Sometimes, the use of website creates new behaviors that are considered corrupt [24], favoring those who know how to operate websites [25]. The use of websites can produce very different results in different countries and cultures [24]. The success of initiatives based on websites as a strategy for social control will depend on issues of implementation, education and acceptance of websites by citizens and local culture [8]. Transparency tools based on websites are often limited by problems of ability, research capacity, language, legal and political context, technological literacy, sufficient technological infrastructure and trust in social institutions [26–28].

3   Design Science Research

Design Science can be understood as the set of researches in the several areas of knowledge, in which the objective is the investigation of artificial, man-made artifacts. In Design Science Research, the objective is to investigate the artificial and its behavior, both from the academic point of view and from the organization [29]. Thus, Design Science Research is a rigorous process of designing artifacts to solve problems, evaluate what has been designed or is in operation and communicate the results obtained.

In this paper, we use the definition of March and Smith [30] and Hevner et al. [31] for artifact: it can be a construct, a model, a method or an instantiation. In this definition, 'methods' are the ways to accomplish the activities directed to the objectives, are the necessary steps to carry out a certain task. They can be represented graphically or in specific heuristics and algorithms.

Hevner et al. [31] proposed seven practical rules for conducting research using the Design Science approach. Such guidelines describe the characteristics for conducting good research, the most important of which is that research must produce an artifact for a specific problem: (1) the object of study is an artifact: in this work the artifact is the method of searching for information of the governmental budget; (2) relevance of the problem: the artifact is relevant to the solution of a problem faced by one civil society organization, CEDIN, how can monitor the achievement of NEP goals using budget information available on the websites; (3) project evaluation: their usefulness, quality and effectiveness must be rigorously evaluated. In this study we perform a black box test, executing the method; (4) research contributions: the research should represent a verifiable contribution, this study contributed for a solution to a specific problem of an organization an give reflections about budget transparency on the websites; (5) rigor of the research: rigor should be applied in the development of the artifact and its evaluation; this is demonstrated in the methodological procedures (6) design as a research process: the development of the artifact was a research process that draws from existing problem and proposal a solution; (7) research communication: finally, the research must be communicated effectively to the interested public, like in this article. Considering that education is a relevant topic for the Brazilian context and that a civil society organization has an interest in monitoring the achievement of the NEP goals, this study proposes to develop a method of monitoring the public budget of education based in information available on the websites and for this was used the Design Science Research approach.

4   Methodological Procedures

The artifacts are potentially constructs, models, methods or instances [31] and thus the study was dedicated to the development of a method. The methodology used in this study for elaborate the method was that of Peffers et al. [32] developed for research in design science which include five stages described below. In the execution of these five stages a qualitative approach was used. Three meetings with a mean duration of 1.5 h each were held with three managers and five CEDIN employees, which allowed for a deeper understanding of the problem and motivation for the elaboration of the method. Three semi-structured interviews were also carried out with two managers and one CEDIN employee with an average duration of 1 h to identify the objectives of the method to be developed. The researcher's field notes and interviews were transcribed and analyzed using a qualitative analysis software. To aid the development of the artifact, construction, justification of relevance and later evaluation of the results, the seven directives proposed by Hevner et al. [31] were followed. However, their description falls outside the scope of this study. The stages of constructing the method were executed over a period of 15 months in 2013 and 2014. We will present the main point of each stage [32]:

1. Identification of problem and motivation. To define the specific research problem and justify the value of a solution.

   Application: Three meetings were held with the technical team and board of directors of CEDIN. All observations made by the team were noted in the researcher's diary. The federal government and basic education were defined as the levels of application. Four goals of the NEP, out of a total of 20, were selected for monitoring (Table 1).

2. Definition of the aims of the method. To deduce the objectives through a definition of the problem and knowledge of what is possible and feasible.

   Application: Semi-structured interviews were conducted with the person responsible for monitoring budgets, with the manager and one of the representatives from CEDIN. The purpose of the interviews was to define the objectives of the method and the views of the interviewees on e-transparency. The interviews were recorded, transcribed and analyzed using Atlas.ti software. The main indicators identified by the interviewees were: (i) efficiency in the search for information; (ii) that the method should be easy to understand and (iii) the reliability of the data collected using the method.

3. Project and development of the method. The creation of the method for monitoring the NEP.

   Application: The method was developed as follows:

   (a) A study of Brazilian public budgets: the three instruments that make up the public budget were analyzed (LOA, LDO and PPA) and the complementary budgeting laws and manuals[1]. We identified the expenses linked to Education in the public budget. We identified some legal changes that compromise the transparency of information.

   (b) Establishment of a link between the budget and the selected goals of the NEP: we analyzed the budgeting instruments and identified the items of budget expenditure that would be earmarked to meet the goals of the NEP. This was the subject of a careful but subjective analysis, as a more adequate way was not found.

   (c) A study of the website to collect information: we analyzed the most important websites[2] where the federal government publishes information regarding the financial execution of the budget (see footnote 2). This was done to become familiar with the websites and to identify the clearest and most objective way of publishing information. Not all the websites have adequate data. We selected the Siga Brasil website.

   (d) Design of the method: The method consists of a succession of steps that have been described and illustrated in the form of a flowchart. The end product was the design of the flowchart for executing the monitoring of the NEP.

---

[1] We refer to the complementary budget laws that guide the preparation of the public budget in Brazil. These include Law 4320/1964, Law 101/2000, the Federal Constitution of 1988, Bulletin 42/1999 and other forms of legislation.

[2] https://www1.siop.planejamento.gov.br/acessopublico/?pp=acessopublico&rvn=1, http://www12.senado.gov.br/orcamento/sigabrasil, http://www.portaltransparencia.gov.br/downloads/, http://simec.mec.gov.br/.

4. Demonstration of the method. To demonstrate the use of the artifact to solve one or more problems.

   Application: After the flowchart, had been designed, it was presented to the CEDIN team. The team was shown how to use it. Following the presentation, the team made some suggestions like an evaluation of the PPA to compare the percentage of expenditure forecast for each with the values executed in the budget. We also identified a limitation of the method, the non-identification of eventual expenditure applied by other public departments that are not subscribe in the education sub functions.

5. Evaluation of the method. To observe and measure how well the artifact handles a solution to the problem.

   Application: Based on the indicators from Stage 2, the effectiveness of the method was evaluated. Following the recommendations of Hevner et al. [31] we conducted functional test (Black Box) to execute the method. The method proved to be quick and efficient at obtaining information, without the need for time to search for data, although there were some limitations due to the problems of transparency identified in Stages 3 and 4.

Table 1. Selected goals of the NEP

Selected goals	Description goal of the NEP
Goal 1	To provide education in pre-schooling centers for all children aged 4 and 5 by 2016 and increase the offer of children's education at crèches for at least 50% (fifty percent) of children under the age of three by the end of this NEP
Goal 2	To provide 9 years of fundamental schooling for all children aged 6 (six) to 14 (fourteen) and guarantee that at least 95% (ninety-five percent) of students conclude this stage of their education at the recommended age by the end of the current NEP
Goal 3	To provide schooling for all young people aged 15 (fifteen) to 17 (seventeen) by 2016 and raise, by the end of this NEP, the net rate of enrollments in high school education to 85% (eighty-five percent)
Goal 6	To offer full-time education in at least 50% (fifty percent) of public school in order to include at least 25% (twenty-five percent) of students in basic education

CEDIN operates in state councils and in partnership with other agencies in making investment decisions for public resources earmarked for education. However, to provide better support for its decisions, CEDIN needs to collect information on the budget execution for education and on this point it has encountered difficulties. To obtain data on budget execution, the technicians need to consult a number of websites and visit public agencies to request information in the form of printed reports. This means unnecessary costs and time wasting. For this reason, it was necessary to develop a method that would facilitate the search for information and organize activities. The expectation of the members of CEDIN is that budget analysis will become more efficient, enabling the monitoring of public education policies and public investments.

From a wider perspective, the interviewees hope that internal actions, such as the method for monitoring the NEP will help citizens to understand budget execution and learn more about it. The interviewees recognize that the method has its restrictions, as it depends on the information available on government websites and that under-standing the budget is a complex matter.

"Our role as a result of all this learning is, along with other organizations, to make the information available to more people [...]. The systematization of the method can act as a guideline for other organizations" (Interviewee 2).

"I believe that the method, besides monitoring data and NEP initiatives, can be replicated for other public policies, I think [...]" (Interviewee 3).

During the document analysis, we analyzed the three instruments that make up the Brazilian public budget, the PPA 2012–2015, the LDO and the LOA. We opted for 2013, as it was the last closed fiscal year, enabling a better analysis of the results. We also analyzed the NEP 2014–2024 and the complementary budget laws. The PPA 2012–2015 of the federal government is structured in the form of programs. The program expresses and guides government action for the delivery of goods and services to society. It is composed of objectives, goals, initiatives, indicators and investment values. The initiative described in the PPA is transcribed for the budget (LOA), where they are unfolded in actions with corresponding forecasts for expenditure. However, the budget actions are very generic and the value forecast for a given action can be applied in numerous ways. The lack of clarity and alignment hampers transparency and social control.

We found that a series of legal alterations in part of the complementary budget legislation that have occurred since 2007 also hindered the listing of expenditure on education. Prior to these changes, each phase of basic education (children's, elementary school and high school) had separate lists of expenditure. Now the entire expenditure is concentrated in one sub-function (368 – Basic education). All the values transferred from the federal government to the states and municipalities are listed in sub-function 847 – Transfers. This makes monitoring more difficult.

When analyzing the link connection between budget tools and the NEP, a subtle relationship is perceived between these instruments. It cannot be said that a certain part of the budget (LOA) is earmarked to achieve a goal of the NEP. We noted that the transparency of public policies is reduced. Consequently, the possibility for society to monitor and control the budget is reduced and compromised, as it is not possible to ascertain how much of the policy is implemented. Any counter argument serves to make it unfeasible to demand more effective action from the state. Another characteristic of the budget is its dynamic nature. To monitor it adequately, it is necessary to analyze the constant legal and financial changes.

Regarding the websites, we identified a series of problems. The websites for planning and budgeting (SIOP) is highly complex, with many filters and no adequate explanation for the purpose of the filters. There were also accessibility problems, with more than three attempts necessary to obtain a password to the site. When we did manage to access the site, the platform presented execution problems. There were no problems in accessing the Transparency Website. However, the reports were very large, making it difficult to analyze them. The website maintained by the Ministry of Education was difficult to access, and despite persistent attempts, it was not possible to access it without a login identification and password. Finally, we accessed the SIGA Brasil website, which allowed facilitated access to the budget databases. With a login ID and password, it was possible to create and save reports with the variables we desired.

In short, all the analyses conducted on the budget and its links with the NEP enabled us to identify gaps for the construction of the budget monitoring model. There was some difficulty in finding the transcription of the NEP in the main instrument for public policies, the PPA 2012–2015. There is no assertiveness in the budget goals and the connection between the budget instruments is loose. The constant changes in legislation also affect the quality of the transparency of public expenditure on education.

5   Discussion of the Results

The result of a study in design science is both an artifact and a process that guides the construction of the artifact [31]. The main findings of this study are concentrated in the construction of the method for monitoring the NEP. We have presented here the findings regarding transparency and the generalized method.

The method developed in this study is specific for CEDIN to monitor the public budget for education. It consists of a first qualitative stage, with 14 steps. In this stage of the method it is explained step-by-step which documents related to the NEP and the public budget should be collected and how to analyze them. At the end of this stage the user can identify in the public budget what expenses need to be monitored and which on are related to the achievement of NPE goals. The second stage is quantitative and consists of 27 steps. This stage explains how the user should consult the transparency website to extract the information about the budget expenses and how to analyze them. In the end, the user is able to compile a report that allows comparisons about which NEP goal receives more financial resources, which receives less financial resources, and makes comparisons between the expenditures planned by the government and the expenditures incurred. It makes possible the user project the future achievement of the NEP goals.

Inspired by the method developed for CEDIN and, based on an abstraction exercise of the researchers, with the validation of the team of specialists and managers of CEDIN, we tried to make a generalization of the method elaborated for a specific problem of an organization. The generalized method is presented in Item 5.2.

5.1   Implications for Transparency

During the five stages of the process of constructing the model, there was evidence that the transparency needs to be advanced, in terms of publicity and in the use of websites to divulge information. The reports that are available are incomplete and no not meet all the legal requirements; nor do they comply with the principles of open government data. E-transparency is recognized by the interviewees from CEDIN as being beneficial to social monitoring and control.

Laws 101/2000, 131/2009 and 12.527/2011 are proof of state guidelines to ensure access to information and transparency. Websites are required to be transparent as a result of Decree 7.185/2010 on the publication of public information, reinforcing the practical application of these laws via the websites. However, although the legislation exists, it is not put into practice under the auspices of transparency.

The transparency of public information depends on a set of factors that go beyond the wording of a law. Transparency is presented in the literature as a potential for access to public information [16–18], which would result in to the empowerment of citizens [9–12] and greater social monitoring and control. However, the way in which information is presented appears to be the main issue. In the case of information on basic education expenditure, from the moment when expenditure was grouped into a single sub-function it became more difficult to monitor expenditure by stage of education. In a way, this is a step backwards for transparency. Even though budget information is widespread, it does not meet the levels of transparency required by society.

In the interviews with the members of CEDIN, transparency is identified by the interviewees and positively evaluated when it exists. The interviewees recognize open data and publicity as important aspects of transparency. But transparency is also associated with other elements that form the macro environmental context. Another element that appears in the analysis is that e-transparency can also be the result of an initiative by society, mainly actors in organized civilian society.

The source of data is varied, generally obtained from government transparency websites, but not limited to them. Public agencies can also be sources of data. The publicity for public information is still viewed as insufficient, first of all because the information is difficult to access, the transparency websites are difficult to handle and the information available for download is incomplete or non-existent. The interviewees recognize that there are differences in the publicity of information from one branch of government to another, with some being more advanced.

Transparency is linked to several variables of the macro environmental context. The variables for society, knowledge, technology, access to information and the political and legal context were identified. Society is understood as the diversity of the actors of which it is composed, citizens and civilian society organizations acting together to influence transparency. Transparency depends on a critical analysis of these actors, and for this it is necessary to acquire knowledge of transparency. The context of knowledge has to do with this, i.e., the development of capabilities to analyze and assess information. Technology can influence transparency, as it enables broad access to information. Finally, the political and legal context should provide transparency mechanisms. Transparency is possible only if it is enabled through access to basic information. Even if public information is widely available, if the way in which it is presented is not adequate, websites will not ensure transparency.

This was confirmed during the construction of the method. Although information on basic education expenditure is available through the transparency websites, the way the expenditure is grouped does not show exactly how the federal government spends this money. The political and legal context once again appears as a determining factor for the existence of transparency, in the willingness of the state to adopt measures that ensure transparency of public information. The recognized benefits of websites transparency are the broadening access to public information, the massification of access and growing efficiency when the information is analyzed by interested parties. With the information available online, transparency actors do not need to seek information directly from public agencies in printed format. This means more efficient analyses and faster decision making.

5.2   Attempt to Generalize the Method for Monitoring Public Policies

Using the method for monitoring the National Education Plan created for CEDIN, an attempt was made to generalize to one class of problems 31, which is need to monitor the projection and execution of public policies. The generalization stemmed from the research results, which contained the demands of organized social society to have social control over public policies. The main motivation for this control is to project whether the goals of public policy will be achieved. For instance, CEDIN is concerned about whether the investments for the NEP will be sufficient for achieving the goals of the ten year plan. Six steps were established for the MONITORE method for the monitoring and projection of the execution of a public policy.

- **Define which public policy to monitor/project:** From the demands of society or a specific interest group, it should be decided which policy to monitor. For this it is necessary to understand the public policy, whether there are long-term plans, goals or specific points to be monitored. This activity should be done in collaboration with a multidisciplinary work group and the final goal to be achieved should be stated clearly.
- **Understand the public budget:** The public budget is complex. To understand how it is prepared, executed and which tools are used is a fundamental step in the MONITORE method. Budgeting tools and complementary documentaries should be sought and studied.
- **Connect the public budget to public policy:** This is a critical step in monitoring and projection and should be done rigorously. A qualitative analysis is recommended, connecting the goals or points of public policy to budgetary actions. These connections will serve as a basis for analyzing future projections and for this reason the connections that are found should be validated by a multidisciplinary team.
- **Supply information:** Select the source of data and identify the reports with budget information. The use of government sub-functions is recommended as information filters to ensure greater reliability and traceability of data. For this reason, it is important to supply the goals or points of the policy with information gleaned from the reports.
- **Projection and execution of public policy:** Public policy is generally medium or long term. Analyzing past and current budget execution can provide evidence regarding long-term goals. An analysis of budget execution information is recommended for each selected point of public policy is recommended, as is a projection of the future situation. In this step, there is feedback, as the public budget constantly undergoes change. It should be remembered that budget execution alone does not guarantee the execution of the policy. Other factors of the context can make an impact, such as laws.

- **Disseminate:** One of the main purposes of the Monitore method is to support the social control of public policies through transparency concerning public expenditure. For this purpose, the projections made regarding the execution of the policy must be available to the interested parties. By disseminating the info, society will have access to it to aid its decision making and social control.

6 Conclusions

This study was guided by the following research question: how can a civil society organization monitor the achievement of public policy goals using information available on transparency websites? In this study, a method was constructed for monitoring the financial and budgetary execution of the NEP. We thus proposed a more generic method, the Monitore, for monitoring the execution and projection of public policies in Brazil. We also investigated the implications of e-transparency for the monitoring and projection of public policy in the Brazilian context. We have concluded that is possible a civil society organization monitor the achievement of public policy goals using information available on transparency websites, following the method developed. Although, there are some limitations of websites, in example, difficulty of accessibility, incomplete information, lack of open data, etc., and context limitations like changes in budget legislation.

The results of the model indicate that web sites transparency does not achieve the goals of a tool that acts as an aid to the empowerment of citizens. In our contribution to the paradox of views, e-transparency remains at a phase of more rhetoric than practice when we compare the results with the recommendations found in the literature. In the present study, the political and legal context, with the changes in legislation and non-compliance with transparency laws results in inadequate e-transparency. Furthermore, the way in which information is made available hampers e-transparency. The websites that we consulted did not adhere to the best e-transparency practices. We can infer that the potential of e-transparency for monitoring and projecting public policies in the context we analyzed remains small. More effective mechanisms are required to promote transparency. It would be interesting to propose sanctions for state representatives for non-compliance with the transparency laws and demand an agenda for more concrete actions to be taken.

We concluded that monitoring the budgetary goals of the NEP using the current transparency structure is almost impossible. More effort is required on the part of organized society to understand information and documents and connect them with the public budget and analyze whether the expenditure is adequate for achieving the goals that have been set. Civilian society should adopt a stance of political incidence and request greater transparency in terms of public expenditure.

It is also suggested that the budget tools should be prepared so as to enable clear and easy reading. The study found that it was difficult to make connections between the tools of the budget and those of the NEP: For the budget to become subject to social control and for the NEP to become more effective in the next ten years, there should be greater compatibility between the budgetary tools and the NEP. The budgetary tools need to be better aligned with each other and enable the monitoring and tracing of public expenditure.

E-transparency for budget expenditure by the federal government has evolved in recent years with the passing of Laws 131/2009 and 12.527/2011, the availability of reports and data on websites. Despite this willingness on the part of the state to make its actions more transparent, differences in this evolution were found between the branches of government. Some points require more effort: (i) the availability of complete information and compliance with legislation; (ii) accessibility, as the websites are not easy to access and difficult to use; and (iii) the complexity of reports and filters for obtaining information is another sticking point. The websites are not very intuitive and using them requires considerable knowledge of the budget structure before the desired information can be obtained.

The origin of the information, in this case the public budget, also requires advances and improvements in terms of transparency. The alterations that the budgetary sub-functions for education undergo to a certain extent reflect the lack of transparency on the expenditure for this public policy. The results show that ICT is a tool for accessing information, but does not ensure transparency.

The most relevant contribution of the study, and one which can open up new possibilities for research, is that e-transparency in the budget execution of a public policy begins a projection of the goals of this policy. E-transparency can initiate a cycle of projection and dissemination among the various actors in society and contribute to participation in the political and democratic sphere, demanding more efficient government actions. A limitation of the study is that the generalization of the method is limited to the Brazilian context. The findings on e-transparency are anchored in the view of an organization of society and need to be investigated in other contexts.

References

1. Grönlund, A.: Democracy in an IT-framed society. Commun. ACM **44**, 22–26 (2001)
2. Macintosh, A.: Characterizing e-Participation in policy-making. In: Proceedings of the 37th Annual Hawaii International Conference on System Sciences. IEEE Press (2004)
3. Romme, A.G.L.: Making a difference: organization as design. Organ. Sci. **14**, 558–573 (2003)
4. Avgerou, C.: Information systems in developing countries: a critical research review. J. Inf. Technol. **23**, 133–146 (2008)
5. Giacomoni, J.: Orçamento público, 16th edn. Atlas, São Paulo (2012)
6. Pires, J.S.D.B., Motta, W.F.: A evolução histórica do orçamento público e sua importância para a sociedade. Enfoque: Reflexão Contábil, **25**, 16–25 (2006)
7. de Oliveira, M.H.N.: Financiamento da educação, plano nacional de educação (2011–2020) e agenda governamental: desafios e perspectivas. Revista Científica CENSUPEG **1**, 135–152 (2013)
8. Bertot, J.C., Jaeger, P.T., Grimes, J.M.: Using ICTs to create a culture of transparency: E-government and social media as openness and anti-corruption tools for societies. Gov. Inf. Q. **27**, 264–271 (2010)
9. Negroponte, N.: Being Digital. Hodder and Stoughton, London (1995)

10. Lopes, C.A.: O uso das Tecnologias da Informação e Comunicações nas políticas de acesso à informação pública na América Latina. In: Congresso da associação brasileira de pesquisadores em comunicação e política (2009)
11. Bezerra, H.D.: Atores políticos, informação e democracia. Opinião Pública **14**, 414–431 (2008)
12. Merry, M.K.: Interest group activism on the web: the case of environmental organizations. J. Inf. Technol. Politics **8**, 110–128 (2011)
13. Akutsu, L., Pinho, J.A.G.: Sociedade da informação, accountability e democracia delegativa: investigação em portais de governo no Brasil. Revista de Administração Pública **36**, 723–745 (2002)
14. Hall, M.: Virtual colonization. J. Mater. Cult. **4**, 39–55 (1999)
15. Dreyfus, H.L.: On the internet. Routledge (2008)
16. Cunha, M.A., de Miranda, P.R.M.: A pesquisa no uso e implicações sociais das tecnologias da informação e comunicação pelos governos no Brasil: uma proposta de Agenda a partir de reflexões da prática e da produção acadêmica nacional. Organizações Sociedade **66**, 543–566 (2013)
17. Heald, D.: Varieties of transparency. In: Hood, C., Heald, D. (eds.) Transparency: the key to better governance? Oxford University Press, New York (2006)
18. Ribeiro, M.M.: Monitoramento de políticas públicas de governo eletrônico. VI Congresso CONSAD de Gestão Pública, Brasília (2013)
19. Relly, J.E., Sabharwal, M.: Perceptions of transparency of government policymaking: a cross national study. Gov. Inf. Q. **26**, 148–157 (2009)
20. Bimber, B.: Information and political engagement in America: the search for effects of information technology at the individual level. Polit. Res. Q. **54**, 53–67 (2001)
21. Kakabadse, A., Kakabadse, N.K., Kouzmin, A.: Reinventing the democratic governance project through information technology? A growing agenda for debate. Public Adm. Rev. **63**, 44–60 (2003)
22. Bhatnagar, S.: E-government and access to information. Global Corruption Report, pp. 24–32 (2003)
23. Reddick, C., Frank, H.: The perceived impacts of e-Government on U.S. cities: a survey of Florida and Texas city managers. Gov. Inf. Q. **24**, 576–594 (2007)
24. Heeks, R.: e-Government as a carrier of context. J. Public Policy **25**, 51–74 (2005)
25. Wescott, C.G.: E-Government in the Asia-Pacific region. Asian J. Polit. Sci. **9**, 1–24 (2001)
26. Bertot, J.C.: Public access technologies in public libraries: impacts and implications. Inf. Technol. Libr. **28**, 84–95 (2009)
27. Jaeger, P.T., Thompson, K.M.: E-government around the world: lessons, challenges, and new directions. Gov. Inf. Q. **20**, 389–394 (2003)
28. Singh, A.K., Sahu, R.: Integrating internet, telephones, and call centers for delivering better quality e-governance to all citizens. Gov. Inf. Q. **25**, 477–490 (2008)
29. Bayazit, N.: Introduction to Design Methods in Industrial Product Design and Architecture. Literatur Yayinevi, Istanbul (1994)
30. March, S.T., Smith, G.F.: Design and natural science research on information technology. Decis. Support Syst. **15**, 251–266 (1995)
31. Hevner, A.R., et al.: Design science in information systems research. MIS Q. **28**, 75–105 (2004)
32. Peffers, K., et al.: A design science research methodology for information systems research. J. Manag. Inf. Syst. **24**, 45–77 (2007)

Enabling Business Domain-Specific e-Collaboration: Developing Artifacts to Integrate e-Collaboration into Product Costing

Diana Lück[⊠] and Christian Leyh

Chair of Information Systems, esp. IS in Manufacturing and Commerce,
Technische Universität Dresden, Helmholtzstr. 10, 01069 Dresden, Germany
Diana.Lueck@mailbox.tu-dresden.de,
Christian.Leyh@tu-dresden.de

Abstract. With the rise of digitalization and knowledge work, the relevance of e-collaboration in and among enterprises continues to increase. However, in the discrete manufacturing industry, whose product costing requires ample communication, coordination, and information exchange, we detected a particular lack of collaboration support in product costing. In response, we established the concept of Business Domain-Specific e-Collaboration, which focuses on integrating e-collaboration into the core process of product costing. In this paper, we present how we developed and evaluated that concept from the perspective of design science.

Keywords: Business Domain-Specific e-Collaboration · Product costing · Accounting systems · Enterprise systems integration · Design science research

1 Motivation

In the discrete manufacturing industry, product costing is crucial to determine the costs of new products as their development cycles begin. In general, the more complex and uncertain the composition of a product is, the more extensive is the process of assessing the costs in advance [1]. Given the high degree of information exchange and communication among parties involved in that process, product costing represents a collaborative business activity [2]. In the first study of our long-term research project, we focused on identifying problems and challenges in product costing [3]. Ultimately, we detected severe deficits, especially in the collaborative processes of product costing, even though exchanging information and sharing knowledge digitally have become vital activities for companies [4, 5].

In that first study, we revealed that collaboration in product costing is highly complex due to the multitude of participants and their distribution across numerous divisions and locations. Participants expressed their dissatisfaction with current information technology (IT) solutions available for collaborating on product costing and that appropriate (software) support is typically unavailable. They often reported, among other problems, a lack of clarity about which parties were involved in the costing

© Springer International Publishing AG 2017
A. Maedche et al. (Eds.): DESRIST 2017, LNCS 10243, pp. 296–312, 2017.
DOI: 10.1007/978-3-319-59144-5_18

process and a lack of transparency regarding its progress. Currently, data sources remain unintegrated, meaning that data management requires considerable manual effort, given media breaks and either redundant or inconsistent data. We also showed that generic e-collaboration solutions (e.g., email, chat platforms, and workflow management [5]) are not specifically designed to integrate collaboration support into the work process [3].

Although researchers frequently investigate e-collaboration in terms of its business impacts and benefits [6, 7], in cases such as product costing, the fusion of e-collaboration and the specific business process targeted, with all of its activities and workflows, remains neglected [3]. To address that gap in the research, we developed a requirements model - namely, Business Domain-Specific e-Collaboration (BDSpeC) - for e-collaboration support designed specifically for adoption in business domains. With this artifact, we intend to overcome the abovementioned challenges in product costing by supporting actors involved in the costing process when and where they need help. We also constructed a design prototype for our BDSpeC concept as an instantiation of integrated e-collaboration in product costing and evaluated both artifacts in iterative cycles.

In this paper, we present how we applied design science approaches during the development and evaluation of our BDSpeC concept, and therefore, we have structured our paper according to the recommendations of Gregor and Hevner [8]. The next section offers related work on the fields of product costing and e-Collaboration. Section 3 presents our research approach and its steps, including the development of the requirements model, the instantiation of BDSpeC, and the evaluation cycles. After a discussion, the paper closes with our conclusions and outlook on future research.

2 Related Work

As corporate management demonstrates, adequate instruments and methodologies are required to lead, manage, and direct a company. To establish the foundations for corporate decision making, both financial and nonfinancial data are used to inform managerial accounting [9]. As part of managerial accounting, product costing enables companies to estimate the costs that a product will generate in the future. In such efforts, preliminary costing is crucial since 70% of the costs of goods sold are already fixed during product development and can exert great influence on costs [1].

In product costing, the calculation of realistic costs should provide a reliable financial assumption. Especially in the discrete manufacturing industry, product costing is a highly relevant task, since the industrial products consist of numerous parts that can be produced in-house or in a different plant of the company or else purchased from suppliers. Furthermore, every product needs to be assembled, often according to complex procedures [2]. In today's globalized world, new sources of procurement and markets evolve daily and manufacturing processes change constantly in response to new innovative technologies. As such, diverse factors influence the costs of a product. Especially when profit margins are low, as they are for automotive suppliers, cost calculations need to be exact, for even minor deviations from the calculated future real costs per piece add up rapidly and can easily spell financial losses for the business [10]. In short, accurate cost calculations are essential in discrete manufacturing.

Product costing involves collaborative activities. Sales management organizes communications with customers regarding new products, and as soon as a cost quote for the product is needed, the product costing department is contacted. Product engineering begins to design the product and issue feedback about the possible composition of the product. If parts for the product need to be purchased, then the procurement department has to negotiate purchase prices for the parts with the company's suppliers, and manufacturing has to validate the specifications regarding production before the cost quote can be issued to the customer. To execute those various tasks of the costing process efficiently, collaboration is essential given the number of participants and the array of information that has to be exchanged. Due to the expansive amount of data in management accounting, IT is also essential [11], and to estimate product costs, spreadsheets created in programs such as Microsoft Excel are often used. As a result, problems are liable to arise, including costly manual data administration, inconsistency, and missing documentation, as well as a dismal degree of integration [3, 12].

It is surprising that such problems still exist despite the wide possibilities how technology can be used to support people in their work. Web 2.0 has enabled to work together via the Internet in virtual social networks, using real-time collaboration, instant communication, and collaborative authoring tools [5]. E-Collaboration, also referred to as Enterprise 2.0 or Social Enterprise [4], covers collaboration within and between organizations based on information and communication technology and describes practices of communication, coordination, and collaboration between people in distributed contexts like projects, teams, or processes within and between organizations [5]. The implementation of such tools can improve communication, enable collaboration, and provide more flexibility for employees to work together. Accordingly, e-Collaboration can benefit a company's work productivity [6]. Although numerous software products exploit these collaborative technologies, e-Collaboration is a complex, risky, and often-ineffective undertaking in practice. As the general adoption of e-Collaboration has been investigated in numerous research studies [5, 6], a new aspect is the business domain specific adoption. In several business domains, the level of collaboration is very high, but the usage of generic e-Collaboration tools is not appropriate. Product costing and collaboration are highly linked, which means a specific division has to be contacted at an exact point in time that is business driven, e.g. when the supplier has announced the new price for a purchasing part. Therefore, in the next section we present how this deep integration of the costing process with e-collaboration can be established based on our concept of BDSpeC.

3 Development of the Artifact "BDSpeC"

3.1 Research Approach

For research projects seeking to generate new artifacts for the knowledge base of information systems (IS), examining design science research (DSR) and design theories regarding IS is critical for project positioning. Hevner et al. [13] provide seven guidelines for DSR: (1) Design as an artifact, (2) Problem relevance, (3) Design evaluation, (4) Research contributions, (5) Research rigor, (6) Design as a search, and (7) Communication of research. Additionally, Hevner's [14] three-cycle view of DSR demonstrates how relevance, design, and rigor help to clearly position a project within the design science paradigm. Gregor and Jones [15] claim that IS design theories (ISDT) are an output of DSR for IS and stress that ISDT postulate a certain degree of generalizability in order to address not only specific instances of types of solution, but also classes of problems. The simplified version of ISDT as suggested by Venable [16] provides recommendations concerning the form and use of design theory in order to advance the development of clearer, more useful formalizations of IS knowledge. In contrast to Gregor and Jones [15], Venable [16] argues that explanatory theories, called *kernel theories*, should not be deemed necessary. In a similar vein, Fischer et al. [17] show how different DSR approaches to design and kernel theory correlate.

For our long-term research project, we considered four research steps observing Hevner et al.'s [13] guidelines and Hevner's [14] research cycles. Our steps also correspond to the thinking of March and Storey [18], who summarize four required steps for design science in IS research: Identifying the problem, Demonstrating a novel artifact, Evaluating the artifact, and Communication.

With the problem identification demonstrated in Sect. 3.2, we verify the relevance of the topic and articulate the problems addressed in our research project. In this paper, we present our concept for BDSpeC in the form of two novel artifacts: a requirements model (Sect. 3.3) and a design prototype representing the instantiation of BDSpeC (Sect. 3.4). To achieve both rigor and relevance, Nunamaker et al. [19] advise providing a proof of concept to confirm the functional feasibility of a potential solution, which we observe by providing our design prototype. We executed the evaluation of the artifacts over the course of several iterations, thereby conforming to Hevner's [14] design cycle and the demand for constant evaluation activities in the DSR process recommended by Sonnenberg and vom Brocke [20]. Along with the general evaluation of the requirements model for BDSpeC, we evaluated how our model supports specific use cases for collaboration in product costing. In a second cycle, we validated the design prototype for a specific use case with a usability test. As Venable et al. [21] show, evaluation in DSR can follow different strategies; however, we focus on human risk and effectiveness, as recommended for cases in which the major design risk is of a social nature and depends on the further continuation of utility. The evaluation cycles also serve as a proof of value that, according to Nunamaker et al. [19], should gauge whether stakeholders can use the solution to create value. We describe the evaluation cycles in Sect. 3.5, and by applying established methodologies (Sects. 3.3–3.5), we ensure the rigor of our research. In Sect. 3.6, we present the ways in which we performed knowledge transfer as recommended by [13, 15, 18]. Table 1 summarizes the overall research process.

3.2 Problem Identification

We began our research project by conducting an exploratory study focused on identifying a problem, as addressed in the motivation section, in order to assure the relevance

Table 1. Research steps.

	Step	Methodology	No. of participants	Outcome
1.	Problem identification	Online survey	N = 28	List of issues faced during product costing
2.	Requirements analysis	Expert interviews	N = 14	Requirements model for BDSpeC
3.	Design prototype	Mock-up modelling	–	Instantiation of BDSpeC (Proof of concept)
4.	Evaluation cycle I	Focus groups	N = 7	Model validation regarding use cases (proof of value)
5.	Evaluation cycle II	Usability test	N = 8	Prototype validation (proof of value)

of the project's field. In that study, we investigated the collaborative process in product costing, along with its participants and organizational IT support, to identify relevant problems and challenges. Further details appear in our corresponding paper [3].

Methodology. The goal of our first step was to identify whether a lack of collaboration support exists in product costing. To that end, we designed an online survey to collect data to simplify the data collection process [22]. We divided the questionnaire into three topic areas: the collaborative process, its participants, and IT support for collaboration. We selected an international sample of participants for the questionnaire; since discrete manufacturing consists of several industrial sectors, we included companies from the automotive industry, the machine building industry, and the industrial sector of consumer goods. We considered different perspectives to provide an overall understanding of the process, which encompassed managerial accounting, product controlling, marketing, sales and procurement as well as engineering and IT.

Based on those requirements, we contacted companies with potential interest in research regarding product costing and attracted 26 cooperation partners that signaled their willingness to participate - seven companies from Germany and 19 from the United States - from which we contacted 26 German and 55 US employees. We conducted the study in April 2015, and altogether, 15 companies took part: six from Germany and nine from the United States. Of the 81 invitees, 28 participated: half from US companies and half from German ones.

Results. Our results underscore the importance of product costing in the discrete manufacturing industry. A whopping 96% of participants deemed product costing to be relevant for running their business successfully. On average, 87% of the overall workload in product costing was reported to consist of communication and information exchange, for which traditional methods (e.g., in-person meetings and telephone calls) and generic tools (e.g., email and online conferencing) are primarily used. Data management was often reported to be detached from the collaborative process, since using spreadsheet programs remains common. Overall satisfaction with IT support in product costing demonstrated the need for action to improve the current situation, and 46% of participants (13/28) stated being unsatisfied with the IT support for collaboration. No respondent reported that the costing process was operated in a completely unstructured way, although it was usually reported that completing the necessary steps simultaneously was common, which indicates the potential to automate and accelerate the process. Moreover, agreements with colleagues and external partners were reported to often prompt the modification of costing goals that needed to be reflected in the product cost assessment. Participants stated that usually one person manages the entire process and takes responsibility for its coordination.

We also analyzed the extent to which the current use of IT supports the collaborative process. 39% of participants (11/28) had little awareness of their tasks and the status of the process, while 29% of participants (8/28) did not feel informed about the data that they needed to use for certain calculations. Accordingly, the ability of IT support to effectively integrate data for the process merits further investigation. The results additionally demonstrate that collaboration support of 46% of participants (13/28) was not directly integrated into the system used for product costing. 46% of participants also stated that the IT support for product costing provided inadequate support in helping to prevent miscommunication and ensure consistency in the company process.

DSR Perspective. With our study, we identified problems in the field per Hevner et al.'s [13] second guideline and verified the relevance of addressing and solving those problems in future research per Hevner's [14] recommendations. Ultimately, we opted to pursue an investigation of the requirements for collaboration in product costing (Sect. 3.3).

3.3   Requirements Analysis

In this step of our research, we developed and validated a requirements model for e-collaboration in the business domain of product costing as a possible solution for the identified problems. The requirements analysis is described in detail in [23].

Methodology. To deepen our understanding of the collaborative practices in the product costing process and how they are supported by IT, we invited experts with diverse business roles and from various industrial sectors to participate in semi-structured interviews. We selected 14 participants with a high level of professional experience and who declared specific interest in the topic. Since participants were located around the world, we conducted interviews using a web-conferencing solution. During each interview, the interviewer introduced herself and explained the research, the purpose and structure of the interview, and how the researchers would use the results. She asked the interviewee to describe his or her professional career and expertise in the field, largely to clarify his or her relation to product costing. The following part of the interview addressed the collaborative process and IT support systems in terms of product costing by asking the interviewee to characterize all steps in the process and their participants. The interviewer also asked each interviewee to describe how IT supports the process as well as what shortfalls exist and what improvements, if any, are possible. Each interview took one to two hours.

After data collection, we conducted qualitative data analysis in order to identify requirements for e-collaboration in product costing. We coded and analyzed the interview protocols using AQUAD 7 [24], and all coding was structured to systematically examine data content. Our tool-based approach enabled us to derive specific requirements for collaboration in product costing [25], and by classifying those requirements, we formulated a requirements model for BDSpeC. To evaluate the model, we lastly organized a face to face expert session where we presented the requirements model to 11 product costing specialists who did not participate in the interviews.

Results. Based on the expert interviews, we established a requirements model for collaboration in product costing. The model represents our concept for BDSpeC for integrating e-collaboration into a particular business area and the respective domain-specific application, such as an accounting or enterprise system. By incorporating collaboration support directly into the core processes of a business domain, we address the potential to enable teams to cooperate based on a connection between daily work routines, data sources, and need for collaboration. The requirements model for BDSpeC in product costing is illustrated in Fig. 1.

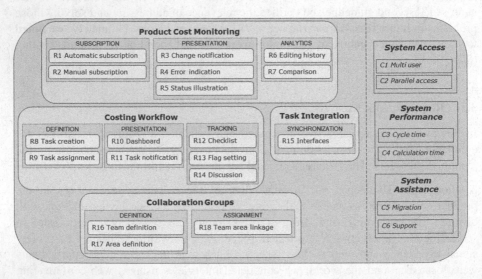

Fig. 1. Requirements model for collaboration in product costing

The model consists of four requirement areas that encompass 18 requirements (R in the model), as well as three system prerequisite areas comprising six constraints necessary to enable IT-based collaboration support (C in the model). First, the requirement area termed *Product Cost Monitoring* should give experts a clear overview of the costing process. In product costing, a goal of collaboration support is to keep the participants informed about the process status. Hence, a necessary component of Product Cost Monitoring is the subscription to objects. To track an object, users should be able to subscribe to it, both manually and automatically. The presentation of which tasks have been completed, what has yet to be done, and whether any issues remain unaddressed enables product costing experts to understand and control the process. To alert users of the status of the process, they have to be provided with exact, up-to-date information about the progress. Furnishing information about the status, errors, and changes enables system-based monitoring, simplifies coordination, and improves control over the process. Product Cost Monitoring should also provide analytical functionality. Since the results of product costing analyses can influence ways of collaborating on the team, analytics also need to be embedded.

The second requirement area is the *Costing Workflow*. To collaborate virtually in product costing, every user should be able to participate in a self-initiated, ad hoc workflow. Costing Workflow should be a flexible tool for coordinating tasks, the statuses of which should then be summarized and presented in Product Cost Monitoring. Since the execution of collaborative tasks needs to be highly flexible, in the Costing Workflow users need to define necessary steps themselves instead of imposing a predefined workflow. The presentation of information in form of a dashboard and via notifications helps to raise awareness of the actions that each user has to perform, since the system automatically informs participants about their workload and the tasks that they need to complete. Furthermore, tracking functions are required in order to automate and facilitate steps necessary in the collaboration process.

Third, the requirement area of *Task Integration* extends the task concept of Costing Workflow to other IT systems used for product costing. To obtain data necessary in the collaboration process, it is common for participants to determine information from several information systems, and to prevent inconsistencies, relevant data input has to be synchronized among the different IT systems. To coordinate tasks handled externally, interfaces connecting the relevant IT systems need to be provided in order to manage and automatically integrate data from other sources.

The fourth and final requirement area, *Collaboration Groups*, should support the definition of teams and the areas that each team may access. Since Collaboration Groups authorize the collaboration system and make it accessible, it is necessary to manage members of the collaboration teams as well as the areas that team members may access. To determine who may contribute and where they may collaborate, the assignment of teams to access areas is also necessary.

The requirements model additionally reveals preconditions for e-collaboration in product costing. Without comprehensive access to the system, the potential of collaboration support is limited. Thus, *System Access* for all participants of the collaboration process is necessary to realize the system's full capabilities. Another precondition is *System Performance*. Since users have to wait for results in order to proceed to the next step, when there are time restrictions in the system, performance is critical. Since *System Assistance* is a major asset of standardized systems, implementation and operation knowledge from experts is another precondition for the success of collaboration support.

DSR Perspective. Since our model addresses product costing, which encompasses diverse sectors of the discrete manufacturing industry, the artifact not only addresses the requirements of a specific instance, but a class of problems, as claimed by Gregor and

Jones [15] regarding ISDT. Given Hevner's [14] recommendation that the design cycle should include the iterative construction and evaluation of the artifact, we conducted an initial demonstration and evaluation of our BDSpeC concept by presenting the requirements model to business experts. In doing so, we comply with Sonnenberg's and vom Brocke's proposal to conduct evaluation cycles in the early phase of research [20].

In the evaluation session of the model, all 11 participating product costing specialists agreed on the structure of the model, its requirement areas, and their subdivisions, and nobody indicated that any additional requirement area was missing. Evaluation revealed that all constructs of our model have significance for e-collaboration in product costing. No changes to the model were deemed necessary, and the modular composition was evaluated quite positively. The holistic approach to BDSpeC received excellent feedback, and participants confirmed that the requirements represented the demand for collaboration in product costing. Evaluation also represented our first applicability assessment, as recommended by Rosemann and Vessey [26] to investigate the relevance of our research to practical needs, which was confirmed. The requirements presented serve as the foundation for the design prototype of BDSpeC that we describe in the next section.

3.4   Design Prototype

The following design prototype presents the instantiation of BDSpeC for integration into an enterprise system based on the requirements model described earlier. Detailed information about the prototype appears in our corresponding research paper [27].

Methodology. With the design prototype, we sought to develop a system design in form of screens that would fulfill all requirements for collaboration in product costing to create a comprehensive instantiation of BDSpeC. Following, we illustrate how each aspect of BDSpeC can be integrated into an enterprise system as a basis for the future implementation of the artifact.

Results. As an entry point for all collaboration-related issues, we designed a screen called **My Home**. The screen enables users to immediately understand the status of all objects and to see all assigned tasks (Fig. 2). A chief objective of the **My Home screen** is to achieve direct integration with the primary application, given our aim to enable users to cooperate directly within the system. Such integration reduces the need for manual effort leading to inconsistencies in data and a lack of transparency.

Clicking on a tile item opens the **Product Cost Monitoring screen**, which provides detailed information about the selected object, e.g., about existing tasks, checklist and flags and their completion status (Fig. 3). The screen also shows unresolved errors for the selected object and allows access to the analytical functions: Editing History displays a chart of the chronological course of all changes made by processors, while the Comparison function enables users to match different objects as a means to analyze differences. Here, collaboration steps can also be initiated by creating new tasks and checklists. When external systems are used, synchronization can be activated, which enables the external processing of tasks. Such integration benefits automation.

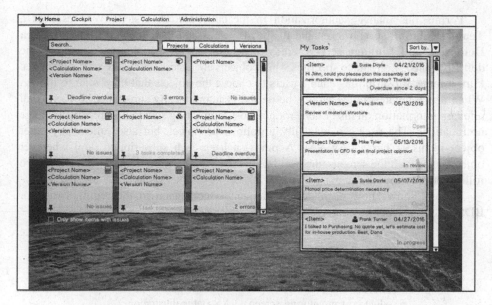

Fig. 2. Screenshot of my home

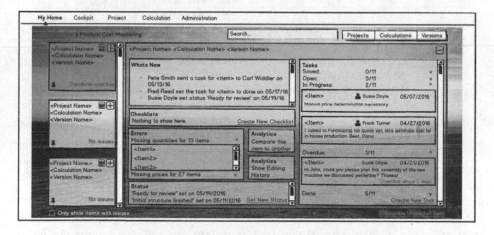

Fig. 3. Screenshot of product cost monitoring

The central element of collaboration execution is the **My Tasks screen** for users to gain detailed insights into tasks assigned to them. It helps to raise awareness and to keep each user informed about his or her workload. When a user changes the status of a task, a notification is sent automatically. So, everyone involved in the process is immediately informed about the change. A similar procedure is triggered whenever a new task is sent or a new checklist is activated. Users can also set flags to communicate the status of an object and leave comments to discuss issues.

Permissions manage authorization in the collaboration system. We designed a **Team Definition screen** to enable to specify teams and their members. On the **Area Definition and Linkage screen**, areas of access can be specified and linked to the defined teams. A reference specifies which objects are accessible by the respective area. Furthermore, subscriptions enable users to choose the objects that they want to follow. When a user creates a new object, he or she is automatically subscribed to it, sees all relevant information on his or her Product Cost Monitoring screen, and receives change notifications. The user can manually unfollow the object, but also follow any other object in his or her access area. A pin visualizes each subscription, and wherever objects appear on the screens, the user has the opportunity to click on the pin in order to follow or unfollow the item.

Table 2 shows how each design element is connected to the requirements for BDSpeC in product costing.

Table 2. Mapping of design elements and requirements.

Design element	Requirement addressed
Monitoring and Initiation •Product cost monitoring screen •My home screen	R4 Error indication R5 Status illustration R6 Editing history R7 Comparison R8 Task creation R9 Task assignment R12 Checklist R15 Interfaces
Execution and Progression •My tasks screen •Product cost monitoring screen	R3 Change notification R10 Dashboard R11 Task notification R13 Flag setting R14 Discussion
Permissions and Subscriptions •Team definition screen •Area definition and linkage screen •My home screen •Product cost monitoring screen	R1 Automatic subscription R2 Manual subscription R16 Team definition R17 Area definition R18 Team area linkage

DSR Perspective. Following Nunamaker et al. [19], we can demonstrate the functional feasibility of our solution by providing a proof of concept. With the design prototype, we have addressed collaboration in product costing holistically; since it covers not only problems of a specific instance, but the entire discrete manufacturing industry, it bears the potential to derive an ISDT [15, 16] at later stages.

3.5   Evaluation Cycles

In design science, evaluation methods should demonstrate the usefulness, quality, and efficacy of a design artifact [13]. To that end, we evaluated our artifacts in several iterations. Along with the initial evaluation of the requirements model for BDSpeC, we evaluated how our model supports the use cases for collaboration in product costing. In a second cycle, we validated the design prototype for a specific use case with a usability test. Details about each evaluation cycle appear in our papers [28, 29].

Methodology. In our first evaluation cycle, we investigated how our requirements model for BDSpeC for integrated e-collaboration supports and improves the product costing process. To do so, we examined related use cases and validated the relevance of the research artifact by analyzing whether and, if so, then how the model for BDSpeC addresses the detected collaborative use case. We evaluated the potential improvements that BDSpeC provides for each use case with the focus group technique [30, 31]. Tremblay et al. [32] adapt that same method to design research projects and demonstrated how exploratory focus groups can be used to study an artifact to propose improvements, after which an artifact can be tested in confirmatory focus groups to prove its usefulness in the field. Correspondingly, we discussed our use case analysis first with an exploratory focus group of four business experts in product costing and collaboration. Each participant had a professional background in project management and software development for product costing. Based on the feedback, we were able improve our artifact and discuss it in a confirmatory focus group consisting of three experts with backgrounds in consulting and go-to-market strategies related to product costing.

In the second evaluation cycle, we conducted a usability test for a prototype that instantiated BDSpeC for the use case we identified as a basis in our first evaluation cycle: the coordination of component calculations. During the usability test, business experts tested BDSpeC in the scenario based on the design prototype [27]. Eight experts from five different German companies in the automotive or machine building industries participated; each had a professional background in product costing and an extraordinary level of expertise in the field. During the test, each participant followed a test script with instructions explaining which steps to take and how to proceed. The usability test concluded with a feedback survey and a discussion, following Kriglstein et al. [30].

Results. In our use case analysis representing the first evaluation cycle, we identified five use cases, all of which we presented to the exploratory focus group. The use cases for data enrichment and the sourcing process sparked discussion about their commonalities. Since participants stated that they both address the same element of the BDSpeC concept (R15 Interfaces), we consolidated them in a single use case (i.e., maturity process). As a fifth use case, we presented the calculation analysis to the focus group; that case was also addressed by BDSpeC in response to R4 Error indication, R6 Editing history, and R7 Comparison. As the group explained, analyzing calculations has to be as a preliminary or follow-up step of collaboration. Although the results of analyses can prompt cooperative activity or vice versa, the use case itself is not defined by collaboration. In reply, we excluded that use case from the session with the confirmatory focus group, meaning that the respective elements of BDSpeC are not major aspects for collaboration in product costing.

Our remaining use cases were the *Coordination of component calculations*, the *Approval process*, and the *Maturity process*. Once we verified that our artifact for BDSpeC addresses all of those points, we discussed them with our confirmatory focus group. With the Costing Workflow, it is possible to distribute tasks ad hoc, which supports the coordination of component calculations. Meanwhile, Product Cost Monitoring enables the tracking of the collaboration process in terms of current tasks and their statuses; consequently, keeping participants informed improves transparency and awareness of the workload. Maintaining cost components is a highly collaborative procedure, and the focus groups confirmed that the automation of that use case provided more accurate results. At the same time, the confirmatory focus group agreed that, with BDSpeC, approval processes can be executed in a simplified way. By setting flags, approvals can be easily communicated, whereas checklists allow for the creation of ad hoc workflows that help to automate approval procedures. Among other findings, the maturity process was considered to be quite complex, for it sums up all scenarios in which data need to be exchanged and information from other data sources integrated. Interfaces that enable the expansion of the Costing Workflow so that tasks can be completed in other systems were thought to be highly relevant. Meanwhile, Task Integration provides several benefits, including the reduction of manual data input and the improvement of data consistency. The focus groups agreed that the user-centricity of BDSpeC supports the need for collaboration in product costing in a robust way.

In the second evaluation cycle, we conducted a usability test for the use case of coordinating component calculations. Half of participants assumed the role of a product manager who coordinated the maintenance of the different components by distributing their tasks to the respective experts. By contrast, the other half played the part of a costing expert who had to impart knowledge about the components and work on assigned tasks. In the feedback session following the usability test, participants had to complete a questionnaire, which segued into a discussion. For the questions, we used a 7-point Likert scale (1 = *Strongly disagree*, 7 = *Strongly agree*) to allow sufficient room for differentiation [22]. In what follows, average responses appear in brackets.

Participants agreed that the scenarios of the usability test were realistic (5.5). The prototype was rated to be easy to use (6.5) and allowed scenarios to be completed quickly (6.25). Participants stated that the design prototype for the use case represented useful support for collaboration (6.375), for it could improve transparency (6.125) and enhance productivity in product costing (5.625). Regarding the visualization, our design prototype for the coordination of component calculations based on BDSpeC received exceptional feedback. The approach of connecting tasks with components of a calculation was rated to be highly useful (6.5), and displaying tasks in the side panel of the Calculation View was considered to be effective (6.5). Participants assessed the overview regarding tasks in the My Home screen to be helpful (5.5), though the discussion revealed a perceived risk of information overload when the number of tasks becomes very high. Another aspect of BDSpeC is the integrated navigation between tasks and business objects in terms of calculation components. Along those lines, the prototype was rated to be easily navigable (6.375) and shifting from tasks to the respective component of the calculation to be very useful (6.5).

In the discussion, we deepened the assessment by asking what participants liked and disliked about the BDSpeC presented and tested in the prototype. Feedback stressed three aspects - for one, that BDSpeC offers a great opportunity to give an overview about the collaboration process and manage it. Due to the intuitive navigation and integrated visualization, the prototype was described as a good tool to quickly assign tasks, gain insights into one's workload, and track the collaborative costing process. Furthermore, participants stressed the importance that the prototype allows the history of a calculation to be tracked in terms of who contributed and which input was given. Several additional feature ideas were also mentioned, especially concerning the My Home screen. In all, the usability test showed that BDSpeC could facilitate the product costing process and improve data consistency due to the direct integration of tasks and components. Data input could be handled directly in the enterprise system used for product costing, and collaboration could be managed and tracked in an integrated way. At the same time, improved transparency and easy navigation afford the potential to accelerate the process.

DSR Perspective. Hevner [14] specifies that the internal design cycle of research activities should iterate between the construction of the artifact and its evaluation. We evaluated our artifacts over the course of several iterations, thereby observing the design cycle of Hevner [14] and the demand for evaluation activities within the DSR process described by Sonnenberg and vom Brocke [20]. As Venable et al. [21] show, evaluation in DSR can follow different strategies, whereas we focus on human risk and effectiveness since the artifact's benefits depend primarily on social aspects, not technical risks. In the second evaluation cycle, we provided a proof of value corresponding to Nunamaker et al. [19] by investigating whether our solution creates value for collaboration in product costing. Taken together, both evaluation cycles represent additional applicability assessments [26] of our concept of BDSpeC.

3.6 Communication

It is important to share knowledge contributions with the research community, and Hevner et al. [13] situate the communication of research as a guideline in design science. Above all, communication should enable an understanding of the value added to the IT knowledge base and the implications for IT management [18]. To that end, we have enabled knowledge transfer with the research community by publishing papers and delivering presentations at conferences, as well as by presenting the results of every step of our project in research papers [3, 23, 27–29]. We have also shared our results regularly with practitioners by conducting expert sessions, focus groups, and a usability test with business experts. Consequently, experts from the discrete manufacturing industry received direct access to the research results related to their domain, and we used their feedback from the evaluation cycles to refine the artifacts. At the same time, the evaluation cycles served as applicability assessments per Rosemann and Vessey [26] and verified the importance of our research to practice. In business environments, future products implementing BDSpeC are planned to be made available.

4 Discussion

For researchers in the IS community, this paper shows how DSR can be applied in a domain-specific environment, namely the discrete manufacturing industry. We present a research approach with a strong practical background represented in the different research steps by the cooperation with various companies from discrete manufacturing. The contribution of this paper is to demonstrate how such a research project can be performed - from problem identification to evaluation of the artifacts we developed - by presenting which research methods we chose for each step and the respective results. By showing how we addressed DSR guidelines in our research project, we share our experience on how DSR can be conducted in strong collaboration with practice.

From a methodological perspective, we next aim to generalize our outcomes in terms of design principles. Gregor and Jones describe those as constructs representing the entities of interest of an ISDT [15]. The requirements model and design prototype for BDSpeC presented in this paper address a class of problems related to collaboration in the domain of product costing in discrete manufacturing which can be generalized for use in other domains sharing similarities with product costing. Yet, we recognize that we did not use explicit kernel theories, which situates us in a design theory school that Fischer et al. [17] call "kernel theory pragmatists." As such, we stress "the importance of artifact impact over artifact grounding" [17] in our upcoming work by aiming for a simplified version of an ISDT, as suggested by Venable [16]. Therefore, the explicit formulation of the design principles for BDSpeC aims to support the design of integrated e-Collaboration solutions for other domains than product costing. They are planned as an outcome of the next phase of our research project.

5 Conclusion

In the research project presented in this paper, we applied design science research in the domain of product costing in the discrete manufacturing industry. Our initial study showed that collaboration in product costing is a relevant topic and that we addressed relevant business problems with our project. With the requirements model and design prototype, our research produced two new artifacts representing our concept for Business-Domain Specific e-Collaboration (BDSpeC). Furthermore, we evaluated our artifacts in several iterations, and the initial validation underscored the relevance and accuracy of the model. We also conducted two evaluation cycles; first, we investigated how our requirements model for BDSpeC addresses the use cases for collaboration in product costing, and focus groups enabled us to prioritize the elements of our model based on the use cases. Second, we conducted a usability test for the design prototype limited to the use case of coordinating component calculations in product costing. The feedback session revealed that with BDSpeC, resources can be used more efficiently, productivity and transparency can be increased, and data consistency can be improved. The iterative evaluation steps enabled us to validate our artifacts early within the DSR process, as suggested by Sonnenberg and vom Brocke [20]. Our evaluation strategy of human risk and effectiveness allowed us to assess user-oriented risks as a focus of our research [21]. As applicability checks recommended by Rosemann and Vessey [26], the user-oriented evaluation steps helped to improve the relevance of our research for practitioners.

Per Nunamaker et al. [19], we completed the first two steps of "the last research mile of IS research": the proof of concept regarding functional feasibility and the proof of value showing that the solution can create value. The next step of our research project is the proof of use to demonstrate that practitioners can gain value from their own instances of our solution [19]. Implementing BDSpeC in a specific enterprise system for product costing will enable employees to use BDSpeC in their everyday work and allow further evaluation of the artifacts in a real-world setting. Furthermore, with the design principles for BDSpeC that we plan to develop as an abstraction from the product costing domain we will provide more generalized knowledge for the IS community to enable integrated e-Collaboration in various other business domains.

References

1. Saaksvuori, A., Immonen, A.: Product Lifecycle Management. Springer, Berlin (2004)
2. Hansen, D.R., Mowen, M.M., Guan, L.: Cost Management - Accounting and Control. Cengage Learning, Mason (2009)
3. Lück, D., Leyh, C.: Integrated virtual cooperation in product costing in the discrete manufacturing industry: a problem identification. In: Proceedings of the Multikonferenz Wirtschaftsinformatik 2016 (MKWI 2016) (2016)
4. McAfee, A.P.: Enterprise 2.0: the dawn of emergent collaboration. MIT Sloan Manag. Rev. **47**, 21–28 (2006)
5. Riemer, K., Steinfield, C., Vogel, D.: eCollaboration: on the nature and emergence of communication and collaboration technologies. Electron. Mark. **19**, 181–188 (2009)
6. Alqahtani, F.H., Watson, J., Partridge, H.: Organizational support and enterprise web 2.0 adoption: a qualitative study. In: Proceedings of the 20th Americas Conference on Information Systems (AMCIS 2014) (2014)
7. Andriole, S.: Business impact of web 2.0 technologies. Commun. ACM **53**, 67–79 (2010)
8. Gregor, S., Hevner, A.R.: Positioning and presenting design science research for maximum impact. MIS Q. **37**, 337–355 (2013)
9. Warren, C.S., Reeve, J.M., Duchac, J.E.: Financial and Managerial Accounting. Cengage Learning, Boston (2014)
10. Drury, C.: Management and Cost. Cengage Learning, London (2008)
11. Fiedler, R., Gräf, J.: Einführung in das Controlling, Methoden, Instrumente und IT-Unterstützung. Oldenbourg Wissenschaftsverlag, München (2012)
12. Schicker, G., Mader, F., Bodendorf, F.: Product Lifecycle Cost Management (PLCM): Status quo, Trends und Entwicklungsperspektiven im PLCM – eine empirische Studie. Arbeitspapier Wirtschaftsinformatik II. Universität Erlangen-Nürnberg (2008)
13. Hevner, A.R., March, S.T., Park, J., Ram, S.: Design science in information systems research. MIS Q. **28**, 75–105 (2004)
14. Hevner, A.R.: A three cycle view of design science research. Scand. J. Inf. Syst. **19**, 87–92 (2007)
15. Gregor, S., Jones, D.: The anatomy of a design theory. J. Assoc. Inf. Syst. **8**, 312–335 (2007)

16. Venable, J.R.: Rethinking design theory in information systems. In: vom Brocke, J., Hekkala, R., Ram, S., Rossi, M. (eds.) DESRIST 2013. LNCS, vol. 7939, pp. 136–149. Springer, Heidelberg (2013). doi:10.1007/978-3-642-38827-9_10

17. Fischer, C., Winter, R., Wortmann, F.: Design theory. Bus. Inf. Syst. Eng. **2**, 387–390 (2010)

18. March, S.T., Storey, V.T.: Design science in the information systems discipline: an introduction to the special issue on design science research. MIS Q. **32**, 725–730 (2008)

19. Nunamaker, J.F., Briggs, R.O., Derrick, D.C., Schwabe, G.: The last research mile: achieving both rigor and relevance in information systems research. J. Manag. Inf. Syst. **32**, 10–47 (2015)

20. Sonnenberg, C., vom Brocke, J.: Evaluations in the science of the artificial – reconsidering the build-evaluate pattern in design science research. In: Peffers, K., Rothenberger, M., Kuechler, B. (eds.) DESRIST 2012. LNCS, vol. 7286, pp. 381–397. Springer, Heidelberg (2012). doi:10.1007/978-3-642-29863-9_28

21. Venable, J., Pries-Heje, J., Baskerville, R.: FEDS: a framework for evaluation in design science research. Eur. J. Inf. Syst. **25**, 77–89 (2014)

22. Bethlehem, J., Biffignandi, S.: Handbook on Web Surveys. Wiley, Hoboken (2012)

23. Lück, D., Leyh, C.: Toward business domain-specific eCollaboration: requirements for integrated virtual cooperation in product costing. In: Proceedings of the 22nd Americas Conference on Information Systems (AMCIS 2016) (2016)

24. Huber, G.L.: AQUAD7 - Analysis of qualitative data. http://www.aquad.de/en/

25. Miles, M.B., Huberman, A.M., Saldana, J.: Qualitative Data Analysis: A Methods Sourcebook. Sage, London (2013)

26. Rosemann, M., Vessey, I.: Toward improving the relevance of information systems research to practice: the role of applicability checks. MIS Q. **32**, 1–22 (2008)

27. Lück, D., Leyh, C.: Enabling business domain-specific eCollaboration - how to integrate virtual cooperation in product costing. In: Proceedings of the 19th International Conference on Enterprise Information Systems (ICEIS 2017) (2017)

28. Lück, D., Leyh, C.: Evaluating business domain-specific e-Collaboration - how integrated e-Collaboration improves the product costing process. In: Proceedings of the 19th IEEE Conference on Business Informatics 2017 (CBI2017) (2017)

29. Lück, D., Leyh, C.: Evaluating business domain-specific e-Collaboration: the impact of integrated e-Collaboration on the coordination of component calculations in product costing. In: Proceedings of the 20th International Conference on Business Information Systems (BIS 2017) (2017)

30. Kriglstein, S., Leitner, M., Kabicher-Fuchs, S., Rinderle-Ma, S.: Evaluation methods in process-aware information systems research with a perspective on human orientation. Bus. Inf. Syst. Eng. **58**, 397–414 (2016)

31. Stewart, D.W., Shamdasani, P.N., Rook, D.W.: Focus Groups: Theory and Practice, 2nd edn. Sage, London (2007)

32. Tremblay, M.C., Hevner, A.R., Berndt, D.J.: Focus groups for artifact refinement and evaluation in design research. Commun. Assoc. Inf. Syst. **26**, 599–618 (2010)

Domain-Specific Reference Modeling
in the Telecommunications Industry

Christian Czarnecki[1](✉) and Christian Dietze[2]

[1] Hochschule für Telekommunikation Leipzig, Leipzig, Germany
czarnecki@hft-leipzig.de
[2] Detecon Consulting FZ-LLC, Abu Dhabi, UAE
christian.dietze@detecon.com

Abstract. The telecommunications industry is currently going through a major transformation. In this context, the enhanced Telecom Operations Map (eTOM) is a domain-specific process reference model that is offered by the industry organization TM Forum. In practice, eTOM is well accepted and confirmed as de facto standard. It provides process definitions and process flows on different levels of detail. This article discusses the reference modeling of eTOM, i.e., the design, the resulting artifact, and its evaluation based on three project cases. The application of eTOM in three projects illustrates the design approach and concrete models on strategic and operational levels. The article follows the Design Science Research (DSR) paradigm. It contributes with concrete design artifacts to the transformational needs of the telecommunications industry and offers lessons-learned from a general DSR perspective.

Keywords: enhanced Telecom Operations Map (eTOM) · Process reference model · Process design · Telecommunications industry

1 Introduction

Telecommunications operators are confronted with extensive transformations of market conditions, value chains, and services, e.g., [9, 17, 32, 33]. The Information Systems (IS) discipline contributes with various design artifacts to support the transformational needs of telecommunications operators, e.g., [7, 10, 16, 25, 27, 28, 56]. In this context, reference models are a common approach to generalize knowledge and to offer a point of reference for a whole domain [13]. In the telecommunications industry the non-profit organization TM Forum offers – amongst other content – the domain-specific process reference model *enhanced Telecom Operations Map* (eTOM) [23, 28, 38]. It was confirmed by the International Telecommunications Union (ITU) as de facto standard [21], and is well-accepted within the whole industry. Its usage has been documented in a broad range of project cases [11].

Hence, eTOM is a domain-specific reference model with a high practical relevance. This article illustrates the reference modeling (i.e., design and application) of eTOM following the Design Science Research (DSR) paradigm [18, 30]. After a discussion of the problem domain, the design and the resulting artifact are described. Its evaluation is illustrated based on three project cases. In this context, designing concrete models

© Springer International Publishing AG 2017
A. Maedche et al. (Eds.): DESRIST 2017, LNCS 10243, pp. 313–329, 2017.
DOI: 10.1007/978-3-319-59144-5_19

based on eTOM are again DSR projects. Therefore both the reference model and the concrete models are described based on the DSR publication scheme proposed by [15]. The content of this article is based on the authors' involvements in the eTOM development and project cases.

The contribution of this article is twofold. First, the designed artifacts address the practical requirements of telecommunications operators – a major goal of DSR. Second, eTOM and the three project cases can be used as examples for broad design artifacts in the context of general DSR.

The structure of the article is as follows: Sect. 2 briefly explains the research goal and the methodology with respect to DSR. Section 3 describes the design artifact eTOM and its application following the DSR scheme: problem domain containing literature discussion on its relevance (cf. Sect. 3.1), design method (cf. Sect. 3.2), artifact description (cf. Sect. 3.3), and artifact evaluation (cf. Sect. 3.4). Section 4 discusses lessons-learned and further research steps.

2   Research Goal and Methodology

The topic of this article is the design and application of a process reference model in the telecommunications industry. Reference models are a common research artifact of the IS discipline, e.g., [2, 29, 44, 50, 53]. A concrete model is a solution to a clearly defined situation, while a reference model is a point of reference for a whole range of situations [13]. Subject of this paper is the process reference model eTOM. Various publications show the relevance of eTOM in the telecommunications industry, e.g., [11, 23, 37, 57]. The importance of researching the design process and the resulting design artifacts as part of the IS discipline has been underlined by multiple authors, e.g., [15, 18, 30].

Furthermore, understanding and improving the IS design in practice is a major goal of DSR [15]. This article contributes to DSR by describing the design and application of a domain-specific process reference model that is well-accepted in practice. This article follows the DSR paradigm [18, 30] and proposed DSR publication scheme [15]: (1) problem description, (2) design method, (3) artifact description, (4) artifact evaluation, and (5) discussion and conclusion. With respect to reference modeling both the design of the reference model itself as well as the design of a concrete (application) model based on the reference model can be seen as design artifacts. Hence, the description of the reference model eTOM (cf. Sect. 3) and the evaluation through the application in three concrete project cases (cf. Sect. 3.4) follow the above DSR scheme.

According to the *DSR Knowledge Contribution Framework* proposed by [15] the design of eTOM is located in the improvement quadrant, i.e., development of new solutions for a known problem domain (cf. Sect. 3.1). DSR projects are typically producing design artifacts on different levels of detail, also dependent on the maturity of the design artifact [15]. eTOM is a mature reference model and its application has been discussed in various publications, e.g., [23] explains the initial process definitions, [37] proposes the application of eTOM for a Next Generation Network (NGN), and [57] uses eTOM for an integrated network management system. Furthermore, the details of eTOM are published by the TM Forum [46]. The authors research eTOM from the reference modeling perspective, and selected parts of their work has been discussed in prior publications: [12] discusses the extension of eTOM through reference process flows, [11] provides an empirical study of the eTOM usage, [10] discusses eTOM in the context of NGN, and [8, 9] uses eTOM in the broader context of an enterprise architecture. In this context, this is the first article that summarizes and illustrates the current state of the whole eTOM development from a reference modeling perspective. The own empirical analysis of the eTOM usage [11] shows that its application requires further guidelines. Therefore, this article discusses three project cases that provide exemplary artifacts on a more detailed level.

eTOM is continuously updated by the respective working group within the TM Forum. The latest version of eTOM and details about contributing companies and persons are available there (cf. www.tmforum.org). The authors have been involved for many years in the development as part of the TM Forum. The described three project cases are summarized and anonymized illustrations of real-life projects that the authors have accompanied in leading roles (such as project manager). Project cases based on direct observations and official documentations are a valid approach for researching real-life phenomena [58].

3 Reference Modeling in the Telecommunications Industry

3.1 Problem Domain

The telecommunications industry is currently going through a major transformation that impacts strategy, structure, and technology of the players along the whole value chain, e.g., [9, 17, 32, 33]. Understanding the transformational needs and proposing solutions for telecommunications operators are intensively researched with different topical focus, including overall market research [33], value creation and market players [17, 31, 32, 36, 43, 54], structures and processes [6, 12, 34] as well as various functional or technical solutions [7, 10, 16, 25, 27, 28, 56]. The challenges for today's telecommunications operators can be summarized into (1) changed market conditions, (2) restructured value chains, and (3) new products and services [9]:

Looking at the *changed market conditions* the telecommunications industry is an important part of the ICT sector with a global yearly revenue of approximately 5 trillion USD [33, 43]. Even though the next years forecast a slight revenue growth, the telecommunications industry is a stagnating market. However, the market development differs based on the transmission technology. The total number of fixed telephone subscriptions is declining, and also the growth rate of mobile-cellular telephone subscriptions is decreasing, while mobile-broadband subscriptions have shown a tremendous growth [19]. Those changed usage behaviors are combined with an overall price decrease for most communication services [20, 33]. On the one hand, the increasing demand for high transmission bandwidths requires extensive investments in network infrastructure, but on the other hand, the transmission itself becomes a commodity. Customers relate the value proposition more with the communication service. Over-the-Top (OTT) providers offer new communication services without owning network infrastructure [14], and create a new competition for traditional telecommunications operators. Some new services offered by OTT providers have even replaced equivalent communication services – for example, *WhatsApp* has replaced the traditional Short Messaging Service (SMS). While the pure transmission business is stagnating, there is a growth potential for telecommunications operators in vertical markets, e.g., automotive, banking, healthcare, insurance, transportation and logistics as well as smart home [9]. In summary, from a market perspective telecommunications operators have to combine more *customer orientation* with *increased efficiency*.

The *restructured value chain* is influenced by new market players [31, 35]. Technical transmission becomes a minor part of the overall value chain, which is now confronted with new players, mergers, and acquisitions [42, 55]. The convergence of communication services [4], new mobile devices (i.e., smartphones) with high performance operating systems [1], and virtual business models [36] are impacting the value creation. The telecommunications value chain evolves into a value network consisting of network operators, software intermediaries, financial intermediaries, content providers, portals, and resellers [26]. For traditional telecommunications operators the shift from usage-dependent to flat-rate tariffs was the starting point for a complete rethinking of their business models. A possible strategic option is the combination of transmission services with application services, which allows differentiated pricing and new revenues (e.g., advertisement). For traditional telecommunications operators own developments, acquisitions, or partnerships with new market players are required, which leads in most cases to a *fragmented value creation*.

New products and services are strongly linked with the changed market conditions and value creation. For example, a smartphone generates more than 14 times the data volume of a basic mobile phone [49]. Telecommunications operators are confronted with continuous innovations [32] and shorter product development cycles [6]. Convergence on the application as well as on the technology side impacts the production structure [52]. For example, the strong link between the telephone network and the assigned telephony service is no longer valid. Nowadays Internet Protocol (IP) services realize telephony services independent from the transmission network. Hence, a flexible coupling between application services and transmission services is required. Furthermore, the commercial perspective of a communication product should be differentiated from its realizing services [6]. Both require a complete rethinking of product and production structure of traditional telecommunications operators [6, 10], which is related to an *abstraction from technical complexity* and *flexibility of the production*.

In practice, telecommunications operators have been adapting their strategies, structures, and technologies due to the described industry changes [6, 42, 55]. Therefore, a need for domain-specific reference solutions supporting those transformations has been arisen.

In this context, the industry organization TM Forum offers reference models for the telecommunications industry [23, 28, 38]. The TM Forum is an international well-accepted non-profit organization and was founded by major telecommunications operators. Today, it has more than 900 member companies that range from communication service providers to software vendors and system integrators. With working groups, workshops, and conferences it provides an ecosystem for joint development and research activities. The TM Forum is headed by a board of directors. Membership is open to companies and research institutes. Members can contribute in the working groups and use all the provided content in their companies' projects. The TM Forum offers the following three references for processes, data, and applications [45]:

1. *enhanced Telecom Operations Map* (eTOM), provides process definitions and process flows based on a hierarchical structure [46].
2. *Shared Information/Data Model* (SID), provides a data structure and detailed entity relationship models (ERM) [47].
3. *Telecom Application Map* (TAM), focuses on functionalities for applications [48].

With respect to the discussed challenges and requirements those TM Forum reference models support telecommunications operators through customer-centric processes and consequent decoupling between market requirements and technical realizations. The proposed models differentiate between product, service, and resource. They are combined with clear process domains, and therefore those reference models help to increase flexibility and generalize from technical complexity. Furthermore those reference models are applied by industry-specific standard software systems. This interrelation between challenges, requirements, and TM Forum reference models is summarized in Fig. 1. For the reference process model eTOM a more detailed explanation is provided in Sect. 3.3.

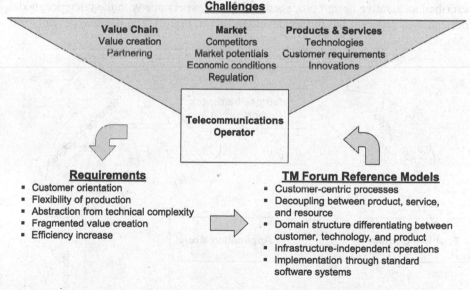

Fig. 1. Summary of problem domain (upper part according to [9])

All three reference models are continuously updated in working groups belonging to the TM Forum. They reflect a consensus within the industry. Furthermore, the ITU has confirmed parts of the TM Forum reference models as de facto standard [21, 22].

This publication focuses on the process reference model eTOM. The application of eTOM is described in various publications with different topical scope [12, 23, 24, 28, 37, 40, 57]. Furthermore, an own analysis of 184 transformation projects in the telecommunications industry shows an extensive usage of eTOM [11]. In this context, this article contributes a comprehensive description of eTOM, its development, and its application with a clear link to DSR.

3.2 Design Method

The design of eTOM follows an iterative process that is mainly based on contributions by member companies based on their experiences in practice, i.e., requirements from the problem domain. The eTOM working group discusses in regular conference calls as well as during on-site workshops those contributions (e.g., Team Action Week). The whole development follows a hierarchical structure. All new contributions or changes are mapped to the high-level structure (eTOM level 0–1). Furthermore, general design principles have been defined as a common basis [46]. Those design principles, e.g., define that eTOM "is decomposed from notional Level 0 to more granular levels – Levels 1, 2 and 3 (and some of level 4)" [46] and that "the goals, inputs, outputs, and activities of decomposed Process Elements at a lower level are consistent with the higher level" [46].

From a general perspective, the real value of a reference model can only be observed after using it in a concrete implementation [5]. In this context, [41] has described an iterative design process that uses the experience with the reference model application as input for the further development (cf. Fig. 2). The iterative development

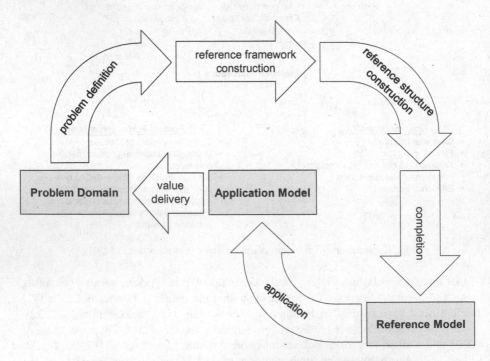

Fig. 2. General reference model design method ([9] according to [41])

process of eTOM is comparable with this general approach [9]. The specific requirements of the telecommunications industry (problem domain) as well as the concrete experiences with the application of eTOM are used as input for a continuous development by the TM Forum. The high-level eTOM structure can be seen as reference framework, while the regular contributions and updates are constructions and completions according to this structure.

Furthermore, the design method includes an evaluation that is mainly based on a consensus within the TM Forum [12]. First, the development team decides that a concrete design artifact is ready for its publication, i.e., the artifact has reached "team approval". Second, the whole eTOM working group – consisting of industry representatives – evaluates the artifact. Third, a technical committee of the TM Forum checks the overall quality and consistency of the new artifact. Fourth, the new artifact is provided to all TM Forum members for their comments. During the whole evaluation process changes are documented and incorporated in the artifact. Afterwards, the design artifact is officially published as part of the next eTOM version which is available through the TM Forum website.

3.3 Artifact Description

The core elements of eTOM can be structured into (1) *process definitions* which provide a collection and categorization of business processes specific for telecommunications operators [23] and (2) *reference process flows* which propose a sequence for those process definitions [12]. Both are structured in a hierarchical manner on different levels of detail (cf. Fig. 3) [9]. Each part of eTOM contains specific design artifacts, e.g., on level 0–1 a process framework is proposed and on level 3 detailed reference process flows are provided. Those design artifacts are interrelated with each other, e.g., the process definitions level 3 are categorized according to level 2 and used as input for the detailed reference process flows on level 3. Furthermore, eTOM contains various methodical guidelines, a general concept description, and application notes describing specific implementations. Hence, eTOM consists of many different documents, an XML-based representation and model files in various formats.

The eTOM *process definition* distinguishes on the highest level the following three process groups [23]:

1. *Operations* contains all processes that are required to run a telecommunications operator under the assumption of existing infrastructure and products. Those processes cover, e.g., sales, after-sales, incidents, and billing.
2. *Strategy, Infrastructure and Products (SIP)* cover all other domains-specific processes that are a necessity for a telecommunications operator – i.e., planning and implementing its infrastructure and products from strategy development to technical realization.
3. *Enterprise Management* provides general supporting processes, e.g., human resource management, finance, and communication.

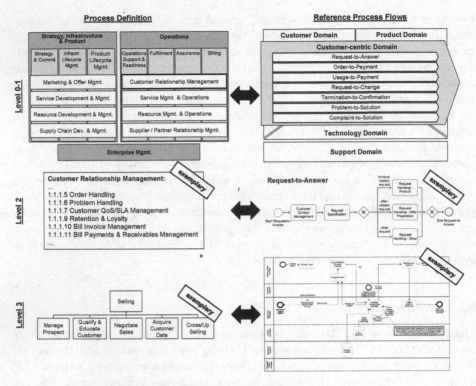

Fig. 3. Structure of eTOM artifact

The process groups Operations and SIP cover the industry-specific content that is required for the core value creation [9]. Both are further horizontally structured by the involved entities [23]:

- *Market* summarizes the general view of market requirements and opportunities.
- *Products* are service capabilities combined with commercial offers. They are sold to customers.
- *Customers* are the interface to individual consumers or business entities that are interested in or have bought products.
- *Services* are a logical view on capabilities that are relevant to sell products.
- *Resources* provide a technical realization of services.
- *Suppliers/partners* might deliver capabilities with respect to products, services, or resources.

The three process groups Operations, SIP, and Enterprise Management are combined with the six horizontal entities from the eTOM framework (level 0–1). Based on this structure process decompositions are provided (cf. left part of Fig. 3). Hence, the process definition of eTOM is a hierarchical collection of business processes. For a concrete process design, this collection can be used as a common terminology as well as a checklist to identify all relevant processes. However, the process definitions proposed in the initial eTOM publications (i.e., GB921-D and GB921-DX) do not include any reference for a process flow, i.e., they do not make any statement about the sequence. As part of the continuous development of eTOM (cf. Sect. 3.2), reference process flows were developed [12]. The reference process flows are published as an official extension to eTOM in GB921-E.

The *reference process flows* are based on the following domains providing an end-to-end perspective on the process sequence [8, 9, 12]:

- *Customer-centric domain* contains all interactions that are directly initiated by the customer.
- *Technology domain* includes the realization and operations of communication services and network resources.
- *Product domain* ranges from product development to product elimination.
- *Customer domain* covers interactions that deal with customers but are not directly initiated by the customer (e.g., marketing campaigns).
- *Enterprise support domain* includes general support processes (e.g., finance or human resource management).

For each domain, end-to-end process flows are defined. These end-to-end process flows are then mapped to eTOM. With this mapping the sequence is added to the process definition. Furthermore, the reference process flows are defined on different levels following the eTOM hierarchy (cf. right part of Fig. 3). The customer-centric domain, for example, contains the end-to-end process flow *Request-to-Answer* that covers all process steps from the customer contact to the answering of the request [8, 9, 12].

By combining the hierarchical process definitions with end-to-end process flows, eTOM provides an extensive process reference model for telecommunications operators. Through its hierarchical structure, it can be used for strategic and planning purposes as well as for operational implementations. With the end-to-end process flows, interrelations between organizational and technical entities are transparent.

3.4   Artifact Evaluation

Even though the evaluation is an indispensable part of DSR [18], the evaluation of a reference model is a methodical challenge [39]. The reference model should be generalizable for a certain problem domain, and its application is decoupled from its development [41, 51]. Hence, its general validity cannot be proven, however it becomes more likely with each application [3]. The application of a reference model can be illustrated through project cases which are seen as a valid evaluation of design artifacts [18].

The focus of this article is on the evaluation of the eTOM process reference model through real-life project cases. It follows an illustration of three project cases. All three cases were accompanied by the authors and are illustrated here in a summarized and anonymized manner. Their descriptions are based on direct observations and official project documents which are valid methods for researching real-life phenomena [58].

Project Case 1: Improvement of Problem-to-Solution Process

Purpose and Scope

Subject of this first project case is a well-established telecommunications operator in the Middle East. It offers fixed line and mobile products. The former monopolist faced increased competition combined with declining customer satisfaction. The telecommunications operator started an extensive transformation program. The improvement of the Problem-to-Solution process was part of this program and integrated in a broader Business Process Management (BPM) project [8, 9].

Project Approach

First, the existing processes related to problem reporting, analysis, and resolution were analyzed. Second, an improved target process was designed and implemented. In both parts eTOM was used as a reference. During the analysis the process framework (level 0–1) supported the identification of relevant processes and their interfaces. Based on the process framework interviews with responsible persons were conducted in order to understand the currently implemented process. For the target process design the detailed charts of the eTOM reference process flows (level 3) were used as starting point. They were mapped to the organizational structure and adapted according to specific requirements based on workshops with the responsible persons. Some process parts were further detailed on level 4.

Artifact Description

As a result detailed target processes were designed for the Problem-to-Solution process. In total, 35 detailed target process charts were developed. All target processes were based on the process reference model eTOM. Figure 4 shows an example of a detailed target process (level 3).

Artifact Evaluation

The target Problem-to-Solution process was implemented within a project duration of 8 months. In comparison to the initial situation concrete performance improvements were measured one month after process implementation. For example, the working hours related to the process were reduced by 39%. Furthermore, the total number of reported incidents was decreased by 23% due to faster problem resolution and less repeated problem reports. The evaluation of the long-term performance development would require further studies that are not planned so far.

Project Case 2: Implementation of a Network Operations Center

Purpose and Scope

Subject of this second project case is an African telecommunications operator offering fixed line and mobile products. Due to historically grown network infrastructures, a new overall Network Operations Center (NOC) was implemented. One part of this implementation was the design of target processes for the NOC.

Project Approach

The project was structured into three phases. In phase 1, the existing processes were collected and analyzed. Phase 2 covered the definition of a high-level framework for the target processes. In phase 3, detailed processes were designed and mapped to the

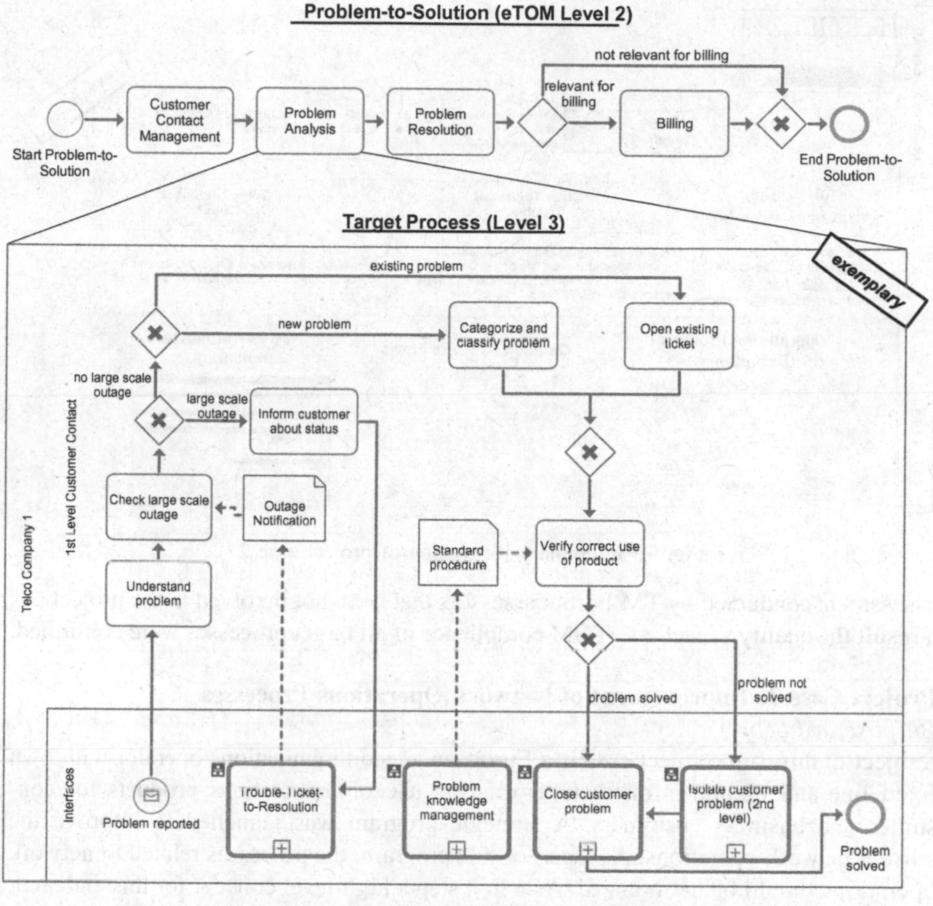

Fig. 4. Exemplary illustration of project case 1

existing organization. In all three phases eTOM and especially the reference process flows of the technology domain were used as a reference.

Artifact Description

As a result, a complete process design from level 0 to level 5 was developed for the NOC implementation (cf. Fig. 5). The reference process flows of the technology domain from eTOM were adapted based on the specific requirements. On level 3–5 process definitions and process flows provide a clear mapping to organizational responsibilities on an operational level. Furthermore, detailed Key Performance Indicators (KPI) were defined.

Artifact Evaluation

All designed target processes were discussed and agreed with the persons responsible for the execution of these processes. After the NOC implementation, the TM Forum assessed all NOC processes as part of an eTOM certification, which is a formal

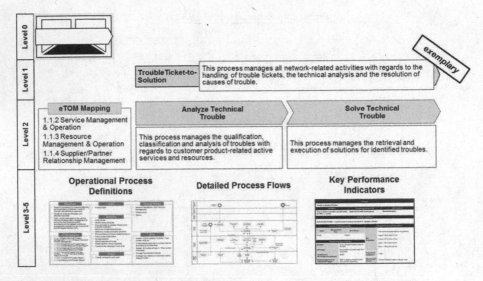

Fig. 5. Exemplary illustration of project case 2

assessment conducted by TM Forum assessors that were not involved in the project. As a result the quality as well as eTOM compliance of all target processes were confirmed.

Project Case 3: Improvement of Network Operations Processes

Purpose and Scope

Subject of this third project case is a European telecommunications operator with own fixed line and mobile infrastructures offering telecommunications products for consumer and business customers. A strategic program was launched to improve the current network operations. As a part of this program, the processes related to network operations should be harmonized. As a first step a high-level concept for this endeavor was developed.

Project Approach

The eTOM framework level 0–1 was used as starting point. Specific requirements were collected, evaluated and mapped to eTOM. The identified processes and requirements were discussed with the responsible persons and summarized in a high-level concept.

Artifact Description

The result contains a process framework (level 0–1) with a definition of all relevant core processes (cf. Fig. 6). The definition included a detailed description as well as a mapping to the organizational structure. Those core processes were based on the reference process flows of the technology domain. Furthermore, support processes and the interfaces were identified based on the eTOM framework.

Artifact Evaluation

The designed results were confirmed by the responsible persons and the steering committee of the overall program. In a next step, the outcomes were used for the planning and implementation of the improved network operations. This task also

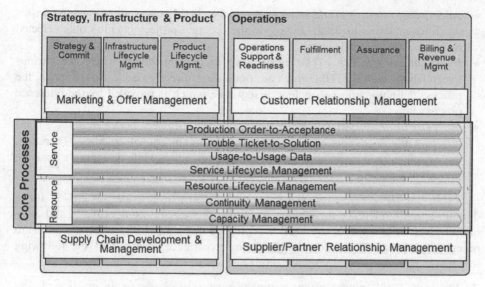

Fig. 6. Exemplary illustration of project case 3

included more detailed process flows and operational process implementations. However, the implementation is still work in progress.

4   Discussion and Outlook

This article describes the design and application of the domain-specific process reference model eTOM. Following the DSR paradigm, it contributes to the development of new solutions for the known problem domain telecommunications industry. As starting point, the requirements of the telecommunications industry are summarized. eTOM is a mature design artifact that is well-accepted in practice. Both the design of eTOM as well as the resulting artifact are illustrated. As an evaluation three projects are described that apply eTOM in a practical context. Also the illustrations of those three projects follow the DSR paradigm and are structured accordingly. Due to the complexity of the topic, the explanation of eTOM is limited to an abstract level, and the illustrations of the project cases provide summaries of selected parts. Further details would be required to apply the results in practice.

From the *perspective of the telecommunications industry* the article proposes domain-specific artifacts for the current transformational needs. Both the process definitions as well as the reference process flows provide reference solutions on different levels of detail. The project cases illustrate the usage of eTOM on strategic and operational levels. The examples show the identification and mapping of the different parts of eTOM to solve concrete practical problems. The following lessons-learned for using eTOM in a practical context can be summarized:

- *Selection of relevant eTOM parts is essential.* eTOM covers all possible processes on different levels of detail. Based on the concrete project situation only selected parts of eTOM are relevant.
- *Interrelations between eTOM parts have to be considered.* There are various interrelations within eTOM which are not always directly visible. For example, the process definitions do not include a sequence which is provided by the reference process flows.
- *Mapping to organizational structure is a prerequisite for implementation.* eTOM provides reference processes independent from organizational structures. Therefore, the organizational mapping is part of the customization while designing a concrete model.

From the *perspective of general DSR* the article provides examples for a domain-specific reference modeling, i.e., design process, resulting artifacts, and evaluation. Reference models are well-accepted contributions of the IS discipline to practical problems. Based on the exemplary experience with eTOM the following lessons-learned for general research on design science can be summarized:

- *Illustration of comprehensive design artifacts is a challenge.* In practice, design artifacts are typically complex, e.g., the process definition of eTOM encompasses several hundreds of pages.
- *Evaluation of reference models requires further guidelines.* The project cases show that the application of eTOM is related to different parts and require specific customizations. Hence, the evaluation with project cases is mainly related to the applicability.

With respect to the continuous enhancement of eTOM, the presented results can be used in future developments. Especially the experience with ongoing virtualization of network operations (project case 3) as well as the harmonization of operations processes due to technical innovations (project cases 1 and 2) are important inputs for eTOM. In addition, future research could be related to the following questions: What is the relation between eTOM processes and different types of organizational structures? How is a concrete model derived from eTOM, and which interrelations (also between processes, data, and applications) should be considered? How can those concrete project cases be used for the evaluation of reference models? These questions are a starting point for further research on domain-specific design artifacts supporting the practical transformational needs in the telecommunications industry as well as general research on guidelines for designing and evaluating reference models in the context of DSR.

References

1. Basole, R.C., Karla, J.: On the evolution of mobile platform ecosystem structure and strategy. Bus. Inf. Syst. Eng. **3**, 313–322 (2011). doi:10.1007/s12599-011-0174-4
2. Becker, J., Delfmann, P.: Reference Modeling Efficient Information Systems Design Through Reuse of Information Models. Physica Verlag, Heidelberg (2007)

3. Becker, J., Schütte, R.: Handelsinformationssysteme. MI-Wirtschaftsbuch, Munich (2004)
4. Bertin, E., Crespi, N.: Service business processes for the next generation of services: a required step to achieve service convergence. Ann. Telecommun. **64**, 187–196 (2009)
5. Böhmann, T., Schermann, M., Krcmar, H.: Application-oriented evaluation of the SDM reference model: framework, instantiation and initial findings. In: Becker, J., Delfmann, P. (eds.) Reference Modeling, pp. 123–144. Physica-Verlag, Heidelberg (2007)
6. Bruce, G., Naughton, B., Trew, D., et al.: Streamlining the telco production line. J. Telecommun. Manag. **1**, 15–32 (2008)
7. Copeland, R.: Converging NGN Wireline and Mobile 3G Networks with IMS. CRC Press, Boca Raton (2009)
8. Czarnecki, C.: Entwicklung einer referenzmodellbasierten Unternehmensarchitektur für die Telekommunikationsindustrie. Logos-Verl, Berlin (2013)
9. Czarnecki, C., Dietze, C.: Reference Architecture for the Telecommunications Industry: Transformation of Strategy, Organization, Processes, Data, and Applications. Springer, Heidelberg (2017)
10. Czarnecki, C., Spiliopoulou, M.: A holistic framework for the implementation of a next generation network. Int. J. Bus. Inf. Syst. (IJBIS) **9**, 385–401 (2012)
11. Czarnecki, C., Winkelmann, A., Spiliopoulou, M.: Transformation in telecommunication – analyse und clustering von real-life projekten. In: Mattfeld, D.C., Robra-Bissantz, S. (eds) Multi-Konferenz Wirtschaftsinformatik 2012, pp. 985–998. GITO Verlag, Braunschweig (2012)
12. Czarnecki, C., Winkelmann, A., Spiliopoulou, M.: Reference process flows for telecommunication companies: an extension of the eTOM model. Bus. Inf. Syst. Eng. **5**, 83–96 (2013). doi:10.1007/s12599-013-0250-z
13. Fettke, P., Loos, P.: Perspectives on reference modeling. In: Fettke, P., Loos, P. (eds.) Reference Modelling for Business Systems Analysis, pp. 1–21. IGI Global, Hershey (2007)
14. Fritz, M., Schlereth, C., Figge, S.: Empirical evaluation of fair use flat rate strategies for mobile internet. Bus. Inf. Syst. Eng. **3**, 269–277 (2011). doi:10.1007/s12599-011-0172-6
15. Gregor, S., Hevner, A.R.: Positioning and presenting design science research for maximum impact. MIS Q. **37**, 337–356 (2013)
16. Grishunin, S., Suloeva, S.: Project controlling in telecommunication industry. In: Balandin, S., Andreev, S., Koucheryavy, Y. (eds.) ruSMART 2015. LNCS, vol. 9247, pp. 573–584. Springer, Cham (2015). doi:10.1007/978-3-319-23126-6_51
17. Grover, V., Saeed, K.: The telecommunication industry revisited. Commun. ACM **46**, 119–125 (2003). doi:10.1145/792704.792709
18. Hevner, A.R., March, S.T., Park, J., Ram, S.: Design science in information systems research. MIS Q. **28**, 75–105 (2004)
19. ITU: Key ICT indicators for developed and developing countries and the world (2015)
20. ITU: ICT facts and figures – the world in 2015 (2015)
21. ITU: ITU-T recommendation M.3050.0: enhanced Telecom Operations Map (eTOM) – introduction (2007)
22. ITU: ITU-T recommendation M.3190: shared information and data model (SID) (2008)
23. Kelly, M.B.: The telemanagement forum's enhanced Telecom Operations Map (eTOM). J. Netw. Syst. Manag. **11**, 109–119 (2003)
24. Kwak, E., Chang, B.-Y., Hong, D.W., Chung, B.: A study on the service quality management process and its realization strategy for capturing customer value. In: Ma, Y., Choi, D., Ata, S. (eds.) APNOMS 2008. LNCS, vol. 5297, pp. 297–306. Springer, Heidelberg (2008). doi:10.1007/978-3-540-88623-5_30
25. Lewis, L.: Managing Business and Service Networks. Kluwer Academic Publishers, New York (2001)

26. Li, F., Whalley, J.: Deconstruction of the telecommunications industry: from value chains to value networks. In: Telecommunications Policy, pp. 451–472. Elsevier Science Ltd. (2002)
27. Mikkonen, K., Hallikas, J., Pynnönen, M.: Connecting customer requirements into the multi-play business model. J. Telecommun. Manag. 2, 177–188 (2008)
28. Misra, K.: OSS for Telecom Networks: An Introduction to Network Management. Springer, London (2004)
29. Otto, B., Ofner, M.: Towards a process reference model for information supply chain management. In: 18th European Conference on Information Systems. Pretoria, South Africa (2010)
30. Peffers, K., Tuunanen, T., Rothenberger, M.A., Chatterjee, S.: A design science research methodology for information systems research. J. Manag. Inf. Syst. 24, 45–77 (2007). doi:10.2753/MIS0742-1222240302
31. Peppard, J., Rylander, A.: From value chain to value network. Eur. Manag. J. 24, 128–141 (2006). doi:10.1016/j.emj.2006.03.003
32. Picot, A. (ed.): The Future of Telecommunications Industries. Springer, Heidelberg (2006)
33. Plunkett, J.W.: Plunkett's telecommunications industry almanac 2015: the only comprehensive guide to the telecommunications industry (2014)
34. Pospischil, R.: Reorganization of European telecommunications: the cases of British Telecom, France Télécom and Deutsche Telekom. Telecommun. Policy 17, 603–621 (1993)
35. Pousttchi, K., Hufenbach, Y.: Value creation in the mobile market: a reference model for the role(s) of the future mobile network operator. Bus. Inf. Syst. Eng. 3, 299–311 (2011). doi:10.1007/s12599-011-0175-3
36. Pousttchi, K., Hufenbach, Y.: Analyzing and categorization of the business model of virtual operators. In: IEEE, pp. 87–92 (2009)
37. Raouyane, B., Bellafkih, M., Errais, M., Leghroudi, D., Ranc, D., Ramdani, M.: eTOM business processes conception in NGN monitoring. In: Lin, S., Huang, X. (eds.) CESM 2011. CCIS, vol. 176, pp. 133–143. Springer, Heidelberg (2011). doi:10.1007/978-3-642-21802-6_22
38. Reilly, J.P., Creaner, M.J.: NGOSS Distilled: The Essential Guide to Next Generation Telecoms Management. The Lean Corporation, Cambridge (2005)
39. Riege, C., Saat, J., Bucher, T.: Systematisierung von Evaluationsmethoden in der gestaltungsorientierten Wirtschaftsinformatik. In: Becker, J., Krcmar, H., Niehaves, B. (eds.) Wissenschaftstheorie und gestaltungsorientierte Wirtschaftsinformatik, pp. 69–86. Physica-Verlag, Heidelberg (2009)
40. Sathyan, J.: Fundamentals of EMS, NMS, and OSS/BSS. CRC Press, Auerbach Publications, Boca Raton (2010)
41. Schütte, R.: Grundsätze ordnungsmässiger Referenzmodellierung: Konstruktion konfigurations- und anpassungsorientierter Modelle. Gabler, Wiesbaden (1998)
42. Tardiff, T.J.: Changes in industry structure and technological convergence: implications for competition policy and regulation in telecommunications. Int. Econ. Econ. Policy 4, 109–133 (2007). doi:10.1007/s10368-007-0083-7
43. Telecommunications Industry Association: TIA's 2015–2018 ICT Market Review and Forecast (2015)
44. Thomas, O.: Reference model management. In: Fettke, P., Loos, P. (eds.) Reference Modeling for Business Systems Analysis, pp. 288–309. Idea Group Publishing, Hershey (2007)
45. TM Forum: Frameworks Release 15.0.0: Release Notes (RN354), Version 15.0.0 (2015)
46. TM Forum: Business Process Framework (eTOM): Concepts and Principles (GB921 CP), Version 15.0.0 (2015)

47. TM Forum: Information Framwork (SID): Concepts and Principles (GB922), Version 15.0.0 (2015)
48. TM Forum: Application Framwork (TAM): Concepts and Principles (GB929 CP), Version 14.5.1 (2015)
49. Verma, D.C., Verma, P.: Techniques for surviving the mobile data explosion (2014)
50. vom Brocke, J.: Design principles for reference modeling: reusing information models by means of aggregation, specialisation, instantiation, and analogy. In: Fettke, P., Loos, P. (eds.) Reference Modeling for Business Systems Analysis, pp. 47–75. Idea Group Publishing, Hershey (2007)
51. vom Brocke, J.: Referenzmodellierung: Gestaltung und Verteilung von Konstruktion-sprozessen. Logos, Berlin (2015)
52. Wieland, R.A.: Konvergenz aus Kundensicht. In: Picot, A., Freyberg, A. (eds.) Infrastruktur und Services - Das Ende einer Verbindung?, pp. 43–67. Springer, Heidelberg (2007)
53. Winkelmann, A.: Reference model maintenance based on ERP system implementation. AIS Trans. Enterp. Syst. 3(1), 27–35 (2012)
54. Wulf, J., Zarnekow, R.: Cross-sector competition in telecommunications: an empirical analysis of diversification activities. Bus. Inf. Syst. Eng. 3, 289–298 (2011). doi:10.1007/s12599-011-0177-1
55. Wulf, J., Zarnekow, R.: How do ICT firms react to convergence? An analysis of diversification strategies. In: ECIS 2011 Proceedings, paper 97 (2011)
56. Yahia, I.G.B., Bertin, E., Crespi, N.: Next/new generation networks services and management. In: Proceedings of the International Conference on Networking and Services, Washington, DC, USA, p. 15. IEEE Computer Society (2006)
57. Yari, A.R., Fesharaki, S.H.H.: A framework for an integrated network management system base on enhanced Telecom Operation Map (eTOM). In: Ata, S., Hong, C.S. (eds.) APNOMS 2007. LNCS, vol. 4773, pp. 587–590. Springer, Heidelberg (2007). doi:10.1007/978-3-540-75476-3_72
58. Yin, R.K.: Case Study Research: Design and Methods. Sage Publications, Los Angeles (2009)

Finding Evidence for Effectual Application Development on Digital Platforms

Onkar Malgonde[✉] and Alan Hevner

Information Systems and Decision Sciences, Muma College of Business,
University of South Florida, Tampa, USA
{omalgonde, ahevner}@usf.edu

Abstract. The development of novel software applications on digital platforms differs from traditional software development and provides unique challenges to software development managers and teams. Platform-based applications must achieve application-platform match, application-market match, value propositions exceeding platform's core value propositions, and novelty. These desired properties support a new vision of the software development team as entrepreneurs with a goal of developing novel applications on digital platforms. In this research study, we look for evidence on an open-source software development project – Apache Cordova – that development teams use effectual thinking. Over one thousand user stories are analyzed for the use of constructs from a proposed effectual software development research model. The findings provide an initial confirmation that effectual development methods hold promise for the definition of new process models that better support application development on digital platforms. We conclude with a discussion on the implications of our results, research contributions, and future directions.

Keywords: Software development · Platform · Innovation · Effectuation

1 Digital Innovations on Software Platforms

Digital innovations are new combinations of digital and physical components characterized by reprogrammability, homogenization of data, and use of digital technology [1]. The application platform, as shown in Fig. 1, is a pervasive digital technology that is rapidly transforming the ways in which products and services are produced and consumed in our market economy [2].

The *platform ecosystem* consists of the platform infrastructure and the applications that are available via the platform (or connect to the platform via the interfaces offered by the platform) in a contextual *environment* of regulations and competitors [3, 4]. Platforms enable value-creating interactions among organizations with disparate resources and specializations [2]. This transfers the locus of innovation, which traditionally has been within the organization, to a diverse set of external organizations that develop applications available via the platform.

A platform *owner* is the organization or group of organizations that determine the architecture, governance, and curation mechanisms for the platform. *Producers* are the organizations that develop applications (extensions to the core functionality offered by

© Springer International Publishing AG 2017
A. Maedche et al. (Eds.): DESRIST 2017, LNCS 10243, pp. 330–347, 2017.
DOI: 10.1007/978-3-319-59144-5_20

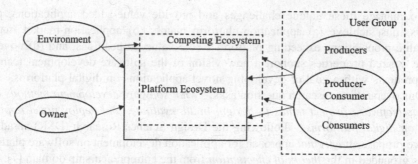

Fig. 1. The digital platform ecosystem

the platform) that are available via the platform. *Consumers* are the organizations that use applications offered via the platform. Examples of well-known software platforms include Apple's iTunes, Google's Play, Salesforce's appexchange, SAP's HANA, Valve's Steam, and Instructure's Canvas, among others.

Development of novel software applications on a digital platform differs from traditional software development. The following platform characteristics support a new and challenging application development environment:

- A platform offers a compelling set of *core value propositions* to its consumers [2]. Applications on the platform play off the core values and add novel extensions to the platform's capabilities.
- Over time, these core values evolve based on consumer demands and goals and, as a result, platform applications are added, updated, and dropped.
- All applications must adhere to connection specifications and development procedures determined by the platform [4]. Platforms provide standard connection interfaces in the form of application programming interfaces (API's) that are used by applications to access common features within the platform. Thus, platform owners and user groups often require that application producers follow certain best practices such as 'look and feel' interactions. In many cases, the platform owners evaluate and approve new applications (curation mechanisms) before they are offered to consumers via the platform.
- As the number of similar applications on a software platform increases, investment incentives for individual producers are crowded out [5]. Similarity of applications available via a platform limits the platform's value proposition and incentivizes the platform to assimilate those features into the core value proposition of the platform. Consequently, applications whose value proposition is assimilated into the core offering of the platform are discontinued.
- Application developers may request changes in platform interfaces and protocols based on environmental changes or new customer demands.
- Platforms exhibit different levels of maturity over time. Changes to platform architecture and governance mechanisms require application producers to adapt their applications and routines to comply with updated platform regulations.

To manage these unique challenges and provide value-added applications, producers must achieve (a) application-platform match, (b) application-market match, (c) value propositions exceeding platform's core value propositions, and (d) novelty. These desired properties support a new vision of the software development team as entrepreneurs with a goal of developing novel applications on digital platforms.

Our overarching research question asks, *"What software development methods best support software project teams to design, build, evaluate, and deploy novel applications on digital platforms?"* Following the Design Science Research (DSR) paradigm [6], we propose an *effectual* approach for application development on software platform that is grounded in the *theory of effectuation* from the entrepreneurship domain [7]. The goal of this paper is to investigate existing application development projects on digital platforms to see if the concepts of effectual thinking are present. We structure the paper as follows. First, we will review the theory of effectuation and discuss the need for effectuation thinking for application development on platforms. Drawing from the theory of effectuation, we develop a research model of effectual software development. Section 3 presents our research design of qualitative data analysis conducted on secondary data from Apache Cordova project—an open source software development environment that supports multiple platforms. Section 4 will discuss the findings and results of the analysis. Section 5 will discuss qualitative data that address the need for effectual thinking in software development. We conclude with a discussion of implications of this study for application development on platforms in Sect. 6 and contributions and future research directions in Sect. 7.

2   An Effectual Software Development Process

The consumer demand for new and interesting applications on ubiquitous digital platforms has energized the software development world to greater requirements for delivery speed and higher quality user experiences. Existing agile approaches often fail to provide the right types of design thinking, concepts, and processes to support the challenges of digital platform application development [7]. Thus, we propose a new approach of effectual software development.

2.1   Effectuation

Sarasvathy [8] conceptualizes effectuation as the opposite of causation. Unlike causation, effectuation does not focus on finding causes that explain or achieve a given (intended) effect, but considers available actions through given means and their spectrum of possible effects. Effectuation therefore is about designing and evaluating alternatives with differing effects (and choosing one of them) instead of choosing among given alternatives which all lead to the same effect. Thus, effectuation logic constitutes a logic of controls; specifically controlling the future by actively shaping one's environment within one's possibilities.

In effectuation, the choice of action depends on the three given means of (1) the actors (effectuators) themselves and their traits ("who I am"), (2) their knowledge ("what I know"), and (3) their social connections ("whom I know"). It also depends on what the effectuators can imagine to be possible effects and what they perceive the corresponding risks or potential losses to be. These risks and losses are matched with effectuator's set of aspirations, leading to the eventual choice of action. Neither the means nor the aspirations are treated as invariant, leading to a concept that embraces flexibility and dynamism, allowing the exploitation of emerging contingencies [8]. Figure 2 illustrates the basic concepts of effectuation.

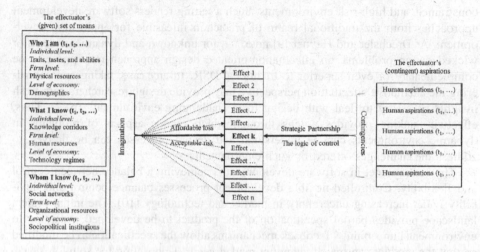

Fig. 2. Theory of effectuation (Sarasvathy [8])

Two decision heuristics are employed when the entrepreneur pursues possible actions: *acceptable risk/affordable loss* and *logic of control*. Acceptable risk/affordable loss favors those actions which carry a degree of risk that is acceptable to the entrepreneur. It avoids actions that carry existential risk to the enterprise. This is in contrast to causation where decision making is based on expected returns of the alternative actions. Logic of control involves decision making based on factors that the entrepreneur can control as opposed to prediction of future events. As the iterative process of effectuation evolves, the entrepreneur accumulates new means and goals, and converges to a set of effects resulting in an artifact that embodies the desired aspirations and goals.

2.2   Applying Effectual Thinking to Software Development

Drechsler and Hevner [9] provide guidance for incorporating the concepts of effectuation into the design science research (DSR) paradigm. They argue that effectuation-oriented DSR may provide superior lens to examine problem spaces that are characterized with uncertainty and dynamic evolution. In our research, we take this conceptualization one step further to propose an effectual process to develop novel applications on software-based platforms. Effectual thinking aligns with software development on digital platforms due to the limitations of causal based approaches in the literature [10] and the challenges offered by digital platforms. Causation based approaches to software development identify a particular goal and realize it through a linear and/or iterative process. These are prediction based approaches, where the application's ultimate fit and utility in the platform context is identified a priori [11]. Such a priori identification of application's utility is possible in environments that are characterized by certainty and stability.

However, software development on digital platforms provide uncertain, resource constrained, and high-risk environments. Such a setting renders software development approaches from the traditional realm of prediction infeasible for application development. As Drechsler and Hevner [9] note, "... for unknown and dynamic contexts or wicked design problems, an effectuation-oriented design approach may prove to be complementary or even superior to traditional DSR. In any case, taking and considering the alternative effectuation perspective may provide design researchers with fresh insights necessary to deal with design for a challenging environment" (p. 7). Thus, effectual thinking provides a lens through which unique aspects of problems in dynamic environments can be understood and design processes can be derived to address the challenges offered by such environments.

The central tenet in software development is achieving a balance between control and flexibility. Controlled-flexible development processes balance control and flexibility under increasing uncertainty in market and technology [10]. The initial project landscape provides partial specification of the product to be developed. Adapting to environmental uncertainty, feedback mechanisms allow the specification to be modified so that the product can match changing market needs. Controlling the solution space, scope boundaries allow exploration of solution by the project team while constraining their space to align with organizational goals. Thus, iterative development, scope boundaries, and feedback mechanisms allow the software product to be relevant upon completion [10]. Though a controlled-flexible approach develops a relevant product in uncertain environment, none of the prior literature has explored its applicability to the development of novel software products on digital platforms.

We contend that current agile development processes and methods do not effectively address the challenges of digital platforms because (a) any form of prediction in highly dynamic environments is suspect, (b) fixed development constraints on platforms are not conducive to agile thinking, (c) risk and loss tolerance are key factors in whether or not to build an application in a risky environment and are not highlighted in agile processes, and (d) the platform development process must go beyond just product-market match to consider the factors of product-platform match, value add beyond the core platform values, and novelty of offering. Consideration of these issues requires a software development approach that treats the uncertain environment as endogenous and shapes it.

Digital platforms represent socio-technical, dynamic, and challenging contexts for software development teams. Using effectual thinking allows software development teams to identify multiple possible effects based on their available means. Through market and stakeholder feedback, the development team can iteratively attenuate their aspirations and identify an appropriate effect that embodies their aspirations, fits the application context, and provides utility to its users. This approach is in contrast to the causal approach since the team does not identify a particular goal; rather they iteratively attenuate their aspirations to arrive at the desired effect (artifact).

2.3 A Model of the Effectual Development Process

An investigation of an effectual application development process begins with a fuller understanding of components of the process and their relationships as presented in Fig. 3. The three key components of the effectual model are:

- *Means* for the project manager (PM) and development team are the existing resources that are available to them. Means consist of technology and skills (programming language, API's, tools), market knowledge (customer orientation, seasonal trends, patterns from archival data), platform knowledge (connection interface, tools and technology, best practices, available API's on the platform), control mechanisms (scope boundaries, stakeholder feedback), and the social capital that the development team can draw upon.
- The *software platform* provides a set of resources and constraints. For example, the connection interfaces to the platform, development guidelines, tutorials, and development standards that provide resources for the project to draw upon while constraining them to those specific alternatives.
- Four *aspirations* for the project team are identified – application-platform match, application-market match, value proposition of the application should exceed the core value proposition of the platform, and novelty of the application.

For the development team, means, platform, and aspirations exist a priori to the development process. However, they evolve over time as intermediate effects identify new means, constraints, and aspirations. The PM and development team act towards developing the partial specification for the application. Actions utilize available means, current state of the platform, and aspirations of the team as the input. An *effect* is the operationalization of abstract aspirations [8]. Effects give rise to new means and constraints for the development team. New means stem from an improved understanding of the problem space. Similarly, new constraints are identified that help retain appropriate and promising aspects of the aspiration. The *Artifact* (application product or service) is the realization of team's aspirations.

Given the means and aspirations of the project team, alternative actions are possible. The mechanism to select appropriate actions is provided by two heuristics: *acceptable risk* and *logic of control*. According to classical decision theory, risk associated with an alternative is the variation in its possible outcomes [12]. The larger the variation in possible outcomes, the larger is the risk associated with the alternative. Thus, evaluation of decision alternative is based on the trade-off between its expected return and associated risk. This perspective is in line with the causation logic, where decision alternatives are chosen based on their expected returns and risks. With an effectual approach, a managerial perspective on risk suggests that risk is associated with negative outcomes of the decision alternative. Further, the managerial perspective notes that risk is *controllable* and *modifiable* through skills and information [13]. The logic of control emphasizes controllable aspects of future events i.e., a focus on

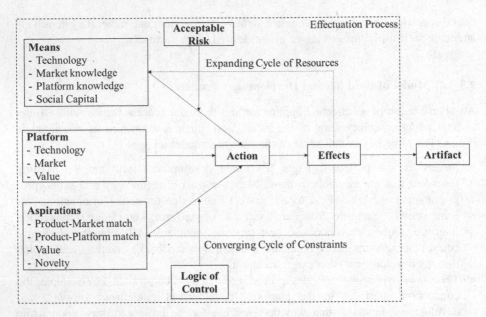

Fig. 3. Components and relationships of the effectual development process

aspirations that can be controlled by the project team [8]. A focus on controllable aspects allows the project team to identify alternative actions that in turn lead to multiple effects.

The project team conducts a risk analysis [14–16] on the set of possible action alternatives based on the means. Action alternatives that have an acceptable risk are identified. Platform state, existing portfolio of controls [10, 17], and aspirations of the project team identify the controllable aspects of the possible actions. Together, these heuristics serve as leverage to the project team to determine appropriate actions that lead to desired effects.

3   Research Method

As an initial investigation of the effectual research model in Fig. 3, we study an existing open source environment that supports the development of applications on digital platforms. We identified *Apache Cordova*[1] as an open-source mobile application development framework (Fig. 4). Following the mantra of Apache Software Foundation (ASF), the Cordova application framework is used by numerous application developers to develop applications and provides tools and interfaces that can be readily used by developers. Apache Cordova provides all the interfaces and plugins that the development team needs to develop the application which can then be published across those platforms. Thus, Cordova acts as an intermediary application which is used by

---

[1] https://cordova.apache.org/docs/en/latest/guide/overview/index.html.

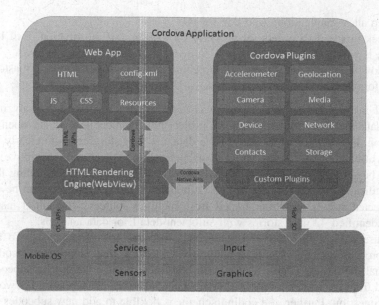

Fig. 4. Apache Cordova architecture from https://cordova.apache.org/docs/en/latest/guide/overview/index.html

the software development team to develop an application such that it is compatible across multiple platforms. Cordova supports seven platforms—Android, iOS, Windows, Ubuntu, Blackberry 10, WP8, and OS X. Web View provides user interface capabilities, *Web App* provides configurational settings for the application, and Cordova *Plugins* allow seamless communication within application components and the platform. The *Mobile OS* platform provides standardized plugins, which are regularly updated by the platform owner.

All Apache projects are required to store and host programming activities, decisions, and status of the project. Projects adhere to these requirements using mailing lists, project management and version control tools, and/or messaging platforms. We extract data from the project management tool. Specifically, we focus on this particular dataset because (a) all data are available, (b) the dataset consists of issues raised by a vast array of active individuals (contributors), and (c) the dataset includes requests for information, bug fixes, feature requests, suggestions, and discussions. We focus on *user stories* that describe a specific feature request and/or issue with the application and/or platform. We select user stories that are marked completed. Story descriptions and related comments for 1,051 stories are extracted. Finally, our data analysis is supported with documents from proposals, board reports, and project documentation.

We analyze the data as follows. First, inspecting all stories in our database, we remove unclear or non-descriptive stories from the database. These include stories that do not discuss any specific issue in depth, provide solely a link or non-conclusive short description, and/or provide a blob of program code without accompanying discussion. For example, consider following three stories and their descriptions that were discarded from the database.

(a) Keep allow-navigation; Add doc for iOS
(b) Check to see if date gets set properly on writing exif information. Exif info for date is wrong
(c) Following steps at https://github.com/apache/cordova-coho/blob/master/docs/platforms-release-process.md; Cordova-Ubuntu Platform Release

Initial inspection of the database was necessary because we are analyzing secondary data that are extracted from a project management tool of an open-source application. In order for us to analyze the data, the user story needs to clearly present the issue at hand. Also, as the initial inspection retained clear and descriptive stories, they can be subjected to qualitative analyses. These analyses include coding the data and identification of relevant terms and definitions. Finally, inferences can be derived from selected stories and triangulated from multiple sources. The initial inspection process identified 42 user stories with sufficient detail for data analysis.

We use Atlas.ti qualitative data analysis software for our analysis. To aid our coding procedure, we develop a qualitative codebook that identifies subcodes and operational definitions (Table 1) for each construct in our model. The subcodes are identified from the research context, theoretical constructs, conceptual framework, and research question. Further, the coding scheme is flexible to add new subcodes as they

Table 1. Operational definitions

Construct	First cycle code	Operational definition
Means (existing resources at hand)	Technology	Existing technological capability within the team (in this case, the community) – programming languages, tools, configuration, testing, documentation, etc.
	Market knowledge	Existing knowledge about the platform market (alternatives, competitors)
	Platform knowledge	Existing knowledge about the technological state of the platform
	Social capital	Capital that the team can draw upon to append existing means
Platform (resources and constraints provided by the platform)	Technology (API)	Technological resources and constraints provided by the platform (APIs, programming language, setup, features)
	Market	Existing offerings on the platform market
	Value	Existing value offered by the platform to its customer (in terms of features that the users can use – tangible)
Aspirations	Product-market match	The features to be built in the product should match the requirement of the market
	Product-platform match	The product should be technologically compatible and functional on the platform
	Exceed platform value	The features being built in the application should help exceed the application the core set of value provided by the platform

(continued)

Table 1. (*continued*)

Construct	First cycle code	Operational definition
	Novelty	Technological or feature based novelty of the application that the existing applications and platform do not cover
Acceptable risk	Commit limited resource	Commit limited technological and people resources to any given feature
	Application recoverable after failure	If implementation of the given feature results in failure, it should not jeopardize entire application
	Risk analysis	Risk portfolio of an alternative are determined before decision-making
Logic of control	Logic of control	Decision making based on factors that the team can control as opposed to prediction of future events
Action	Fixed bugs	The issues that were identified based on means and fixed
	Completed tasks	Feature requests which were identified and completed using means and acceptable risk
Effects	NA	Collective documentation and understanding of which features and issues are to be addressed in the project
Expanding cycle of resources	New technological knowledge	Identify new API's, tools, and configurations that can be used by the application
	New market knowledge	Identify new requirements that the market needs
	New platform knowledge	Identify new API's, tools, and configurations that are provided by the platform
Converging cycle of constraints	Converging technological (means) constraints	Identify specific API, tool, or configuration for the application from competing alternatives
	Converging feature constraints	Identify specific feature for the application from competing alternatives
	Converging platform constraints	Identify specific API, tool, feature, or configurations competing alternatives provided by the platform

emerge from the data. The codebook guides our first-order coding. Using *descriptive* coding technique [18], subcodes from the codebook are applied to each story. Stories that demonstrate multiple subcodes are simultaneously coded by multiple subcodes. This coding strategy follows the rigorous coding strategy used for analyses of primary data. Finally, using all the data for each code, a matrix is developed to facilitate analyses [18].

To address construct validity, multiple sources of data—stories, documentation, contributor comments, board reports, and proposals—are tapped to ensure that the findings converge. Reliability of the study is addressed with (a) programmatically retrieving and storing analyzed stories locally from the project management tool, (b) maintaining the qualitative codebook of codes and operational definitions, and (c) matrices developed from the labeled data.

4   Results

Table 2 provides the first cycle codes (and related constructs identified in Fig. 3) and the frequency of the codes identified in the data. As the secondary data used for this analysis consists of contributors' descriptions of issues and feature requests for the Cordova application, the data are characteristically technical in nature. This readily translates into identification of technological means available to the application development team that is specific to the application and platform. We identified 40 stories that show technological means for the development team. Available means include knowledge about market needs (feature requests), value proposition provided

Table 2. Constructs and their frequency in the data

Construct	First cycle code	Frequency
Means	Technology	40
	Market knowledge	5
	Platform knowledge	20
	Social capital	2
Platform	Technology	23
	Market	7
	Value	8
Aspirations	Product-market match	8
	Product-platform match	24
	Exceed platform value	14
	Novelty	15
Acceptable risk	Commit limited resource	33
	Application recoverable after failure	5
	Risk analysis	21
Logic of control	Logic of control	32
Action	Fixed bugs	20
	Completed tasks	11
Expanding cycle of resources	New technological knowledge	37
	New market knowledge	5
	New platform knowledge	21
Converging cycle of constraints	Converging technological constraints	24
	Converging feature constraints	9
	Converging platform constraints	11

by the platforms, and new features that are introduced by platforms or competing applications (through developer conferences or official press releases). Similarly, the technological opportunities and limitations by platforms are discussed by contributors. Current working of API's and the value they provide to the user are discussed and coded in 23 stories. This leads to identification of limitations and opportunities that serve as value additions to the current value proposition of the platform and serve the market need.

The analysis also leads to identification of aspirations in the team's decision making and actions. Specifically, the application-platform match is one of the central driving forces across these stories since contributors focus on technical aspects that lead to seamless operation between the application and platform. 24 stories are coded to identify application-platform match. Further, the analysis finds support for the aspiration of introducing novelty to the application (15 stories) and ultimately adding value to the existing value proposition provided by the platforms (14 stories). The common theme in these aspirations is identification of opportunities (limitations and/or enhancements) for value addition through existing means and platform knowledge, and introducing novel features that take advantage of the platform's opportunities.

The heuristics of acceptable risk and logic of control also find strong support in our analysis. Each story is identified and addressed by (typically) one contributor. Thus, the team is devoting limited resources for each issue and feature, and 33 stories are coded for this sub code. Alternatives identified—do feature A or B or C—accompany risk analyses that discuss technological implications on the application and platform, novelty, and extending the platform's value proposition. 21 stories are coded to show risk analysis and identify alternatives that have acceptable risk associated with them. Further, actions identified by the team embody the logic of control and are coded in 32 stories. These include decisions based on the current means, platform knowledge, and the aspirations of the team, rather than predicting which actions would enhance the application. Finally, the application is already in use by an array of users which provide feedback to the development team. This represents a control driven approach rather than prediction based approach that would identify the goals of an application a priori.

Actions (32 stories coded) lead to intermediate effects, which are the operationalization of team aspirations. Each iteration of the Cordova application served as an intermediate effect that, in turn, expanded means and attenuated aspirations. Specifically, intermediate effects help identify technological avenues, tools, limitations, and features, that increase the fit and utility of the artifact. 37 stories are coded to identify expanding technological knowledge. In addition, intermediate effects improve the platform knowledge for the overall team, as new features are implemented that connect to the platform and add new value to its existing value proposition.

Overall, the frequency of subcodes identified in our analyses justifies the conjecture that software development teams developing novel applications on digital platforms use effectual thinking even when the terms used in the processes may not align with those used in effectuation context. In what follows, we look at several specific examples of user stories to show how we coded and interpreted them in our analyses.

5   Qualitative Evidence for the Effectual Model

In this section, we present and discuss specific instances of qualitative secondary data from the Cordova platform repository and the constructs identified in the effectual software development model.

5.1   Means

Means represent the overall existing knowledge about the current state of the application, platform, market, and social capital that the project team draws upon. Means for the development team consists of software development kits, documentations, discussion boards, mailing lists, and so on. These resources provide a set of means that are collectively identified and referred to by the team to generate alternatives for actions that develop intermediate effects. However, the qualitative data available in this analysis consists of story descriptions of issues and features identified by the contributors. This leads us to means that are not explicitly stated in the descriptions but implied in the discussions. For example, consider the following description of a story:

> Under Adobe AIR, you can open a connection to a SQLite db and point to an existing file. The benefit of this is that your application can ship a database seeded with data. Without this support, your application has to initialize the db via scripting. While not difficult, it does increase the application's first run time and also complicates the code unnecessarily. I understand that this isn't per the Web SQL spec, http://dev.w3.org/html5/webdatabase, but it could certainly be useful.

The contributor is discussing a feature that is introduced in the application. The technological and platform-specific means posed by the contributor identifies this enhancement and the team relies on its means (tools, programming language, design, architecture, platform interface, and market) to evaluate possible alternatives and introduce it in the application. Specifically, the contributor identifies a specific plugin that enhances value to the existing framework. The risks associated with standards (W3C) are also discussed. Consider another example of means-driven approach as illustrated in the following story description, where tools are identified to develop test cases.

> Most of automatic geolocation tests were pended on Android because we didn't have the tool to detect if the tests are running on a simulator or on a real device. Now we have device.isVirtual and can use it to pend the tests only on an emulator.

5.2   Platform

The Platform is the centerpiece around which decisions and choices are made for the application. Platforms provide and constrain the application development context. In the following story, the contributor identifies a specific framework in the iOS platform that is deprecated. Demonstrating reusability and modularity of the platform design, the framework is used across multiple plugins within the platform (as listed by the contributor). However, it constraints application developers because updates to platform components may often require significant change to the application.

> The ALAssetsLibrary framework has been deprecated in iOS 9, replaced by the Photos. framework. Once our minimum dependency is iOS 9, move to it. Usage: 1. iOS (CDVURLProtocol); 2. Camera plugin; 3. File plugin; 4. File Transfer plugin; 5. Local-Webserver plugin (cordova-plugins).

5.3 Aspirations

The aspirations of 'product-market match' and 'product-platform match' are implicit in team's actions. It follows that the application design and development should ultimately ensure that the application works with the platform. Also, feature requests are accompanied with the limitations of the platform's value proposition and the added value proposed by the contributor. As an illustration, consider the following story where the contributor identifies (a) the value provided by the platform (Android and iOS), (b) a platform-market need that is not satisfied and subsequently the value that is added through this feature, and (c) using technological and platform means, possible actions are suggested for both of these platforms.

> The use case is when an app/user needs to access geoposition while device's location services are disabled. Let's say for the first time/attempt. While I've been able to find a way to send the user directly to the system setting on Android (via cordova-diagnostic-plugin's switchToLocationSettings), it seems to be no obvious way to achieve the same on iOS with the plugin(s) at present. ... I thus suggest extending getCurrentPosition with an option for a better UX in case the device's location services are disabled. ... I would suggest covering the same for Android, even though this issue is concerned mainly with the UX on iOS.

5.4 Acceptable Risk

Feature requests and issues are accompanied with risk analysis. Typical areas of risk analysis include identification of alternatives—technological, platform, and/or market, risk associated with the alternatives, and the resources required to realize the alternatives that have been identified. Consider the following story description (listing added) where the contributor identifies an issue in dynamic programmatic calls for specific platform. The issue is identified, elaborated, and alternatives are discussed. Finally, the committer narrows to a specific plan of action.

> We have a logic in Windows/wp8 parsers that fires a hooks, specific for these particular platforms. There is some problems with this: (a) This doesn't fits well into the concept of PlatformApi (b) The original purpose of the hook is now lost. ... So the proposed plan is: (a) Do not touch 'pre_package' if 'old' platform is used (via PlatformApi polyfill); (b) If the 'new' platform is used, 'pre_package' doesn't emitted by platform, so we need to emit it manually (right before 'after_prepare' - to keep the order of hooks unchanged); (c) Move bomify from prepare to build in Windows PlatformApi, so www sources will be not-yet-bomified in 'pre_package'; (d) Add a notice about 'pre_package' deprecation and removal to HookRunner

5.5   Logic of Control

With logic of control, the project team is selecting actions that they have control over rather than predicting if and when the features and/or issues will be identified and resolved on the platform. Story descriptions do not speculate on the possible directions in which platforms will change. Rather, alternatives are identified based on the means and aspirations of the team. Consider, for example, the following story which discusses an issue with two platforms. Relying on the means (technological and platform) and the knowledge about platform leads to the identification of this issue. Instead of reporting the issue to platform and waiting for a fix in its next version, the contributor has provided a fix and tested it across multiple devices.

> MediaFile.getFormatData result data was empty (filled with default "0" values) for all types of capture: image, video audio. Problem encountered on Android iOS. I solved this by changing the url passed to native code from localURL to fullPath. Tested with two different Android phones (5.1 4.4) one iPhone 5 (iOS 9). The fix works!

5.6   Action, Expanding Cycle of Resources, and Converging Cycle of Constraints

All stories within our dataset are marked as complete because the issue/request has been resolved. These completed stories represent the actions of the project team to generate intermediate effects in the project. In the Cordova project, *effect*, which is the operationalization of team's aspirations, is the collective documentation of which features and issues are to be addressed in the Cordova project. Each intermediate release of the project represents an *effect* for the overall effectuation process in the Cordova project which converges constraints and expands means. Consider another story's description from our dataset. The story is discussing a flexible cropping feature unavailable on iOS platform (an *effect* that provides novelty, platform-market match, and value to that provided by the platform) for pictures.

> On iOS there's only that very insufficient inflexible cropping square compared to Android or WinMobile which moreover obviously doesn't work properly (see CB-9930, CB-2648). As we need a flexible, sizable rectangle, we implemented that in our fork of the camera plugin. ... To be downward compatible and to not urge others, for whom that square may be sufficient, it is made parameterizable via a new preference (as this is iOS specific and nothing that has to be changeable at runtime), defaulting to false. If the plugin is called with option allowEdit == true, then setting this new preference to true suppresses that standard (fairly useless) square for cropping the photo, even suppresses the (then also useless) view of the photo with the "Retake"- and "Use Photo"-buttons, but instead offers a resizable cropping rectangle (with "Redo" and "Save). ...

As the effect is identified, project teams converge constraints on application design, technology, and platform match. Similarly, these intermediate effects lead to identification of additional effects, and technological, platform-specific, and application-specific means to the team.

6 Discussion

Pervasive digital technology (digital platforms) has led to the development of challenging environments for the design, implementation, and deployment of innovative software applications. Our research proposes an effectual approach that support new ways of thinking about software development on digital platforms. Although the overall goal of developing software for a specific market on a platform may be identified a priori, the challenges offered by dynamic environments like platform ecosystems requires development teams to focus on their existing means, attenuate aspirations, and employ emergent controls that fit the platform context and provide the desired solution utilities.

It is important to note the coexistence of prediction and control based approaches that our study has presented. In our data analysis, the broader goal of Cordova application is known a priori—develop the Cordova environment that can be used by developers to build applications on multiple platforms. In addition, this goal is pursued through iterations and ultimately is embodied by the artifact. However, the dynamic nature of the platform environment promotes an effectual approach to develop an artifact that satisfies the goal, fits the platform context, and provides utility in a dynamic and challenging environment.

In our discussions so far, we have refrained from exploring specific software development methods (Scrum or XP) in use today because the focus of this research is the broader software development approaches and the underlying theoretical underpinning adopted by these approaches. While specific software development methods have been shown to provide innovation [19] in fast-paced environments, we contend that the unique challenges and dynamic environment provided by platform ecosystems exceed the fast-paced environments that were of interest in prior work.

Control-based effectual approaches have the potential to more clearly represent the software development thinking and methods that can be used to develop products that are relevant in changing platform environments. Initial means are iteratively expanded to identify new goals that encompass changing platform proposition. As intermediate effects (intermediate products) are trialed in the market, development teams attenuate their goals for developing the product.

The focus of the analysis in this paper is to identify evidence that supports the use of effectual thinking in current development projects in the Apache Cordova environment. Our qualitative data analyses provide prima facie evidence of the usefulness of an effectual approach to novel application development on software platforms. A limitation of this study is that our data analysis is limited to qualitative secondary data for an open source project. Specifically, the software development projects studied did not use effectual concepts and terms directly. Thus, the user stories required subjective coding and interpretation via an effectual lens. In order to address these limitations, we developed operational definitions for effectuation constructs in the software development context and updated them as the data were analyzed. Also, stories selected for analyses provided extended discussion on the issue at hand. Based on these analyses, however, we did find considerable evidence that demonstrates the wide-spread use of effectual thinking in the projects.

7 Conclusion

This research has identified unique application development challenges for producers on digital platforms. To address these challenges, an effectual approach to software development has been proposed which is grounded in the theory of effectuation. A conceptual model is developed and analyzed using qualitative secondary data from an open-source project.

This study has important contributions and implications for research and practice. Building on the challenges identified for the development of novel applications on software platforms, this paper advances a new vision of software development where the software development project is envisioned as an entrepreneurial endeavor with the project manager and development team as entrepreneurs. An effectual approach to development of novel applications on software platforms is proposed and described. Grounded in the theory of effectuation, the approach introduces context specific constructs (platform) and theorizes and adapts existing effectuation constructs to the software development context.

The effectual approach to software development introduces new constructs and feedback processes in software development research – aspirations, focus on existing resources, decision heuristics, and expanding and converging cycles. These effectual processes provide improved explanations for novel application development on software platforms where existing approaches have failed.

This research also contributes to practice. First, we draw attention to the development approach for novel applications on software platforms which has received limited attention in the information systems literature. Attention to development approaches on software platforms is particularly important and timely, given the proliferation of platforms [2]. Second, application producers have a direct interest in development approaches that specifically address the unique challenges offered by platform ecosystems. These interests extend beyond development of novel applications, and include development of novel new applications and maintenance of existing applications. Third, platform owners also benefit from the introduction of novel applications on software platforms. As the locus of innovation shifts from within the organization to a heterogeneous base of application producers, introduction of novel applications allows the platform to serve diverse consumer segments and introduces new demand within the user group.

Our future directions for this research will include in depth interviews as part of case study designs at two local organizations that are developing novel applications on digital platforms. Together, these research sites will allow us to evaluate the effectual approach to develop a critical mass of novel applications on software platforms. The identified case study design should provide additional insights to augment the research model developed in this paper. In addition, they offer different perspectives (producer and owner) on the appropriate development approach for novel applications on software platforms.

Further research directions include the development of application development processes and metrics that embody effectual thinking and support such processes. Future research initiatives that compare effectual approaches with existing approaches to software development can expand on the boundary conditions for these competing approaches. Finally, as our study shows the coexistence of prediction-based and control-based approaches for a project, future research endeavors can design processes that integrate the best features these differing approaches into hybrid development methods that incorporate both predictive and control-based development techniques.

References

1. Yoo, Y., Henfridsson, O., Lyytinen, K.: The new organizing logic of digital innovation: an agenda for information systems research. Inf. Syst. Res. **21**, 724–735 (2010)
2. Parker, G.G., Van Alstyne, M.W., Choudary, S.P.: Platform Revolution. W. W. Norton & Company, New York (2016)
3. Tiwana, A., Konsynski, B., Bush, A.A.: Platform evolution: coevolution of platform architecture, governance, and environmental dynamics. Inf. Syst. Res. **21**, 675–687 (2010)
4. Tiwana, A.: Platform Ecosystems. Morgan Kaufmann, Burlington (2013)
5. Boudreau, K.: Let a thousand flowers bloom? An early look at large numbers of software app developers and patterns of innovation. Organ. Sci. **23**, 1409–1427 (2012)
6. Hevner, A.R., March, S.T., Park, J., Ram, S.: Design science in information systems research. MIS Q. **28**, 75–105 (2004)
7. Malgonde, O., Hevner, A.: An effectual approach for the development of novel applications on digital platforms. In: Workshop on Information Technology and Systems (WITS), Dublin (2016)
8. Sarasvathy, S.: Causation and effectuation: toward a theoretical shift from economic inevitability to entrepreneurial contingency. Acad. Manag. Rev. **26**, 243–263 (2001)
9. Drechsler, A., Hevner, A.R.: Effectuation and its implications for socio-technical design science research in information systems. In: DESRIST, Dublin (2015)
10. Harris, M.L., Collins, R.W., Hevner, A.R.: Control of flexible software development under uncertainty. Inf. Syst. Res. **20**, 400–419 (2009)
11. Gill, T.G., Hevner, A.R.: A fitness-utility model for design science research. ACM Trans. Manag. Inf. Syst. **4**, 5 (2013)
12. March, J., Shapira, Z.: Managerial perspectives on risk and risk taking. Manag. Sci. **33**, 1404–1418 (1987)
13. MacCrimmon, K., Wehrung, D.: Taking Risks: The Management of Uncertainty. Free Press, New York (1986)
14. Benaroch, M., Lichtenstein, Y., Robinson, K.: Real options in information technology risk management: an empirical validation of risk-option relationships. MIS Q. **30**, 827–864 (2006)
15. Lyytinen, K., Mathiassen, L., Ropponen, J.: Attention shaping and software risk—a categorical analysis of four classical risk. Inf. Syst. Res. **9**, 233–255 (1998)
16. Flyvbjerg, B., Budzier, A.: Why your IT project may be riskier than you think. Harv. Bus. Rev. **89**, 23–25 (2011)
17. Kirsch, L.J.: Portfolios of control modes and IS project management. Inf. Syst. Res. **8**, 215–239 (1997)
18. Miles, M., Huberman, A.M., Saldana, J.: Qualitative Data Analysis: A Methods Sourcebook. SAGE Publications, Thousand Oaks (2013)
19. Highsmith, J., Cockburn, A.: Agile software development: the business of innovation. Computer **34**, 120–127 (2001)

GreenCrowd: An IoT-Based Smartphone App for Residential Electricity Conservation

Olayan Alharbi(✉) and Samir Chatterjee

Innovation Design and Empowerment Applications Lab (IDEA),
Center for Information Systems and Technology,
Claremont Graduate University, 130 E. 9th Street, Claremont, CA 91711, USA
{Olayan.alharbi,samir.chatterjee}@cgu.edu

Abstract. Energy is a scarce commodity. Diffusion of responsibility, forgetfulness, lack of knowledge and motivation are reasons for families' electricity waste. GreenCrowd is a smartphone application and IoT system to help families to decrease their electricity consumption. GreenCrowd incorporates educational, motivational and supportive features. The IoT device (smart LED lamp) reports previous consumption with a comparison to each family baseline. The smart LED lamp works as a notification tool that targets all house members. The current study presents preliminary results for electricity reduction during an intervention experiment. Also, it presents result about the effectiveness of the smart LED lamp as a notification tool.

Keywords: Design science · Energy informatics · Internet of Thing (IoT) · Persuasive technology

1 Introduction

Household energy consumption accounts for 22% of total energy consumption in the U.S. Almost half of that is electricity use, which accounts for approximately 4.39 Quadrillion Btu [1]. Producing one Quadrillion Btu requires 45 million tons of coal, 1 trillion cubic feet of natural gas, or 170 million barrels of crude oil. The household and/or residential sector includes multiple small energy consumers: houses, mobile homes, and apartments. In the U.S., these small consumers spent on average $1,419 annually for electricity in 2010. This amount is more than the average spent in 2006 by about $300 [1].

Regarding environmental concerns in the U.S., residential energy consumption is responsible for about 5.7 billion metric tons of CO2 annually [2]. From 1950 to 2009, the amount of residential carbon dioxide emissions tripled [3]. Electricity consumption in particular accounts for over 70% of household CO2 emissions. Thus, residential electricity consumption serves as a catalyst in increasing living costs and environmental threats. Electricity waste is not only affecting individual budgets but also simultaneously increasing CO_2 production rates globally.

Excessive electricity consumption at homes is a result of the usage by all members within the household. However, Utility provider portals and messages usually are solely accessed by homeowners only (e.g. parents). Therefore, other members

© Springer International Publishing AG 2017
A. Maedche et al. (Eds.): DESRIST 2017, LNCS 10243, pp. 348–363, 2017.
DOI: 10.1007/978-3-319-59144-5_21

(e.g. children) do not regularly track the recent electricity consumption of their homes. According to [4, 5], forgetfulness and diffusion of responsibility limit electricity saving actions although residents are aware of the risk of excessive electricity consumption. Thus, uniting all house members' electricity saving effort is essential to limit electricity waste.

Besides diffusion of responsibility as a barrier for people who live in groups, there are other reasons for electricity waste such as lack of knowledge, motivation and continuous support to maintain their conservative habits in consuming electricity [4]. This study presents an IoT system and a smartphone application to provide members of a household with an educational, motivational, and a family-wide notification tool for the purpose of reducing electricity waste.

Internet of Thing (IoT) is defined as objects with connectivity capability. IoT devices are capable of connecting to local devices and internet resources [6]. IoT devices are utilized to sense, collect and/or display information. The rapid growth of IoT presents standalone devices that have internet connectivity (e.g. Wi-Fi adaptor). These devices can be installed in homes to communicate directly with a cloud-based system. A standalone IoT device does not rely on Bluetooth or Infrared technology that requires a middle device (such as a smartphone) to be connected. Thus, it is suitable to be installed and communicate directly through any available Wi-Fi.

GreenCrowd presents a novel notification method that easily allows entire households to be informed about their previous day's consumption rather than notifying only those who have access to the utility provider portal. A smart LED lamp (standalone IoT device) was developed to illuminate certain colors based on electricity consumption. This comprehensive notification device is a support intervention to help participants to maintain their actions toward reducing electricity consumption. In addition, Green-Crowd includes a smartphone application that presents daily informative feedback, educational and motivational tips, peer comparison, and social facilitation services. Both interventions are developed with purpose of helping family reduce their electricity consumption. Since, the smart LED lamp is a standalone IoT device, the lamp does not need to be around the GreenCrowd app to be connected.

Following Gregor and Hevner 2 × 2 framework [7] and their classification for DSR knowledge contribution, this study has two level-1 instantiations (The Green-Crowd App, and the LED lamp as a novel notification technology). We next describe the design, build and evaluation phases. The evaluation phase measures the effectiveness and usability of the solution in reducing electricity consumption.

2   Research Method

Design Science Research (DSR) is an iterative research approach to design, develop and evaluate IT-based artifacts. DSR has two phases: design, build, and evaluate artifacts [8]. DSR has three iterative cycles: the rigor cycle, the design cycle, and the relevance cycle. The rigor cycle helps in accessing existing knowledge and the relevance cycle ensures the problem has societal relevance.

According to Gregor and Hevner [7], a DSR work should follow a specific DSR methodology. This study follows Peffers et al. [9] method. It is called a Design Science

Research Methodology (DSRM) for Information Systems Research. DSRM includes six activities: (1) identify problem and motivate; (2) define objectives of a solution; (3) design and development; (4) demonstration; (5) evaluation; and (6) communication. In this paper, the Introduction Section identifies the problem and motivation. It presents the study objectives (activity 1). In addition, Sect. 1 explains the objective of this research and the developed solutions (activity 2). Section 2.2 presents the Design and Build phase (Activity 3) of the research. Section 3 explains how the pilot study and field experiments are conducted to demonstrate the research solutions (Activity 4 & 5). Then, Sect. 4 is the evaluation of the research solutions. Finally, the entire paper carries out activity 6 which is publishing the results of the research in a scholarly or professional publication.

2.1 Theoretical Framework

The GreenCrowd system includes a smartphone application and an IoT device (Smart LED lamp). GreenCrowd has several persuasive techniques (e.g. peer comparison and self-tracking) that aim to form sustainable pro-environmental behavior.

Brynjarsdóttir et al. proposed three guidelines for designing an energy conservation solution [10]:

1. *Broaden our understanding of persuasion:* Brynjarsdóttir et al. [10] stated that most of the available studies are developing persuasion solutions just to provide monitor, feedback and control solutions. Most research focuses on showing users risky habits without enough information about the desired behavior (alternative behavior). Digital rhetorical solutions are suggested to present the consequences of excessive electricity consumption and alternative behaviors. An example for a digital rhetorical solution is using media to design an informative, inspirational, and persuasive solution.
2. *Include users in the design process*: Brynjarsdóttir et al. [10] assert the importance of including users in the design process. Including users is important for two reasons: solution acceptance and persuasive features. Meeting users requirements increases their acceptance chances. Likewise, personalizing and customizing persuasion solutions are recommended to increase solution effectiveness [11].
   According to Stokes et al. [4], there are several barriers that limit people from taking action when they are aware of the risk of electricity waste. The report includes barriers that can be handled by behavioral interventions such as lack of knowledge, diffusion of responsibility, futility, and laziness. Moreover, Barreto et al. [12] list six main motivations for the family to reduce their electricity consumption. Besides the two most common motivations (cost and environment concerns), Barreto et al.'s [12] study reveal four other motivations: self and family identity, parenting, routines, and sense of control.
3. *Move beyond the individual:* excessive electricity consumption is different from other behavioral issues. To gain results, group efforts are necessary. For example, within homes, if only one member is concerned about energy saving, usually very little changes. Energy sustainability needs to be an interaction between end users

(residents, employees), communities, organizations, energy providers, governments, etc. Most of the current sustainable persuasive solutions are targeted at individuals [10]. Brynjarsdóttir et al. [10] suggests including a community-oriented approach in providing sustainable persuasive solutions. For instance, motivating the entire community to unite their efforts in reducing electricity waste.

Based on Brynjarsdóttir et al.'s [10] suggestions, narrowing the persuasion intervention to only motivate individuals or educate them about some saving tips limits the effects of persuasion technology as a solution for sustainability. Sustainability requires more comprehensive interventions including two levels: individual and community. Individuals need customized solutions that address their own barriers and motivations. Moreover, individuals need to be involved in a social movement to sustain their new conservative and efficient behavior. Thus, this study is broadening its interventions to include individual- and community-based approaches. The individual-oriented approach is essential to educate people about how to reduce electricity waste. The community-oriented approach is applied to the motivational and supportive interventions.

2.2 GreenCrowd Design and Build Phase

The overall GreenCrowd architecture is shown below in Fig. 1. GreenCrowd includes a smartphone (Android) application, an IoT-enabled LED lamp, and the cloud. The smartphone application presents information about recent electricity consumption, peer comparison, motivational and educational features. The LED lamp works as a notification tool. Moreover, the lamp reports the result of the previous day's consumption in comparison with the family's baseline. The cloud serves as the backend for the data store and analysis.

Electricity consumption has several determinants (e.g. household size, income, weather etc.). Therefore, having the same baseline for all participants is not ideal. Similarly, setting the last month consumption is not a better option because of the weather changes. Therefore, for having a baseline that may have similar circumnutates, GreenCrowd is using the average consumption of the same month a year prior.

GreenCrowd Smartphone Application
The smartphone application educates and motivates households to start the new conservative behavior. Therefore, it provides three feedback and comparison services. These services work as educational and motivational interventions. Oinas-Kukkonen and Harjumaa [13] list self-tracking and social comparison as motivation techniques for designing persuasive technology. In addition, each of the services is combined with an educational or motivational feed. These feeds are written based on Stokes et al. [20], and Barreto et al. [12] findings of family barriers and motivation toward energy conservation.

Self-tracking: Provides households with their electricity consumption for last seven days. A self-tracking service presents the consumption for last seven days in a line

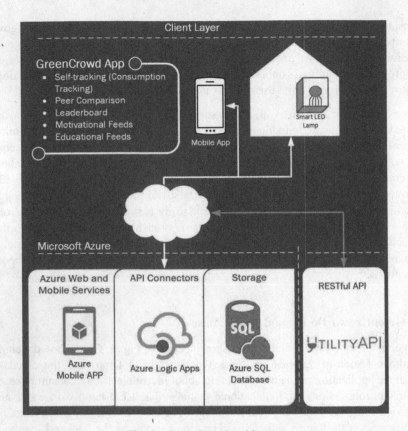

Fig. 1. GreenCrowd architecture

chart format. Self-tracking service is a self-comparison method that allows households to compare their own electricity consumption for the last seven days (see Fig. 2).

Peer Comparison Service: Is a visual method to compare electricity consumptions among participants. It presents a comparison for a participant's consumption the previous day with average consumption for the entire group on that day (see Fig. 3).

Leaderboard: Presents the five families who have the highest savings rate in the cohort since the beginning of the study. The savings rate is the ratio between the amount of saving and a calculated baseline. Hence, the baseline represents the average daily consumption during the same month a year prior. The calculated baseline equals the baseline multiplied by the number of days since the beginning of the experiment. Therefore, a calculated baseline is used to calculate the saving amount over the number of days since the beginning of the study. The saving amount is the difference between the calculated baseline of each family and their consumption since the beginning of the study (current consumption). Below is the saving rate pseudo code.

```
Set x = Today date - Experiment start date
Set i = current month
Set consumption(x) = Consumption since the beginning of
the experiment
Set baseline(i) = average consumption of month(i) a year
prior
Set baseline(x,i) = baseline(i)*x
Set amount of saving (x,i) = baseline(x,i) - consumption(x)
Set Saving Rate(x,i) = Saving amount(x,i) / baseline(x,i)
```

Leaderboard helps users compare their results with the top five participants. If a participant's result is not among the top five, their rank and their saving rate results are showed below the leaderboard table. As advised by Brynjarsdottir et al. [10], the community-oriented approach is needed to help households maintain their new behavior and create a social movement toward electricity saving.

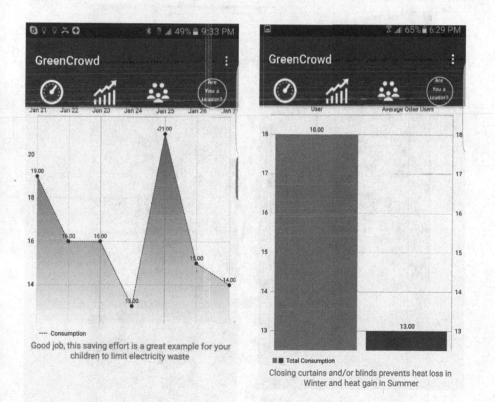

Fig. 2. GreenCrowd self-tracking and customized motivational feeds

Fig. 3. GreenCrowd peer comparison and customized educational feeds

Recognitions Feeds: The Leaderboard screen contains a recognitions feed. The feed presents the leading five families ranked by their savings rate. All users view the same leaderboard, thus, top five families are recognized among the cohort.

Educational and Motivational Feeds: The Self-tracking and Peer comparison screens include a feed area (see Figs. 2 and 3.). Based on the comparison service result, a participant receives a text or a visual feed. The feed can be a motivational or educational feed. The App presents an educational feed when a family consumption is increasing or more than the average of the other participants. Otherwise, the app shows a motivational message.

GreenCrowd Notification Device (Smart LED Lamp)
The smart LED lamp is equipped with wireless capability to exchange commands with the corresponding server. The smart LED lamp is an intervention for the entire household to notify member about their consumption the day prior. It is placed in a highly visible place for everyone to see (see Fig. 4).

Fig. 4. The smart LED lamp (best seen in color)

This novel LED notification targets everyone in the home rather than just the smartphone application users. Stokes et al. [4] find diffusion of responsibility as one of family barriers to reduce their electricity waste. Building a smart LED Lamp, that simply lights a certain color based on the family's previous day's consumption, is an innovative notification method that targets the entire family. Children, parents, and other house members do not need to download a smart application to view their consumption for yesterday. The smart LED lamp informs them all. The smart LED lamp uses three colors to notify families about their consumption compared to their baseline.

- Red color: if the previous day consumption is more than the baseline.
- Green color: if the previous day consumption is less than the baseline.
- White color: if the previous day consumption and the baseline are equal.

Daily Consumption Tracking

Most of GreenCrowd functions and services (self-tracking and peer comparison, and the smart LED Lamp) require access to participants' daily electricity consumption rate. In the early stage of designing GreenCrowd, there were two suggested methods to collect participants' daily electricity consumption: a collaborative partnership with a utility provider to evaluate GreenCrowd was considered or installing third party devices that are authorized to track daily electricity consumption (e.g. Radio Adaptor for Viewing Energy (RAVEn))

However, during the design process, the research team found a company named UtilityAPI. UtilityAPI collects historical and almost real time data (15 min' interval data) from utility providers and makes the data available to be retrieved through a RESTful API. Data retrievers should obtain home owner agreement to retrieve their family consumption rate. UtilityAPI provides a secured electronic document that can be sent by data retrievers to be signed by householders. UtilityAPI and the utility provider (e.g. Southern California Edison) then automatically receive the household agreement form. UtilityAPI has an agreement with the Utility provider at the study location. In addition, UtilityAPI agreed to grant this study with 40 accounts to be tracked.

UtilityAPI was chosen to be the provider of daily electricity consumption for the project. The process of obtaining the agreement required reasonable effort and did not require installing extra devices at participants' house.

GreenCrowd System Architecture

Infrastructure as Services (IaaS) is a cloud infrastructure to deliver computing services such as storage, network, and operating systems. Microsoft Azure is a trademark for Microsoft's cloud-computing services [14]. Microsoft Azure provides a wide-range of services that include data, application, integration, and client (on-premise) layers. GreenCrowd's entire system was developed and implemented using Microsoft Azure (see Fig. 1). Microsoft SQL Azure was utilized as the data center for GreenCrowd. Azure Web App and Mobile App were hosting backend services for the smartphone application and the required web services. Azure Logic Apps was used to create communication channels between GreenCrowd backend services, UtilityAPI, the Smart LED Lamp. Azure Logic App offers a method to simplify, schedule, and run a workflow. Azure Logic App provides a timing schedule or a schedule based on certain actions (e.g. HTTP PUT request).

3   Research Study

GreenCrowd aims to support families to obtain a sustainable energy behavior. The smartphone App and the LED provide educational, motivational interventions, and reminders. Hence, we paper focus on evaluating GreenCrowd usability, the effectiveness of the smart LED lamp as a notification method, and measuring the entire system effectiveness in reducing electricity consumption.

3.1   Pilot Study

The pilot study was conducted to test the GreenCrowd App and the Smart LED lamp. The aim of the pilot study was to run a functional testing. The functionality test was to ensure that GreenCrowd was working correctly. Three families were recruited for the pilot study and the pilot study lasted for two weeks. During the pilot study, two issues were identified and resolved.

First, the system was planned to be updated at 9 am (Pacific Standard Time) based on the utility provider schedule for releasing the last 24 hours' consumption. However, during the pilot study, the utility provider (Southern California Edison (SCE)) changed the schedule to 4:00 PM. The Azure Logic App schedule was updated accordingly.

Secondly, the smart LED lamp brightness was initially set at 30%. However, during the pilot, all families claimed that it was too bright. Therefore, the lamp brightness was lowered to 10%. This adjustment allowed the lamp to be a colored bulb without strong light.

Finally, during the pilot study, the smart led lamp was left on all the time. However, for meeting the study ultimate goal of using less electricity, in the actual study, the lamp was set to be on for five hours only (4:00 PM to 9:00 PM).

3.2   GreenCrowd Field Deployment

GreenCrowd implementation required three specifications: (1) household members' agreement to install the LED lamp within their homes, (2) Filling out the utility provider agreement form to share their consumption data with GreenCrowd, (3) access to an android device to install the smartphone application (GreenCrowd was built on an android environment). The experiment started by disseminating an electronic invitation form. 46 families filled out the invitation form. Then, these 46 families received the agreement document from UtilityAPI after submitting their information to UtilityAPI by the research team. UtilityAPI allows having a landing page for participants after completing the sharing form. Therefore, the landing page was the pre-survey page.

The invited participants were allowed three weeks to complete the agreement document and the pre-survey. 26 families filled out the agreement form and completed the pre-survey. Only 16 families have access to an android device. 10 families agreed to install the smart LED lamp. The remaining 6 families agreed to use the GreenCrowd App only.

Below is how the study groups are divided:

- (Group L): 10 households with the smartphone app and the LED lamp.
- (Group A): 6 households with the smartphone app only.
- (Group C): 10 in the control group that receives email only.

(Group C) receives an email every Thursday. The email contains information about their last consumption and a list of educational or motivational tips for electricity saving.

(Group A) does not have a notification that informs everyone at home. Therefore, a text messaging system was adopted (BulkSMS) to send a daily message for (Group A). The head of each family receives a text message daily. The text message includes information about the comparison result of yesterday's consumption with the baseline (e.g. Dear Bob, Your consumption for Jan 18th was more than your baseline).

The duration of the study was 14 days. Each day during the study, the smart LED lamp was turned on at 4:00 PM PST. Between 4:00–5:00 PM the LED lamp color remained as same the color of previous day. The LED lamp color was updated daily at 5:00 PM PST based on the result of a comparison between yesterday's consumption and the baseline. Daily at 9:00 PM PST the smart LED lamp was deactivated.

In addition, Three of the GreenCrowd App screens (Dashboard, Self-tracking, and Peer-Comparison) were updated daily at 5:00 PM PST. Whereas, the leaderboard was updated every Monday. GreenCrowd App information was updated daily at 5:00 PM PST. At the end of the study, participants were asked to fill out a post-study survey.

4   Evaluation

According to Hamilton and Chervany [15], system effectiveness can be evaluated with two approaches: summative and formative.

Summative evaluation determines whether the system has accomplished objectives. Formative evaluation assesses the quality of the system and related support. The distinction between summative and formative evaluation approaches is analogous to the evaluation of ends versus means, or outcomes versus process [15].

Therefore, evaluating GreenCrowd is divided into two phases. First, evaluating the entire system effectiveness in changing families' behavior to save electricity. Second, evaluating the GreenCrowd application and the smart LED Lamp usability. The following points summarize the evaluation phase objectives:

1. Evaluating GreenCrowd effectiveness in reducing electricity consumption.
2. Evaluating the smart LED Lamp effectiveness as a notification method for the entire house members.
3. Measuring the usability of the GreenCrowd system.

4.1   Measures

Electricity Consumption Reduction

The consent form allows GreenCrowd to collect historical data (for the past year) and daily real-time data. The historical data was collected to establish the baseline for each participant/household. The baseline is used to measure the difference in electricity consumption before and after the GreenCrowd intervention. Here, the amount of saving for (Group L & A) is compared to the amount of saving for (Group C).

System Usability Scale (SUS)

System usability scale is a well-known scale for measuring system usability. It is suitable for small size of participants [16]. SUS is adopted to measure the GreenCrowd app usability from the users perspective. It contains 10 items. Users rate their level of agreement on a five-point Likert scale.

Perceived Effectiveness of Smart LED Lamp as a Notification Tool

We adopted a perceived effectiveness scale from [17] with (Cronbach's alpha = 0.894). The measure includes four items: The items were edited to be suitable for the LED lamp. The items asked if the smart LED lamp was useful, informative, annoying, and confusing. In addition, an extra item was added to measure the LED effectiveness in reaching all the members of the household.

Comparative feedback

The GreenCrowd App provides comparative feedback (peer comparison, and leaderboard screens). The effectiveness of GreenCrowd App comparison features was measured by four questions (1 = strongly disagree, 7 = strongly agree): "I am curious to know about the saving results of other households [18] ", "I prefer not to receive a comparative feedback.", "The comparative feedback (your consumption relative to other people's average consumption) is motivating, and "The comparative feedback (your consumption relative to other people's average consumption) is useful". For comparison purposes between the GreenCrowd app and the LED lamp, participants were asked to report the usefulness of each one.

4.2   Results and Discussion

The sample was 23 men, 3 women. Household size was between two members to five members. Only two households with only 2 members. Nine of the families had five members. There were three family who did not report the number of households (See Table 1.)

Reducing residential electricity consumption is one of the intended outcomes of this study. Changing participants' behavior are the means to reduce electricity consumption. According to [19], interventions may succeed in changing behavior but it requires time to notice a sustainable reduction in energy consumption. However, the GreenCrowd interventions were able to help (Group A & L) to save an average of 7 kWh, while the average of electricity consumption for (Group C) increased by 19 kWh.

Table 1. How many people are living or staying at this address?

Household members		Frequency	Percent	Valid percent	Cumulative percent
Valid	2	2	8.3	8.7	8.7
	3	4	16.7	17.4	26.1
	4	8	33.3	34.8	60.9
	5	9	37.5	39.1	100.0
	Total	23	95.8	100.0	
Missing	System	1	4.2		
Total		24	100.0		

Electricity consumption is influenced by changes in seasons. The consumption is affected by the weather. Therefore, to limit the weather effects on the differences between the baseline and current consumption, the baseline for each family was chosen based on the same month consumption of the prior year. Although, Southern California (the study location), experienced the most raining and snowing season since 1995 [20]. Nevertheless, during the research experiment, (Group L & A) were able to reduce their consumption while (Group C) consumption increased.

(Group L & A) were able to save in average 7 kWh comparing to their baseline. If we consider the increasing consumption for (Group C) because of the weather changes, (Group L & A) approximately saved 26 kWh.

The System Usability Scale (SUS) [21] was adopted to measure the GreenCrowd smartphone App usability. The SUS is a 5-point Likert scale containing 10 questions. All even questions are negatively worded items. To calculate each response, five points are subtracted from the even number responses and one point is subtracted from odd responses. Then, the total is multiplied by 2.5. Thus, the SUS score for each response ranges between 0 and 100. According to [22] scores that above 68 is above the average. The GreenCrowd smartphone app SUS was 87.5. This suggests that users found the app is very useful. In addition, the total rate of GreenCrowd app's ease of use was 95 out of 100. These results are for all users' feedback (the app and LED lamp group the app only group)

A further step in investigating the GreenCrowd app usability was made to compare SUS results of participants, who has the app and the LED lamp, with SUS results of participants who use the app only. Interestingly, average of SUS responses that made by people with the app only is 93 out of 100 while the average responses of the LED lamp group was 83 out of 100. Although the GreenCrowd app provides extra information compare to the LED lamp, more people in the App only group would like to use this system frequently. This interesting point could be because the LED lamp was providing enough information for participants about their previous day's consumption. The smart LED lamp provides electricity consumption at glance. Users of the smart LED lamp need a minimum effort to be informed about the previous day's consumption. A participant is altered about the rate of the previous day's consumption with the comparison to their own baseline by just looking to the smart LED lamp once a day.

For measuring the effectiveness of the smart LED lamp as a notification tool, participants were asked to report their feedback in the form of a 7-point Likert scale. In general, all participants found the LED lamp to be effective in reporting the previous day's consumption. A one-sample t-test has been implanted to verify if the average of responses differs from the scale median of 4 (see Fig. 5) [23]. Participants' feedback about the smart LED lamp's effectiveness in reaching all members of the household is 2.6 points above the median (Q1 mean = 6.7, SD = .6, P < .001). This significant positive result indicates that participants believed the LED lamp was effective in informing all members of each household about their energy consumption. Similarly, participants found the smart LED lamp to be informative and useful as a tool that reports their pervious consumption in comparison to their baseline (Q2 mean = 6.5, SD = .8, P < .001) and baseline (Q3 mean = 6.7, SD = .4, P < .001).

On the other hand, no users found the lamp to be confusing (Q4; mean = 1.4, SD = .8, P < .001). These results can be linked to the fact that the colors were chosen based on the common utilization for red, green, and white (e.g. red is known for signaling caution or warning). Finally, no users found LED lamp to be annoying (Q5; mean = 2.4, SD = 2.2, P = .053).

Finally, all Participant (Group L & A) were asked to rate the comparative feedback (e.g. peer comparison). The comparative feedback is one of the GreenCrowd app features. Results agree with previous study that believes comparative feedback is a motivation technique for persuasive interventions [12, 13, 24].

Both the LED effectiveness scale and the comparative scale include a statement about the usefulness of each one of them ("The comparative feedback is useful" and "The LED as a notification tool is useful"). Participants believe the comparison to their baseline through the LED lamp is more useful than the comparison to their peers through the app (mean = 1.6, SD = .7, P = .05). The ease of observing the consumption information through the LED lamp and its ability to inform all house members can be a reason for the variation in rating.

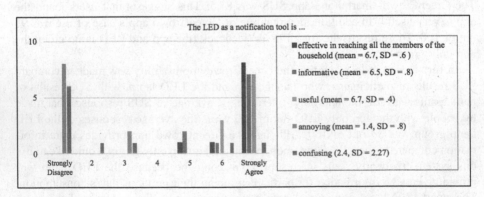

Fig. 5. Participants' feedback regarding the LED effectiveness as a notification tool (best seen in color)

On the other hand, it is noticed that the number of recruited families dropped by 50% before starting the project. During the early stage of the project, the utility provider updated the sharing form. Therefore, the families were instructed to fill out the updated form. Only 26 families filled out the new form. GreenCrowd is allowed to retrieve the daily consumptions for only those families who filled out the updated form. Therefore, only 26 families were eligible to be part of this study.

5 Conclusion and Limitations

Previous studies [4, 10, 12] provide three important findings to help families adopt sustainable energy conservation behavior. These findings include family barriers, motivations and design principles toward sustainability. GreenCrowd provides interventions to overcome family barriers and emphasize family motivations. Also, the interventions are designed by following three important design principles: broaden our understanding of persuasion, include users in the design process, and Move beyond the individual.

Therefore, from a technology perspective, this study contributes to the field by providing two level-1 instantiations [7] (the GreenCrowd App and LED lamp). Both instantiations use customized content and community-approach simultaneously. A GreenCrowd app user is receiving an educational feed when his/her consumption is increasing whereas a motivational feed is displayed when there is a reduction in consuming electricity. These feeds were written specifically based on the family barriers and motivations that were found in the previous study [4, 12].

On the other hand, the peer comparison and leaderboard services provide community-approach for reducing electricity consumption. Social comparison and comparison feedback are well-established persuasion techniques that involve social facilitation for changing an existing behavior or adopting a new behavior. Thus, the GreenCrowd App compares a household consumption with the average of other participants. In addition, every Monday the GreenCrowd App presents the best five families in saving electricity for a previous week. It is a public recognition that viewed by all participants.

Our research provides a novel feedback method that informs the entire house members regarding their consumption status. The contribution here is divided into two parts: (1) the actual artifact development and (2) the artifacts effectiveness evaluation. The GreenCrowd system was designed and built to retrieve electricity consumption on a daily basis. Then, the color of the smart LED lamp is updated base on the consumption level. Three colors are used to indicate the result of a comparison between the previous day's consumption and each family's baseline.

However, increasing the number of participants could improve the evaluation of this study. Considering the pre-requirements for participating in the GreenCrowd project, such as filling out the agreement form, 26 participants is acceptable number to evaluate the GreenCrowd project. Nielsen and Lauder [25] states that the system can be tested by three to five users as a minimum number for the experiment size.

Furthermore, the full duration of the study is limited to one month. UtilityAPI, as the third party that provides the GreenCrowd system with daily electricity consumption, granted us a 60 day subscription only. The first month was utilized for the pilot study and internal testing; the second month was the actual experiment. However, the results of the current report are based on a midway survey that measures the GreenCrowd usability, effectiveness and report any change in electricity consumption.

Creating a significant behavioral change can be achieved through short or long-term intervention. However, the measurement of sustainability requires a thorough follow-up evaluation. This study reported results collected from the experiment evaluation. After the conclusion of this evaluation, a thorough examination and more extensive evaluation are planned for the future.

Acknowledgment. The research team would like to acknowledge with thanks the financial and technical support granted to this research project by UtilityAPI.

References

1. Cauchon, D.: Household electricity bills skyrocket. http://www.usatoday.com/money/industries/energy/story/2011-12-13/electric-bills/51840042/1
2. Weber, C.L., Matthews, H.S.: Quantifying the global and distributional aspects of American household carbon footprint. Ecol. Econ. **66**, 379–391 (2008)
3. Energy Information Administration: International Energy Outlook (2014). http://www.eia.gov/forecasts/ieo/index.cfm
4. Stokes, L.C., Mildenberger, M., Savan, B., Kolenda, B.: Analyzing barriers to energy conservation in residences and offices: the rewire program at the University of Toronto. Appl. Environ. Educ. Commun. **11**, 88–98 (2012)
5. Frantz, C.M., Mayer, F.S.: The emergency of climate change: why are we failing to take action? Anal. Soc. Issues Publ. Policy **9**, 205–222 (2009)
6. Mattern, F., Floerkemeier, C.: From the internet of computers to the internet of things. In: Sachs, K., Petrov, I., Guerrero, P. (eds.) From Active Data Management to Event-Based Systems and More. LNCS, vol. 6462, pp. 242–259. Springer, Heidelberg (2010). doi:10.1007/978-3-642-17226-7_15
7. Gregor, S., Hevner, A.R.: Positioning and presenting design science research for maximum impact. MIS Q. **37**, 337–356 (2013)
8. Hevner, A., Chatterjee, S.: Design Science Research in Information Systems. Springer, New York (2010)
9. Peffers, K., Tuunanen, T., Rothenberger, M.A., Chatterjee, S.: A design science research methodology for information systems research. J. Manag. Inf. Syst. **24**, 45–77 (2007)
10. Brynjarsdottir, H., Håkansson, M., Pierce, J., Baumer, E., DiSalvo, C., Sengers, P.: Sustainably unpersuaded: how persuasion narrows our vision of sustainability. In: Proceedings of the SIGCHI Conference on Human Factors in Computing Systems, pp. 947–956. ACM (2012)
11. Oinas-Kukkonen, H., Harjumaa, M.: A systematic framework for designing and evaluating persuasive systems. In: Oinas-Kukkonen, H., Hasle, P., Harjumaa, M., Segerståhl, K., Øhrstrøm, P. (eds.) PERSUASIVE 2008. LNCS, vol. 5033, pp. 164–176. Springer, Heidelberg (2008). doi:10.1007/978-3-540-68504-3_15

12. Barreto, M.L., Szóstek, A., Karapanos, E., Nunes, N.J., Pereira, L., Quintal, F.: Understanding families' motivations for sustainable behaviors. Comput. Hum. Behav. **40**, 6–15 (2014)
13. Oinas-Kukkonen, H., Harjumaa, M.: Persuasive systems design: key issues, process model, and system features. Commun. Assoc. Inf. Syst. **24**, 28 (2009)
14. Copeland, M., Soh, J., Puca, A., Manning, M., Gollob, D.: Microsoft azure and cloud computing. In: Microsoft Azure, pp. 3–26. Apress (2015)
15. Hamilton, S., Chervany, N.L.: Evaluating information system effectiveness-Part I: Comparing evaluation approaches. MIS Q. 55–69 (1981)
16. Bangor, A., Kortum, P.T., Miller, J.T.: An empirical evaluation of the system usability scale. Int. J. Hum. Comput. Interact. **24**, 574–594 (2008)
17. Cho, V., Hung, H.: The effectiveness of short message service for communication with concerns of privacy protection and conflict avoidance. J. Comput. Mediat. Commun. **16**, 250–270 (2011)
18. Siero, F.W., Bakker, A.B., Dekker, G.B., Van Den Burg, M.T.: Changing organizational energy consumption behaviour through comparative feedback. J. Environ. Psychol. **16**, 235–246 (1996)
19. Kurisu, K.: Pro-environmental Behaviors. Springer Japan, Tokyo (2015)
20. Daniel, S.: Remarkably wet winter so far in California...and more storms to come. http://weatherwest.com/
21. Brooke, J., et al.: SUS-a quick and dirty usability scale. Usability Eval. Ind. **189**, 4–7 (1996)
22. Sauro, J.: A practical guide to the system usability scale: background, benchmarks & best practices. Measuring Usability LLC (2011)
23. Noyen, K., Wortmann, F.: Travel safety: a social media enabled mobile travel risk application. In: Tremblay, M.C., VanderMeer, D., Rothenberger, M., Gupta, A., Yoon, V. (eds.) DESRIST 2014. LNCS, vol. 8463, pp. 373–377. Springer, Cham (2014). doi:10.1007/978-3-319-06701-8_28
24. Geller, E.S.: The challenge of increasing proenvironment behavior. Handb. Environ. Psychol. 525–540 (2002)
25. Nielsen, J., Landauer, T.K.: A mathematical model of the finding of usability problems. In: Proceedings of the INTERACT 1993 and CHI 1993 Conference on Human Factors in Computing Systems, pp. 206–213. ACM (1993)

On the Design of Digitized Industrial Products as Key Resources of Service Platforms for Industrial Service Innovation

Matthias M. Herterich[1,2(✉)]

[1] Institute for Information Management (IWI-HSG), St. Gallen, Switzerland
matthias.herterich@unisg.ch
[2] Center for Design Research (CDR), Stanford University, Stanford, USA
matthias.herterich@stanford.edu

Abstract. The pervasive infiltration of digital technology into physical products fundamentally changes the requirements regarding the design of physical products and their potential for service innovation. To effectively leverage the generative capacity of digitized industrial products in future smart service offerings, proper design decisions must be made when designing today's products. The purpose of this paper is to report on a 2.5-year action design research project with an industrial forklift manufacturer, a software company, and an IoT consultancy. I elicit meta-requirements of digitized products arising from the industrial service business and derive design principles for digitized industrial products. This work empowers researchers to better understand the importance of generative product design to enable opportunities to innovative services. For managers, this work provides a blueprint for the design of digitized industrial products and raises awareness for generative product design in the digital age.

Keywords: Digital product innovation · Service innovation · Generativity · Manufacturing industry · Servitization in manufacturing · Design principles · Action design research

1 Introduction

The pervasive infiltration of digital technology into products that so far have been solely physical, fundamentally changes the way how product-centric organizations co-create value [1–4]. Innovation is no longer bound to physical product design and no longer follows the traditional goods-dominant logic [5]. Instead, tangible products are increasingly understood as distribution mechanisms [6] and endpoints for service to co-create value with customers as actors in service ecosystems [3]. As a result, original equipment manufacturers (OEMs) increasingly shift from selling products to selling integrated product-service offerings [7–9]. Specifically, industrial OEMs have recognized the importance of the service business among the long lifecycles of their products [10]. High requirements in terms of product reliability and uptime make product operators pay for services offered by OEMs to ensure stress-free and failure-free operations. The term servitization in manufacturing was coined to describe this trend

A. Maedche et al. (Eds.): DESRIST 2017, LNCS 10243, pp. 364–380, 2017.
DOI: 10.1007/978-3-319-59144-5_22

[7, 9]. Thus, product design and digital technology incorporated in today's industrial products is one of the key competitive advantages to offer differentiating smart services tomorrow [11–13]. The structure and architecture of digitized products affect how they behave, function, and evolve over time [14]. Because of the added digital materiality of products, product design goes beyond the pure physical representation [4, 15]. Traditionally rooted in mechanical engineering, OEMs face the challenge to build up adequate expertise as well as digitized products and digital infrastructure as platforms for service innovation. They therefore struggle in designing digitized industrial products that are characterized by a high generative capacity, which means that they offer the potential to be leveraged in a multitude of unanticipated and innovative industrial services [16].

The IS community picks up this trend and calls for design-oriented research on the generative design of digitized products [17–20] and their innovative uses in smart service systems [1, 3, 13, 21, 22]. So far, no research on the actual design and implementation of digitized products that are used as resources for service innovation exist. Therefore, the objective of this paper is to close this gap by (1) identifying meta-requirements of digitized products that arise in the context of the industrial service business and (2) formulating design principles for digitized products as resources in digitized service systems. Accordingly, the following two research questions are formulated:

(1) *What are meta-requirements of digitized industrial products in the industrial service business?*
(2) *How should digitized industrial products be designed to address these requirements?*

The remainder of this paper is structured as follows. In Sect. 2, I provide the relevant theoretical foundation and introduce relevant terms and concepts for this work. Section 3 outlines the research approach. In Sect. 4, the identified meta-requirements and the design are presented. Section 5 reports on the generalizable design principles. The paper closes with discussing and summarizing the results and a conclusion.

2 Theoretical Foundation and Related Work

Existing research on digitized products is highly interdisciplinary and scattered across various disciplines. Among scholars, different conceptualizations of the emerging digital and physical materiality [23] of digitized products exist. As research on this topic is still at its infancy, Herterich and Mikusz [17] identify two dominant research streams with major scientific impact, namely (1) 'digital product innovation and digitized products' [4, 20, 24] and (2) 'digitized service innovation' [1, 3, 25, 26].

First, focusing on digital product innovation and digitized products, the concept of 'digital product innovation' can be considered as the most comprehensive and scholarly recognized vocabulary for describing the phenomenon [20, 24]. Yoo et al. [4] define digital product innovation as 'the carrying out of new combinations of digital and physical components to produce novel products' [4]. The layered modular architecture is considered as a framework for describing the design of digitized products [4]. The paper at hand draws on this conceptualization and understands digitized products consisting of four layers. The *device layer* deals with physical machinery properties and logical issues at operating system level. The *network layer* focuses on the physical aspects of data transmission. The *service layer* addresses application functionality enabling actions such as create, manipulate, store, and consume contents. The *contents layer* finally addresses the digital content related to the digitized product. Unlike traditional physical products, digitized products that follow the principles of the modular layered architecture hold a high generative capacity as potential foundation for innovative services [16, 27, 28]. The term generativity refers to "a system's overall capacity to produce unprompted change driven by large, varied, and uncoordinated audiences" [28]. The concept recently got attention in the context of digital innovation research [29]. Eck and Uebernickel [30] identify two perspectives on generativity: (1) generativity as consequence of system design and (2) generativity as consequence of system evolution. Existing work on product innovation largely omits this generative capacity although acknowledging the related explorative and iterative innovation processes [31, 32] and recognizing the importance of generative for innovation [33, 34]. For this paper, I draw on the first perspective and focus on investigating the generative design of digitized industrial products and the consequent capacity of generating a multitude of surprising uses of within the given context of the industrial service business.

Second, research on service systems and service innovation goes beyond the digital and physical materiality and focuses on leveraging the generative capacity of digitized products in smart service systems [1, 3, 21]. Service innovation literature understands digitized products as service platforms consisting of tangible and intangible components (resources) [3]. Barrett et al. [1] recognize the increasing focus on service in different industries and argue that pervasive digitization and the generative capacity of digital technology afford dramatic new opportunities for service innovation. Particularly the manufacturing industry is dominantly focused on physical products and the traditional principle of value in exchange [6, 9]. Thus, the generative capacity of digitized artifacts allows unanticipated potential for service innovation [27]. As an example, imagine a manufacturer of forklifts. Instead of selling forklift trucks as one-time transactions and additionally offering traditional ad hoc maintenance and repair services, digitized industrial products afford the OEM to implement service-oriented pay-per-use business models and draw on the concept of value-in-use [6] to eventually outpace traditional goods-dominant competitors.

In between these two fields of research, the need for design knowledge on digitized products [35], the necessary information architecture [36], and digital service platforms [37] arises. The generative nature of digitized products, however, makes it challenging to design these products, because requirements originate from unanticipated smart industrial services and cannot be defined yet. So far to the best of my knowledge, no research exists that focuses on the design of digitized products considering their generative nature. Therefore, the aim of this paper is to elicit design principles as guidelines for generative digitized industrial products that form platforms for industrial service innovation in the digital age.

3   Research Approach

Within this article, I report on the elicitation of meta-requirements (MRs) and elaboration of design principles (DPs) of digitized industrial products as service platforms for industrial service innovation. The interdisciplinary nature of this research between digitized products [38] and service innovation [1] demands for authentic and concurrent evaluation activities [20, 39]. Action design research (ADR) is identified as an adequate emerging methodology with the goal to obtain relevant results by means of a rigorous yet pragmatic approach [40]. I chose ADR over other design-oriented research approaches since they relegate evaluation to a subsequent project phase exclusively [40]. By drawing on the existing body of knowledge, ADR aims to develop prescriptive design knowledge by building and evaluating innovative IT artifacts. It furthermore aims to develop innovative and useful solutions for classes of problems that are relevant for practice solve an identified class of problems [40–42]. Therefore, a 2.5-year lasting ADR project was set up following the guidelines of Sein et al. [40].

Following the ADR methodology, initially the problem is formulated by eliciting MRs. MRs are addressed by solving one specific problem instance and come up with a concrete solution design. This approach is in line with Böhmann et al. [21], who propose that research related with interdisciplinary service systems engineering should draw on a real-world problem instance. The built solution is refined in an authentic and concurrent manner within a reflection and learning stage. Finally, learnings are formalized as generic DPs. DPs are the most common form of prescriptive design knowledge and describe how a system or product should be built in order to fulfill MRs as identified and theorized attributes of an aspired system or product [41, 43]. Figure 1 provides an illustrative overview of the ADR project.

Three interdisciplinary industrial partners were selected for the ADR project based on their willingness to gain practical experiences on the augmentation of industrial products with digital technology with the goal to offer innovative services. Considering

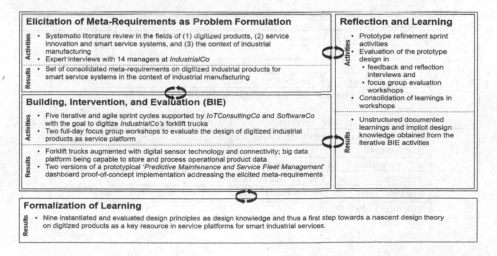

Fig. 1. Overview of ADR stages with key activities and results adapted from Sein et al. [40]

the interdisciplinary nature of this project, *IndustrialCo* is a leading multinational intra-logistics and materials handling OEM organization mainly focusing on industrial trucks and warehouse equipment. *IoTConsultingCo* is a €-700-million-revenue technology consultancy involved in this study focusing topics like 'Internet of Things (IoT)', 'Big Data Analytics', and 'Machine Learning'. *SoftwareCo* is a €20-billion-revenue software company with around 75000 employees worldwide. A strategic goal of the organization is to develop a software platform for the context of the 'Industrial Internet of Things and Services'.

The ADR method initially focuses on problem formulation with the goal to elicit MRs. Addressing not only the problem instance but a class of problems, ADR focuses on generating generalized knowledge [40]. To define the problem space, I elicit MRs that apply for the class of problems that the ADR project aims to address. MRs reflect generic requirements that should be followed when implementing a specific kind of information system [44]. I use triangulation and rely on rich data from both (1) a systematic literature review (SLR) and (2) data obtained from expert interviews with managers from *IndustrialCo* to gather MRs. Obtained MRs were discussed and refined in a focus group workshop with participants from all three organizations.

First, a SLR is conducted to identify existing knowledge on the problem. For conducting the review, I follow the well-established principles of Webster and Watson [45] and vom Brocke [46]. I perform keyword searches as depicted in Table 1. Due to the interdisciplinary nature of the work, I draw on (A) literature on 'digitized products' to consider existing work in the field of digital product innovation and engineering design technology, (B) 'service innovation, smart service systems, and servitization' to focus on the business process implications, and (C) literature that focuses on 'industrial manufacturing and the industrial service business' to consider the requirements arising from the industrial manufacturing context and industry characteristics. I limit the results

Table 1. Search terms among the three relevant fields of research

Stream	Search term	Hits	Net hits
A	digit* OR Smart OR Platform	1189	Elimination of duplicates and application of exclusion criteria 36
	pervasive* OR ubiqu*	177	
	generativ*	245	
	"internet of things" OR "internet of services"	51	
	(platform* OR product* OR service* OR software* OR technolog*) AND convergen*	88	
	"Product Service" OR "Product/Service" OR PPS	120	
B	("SD" OR "Service Dominant") And "Logic	8	
	"Service Innovation*"	60	
	"service system*" OR ecosystem*	188	
C	"Industrial Service*" OR "Industrial Internet"	25	
	"Installed Base" OR "Heavy Equipment"	17	
	"Machine Data"	21	

to contributions published in the journals of the IS basket of 8 and in the top 10 journals on innovation as defined by Linton and Thongpapanl [47]. Additionally, proceedings of the *International Conference on Information Systems (ICIS)* were included. The search is restricted to articles published within the last 10 years. Out of the total of 2189 hits, 36 were considered after reading the abstract and applying firm inclusion (i.e., focus on physical goods getting augmented with digital technology, focus on digitization in industrial context, focus on innovative services based on digitized industrial products) and exclusion criteria (i.e., focus on product with solely physical or digital materiality, no link or transferability to industrial context, interview or editorial, no link to product- and service innovation).

Second, interviews with industrial manufacturing experts were the main source of data collection to obtain deeper insights at one instance of the problem at *IndustrialCo*.

Within the scope of the servitization trend [7, 8], the overall goal of *IndustrialCo* is to pivot the existing, product-focused business models towards outcome-based service offerings and overcome the traditional goods-dominant logic [13]. Due to the long lifecycles of industrial products, however, *IndustrialCo* must set up the service platform as foundation for service innovation within the course of designing the next forklift truck generation today. Interview partners were selected by snowball sampling in the context of the case organizations [48]. Specifically, 14 digitization and service innovation managers of *IndustrialCo* were interviewed that aim at leveraging digitized industrial products in innovative service offerings. This ensured a high level of diversity for work context regarding the interview participants. NVivo 11 was used for analyzing and coding interview transcripts as well as secondary sources that were provided by the interviewees. MRs obtained from (1) the SLR and (2) expert interviews were consolidated and generalized resulting in generic MRs that abstract from the dedicated case context.

In the 'Building, Intervention, and Evaluation (BIE)' stage, MRs were addressed by means of a prototypical implementation in the context of *IndustrialCo's* service business. Expert interviews and a full-day ideation workshop with innovation mangers, service staff, digitization and product experts allowed the ADR team to identify (1) predictive maintenance and (2) fleet management as two innovative service offerings that instantiate the identified design principles. These two use cases were chosen to demonstrate the generative capacity of the digitized forklift trucks and the big data architecture. The implementation of the prototypes was highly iterative and organized in five agile sprints cycles supported by *IoTConsultingCo* and *SoftwareCo*.

4   Elicitation of Meta-Requirements and Solution Design

4.1   Elicitation of Meta-Requirements

According to a seminal paper on service innovation, Lusch and Nambisan [3], service platforms conceptualize the venue for value co-creation within service ecosystems and thus lead to service innovation. Specifically, resource liquefaction, resource density, and resource integration represent foundational elements of a service platform.

Existing literature considers resource liquefaction as a key concept for service innovation [3]. It is suggested that operational data arising from digitized products should be detached from the physical product representation [3, 49]. Operational data of digitized industrial products need to be integrated in existing information systems and made available to various organizational actors of the service ecosystem in a timely manner [1, 3]. Besides operational data originating from the product itself, context information is equally important to understand how the product is used. Resource liquefaction unleashes generativity and thus enables opportunities for service innovation [3, 15]. Terms like 'digital twin' or 'thing shadow' emerge to describe the duality of the physical and material representation of digitized industrial products [18]. Insights obtained from case study research specify this even more precisely. *"Right now, we collect [operational product] data only in a limited manner. We seek to add telematics parameters to our web and e-business platform and collect these operational truck data."* Head of IoT Development and Integration, IndustrialCo. Thus, based on insights from literature and case study research, the first MR is theorized. *MR01: The design of digitized industrial products should provide open accessibility to exchange operational product data among actors in the service ecosystem.*

Second, *resource density* addresses the need to gain access to a sustainable combination of resources. Because of (1) the generative capacity of digital technology [16, 24, 27] and (2) the long lifecycles of industrial products [10], potential future affordances of digitized industrial products cannot be anticipated today [13]. Hence, the material properties of digitized industrial products need to be flexible to be prepared to support potential changes in requirements. To effectively integrate new resources, literature suggests that layered modular product structures enhance the level of resource density and generativity compared to integrated structures or simple modular structures [3, 4]. Thus, these aspects can be aggregated as a second MR. *MR02: The design of digitized industrial products should harness the generative capacity of digital technology to foster resource density.*

Third, *resource integration* addresses the rebundling and recombining of existing resources with new resources [1, 3]. Especially in interdisciplinary contexts such as industrial manufacturing or smart cities, integration with existing systems is key as data from various actors has to be taken into account to realize innovative service offerings [18, 36, 50]. Consequently, digitized industrial products must be built in a way that allows for structural flexibility to interact with existing information systems, actors and changing product configurations. *"We must expect that what we are developing right now must be understood as a platform although it will be outdated very quickly - but we also need to think about the next steps."* Global Director Sales and Service and Head of IoT Development and Integration, IndustrialCo.

Industrial products are characterized by long lifecycles [10]. This results in a heterogeneous installed base in the field with disparate material properties. A key challenge is to collect operational data in a consistent way and derive steady and reliable insights [51]. Standardized interfaces are needed to make the different systems work together [52]. Based on insights obtained from existing work and interviews, the following MR emerges. *MR03: The design of digitized industrial products should allow for integration and recombination of data from different actors and information systems to support resource integration.*

Besides just monitoring the products, dedicated use cases require remote control functionalities to detect and resolve defects. Some smart services require switching industrial products into analysis or debugging mode or send other commands to the products to alter its mode of operation. Thus, requirement that digitized industrial products must offer the possibility to connect to the product remotely and control dedicated product functionality was identified when talking to interviewees. *"In some way, we not only have communication from the sensor to us. We also need to be able to log in on these trucks and run diagnostic software on it [...] If we had such a debug-mode, I could just log in on this truck and debug it no matter where the truck is."* *Director Connectivity and Digital Product Platform, IndustrialCo.* Consequently, the need for remote accessibility and bidirectional communication is formalized as follows. *MR04: The design of digitized industrial products should consider remote access functionalities to control, configure and debug digitized industrial products.*

Apart from shop floors and production facilities, industrial products are situated in remote locations and often connected via limited connectivity. Imagine off-shore wind turbines, forklift trucks, or elevators or within massive buildings that are characterized by bad reception of mobile internet. *"Because these trucks are sometimes not within the range of our local connections but the customer needs this data, we have to evaluate alternative connection possibilities."* *Head of IoT Development and Integration, IndustrialCo.* In such a setting, it is even more challenging to work with real-time data when required by the smart service. *"It's always difficult to work with real-time data because you need to send this data to the platform and the connection is not always reliable and able to transmit data in real-time"* *Head of IoT Development and Integration, IndustrialCo.* In terms of connectivity, the fifth MR is theorized as follows. *MR05: The design of digitized industrial products should consider limited connectivity and data transmission bandwidth.*

To obtain relevant insights and derive decisions based on operational product data, data analytics technology needs to be in place that can cope the enormous amounts of data. Literature distinguishes between two modes of data analytics that is also reflected in empirical data form the context of [53, 54]. First, incoming data must be analyzed in a timely manner to react to unforeseen events. *"When I get an error, I can immediately tell the customer to stop the operations to prevent any damages."* *Head of Field Service, IndustrialCo.* Second, pattern detection and advanced statistical analysis can be applied to substantial amounts of historic data. *"We need an exact analysis of historic operational data to understand how a truck is used and then define measures to make the next generation more cost efficient."* *Head of Product Marketing, IndustrialCo.* To support both modes of data analysis, the sixth MR is theorized as follows: *MR06: The design of digitized industrial products should allow for mechanisms to analyze (1) timely incoming operational data to immediately react to unforeseen events and (2) massive quantities of historic operational product data to generate insights from patterns in this data.*

In total, six MRs were elicited based on existing literature and insights from the problem formulation stage of the ADR project with *IndustrialCo.* Furthermore, meta-requirements were evaluated and refined in focus group workshops. Table 2 presents an overview of theorized MRs.

Table 2. Overview of identified meta-requirements with frequencies

ID	Meta-requirement	Absolute and (relative) frequency	
		SLR	Interviews
01	The design of digitized industrial products should provide open accessibility to exchange operational product data among actors in the service ecosystem	21 (0.583)	14 (1.000)
02	The design of digitized industrial products should harness the generative capacity of digital technology to foster resource density	11 (0.306)	4 (0.333)
03	The design of digitized industrial products should allow for integration and recombination of data from different actors and information systems to support resource integration	12 (0.333)	14 (1.000)
04	The design of digitized industrial products should consider remote access functionalities to control, configure and debug digitized industrial products	14 (0.389)	10 (0.714)
05	The design of digitized industrial products should consider limited connectivity and data transmission bandwidth	15 (0.417)	9 (0.643)
06	The design of digitized industrial products should allow for mechanisms to analyze (1) timely incoming operational data to immediately react to unforeseen events and (2) massive quantities of historic operational product data to generate insights from patterns in this data	16 (0.444)	14 (1.000)

4.2 Building, Intervention, and Evaluation (BIE) of the Solution Design

In the BIE stage, electronic forklift trucks were augmented with digital technology based on open-source commodity hardware to continuously collect more than 100 distinct signals from the central control unit (i.e., CAN bus) of forklift trucks. In addition, longitudinal information (i.e., GPS data) and operational data on the battery of the trucks were collected. Since forklift trucks represent 'moving assets', wireless data transmission was implemented by leveraging the existing corporate wireless network of *IndustrialCo*. Drawing on public cloud service offerings, a 'big data platform' was set up to store and process the gathered data centrally. In agile and iterative sprint cycles, the prototypical implementation was refined until continuous reliable data collection and central data storage were possible continuously over a period of one month. In total, approximately 200 Gigabytes of operational product data was collected from both working and malfunctioning forklift trucks. Initially, *Kibana* was used as an explorative visualization tool to implement first queries and deep-dive into the data in data-exploration workshops with interdisciplinary participants.[1] An initial set of MRs was addressed by continuously collecting data and digitizing the forklift trucks. Unlike specified by MR06, analytical capabilities on the trucks themselves were not

---

[1] Kibana is a state-of-the-art open source data visualization tool for Elasticsearch. It provides visualization capabilities on top of the content indexed on an Elasticsearch cluster.

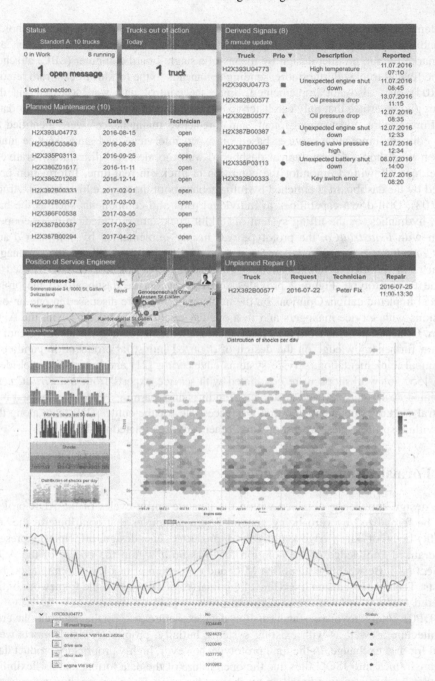

Fig. 2. 'Real-time predictive maintenance and fleet management' dashboard after five iterative and agile sprint cycles

implemented initially, since this requirement did not arise from the service of choice. Capabilities in terms of processing power and execution environment, however, are earmarked in the product design by means of a single-board computer (SBC) attached to the forklift trucks. Furthermore, sending commands to the forklift trucks from remote (MR04), was also not implemented, since the control unit was accessed via the debugging interface that only can listen to onboard control unit signals and sensor data.

Furthermore, 'fleet management' and 'predictive maintenance' were identified as two concrete innovative services based on expert interviews and smart service innovation workshops. A prototypical dashboard with mobile capabilities was iteratively developed allowing to monitor the condition of trucks in real-time. Information provided by the dashboard is enriched by information about the service history of the truck (MR03). Drill-down capabilities to individual parts and components such as the battery, hydraulics, or the lifting system of forklift trucks are provided. In close cooperation with *IndustrialCo,* the prototype was mainly implemented by *SoftwareCo* and *IoTConsultingCo* as a foundation for service offerings in the fields of 'fleet management' and 'predictive maintenance'. Agile and iterative sprint cycles were used to refine the prototype. Figure 2 provides an overview on the dashboard of the prototypical implementation. Opinions on the implementation were discussed in one-on-one sessions with service managers and in a one-day evaluation workshop with the ADR team. Obtained insights from the prototypical implementation helped the ADR team to obtain further knowledge on the design of digitized industrial products. In parallel to technical implementation, service systems engineering [21] and business model ideation [55, 56] workshops were conducted with service experts from *IndustrialCo,* its affiliated dealer network and customers. Findings and learnings were documented in a central working documentation that was accessible for the entire ADR team along the individual sprint cycles, workshops and other activities related to the project.

5   Formalization of Learnings

The design knowledge obtained within the iterative sprint cycles of the ADR project can be formalized by verbalizing general design principles that contribute to the scientific body of knowledge on digitized products. The design principles represent generalized knowledge of the solution that was built within the course of the ADR project [40]. Between the identified MRs and the design principles, a m:n relationship exists. Table 3 presents an overview of the final set of DPs within the framework of the layered modular architecture of digitized products [24].

DP01 refers to open standards for data exchange within the modular layered architecture as well as with existing systems. Initially, proprietary data formats were used for data exchange. In the final prototype, however, highly proprietary product data is transformed into JSON files due the open nature of the data format and its flexibility in terms of data structure based on attribute-value pairs. Furthermore, it was discussed to use MQTT as a lightweight messaging protocol. DP02 originates from the long lifecycles of industrial products. This implies that (1) various product models are in the field that must be compatible and (2) parts must be replaced over time. Loosely coupled modules and standardized interfaces (DP03) take this into account. In a later stage, the

Table 3. Design principles of digitized industrial products for smart industrial service systems

ID	Design principle	Addressed MRs	Device layer	Network layer	Service layer	Contents layer
01	To allow for open data accessibility and data exchange among actors, interfaces should be based on open protocols and standards	MR01	•	•	•	•
02	To foster resource density and provide structural flexibility, the principles of a layered modular architecture should be adapted	MR02	•	•	•	•
03	To connect to a broad variety of product models and generations, the interfaces between the layers must support open interfaces and standards	MR01 MR02	•	•	•	•
04	To combine operational product data with other existing contextual business data from the own organization and other actors, operational product data need to be integrated with existing information systems via standardized interfaces to integrate resources and co-create value	MR03			•	•
05	To have the possibility to control, configure and debug digitized products remotely, digitized industrial products must be designed in a way that allows secure bidirectional communication	MR04	•	•		
06	To analyze large amounts of operational data that is relevant for product operations despite low network bandwidths, digitized industrial products should be able to analyze operational data on the edge in addition to analytical capabilities on a central digital platform	MR05			•	•
07	To process both timely incoming operational data and massive quantities of historic data, the principles of the lambda architecture should be adapted	MR06			•	•
08	To being able to react to unforeseen events in a timely manner, operational product data must be collected and analyzed in an adequate velocity	MR06	•	•	•	
09	To generate insights from patterns in this data, operational product data must be collected continuously and in an adequate volume	MR06	•	•	•	

importance of open interfaces was furthermore considered as being relevant for smart service systems that incorporate additional actors in the service ecosystem. DP04 was formulated since operational product must be integrated and enriched with data from existing systems. Predictive maintenance services, for instance, can only be offered, if operational product data is contextualized with data about product master data, pervious maintenance activities, and customer data. DP05 came up when discussing an intermediate architecture of digitized forklift trucks with service managers in a focus group evaluation workshop. As more and more truck components have a digital materiality, it was noted that it must even be possible to send firmware updates to trucks to solve software-related issues remotely. DP06 focuses on the idea of 'edge analytics'. It must be possible to analyze massive amounts of operational sensor of a single product instance without sending the data to a central platform because of bandwidth and connectivity limitations at the network layer. Thus, code (i.e., algorithms) can be sent to and run on industrial products in the field. Only the results of the in-depth (long-term) monitoring are transmitted to a central platform. DP07-09 refer to the back-end design of an analytics platform. To trigger timely events and recognize trends in historic data, the lambda architecture was finally identified as a valid data-processing architecture enabling two fundamental kinds of data processing for data-driven services.[2]

6 Discussion and Conclusion

This paper reports on a 2.5-year lasting ADR project on designing digitized products to be used in innovative industrial service offerings. It contributes to the increasingly important body of knowledge on the generative design of physical products augmented with digital technology. Generic design knowledge is formalized as principles of form and function (causa formalis) [57]. The final set of derived design principles can be considered as a first step towards a nascent design theory [58] and extend the existing state of knowledge on digitized products for several reasons. First, the elicited and evaluated DPs allow to publish design knowledge at an intermediate level and thus lays the foundation of a nascent information systems design theory (ISDT) of digitized industrial products [59]. Second, the results concretize the existing state of knowledge on the material properties and design of digitized products [16, 20, 35, 60]. Finally, this work contributes to the ongoing conceptual convergence of literature on service innovation and the generative capacity of digitized products [1, 14, 17]. The paper raises awareness that the generative capacity of digitized products is based on adequate design decisions. Besides the theoretical contributions, the formalized design knowledge might help practitioners to design digitized products that effectively can be leveraged in the growing industrial service business. Specifically, managers must make adequate investment decisions today to build the foundation for future service innovation. Only if managers understand the implications of generative product design for the service innovation, proper investment decision can be made. Managers are required to consider generative digitized products as foundation for service innovation and smart service systems.

Although crafted from a thoroughly conducted ADR project and a solid foundation in existing literature, this study is not without limitations. First, I only had extensive access to *IndustrialCo* as one OEMs that aim at augmenting their industrial products with digital technology to be used in the industrial service business. Therefore, the DPs

---

[2] The lambda architecture is a data-processing architecture to manage massive amounts of operational product data in an effective way. It distinguishes between a batch layer and a speed layer combining the advantages of both processing designs.

are still tentative and additional corroboration is needed. Second, although the guideline for the explorative interviews is based on an in-depth literature review in the field of potential organizational capabilities as well as the review of two experts within the field, it might still contain personal inclinations of the author. Third, derived MRs and DPs are valid for all kinds of industrial products and resulting service innovation. However, there might be need to adapt both the MRs and DPs depending on industry specifics. For instance, design decisions for digitizing forklift trucks being 'moving assets' might differ from off-shore wind turbines or elevators. Future research is needed to corroborate the identified MRs and derived design principles with additional organization in the manufacturing industry and additional literature in the realm of engineering design technology. The validity of the results could be improved by using a quantitative approach.

Acknowledgements. This work has been supported by the *Swiss National Science Foundation (SNSF)*. I furthermore would like to thank the project partners and member organizations of the *Competence Center Industrial Services and Enterprise Systems (CC ISES)* at the *Institute for Information Management (IWI-HSG)* at *University of St. Gallen* and Michael Spori for his valuable support throughout this ADR project.

References

1. Barrett, M., Davidson, E., Prabhu, J., Vargo, S.L.: Service innovation in the digital age: key contributions and future directions. MIS Q. **39**, 135–154 (2015)
2. Lakhani, K.R., Iansiti, M.: Digital ubiquity: how connections, sensors, and data are revolutionizing business. Harvard Bus. Rev. **92**, 91–99 (2014)
3. Lusch, R.F., Nambisan, S.: Service innovation: a service-dominant (SD) logic perspective. MIS Q. **1**, 155–175 (2015)
4. Yoo, Y., Henfridsson, O., Lyytinen, K.: The new organizing logic of digital innovation: an agenda for information systems research. Inf. Syst. Res. **21**, 724–735 (2010)
5. Sawhney, M., Wolcott, R.C., Arroniz, I.: The 12 different ways for companies to innovate. Sloan Manag. Rev. **47**, 28–34 (2006)
6. Vargo, S.L., Maglio, P.P., Akaka, M.A.: On value and value co-creation: a service systems and service logic perspective. Eur. Manag. J. **26**, 145–152 (2008)
7. Lightfoot, H., Baines, T., Smart, P.: The servitization of manufacturing: a systematic literature review of interdependent trends. Int. J. Oper. Prod. Manag. **33**, 1408–1434 (2013)
8. Neely, A.: Exploring the financial consequences of the servitization of manufacturing. Oper. Manag. Res. **1**, 103–118 (2008)
9. Ulaga, W., Reinartz, W.J.: Hybrid offerings: how manufacturing firms combine goods and services successfully. J. Market. **75**, 5–23 (2011)
10. Blinn, N., Nüttgens, M., Schlicker, M., Thomas, O., Walter, P.: Lebenszyklusmodelle hybrider Wertschöpfung: Modellimplikationen und Fallstudie an einem Beispiel des Maschinen- und Anlagenbaus. In: Proceedings of the Multikonferenz Wirtschaftsinformatik (MKWI), München, Germany (2008)
11. Medina-Borja, A.: Editorial column - smart things as service providers: a call for convergence of disciplines to build a research agenda for the service systems of the future. Serv. Sci. **7**, ii–v (2015)

12. Maglio, P.: Editorial—smart service systems, human-centered service systems, and the mission of service science. Serv. Sci. **7**, ii–iii (2015)
13. Herterich, M.M., Eck, A., Uebernickel, F.: Exploring how digitized products enable industrial service innovation - an affordance perspective. In: Proceedings of the 24th European Conference on Information Systems (ECIS), Istanbul, Turkey (2016)
14. Tiwana, A.: Platform Ecosystems: Aligning Architecture, Governance, and Strategy. Morgan Kaufman, Amsterdam (2014)
15. Tilson, D., Lyytinen, K., Sørensen, C.: Digital infrastructures: the missing is research agenda. Inf. Syst. Res. **21**, 748–759 (2010)
16. Yoo, Y.: The tables have turned: how can the information systems field contribute to technology and innovation management research? J. Assoc. Inf. Syst. **14**, 227–236 (2013)
17. Herterich, M.M., Mikusz, M.: Looking for a few good concepts and theories for digitized artifacts and digital innovation in a material world. In: Proceedings of the 37th International Conference on Information Systems (ICIS), Dublin, Ireland (2016)
18. Porter, M.E., Heppelmann, J.E.: How smart, connected products are transforming companies. Harvard Bus. Rev. **93**, 96–114 (2015)
19. Porter, M.E., Heppelmann, J.E.: How smart, connected products are transforming competition. Harvard Bus. Rev. **92**, 64–86 (2014)
20. Yoo, Y.: Computing in everyday life: a call for research on experiential computing. MIS Q. **34**, 213–231 (2010)
21. Böhmann, T., Leimeister, J.M., Möslein, K.: Service systems engineering: a field for future information systems research. Bus. Inf. Syst. Eng. **6**, 73–79 (2014)
22. Herterich, M.M., Uebernickel, F., Brenner, W.: Stepwise evolution of capabilities for harnessing digital data streams in data-driven industrial services. MIS Q. Executive **15**, 297–318 (2016)
23. Leonardi, P.M., Barley, S.R.: Materiality and change: challenges to building better theory about technology and organizing. Inf. Organ. **18**, 159–176 (2008)
24. Yoo, Y., Boland, R.J., Lyytinen, K., Majchrzak, A.: Organizing for innovation in the digitized world. Organ. Sci. **23**, 1398–1408 (2012)
25. Lusch, R.F., Vargo, S.L.: Service-Dominant Logic: Premises, Perspectives Possibilities. Cambridge University Press, Cambridge (2014)
26. Vargo, S.L., Lusch, R.F.: Institutions and axioms: an extension and update of service-dominant logic. J. Acad. Market. Sci. **44**, 5–23 (2016)
27. Zittrain, J.: The Future of the Internet and How to Stop it. Yale University Press, New Haven (2006)
28. Zittrain, J.L.: The generative internet. Harvard Law Rev. **119**, 1974–2040 (2006)
29. Eck, A., Uebernickel, F., Brenner, W.: The generative capacity of digital artifacts: a mapping of the field. In: Proceedings of the 19th Pacific Asia Conference on Information System (PACIS), Singapore (2015)
30. Eck, A., Uebernickel, F.: Untangling generativity: two perspectives on unanticipated change produced by diverse actors. In: Proceedings of the 24th European Conference on Information Systems (ECIS), Istanbul, Turkey (2016)
31. Henderson, R.M., Clark, K.B.: Architectural innovation: the reconfiguration of existing product technologies and the failure of established firms. Adm. Sci. Q. **35**, 9–30 (1990)
32. Eisenhardt, K.M., Tabrizi, B.N.: Accelerating adaptive processes: product innovation in the global computer industry. Adm. Sci. Q. **40**, 84–110 (1995)
33. Woodard, C., Clemons, E.: Modeling the evolution of generativity and the emergence of digital ecosystems. In: Proceedings of the 35th International Conference on Information Systems (ICIS), Auckland, New Zealand (2014)

34. Piccinini, E., Hanelt, A., Gregory, R., Kolbe, L.: Transforming industrial business: the impact of digital transformation on automotive organizations. In: Proceedings of the 36th International Conference on Information System (ICIS), Fort Worth, TX (2015)
35. Hylving, L., Henfridsson, O., Selander, L.: The role of dominant design in a product developing firm's digital innovation. J. Inf. Technol. Theory Appl. 13, 5–21 (2012)
36. Dreyer, S., Olivotti, D., Lebek, B., Breitner, M.: Towards a smart services enabling information architecture for installed base management in manufacturing. In: Proceedings of the 13th International Conference on Wirtschaftsinformatik (WI), St. Gallen, Switzerland (2017)
37. Göbel, H., Cronholm, S.: Nascent design principles enabling digital service platforms. In: Parsons, J., Tuunanen, T., Venable, J., Donnellan, B., Helfert, M., Kenneally, J. (eds.) DESRIST 2016. LNCS, vol. 9661, pp. 52–67. Springer, Cham (2016). doi:10.1007/978-3-319-39294-3_4
38. Lyytinen, K., Yoo, Y., Boland, R.J.: Digital product innovation within four classes of innovation networks. Inf. Syst. J. 26, 47–75 (2015)
39. Fichman, R.G., Dos Santos, B.L., Zheng, Z.E.: Digital innovation as a fundamental and powerful concept in the information systems curriculum. MIS Q. 38, 329–353 (2014)
40. Sein, M., Henfridsson, O., Purao, S., Rossi, M., Lindgren, R.: Action design research. MIS Q. 35, 37–56 (2011)
41. Hevner, A.R., March, S.T., Park, J., Ram, S.: Design science in information systems research. MIS Q. 28, 75–105 (2004)
42. March, S.T., Smith, G.F.: Design and natural science research on information technology. Decis. Support Syst. 15, 251–266 (1995)
43. Walls, J.G., Widmeyer, G.R., El Sawy, O.A.: Building an information system design theory for vigilant EIS. Inf. Syst. Res. 3, 36–59 (1992)
44. Walls, J.G., Widmeyer, G.R., El Sawy, O.A.: Assessing information system design theory in perspective: how useful was our 1992 initial rendition? J. Inf. Technol. Theory Appl. 6, 43–58 (2004)
45. Webster, J., Watson, R.T.: Analyzing the past to prepare for the future: writing a literature review. MIS Q. 26, xiii–xxiii (2002)
46. vom Brocke, J., Simons, A., Riemer, K., Niehaves, B., Plattfault, R., Cleven, A.: Standing on the shoulders of giants: challenges and recommendations of literature search in information systems research. Commun. Assoc. Inf. Syst. 37, 205–224 (2015)
47. Linton, J.D., Thongpapanl, N.: Ranking the technology innovation management journals. J. Prod. Innov. Manag. 21, 123–139 (2004)
48. Patton, M.Q.: Qualitative Evaluation and Research Methods. Sage Publications, Thousand Oaks (1990)
49. Norman, R.: Reframing Business: When the Map Changes the Landscape. Wiley, Chichester (2001)
50. Parmar, R., Mackenzie, I., Cohn, D., Gann, D.: The new patterns of innovation. Harvard Bus. Rev. 92, 86–95 (2014)
51. Lerch, C., Gotsch, M.: Digitalized product-service systems in manufacturing firms. Res. Technol. Manag. 58, 45–52 (2015)
52. Kees, A., Oberlaender, A.M., Roeglinger, M., Rosemann, M.: Understanding the internet of things: a conceptualisation of business-to-thing (B2T) interactions. In: Proceedings of the 23rd European Conference on Information Systems (ECIS), Münster, Germany (2015)
53. Davenport, T.H.: Competing on analytics. Harvard Bus. Rev. 84, 98–107 (2007)
54. Chen, H., Chiang, R.H., Storey, V.C.: Business intelligence and analytics: from big data to big impact. MIS Q. 36, 1165–1188 (2012)

55. Gassmann, O., Frankenberger, K., Csik, M.: The Business Model Navigator: 55 Models That Will Revolutionise Your Business. FT Press, Harlow (2015)
56. Osterwalder, A., Pigneur, Y., Clark, T.: Business Model Generation: A Handbook for Visionaries, Game Changers, and Challengers. Wiley, Hoboken (2010)
57. Gregor, S., Jones, D.: The anatomy of a design theory. J. Assoc. Infor. Syst. **8**, 312–335 (2007)
58. Gregor, S.: Building theory in the sciences of the artificial. In: Proceedings of the 4th International Conference on Design Science Research in Information Systems and Technology (DESRIST), New York, NY (2009)
59. Heinrich, P., Schwabe, G.: Communicating nascent design theories on innovative information systems through multi-grounded design principles. In: Tremblay, M.C., VanderMeer, D., Rothenberger, M., Gupta, A., Yoon, V. (eds.) DESRIST 2014. LNCS, vol. 8463, pp. 148–163. Springer, Cham (2014). doi:10.1007/978-3-319-06701-8_10
60. Henfridsson, O., Bygstad, B.: The generative mechanisms of digital infrastructure evolution. MIS Q. **37**, 896–931 (2013)

Emerging Themes and New Ideas

A Design Science Approach to Information Systems Education

Göran Goldkuhl[1,2(✉)], Pär Ågerfalk[1], and Jonas Sjöström[1]

[1] Department of Informatics and Media, Uppsala University, Uppsala, Sweden
goran.goldkuhl@liu.se,
{par.agerfalk,jonas.sjostrom}@im.uu.se
[2] Department of Management and Engineering, Linköping University,
Linköping, Sweden

Abstract. Information systems (IS) education is concerned with design and management of information systems. To be prepared to work as an IS practitioner, there is a need for training in design issues during education. This paper investigates what a design science approach would imply for IS education. Such an IS education approach is elaborated and synthesized in eight principles: (1) Exploit resonance between IS research and IS development, (2) conduct theory-informed design-exercises, (3) conduct practice-inspired design-exercises, (4) alternate between the concrete and the abstract, (5) reflect based on experiences for own design-theoretical synthesis, (6) evaluate design processes and design products, (7) archive design reflections in a knowledge diary, (8) compile design artifacts into a portfolio. One key characteristic of design science (DS) is the integration of research and design. A DS approach to IS education means an integration of design and learning. This education approach is theoretically grounded in IS design science literature and also broader in literature of design inquiry (Dewey), experiential learning theory (Kolb) and education of the reflective practitioner (Schön).

Keywords: Information systems education · Design science · Design · Learning · Design inquiry · Concrete design experiences · Abstract design knowledge

1 Introduction

Although the emphasis may vary across programs, information systems (IS) education typically covers different aspects of the planning, design and management of information systems [33]. The purpose of IS education is to prepare students for professional work with information systems – either as IS practitioners or, after further postgraduate education, as IS researchers. These purposes are achieved through different types of educational activity. As an academic education, such activities involve, of course, the reading of pertinent academic literature. However, being an applied discipline, IS education comprises not only learning through reading but also learning by doing. Different kinds of exercises prepare students for practical work in their future careers. Such exercises often involve design tasks. IS education trains students in

© Springer International Publishing AG 2017
A. Maedche et al. (Eds.): DESRIST 2017, LNCS 10243, pp. 383–397, 2017.
DOI: 10.1007/978-3-319-59144-5_23

different aspects of the design of IS and aims to provide both conceptual knowledge and relevant skills [4]. The concepts and skills taught through IS education cover both IS practice (ISP) and IS research (ISR), with a clear progression from undergraduate to postgraduate levels. Undergraduate education typically emphasizes foundational ISP concepts and skills whereas postgraduate (masters and PhD) education emphasizes ISR concepts and skills. Figure 1 depicts this structure.

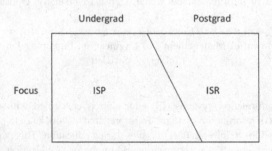

Fig. 1. Typical IS education foci and targets.

Certainly, many undergraduate programs introduce also research concepts and skills and conclude with the crafting of a bachelor's dissertation. However, the main emphasis throughout these programs is on practical skills and supporting concepts. Our experience from many years of teaching at all levels and at different universities in different countries confirms this general structure, as does the ACM/AIS Model Curriculum [33]. Including research components in IS education prepares students for postgraduate studies and research. Another reason is that research skills also provide a foundation for becoming a reflective IS practitioner [21, 27]. Higher education aims to develop the students' ability to think critically about IS phenomena. Therefore, research skills should be integrated early in the education to prepare students for a professional life as researcher or reflective practitioner. Traditionally, though, research concepts and skills are introduced in the final year. In our experience, this has two major drawbacks. First, students are not given the required time to internalize research skills in a way that will help them become reflective practitioners. Second, students find research concepts and skills to be alien and hard to comprehend.

In our search for a solution to the problem of how and when to introduce students to research concepts and skills, we turn our attention to design science (DS). DS has over the last decade grown as a vital research approach within the IS discipline. Hevner et al. [14] articulated it as a distinct research paradigm in IS based on forerunners such as [20, 23, 30]. Its legitimacy as a research approach has grown through many applications and further elaborations. DS is not only research about design, but also *research through design* [15]. DS is a research approach that aims to integrate design and science [2].

IS education is learning about design, but also *learning through design*. In that sense, there is some affinity between design science as a research approach and IS education. The purpose of this paper is to explore such affinities and connections. The driving research question is: "What would a design science approach imply for IS education?" With inspiration from DS (as an integration of research and design) this paper explores *IS education as integration of learning and design.* To do this, the analysis uses certain characteristics from DS; for instance, alternations between abstract and concrete design knowledge.

To complement recent work on DS as an approach for curriculum development [41], this paper thus focuses on applying DS within the curriculum itself.

In the next Sect. 2 we lay out some fundamentals for a DS inspired approach to IS education. Some essentials of DS are described followed by a discussion on design and learning as a basis for the following section that outlines a DS approach to IS education (Sect. 3). This section starts with eight principles for a DS inspired IS education, which are further elaborated in the following. This section ends with an explicit theoretical grounding of the eight DS educational principles. In Sect. 4, the approach is crystallized in a DS model of IS education. The paper ends with a concluding discussion (Sect. 5).

2 Design, Science and Learning

While *science* is concerned with contributing new knowledge *to the world*, *learning* regards the acquisition of new knowledge *to oneself.* In this section, we first address the relationship between design and science, followed by a discussion on the relationship between design and learning.

2.1 Knowledge Development Through Design Science Research

The essence of design science in IS is knowledge development through the design of artifacts. Research activities in DS are performed in interaction with an established knowledge base and a practice environment [14]; see Fig. 1 for a principal overview. Essentially, practical problems and needs together with the use of extant academic knowledge drive research in a DS approach. Results from design research are fed both to the practice (through designed artifacts as solutions to stated problems) and, as additions, to the knowledge base [13].

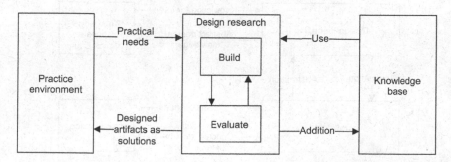

Fig. 2. Research within design science (with inspiration from [14])

The design of artifacts is done through iterations of build and evaluate activities [13, 14, 20]. The iterative approach follows the view of design as a search process, through which we both learn more about the problem domain, innovation opportunities and possible solutions [12]. Evaluation can be done at several stages and with different purposes throughout the DS process [35].

As mentioned above, the design process should be informed by the knowledge base. Kuechler and Vaishnavi [17] describe a process of selecting and translating general theories into design relevant theories that are adapted to the design task at hand. Sein et al. [29] also emphasize an active use of theories in the design process. Such an active use should lead to a "theory-ingrained" artifact, i.e. to a designed artifact that is heavily influenced by some theories during its design and thus certain theory elements become inscribed into the artifact.

It has been noted that not all design science is conducted with a clear reference to practical problems [15, 40]. Some design oriented research seems to be conducted in a more laboratory-oriented manner [15, 40]. There are arguments raised emphasizing the need for design science to be "practice-inspired research" [29, 39].

The seminal article of Hevner et al. [14] showed a reluctance to see theory as a result from a DS process. A designed artifact was considered as the main outcome from the DS process. Theory was rather seen as a result from "behavioral science", which was differentiated from DS. However, many scholars have later argued for acknowledging theory as an important outcome from DS [12, 34]. This could be in the form of an explicit design theory [11] or in design principles [29] or some other kind of abstract design knowledge [9]. Importantly, DS holds a place for both empirical and theoretical contributions [1].

Several authors that have advocated the conceiving of DS as a two-layered process with alternating between concrete design work and abstract design-theorizing [9, 10, 18, 31, 36, 39]. The design process is concerned with artifacts as solutions to specific, situational problems and needs. The abstract layer is the corresponding work with typical problems and typical solutions. Sometimes the notions of "class of problems" and "class of solutions"/"class of artifacts" are used [18, 29]. The abstract layer with analysis and reflection generates abstract design knowledge (as e.g. design principles or design theory). A two-layered approach to design science is depicted in Fig. 3.

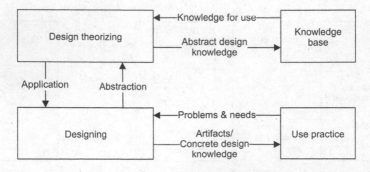

Fig. 3. Research within design science (with inspiration from [9, 10, 39])

Similarly, Baskerville et al. [2] address knowledge production and justification in DS research. They characterize design science research as an alternation between different genres of inquiry—each governed by distinctive goals and scope, knowledge characteristics, and quality criteria. The four genres are conceptualized drawing from two dualities: (1) Science vs. design and (2) nomothetic (abstract) vs. idiographic (situational) knowledge.

2.2 Learning Through Design

The integration of design and learning implies an emphasis on knowledge development in the learning situation. Design-based learning can be framed as design inquiry [26, 39]; i.e. an inquiry process that is conducted (partly) as design. Dewey [5, 6] conceptualized the inquiry process as a movement from a problematic situation to the settlement of such a situation. This process goes through steps of problem formulation and articulation, creation of proposals, reasoning of consequences and testing such proposals and consequences in order to find an adequate response to the initial disturbance of a problematic situation. Design (i.e. creation of suggested solutions) is thus seen as response to a problematic situation of practice. In order to be prepared to create solutions, the learner/designer needs to build a proper understanding of the problematic situation as a starting point of design. This view of the inquiry process (as a practice-oriented knowledge development process) is in line with contemporary views of creativity [19] and design thinking [7].

The inquiry is characterized as a movement back and forth between concrete and abstract and this movement helps to build a proper understanding. Dewey [5, p. 40] writes, "A complete act of thought involves ... a fruitful interaction of observed (or recollected) particular considerations and of inclusive, and far-reaching (general) meanings". This is also well described by Strübing [32] in his interpretation of Dewey's inquiry notion in relation to grounded theorizing, "as moving in a series of loops between the empirical process under scrutiny and the stream of conceptual thinking or theorizing about it" [32, p. 594]. The interaction and dialectics between the concrete and abstract is also theorized in the experiential learning theory by Kolb [16]. A learning circle of four iterative steps are described: (1) Concrete experiences, (2) observation and reflection, (3) abstract conceptualization and (4) active experimentation. One axis in this model is between the concrete (experiences) and the abstract (conceptualizations). A design inquiry in a learning situation should ideally be such a back and forth movement between concrete design exercices (producing concrete experiences) and abstract reflection on such design issues (internalizing and producing relevant abstract meanings). The other axis in Kolb's model harmonizes with this idea; an interaction between active experimentation (doing) and observing/reflecting.

One important aspect of Dewey's inquiry process is the dual outcome. Miettinen [22, p. 67] has described this inquiry result in the following way, "the process has two kinds of result. The direct, immediate outcome is that the situation becomes reconstructed in such a way that the initial problem becomes resolved. This outcome means the increased control over the activity. Another, indirect and intellectual outcome is the production of a meaning that can be used as a resource in forthcoming problem situations." The first outcome is the thus the accomplished design task. The second outcome is the conceptualized learning from this design endeavor as action dispositions for future work. It is vital that a learning environment stimulates the learners to embark on this secondary task; i.e. not only conducting design exercises, but also to create meaningful and useful design principles that connect the conducted design with theorized design knowledge.

In his work on educating the reflective practitioner, Schön [27, p. 160] described such a continuous articulation of design knowledge, "Designers can learn to make better descriptions of designing – more complete, accurate, and useful for action – by continued reflection on their own skillful performances". Schön [27, p. 164] descibes the teaching and learning of design as two related practices; one concerned with "the substantive designing" and one concerned with "the reflection-in-action by which she tries to learn it". One important outcome from the learning process, according to Schön, is an internalized design vocabulary related to skillful design actions and design results.

3   How to Apply Design Science Thinking in IS Education

Following the theoretically informed account of design and learning, we here propose an explicit DS approach to IS education building on a conscious *integration of learning and design*. The design process is not limited to mere concrete design. It is part of a broader knowledge development process. There should be continual *interplay between design and knowledge* for the sake of learning. Knowledge is both an antecedent to design and a reflective consequence of design. In the remainder of this section, we draw from DS in IS to conceptualize a set of aspects to promote learning in IS education.

This DS approach to IS education is synthesized in a "Design science model of IS education" (to be found in Sect. 4) and eight DS-inspired IS education principles. These principles are described in the text below when elaborating the DS approach. The principles rely on DS knowledge (summarized in Sect. 2.1) and knowledge of design inquiry and learning (summarized in Sect. 2.2). We explicate the connections between the education principles and these different types of theoretical base in Sect. 3.7. The eight principles for DS inspired IS education read as follows:

1. Exploit resonance between IS research and IS development
2. Conduct theory-informed design-exercises
3. Conduct practice-inspired design-exercises
4. Alternate between the concrete and the abstract
5. Reflect based on experiences for own design-theoretical synthesis
6. Evaluate design processes and design products
7. Archive design reflections in a knowledge diary
8. Compile design artifacts into a portfolio

There is a fundamental difference between research and learning that needs to be kept in mind. Research is supposed to produce knowledge that is *"new-to-the-world"*, while learning creates knowledge that is *"new-to-me"* (as a learner). However, that what is new-to-the-world (in research) is of course also new-to-me. There might also be cognitive breakthroughs in learning processes that might produce knowledge that is not only new-to-me but also new-to-the-world.

3.1 Design Research and Design Practice

Acknowledging that information systems practice (ISP) and information systems research share many concepts and methods is fundamental when adopting DS as a model for IS education. This resonance between ISR and ISP should be utilized in IS education (Principle #1). The similarity between the two is evident from the build and evaluate cycle, which draws on research based knowledge. It is also evident in terms of how heavily influenced IS design methods are by research methods in general. For instance, when we teach requirements elicitation techniques, we often adopt qualitative data collection methods (as e.g. interviewing, observation, document studies). When we analyze those data by means of conceptual modelling and other techniques, we draw heavily on various qualitative analysis approaches (for conceptualization and abstraction). When we advocate test-first-programming we are using Popper's falsification principles. When we talk about software process improvement, we rely on empirical research methods. The list goes on. The issue at stake here is to explain those IS concepts and techniques using ISR terms and to focus our attention on the intersection between ISR and ISP, see Fig. 4.

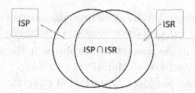

Fig. 4. IS education at the intersection of ISP and ISR.

3.2 Design Exercises and Knowledge

Design exercises are fundamental means for learning. However, conducting design exercises does not automatically qualify an IS education as a DS application. If so, most IS education programs would be seen as DS applications. There is more than just design exercises when applying DS thinking in IS education.

Literature forms a *knowledge base* for students in design exercises. Different kinds of knowledge should be applied by the students in their design exercises. Certainly, this is fundamental to any academic education. The conduct of design exercises should have a clear vantage point in the knowledge base of the education program. This follows the principle of a *theory-informed design* (Principle #2). However, the students should not only read through the literature before application in design exercises. In order to reach a theory-informed design, the students should engage in studying the literature in such a way that theoretical abstractions and principles are made intelligible for the student in order to apply. The initial student's interpretations of theory/literature should be documented in a knowledge diary (to be explained below in Sect. 3.6).

3.3   Design and Business Practice Environments

Design science is not seen as an internal scientific affair. Rather, DS should be related to a practice environment outside academia [14, 29]. DS gets motivation, direction and scope from practical problems and needs (Figs. 2 and 3). DS aims at delivering artifacts as solutions to practice environments. There is thus both input from and output to business practice from design science.

IS education stands in a similar relation to practice environment as does DS. IS education is based on needs in practice for a competent workforce and education should produce students with potential to start working and evolving into competent employees or entrepreneurs. It is important that an IS education trains students to address problems and needs in practice. The design exercises should be practice-inspired (Principle #3). They should contain realistic features of diverse kinds. They should at least be inspired by typical problems and needs in practice and thereby simulating real design tasks. The outcome from design exercises should be solutions that in some sense correspond to real solutions although they might be idealized due to educational circumstances and limitations. In some cases it might be that the students get possibilities to work with real situations in organizations in order to strengthen the academia-practice link.

3.4   Reflection and Abstraction for Design-Theoretical Synthesis

A DS application should imply a movement from the abstract to the concrete, following the principle of theory informed design exercises (Principle #2). It should, however, also imply a movement from the concrete to the abstract. There should be an alternation between concrete and abstract knowledge (Principle #4).

Learning through design produces artifacts and concrete design knowledge. A DS approach to learning through design implies that *abstraction* and *reflection* should occur after the design process (and possibly also concurrent to the concrete design process). The student should reflect about the conducted design, about what abstract knowledge was used in the design process. This can comprise which design principles were used. The idea here is that the student should not only, in a passive way, check off the abstract knowledge used from the knowledge base (literature). An active reflection should imply a formulation (in own words) of abstract design principles and let this be done through filtering of the student's *own design experiences*. This can imply (1) a selection of already stated extant design principles and/or (2) a re-formulation of extant design principles (in ways that are more appropriate for the student and his/her experiences) and/or (3) a formulation of design principles not expressed in the available knowledge base. This means that the student formulates *abstract design knowledge that is personally relevant* for him/her. This should be done in a *knowledge diary*; see Sect. 3.6 below. This experience-based reflection should be a continuation of the active reading and interpretation of literature that was conducted prior to design exercises (Sect. 3.2 above). The reflection after a design exercise gives more flesh to the initial interpretations of theory. The student should be encouraged to work continually during the education with *design-theoretical synthesis*; i.e. a synthesis of the general abstract design knowledge from the literature with the student's own experiences from design exercises (Principle #5). This corresponds to the formulation of design principles as an explicit outcome from DS studies besides designed artifacts [9, 11, 29].

3.5 Evaluation

Evaluation plays a significant role in design science. The building of artifacts is supported by re-current evaluation efforts [14, 29, 35]. In a DS approach to IS education, evaluation should also play a significant role. Evaluation can be conducted by the students themselves, by fellow-students and by teachers in supervision and examination. Evaluation can concern the design process and/or the design product (i.e. the designed artifacts). Evaluation should be used as an instrument for developing design artifacts and as fuel for the reflection and abstraction process. In a DS approach to IS education, evaluation should be actively encouraged and integrated into the learning process (Principle #6). This means also that there should be an emphasis on *evaluation criteria*. Such criteria can concern both design process and design product. Since there are diverse knowledge demands in a design inquiry, there needs to be a varied set of criteria for evaluation and justification [2]. The knowledge base used should contain such different kinds of criteria. These criteria are not only meant to be used in evaluation, but as desired qualities and values, they should also govern design processes. The students should, through such explicit criteria, be more aware of different types of artifact values; implying a value-sensitive design [8, 24].

Values and criteria should be actively used by students and teachers; and they should also be evaluated (in a *meta-evaluation*) leading to reformulated and added criteria. Such meta-evaluation might result in additions in students' knowledge diaries (see below Sect. 3.6) and possibly also in the knowledge base of the education program.

3.6 Design Learning Archives: Knowledge Diary and Design Artifact Portfolio

Each student should work with a personal knowledge diary. Such a knowledge diary, evolving through the education program, should be an expression of the student's internalization of abstract design knowledge (Principle #7). A DS approach to IS education should encourage students to actively work with reflection and abstraction related to conducted design exercises. To keep a knowledge diary should be an instrument for such reflection and abstraction. It should be a way to connect abstract principles from the literature (knowledge base) with the student's own design experiences. It should also be seen as a way for the student to reflect on and articulate his/her evolving tacit design knowledge. The role of the educators should, in this sense, be to stimulate the students to reflect on their own experiences from design [21].

The knowledge diary contains a collection of abstracted design experiences. It corresponds to conducted design exercises in the education program. In design science, the results from the concrete design work are diverse kinds of artifacts. It might e.g. be process models, conceptual models, use-case models, prototypes of user-interfaces, database models, architecture sketches and computer programs. These are also typical artifacts that might be produced in an IS education. A proposal here is that such artifacts (as results from design exercises) are compiled together and form a "*portfolio*" of each student (Principle #8). The concept of a portfolio (student portfolio, career portfolio) is established in education contexts [3, 4, 25, 37]. Portfolios are created, sometimes through the support of academic organizations, as career instruments for students. The suggestion is that each student should keep a "design artifact portfolio" as *an archive of created design artifacts* through the education program's different design exercises. The point is to have this as concrete reference material that corresponds to the evolving knowledge diary. Such a design artifact portfolio can also be one basis for the student in creating a career portfolio.

3.7   Theoretical Grounding of IS Education Principles

The IS education principles described above were informed by design science knowledge (summarized in Sect. 2.1) and knowledge on design inquiry and learning (summarized in Sect. 2.2). We will here relate the eight IS education principles to referred knowledge bases as an explicit theoretical grounding (Table 1).

Table 1. Theoretical grounding of IS education principles

IS education principles	Design science principles	Design inquiry principles
1. Exploit resonance between ISR and ISP	Proper data collection is needed in DS processes [14, 35]	Inquiry principles and methods are generic and valid for all types of knowledge development [6]
2. Conduct theory-informed design-exercises	Design should be informed by knowledge base [14], which can include selected and adapted theories [17, 29]	Pre-understanding is utilized in inquiry processes [6, 27]
3. Conduct practice-inspired design-exercises	Design should be a response to practical problems and needs [14, 29, 39]	A problematic situation is the starting point for inquiry [6]
4. Alternate between the concrete and the abstract	Design science should alternate between situational design and abstract design theorizing [2, 9, 18, 39]	Iterate between concrete observations and abstract meanings [6, 16, 32]
5. Reflect based on experience for own design-theoretical synthesis	Design science should produce empirically based abstract design knowledge as a result [9, 29]	Concrete experiences are basis for reflection, abstraction and reasoning [6, 16, 27]
6. Evaluate design processes and design products	There should be a continual interplay between building and evaluating in design processes [14, 35]	Practical validation is needed for judgement of solution proposals [6, 7, 19]
7. Archive design reflections in a knowledge diary	Design science should produce abstract design knowledge as a result [9, 29]	New meanings (new conceptualizations) are important results from inquiry [6, 16, 27]
8. Compile design artifacts into a portfolio	Design science should produce artifacts as a result [14, 20]	The inquiry ends with resolution of the problematic situation [6]

4   A Design Science Model of IS Education

The description above with characteristics of a DS based IS education will now be summarized. A model depicting important features is found in Fig. 5. As seen from the figure, design exercises play an important role for training students in conducting various design tasks. Design exercises should always contain a mix of building and evaluating artifacts. The design exercises should be arranged based on (1) relevant academic knowledge (course literature) and (2) typical design challenges from practice. In design exercises, students should actively apply different kinds of knowledge from the knowledge base (e.g. models, methods, design language, design principles, design theories).

Based on the design exercises, students should be encouraged to reflect on design processes and achieved design results (artifacts). They should relate what has been done in design exercises to different elements in the knowledge base. The knowledge base contains abstract design knowledge. The reflection process aims at working with this abstract design knowledge and doing this based on experiences from the conducted design exercises. The reflection and abstraction process should produce knowledge that is relevant for the student based on performed design exercises. This abstract design knowledge (that is relevant to the student and formulated by the student in words meaningful to that specific student) should be expressed as parts of the individual knowledge diary of that student. The knowledge diary is thus an output from the

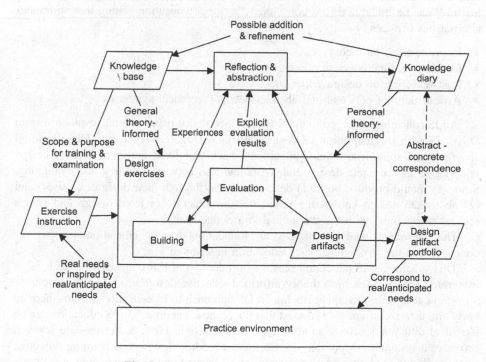

Fig. 5. A design science model of IS education

reflection process and it should correspond to the output from the design exercises, which should be compiled into a design artifacts portfolio. The knowledge diary should not only be an output from the student's work with abstraction. The knowledge diary should be used as an own "knowledge base" for the student (as input) in further design exercises when relevant. The knowledge diary becomes a "personal theory" to be used in design tasks. If "new-to-the-world" insights emerge and become recorded in a student's knowledge diary, teachers should, in a feedback loop, assess and take care of such insights as possible additions to the knowledge base (adapted course material).

5   Concluding Discussion

With reference to the inquiry perspective, Schön [28, p. 131] states, "Because learning is essential to designing, there is a great potential for learning through designing". In his book, *Educating the reflective practitioner*, Schön [27] develops the notion of a "practicum", i.e. "a setting designed for the task of learning a practice" [27, p. 37]. A practicum is characterized as a learning arrangement where students, under supervision, are engaged in learning by doing and reflecting on process and outcome of this doing. Schön uses the designer as the role model for students in a practicum; "all professional practice is designlike, must be learned by doing" [27, p. 157]. In the views of inquiry and design as practice-oriented knowledge development [6, 27], there is an intrinsic learning component. Progression is made through acting informed by action-relevant knowledge and a reflective assessment of achievements. Design and learning can be integrated in a consciously arranged education setting that stimulates alternations between

- Pre-reflections on theory
- Conduct of concrete design exercises
- Post-reflection on design experiences
- Articulations of personal and abstract design-theoretical syntheses

An IS education arranged in the ways outlined in this paper obtains inspiration from DS in IS with its integration of design and knowledge development. The education arrangements should stimulate movements back and forth between abstract design knowledge and concrete design endeavors and also between building and evaluating. Students should produce both (1) design artifacts (through their design exercises) and (2) abstracted design knowledge based on (2a) experiences from design and (2b) a critical engagement with the theoretical knowledge base.

The presented analysis of DS as foundation for IS education lets us reconceptualize the structure of such education in terms of Fig. 6.

This structure of IS education sees the introduction of ISR concepts and skills as an integrated aspect of teaching theory-informed reflective design practice. To paraphrase an often cited Agile methods principle, a DS approach to IS education would 'theorize early and theorize often.' We suggest that the proposed approach to IS education can be useful at different levels of module and course design. First, at the module level, it provides a systematic approach to reflect about module design, e.g. learning outcome, exercise design, and examination requirements. Second, at the course level, it supports

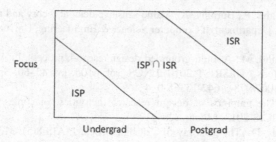

Fig. 6. A model of DS based IS education in terms of focus on ISP and ISR.

a systematic aproach to student progression; incorporating theory and theorizing early facilitate seamless progression towards more advanced research concepts. Similarly, we suggest that students should be confronted with increasingly sophisticated evaluation methods during a module. Drawing explicitly on DS research principles also provides grounding of development skills in ISR, such as behavioral methods for design evaluation.

Finally, especially in the DS context, there is a need to address the issue of evaluation. We have proposed a DS model of IS education and eight IS education principles. While drawing from our own practical experiences as DS researchers and teachers, this paper has provided a theoretical justification of its propositions. Our future work aims at implementing these ideas into education practice, managing curriculum coherence over time and studying the impact on students' research abilities and their progression as reflective practitioners. Given the systematic approach to learning facilitation outlined here, our approach needs to be adopted in concert with a governance model for education [e.g. 38], addressing planning, maintenance and human aspects of education organisation.

References

1. Ågerfalk, P.J.: Insufficient theoretical contribution: a conclusive rationale for rejection? Eur. J. Inf. Syst. **23**(6), 593–599 (2014)
2. Baskerville, R., Kaul, M., Storey, V.: Genres of inquiry in design-science research: Justification and evaluation of knowledge production. MIS Q. **39**(3), 541–564 (2015)
3. Cambridge, D.: Audience, integrity, and the living document: eFolio Minnesota and lifelong and lifewide learning with ePortfolios. Comput. Educ. **51**, 1227–1246 (2008)
4. Carlsson, S., Hedman, J., Steen, O.: Integrated curriculum for a bachelor of science in business information systems design (BISD 2010). Commun. AIS **26**, 525–546 (2010). Article 24
5. Dewey, J.: How We Think. DC Heath & Co, Boston (1910)
6. Dewey, J.: Logic: The Theory of Inquiry. Henry Holt, New York (1938)
7. Dorst, K.: The nature of design thinking. In: Dorst, K., Stewart, S., Staudinger, I., Paton, B., Dong, A. (eds.) Design Thinking Research Symposium 8. DAB Documents, Sydney (2010)

8. Friedman, B., Kahn, P., Borning, A.: Value sensitive design: theory and methods. Technical report 02-12-01, Department of Computer Science & Engineering, University of Washington (2002)

9. Goldkuhl, G., Lind, M.: A multi-grounded design research process. In: Winter, R., Zhao, J. Leon, Aier, S. (eds.) DESRIST 2010. LNCS, vol. 6105, pp. 45–60. Springer, Heidelberg (2010). doi:10.1007/978-3-642-13335-0_4

10. Goldkuhl, G.: The empirics of design research: activities, outcomes and functions. In: Proceedings of ICIS-2013, Milano (2013)

11. Gregor, S., Jones, D.: The anatomy of a design theory. J. AIS **8**(5), 312–335 (2007)

12. Gregor, S., Hevner, A.R.: Positioning and presenting design science research for maximum impact. MIS Q. **37**(2), 337–355 (2013)

13. Hevner, A.R.: A three cycle view of design science research. Scand. J. Inf. Syst. **19**(2), 87–92 (2007)

14. Hevner, A.R., March, S.T., Park, J., Ram, S.: Design science in information systems research. MIS Q. **28**(1), 75–115 (2004)

15. Iivari, J.: Distinguishing and contrasting two strategies for design science research. Eur. J. Inf. Syst. **24**, 107–115 (2015)

16. Kolb, D.A.: Experiential Learning. Experience as the Source of Learning and Development. Prentice Hall, Englewood Cliffs (1984)

17. Kuechler, B., Vaishnavi, V.: A framework for theory development in design science research: multiple perspectives. J. AIS **13**(6), 395–423 (2012)

18. Lee, J.S., Pries-Heje, J., Baskerville, R.: Theorizing in design science research. In: Jain, H., Sinha, Atish P., Vitharana, P. (eds.) DESRIST 2011. LNCS, vol. 6629, pp. 1–16. Springer, Heidelberg (2011). doi:10.1007/978-3-642-20633-7_1

19. Lubart, T.: Models of the creative process: past, present and future. Creativity Res. J. **13**(3 & 4), 295–308 (2000)

20. March, S.T., Smith, G.F.: Design and natural science research in information technology. Decis. Support Syst. **15**(4), 251–266 (1995)

21. Mathiassen, L., Purao, S.: Educating reflective systems developers. Inf. Syst. J. **12**(2), 81–102 (2002)

22. Miettinen, R.: The concept of experiential learning and John Dewey's theory of reflective thought and action. Int. J. Lifelong Educ. **19**(1), 54–72 (2000)

23. Nunamaker, J., Chen, M., Purdin, T.: Systems development in information systems research. J. Manag. Inf. Syst. **7**(3), 89–106 (1991)

24. Pereira, R., Baranauskas, C.: A value-oriented and culturally informed approach to the design of interactive systems. Int. J. Hum.-Comput. Stud. **80**, 66–82 (2015)

25. Reardon, R.C., Lumsden, J.A., Meyer, K.E.: Developing an e-portfolio program: providing a comprehensive tool for student development, reflection, and integration. NASPA J. **42**(3), 1–13 (2005)

26. Richter, C., Allert, H.: Moves beyond critique: Design as inquiry as a form of critical engagement. In: Professional Practice, Education and Learning International Conference, University of Stirling, Stirling (2014)

27. Schön, D.: Educating the reflective practitioner. Toward a new design for teaching and learning in the professions. Jossey-Bass Publishers, San Francisco (1987)

28. Schön, D.: The theory of inquiry: Dewey's legacy to education. Curriculum Inq. **22**(2), 119–139 (1992)

29. Sein, M., Henfridsson, O., Purao, S., Rossi, M., Lindgren, R.: Action design research. MIS Q. **35**(1), 37–56 (2011)

30. Simon, H.A.: The Sciences of the Artificial. MIT Press, Cambridge (1969, 1996)

31. Sjöström, J., Ågerfalk, P.J.: An analytic framework for design-oriented research concepts. In: Proceedings of AMCIS-2009, San Francisco (2009)
32. Strübing, J.: Research as pragmatic problem-solving: the pragmatist roots of empirically-grounded theorizing. In: Bryant, A., Charmaz, K. (eds.) The SAGE Handbook of grounded theory. SAGE, London (2007)
33. Topi, H., Valacich, J., Wright, R., Kaiser, K., Nunamaker, J., Sipior, J., de Vreede, G.-J.: IS 2010: curriculum guidelines for undergraduate degree programs in information systems. Commun. AIS 26(18), 359–428 (2010)
34. Venable, J.: The role of theory and theorising in design science research. In: Proceedings of DESRIST-2006, Claremont (2006)
35. Venable, J., Pries-Heje, J., Baskerville, R.: FEDS: a framework for evaluation in design science research. Eur. J. Inf. Syst. 25, 77–89 (2016)
36. Winter, R.: Towards a framework for evidence-based and inductive design in information systems research. In: Helfert, M., Donnellan, B., Kenneally, J. (eds.) EDSS 2013. CCIS, vol. 447, pp. 1–20. Springer, Cham (2014). doi:10.1007/978-3-319-13936-4_1
37. Wright, A.: The Dalhousie Career Portfolio programme: a multi-faceted approach to transition to work. Qual. High. Educ. 7(2), 149–159 (2001)
38. Hatzakis, T., Lycett, M., Serrano, A.: A programme management approach for ensuring curriculum coherence in IS (higher) education. Eur. J. Inf. Syst. 16(5), 643–657 (2007)
39. Goldkuhl, G., Sjöström, J.: Closing the practice loop: practice design research. In: AIS SIGPRAG Pre-ICIS Workshop Practice-based Design and Innovation of Digital Artifacts, Fort Worth (2015)
40. Zimmerman, J., Forlizzi, J.: Research through design in HCI. In: Olson, J., Kellogg, W. (eds.) Ways of Knowing in HCI. Springer, New York (2014)
41. Sjöström, J., Ågerfalk, P., Tuunanen, T.: Five principles for DSR based curriculum development. In: Proceedings of the AIS SIGED 2016 Conference, Dublin (2016)

Knowledge Accumulation in Design-Oriented Research

Developing and Communicating Knowledge Contributions

Ana Paula Barquet[(⊠)], Lauri Wessel, and Hannes Rothe

Freie Universität Berlin, Garystr. 21, 14195 Berlin, Germany
ana.barquet@fu-berlin.de

Abstract. In this paper, we problematize a relative absence of established ways to develop and communicate knowledge contributions (KC) from Design-oriented research (DOR) within information systems. This is problematic since it hinders the potential for knowledge accumulation within the field. Thus, for communicating KC, we propose a framework, dubbed PDSA (Prescriptive, Descriptive, Situated, and Abstract). To develop KC especially from empirical data, we suggest the use of qualitative process methods. The framework is illustrated by revisiting a published DOR study. Finally, we show how the PDSA framework serves as a template to establish firm KC in DOR. In addition, we explore contributions generated from empirical data and suggest possibilities to use qualitative process methods as means to increase transparency and rigor of KC development and communication.

Keywords: Knowledge contribution · Qualitative process methods · Empirical data · Design theory · Design-oriented research

1 Introduction

The design of information systems (IS) has been an important topic within the IS research community for many years [1–3]. Studies in this domain have improved means for organizations to confront challenging issues, such as managing diffuse knowledge processes [2], aligning individual and organizational competencies [4], or exploiting potentials of secondary design in emergent IS [5]. Such design-oriented studies typically aim to generate prescriptive knowledge on how organizations design IS, while the development of explanatory or predictive knowledge might assume a secondary role [6, 7]. Therefore, design-oriented works are relatively well geared for contributions to solving important problems in organizational practice [8–10].

Research on how to design artifacts has indeed become such an important topic in IS that it is now widely acknowledged as the 'Design Science (DS) paradigm' [11]. It has grown significantly in volume throughout the last decades, comprising different streams of literature that we summarize by using the umbrella term 'design-oriented research' (DOR). The main aim in DOR is to understand how effective artifacts can be designed and how design-oriented knowledge can be utilized for theorizing [12].

© Springer International Publishing AG 2017
A. Maedche et al. (Eds.): DESRIST 2017, LNCS 10243, pp. 398–413, 2017.
DOI: 10.1007/978-3-319-59144-5_24

To this end, DOR usually draws on design processes that unfold over different stages such as problem identification, development and evaluation of artifacts [13–15]. In this context, evaluation of the utility of artifacts is typically central [16–18]. Yet, this has led to the criticism that DOR is too narrowly concerned with designing and evaluating artifacts and circumventing questions about generalizable knowledge [19, 20]. Therefore, while there is a wellspring of work on how to design and evaluate the quality and utility of artifacts, little is known about how to develop and communicate knowledge contributions (KC). This is problematic since one important aspect of KC in DOR comprises gradual abstraction of knowledge about particular instantiations into more general 'design principles' and 'design theories' [12]. Yet, this abstraction demands careful attention to how researchers collected and used empirical data when interacting with organizations and how this affected formulation of 'design principles' or 'design theories.'

In this paper, we constructively engage with the aforementioned challenges and discuss how usage of empirical data within a DOR project affects KC. In this regard, we propose that an increasing importance of theorizing from DOR [21, 22] demands critical engagement with procedures for data collection and analysis, which are carried out as part of DOR. As DOR projects are typically seen as processes where researchers enact multiple cycles and stages, we promote that reliance on procedures for the analysis of process-data, which are known from innovation research [23], increases potentials to clearly communicate how KC were formulated. In this spirit, we follow recent calls to extend use of these particular procedures within DOR [24]. Mandviwalla [24] recently stressed that techniques for analyzing process-data could be fruitfully used to build design theories. By extension, we propose that use of these methods is not limited to develop design theory but also to other types of KC. Our first research question is thus (RQ1): *How do qualitative process methods help to develop knowledge contributions in DOR?*

Through engagement with this question, we gradually discovered a second related issue that demands careful consideration, i.e., what 'knowledge contributions' really are. Gregor and Hevner [12] have provided first insights by introducing a differentiation of three levels of generalizability of KC. They also propose a rather generic typology of KC, which considers a relevant but not complete selection of KC. For instance, it does not cover some types of KC, such as the ones depicted from empirical data. Accordingly, we ask (RQ2): *How do we present and communicate 'knowledge contributions' created in DOR?*

By taking Gregor and Hevner [12] as a starting point, we elaborate on their contribution by further detailing what KC are and how they can be developed during DOR projects. Our study, thus, offers two main contributions. On the one hand, we offer a framework, called PDSA (Prescriptive, Descriptive, Situated, Abstract), that is conducive to communicate and capture the dynamic evolution of novel knowledge in DOR projects over time. Furthermore, we contribute by showing that techniques for analysis of qualitative process methods [23] have significant potentials to inform the development of cumulative KC, especially when DOR covers empirical cases.

We proceed by a brief review of the fundamentals in DOR, followed by a presentation of dominant procedural models to carry out DOR. This sets the basis to define the problem, which addresses the lack of prescriptions on how to develop and communicate KC from DOR. Subsequently, we introduce the PDSA framework to support the communication of KC and show how techniques for analysis of qualitative process data supports the development of KC in DOR. We indicate the potentials of this idea through an illustrative case. In closing, we discuss our contributions, limitations and further research opportunities.

2 Relevant Literature on Design-Oriented Research (DOR)

Design-oriented research within IS can broadly be seen as a problem solving paradigm that aims to extend human and organizational capabilities by developing artifacts [11]. Thus, development of IS artifacts is of central concern to DOR [3, 12, 20, 25], which has its intellectual roots in engineering and architecture [3, 24, 25]. Various perspectives from behavioral sciences have been used in DOR over time (see for example [2, 5, 26]). While this undoubtedly increased the prominence of DOR within the IS discipline [18, 20, 27], the broad label 'design-oriented research' has also become sub-divided into different branches of literature that, while mostly similar, differ in details [12, 25, 27]. First, 'design research' refers to constructing artifacts in order to solve a specific class of problems [22, 27]. Second, 'design science' in the narrower sense is concerned with general rigor standards for conducting research projects [20]. Thus, design science aims at "explicitly organized, rational and wholly systematic approach[es] to design" [28] (p. 53) of IS artifacts. Third, 'design theory' refers to theorizations of knowledge about how specific classes of artifacts should be designed [3, 7, 24]. This means that design theories put a strong emphasis on how design-oriented knowledge can be formalized and made subject to replication [3, 12, 24].

2.1   The Roles of Artifacts and Knowledge Contributions in DOR

The outputs of DOR encompass IS artifacts and KC. Recently, KC in the form of design theories have become increasingly important [12]. In contrast, earlier works highlighted that contributions of DOR largely comprise 'design artifacts' [29] like constructs, models, methods, and instantiations [7, 30, 31]. Even though many of these artifacts carry certain degrees of abstraction [25, 31], scholars in DOR expressed their concern that it is sometimes hard to identify abstract knowledge contributions which arise from a DOR project [12]. In this context, Gregor and Hevner [12] categorized DOR contributions by their level of abstractness. Instantiations can be seen as most concrete and particular contributions ('Level 1'), 'Level 2' contributions comprise abstractions of a 'mid-range', such as design principles [32, 33]. They reach beyond a particular application context, but are themselves insufficient to be seen as 'design theories' [24, 26]. Finally, design theories would be the most general and abstract contribution of DOR ('Level 3'). Table 1 reviews these contributions.

The introduction of these levels '1–3' coincides with a general concern to develop theory through DOR [24, 34–36]. The reason is that the levels are cumulative, i.e. level 1 contributions can be developed into level 2 contributions, which may be the basis for building level 3 contributions [24, 26, 37–39]. Accumulation is a key idea in this regard

Table 1. Examples of contributions from DOR according to their level of abstractness

Contributions	Definition	Level
Instantiation	The realization of an artifact in its environment	Level 1
Constructs	The conceptualization used to describe problems and solutions within a certain domain	Level 2
Model	Set of propositions or statements that express relationships between constructs	Level 2
Method	Set of steps used to perform a task. It is based on constructs and the solution space representation	Level 2
Design principles	Knowledge captured in the process of creating solutions and building instances for same problems class	Level 2
Design theory	Covers "explanatory, predictive, normative aspects" into a design for achieving a specific goal	Level 3

because moving from level 1 to level 3 will unlikely be possible within a single research project or one paper [24]. Instead, systematic design theory-building is likely to be a process that emerges across publications of different scholars interested in related phenomena [3]. Therefore, if DOR is to exploit these potentials for systematic KC development, it needs a toolkit to explicate how knowledge was developed as well as a clear way to communicate it so that succeeding studies can carry on in a systematic way. Next, we review procedure models in DOR to assess whether and how they incorporate such thinking.

2.2 Procedure Models in DOR

In this section, some of the commonly accepted procedure models for DOR are explored with the goal to highlight how they address KC. The model of Hevner et al. [11] aims to support the understanding, execution and evaluation of DOR. This particular framework was later revised as a model comprising three cycles [14]: (i) the "relevance cycle" draws on business' needs and introduces the artifact into the application domain, (ii) the "design cycle" comprises artifact building and evaluation and, (iii) the "rigor cycle" receives applicable knowledge as input and adds contributions to the knowledge base as output. Hevner et al. [11] also emphasized guidelines for creation of useful artifacts. They highlight research contributions in the form of designed artifacts, foundations or methodologies as well as the importance to communicate results.

Peffers et al. [15] proposed a methodology within steps from problem identification to the development of a solution, demonstration, evaluation and communication. The authors illustrated the latter as a part of an iterative DOR process, however it is not further explained how 'communication' informs further design iterations. Nunamaker et al. [13] developed an iterative and prototypical process for system development in IS, which covers fives phases: construct of a conceptual framework, development of a system architecture, analysis and design of the system, building of a (prototypical) system, and observing and evaluating the system.

Mandviwalla [24] developed a set of processes to support the development of design theory. Goals, kernel theory and existing artifacts inform the prototyping cycle, which includes a concurrent iteration of design, evaluation, and appropriation/ generation. Last, Sein et al. [26] proposed a method called 'action design research', which treats the artifact creation and evaluation as inseparable and interrelated activities, differently from traditional DOR, which separates artifact building and evaluation. Action design research addresses four inter-related stages: problem formulation, building, intervention and evaluation, reflection and learning and formalization of learning.

Even though KC play a role for these procedure models, they provide limited prescriptions on how to develop or communicate them. For example, the importance of knowledge contributions is echoed in the method of Sein et al. [26] within "formalization of the learning"; within Hevner et al. [11], in "Guideline 4: Knowledge Contributions"; and in studies that stressed (partial) design theories as outcomes of DOR [12, 24], including theory building or refinement [13].

3   Towards Development and Communication of KC

3.1   Knowledge Contribution in DOR

Claims on how to develop and communicate knowledge contributions demand a clarification of what knowledge represents in lieu of epistemological and ontological considerations. The epistemological position of this study sees DOR knowledge contributions as "knowing by making" [39] (p. 4). Thus, knowledge embraces creation of artifacts as well as understanding the more abstract idea that guided the design of the artifact, regardless if this is theory building or testing. Ontology addresses nature and components of theory [7]. Our ontological position coincides with DOR (see [7, 37, 40]), which separates theory from understanding of individuals through Popper's [41] three worlds classification. He discerns an objective/material (1), from a subjective/ mental (2), and an abstract world (3). The latter embraces human-made entities, e.g. language, theories, models, and constructs. According to this view, artifacts instantiations are part of world 1, abstract knowledge is part of world 3 and ideas and experiences of design science researchers belong to world 2 [12].

3.2   Types of Knowledge Contribution in DOR

In order to structure and understand better KC from DOR, we considered publications which addressed topics such as design knowledge, theory development or theorizing in DOR as well as knowledge contribution itself [7, 12, 21, 32, 40, 42–44]. Additionally, we investigated DOR procedure models, as presented in Sect. 2.2, and possible KC mentioned by them. In the end, a set of types of KC were identified, as exemplified in Table 2.

Table 2. Examples of knowledge contributions from DOR identified on the review

Examples of KC from DOR
Constructs, statements of relationship, causal explanations, testable propositions (hypothesis), prescriptive statements, frameworks, classification schema, taxonomies [7]
Patterns, principles, laws of a phenomenon [12]
Observational, predictive and explanatory statements [37]
Instantiated artefacts, empirical data and data triggers (e.g. interview questions and observation protocols); models that works only in a specific situation [45]
Constructs, models, methods and instantiations [29]
[29], evaluation methods and metrics [11]
[29], design principles and technological rules, design theory [12]
Instantiations, design principles, technological rules [24]
Descriptive knowledge, hypotheses, mechanisms, conceptual knowledge (ontologies, concepts or constructs) [13]

The authors of this paper worked together in a set of discussion rounds to clarify the similarities and differences of the identified KC. Relying on Gregor and Hevner [12], our first insight was to classify KC according to descriptive and prescriptive knowledge. While this was a feasible alternative, we also realized that some of the KC differ according to its level of abstractness, i.e. some KC are context-related or data-driven while others are more abstracts or theory-driven, e.g. theories [45, 46]. Therefore, we propose four dimensions for a KC typology: descriptive, prescriptive, situational and abstract.

Descriptive vs. Prescriptive Knowledge. Based on Aristotle's terms "episteme" and "techne", Gregor and Hevner [12] suggest to classify knowledge as descriptive and prescriptive. Descriptive knowledge describes natural, artificial and human phenomena as well as relationships among them. By classifying, observing, measuring and cataloging, these descriptions can be made accessible to the human mind [47]. Prescriptive knowledge addresses artifacts created to improve reality. Gregor and Hevner [12] have added design theories arguing that they are formed from prescriptive knowledge that can also include other types of knowledge. In this sense, while prescriptive research focuses on improvement through the "how" knowledge, descriptive research focus on understanding via the "what" knowledge [12, 29, 36]. Yet, descriptive knowledge might evolve into prescriptive knowledge, e.g., when explanatory statements are combined with goals into prescriptive statements [48] or when little is known about the phenomena and classification schema or taxonomies [7] prompt future research.

Situational vs. Abstract Knowledge. Goldkuhl and Lind [45] proposed to classify DOR-related knowledge as abstract versus situational. Abstract knowledge refers to general knowledge enhancing understanding phenomena so that this knowledge can be used as foundation for DOR in a variety of contexts. Situational knowledge refers to specific knowledge generated in specific contexts and produced during empirical design practice. In this sense, a set of data about single facts are generated by not yet considered theory, although they might be foundations for future theories [7]. Against this background, situational outcomes are more empirical outcomes or exploratory results. Abstract knowledge embraces design theories but also other knowledge contributions developed throughout iterative cycles of (i) generation and validation of knowledge and (ii) between different types of knowledge sources, such as empirical data, design theory, other knowledge and theories [17, 45]. Abstract knowledge can be extracted from as well as empirically grounded in situational knowledge and adapted to be applied in situational contexts, which might lead to modification of the abstract knowledge. On the other hand, situational knowledge is grounded in abstract knowledge and can also evolve into generalized abstract knowledge [45].

Both attempts to classify knowledge, i.e. the descriptive vs. prescriptive as well as the situational vs. abstract dichotomies, share much in spirit yet differ in important ways. In terms of similarity, both ideas allow that a focal project uses and generates both types of knowledge per respective dichotomy and that cumulative research helps to develop one type of knowledge out of the other. In terms of differences, the dichotomies refer to different claims. Where prescriptive (P) vs. descriptive (D) addresses the knowledge base on DOR [7], situational (S) vs. abstract (A) is more concerned with the knowledge reach (design knowledge of a specific context or more generalizable) but less with whether that is prescriptive or descriptive. In this sense, synthesis of both views helps to systematically understand and classify knowledge generated in DOR, therefore supporting to answer our second research question.

After defining dimensions for a KC typology, we separately placed the set of identified KC into the typology to be sure that the four dimensions could comprise all types properly. In another round of discussion, we compared the individual classifications and discussed them until we found a common decision. Figure 1 presents the result of this discussion by illustrating examples of different knowledge contribution types classified according to the KC typology.

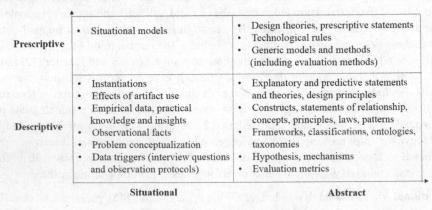

Fig. 1. Typology of KC from DOR

3.3   Communication of Knowledge Contributions: The PDSA Framework

As KC in DOR emerge throughout a research process, it is important to consider time when classifying and presenting them. To this end, we introduce a framework drawing

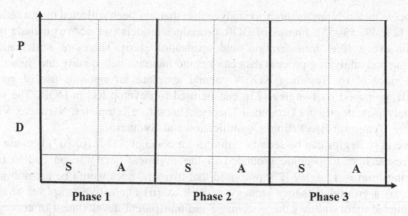

Fig. 2. PDSA framework

on the aforementioned typology and incorporate the time dimension, represented by the phases of a DOR project. Figure 2 shows the framework.

The procedure models for DOR cover different number of phases and labelling. For Peffers et al. [15], phase 1 is "problem identification and motivation", phase 2 "definition of the objectives for a solution", phase 3 "design and development", phase 4 "demonstration", phase 5 "evaluation" and phase 6 "communication". For Sein et al. [26], phase 1 is "problem formulation", phase 2 "building, intervention and evaluation", phase 3 "reflection and learning" and phase 4 "formalization of learning". Therefore, the three phases showed in Fig. 2 have illustrative purposes.

Figure 2 provides a backdrop to propose means to communicate KC in DOR. As scholars generally see DOR as a process [13–15, 24, 26], KC likely emerge through phases like those in Fig. 2. Moreover, as they emerge through these phases, they likely fall into different quadrants over time. Providing transparency about these dynamics, we believe, is central to clearly communicate KC in DOR and support the reuse and accumulation of knowledge over time.

4 Development of Knowledge Contributions from Empirical Data: Potentials of Qualitative Process Methods

In this section, we draw on templates for analyzing process data in order to suggest a frame of reference for how DOR researchers could develop KC especially in DOR covering empirical cases. In doing so, we draw on qualitative process methods [23, 49], prominent in behavioral IS and management studies [50, 51] but comparatively under-utilized in DOR [52]. By doing that, we follow the suggestion of Mandviwalla [24], who proposed the use of these methods to develop design theory. Design theory not only represents the prominent KC generated in DOR, but may also represent the final outcome of knowledge accumulation steps throughout several projects and publications. Our intention is to show that such methods do not only help to develop design theory, but also other types of KC.

Process methods are methods to analyze data that has been collected over a series of events [23, 49, 53–55]. Phases of DOR procedure models (see above) include many potential events like 'formalization' and 'evaluation' [26]. Therefore, systematically collecting and analyzing process data can help to increase data quality and, hence, the overall rigor of the resulting KC. A general template for rigorous use of process methods, proposed by Langley [23], can be used to develop KC in DOR. The seven data analysis strategies are Grounded Theory, Alternative Templates, Narrative, Visual Mapping, Temporal Bracketing, Quantification and Synthesis.

Several strategies can be seen as "sources for concepts" [23] (p. 707) because they allow researchers to become grounded in the empirical phenomenon and to begin theorizing from it. Langley [23] proposed that two strategies would be helpful in this regard: (i) a grounded theory strategy as well as (ii) alternative templates strategy. (i) Grounded theory allows the systematic and transparent development of conceptual categories from the empirical data. The alternative templates strategy (ii) is more deductive in that it proposes to use different pre-existing theoretical premises to explain data and assess which premise performs best [23]. As such, these two strategies have a lot in common with the process of formalizing problems in DOR.

Even though they did not use this language, Giessmann and Legner [56] seemed close to the grounded theory approach since they engaged with the field to formalize the design problem as prescribed by Sein et al. [26]. In contrast, Peters et al. [57] surveyed existing literature, i.e. theoretical templates, to justify their solution. Accordingly, the source chosen to formalize or ground a problem in DOR depends on the individual study. This coincides with Gregor and Hevner's [12] proposal that different types of problems imply KC that differ in scope. However, how to assess that scope is a relatively under-developed in DOR. Hence, reliance on a more standardized procedure could help to increase validity and transparency in qualitative DOR.

The organization of data can be seen as a crucial step in DOR. With organizing data, Langley [23] refers to means of "descriptively representing process data in a systematic organized form." We believe that such systematic engagement with the data is important when researchers build artifacts, intervene in the field and evaluate outcomes of this intervention. At this stage, numerous encounters with the field happen, and empirical data gathered in this encounters affect the formulation of KC [17, 20, 36]. Thus, a transparent and organized way to report on the development of the processes of building, intervening and evaluating could help external audiences to trace how immersion with the field affected KC. Two other strategies could help here: (iii) a narrative strategy as well as a (iv) visual mapping strategy [23].

The narrative strategy (iii) comprises writing a detailed narrative about the research process to provide numerous contextual details about how a DOR process unfolded, putting more focus on the situational knowledge. This level of detail can help to disentangle which encounters affected the formulation of KC in a highly granular manner. The visual mapping strategy (iv) is more reductionist. While narratives capture many details in words, visual maps are abstract representations of the building, intervention and evaluation processes that took place. Such maps should include clear denominations, i.e. "arrows and boxes", effects of one element on another (positive/negative) as well as brief descriptions of the involved elements. Both strategies could also be used in high and low n studies. For n > 1, it seems possible to compare narratives and visual maps across cases in order to search for regularities. For n = 1 narratives and maps could be compared across design cycles in the form of within-case analysis. Practically, narratives and maps could be made available as research supplements, which would increase transparency over the process of developing KC.

Because increasing attention has been paid to formalizing KC and making them replicable and testable [3, 24], it is important to understand how qualitative methods can serve this purpose. In this context, three of Langley's [23] strategies can be helpful: (v) temporal bracketing, (vi) quantification as well as (vii) synthesis. Temporal bracketing (v) means to structure a DOR process into distinct phases, which arise due to a "certain continuity in the activities within each period and there are certain discontinuities at its frontiers" [23] (p. 703). Temporal bracketing is in a sense evident in DOR procedure models since labels such "building, intervention, evaluation" [23] (p. 559) are used to structure the process. This provides a significant opportunity for replicating DOR studies because if researchers document how each phase affected the development of the KC (for example by visual maps), other researchers could replicate studies or modify them by bringing them to other contexts or by holding certain factors constant while variating others. This may not be a 'hard control' in the statistical sense but nonetheless an insightful inquiry into the maturity of KC that allows to assess whether these are 'design theories' or 'design principles' [12].

The quantification strategy (vi) fosters quantitative analysis of the data and, hence, formalization of design principles as hypotheses that enable testing and replication. Specifically, this strategy involves systematically coding the data, for example visual maps or narratives, according to sets of pre-defined codes, which could be results of the formalization phase. For process theorists [23, 49, 53–55], one important coding in this regard is to capture whether intended changes in each phase of the process really occurred. This ties in nicely with high-level KC, i.e. design theory, because theoretical predispositions about why a design should work can be coded as well as whether the design really had such outcomes. This involves tests of the design propositions and thus yields more robust propositions as outcomes. Therefore, this is a means to formalize qualitative DOR and make it conducive to replication.

The last strategy, synthesis (vii), is related to quantification, perhaps most reductionist and least suited for low n case. Synthesis "attempts to construct global measures from the detailed event data" [23] (p. 704). The main goal of this approach is to identify larger regularities across processes that allows the formulation of a more predictive theory in the statistical sense. Thus, this approach aims to synthesize qualitative process data into a more abstract statement on how certain independent variables affect dependent variables. This could be done if sufficient information is available (like narratives or visual from multiple cases). For this reason, this approach is the most suitable in terms of making a qualitative design theory generalizable.

Through the description of these strategies, we attempted to unpack that qualitative process methods [23] have potentials to inform how DOR develops KC. Next, in order to illustrate how the PDSA framework can communicate DOR knowledge as well as how qualitative processes methods can be used to develop KC from empirical data, we present an illustrative case.

5 Development and Communication of KC: Illustrative Case

To illustrate our contributions, a published DOR by Ebel et al. [58] was chosen after a literature search on development of design theories from empirical cases. Search of relevant literature was done using the template by von Brocke et al. [59] in the journals listed in the AIS' "Basket of Eight". Because of space constrains, we only mention the 11 papers selected: [5, 21, 34, 35, 56–58, 60–63]. Ebel et al. [58] is an interesting example of empirical data use in different phases of a DOR project as well as for the communication of KC in the "formalization of learning" phase.

In order to illustrate the use of the framework in this case, each of the DOR phases are briefly explained and a number is given for the sequence of activities carried out within these phases. Subsequently, in order to understand the development of KC from empirical data, an analysis of the situated knowledge is done with the goals to present how deep this knowledge was addressed, how it was presented and similarities and opportunities of developing it according to Langley's [23] strategies.

5.1 Communication of KC: Application of the PDSA Framework

Drawing on action design research, Ebel et al. [58] developed a solution for systematically designing business models based on theoretical and empirical knowledge about business models. Figure 3 shows the application of the PDSA framework to their study. Note that despite the fact that Sein et al. [26] suggest to carry out the phases development and evaluation together, we separate them for illustrative purposes, i.e. to better represent the time sequence of activities and the KC emerging from them.

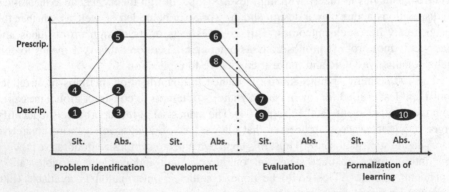

Fig. 3. DOR from Ebel et al. [54] applied in the PDSA framework

Problem identification was done by reviewing the existing product portfolio of a specific company (1) and investigating literature. Both led to the formulation of a set of processes relevant to develop and manage business models (2) as well as identification of gaps in the literature (3). Aiming to assess the processes they developed as well as to contribute to the literature, interviews with experts were performed using semi-structured questionnaires (4). Analysis of this data occurred in three phases: immersion, reduction and interpretation. During immersion, data were transcribed and analyzed. In the reduction phase, data was reduced to what was considered relevant to the research. To reach that, a coding scheme and codebook were created in order to enable the rearrangement of data into meaningful categories. The process of creating the codes are explained in detail, however the data itself was not presented. During interpretation, codes were then used to reassemble data in a coherently and concisely. From the analysis, the authors stated they could confirm the processes they developed in (2).

In order to build their artifact, kernel theories used to solve similar problems were investigated (5). Next steps concerned the creation of an alpha-version (6) and its evaluation within an organizational setting (7) drawing on 27 test users. With the aim of evaluating the usability of the artefact, the Questionnaire for User Interaction Satisfaction (QUIS) was used and the data analyzed through an independent-samples t-test (M > 5). Some insights of the evaluation are given: "... a major weakness of the artifacts is that the used terminology does not relate well to the work situation..."; "[t]he testers also criticized the system as being too dull (...) and too rigid to cope with their needs" (p. 17). When reporting the refinement of the functionalities, the authors described how they improved the tool (8) according to the weaknesses pointed out during the first evaluation. The second evaluation (9) aimed at assessing the tool efficacy. To this end, six project teams were formed with the goal of developing business models with the tool. Based on literature, six dimensions (novelty, originality, feasibility, acceptability, effectiveness and elaboration) were used to assess the results.

In "formalization of learning", two aspects of the framework that extend the existing literature were pointed out: the shared material sections and the community Section (10). While the former includes guides on how people from outside the project can contribute to the design of the business model, the first provides training material to support the development of business models. Finally, by stating, "the artefact itself produces knowledge as constructs and instantiations that may or may not lead to the level of abstraction that constitutes a design theory" (p. 26), the authors concluded that they created three major contributions to the knowledge base for the specific problem domain. A conceptual classification (2), which is "...descriptive knowledge in the problem domain" (p. 26), additional descriptive knowledge that extends current literature (10) and the development of a framework to create business models, a nascent design theory (8), cover these contributions.

5.2 Development of KC from Empirical Data: Qualitative Process Methods

Despite the sophisticated use of data in DOR, it seems sometimes difficult to build on earlier studies because little is known about how data was used. In terms of this study in particular, situated knowledge is generated in problem identification (1), through expert interviews (4), as well as evaluation (7, 9) and it is here were use of Langley's [23] strategies could amplify transparency. For example, details of the problem identification (1) can be made more widely known through either using grounded theory or alternative templates. Choice between the two likely varies with maturity of design theorizing in a particular domain, as more mature domains are likely to offer more firmly established templates to identify and analyze problems. In case of developing 'nascent' design theories, grounded theory is likely helpful as 'nascence' of design theories indicates that they were developed in partially unknown contexts that become more known through the nascent design theory.

Similarly, regarding evaluation with experts (4), while this particular study explains the coding process, it does provide little insights on data itself. While insights gathered from interviews are presented, they lack links to the raw data. It is interesting that provision of such links seems key for papers in behavioral IS, which implies that it should also be seen as such in the DOR context. To facilitate the formulation of these links, we propose the use of narratives or visual mapping. Narratives may accrue more to cases that began with grounded theory while visual mapping may facilitate to show how codes, which were developed from literature [58], can be related to each other on the basis of the analysis of empirical material. This could help to show how comments made in interviews converged towards KC. Concerning evaluation (7; 9), a statistical analysis is presented, which suggests that linking earlier, more qualitative insights to the 'synthesis' strategy [23] could be helpful to also use mixed-methods in DOR.

6 Discussion

Within this article, we highlighted the role of designing and communicating KC in DOR, a current gap in the literature [12, 17, 37]. Our first contribution is the PDSA framework, suitable to systematically communicate KC from the entire DOR process. PDSA goes beyond existing research by synthesizing somewhat isolated understandings of knowledge contributions in DOR (e.g. [12, 45]) and by providing a backdrop to map and understand how KC emerge over time. In addition, by considering the time dimension, the framework can be used complementary to different existing procedure models in DOR. The second contribution of this study is to offer suggestions on how to develop KC from empirical data. To this end, we leveraged the techniques for analyzing qualitative process data proposed by Langley [23] and pointed out that these can be used to report how empirical data was collected and analyzed. Through a somewhat more formalized approach to justify KC generated from empirical data, we hope to offer a toolkit that enables researchers to more easily explicate and document what they did, how they did it, and what the limitations of these approaches were. In turn, this will enable audiences to better assess the rigor of KC emerging from DOR.

While hopefully thought provoking, our work is not without limitations. First, our work has not been formally evaluated, a limitation that needs to be overcome in the future. In addition, only one application of the framework is presented, despite the fact that we applied it in several of the papers selected from the literature review. Therefore, we see multiple options for future research. By increasing the number of illustrative cases to which the framework is applied, we can find associations between types of KC in different phases of DOR. For instance, we can depict how descriptive and situational knowledge of one phase is linked to abstract and prescriptive knowledge in another. Therefore, the framework may be helpful in specifying the role, validity, and boundary conditions of these associations. Furthermore, it may enable us to explore patterns for

KC developed, methods applied, and quality standards in their evaluation in accordance with different research aims, e.g. varying artifacts.

References

1. Walls, J.G., Widmeyer, G.R., El Sawy, O.A.: Building an information system design theory for vigilant EIS. Inf. Syst. Res. **3**, 36–59 (1992)
2. Markus, M.L., Majchrzak, A., Gasser, L.: A design theory for systems that support emergent knowledge processes. MIS Q. **26**, 179–212 (2002)
3. Jones, D., Gregor, S., Jones, D., Gregor, S.: The anatomy of a design theory. J. Assoc. Inf. Syst. **8**, 312–335 (2007)
4. Lindgren, R., Henfridsson, O., Schultze, U.: Design principles for competence management systems: a synthesis of an action research study. MIS Q. **28**, 435–472 (2004)
5. Germonprez, M., Hovorka, D., Gal, U.: Secondary design: a case of behavioral design science research. J. Assoc. Inf. Syst. **12**, 662–683 (2011)
6. Davison, R.M., Martinsons, M.G., Ou, C.X.J.: The roles of theory in canonical action research. MIS Q. **36**, 763–786 (2012)
7. Gregor, S.: The nature of theory in information systems. MIS Q. **30**, 611–642 (2006)
8. Zmud, B.: Editor's comments. MIS Q. **20**, 257 (1996)
9. Davison, R.M., Martinsons, M.G., Kock, N.: Principles of canonical action research. Inf. Syst. J. **14**, 65–86 (2004)
10. Straub, D., Ang, S.: Editor's comments: rigor and relevance in IS research: redefining the debate. MIS Q. **35**, ii–xi (2011)
11. Hevner, A.R., March, S.T., Park, J., Ram, S.: Design science in information systems research. MIS Q. **28**, 75–105 (2004)
12. Gregor, S., Hevner, A.R.: Positioning and presenting design science research for maximum impact. MIS Q. **37**, 337–355 (2013)
13. Nunamaker, J., Chen, M., Purdin, T.: Systems development in information systems research. J. Manag. Inf. Syst. **7**(3), 89–106 (1990)
14. Hevner, A.R.: A three cycle view of design science research. Scand. J. Inf. Syst. **19**, 87–92 (2007)
15. Peffers, K., Tuunanen, T., Rothenberger, M.A., Chatterjee, S.: A design science research methodology for information systems research. J. Manag. Inf. Syst. **24**, 45–77 (2007)
16. Pries-Heje, J., Baskerville, R.L., Venable, J.R.: Strategies for design science research evaluation. Eur. Conf. Inf. Syst. Pap. **87**, 1–13 (2008)
17. Venable, J., Pries-Heje, J., Baskerville, R.: A comprehensive framework for evaluation in design science research. In: Peffers, K., Rothenberger, M., Kuechler, B. (eds.) DESRIST 2012. LNCS, vol. 7286, pp. 423–438. Springer, Heidelberg (2012). doi:10.1007/978-3-642-29863-9_31
18. Venable, J., Pries-Heje, J., Baskerville, R.: FEDS: a framework for evaluation in design science research. Eur. J. Inf. Syst. **25**, 77–89 (2016)
19. Chandra, L., Seidel, S., Gregor, S.: Prescriptive knowledge in IS research: conceptualizing design principles in terms of materiality, action, and boundary conditions. In: 2015 48th Hawaii International Conference on System Sciences (HICSS), pp. 4039–4048 (2015)
20. Winter, R.: Design science research in Europe. Eur. J. Inf. Syst. **17**, 470–475 (2008)
21. Gregory, R.W., Muntermann, J.: Heuristic theorizing: proactively generating design theories. Inf. Syst. Res. **25**, 639–653 (2014)

22. Niehaves, B., Ortbach, K.: The inner and the outer model in explanatory design theory: the case of designing electronic feedback systems. Eur. J. Inf. Syst. **25**, 303–316 (2016)
23. Langley, A.: Strategies for theorizing from process data. Acad. Manag. Rev. **24**, 691–710 (1999)
24. Mandviwalla, M.: Generating and justifying design theory. J. Assoc. Inf. Syst. **16**, 314–344 (2015)
25. Gregory, R.W.: Design science research and the grounded theory method: characteristics, differences, and complementary uses. In: Theory-Guided Model Empiricism Information Systems Research, pp. 111–127 (2011)
26. Sein, M.K., Henfridsson, O., Purao, S., Rossi, M., Lindgren, R.: Action design research. MIS Q. **35**, 37–56 (2011)
27. Baskerville, R.: What design science is not. Eur. J. Inf. Syst. **17**, 441–443 (2008)
28. Cross, N.: Designerly ways of knowing: design discipline versus design science. Des. Issues **17**, 49–55 (2001)
29. March, S.T., Smith, G.F.: Design and natural science research on information technology. Decis. Support Syst. **15**, 251–266 (1995)
30. Iivari, J.: Distinguishing and contrasting two strategies for design science research. Eur. J. Inf. Syst. **24**, 107–115 (2015)
31. Österle, H., Becker, J., Frank, U., Hess, T., Karagiannis, D., Krcmar, H., Loos, P., Mertens, P., Oberweis, A., Sinz, E.J.: Memorandum on design-oriented information systems research. Eur. J. Inf. Syst. **20**, 7–10 (2011)
32. Kuechler, W., Vaishnavi, V.: A framework for theory development in design science research: multiple perspectives. J. Assoc. Inf. Syst. **13**, 395–423 (2012)
33. Merton, R.K.: Social Theory and Social Structure. The Free Press, New York (1968)
34. Kuechler, B., Vaishnavi, V.: On theory development in design science research: anatomy of a research project. Eur. J. Inf. Syst. **17**, 489–504 (2008)
35. Pries-Heje, J., Baskerville, R.: The design theory nexus. MIS Q. **32**, 731–755 (2008)
36. Baskerville, R., Pries-Heje, J.: Explanatory design theory. Bus. Inf. Syst. Eng. **2**, 271–282 (2010)
37. Iivari, J.: A paradigmatic analysis of information systems as a design science. Scand. J. Inf. Syst. **19**, 39–64 (2007)
38. Bunge, M.: Scientific Research II. The Search for Truth. Springer, New York (1967)
39. Purao, S.: Design research in the technology of information systems: truth or dare. Pennsylvania State University (2002)
40. Gregor, S., Jones, D.: The anatomy of a design theory. J. Assoc. Inf. Syst. **8**, 313–335 (2007)
41. Popper, K.: Unended Quest an Intellectual Autobiography. Fontana, Glasgow (1986)
42. William, K., Vijay, V.: A framework for theory development in design science research: multiple perspectives science research: multiple perspectives. J. Assoc. Inf. **13**, 395–423 (2007)
43. Beck, R., Weber, S., Gregory, R.W.: Theory-generating design science research. Inf. Syst. Front. **15**, 637–651 (2013)
44. Holmstrom, J., Tuunanen, T., Kauremaa, J.: Logic for accumulation of design science research theory. In: 2014 47th Hawaii International Conference on System Sciences, pp. 3697–3706. IEEE (2014)
45. Goldkuhl, G., Lind, M.: A multi-grounded design research process. In: Winter, R., Zhao, J.L., Aier, S. (eds.) DESRIST 2010. LNCS, vol. 6105, pp. 45–60. Springer, Heidelberg (2010). doi:10.1007/978-3-642-13335-0_4
46. Fischer, C., Gregor, S., Aier, S.: Forms of discovery for design knowledge. In: Proceedings of the ECIS 2012, p. 64 (2012)

47. Nagel, E.: The Structure of Science Problems in the Logic of Scientific Explanation. Hackett Publishing Co., Indianapolis (1979)
48. Goldkuhl, G.: Design theories in information systems – a need for multi-grounding. J. Inf. Technol. Appl. **6**, 59–72 (2004)
49. Langley, A., Smallman, C., Tsoukas, H., Van de Ven, A.H.: Process studies of change in organization and management: unveiling temporality, activity, and flow. Acad. Manag. J. **56**, 1–13 (2013)
50. Pozzebon, M., Pinsonneault, A.: Challenges in conducting empirical work using structuration theory: learning from it research. Organ. Stud. **26**, 1353–1376 (2005)
51. Ortiz de Guinea, A., Webster, J.: Overcoming variance and process distinctions in information systems research. In: Proceedings of the 35th ICIS, Auckland, NZ (2014)
52. Adomavicius, G., Bockstedt, J.C., Gupta, A., Kauffman, R.J.: Making sense of technology trends in the information technology landscape: a design science approach. MIS Q. **32**, 779–809 (2008)
53. Van de Ven, A.H., Poole, M.S.: Methods for studying innovation development in the minnesota innovation research program. Organ. Sci. **1**, 313–335 (1990)
54. Van de Ven, A.H., Poole, M.S.: Explaining development and change in organizations. Acad. Manag. Rev. **20**, 510–540 (1995)
55. Van de Ven, A.H., Poole, M.S.: Alternative approaches for studying organizational change. Organ. Stud. **26**, 1377–1404 (2005)
56. Giessmann, A., Legner, C.: Designing business models for cloud platforms. Inf. Syst. J. **26**, 551–579 (2016)
57. Peters, C., Blohm, I., Leimeister, J.M.: Anatomy of successful business models for complex services: insights from the telemedicine field. J. Manag. Inf. Syst. **32**, 75–104 (2015)
58. Ebel, P., Bretschneider, U., Leimeister, J.M.: Leveraging virtual business model innovation: a framework for designing business model development tools. Inf. Syst. J. **26**, 519–550 (2016)
59. von Brocke, J., Simons, A., Niehaves, B., Riemer, K., Plattfaut, R., Cleven, A.: Reconstructing the giant: on the importance of rigour in documenting the literature search process. In: 17th European Conference on Information Systems, vol. 9, pp. 2206–2217 (2009)
60. Gregor, S., Imran, A., Turner, T.: A "sweet spot" change strategy for a least developed country: leveraging e-Government in Bangladesh. Eur. J. Inf. Syst. **23**, 655–671 (2014)
61. Papas, N., O'Keefe, R.M., Seltsikas, P.: The action research vs design science debate: reflections from an intervention in eGovernment. Eur. J. Inf. Syst. **21**, 147–159 (2012)
62. Rosenkranz, C., Holten, R., Räkers, M., Behrmann, W.: Supporting the design of data integration requirements during the development of data warehouses: a communication theory-based approach. Eur. J. Inf. Syst. **0**, 1–33 (2015)
63. Spagnoletti, P., Resca, A., Sæbø, Ø.: Design for social media engagement: insights from elderly care assistance. J. Strateg. Inf. Syst. **24**, 128–145 (2015)

Insights into Practitioner Design Science Research

Tadhg Nagle[1]([⊠]), David Sammon[1], and Cathal Doyle[2]

[1] Cork University Business School, Cork, Ireland
t.nagle@ucc.ie
[2] Victoria University of Wellington, Wellington, New Zealand

Abstract. Building on two previous papers that focused on the concept of Practitioner Design Science Research [1, 2], this paper: (i) presents the Practitioners Design Science Research (PDSR) Canvas, a visual guide for practitioners undertaking DSR, and (ii) utilises it as a lens to analyse the insights of 48 practitioners on their DSR journey. Data is primarily gathered from 48 practitioners, of which, 34 have completed a 12-month Design Science Research study, with the other 14 in the final stages of their journey. This unique practitioner perspective further develops the novel concept of PDSR which enables practitioners to engage with the academic community and not the other way around. Key findings show that practitioners have challenges with the practical (relevance) aspects of DSR as well as the research (rigour) aspects. Nonetheless, the analysis indicates that with a clear depiction of DSR, the gap between practice and research may not be as difficult to bridge as previously thought. However, this requires the IS community to rethink their definition of engaged scholarship from one that solely focuses on the academic as the researcher to one that also includes the practitioner.

Keywords: Practitioner research · Design science research · PDSR canvas

1 Introduction

According to Swanson [3] "academic research in the information systems (IS) field is presently under institutional pressure to justify its value by speaking to its actual, not just intended or imagined, impacts on professional practice". Unfortunately, this is not a new phenomenon as in 2006 there was a call to action by a number of IS senior scholars to understand "how to more effectively structure and shape the way that practitioners participate in IS research" [4, p. 343]. But why is this so problematic? One reason noted by Avison *et al.* [5, p. 96], when commenting on Action Research (which associates research and practice) is that "there is a lack of detailed guidelines for novice researchers and practitioners to understand and engage in action research studies in terms of design, process, presentation, and criteria for evaluation". Almost 10 years later, Baskerville [6] in his editorial for the 2008 EJIS special issue on Design Science Research reiterated a similar theme as he stated DSR "is engaged in a discourse of discovery" and void of any "broad agreement on terminology, methodology, evaluation criteria, etc." [6, p. 441]. Some 8 years on (and almost two decades from Avison *et al.*

© Springer International Publishing AG 2017
A. Maedche et al. (Eds.): DESRIST 2017, LNCS 10243, pp. 414–428, 2017.
DOI: 10.1007/978-3-319-59144-5_25

[5]) we are still repeating that same sentiment for DSR, which detailed by Iivari [7, p. 107], notes that "the scientific discourse on DSR is still in a state of conceptual confusion". If this is the case for academics, what chance have practitioners with understanding and engaging in DSR?

To tackle this problem, a guide specifically designed for practitioners was developed (see Fig. 1). The key objective of the canvas is to facilitate a common understanding on the role of research and practice in DSR projects. This is achieved by providing a visual guide with clear language on how to complete a DSR project and a visual template to facilitate communication and collaboration. While a more detailed account of the canvas development is published in an earlier paper [8], this paper utilises the canvas as a lens to analyse the insights of 48 practitioners who have completed or are currently undertaking DSR projects. Data is gathered from two surveys and participant observation of these practitioners undertaking DSR projects. The output of the completed projects has yielded 11 published papers in academic and industry outlets, an estimated €40 million in financial benefits, and 5 of the practitioners have decided to extend their research capability and journey by committing to a part-time PhD, with another 5 in the pipeline.

Building on a wider stream of literature that focuses on the need to bridge the practice-research gap, this paper answers the call of "how to more effectively structure and shape the way that practitioners participate in IS research" [4 p. 343]. As a result, the novel concept of Practitioner Design Science Research (PDSR) is further developed and differentiated from the range of engaged scholarship types as it is primarily aimed at the practitioner undertaking research. For instance, methodologies such as: design science research [9], practice research [10], collaborative practice research [11], and action research [5], all aim to provide the academic community with more effective industry engagement techniques. Moreover, these approaches enable the researcher to become more involved in the practical nature of their areas of expertise and also provide operationalisation guides, which put real world problems at the focal point of academic research [12]. While these approaches have met with a huge degree of popularity they still only view the solution of becoming more relevant as a function of the academic.

2   Guide to Practitioner Design Science Research

Designed with the specific need of facilitating practitioners undertaking DSR, the Practitioner Design Research Canvas evolved from an original focus of clearly depicting the dual imperatives of research and problem solving [13] but was later refined into three parts: (i) clearly depict how rigour and relevance co-exist as an integral part of DSR, (ii) outline both the practical and research tasks to be completed in a DSR project, and (iii) communicate the iterative nature of a DSR project and the philosophy of emergent design with impacts for both research and practice. After two and a half years (see Appendix 1, Table 3 for a summary of its development), the canvas has evolved to the structure seen in Fig. 1. This section details the canvas and provides a basis from which the insights of the practitioners are analysed. The description is structured by the three pillars of the canvas: the practitioner (relevance)

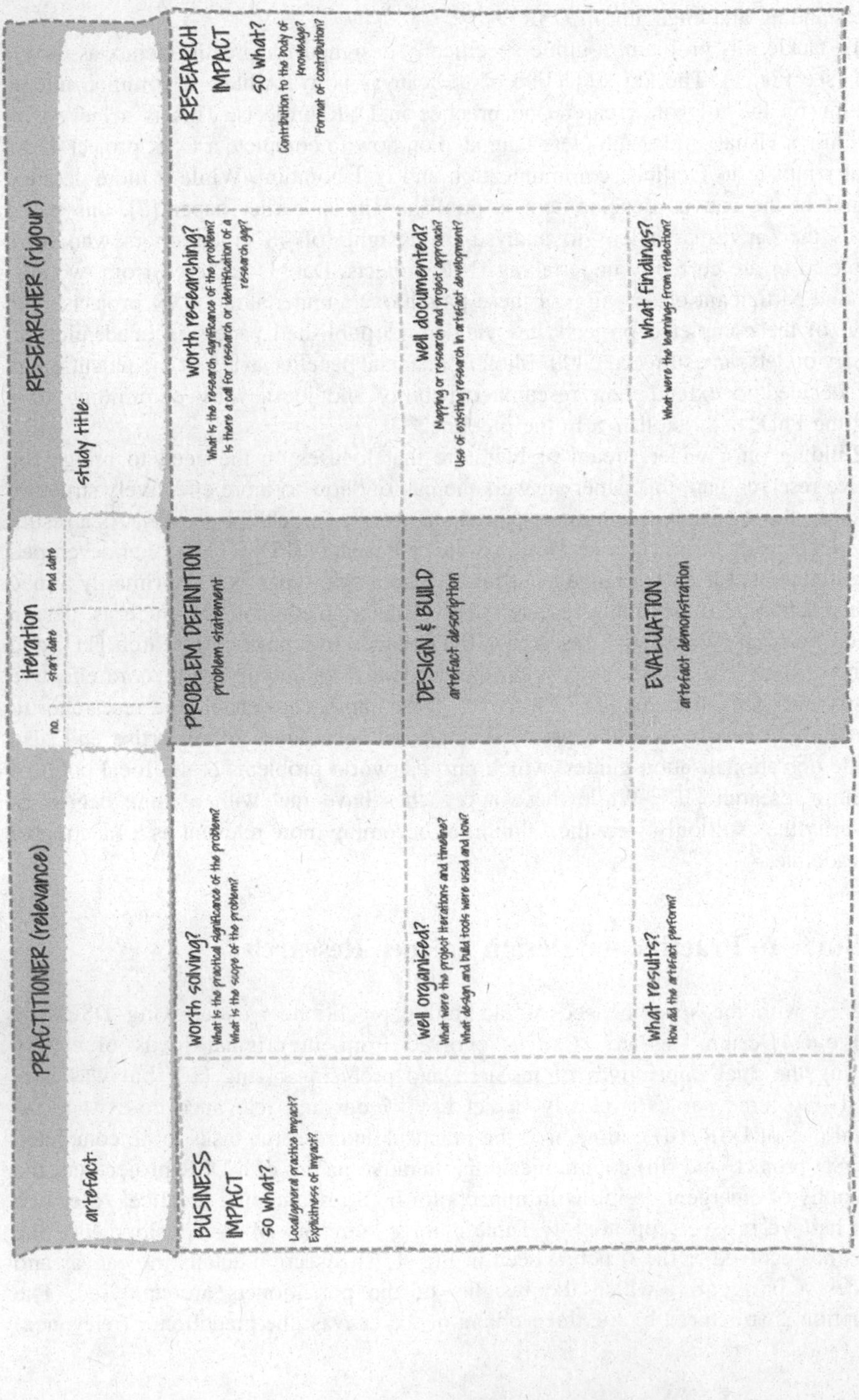

Fig. 1. Practitioner design science research canvas.

pillar, the iteration pillar, and the researcher (rigour) pillar. This is followed by a complete list of supporting questions depicting the DSR tasks required that were validated through literature in DSR and action research domain (see Table 1).

Table 1. Final set of questions with supporting literature.

	Worth solving	
Problem	What is the practical significance of the problem?	Guideline 2: Problem Relevance – "The objective of design-science research is to develop technology-based solutions to important and relevant business problems" [9, p. 83]
	What is the scope of the problem?	Problem needs to be described in a 'holistic fashion' [17, p. 15]
	Worth researching?	
	What is the research significance of the problem?	"When is something really novel or a significant advance on prior work? A DSR project has the potential to make different types and levels of research contributions depending on its starting points in terms of *problem maturity* and *solution maturity*" [19, p. 344]
	Is there a call for the research or identification of a research gap?	In Myers [21] the link between research gap and resulting contribution is made
Design and build	Well organised?	
	What were the project steps, iterations and timeline?	Mathiassen *et al.* [18] highlight the element of "the methods guiding the problem-solving cycle" or M_{PS}
	What design and development frameworks/tools were used and how?	The rigor in design science research must be pursued in the methods employed in the development of the artifact [25]
	Well documented?	
	Was there adherence to a research methods and alignment with project plan?	Mathiassen *et al.* [18] highlight the element of "the methods guiding the research cycle" or M_R
	Was there use of existing research in the artefact development?	"Needs to be informed by principles that both embody a sound theoretical base and are accepted by a research community that supports their reflective and appropriate application in problem contexts" [12, p. 66]
Evaluation	What results?	
	What was the performance of artefact?	Criteria to measure such performance includes: quality of the artefact, utility of the artefact, and efficacy [16]
	What findings?	
	Was there learning from reflection?	Ability to explore through design [22, 23] from which reflection-in-action is key [24]
Impact	So what (for business)?	
	Was there local and/or general practice impact?	Goldkuhl [26] differentiates between local and general practice impact
	What was the explicitness of impact?	Impact can be detailed with four levels of explicitness from observable to financial [20]
	So what (for research)?	

(*continued*)

Table 1. (*continued*)

Worth solving	
What is the contribution to the body of knowledge?	"The main objective is to create knowledge through meaningful solutions that survive rigorous validations through proof of concept, proof of use, and proof of value. Therefore, it is absolutely not a requirement of successful design science manuscripts to have an explicit tie to theory" [25, p. 6]
What is the format of contribution?	Mathiassen *et al.* [18] outlined five contribution formats: (i) experience report, (ii) field study, (iii) theoretical development, (iv) problem-solving method, and (v) research method

Iteration. Being a core aspect to completing DSR, the central pillar sets out to detail the key components of an iteration and incorporates three sections, namely: (i) problem definition, (ii) design and build, and (iii) evaluation, which came from a synthesis of three seminal DSR papers [9, 14, 15]. Focusing on these phases the central pillar provides an area for the core iteration components to be captured, while the rigour and relevance DSR aspects are detailed in the two adjacent pillars. The first section "*Problem Definition*" provides a space to detail the actual problem being solved and with the sub-heading of "problem statement" encouraging its explicit description in the form of a short problem statement. The second section is "*Design and Build*" and emphasises detailing a clear description of the artefact or version of the artefact being developed. This ensures that every iteration has an updated description which should align with the problem statement and provide a basis for setting the evaluation. Finally, the third section is "*Evaluation*" and in line with the steps of Peffers *et al's* methodology [14], 'demonstration' of the artefact is the focus. Guidance on how an evaluation should be planned is provided by Venable *et al.* [16] through their DSR evaluation framework. This allows the context of the evaluation to be discussed before it takes place and documented once decided upon. Evaluation also marks the end of an iteration and once completed should mark the beginning of a new iteration or completion of the project.

Practitioner (Relevance)

The practitioner side of the canvas outlines the components that need to be completed during a DSR project to ensure relevance. It is labelled as "Practitioner" as it contains the aspects of a DSR project that practitioners are most familiar and comfortable with. During the "*Problem Definition*" phase of a DSR project, the key relevance requirement is to ensure that the problem is worth solving. In particular, Hevner *et al.'s* [9, p. 83] Guideline 2 (Problem Relevance) states "the objective of design-science research is to develop technology-based solutions to important and relevant business problems". In addition, for further clarity on the problem and its relevance, it should be described in a 'holistic fashion' [17, p. 15]. For the "*Design and Build*" phase, the practitioner focus is to ensure that the process is well organised. For instance, ensuring there is a clear plan/timeline and outlining the problem solving method [18]. This enables techniques such as agile methods to be included and described as part of the artefact development. From an "*Evaluation*" perspective, the key focus is on the results of the demonstration in relation to the performance of the artefact in solving the problem outlined. Criteria measuring the performance can include: (i) quality, (ii) usability, (iii) efficacy, and (iv) validity [19]. Finally, *"Business Impact"* is highly important because it clearly outlines the practical project contributions in relevant business terminology. For instance, Ward *et al.* [20] outlines four types of explicitness when detailing impacts, namely: (i) financial, quantifiable, measurable, and observable. Using a scale like this or otherwise will provide a clear indication of the impact of the artefact but should also outline where the impact is located, be-it locally within the organisation or at a more general/industry level. In addition, the significance of the component spanning the three phases is to depict the notion that a business impact can come from any of those phases. For instance, the scoping of a problem in itself could unearth potential benefits not seen before the scoping took place.

Researcher (Rigour)

Mirroring the practitioner side of the canvas, the researcher side follows the same principles, but promoting the rigour aspects of a DSR project. Just as *"Problem Definition"* on practitioner side looks at whether the problem is worth solving, the researcher side asks question if the problem is worth researching. To answer this question, Gregor and Hevner [19] developed their problem maturity/solution maturity matrix to determine the research contribution potential from a DSR project. Alternatively, the identification of a research gap or call for research can determine the academic value in researching a particular problem [21]. For the *"Design and Build"* phase, the key rigour focus is on documenting the research process (M_R), which includes the use of: research methods, theories and existing research. Moreover, the mapping of the problem solving method (M_{PS}) and research method (M_R) provides transparency on the alignment and overlapping rigour of each method. For an *"Evaluation"* aspect, the key focus is the findings from reflecting on the DSR process. This type of evaluation is quite different from examining the performance of the artefact as it enables the ability to explore through design [22, 23]. Moreover, to facilitate this type of evaluation, an inductive mind-set and capability for "reflection-in-action" [24] is needed. Finally, the researcher side has *"Research Impact"*, which sets out the contribution to the body of knowledge. Such impact can come from any of the three phases within an iteration. Moreover, an important distinction to make is that the contribution required is to the body of knowledge not necessarily to theory. As stated by Goes [25, p. 6] "it is absolutely not a requirement of successful design science manuscripts to have an explicit tie to theory". However, to ensure contributions are classed correctly the format or style of contribution can be identified using Mathiassen *et al.'s* [18] five contribution formats: (i) experience report, (ii) field study, (iii) theoretical development, (iv) problem-solving method, and (v) research method.

2.1 Canvas Usage

The design of the canvas has evolved to fulfil a number of primary needs for practitioners as they undertake DSR. These needs include: (i) facilitating a common understanding of the role of research and practice in DSR projects, (ii) providing a visual guide with clear language on how to complete a DSR project, and (iii) providing a visual template to facilitate communication and collaboration.

The primary use for the canvas has been to provide a platform for developing a shared understanding on DSR for practitioners. From a very superficial perspective, DSR can look very much like any other project that is executed on a daily basis in industry. This can lead to the misconception that following the same routine will fulfil the requirements of a DSR project. As a result, an understanding on the alignment of research and practice must be first gained before initiating a DSR project. The canvas fulfils this need by providing a mental model from which practitioners can begin to grasp the role of practice and research. By positioning the respective tasks in relation to the central concepts of DSR, it becomes easier to internalise the nature of a DSR project.

Moreover, the canvas provides a visual guide for practitioners for completing a DSR project. Firstly, the canvas provides a simple and visual conceptualisation of all the components of a DSR project and their links to each other. In addition, by using clear and simple language, the definition and role of features such as artefact, evaluation, iterations, and contributions can be operationalised in a more efficient fashion. In using the canvas, it is necessary to complete all the sections of the central pillar for each iteration. However, while the problem has to be defined on the first iteration, upon review in subsequent iterations it may or may not change. In contrast, for the two sides of the canvas it is not necessary to fill out each section for each iteration. For instance, it may not be until iteration 2 or 3 before the research significance of the problem is explored.

Another use of the canvas is to facilitate the communication of the project to interested stakeholders such as: project supervisors (industry/academic), project participants, or future collaborators. Modes of communication can be through the likes of using the canvas as a wall chart onto which sticky notes can be used to record or plan project actions (see Fig. 2 for examples on earlier versions of the canvas). This will primarily involve project supervisors and provide the opportunity to discuss the project's current and future status. The canvas can also be used in the form of a presentation template to facilitate communication to a wider audience.

Fig. 2. Examples of the canvas being used to facilitate communication

3   Research Methodology

Underpinning this research is a longitudinal study, which incorporates data from 48 practitioners over the course of 30 months (still ongoing). Of the 48 practitioners, 34 had completed a 12 month DSR project, with the other 14 in the later stages of completion. The DSR projects were unique to each practitioner and focused on developing artefacts to solve data problems. Examples of the types of artefacts, included: (i) dashboards, (ii) data models, (iii) analytical models, (iv) data strategies, and (v) governance frameworks.

Data was collected through two main methods: (i) participant observation, and (ii) survey. Participant observation was primarily carried out during meetings with the practitioners as they progressed through the DSR process. In these discussions, all aspects of the design research methodology were covered, with particular emphasis on supporting the practitioner achieve a successful outcome. These meetings were an excellent insight into how the practitioners were progressing with the programme, but also into how they were coping with becoming a practitioner-researcher. The meetings amounted to over 150 h of one-to-one/group sessions and were documented in terms of written notes, pictures of white-boarding sessions and follow-up emails. In addition, once the practitioners had completed their DSR project, they were asked to fill out a survey. The survey was in free text format and asked for their views on DSR, namely the key challenges and benefits in going through the process.

Once collected, the data was analysed using the PDSR canvas as a lens. In particular, the data was analysed from two perspectives (i) relevance, and (ii) rigour. Moreover, subcategories within this dichotomy equated to the four outlined components of DSR (problem definition, design and build, evaluation, and impact). Having coded the data to this structure it was then synthesised into Table 3. This further enabled an in depth examination of how practitioners undertake DSR and provided insights into the challenges and benefits of doing so.

4   Findings

This section outlines the resulting findings from the analysis of the data collected. Detailing the challenges and benefits for practitioners undertaking DSR, the findings also provide insights into the role of the academic in facilitating practitioner engagement.

4.1   Relevance Challenges and Benefits

A key relevance challenge for the practitioners when defining if a problem was worth solving was the task of refining the problem. For some this was the first time they went beyond superficial root cause analysis to conduct a rigorous deep dive into the problem. This challenged them in the sense that when it came to DSR it was difficult to grasp if *"you only needed one problem for the whole project or one problem per iteration"*. Moreover, that high level of introspection often put practitioners down paths they had not envisaged, which required them to be very agile in their approach and mind-set. For instance, one practitioner mentioned that "*I found myself changing my approach during the project which I suppose ultimately worked out OK, but was very disconcerting at the time*". However, the key benefit they gained was a number of "*new skills and expertise to consider problems*". In particular, the ability to "*ask the right questions*" while also being "*less inclined to dive into action mode*", demonstrates an increased maturity in taking time to fully understand the problem.

When ensuring the project was well organised (under Design and Build), a key challenge encountered was the alignment of project methodologies, such as agile with the research methodology of DSR. Very similar to the challenge in problem definition, the frequency of agile iterations to DSR iterations was particularly difficult. On the other hand, the benefit gained included an increased ability to solve data problems, which was the focus of all the DSR projects. In addition, the use of DSR along with other project methodologies was deemed useful in keeping the project on track with solving the problem.

From an evaluation perspective, a key challenge was on timing. Practitioners found it difficult to know when they should start evaluating or when an artefact was developed enough to evaluate. This would come from a more traditional waterfall style approach to development where evaluation would always come at the end of development. By promoting the notion of low fidelity artefacts, practitioners began to realise the value of evaluating as early as possible and the range of techniques (formal/informal). One practitioner noted "*it changed the way I think and evaluate*". The benefit was also felt by the organisations of the practitioners as one person noted "*they (the organisation) now understand why I demand rigour*".

From an impact aspect on the relevance side of the canvas, the challenge for the practitioners was the level of evidence needed to support the impact their artefact had. For some, impact would have never been measured after implementation, much less linked back to the original problem. Of concern was the level of insensitivity in some organisations to impact estimates due to a lack of clear and consistent guidelines on impact measurement. Due to the lack of these guidelines, people were able to put any figure on the potential impact with the knowledge that it would never be accurately measured. For others, there was a fear in outlining positive benefits of a project as it would be seen as a current weakness that should have never existed. However, once the practitioners undertook the impact analysis, they found themselves to be "*more critical in evaluating business benefits*" but also uncovering more impacts. For instance, for the last 16 completed projects, a total financial benefit was estimated at €40 million of which 75% was starting to be realised at the time of estimation. In addition, they not only saw the value of a critical assessment of impact at the end of a project, but noted the organisational advantage of doing it at the start of the project.

Finally, it is interesting to note that practitioners have challenges with the practical side of a DSR projects. While they are familiar with managing projects that are focused on solving problems, there seems to be more of an emphasis on action/development tasks and less on problem refinement or critical impact evaluation. Practitioners have no issue with finding problems to solve but don't seem to know if it's the right problem to solve or (in the case that it is) when the problem is solved.

4.2   Rigour Challenges and Benefits

From the research aspect, a key challenge was consuming the literature. Unsurprisingly, one practitioner noted that the *"literature was heavy going"*. In addition, the sourcing of a problem that was worth researching as well as solving was a predictable challenge. However, given that it was a challenge their increased ability to frame or classify problems was noted. This would have come from the requirement of linking a context-specific/local problem to a more generalisable area in literature. Moreover, one practitioner noted the value of doing *"research to see if anyone else solved it or part of it already"*.

When documenting the research being used in the design and build of the artefact, one practitioner noted the challenge in *"leveraging research in a meaningful way"*. However, once familiar with the literature, practitioners appreciated the "value in the existing knowledge base" and the support it provided in *"helping with business problems"*. Moreover, the *"need for documentation"* was often seen as a challenging task, but was overcome quite easily by many through the use of a personal learning journal or through the simple act of writing emails to oneself. For some, they got to realise they were already *"doing research but didn't realise it"*.

It was interesting to note that there was a conscious perception of *"switching mindset from a practitioner to researcher"* during the DSR process, especially in evaluation where they were asked not just to measure the artefact but to reflect on it also. This is itself a major difference from the previous quote which was about *"doing"* DSR versus *"being"* a DSR researcher. However, the benefit from becoming more reflective was noted. For instance, one practitioner learned to not *"settle for the first solution that presents itself"*.

Finally, from an academic impact perspective, the challenge of addressing the contribution to knowledge was highlighted. However, the dual role of practice and research and *"solving a problem and generating knowledge"* was appreciated along with the learning that could be gained from research. Moreover, one interesting benefit that was also mentioned was *"improved writing and storytelling"*, something of vital importance for communicating impacts for the practitioner and academic communities. This ability was further showcased with a yield of 11 published papers in academic and industry outlets. More importantly, 5 of the practitioners have decided to extend their research capability and journey by committing to a part-time PhD, with another 5 in the pipeline.

It is unsurprising to note that the practitioners were challenged with the Researcher (rigour) aspects of DSR. Yet, they were not insurmountable and did provide a lot of benefits once they were overcome. For instance, there is an appetite for research literature, with a value placed on its utilisation in solving real problems. However, when it's hard to consume, it does create an engagement barrier for practitioners. What is also interesting is the fact that some practitioners realised they were already carrying out tasks that were defined as research tasks. This indicates the closeness of DSR to the day-to-day practices, especially as these tasks are located on the researcher side. It also highlights that the gap exists between practice and research within the IS domain may not be that difficult to bridge through the use of DSR. The need to be reflective was also outlined as a challenge, but one that again provided value and marked a changing mind set from practitioner to practitioner-researcher.

Table 2. DSR Challenges and benefits for practitioners

	Practitioner (Relevance)	Researcher (Rigour)
Problem Definition	Challenge: refining the problem	Challenge: research literature hard to consume and finding a suitable problem for research
	Benefit: new skills to consider problems	Benefit: better ability to frame or classify problems
Design and Build	Challenge: aligning project frameworks such as agile with DSR	Challenge: leveraging research in a meaningful way
	Benefit: increased ability to design and build a solution	Benefit: value of existing knowledge base
Evaluation	Challenge: knowing when to start evaluation	Challenge: switching to the mindset of a researcher
	Benefit: better process for evaluating actions	Benefit: being more reflective and objective
Impact	Challenge: the level of evidence needed to demonstrate impact	Challenge: defining contribution to knowledge
	Benefit: more critical in evaluating business impacts	Benefit: improved knowledge dissemination skills

4.3   Role of the Academic in Facilitating Practitioner DSR

As well as observing and reflecting on the challenges and benefits of practitioners, the role of the academic was also examined with particular focus on facilitating the practitioners through the DSR process. In essence, the academic facilitates the practitioner in all aspects of DSR (practitioner and researcher), most of which are formalised in the PDSR canvas and supporting questions/tools. However, there are aspects that are not as easily codified. The following section highlights these aspects to help academics further guide practitioners along the DSR journey.

During the problem definition, the role of the academic mentors facilitated the practitioner by primarily providing an external challenge to the problem defined and the status quo of the organisation. The challenge would mainly come in the form of questioning (i) the value/importance of a problem, (ii) the clarity of its description, or (iii) the cultural norms of the organisation. This facilitated the practitioners in calling out wicked problems in a less unbiased fashion with respect to the local context and practitioners' role. In addition, the academic's knowledge of literature would be leveraged to validate the worthiness of the problem from a research perspective.

While the artefact was being developed, the academic mentors pushed for lo-fi artefacts to enable quicker evaluation and as a result a completed iteration. As already mentioned, the concept and timing of a DSR iteration is a challenge for practitioners. Moreover, this challenge increases the longer a practitioner stays within the first iteration. As a result, the quicker a practitioner gets through an iteration, the quicker they get a handle on the concept of an iteration and how it ties to project methodologies. However, going through an iteration too quickly may result in a poorly defined problem. This in-turn requires a balanced approach. In addition, a key part in facilitating a practitioner doing DSR is to describe the concept of the iteration. The standard understanding of an iteration is that you define the problem, design and build the artefact, and evaluate the artefact (each phase singular in nature). However, a problem can be defined and refined a number of times before a design and build is attempted, multiple versions of an artefact can be built before it is evaluated, and an evaluation can be carried out a number of times. This expands the number of ways in which an iteration can be described from one to eight. More importantly, it allows a more agile approach to completing an iteration and a way of aligning different project methodologies with DSR.

When it comes to evaluation, the academic mentors facilitate a wider range of reflection beyond the performance of the artefact. Such reflection includes: (i) the journey of the practitioner-researcher, (ii) the problem solving process, (iii) the research process, (iv) out of scope impacts, and (v) the surrounding organisational context and culture. The aim is to get the practitioner to look beyond the focus of the solution to appreciate the overall interestingness of the project. Moreover, the ability to communicate this novelty is also facilitated.

Finally, facilitating the practitioner in disseminating project impacts, the academic mentors have provided appropriate channels and opportunities for the practitioners to publish their contributions. These opportunities range from (i) local poster presentations, (ii) international workshops, (iii) special issues in peer reviewed journals, and (iv) co-authorships in industry research outlets. Without providing these opportunities for publication in a format that suits practitioners (e.g. short-form articles and quick publishing cycles), very few of the practitioners would have fully engaged in the dissemination process.

5 Discussion and Conclusion

With access to 48 practitioners undertaking DSR, this paper is unique in the perspective it offers. Indeed, very few papers outside of Mathiassen and Sandberg [27] provide such an insight into practitioners doing IS research. In addition, not only does the paper highlight a successful model of DSR in the form of PDSR, it provides new insights into that success and examines current assumptions around DSR and practitioner engagement.

As expected, finding a problem worth solving was not a challenge for the practitioners, but refining it was. Being such a very practical task, this came as somewhat of a surprise. However, this may be a result of the assumed benefit of being close to the problem area. A characteristic that is paradoxically at the core of DSR [9]. Yet in some cases, practitioners may be too close to the problem area to be objective, or there may be embedded organisational factors that create a culture that does not encourage the calling out of problems in fear of blame or retribution. In contrast, as expected the practitioners did have an issue in resolving the research worthiness of a problem. Difficulty with literature was cited as a key challenge, but once mastered, practitioners appreciated the value of research in their work. This is very positive to hear, as it not only shows an appetite for research, but also a practical appreciation for the research skills/techniques being developed. More specifically, it demonstrated to practitioners that DSR is not just an academic exercise, but has tangible/practical value also. For instance, it not only solved problems of significant extrinsic value, but the practitioners also felt there was intrinsic value in the research techniques they used, which could be applied to their work.

In addition, the success of the practitioners and PDSR indicates the untapped potential of practitioners for the IS research community. In a very welcome and recent call-to-action, Peppard *et al.* [28] highlight the lack of research on the people engaged in "real work" and "actual practices" (p. 3) within an IS strategy context. Their solution is that "researchers will have to get their hands dirty" and deeply immerse themselves in organisations. While wholeheartedly agreeing with this counsel, it doesn't recognise the potential for practitioners in contributing to this resolution. This may be a simple oversight, but it is nonetheless indicative of engaged scholarship in the IS domain [cf. 10]. Moreover, one of the contributions of this paper is that it highlights the potential opportunity that practitioners present to the IS community. Rather than crossing the research-practice divide by focusing entirely on perfecting researcher-led engagement techniques that requires longitudinal immersion, an alternative course of action could be to look at crossing an arguably narrower divide from the practitioner's side. Yet, this is not without it challenges, given the expected style and format by publication outlets in the mainstream IS community.

Appendix

See Table 3

Table 3. Summary of the DSR iterations involved in developing the canvas

	Iteration 1 (May 2014–Jan 2016: 21 months)	Iteration 2 (Feb 2016–July 2016: 6 months)	Iteration 3 (Aug 2016–to-date)
Problem definition	Date: May 2014–Dec 2014	Date: Feb 2016–Mar 2016	Date: July 2016–Aug 2016
	Description: Need to aid practitioners in understanding the dual role (of researcher and practitioner) within DSR projects	Description: After the first iteration, the need was widened to focus on supporting practitioners in conducting DSR projects	Description: Need to support general IS practitioners in conducting DSR projects
Design and build	Date: Jan 2015–Aug 2015	Date: April 2016–May 2016	Date: Aug 2016–Sept 2016
	Description: Built version 1 of the canvas with a focus of enabling practitioners to conduct DSR projects. Key emphasis was to get the practitioners to be mindful the dual role (researcher and practitioner) in DSR and to do more than just routine design	Description: Version 2 of the canvas included a modified structure of that aimed to make it more intuitive to use and aid practitioners to implement the key aspects of DSR	Description: Version 3 (see Fig. 1) of the canvas was designed to align more with the language of DSR in literature and to link to previous research for clear guidelines on how to complete the sections on the canvas (see Table 2). The link to literature was also to make the canvas itself more robust and potentially more consumable by practitioners outside of the reach of the authors
Evaluation	Date: Sept 2015–Jan 2016	Date: June 2016–July 2016	Date: Ongoing
	Data sources: (i) request for comment, (ii) conference paper review, (iii) use in 16 practitioner DSR projects	Data sources: (i) request for comment, (ii) conference presentations, (iii) simulation	Data sources: (i) 14 practitioner DSR projects, (ii) conference presentations to practice research and DSR academic audiences
	Analysis: User evaluation highlighted good usability and impact results. Had issues with the structure and ability of the canvas to represent the iterative nature of design rather than being a waterfall approach ending with contributions as the last phase	Analysis: Expert evaluation highlighted a need for more depth and rigour to verify the emergent structure of the canvas and provide more guidance in utilising the canvas	Analysis: To commence June 2017

References

1. Nagle, T., Sammon, D., Doyle, C.: Meeting in the middle: bridging the practice research divide from both sides. Paper Presented at the European Conference of Information Systems, Istanbul, June 2016
2. Nagle, T., Sammon, D.: The development of a practitioner design science research canvas. Paper Presented at the Pre-ICIS Workshop on Practice-Based Design and Innovation of Digital Artifacts, Dublin (2016)
3. Swanson, E.: A simple research impacts model applied to the information systems field. Commun. Assoc. Inf. Syst. 35(1), 16 (2014)
4. Desouza, K.C., El Sawy, O.A., Galliers, R.D., Loebbecke, C., Watson, R.T.: Beyond rigor and relevance towards responsibility and reverberation: information systems research that really matters. Commun. Assoc. Inf. Syst. 17(1), 341–353 (2006)
5. Avison, D., Lau, F., Myers, M., Nielsen, P.A.: Action research. Commun. ACM 42(1), 94–97 (1999)
6. Baskerville, R.: What design science is not. Eur. J. Inf. Syst. 17(5), 441–443 (2008)
7. Iivari, J.: Distinguishing and contrasting two strategies for design science research. Eur. J. Inf. Syst. 24(1), 107–115 (2015)
8. Nagle, T., Sammon, D.: The development of a design research canvas for data practitioners. J. Dec. Syst. 25(Suppl. 1), 369–380 (2016). doi:10.1080/12460125.2016.1187386
9. Hevner, A., March, S.T., Park, J., Ram, S.: Design science in information systems research. MIS Q. 28(1), 75–105 (2004)
10. Goldkuhl, G.: From action research to practice research. Australas. J. Inf. Syst. 17(2), 57–78 (2012)
11. Mathiassen, L.: Collaborative practice research. Inf. Technol. People 15(4), 321–345 (2002)
12. Davison, R., Martinsons, M.G., Kock, N.: Principles of canonical action research. Inf. Syst. J. 14(1), 65–86 (2004)
13. McKay, J., Marshall, P.: The dual imperatives of action research. Inf. Technol. People 14(1), 46–59 (2001)
14. Peffers, K., Tuunanen, T., Gengler, C.E., Rossi, M., Hui, W., Virtanen, V., Bragge, J.: The design science research process: a model for producing and presenting information systems research. In: S.C., A.H. (eds.) Proceedings of the First International Conference on Design Science Research in Information Systems and Technology (DESRIST 2006), Claremont, California, CGU, pp. 83–106 (2006)
15. Sein, M., Henfridsson, O., Purao, S., Rossi, M., Lindgren, R.: Action design research. MIS Q. 35, 37–56 (2011)
16. Venable, J., Pries-Heje, J., Baskerville, R.: A comprehensive framework for evaluation in design science research. In: Peffers, K., Rothenberger, M., Kuechler, B. (eds.) DESRIST 2012. LNCS, vol. 7286, pp. 423–438. Springer, Heidelberg (2012). doi:10.1007/978-3-642-29863-9_31
17. Baskerville, R.L.: Investigating information systems with action research. Commun. Assoc. Inf. Syst. 2(1), 2–32 (1999)
18. Mathiassen, L., Chiasson, M., Germonprez, M.: Style composition in action research publication. MIS Q. 36(2), 347–363 (2012)
19. Gregor, S., Hevner, A.R.: Positioning and presenting design science research for maximum impact. MIS Q. 37(2), 337–356 (2013)
20. Ward, J., Daniel, E., Peppard, J.: Building better business cases for IT investments. MIS Q. Execut. 7(1), 1–15 (2008)

21. Myers, M.D.: Qualitative Research in Business and Management, 2nd edn. Sage, London (2013)
22. Holmström, J., Ketokivi, M., Hameri, A.P.: Bridging practice and theory: a design science approach. Decis. Sci. **40**(1), 65–87 (2009)
23. Simon, H.A.: Does scientific discovery have a logic? Philos. Sci. **40**(4), 471–480 (1973)
24. Weick, K.E., Sutcliffe, K.M., Obstfeld, D.: Organizing for high reliability: processes of collective mindfulness. In: Research in Organizational Behavior, vol. 21. pp. 81–123 (1999)
25. Goes, P.B.: Editor's comments: design science research in top information systems journals. MIS Q. **38**(1), iii–viii (2014)
26. Goldkuhl, G.: Pragmatism vs interpretivism in qualitative information systems research. Eur. J. Inf. Syst. **21**(2), 135–146 (2012)
27. Mathiassen, L., Sandberg, A.: How a professionally qualified doctoral student bridged the practice-research gap: a confessional account of collaborative practice research. Eur. J. Inf. Syst. **22**(4), 475–492 (2013)
28. Peppard, J., Galliers, R.D., Thorogood, A.: Information systems strategy as practice: micro strategy and strategizing for IS. J. Strateg. Inf. Syst. **23**(1), 1–10 (2014)

Products and Prototypes

Logistics Service Map Prototype

Michael Glöckner[1]([⊠]), Tim Niehoff[1], Benjamin Gaunitz[1], and André Ludwig[2]

[1] Leipzig University, Leipzig, Germany
{gloeckner,gaunitz}@wifa.uni-leipzig.de, niehoff@studserv.uni-leipzig.de
[2] Kühne Logistics University, Hamburg, Germany
andre.ludwig@the-klu.org

Abstract. Concentration on core competencies in logistics requires collaboration between logistics service providers in order to fulfill complex customer demands. The increasing demand for flexibility in logistics is facing the heterogeneity of the providers. This creates a challenging field for planning complex supply chains. Logistics integrators are meeting this challenge. One main issue is the retrieval of the services available in the logistics network and their combination for planning complex supply chains. The prototype presented in this paper supports the retrieval by providing a customizable domain-specific dimension concept for structuring services. With the help of the dimensions and a customizable domain-specific template scheme, a dynamic matrix is created in order to facilitate the retrieval of services matching the selected dimensions. After retrieval, the services can be combined on a canvas via drag and drop in order to plan complex services and simultaneously create both their BPMN diagram and corresponding XML file.

Keywords: Logistics service map · Prototype · Service engineering · Service management · Cloud logistics

1 Introduction

The paradigm of cloud logistics [1] focuses on the combination of logistics services of different logistics service providers (LSP). Based on the concentration on core competencies [2], LSPs have to collaborate in order to fulfill complex customer demands [3]. With a high demand for flexibility on the customer side [4] and a high heterogeneity on the provider side [5], the business model of a 'logistics integrator' (LI) [6] is required to solve the resulting field of tension. Main tasks of the integrator are the retrieval of services available in the logistics network and their combination for planning complex supply chains. Due to the heterogeneity of the services and their description, a common framework requires a high degree of customization. Further, a domain-specific categorization scheme for the structuring of the services is needed in order to facilitate retrieval of suitable services during the planning phase. These issues are taken into account by the *Logistics Service Map* (LSM) [7]. As the LSM is only realized on a conceptual level, this paper's contribution is the incremental advancement of a prototypical implementation by answering the following research question: *How can the concept of the Logistics Service Map be implemented prototypically?*

© Springer International Publishing AG 2017
A. Maedche et al. (Eds.): DESRIST 2017, LNCS 10243, pp. 431–435, 2017.
DOI: 10.1007/978-3-319-59144-5_26

2   Logistics Service Map Prototype Description

The LSM prototype mainly comprises a single page web application for the collaboration of an LI and several LSPs. Customizable concepts of structuring and
visualization support the engineering and management of the logistics services
that are available in a logistics network. In addition to the rather literature-
based functional requirements presented in [1] and the further publications
cited therein, the list of features was extended by empirical-based requirements.
Through workshops with LSP from a logistics network prior to the development
of the prototype, several features were added. Main features are the engineering
of *service templates* that constitute the origin of *services*. The customizable concepts of service templates and *dimensions* are used to structure services. The
management and retrieval of services is realized through a *matrix* as a visual
structured representation that dynamically takes the structuring concepts into
account and facilitates the retrieval of services. The function of combining several services to engineer complex logistics services is essential to the service map
concept. Empirical findings suggested *Business Process Management Notation*
(BPMN) to be the favored way of presenting complex services that shall be used
afterward for process management in the network.

Cooperation with regard to the exchange of information is facing several
issues, such as the LSPs' heterogeneity of IT systems and service description.
The LSM prototype solves this issue by providing a web application, i.e. *cross-
platform solution*, that all network participants can use. Further, different quality levels of service descriptions are an issue. Information gaps can occur that
complicate picking the most suitable services for customers' demand. The LSM
prototype addresses this issue by a shift of responsibility. The LI can create
service templates for certain types of services, e.g. transportation service, with
mandatory and optional attributes. LSP that want to offer their logistics service
through the LSM chose a suitable template and fill in at least the mandatory
information, e.g. mode of transport, area, and range, in order to make their
capability available as a *service* in the LSM. After filling in the attributes, a
new service (e.g. transportation) is created and stored in the database. Hence,
quality standards of the service descriptions can be achieved with regard to the
requirements of the LI. The LSM prototype aims at supporting the management
of the logistics services offered by the participating LSPs. In order to keep track
of a possibly large amount of services, the LSM features a domain driven structuring of services in order to support filtering and visualization of services. For
this issue, the prototype contains a resource named *dimension* that represent
one possible aspect of *services* (e.g. region of provision, range of distance). With
this, the service can be sorted by distinct inherent attributes (e.g. Europe, long
distance). The *matrix* is a table created by selecting two *dimensions* and certain
templates as filters in order to narrow the selection. Underneath the matrix, a
BPMN canvas is integrated. The LI can transfer services from the matrix onto
the canvas easily via drag and drop. *Complex service* that consists of multiple
services can be built, while simultaneously a BPMN diagram and its corresponding XML file are created for further use in other contexts.

The described features and resources can be seen in Fig. 1. The LI, who manages the network and plans the supply chains, is in charge of creating *dimensions* and *service templates* that fit the network's character and the planning style. Afterward, LSPs willing to participate in the network and the inherent supply chains are able to create and submit their *services* to the LSM with the help of mentioned resources. During planning phase, the LI is able to filter and visualize the available submitted services with the help of the *matrix* and to create complex service (in BPMN and XML) with the help of the *BPMN canvas*.

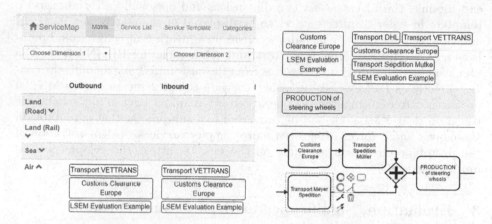

Fig. 1. Screenshot with parts of the prototype. On the left, from top to bottom, are the navigation bar, the *dimension* selection and one top piece of the *matrix* with the *services* represented as radiused rectangles. On the right, from top to bottom, are the bottom piece of the *matrix* and the integrated BPMN editor canvas underneath.

In addition to the identified requirements and features, further non-functional requirements, such as fast development, easy maintenance and customization are defined. Consequently, the *MEAN stack* paradigm [8] is applied to develop the web-based application. This comprises the embedded components MongoDB, Express, AngularJS and Node.js, each supporting Javascript as a single programming language for the whole stack and thus, allows fast development. While MongoDB offers a NoSQL document store to save all the resources, (i.e. services, service templates, and dimensions), the purpose of AngularJS as a front end framework is to build a single page application providing the user interface. In the prototype, Node.js helps to build a back end web server offering a RESTful API along with its framework Express. Thus, a light way of communication between the client and the back end database can be established.

The front end contains three modules to manage the resources, i.e. dimensions, service templates, and services. Each of them features a view to list all resources of the same kind as well as a view to create, update, observe and delete single resources. During creation of service templates it is possible to add mandatory and optional attributes for the creation of services based on these templates as well as the data types of the attributes, i.e. strings, numbers, boolean (via check-boxes and radio-buttons). Further, the prototype allows to inherit attributes, and their state of being mandatory or not, from more general service templates to more specific ones, e.g. attributes from 'transportation service template' are inherited to 'express transportation service template'. During creation of a service, it is necessarily assigned to one of the provided service templates. Thus, all corresponding attributes of the template are shown to the LSP and have to be filled in if mandatory. Before saving a service to the database, required attributes and their data types are validated. In the fourth front end module, the LI can select two dimensions and optionally a certain service template in order to filter services to be displayed in the matrix, see Fig. 1. In addition, the matrix page includes a canvas underneath that comes from bpmn-js as a Javascript rendering framework and web modeler for BPMN 2.0 [9]. The user is able to drag and drop services from the customized matrix onto the canvas directly as BPMN tasks in order to create complex services as BPMN 2.0 processes. After editing, they can be stored as (complex) services in the database based on their XML code and be converted to a sub-process that is reusable in the canvas again for creating even more complex services. A demonstration of the prototype client can be found on the website: https://lldevelopment.wifa. uni-leipzig.de:8093.

3   Evaluation, Significance of Results, and Outlook

The Framework for Evaluation of Design Science Research (FEDS) [10] was applied to the created artifact. Goal is to show its usefulness with the help of a 'Quick & Simple' strategy. The evaluated properties, which have been chosen to be proved by a group of logistics experts, are usability, flexibility, and comprehensibility. The group of four experts had to model logistics services given by written service descriptions and to create a complex logistics service consisting of some of the given services. Finally, an XML file of the complex service for BPMN had to be produced. The evaluation group rated the properties to be fulfilled partly as *comprehensibility* was marked to have further potential. This resulted from the fact that the users first had to acquaint themselves with the structuring approach of the features template, dimension and category. After explaining the features, the properties *flexibility* and *usability* of the prototype were rated high. As a consequence, a detailed documentation of the several features and modules of the prototype and their relations was created in order to improve the comprehensibility of the prototype.

As the paradigm of cloud logistics is not a widespread field of research [1], such a prototypical implementation is an innovative artifact for the research community that enables researchers to conduct further field experiments. Several domain-driven structuring approaches and template variants can be analyzed towards their suitability from a empirical perspective. With the high evaluation of the properties flexibility, usability as well as with the fulfillment of the functional requirements (i.e. the support of engineering and management of simple and complex logistics services from heterogeneous sources) a high significance to practice is confirmed. Especially, the functions of structuring, retrieval and combination of logistics services and the subsequent creation of BPMN graph and XML for further usage are fulfilled. LSP can benefit from such an artifact by a common standard in logistics network that enbales them to collaborate easily. LI benefit from an increased speed of engineering different process alternatives.

Future work comprises multi-user features like authentication or assignment permissions and the automatic creation and structuring of logistics service from electronic description. Eventually, the full integration of the prototype into the logistics service platform of the main research project LSEM is planned.

Acknowledgment. The work presented in this paper was funded by the German Federal Ministry of Education and Research within the project *Logistik Service Engineering und Management* (LSEM). More information can be found under the reference BMBF 03IPT504X and on the website http://lsem.de/.

References

1. Glöckner, M., Ludwig, A., Franczyk, B.: Go with the flow - design of cloud logistics service blueprints. In: Proceedings of the 50th Hawaii International Conference on System Sciences (2017). doi:10125/41776
2. Langley, J., Long, M.: 2017 third-party logistics study: the state of logistics outsourcing: results and findings of the 21st annual study. In: Annual Study of Capgemini, Pennstate and Penske (2017)
3. Subramanian, N., et al.: 4th party logistics service providers and industrial cluster competitiveness. Ind. Manag. Data Syst. **116**(7), 1303–1330 (2016). doi:10.1108/IMDS-06-2015-0248. ISSN: 0263–5577
4. Esmaeilikia, M., Fahimnia, B., Sarkis, J., Govindan, K., Kumar, A., Mo, J.: Tactical supply chain planning models with inherent flexibility: definition and review. Ann. Oper. Res. **244**(2), 407–427 (2016)
5. Franke, M., Becker, T., Gogolla, M., Hribernik, K.A., Thoben, K.-D.: Interoperability of logistics artifacts: an approach for information exchange through transformation mechanisms. In: Freitag, M., Kotzab, H., Pannek, J. (eds.) Dynamics in Logistics. LNL, pp. 469–479. Springer, Cham (2017). doi:10.1007/978-3-319-45117-6_41
6. Jager, K., Ujvari, S.: Hilmola: Operating as a thirdparty logistics integrator without any distribution operations ownership. Int. J. Serv. Standards **3**(2), 154–168 (2007). doi:10.1504/IJSS.2007.012926. ISSN: 1740–8849
7. Glöckner, M., Augenstein, C., Ludwig, A.: Metamodel of a logistics service map. In: Abramowicz, W., Kokkinaki, A. (eds.) BIS 2014. LNBIP, vol. 176, pp. 185–196. Springer, Cham (2014). doi:10.1007/978-3-319-06695-0_16
8. Holmes, S.: Getting MEAN with Mongo, Express, Angular, and Node. Manning Publications, Shelter Island (2016). ISBN: 1617292036
9. Camunda: bpmn-js. BPMN 2.0 rendering toolkit and web modeler (2016). https://bpmn.io/toolkit/bpmn-js/
10. Venable, J., Pries-Heje, J., Baskerville, R.: FEDS: a framework for evaluation in design science research. Eur. J. Inf. Syst. **25**, 77–89 (2016). doi:10.1057/ejis.2014.36. ISSN: 0960–085X

DORA Platform: DevOps Assessment and Benchmarking

Nicole Forsgren[1,3], Monica Chiarini Tremblay[1(✉)],
Debra VanderMeer[1], and Jez Humble[2,3]

[1] College of Business, Florida International University, Miami, USA
nicolefv@gmail.com, {tremblay,vanderd}@fiu.edu
[2] University of California Berkeley, Berkeley, USA
humble@berkeley.edu
[3] DORA, Portland, USA

1 Introduction

In today's business environment, organizations are challenged with changing customer demands and expectations, competitor pressures, regulatory environments, and increasingly sophisticated outside threats at a faster rate than in years past. In order for organizations to manage these challenges, they need the ability to deliver software with both speed and stability. Yearly or even quarterly software releases are no longer the norm. Organizations from technology (e.g., Etsy and Amazon) to retail (e.g., Nordstrom and Target) and others are using integrated software development and delivery practices to deliver value to their users, beat their competitors to market, and pivot when the market demands.

Given the complexity of the modern software and infrastructure landscape, technology transformation is a non-trivial task. Software development and delivery include several key capabilities: strong technical practices, decoupled architectures, lean management practices, and a trusting organizational culture. Technical teams and organizations are left with an increasingly long list of potential capabilities to develop to improve their ability to deliver software. Technology transformation is a portfolio management problem, with technology leaders must allocate limited resources for to a broad spectrum of potential areas for capability improvement to deliver the greatest benefit.

Having a view to an organization's current performance is key to any improvement initiative. Formal assessments are one way to achieve this visibility. Assessments and scorecards are not a new idea (e.g., CMMI [1]), but the industry has yet to find ways to holistically measure and assess technology capabilities in ways that are based in research and are repeatable, scalable, and offer industry benchmarks. Currently, most commercial assessments consist of interviews conducted by a team of consultants [2]. These are heavyweight, expensive, not scalable, and subject to bias from the facilitators (for example, a covert goal can be to try to sell software or continued consulting services). Furthermore, by their nature, these assessments are myopic and only offer a comparison within the firm. Most commercial assessments do not have external data; research shows comparison benchmarks can drive performance improvements.

The DORA (DevOps Research and Assessment) platform presented in this paper seeks to address these limitations. We do this in three stages. First, we build our

© Springer International Publishing AG 2017
A. Maedche et al. (Eds.): DESRIST 2017, LNCS 10243, pp. 436–440, 2017.
DOI: 10.1007/978-3-319-59144-5_27

assessment on prior research that investigates capabilities and drives improvements in the ability to develop and deliver software. Second, we refine our assessment on psychometric methods that are statistically valid, reliable, and therefore consistent and repeatable. Third, we build our platform on a SaaS model that is scalable and provides industry-wide benchmarks.

2 Foundation

The traditional waterfall methodology treats development as a highly structured process that inhibits rapid software development. As a methodology, it does not allow developers to quickly respond to market and needs, nor to incorporate feedback from discoveries during the delivery process. The Agile manifesto and related agile methodologies emerged as an attempt to address limitations to traditional waterfall methods by leveraging feedback and embracing change through short incremental, iterative delivery cycles. While agile methods address aspects of the challenges seen in traditional methodologies and help to speed up the development process, they are often subject to limitations in the planning (i.e., upstream) and deployment (i.e., downstream) stages.

In response to these developments, the DevOps movement was started in the late 2000's. One notable difference of DevOps from agile is its extension of agile processes beyond the development role downstream into IT operations. Additional differences include the application of lean manufacturing concepts, such as WIP limits and visualization of work. Finally, and most importantly, DevOps highlights the importance of communication across organizational boundaries and a high-trust culture [3]. To maintain competitive advantage in the market, enterprise technology leaders are undertaking technology transformations to move from traditional and agile methodologies to DevOps methodologies that are continually improved.

Understanding where an organization currently performs (i.e., measuring and baselining performance) is important to any continuous improvement initiative (e.g., [4]). Many organizations lack the instrumentation or expertise to measure their capabilities in a holistic way, and therefore seek external assessment options.

The research to support this type of assessment exists, both in industry reports (e.g., [5–7]) and in academic papers (e.g., [3, 8]). However, for several reasons, there currently are no direct ways for technology leaders to apply these findings to their organizations with easy, scalable methods. First, current methods focus on qualitative approaches, which are not scalable and are not appropriate for comparison across time periods and organizations. Second, few in industry understand how to apply behavioral psychometric models and methods; nor do they sufficiently understand analysis, research design, and implementation requirements. Third, team members may not feel safe reporting system and environment performance to internal leaders, but do feel safer reporting to an external anonymized SaaS system [9]. Finally, the unavailability of external benchmarking data to drive performance comparisons, and the inability to measure improvement quantitatively over time in relation to changes in the rest of the industry, prevents teams from understanding the dynamic wider context in which they operate. This can lead to teams failing to take sufficiently strong action, and falling further behind the industry over time.

3   The DORA Assessment Tool

To address the aforementioned challenges, the DORA assessment tool was designed to target business leaders, either directly or indirectly (i.e., through channel partners such as consultancies or system integrators, who can offer the assessment as part of a larger engagement). The DORA assessment tool process is illustrated in Fig. 1.

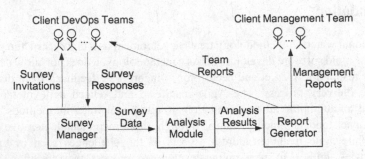

Fig. 1. Assessment tool process

The DORA Assessment Platform is built using PHP and is a SaaS solution hosted in AWS, with the data stored and processed in AWS East Region 1 with two independent availability zones for disaster recovery. The tool collects no personally identifiable information (PII) and stores no IP addresses, making the assessment and analysis appropriate for use in all geographies (for example, the assessment meets UK privacy law guidelines).

3.1   Measurement Components

IT performance is comprised of four measurements: lead time for changes, deploy frequency, mean time to restore (MTTR), and change fail rate. Lead time is how long it takes an organization to go from code commit to code successfully running in production or in a releasable state. Deploy frequency is how often code is deployed. MTTR is long it generally takes to restore service when a service incident occurs (e.g., unplanned outage, service impairment). Change fail percentage are the percentage of changes that result in degraded service or subsequently require remediation (e.g., lead to service impairment, service outage, require a hotfix, fix forward, patch).

Key capabilities are measured among four main dimensions. The *technical dimension* includes practices that are important components of the continuous delivery paradigm, such as: the use of version control, test automation, deployment automation, trunk-based development, and shifting left on security. The *process dimension* includes several ideas from lean manufacturing such as: visualization of work (such as dashboards), decomposition of work (allowing for single piece flow), and work in process limits. The *measurement dimension* includes the use of metrics to make business decisions and the use of monitoring tools. And finally, the *cultural dimension* includes measures of culture that are indicative of high trust and information flow, the value of learning, and job satisfaction.

3.2 Survey Deployment

The DORA assessment surveys technologists along the full software product delivery value stream (i.e., those in development, test, QA, IT operations, information security, and product management). This is different from other assessments in that all technologists are polled and not just a handful, and practitioners on the ground are assessed, not just leadership. The surveys include psychometric measures that capture system and team behaviors along four key dimensions: technical, lean management, monitoring, and cultural practices. Completing the survey takes approximately 20 min, and draws on prior work (see [2, 4–7] for the latent constructs that are referenced in the assessment).

The engagement model for the DORA assessment is one where technology leaders can act on results analysis provided. This may mean looking to internal champions and technical expertise, or it may mean engaging consultants to build out roadmaps and act on the guidance provided. When running an assessment, a survey manager meets with a client to determine the right sampling strategy for optimum data collection. The survey manager then partners with the client to send survey invitations to the client teams, and the platform collects responses.

At the end of data collection, the responses are analyzed, and the reports are generated. These reports are sent to the client management team, and optionally, to the client teams. The DORA assessment tool delivers the following: 1. Measurement of key capabilities described above; 2. Benchmarking these key capabilities against their own organization, the industry, and their aspirational peers in the industry; and 3. Identification of priorities for high impact investments for capability development.

4 Case Study

We present a case study demonstrating the utility of the DORA platform. Fin500 is a Fortune 500 company, and one of the ten largest banks in the United States. The company focuses on an innovative approach to customized services and offerings; this innovative approach requires an ability to develop and deliver quality software with rapidly. The Fin500 team was interested in the DORA assessment platform because the various measurement and assessment tools they had been using were either too narrow, too complicated, didn't offer actionable insights, or didn't show them how they compared against the industry. Crucially, these other tools didn't identify which capabilities were the most important for them to focus on first. Only the DORA platform provided a solution that provided all three things: holistic measurement, an industry benchmark, and identification of most important capabilities.

Following assessments across 17 teams and seven business units, DORA's analysis identified two key areas for capability development: automating change control processes and trunk-based development. Trunk-based development is a coding practice characterized by developers using one single mainline in a code repository; branches have very short lifetimes before being merged into master; and application teams rarely or never having "code lock" periods when no one can check in code or do pull requests due to merging conflicts, code freezes, or stabilization phases.

While the team was aware that their change approval processes were a likely candidate for improvement, the analysis provided an evidence-based second opinion, providing the necessary leverage to prioritize it. Trunk-based development proved to be a bigger challenge: some were skeptical that this would be a key driver for IT performance improvement. But the analysis was clear; these capabilities were key.

Fin 500 created organization-wide working groups and workshops on branching strategies and worked to reduce the amount of manual approvals happening in their change approval processes. In just two months, the team was able to increase the number of releases to production from 40 to over 800. Furthermore, this improvement occurred with no increase in production incidents or outages.

The teams and their leadership also commented on the value of participating in the assessment, since the survey itself highlights and reinforces behaviors and best practices across the dimensions described above. The DORA assessment becomes both a measurement and a learning opportunity, creating a shared understanding of how to drive improvement across the organization. A screencast of the DORA platform can be seen here: http://bit.ly/2k5SYJW.

References

1. Team, C. P.: CMMI® for Development, Version 1.3, Improving processes for developing better products and services, no. CMU/SEI-2010-TR-033. Software Engineering Institute (2010)
2. Shetty, Y.K.: Aiming high: competitive benchmarking for superior performance. Long Range Plan. **26**(1), 39–44 (1993)
3. Forsgren, N., Humble, J.: The role of continuous delivery in IT and organizational performance. In: The Proceedings of the Western Decision Sciences Institute (WDSI) 2016, Las Vegas, NV (2016)
4. Shetty, Y.K.: Aiming high: competitive benchmarking for superior performance. Long Range Plan. **26**(1), 39–44 (1993)
5. Forsgren Velasquez, N., Kim, G., Kersten, N., Humble, J.: 2014 State of DevOps Report (2014)
6. Puppet Labs and IT Revolution: 2015 State of DevOps Report (2015)
7. Brown, A., Forsgren, N., Humble, J., Kersten, N., Kim, G.: 2016 State of DevOps Report (2016)
8. Forsgren, N., Humble, N.: DevOps: profiles in ITSM performance and contributing factors. In: The Proceedings of the Western Decision Sciences Institute (WDSI) 2016, Las Vegas, NV (2016)
9. Lawler, E.E., Nadler, D., Cammann, C.: Organizational Assessment: Perspectives on the Measurement of Organizational Behavior and the Quality of Work Llife. Wiley, Hoboken (1980)

DScaffolding: A Tool to Support Learning and Conducting Design Science Research

Jeremías P. Contell[1]([✉]), Oscar Díaz[1], and John R. Venable[2]

[1] ONEKIN Web Engineering Group,
University of the Basque Country (UPV/EHU), San Sebastián, Spain
{jeremias.perez, oscar.diaz}@ehu.eus
[2] School of Information Systems,
Curtin University, Perth, WA, Australia
j.venable@curtin.edu.au

Abstract. Learning and conducting Design Science Research (DSR) are complex undertakings, for which there is little assistance other than publications describing how to do them. They include many activities which must be mastered and coordinated, sometimes when doing them for the first time. This paper describes a new tool, DScaffolding, developed to support novice DSR researchers in learning DSR while conducting DSR research projects. DSR activities are supported within an existing mind-mapping tool (MindMeister), through the use of features such as (1) integrating MindMeister with literature management and annotation tools, (2) prompting for needed inputs, (3) tracking incomplete tasks, and (4) automatically piping information from one activity to another activity and ensuring consistency of information. An initial version of DScaffolding was evaluated formatively. The prototype is available as a plugin for Google Chrome at the Chrome's Web Store.

Keywords: Strategic reading · Root cause analysis · Mind mapping

1 Introduction

We have developed DScaffolding (**D**esign **S**cience **Scaffolding**), a mind-map template together with companion scripts that guide and partially automate filling this template for a DSR project. This functionality supports approaches for DSR tasks, including Colored Cognitive Mapping (CCM) for DSR [1], an enhanced version of FEDS [2], and RMF4DSR [3], as well as other more general DSR activities, such as requirements identification and definition.

2 Design of the DScaffolding Artifact

Our main insight is to envision support for DSR as a mind mapping activity, based on a template that holistically provides guidance and supports actions. As the research moves ahead, branches of the template map are elaborated as they become relevant. The branches in the template account for the main DSR activities: Describe Practice,

© Springer International Publishing AG 2017
A. Maedche et al. (Eds.): DESRIST 2017, LNCS 10243, pp. 441–446, 2017.
DOI: 10.1007/978-3-319-59144-5_28

Explicate Problem, Formulate Design Theory, Define Requirements, Design Artifact, and Evaluate Artifact (nominally, but not necessarily, in that order). Figure 1 depicts the central part of DScaffolding's *DesignScience* template for a new project. Many details are not shown. DScaffolding significantly extends traditional map mapping to assist researchers in conducting DSR activities. DScaffolding's long aim is at turning the underlying mind-map editor (MindMeister) into a DSR-aware assistant. Assistance is realized in different ways depending on the DSR task at hand: the use cases.

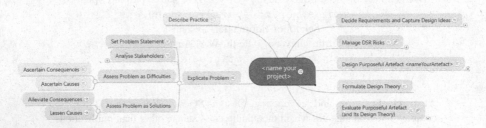

Fig. 1. *DesignScience* template when first opened

2.1   Use Cases: DSR Activities Supported by DScaffolding

Table 1 outlines the main DSR activities (or use cases) and their support in DScaffolding. Support ranges from checklists – that reminds students about the main DSR concerns – to automatic draft generation of some parts of the mind map, to be later elaborated by the student ("head-start rendering"). Next, we provide some details.

Table 1. DScaffolding assistance.

Activity (or use case)	Assistance	Theoretical underpinnings
Problem analysis	Re-arrangement of RCA trees	
Strategic reading	Tracking of annotation repositories	[4]
(Meta-)Requirements identification and determination	Head-start rendering	[5]
Design theorizing	Head-start rendering	[6]
Risk management	CheckList	[3]
Evaluation	CheatSheet	[2]

Root Cause Analysis (RCA). Researchers need to "play around" with causes (and consequences) as they gain insights about the problem. DScaffolding facilitates "playing around" with RCA diagrams. Changing the problem focus or shifting cause for consequences, and vice versa (a common problem for newcomers) is just a drag and drop away. No need for the cumbersome re-arrangement of nodes and arcs. Rather DScaffolding supports these operations as primitives.

(Meta-)Requirements Identification and Determination (Choice). Colored Cognitive Maps (CCMs) have been proposed to derive candidate solutions to the problem [1]. It does so through two CCMs (see Fig. 2). First, a CCM of "the problem as difficulties" where the focus is on what is undesirable about it (i.e. consequences), and what causes the problem. Second, a CCM of "the problem as solutions", which focuses on the solution of the problem, what benefits would accrue from solving the problem, and what causes of the problem might be reduced or eliminated to solve the problem. DScaffolding helps by providing a head-start for the "Assess Problem as Solutions" tree, which is automatically derived from the Assess Problem as Difficulties" tree (see Fig. 2). Both trees are kept in sync so that, e.g., adding a new cause results in creating a new research opportunity by addressing this cause.

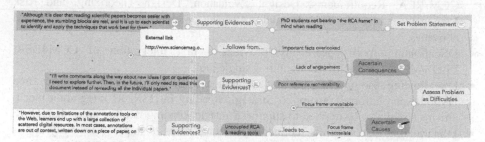

Fig. 2. DScaffolding map. Leaves (quotes) are automatically generated out of user annotations in Mendeley and Hypothes.ls. Map available at https://www.mindmeister.com/830267652

Strategic Reading. "Strategic reading" is the process of extracting evidence from the literature that sustains or informs a DSR project, including literature supporting the RCA, extant solutions, and technologies supporting a designed solution/artefact. Focusing on RCA, we conceive of RCA and reading as two inter-related processes, which feed off each other: RCA progresses as new insights are obtained from the literature while the literature relevant to the concerns that arise during RCA is scrutinized. DScaffolding helps by automatically copying annotations of literature made while reading in Mendeley into the mind map. Annotation nodes are to cause or consequence nodes for which they provide support or evidence (see Fig. 2).

Design Theorizing. Autility theory "makes an assertion that a particular type or class of technology (i.e. a meta-design)... has (some level of) utility (or usefulness) in solving or improving a problematic situation (with specified characteristics)" [6]. An example of a Utility Theory Form would be "Solution technology X (when applied properly) will provide utility A to solve problems of type Y". DScaffolding provides a head-start by suggesting such forms out of the nodes already gathered in the map.

Risk Management. Checklists help ensure that key risks are not overlooked. Pries-Heje et al. propose one such list about things that could go wrong or have gone wrong in other projects (i.e., potential risks) [3]. DScaffolding prompts users to identify relevant risks, analyze the chances of and consequences of incurring any of those risks, assists in prioritizing risks, and integrates selected risks with later risk treatments, e.g. through early formative evaluation.

Evaluation. Evaluation should be in line with the nascent Design Theory. By gathering all information in a single place, DScaffolding helps by checking that evaluation hypotheses serve to back issues relevant to the current Design Theory. Furthermore, it also helps to arrange evaluation scenarios in line with the FEDS framework [2].

3   Significance to Research

DScaffolding could contribute to the area of Design Science Research in the following ways.

- DScaffolding embodies the first conceptual integration of Stakeholder Analysis, CCM/RCA, Requirements, Design, Evaluation, Design Theorizing, and Risk Management in DSR. This then allows piping of inputs to subsequent or related activities.
- DScaffolding more specifically provides a first integration of CCM4DSR, FEDS/MEDS, and RMF4DSR into a single tool.
- DScaffolding also provides the first integration of the MindMeister, Mendeley, and Hypothes.is platforms to support Strategic Reading in DSR. Its integration mechanisms could also be applied to support Strategic Reading in other areas than DSR.
- DScaffolding also supports redundancy in mind maps to improve usability and is the first tool to use of pipes to keep redundant parts in sync (in MindMeister).

4   Significance to Practice

DScaffolding pursues the following benefits to the practice of Design Science Research.

- DScaffolding provides guidance, advice, and support for novice DSR researchers, making it easier to learn.
- DScaffolding operationalizes and supports DSR practices, thereby improving the efficiency and effectiveness of DSR.
- Appropriate use of DScaffolding can improve the documentation of DSR activities, thereby facilitating understanding, replicability and ability to publish, and improving the quality of DSR outcomes.
- DScaffolding facilitates research supervision and collaboration by providing a sharable, Web-accessible, common-ground mind map that makes it easier to monitor progress and spot missing parts.

5   Evaluation

DScaffolding has been taught in workshops and as part of a DSR course in different European and Australian universities. Formative usability evaluations were conducted about first impressions on the use of the tool with positive feedback. Table 2 below shows the aggregate results from four of the questions. All ratings questions in Table 2 were answered on a 0–10 scale, with 0 being not at all and 10 being extremely easy or 100% certain. 16 respondents answered questions 5 and 6 about DScaffolding as a whole. Question 9 asked those respondents who had applied DScaffolding to their own research to rate how likely they were to continue to use DScaffolding on their research project. Fifteen respondents answered question 10 as to how likely they would be to use DScaffolding on a future research project. Detailed results for ratings questions concerning different specialized areas of DScaffolding and open comments will be reported elsewhere.

Table 2. Aggregate results of the formative usability evaluations for DScaffolding.

	5 ease of learning	6 ease of use	9 continue usc	10 future use
Average	7.31	7.25	7.60	7.07
Min.	5	5	6	1
Max.	10	10	9	9
Std. dev.	1.30	1.48	1.34	2.09

6 Availability and Documentation

DScaffolding is available as a Chrome extension at the Chrome's Web Store: https://chrome.google.com/webstore/detail/hkgmnnjalpmapogadekngkgbbgdjlnne. Videos are provided for

- Installation: https://youtu.be/hl6pnJGbVXY
- Root-Cause Analysis: https://youtu.be/kaBTmCr2JWA
- Strategic Reading: https://youtu.be/jHP1MiqjVBM.

Acknowledgments. This work is co-supported by the Spanish Ministry of Education, and the European Social Fund under contract TIN2014-58131-R. Contell has a doctoral grant from the University of the Basque Country.

References

1. Venable, J.R.: Using coloured cognitive mapping (CCM) for design science research. In: Tremblay, M.C., VanderMeer, D., Rothenberger, M., Gupta, A., Yoon, V. (eds.) DESRIST 2014. LNCS, vol. 8463, pp. 345–359. Springer, Cham (2014). doi:10.1007/978-3-319-06701-8_25
2. Venable, J.R., Pries-Heje, J., Baskerville, R.: FEDS: a framework for evaluation in design science research. Eur. J. Inf. Syst. **25**(1), 77–89 (2016)
3. Pries-Heje, J., Venable, J., Baskerville, R.: RMF4DSR: a risk management framework for design science research. Scand. J. Inf. Syst. **26**, 57–82 (2014)
4. McEwan, E.: The power of strategic reading instruction. In: Seven Strategies of Highly Effective Readers: Using cognitive research to boost K-8 achievement. Corwin press (2004)

5. Venable, J.R.: Coloured cognitive maps for modelling decision contexts. In: First International Workshop on Context Modeling and Decision Support, Paris, France (2005)
6. Venable, J.R.: The role of theory and theorising in design science research. In: Proceedings of the 1st International Conference on Design Science Research in Information Systems and Technology (DESRIST 2006), pp. 1–18, Claremont, CA, USA (2006)

DeProX: A Design Process Exploration Tool

Jonas Sjöström[✉]

Department of Informatics and Media,
Uppsala University Campus Gotland, Visby, Sweden
jonas.sjostrom@im.uu.se

Abstract. In exploratory design science research, research questions emerge as the design process progresses. Researchers are faced with the complex task of reconstructing design rationale, i.e. retrospectively scrutinizing certain aspects of the design process. While such a task may be challenging due to social and technical complexities, we present a software prototype to support design process exploration. The software produces visualizations and facilitates exploration by scanning design process data from source code repositories and document collections. We tentatively assess the software by accounting for its use in two design science research projects. Implications for research and practice are discussed.

Keywords: Design science research · Action design research · Design rationale · Repository · Document analysis · Visualization

1 Introduction

Design-oriented research is often exploratory [1]. At the inception phase of a research program, IS researchers may spot several interesting topics that are initially hard to phrase as research questions. While design is often characterized as a search process [2] design science research (DSR) may also be conceived in a similar manner. DSR and other design-oriented approaches such as action design research (ADR) [3] may be based on continual releases of software into a practice environment. The new release may be based on (i) requirements from stakeholders (possibly based on their assessment of the current version), (ii) theory proposed by researchers that ingrain the new release, or (iii) creative work by designers and/or researchers—or a combination of the three. Given a situation where research questions are vague, the documentation of design rationale may be missing or inadequate. In such a research setting, there is a series of naturalistic evaluation activities between each release [4].

Over time, given an increased understanding of the problem domain, vague research interests emerge into well-specified research questions [5]. When this 'shift' occurs, there may be a need for retrospective analysis to reconstruct the design process and the rationale behind design decisions. Such analysis may be required to understand the steps through which the design has evolved. In an ADR context [3], for example, it would be desirable to account for the design cycles through which design principles have evolved. In an action research context, researchers would explain the cycles to show the rationale for each intervention, and how each intervention contributed to

© Springer International Publishing AG 2017
A. Maedche et al. (Eds.): DESRIST 2017, LNCS 10243, pp. 447–451, 2017.
DOI: 10.1007/978-3-319-59144-5_29

knowledge development [6, 7]. In a similar manner, the rigor and relevance of a DSR endeavor relies on the understanding and presentation of the iterative interplay between theory, practice, design and evaluation [2].

As outlined above, design-oriented research highlights the cyclical character of research; how knowledge and its rationale emerge through iterations. As a design-oriented researcher, one must find ways to retrospectively scrutinize a design process. Although there may be existing field notes et cetera, it may still be complex to effectively and efficiently analyze – let's say – a five year long design research effort.

This paper presents a software prototype to support retrospective analysis of design processes. We introduce *Design Process Explorer* (DeProX), a software tool to visualize and explore a design process, thus promoting sensemaking and guidance for further inquiry. DeProX builds on (i) actual code changes in a software repository, and (ii) discussions among stakeholders about requirements, design rationale, *et cetera*.

2   DeProX: The Design Process Explorer

In exploratory research, we may end up in a situation where we need to reconstruct the design rationale in a complex design process. DeProX supports exploring and visualizing past events in design processes. The main idea is to provide design process visualizations that support researchers to quickly make sense of past events. The visualizations are facilitated by an underlying architecture to import design process data from various sources, and index it into a database to prepare for querying. DeProX indexes design documentation and code, thus it brings order to and facilitates inquiry into design history. While there exist several other software tools to analyze software repositories [8, 9], DeProX is novel in the sense that it combines repository analysis with analysis of other data sources, thus facilitating analysis of relations between source code changes and other design activities. An account of the five software modules (Fig. 1) follows.

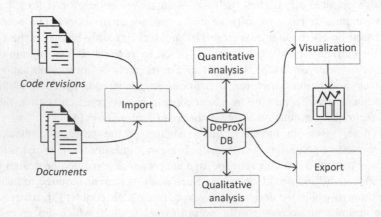

Fig. 1. Overview of DeProX software modules

The Import Module. Fetching data from document collections and source code repositories into the DeProX database. Documents (pdf, word, and text formats) are imported—timestamps and full text data, and links to the original documents. Code revision import includes revision numbers, name of the programmer who committed the code, a revision timestamp, as well as the names the files that were modified in the revision, and the action performed on the file (modify, delete or add). At this stage, DeProX supports import from Subversion repositories. The import module scans the data sources and imports changes only.

The Quantitative Analysis Module. Analysis is based on the setup of an inquiry, including selected keywords related to the current research interest. Identifying appropriate source code repository keywords requires either technical insight into the solution, or a dialogue with knowledgeable developers. Document collection keywords are identified in collaboration with those who are knowledgeable about how various stakeholders would speak about the inquiry topic. The actual analysis – at this point – creates a keyword count for each document grouped by a time interval (typically a day). Experimental improvements of DeProX are being investigated, using Microsoft's Text Analytics API to facilitate sentiment analysis, key phrase extraction, language detection and topic detection when analyzing documents.

The Visualization Module. The dotted line in the visualization (Fig. 2) represents requirements discussions. It shows keyword frequency (grouped by date) in a sprint meeting document repository. The solid line shows how revisions in the code repository contain changes to files matching keywords (keyword matches in change paths in source code revisions, grouped by date). In this case related to the development of peer interaction features such as online forum, chat, and moderation features. At this point, only a few types of visualization have been implemented—two alternative versions of the Fig. 2 type visualization, and a word cloud presentation of document data.

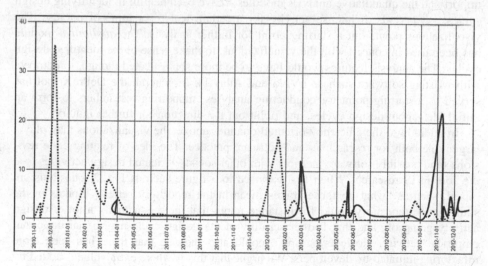

Fig. 2. A chart exported from DeProX showing design activity over a two-year period

The Qualitative Analysis Module. Support for qualitative analysis was implemented in the software, based on an engine to automatically highlight inquiry keywords in pdf documents, and find and open the documents from the software. The feature allows the researcher to get started with a qualitative analysis of documents related to the identified design cycles. The software also allows the researcher to write annotations about documents and about design cycles, facilitating an iterative approach to exploring the design process, fine-tuning inquiry keywords, and constructing design stories with clear links back to the empirical data.

The Export Module. The export module is at a basic stage and only allows for export of data sets and visualizations. A goal is to develop the software to work in concert with other analysis tools such as SPSS, Atlas TI, and nVivo.

3   Evaluation and Concluding Discussion

We have demonstrated a proof-of-concept [10], i.e. a piece of showing the feasibility to implement the ideas into software. The software has been used to support two DSR studies, one concerned with eHealth accountability and one with community translation in software development. Due to the early stage of research on the proposed approach, we may only speculate about the usefulness of the approach in other settings [11]. The approach is however based on mining data sources that are de facto-standards, thus facilitating post-hoc exploration of many design processes.

The experiences so far show that the approach is supportive in navigating a complex design history and making sense of past events and design decisions. The *import* module – storing code revisions and documentation in a database – allows for SQL queries into past events in the design process. Thus it provides a novel opportunity to navigate a messy design process. The *visualizations* – made possible by the import and the quantitative analysis modules – have been helpful in identifying design cycles, i.e. periods of intense activity for a certain feature or topic of interest. The visualizations points out a starting point for further analysis. The *qualitative* module has been used in concert with the visualizations, to make sense of the identified design cycles. The analysis features would have to be more sophisticated though, to compete with existing software such as nVivo and Atlas TI. In general, the DeProX tool has served as a starting point for conducting analyses, supporting researchers to form an initial idea about design cycles, and point out the direction for further inquiry.

In addition to the efficiency-oriented qualities above, the visualizations may play a larger role both for researchers and software practice. The idea of relating code revisions (and possibly software metrics) with other socially oriented design activities is at the fore in IS research. When first exposed to a figure such as Fig. 2, questions are raised, such as "what do these spikes mean in the repository series?" Spikes in the source code repository could for instance imply that there is actually a lot of design activity going on, and that further scrutiny of the design cycle may be an important empirical activity. However, a spike could also indicate that there has been large refactoring initiated by developers. We argue that this is where extra value is added by the other series in the visualization, i.e. the one showing design discussion activity.

When there is activity both in discussion and in code changes, it is fair to assume that further (qualitative) scrutiny of that design episode is highly relevant for research. This is also where the novelty of the approach resides: In the integrated and automated analysis of code and design discussion. In addition to supporting design-oriented researchers 'navigate' design history, it also opens up the possibility to do research on the interplay between domain experts and developers. In essence, the histogram is a novel lens to support a post-hoc view of the dialectics in the design process.

DeProX was originally a desktop application. An emerging web version of DeProX will facilitate collaborative explore design process exploration. Future versions of the tool may thus prove valuable in ways yet unexplored by the authors.

References

1. Goldkuhl, G., Lind, M.: A multi-grounded design research process. In: Winter, R., Zhao, J.L., Aier, S. (eds.) DESRIST 2010. LNCS, vol. 6105, pp. 45–60. Springer, Heidelberg (2010). doi:10.1007/978-3-642-13335-0_4
2. Hevner, A.R., March, S.T., Park, J., Ram, S.: Design science in information systems research. MIS Q. **28**(1), 75–105 (2004)
3. Sein, M., Henfridsson, O., Purao, S., Rossi, M., Lindgren, R.: Action design research. MIS Q. **35**(1), 37–56 (2011)
4. Venable, J., Pries-Heje, J., Baskerville, R.: FEDS: a framework for evaluation in design science research. Eur. J. Inf. Syst. **25**(1), 77–89 (2016)
5. Sjöström, J.: Designing Information Systems. Uppsala University, Uppsala (2010)
6. Susman, G.I., Evered, R.D.: An assessment of the scientific merits of action research. Adm. Sci. Q. **23**, 582–603 (1978)
7. Järvinen, P.: Action research is similar to design science. Qual. Quant. **41**(1), 37–54 (2007)
8. Hassan, A.E.: The road ahead for mining software repositories. In: Frontiers of Software Maintenance, 2008, FoSM 2008, pp. 48–57 (2008)
9. Williams, C.C., Hollingsworth, J.K.: Automatic mining of source code repositories to improve bug finding techniques. IEEE Trans. Softw. Eng. **31**(6), 466–480 (2005)
10. Nunamaker Jr., J.F., Briggs, R.O.: Toward a broader vision for information systems. ACM Trans. Manag. Inf. Syst. **2**(4), 20 (2011)
11. Lee, A.S., Baskerville, R.: Generalizing generalizability in information systems research. Inf. Syst. Res. **14**(3), 221–243 (2003)

A Modeling Environment for Visual SWRL Rules Based on the SeMFIS Platform

Hans-Georg Fill[1]([⊠]), Benedikt Pittl[2], and Gerald Honegger[2]

[1] University of Bamberg, 96047 Bamberg, Germany
hans-georg.fill@uni-bamberg.de
[2] University of Vienna, 1090 Vienna, Austria

Abstract. The representation and processing of semantic information can today be accomplished using a wide range of formalisms. Rule-based approaches are not only a well-known but also easy to use technique. Most approaches rely on a textual specification of rules that can be processed by an according rule engine. For simplifying the specification and understanding of rules by domain experts, we present a visual model editor for rules based on the W3C SWRL recommendation. The goal of this approach is to provide a means for a visual interaction with rule-based systems, while at the same time preserving full expressiveness. The visual language for SWRL rules has been implemented on the SeMFIS platform. In addition, serialization and de-serialization mechanisms have been added for OWLXML and SWRLXML formats. As there are currently no official conformance tests available for SWRL, the approach has been evaluated using W3C sample set for SWRL rules.

Keywords: SWRL · Semantic Web · Visual rule representation · Conceptual modeling

1 Introduction

Rule-based formalisms have been used in the past as a foundation for creating expert systems [15] and have recently come to a revival in the context of web-based applications and linked data [14]. In the context of business information systems, rules have amongst their many applications been used for detailing the branching in business processes, allocating resources, or constraint and compliance checking [2,13]. They are thus an established and sound technique for the declarative specification of decisions based on given facts. Furthermore, rules are one of the main pillars for realizing the semantic web [11]. The rule standardization effort of the W3C resulted in the SWRL (Semantic Web Rule Language) recommendation with the special aim on inferring new knowledge ontologies [11].

For specifying SWRL rules it is common to use text-based editors like the Protégé SWRL tab [11]. An alternative is the use of visual languages [9]. In this way, rule languages can be integrated in enterprise modeling environments, thus leveraging the burden from business users to express rules in a textual syntax.

© Springer International Publishing AG 2017
A. Maedche et al. (Eds.): DESRIST 2017, LNCS 10243, pp. 452–456, 2017.
DOI: 10.1007/978-3-319-59144-5_30

We thus decided to create a visual modeling language for rules according to the most recent SWRL standard [6] and implement it in the form of a prototype.

The remainder of the paper is structured as follows: In Sect. 2 the design of the modeling language is described followed by elaborations on it significance to research and practice in Sects. 3 and 4. A first evaluation of the language is presented in Sect. 5. The paper ends with a conclusion in Sect. 6.

2 Design

In this section we will motivate the design, potential use cases, intended user groups and features of our prototype. To the best of our knowledge, a visual language for a complete representation of SWRL rules is still missing. The visual language for SWRL proposed in [7,8] took a first step in this direction. However, it did not provide explicit support for the different types of built-ins available in SWRL and neither dealt with the import of SWRL rules as models. Also the implementation introduced in [1] is incomplete as it misses the representation of atoms and OWL constructs. It neither includes export mechanisms. The Protégé plugin Axiome visualizes SWRL rules in the form of graphs [5]. However, it is a pure visualization tool, i.e. modifications of rules in the graphical representation are not possible.

It thus seems favorable to develop a modeling language for SWRL that covers all aspects of this language. Such a modeling language can be used both for use cases dealing with the analysis of existing SWRL rules, as well as for use cases where rules have to be specified by non-technical experts, e.g. for compliance checking by business users [13]. As the user group for which we intended to provide the visual modeling language for SWRL were people familiar with enterprise modeling but not necessarily rule modeling, the goal was to realize a language that includes all necessary constructs in a visual form. This led to the following features in our prototype: (i) Visual modeling of all atoms as defined in the SWRL standard (ii) Explicit representation of variables and data values (iii) Linkage to visually represented OWL ontologies using the SeMFIS modeling language [3] (iv) Import and export of visual SWRL models to SWRL-XML and OWL-XML (v) Implementation of the approach on the SeMFIS platform.

Due to the space limits we omit the detailed metamodel here. The most important classes are shown in Table 1. For the design of the visual notation we referred to the principles of Moody [10]. For example, to ensure semiotic clarity we mapped each core concept of SWRL to one modeling element. Therefore, each atom defined in the SWRL standard is represented with a single modeling element in our visual language. We applied the dual theory which enforces that graphical elements are enriched with textual descriptions [10]. This resulted in the visual notation shown in Table 1. The textual information is dynamically added at run time – see Fig. 1. The shown sample is taken from the W3C SWRL specification and would be specified in traditional textual syntax as follows:
hasStatus(?customer, Gold) ∧ hasTotalPurchase(?customer, ?total)
∧ swrlb:greaterThanOrEqual(?total, 500) -> hasDiscount (?customer,

Table 1. Excerpt of the elements used for the SWRL modeling language

Antecedent	The antecedent (condition) of a rule	(A_C)	Class atom, e.g. Person(?x)	(A_≠)	Different Individuals Atom, e.g. differentFrom(?x,?y)
Consequent	The consequent of a rule	(A_i)	Individual-valued Property Atom, e.g. hasRisk(?x,?y)	(A₌)	Same Individuals Atom, e.g. sameAs(?x,?y)
IndividualConstant	Constant representing a data value	(A_d)	Datavalued Property Atom, e.g. hasName(?x,?y)	⚙	MetaInfo for describing meta information about a rule, e.g. about imports
IndividualVariable	Variable for storing individual values	(A_D)	Datarange Atom with datatype	TERM ▶	Built-in Term used as reference for composing built-in parameters
DataVariable	Variable for storing data values	(A_{DL})	Datarange Atom with literal list	●──→	Relation for connecting atoms to antecedents and consequents
DataConstant	Constant representing a data value	(A_B)	Built-in Atom, e.g. greaterThan(?age, 17)	⇗	Relation for connecting antecedents and consequents

10). In addition to the atoms connected to the antecedent and consequent elements, also the separate elements for representing variables, data values and builtIn-terms are shown.

3   Significance to Research

Our work has the following two main contributions to research. First, it extends previous research on visual languages for SWRL rules - e.g. in [1,5,8] - by providing a visual representation of SWRL rules that includes all elements of the W3C recommendation in a formal manner. Second, the prototypical implementation will be integrated in the SeMFIS platform and provided as open-source to the scientific community via the OMiLAB initiative [4]-http://semfis-platform.org. In this way, other researchers will be able to use the modeling language or extend it for their purposes.

4   Significance to Practice

From an industry perspective, the simplification of user interfaces for interacting with complex formalisms is considered as essential for supporting non-technical business users. This is also the case for the described prototype that enables users to specify SWRL rules by using a set of pre-configured elements instead of having to compose rules in a textual syntax. Furthermore, the described prototype includes mechanisms for importing and exporting SWRL rule models to the SWRL XML and OWL XML formats. This enables the interoperability with applications such as Protégé that build upon these standards, which is one of the core requirements of industrial applications.

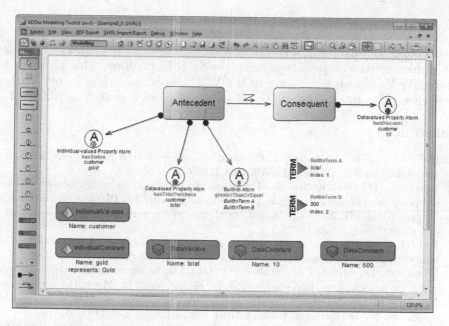

Fig. 1. Example model for a SWRL rule from the W3C sample set in the SeMFIS modeling environment

5 Evaluation

For the evaluation of artifacts in design-oriented and engineering research, it can be chosen from several paths [12]. In the case of our prototype, the most important aspect was to assess whether the models created with it conform to the recommendation by W3C for SWRL[1]. Therefore, we evaluated the completeness of our approach by creating the sample models specified in the W3C recommendation[2] and compared their XML serialization to the original code samples. Thereby, it could be verified that all examples were correctly represented. However, SeMFIS' OWL language requires an update in order to represent datatype attributes within restriction elements (see example 4 in the specification). For evaluating the completeness of our visual language we compared the supported language concepts to the concepts described in the SWRL specification. Currently, the support of annotation elements is limited. We will add this functionality within the next SeMFIS release. Further evaluations will include aspects such as the performance of the transformation algorithms as well as user-related aspects, e.g. to assess the ease of use of the modeling language.

---

[1] A screencast illustrating the usage can be found here: http://semfis-platform.org/swrl/Screencast/.

[2] The examples can be found at: https://www.w3.org/Submission/SWRL/#5.1.

6   Conclusion and Outlook

In this paper we introduced a visual modeling language for SWRL. The language was implemented as a prototype using the SeMFIS platform. This allows us to create SWRL models complying to the W3C recommendation. In our further research we plan to support additional serialization formats such as RDF-XML.

References

1. Bak, J., Nowak, M., Jedrzejek, C.: Graph-based editor for SWRL rule bases. In: RuleML@ChallengeEnriched 2013, CEUR (2013)
2. Feldkamp, D., Hinkelmann, K., Thönssen, B.: KISS – knowledge-intensive service support: an approach for agile process management. In: Paschke, A., Biletskiy, Y. (eds.) RuleML 2007. LNCS, vol. 4824, pp. 25–38. Springer, Heidelberg (2007). doi:10.1007/978-3-540-75975-1_3
3. Fill, H.-G.: SeMFIS: a flexible engineering platform for semantic annotations of conceptual models. Semant. Web (SWJ) 8(5), 747–763 (2017)
4. Götzinger, D., Miron, E.L., Staffel, F.: OMiLAB: an open collaborative environment for modeling method engineering. In: Karagiannis, D., Mayr, H.C., Mylopoulos, J., et al. (eds.) Domain-Specific Conceptual Modeling Concepts, Methods and Tools, pp. 55–76. Springer, Cham (2016). doi:10.1007/978-3-319-39417-6
5. Hassanpour, S., O'Connor, M.J., Das, A.K.: A rule management and elicitation tool for SWRL rule bases. In: RuleML Challenge (2009)
6. Horrocks, I., Patel-Schneider, P., Boley, H., Tabet, S., Grosof, B., Dean, M.: SWRL: A Semantic Web Rule Language Combining OWL and RuleML, W3C (2004). https://www.w3.org/Submission/SWRL/. Accessed 10 May 2017
7. Leutgeb, A., Utz, W., Woitsch, R., Fill, H.-G.: Adaptive processes in e-government - a field report about semantic-based approaches from the EU-Project FIT. In: ICEIS 2007, pp. 264–269, INSTICC (2007)
8. Leutgeb, A.: The business rules method: a modeling method for adaptive processes - Master Thesis. University of Vienna, Wien (2007)
9. Lukichev, S., Wagner, G.: Visual rules modeling. In: Virbitskaite, I., Voronkov, A. (eds.) PSI 2006. LNCS, vol. 4378, pp. 467–473. Springer, Heidelberg (2007). doi:10.1007/978-3-540-70881-0_42
10. Moody, D.: The physics of notations: toward a scientic basis for constructing visual notations in software engineering. IEEE Trans. Softw. Eng. 35(6), 756–779 (2009)
11. O'Connor, M., Knublauch, H., Tu, S., Musen, M.: Writing rules for the semantic web using SWRL and Jess. In: Protégé With Rules WS, Madrid (2005)
12. Peffers, K., Tuunanen, T., Rothenberger, M., Chatterjee, S.: A design science research methodology for information systems research. JMIS 24(3), 45–77 (2007)
13. Pham, T.A., Thanh, N.: Checking the compliance of business processes and business rules using OWL 2 ontology and SWRL. In: Abraham, A., Wegrzyn-Wolska, K., Hassanien, A.E., Snasel, V., Alimi, A.M. (eds.) Proceedings of the Second International Afro-European Conference for Industrial Advancement AECIA 2015. AISC, vol. 427, pp. 11–20. Springer, Cham (2016). doi:10.1007/978-3-319-29504-6_3
14. Stadtmueller, S., Speiser, S., Harth, A., Studer, R.: Data-fu: a language and an interpreter for interaction with read/write linked data. In: WWW Conference, pp. 1225–1236 (2013)
15. Studer, R., Benjamins, R., Fensel, D.: Knowledge engineering: principles and methods. Data & Knowl. Eng. 25, 161–197 (1998)

brAInstorm: Intelligent Assistance in Group Idea Generation

Timo Strohmann[✉], Dominik Siemon, and Susanne Robra-Bissantz

Technische Universität Braunschweig, Braunschweig, Germany
{t.strohmann, d.siemon,
s.robra-bissantz}@tu-braunschweig.de

Abstract. In order to generate valuable innovations, it is important to come up with potential beneficial ideas. A well-known method for collective idea generation is Brainstorming and with Electronic Brainstorming, individuals can virtually brainstorm. However, an effective Brainstorming facilitation always needs a moderator. In our research, we designed and implemented a virtual moderator that can automatically facilitate a Brainstorming session. We used various artificial intelligence functions, like natural language processing, machine learning and reasoning and created a comprehensive Intelligent Moderator (IMO) for virtual Brainstorming.

Keywords: Artificial intelligence · Brainstorming · Creativity

1 Introduction and Motivation

Computer tools that allow real-time collaboration over the internet can support the process of idea generation [1], as team members can work together from almost any place in the world [2]. One well-known method for idea generation is Brainstorming, which is a creativity technique for groups with the purpose to produce many ideas that may solve a given problem [3]. In order to accomplish this, it is important to follow basic rules and principles, like no criticism, the generation of unusual ideas, quantity breeds quality and the combination and improvement of ideas. With the help of information technology, Brainstorming has already been successfully digitized [4] and been identified to even outperform conventional face-to-face Brainstorming [5, 6]. However, the key to an effective Brainstorming is good facilitation [7], which is fulfilled by a moderator in face-to-face sessions. A moderator executes several tasks, like the encouragement to contribute or the intervention when Brainstorming rules are not obeyed [7]. Besides of the organization and observation of the Brainstorming session, the moderator also acts as an active facilitator by stimulating the participants to spark new ideas. Hence, a moderator usually needs special skills and knowledge on how to facilitate a Brainstorming session. Therefore, in virtual teams and so-called Electronic Brainstorming (EBS), a moderator always has to be present. In our research, we approach this, by developing a virtual moderator, who can facilitate an EBS session by both, organizing a session and providing creativity stimulating content. Even so, different agent-based Brainstorming support systems exist [8, 9], no research on comprehensive virtual Brainstorming moderation and facilitation was found that uses

A. Maedche et al. (Eds.): DESRIST 2017, LNCS 10243, pp. 457–461, 2017.
DOI: 10.1007/978-3-319-59144-5_31

features of artificial intelligence (AI). Following the Design Science Research Methodology, we designed and implemented a novel artifact in order to approach this problem in an innovative matter [10, 11]. We strive to create a useful artifact for practice that can fulfill automated Brainstorming sessions. In addition, we aim to deeper understand the interaction between an AI and individuals within a group creativity processes. With our developed prototype, we will provide a first approach on how computer tools can be designed to automatically moderate Brainstorming, which can lead to new insights for research and practice.

As Plucker and Makel show, creativity has various similar, overlapping and synonymous terms, such as imagination, innovation, novelty or uniqueness [12]. Guilford, who initiated the modern creativity era in psychological thinking, describes creativity as problem solving [13] and examined the characteristics of creative individuals. This led to the challenge, if it is possible to design and implement a computer-tool that exhibits creative thinking abilities. As one of the first who looked at creativity and AI, Boden stated why AI must try to model creativity [14]. Today, computational creativity is a multidisciplinary endeavor, overlapping with cognitive science and other areas [15, 16]. According to Besold et al., the target of computational creativity is to model, simulate or replicate creativity to achieve one of the following ends: (1) create a program or computer capable of human-level creativity, (2) help to understand human creativity or (3) construct a program enhancing human creativity without necessarily being creative itself [15]. In the first step of our research, we designed a computer-tool to enhance human creativity without necessarily being creative itself. Our artifact, "brAInstorm", is a web-based tool for collective EBS, with an Intelligent Moderator (IMO), who fulfills various functions of a Brainstorming moderator and addresses a number of current issues in EBS. One benefit of EBS is, that many participants can share their ideas without having to wait for their turn like in face-to-face Brainstorming [17]. This so-called production blocking is effectively addressed with EBS, even so, without a moderator, no feedback can be given to the individuals. However, IMO can reply to every participant simultaneously and provide individual feedback and stimulating content [18, 19]. This additionally implies, that a number of Brainstorming sessions can be conducted at the same time, without the need for more moderators. Another issue in EBS is the use of anonymity to tackle evaluation apprehension (fear of criticism). Even so, anonymity has been proven to be beneficial [20], its effectiveness is still controversial. However, interacting with an AI could solve the problem of evaluation apprehension, as interacting with an AI does not cause evaluation apprehension [18]. Even so, research on AI and group creativity is still at the beginning, our artifact can lead to valuable insights.

2   Design of the Artifact

For the implementation of brAInstorm, we derived basic user interface principles of prior EBS implementations [21–23]. A chat is used, to allow the users to communicate with each other. In addition, participants can add and edit ideas and view other ideas.

For this feature, we used the open-source chat platform Rocket.Chat[1], where we added additional functionalities, like adding and editing ideas. For the essential Brainstorming phases, we adopted the process by Gallupe et al. and implemented it into the system [6]. The process is divided into an individual idea generation and a collective idea evaluation. These phases are facilitated and organized by IMO (see Fig. 1), a chatbot based on Hubot, an open-source chatbot, developed by GitHub, Inc[2]. Besides of organizing the EBS process, the moderator additionally intervenes, if participants use so-called killer phrases, get impertinent or talk too much. The killer phrases are adopted from Dave Dufour, who defined 50 phrases, which can heavily impair a Brainstorming process [24]. IMO is capable of identifying these phrases and intervenes, even if they are alternated. In addition IMO, intervenes, when the group drifts away from the topic or the group stagnates. Even so, Hubot has hearing and responding functions (text/voice input and output), it does not offer conversations, context understanding or machine learning. For this reason, Hubot is extended with wit.ai's Bot Engine. Wit.ai[3] is an open-source and extensible natural language platform, offering various functionalities for building applications, a user can text or talk to. An Intent Parser, which converts user texts or voice into structured data, extracts the intent and other parameters of a user's input. A bot engine combines machine learning with a rule-based behavior, consisting of three key concepts: Stories, actions and an inbox. Stories are rule-like example conversations between the bot and a user, specifying how the bot should react on a certain statement. With the help of wit.ai's predictions, Hubot can execute an action at the needed points in the conversation. Wit.ai's Inbox allows machine learning by collecting all users' expectations. Using this, brAInstorm can be optimized through continuous learning, based on actual usage. With these functionalities, brAInstorm can be seen as a highly novel contribution that offers a comprehensive automated moderation for EBS. Figure 1 shows the adopted Brainstorming process within our artifact and the underlying technology behind each function. A screencast of the artifact is available on https://vimeo.com/203283219 (pw: desrist2017).

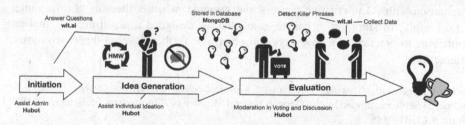

Fig. 1. The Brainstorming process within our artifact, "brAInstorm".

---

[1] https://rocket.chat/.

[2] https://hubot.github.com/.

[3] https://wit.ai/.

3 Evaluation of the Artifact and Outlook

Our planned evaluation can be divided into two parts. First, we plan to conduct a set of experiments, where we will specifically assess the effectiveness of brAInstorm. We will measure the perceived effectiveness and the perceived satisfaction of the users [6, 25] with the functionalities of IMO and whether the Brainstorming process was successfully executed. Following prior research on group creativity and artificial intelligence [18], we aim to examine, whether specific enhancing and impairing group factors apply, when interacting with an AI. Additionally, we plan to examine the specific functions of IMO, e.g. whether IMO is able to maintain the rules of Brainstorming and if IMO is even able to encourage the participants to contribute. The second part of our evaluation is a long-term case study, where we will implement the artifact in an on-going Design Thinking project. Within the Ideation phase of the Design Thinking mind-set, Brainstorming is often used to generate ideas. We will use brAInstorm for ideation and examine, whether our artifact can be used in virtual teams and effectively substitute a real moderator. Both evaluations can lead to valuable insights, for research and practice. Practice can benefit from an innovative artifact that can be used in creative problem solving in virtual teams. New insights on group ideation and the interaction with an artificial intelligence can contribute to current issues in computer-supported collaborative work, group support systems and collaborative creativity support like production blocking and the use of anonymity [18].

With our artifact, we created an innovative solution for virtual Brainstorming that can be supported, organized and executed with the help of a virtual moderator. With our evaluations, we plan to examine the applicability of our prototype. Furthermore, we plan to examine the interaction between individuals and an AI, which can contribute to the understanding of group interaction theories. In this context, we take our artifact to the next level, by developing an independent artificial participant, a Creative Artificial Intelligence (CAI). Currently we are implementing CAI, a creative and active participant that is capable of human-level creativity. We plan on further investigating the interaction with AI in creative process and examine, whether theories of group interaction apply. In summon, it can be said, that we designed a novel artifact, that can contribute to practice in many ways and change or further develop theories on group interaction.

Acknowledgement. This paper is part of a project called DETHIS – Design Thinking for Industrial Services, funded by the German Federal Ministry of Education and Research (BMBF); Grant # 01FJ15100.

References

1. Gera, S., Aneeshkumar, G., Fernandez, S., Gireeshkumar, G., Nze, I., Eze, U.: Virtual teams versus face to face teams: a review of literature. IOSR J. Bus. Manag. **11**, 1–4 (2013)
2. Gumienny, R., Hampel, S., Gericke, L., Wenzel, M., Meinel, C.: Transferring traditional design work to the digital world: does it work. In: Proceedings of the 2012 Design Research Society International Conference (DRS 2012) (2012)

3. Osborn, A.F.: Applied imagination, Scribner'S, Oxford, England (1953)
4. Dennis, A.R., Valacich, J.S.: Computer brainstorms: more heads are better than one. J. Appl. Psychol. **78**, 531–537 (1993)
5. Mullen, B., Johnson, C., Salas, E.: Productivity loss in brainstorming groups: a meta-analytic integration. Basic Appl. Soc. Psychol. **12**, 3–23 (1991)
6. Gallupe, R.B., Dennis, A.R., Cooper, W.H., Valacich, J.S., Bastianutti, L.M., Nunamaker, J. F.: Electronic brainstorming and group size. Acad. Manage. J. **35**, 350–369 (1992)
7. Kramer, T.J., Fleming, G.P., Mannis, S.M.: Improving face-to-face brainstorming through modeling and facilitation. Small Group Res. **32**, 533–557 (2001)
8. Graesser, A.C., Person, N., Harter, D., Group, T.R., et al.: Teaching tactics and dialog in AutoTutor. Int. J. Artif. Intell. Educ. **12**, 257–279 (2001)
9. Wang, H.-C., Rosé, C.P., Chang, C.-Y.: Agent-based dynamic support for learning from collaborative brainstorming in scientific inquiry. Int. J. Comput.-Support. Collab. Learn. **6**, 371 (2011)
10. Hevner, A.R., March, S.T., Park, J., Ram, S.: Design science in information systems research. MIS Q. **28**, 75–105 (2004)
11. Gregor, S., Hevner, A.R.: Positioning and presenting design science research for maximum impact. MIS Q. **37**, 337–356 (2013)
12. Plucker, J.A., Makel, M.C.: Assessment of creativity. In: The Cambridge Handbook of Creativity, pp. 48–73 (2010)
13. Guilford, J.P.: Creativity. Am. Psychol. **5**, 444–454 (1950)
14. Boden, M.A.: Creativity and artificial intelligence. Artif. Intell. **103**, 347–356 (1998)
15. Besold, T.R., Schorlemmer, M., Smaill, A., et al.: Computational Creativity Research: Towards Creative Machines. Springer, Heidelberg (2015)
16. Colton, S., Wiggins, G.A.: Computational creativity: the final Frontier? In: Proceedings of the 20th European Conference on Artificial Intelligence, pp. 21–26. IOS Press, Amsterdam (2012)
17. Paulus, P.B.: Electronic brainstorming research and its implications for e-planning. Int. J. E-Plan. Res. IJEPR. **4**, 42–53 (2015)
18. Siemon, D., Eckardt, L., Robra-Bissantz, S.: Tracking down the negative group creativity effects with the help of an artificial intelligence-like support system. In: 2015 48th Hawaii International Conference on System Sciences (HICSS), pp. 236–243 (2015)
19. Siemon, D., Rarog, T., Robra-Bissantz, S.: Semi-automated questions as a cognitive stimulus in idea generation. In: 2016 49th Hawaii International Conference on System Sciences (HICSS), pp. 257–266 (2016)
20. Connolly, T., Jessup, L.M., Valacich, J.S.: Effects of anonymity and evaluative tone on idea generation in computer-mediated groups. Manage. Sci. **36**, 689–703 (1990)
21. Link, G.J., Siemon, D., de Vreede, G.-J., Robra-Bissantz, S.: Anchored discussion: development of a tool for creativity in online collaboration. J. Univers. Comput. Sci. **22**, 1339–1359 (2016)
22. Javadi, E., Gebauer, J., Mahoney, J.: The impact of user interface design on idea integration in electronic brainstorming: an attention-based view. J. Assoc. Inf. Syst. **14**, 1–21 (2013)
23. Nunamaker Jr., J.F., Applegate, L.M., Konsynski, B.R.: Facilitating group creativity: experience with a group decision support system. J. Manag. Inf. Syst. **3**, 5–19 (1987)
24. Dufour, D.: Fifty Phrases That Kill Creativity. http://creativelicensepodcast.com/fifty-phrases-that-kill-creativity/
25. Dennis, A.R., Valacich, J.S., Connolly, T., Wynne, B.E.: Process structuring in electronic brainstorming. Inf. Syst. Res. **7**, 268–277 (1996)

Making Gamification Easy for the Professor: Decoupling Game and Content with the StudyNow Mobile App

Matthias Feldotto[(✉)], Thomas John, Dennis Kundisch, Paul Hemsen, Katrin Klingsieck, and Alexander Skopalik

Paderborn University, Paderborn, Germany
{matthias.feldotto,thomas.john,dennis.kundisch,
paul.hemsen,katrin.klingsieck,
alexander.skopalik}@uni-paderborn.de

Abstract. Many university students struggle with motivational problems, and gamification has the potential to address these problems. However, gamification is hardly used in education, because current approaches to gamification require instructors to engage in the time-consuming preparation of their course contents for use in quizzes, mini-games and the like. Drawing on research on limited attention and present bias, we propose a "lean" approach to gamification, which relies on gamifying learning activities (rather than learning contents) and increasing their salience. In this paper, we present the app StudyNow that implements such a lean gamification approach. With this app, we aim to enable more students and instructors to benefit from the advantages of gamification.

Keywords: Gamification · Limited attention · Present bias · Mobile app · Education

1 Introduction

Gamification, the "use of game design elements in non-game contexts" [2], has received great interest in education research. There is ample evidence that gamification may help to enhance a learner's motivation and engagement, which are important antecedents of academic performance [3]. The actual use of gamification in the education sector, however, is very rare primarily due to the enormous effort that gamifying courses demands from instructors (e.g., [4, 7]). Typically, gamifying a course so far involves that course contents have to be specifically prepared for use in quizzes, mini-games and the like.

In contrast, we propose a "lean gamification" approach in which (abstract) learning activities (e.g., attend lectures, read assignments, write essays) are gamified, and not course contents. Obviously, this comes with a much lower effort for the instructors compared to previous approaches, because most of the gamification effort is already accomplished by creating the course concept and the corresponding syllabus. At the same time, such a lean gamification approach lends itself to a better learning experience in combination with a mobile app (called StudyNow). Hence, we may expect a much

© Springer International Publishing AG 2017
A. Maedche et al. (Eds.): DESRIST 2017, LNCS 10243, pp. 462–467, 2017.
DOI: 10.1007/978-3-319-59144-5_32

broader diffusion of gamified courses by introducing StudyNow. Still, the question arises how such a mobile app has to be designed in order to cause a substantial increase in the academic performance of students. The proposed solution approach is based on the increase of the salience of learning activities through gamifying these learning activities. With this approach we aim to alleviate the limited attention [6] on and the present bias [1] against pending learning activities. Consequently, marginal learning effort should increase, which expectedly results also in an increase in the overall learning effort and, ultimately, the academic performance of students.

In our research we follow the design science research paradigm [5] and have two general objectives: (1) Creation of an innovative technological artifact which has the capacity to increase the academic performance of its users. (2) Utilization of the artifact to evaluate the gamification of learning activities. In this product and prototype paper we focus on objective (1).

2 Design of the Artifact

The main part of our artifact has been implemented as an app. It is supplemented by a backend for data handling and a web application for instructors to maintain their courses. The choice of smartphones as our target devices is based on our main theoretical foundation: We want to make the learning activities more salient. This means that students should be able to access the learning activities with the least possible effort, independent of time and place.

The app use starts with a registration with email and password and the choice of the university. After the registration, the user stays logged in. A logout has to be performed explicitly and additional components for change of email address and password as well as a forgotten identity management complete the authentication features. The users can select the courses they are enrolled for in the current semester based on the name of the lecturers and the course titles. Having selected their courses, the students see all the learning activities which they have to perform in these courses, they can tick off finished activities and they can see different aggregated statistics of their behavior in specific courses, over specific time frames and in total. For this purpose the app employs two main views specifically designed to increase the salience of learning activities: A week and a semester overview (see Fig. 1). In the week overview the students see pending learning activities and the performance in the current week (or also of any selected week chosen by swipe gestures). Structured by the different courses (given by name and lecturer), all learning activities are listed including the current status (done/not done) which can be switched directly by a tick. Each type of learning activity is visualized by a shortcut symbol. Additionally, the users see aggregated performance values in the form of the number of finished and total activities as well as circular progress bars grouped by the courses and statistics for the whole week grouped by activity types. In the semester overview the students get a higher-level overview of their performance. For each course there is an aggregated performance value based on the relative number of performed learning activities in comparison to the number of pending learning activities. Additionally, the total number of missed learning activities is provided explicitly. The view is completed by an overview

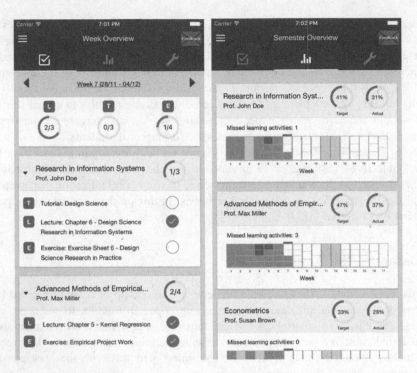

Fig. 1. Main screens of the artifact: week overview (left) and semester overview (right). (Color figure online)

over all semester weeks. For each activity a colored box is used (green = completed, red = overdue, white = in future, grey week = no activities). A tap on a specific week switches to the corresponding week overview.

The artifact addresses students in higher education as the primary user group. These students are heterogeneous in terms of their level of procrastination, their preferences for gamification as well as their capabilities for motivational and volitional control. To account for this heterogeneity, and because so far theoretical guidance for addressing different user types with gamification is largely unavailable, we engaged in an agile, user-driven design process. We conducted short interviews with 41 Students before the start of our project to learn more about students' learning and planning preferences. Subsequent design decisions were invariably made after several iterations of intense user testing with PowerPoint-based click prototypes. Furthermore, design decisions were triggered and backed up by the feedback we received through a prominently placed in-app-feedback feature and the concurrent evaluation studies (see Sect. 4). Additionally, our artifact addresses the instructors of the courses. We were already able to win 46 instructors before the start of the project with a letter of intent. They are valuable talking partners and support our whole design process.

The mobile application is implemented in the cross-platform technology Ionic[1]. At the moment iOS and Android devices are supported. The application is connected with a well-defined REST interface to our backend, which is based on an open-source gamification engine[2] to easily support common gamification related issues (like events, progress and statistics). An additional web interface is available for the management of universities, lecturers, courses and learning activities. Piwik[3] is used to track the users' in-app behavior for reasons of continuous improvement and research purposes (e.g., how often the different views are accessed). Together with the data protection officer of our university we have developed an anonymization concept to comply with German data privacy law. This concept prescribes a two-database approach with one live database and one research database. All our research is to be based on data in the research database, which is generated from the live database by considering the concept of k-anonymity [10]. This dual-database approach assures that single users cannot be identified from the data stored in the research database. While our artifact focuses on progress bars at the moment, it will be extended by further gamification elements like badges and leaderboards in the near future.

3 Significance to Research and Practice

From a research perspective it is noteworthy that most empirical research in gamification lacks a sound theoretical foundation [8]. One reason for this lack of theoretical foundation is that, as mentioned earlier, gamifying a course involves considerable effort. Hence, conducting experiments to identify effective configurations of game design elements involves considerable effort, which limits the number of experiments that can reasonably be conducted. In the future, therefore, we would like to leverage the major strength of our app – that it allows gamifying courses with little effort – to conduct series of field experiments. Through these field experiments it is possible to contribute to gamification research by exploring which game design elements and which combinations thereof are effective in countering student procrastination. From a practice perspective, the resulting knowledge can support instructors in using gamification efficiently and effectively in their courses. For app users (i.e., the students), the artifact is a tool that helps to prevent or reduce procrastination and thereby can contribute to increasing academic performance.

4 Evaluation of the Artifact

To evaluate the merits of the lean gamification approach, we are currently conducting a mixed-methods study that focuses on procrastination, which is a very prevalent problem among students and has highly detrimental effects on academic achievement.

---

[1] http://ionicframework.com.

[2] https://github.com/ActiDoo/gamification-engine.

[3] https://piwik.org.

Academic procrastination is "the voluntarily delay of an intended course of action related to learning or studying despite expecting to be worse off for the delay" [9]. For the quantitative part of our study, we conduct a pretest-posttest-(control-group) design. Participants were asked to participate in an online survey that comprised self-report measures for different forms of procrastination (academic procrastination, general procrastination) and the use of mobile devices. The pretest took place at the beginning of the current semester, the posttest will take place at the end of this semester. Prior gamification research emphasizes that a multiplicity of individual and context factors are likely to be important in gamification studies [8], therefore we complement our experimental study with a qualitative study that is based on the personal diary method [11]. For our diary study, students of two Master's courses (n = 11 & n = 15) were asked to use the mobile application and to report on their experience through three diary entries throughout the current semester. The results of our qualitative study are encouraging. A number of students reported that they could not meaningfully use the app because they are in their final semester and hence only enrolled to one or two courses (i.e., too few courses to lose track of pending learning activities). However, other students reported they would "feel bad" when seeing in the app that missed learning activities accumulate, and would "feel good" when they can tick off finished learning activities. However, these results are largely tentative, and further work is needed to establish the validity and generalizability of these indicative and encouraging statements.

The mobile application was published in the Apple App Store and Google Play Store in November 2016 (see project homepage https://studynow.uni-paderborn.de).

References

1. Akerlof, G.A.: Procrastination and obedience. Am. Econ. Rev. **81**(2), 1–19 (1991)
2. Deterding, S., Dixon, D., Khaled, R., and Nacke, L.: From game design elements to gamefulness: defining gamification. In: Proceedings of the International Academic MindTrek Conference: Envisioning Future Media Environments, pp. 9–15 (2011)
3. Dicheva, D., Dichev, C., Agre, G., Angelova, G.: Gamification in education: a systematic mapping study. J. Educ. Technol. Soc. **18**(3), 75–88 (2015)
4. El-Masri, M., Tarhini, A.: A design science approach to gamify education: from games to platforms. In: Proceedings of the European Conference on Information Systems (2015)
5. Hevner, A., March, S., Park, J.: Design science in information systems research. MIS Q. **28**(1), 75–105 (2004)
6. Kahneman, D.: Attention and Effort. Prentice-Hall, Englewood Cliffs (1973)
7. Sánchez-Mena, A., Martí-Parreño, J.: Gamification in higher education: teachers' drivers and barriers. In: Proceedings of the International Conference the Future of Education, pp. 180–184 (2016)
8. Seaborn, K., Fels, D.: Gamification in theory and action: a survey. Int. J. Hum. Comput. Stud. **74**, 14–31 (2015)
9. Steel, P., Klingsieck, K.B.: Academic procrastination: psychological antecedents revisited. Aust. Psychol. **51**(1), 36–46 (2016)

10. Sweeney, L.: k-anonymity: a model for protecting privacy. Int. J. Uncertain. Fuzziness Knowl.-Based Syst. **10**(5), 557–570 (2002)
11. Symon, G.: Qualitative research diaries. In: Symon, G., Cassell, C. (eds.) Qualitative Methods and Analysis in Organizational Research: A Practical Guide, pp. 94–117. Sage, London, UK (1998)

Designing a Crowd Forecasting Tool to Combine Prediction Markets and Real-Time Delphi

Simon Kloker[✉], Tim Straub, and Christof Weinhardt

Institute of Information Management and Marketing,
Karlsruhe Institute of Technology, Karlsruhe, Germany
{simon.kloker,tim.straub,weinhardt}@kit.edu

Abstract. The FAZ.NET-Orakel is a crowd forecasting tool, made available to readers of the German-based *Frankfurter Allgemeine Zeitung*. Its main component is a prediction market used for forecasting economic indices as well as current political events. A shortcoming of prediction markets is their inability to exchange qualitative information. Therefore, we elaborate the combination of prediction markets with the Real-time Delphi method. We argue that several synergy effects may be achieved by this approach: First, prediction markets can be used to select experts for the Delphi survey. Second, valuable information and debates, which may be of interest, can be collected qualitatively. Third, the gamified approach of the prediction markets can raise commitment to the survey.

1 Introduction

Copious forecasting errors made during the global financial crisis are exemplary of the failure of traditional time series based forecasting methods to deliver accurate results when unexpected and sudden events occur. In recent years, however, new methods in forecasting, based on "the wisdom of the crowd", i.e., prediction markets, have sprung up. Prediction markets have proven to create reliable and continuous forecasts in rapidly changing environments and, in addition, are also suitable for corporate decision-making [2,9]. They provide a simple and convenient way of revealing and aggregating private and/or dispersed information from a large number of people. However, in areas where expertise from different fields is required, or conflicting goals and values have to be considered, prediction markets prove less suitable [11]. This can be attributed to the fact that information is conveyed in prices and quantities and therefore no exchange of qualitative information is made possible. In addition, indeterminable outcomes (their realization may be unobservable or lie in the distant future) are a challenging factor. The Delphi method (or its offspring, Real-time Delphi, RTD) is the tool of choice when considering such problems. It offers experts a structured communication method free of inter-personal and hierarchical effects or social pressures [10]. However, the Delphi method has some challenges, such as high drop-out rates, or the difficulty to select so-called "experts" [14]. The aforementioned factors may have a strong influence on the forecast and may define which

© Springer International Publishing AG 2017
A. Maedche et al. (Eds.): DESRIST 2017, LNCS 10243, pp. 468–473, 2017.
DOI: 10.1007/978-3-319-59144-5_33

points of view are considered [17]. The current prototype intends to evaluate how both methods can be combined to overcome some of the weaknesses of each method: For the prediction market this is the lack of qualitative feedback and for RTD it is the drop-out rates and the problem of selecting appropriate experts.

2 Design of the Artifact

2.1 Approach and Design Process

The proposed approach that seeks to combine prediction markets and RTD is based on the exchange of users. We argue that the market mechanism is capable of selecting/revealing all relevant experts: traders carrying the most prominent information, private information, and outsider views (see Sect. 2.2). These traders are invited to take part in the RTD and discuss their opinions. Traders may alter their opinion and bring their new information into the market (and the public) by trading according to their newfound knowledge (Fig. 1).

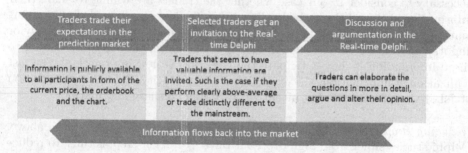

Fig. 1. Selected traders change their estimations in the discussion, seeing as they are confronted with opinions from without and trade according to their new estimations.

For the Requirements and Design Principles we keep with [16], who formulated a Design Theory for the class of Group Wisdom Support Systems (GWSS). As we fit the requirement "the creation of a heterogeneous pool of beliefs", we can, subsequently, regard our tool as a GWSS in contrast to standard prediction markets. The design of the prediction market is heavily based on its predecessor, the Economic Indicator Exchange (EIX), and therefore has a four-year validity period in the field. The Design Principles for the RTD have been formulated based on a literature review of former RTD implementations.

2.2 Key Features

Selection of the "Experts" - One key aspect of the combination is the selection of the experts, that is to say, traders with information worthwhile of being collected qualitatively. Our IT-Artifact implements three algorithms (named according to the selected trader): **(i) The Topscorer:** This algorithm invites the top n persons of the ranking. According to the Hayek Hypothesis [5] in the long run only the trader that holds factual and new (private) information will perform well in a market. **(ii) The Potential:** Based on the data of the EIX, collected over four years, we related different trading patterns to the trader's success in the ranking. The algorithm may therefore predict sooner which trader will probably perform well and should, subsequently, be invited as soon as possibly in order to present their qualitative arguments. **(iii) The Bohemian:** This algorithm selects traders that trade distinctly different from the mainstream – either holding valuable new information or offering an interesting and/or different point of view.

Collecting Qualitative Information - Qualitative information, explaining single estimations and opinions, is essential, when trying to understand better, risks and relationships between different factors. The structured discussions of RTD can help forecasters to relate, challenge, and reconsider their point of view based on additional, convincing information from other participants. It is, however, necessary to consider in our case whether the traders are willing to share their information in the RTD survey. In the market, traders usually realize their information very quickly (until their potential is exhausted due to limited money or depots) and before they access the survey. Therefore, they may be willing to share information if they anticipate the reception of new information. The fast realization of information, the expectation of reciprocity, but also the evolution of "shared artifacts" [8] may incentive the trader to share information.

Reducing Drop-Outs by Gamification and Social Interaction - As stated above, Delphi studies suffer from high drop-out rates. A further step, is thus, to reduce drop-outs. We address this issue using several different means: First, the combination with the prediction market adds to the idea of gamifcation to the platform, which is already seen as a strong incentive to take part and share information [13]. Second, we introduce MicroMarkets. They feature a hidden market design, optimized to reduce cognitive load in order to observe the effect of complexity on forecasting performance and cognitive biases. [3] argues that this may raise participation rates, as users may be deterred due to the high complexity or lack of knowledge about markets. Third, we enhanced the basic features of a RTD survey with social elements, at the same time ensuring anonymity, as suggested in [10]. The latter two points will be addressed in detail in other publications.

3   Significance to Research and Practice

Research - According to [7], Design Science research differs from standard software development in terms of its significant scientific contribution. The combination of prediction markets with other forecasting methods has been considered most recently. Amongst others, [1,4,15] combined either the forecasts or the methods of diverse forecasting tools, which have produced higher-quality results.

Most put a focus on the combination with polls. [12] "combined" prediction markets and Delphi studies, which in his case only meant preselecting the trader for a prediction market and using a hidden market interface. To the best of our knowledge, FAZ.NET-Orakel is the first tool that combines prediction markets and RTD in such a way that the prediction market is used to select experts (or traders with potentially valuable information), invites them to share their knowledge in a RTD survey, and at the same time allows (and tries to quantify) information to flow back into the market. Our research therefore contributes to the understanding of information extracted by crowds and user behaviour in estimation tasks. In addition, the results may better inform our understanding of whether or not the combination of methods improves forecasts.

Practice - The result of our research will be an evaluated artifact potentially capable of combining the advantages of prediction markets and RTD surveys. This may add value to its users and operators by providing better forecasts regarding politics, organizations, companies, or the wider public. Especially when qualitative information behind the probability is of interest – as in idea evaluation and forecasting tasks with high dissent – our tool may be a means of combining the "crowd intelligence" of a large panel and qualitative information.

4   Evaluation of the Artifact

The evaluation of the hypotheses related to the artifact will take place in a field study together with the *Frankfurter Allgemeine Zeitung* aimed at forecasting both economic indices and upcoming political events. As already mentioned, the preliminary evaluation of the prediction market component took place during a four-year field study. Several publications, some of them summarized in [14], report on the performance of EIX. The "social" RTD component, itself subject to a three cycle Design Science project [6], was already evaluated (in the first cycle) in a small online experiment. The results have been submitted for publication. To evaluate the combination of the forecasting methods, we plan to quantify the information flow from the market to the survey and back. In keeping with the latter, we will track both directions with underlying hypotheses: *H1: Selected traders share and discuss information in the survey. H2: Selected traders change their trading behaviour after visiting the survey.* H1 is rejected if traders are not willing to share their information in the survey. H2 is rejected if at least some traders do not change their trading behaviour directly after visiting the survey. A change in trading behaviour is defined to happen if the limit prices or trading intensity (up) changes significantly.

5   Conclusions

The work at hand contributes to the research on the combination of prediction markets and other forecasting methods. Our approach introduced and implemented an artifact that integrates prediction markets and RTD on a trader level. Weaknesses found in both methods are tackled by the proposed solution and current work therefore makes a good contribution to the research of GWSS. The most important contributions addresses the lack of qualitative information in prediction markets and the problem of selecting experts in Delphi studies.

References

1. Atanasov, P., Rescober, P., Stone, E., Swift, S.A., Servan-Schreiber, E., Tetlock, P., Ungar, L., Mellers, B.: Distilling the wisdom of crowds: prediction markets vs. prediction polls. Manag. Sci., April 2016. http://dx.doi.org/10.1287/mnsc.2015.2374
2. Buckley, P.: Harnessing the wisdom of crowds: decision spaces for prediction markets. Bus. Horiz. **59**(1), 85–94 (2016). http://www.sciencedirect.com/science/article/pii/S0007681315001172
3. Chen, W., Li, X., Zeng, D.D.: Simple is beautiful: toward light prediction markets. IEEE Intell. Syst. **30**(3), 76–80 (2015). http://ieeexplore.ieee.org/stamp/stamp.jsp?tp=&arnumber=7111878
4. Graefe, A.: German election forecasting: comparing and combining methods for 2013. Ger. Polit. **24**(2), 195–204 (2015). http://dx.doi.org/10.1080/09644008.2015.1024240
5. Hayek, F.A.: The use of knowledge in society. Am. Econ. Rev. **35**(4), 519–530 (1945)
6. Hevner, A.R.: A three cycle view of design science research. Scand. J. Inf. Syst. **19**(2), 4 (2007)
7. Hevner, A.R., March, S.T., Park, J., Ram, S.: Design science in information systems research. MIS Q. **28**(1), 75–105 (2004). http://www.jstor.org/stable/25148625
8. Kaye, A.: Learning together apart. In: Kaye, A.R. (ed.) Collaborative Learning Through Computer Conferencing. NATO ASI Series (Series F: Computer and Systems Sciences), vol. 90, pp. 1–24. Springer, Heidelberg (1992). doi:10.1007/978-3-642-77684-7_1
9. Klein, M., Garcia, A.C.B.: High-speed idea filtering with the bag of lemons. Decis. Support Syst. **78**, 39–50 (2015). http://www.sciencedirect.com/science/article/pii/S0167923615001190
10. Kloker, S., Kranz, T.T., Straub, T., Weinhardt, C.: Shouldn't collaboration be social? - proposal of a social real-time delphi. In: Proceedings of the Second Karlsruhe Service Summit Research Workshop (2016). http://service-summit.ksri.kit.edu/downloads/Session_3B2_KSS_2016_paper_19.pdf
11. Linstone, H.A., Turoff, M.: Introduction. In: The Delphi Method: Techniques and Applications, chap. 1, pp. 3–12. Addison-Wesley Educational Publishers Inc. (2002)
12. Prokesch, T., von der Gracht, H.A., Wohlenberg, H.: Integrating prediction market and delphi methodology into a foresight support system - insights from an online game. Technol. Forecast. Soc. Change **97**, 47–64 (2015). http://www.sciencedirect.com/science/article/pii/S0040162514000857
13. Scheiner, C.W., Haas, P., Leicht, N., Voigt, K.I.: Accessing knowledge with a game - a meta-analysis of prediction markets (2013)
14. Teschner, F.: Forecasting economic indices: design, performance, and learning in prediction markets. Karlsruhe Institute of Technology (KIT) (2012). http://digbib.ubka.uni-karlsruhe.de/volltexte/1000029512

15. Tetlock, P.E., Mellers, B.A., Scoblic, J.P.: Bringing probability judgments into policy debates via forecasting tournaments. Science **355**(6324), 481–483 (2017). http://science.sciencemag.org/content/355/6324/481.abstract
16. Wagner, C., Back, A.: Group wisdom support systems: aggregating the insights of many trough information technology. Issues Inf. Syst. (IIS) **9**(2), 343–350 (2008). http://iacis.org/iis/2008/S2008_992.pdf
17. Welty, G.: Problems of selecting experts for delphi exercises. Acad. Manag. J. **15**(1), 121–124 (1972)

Trading Stocks on Blocks - Engineering Decentralized Markets

Benedikt Notheisen[✉], Magnus Gödde, and Christof Weinhardt

Institute of Information Systems and Marketing,
Information and Market Engineering, Karlsruhe Institute of Technology,
Fritz-Erler-Str. 23, 76133 Karlsruhe, Germany
{benedikt.notheisen,christof.weinhardt}@kit.edu,
magnus.goedde@student.kit.edu
http://im.iism.kit.edu

Abstract. As an infrastructure for economic systems, blockchain technology challenges the role of traditional intermediaries and enables the creation of novel market designs and value chains. We utilize this potential and design a decentralized market framework that allows users to trade complex financial assets, such as stocks, in an intermediary-free setup. Overall, our prototype implements the basic software structure of this market framework, illustrates the feasibility of decentralized market mechanisms, and highlights potential use cases as well as limitations.

Keywords: Blockchain-based economic systems · Market design · Decentralized market platforms · Securities trading

1 Introduction

Since its introduction in 2008, the blockchain has emerged from its use in cryptocurrencies and prepares to revolutionize a multitude of economic applications. In the context of markets, the combination of a distributed database, a decentralized consensus mechanism, and cryptographic security measures allows distributed system architectures and intermediary-free market designs by algorithmically enforcing agreements on the basis of predefined rules [10]. In addition, the absence of centralized institutions facilitates disintermediation and allows more cost-efficient transactions [1]. As a result, blockchain-based economic systems announce disruptive changes in financial markets and question the role of traditional financial institutions and market intermediaries, such as banks, exchanges, or central securities depositories. To illustrate and evaluate such market platforms, we build on the growing body of literature on blockchain-based economic systems and implement a proof-of-concept prototype of a decentralized securities exchange.

B. Notheisen—Financial support of Boerse Stuttgart is gratefully acknowledged.

© Springer International Publishing AG 2017
A. Maedche et al. (Eds.): DESRIST 2017, LNCS 10243, pp. 474–478, 2017.
DOI: 10.1007/978-3-319-59144-5_34

2   Artifact Relevance

2.1   Significance to Research

Our prototype comprises a blockchain-based market platform that adopts the notion of trust-free economic systems [4] and extends current knowledge on cryptographic transaction systems [1] with a crucial prerequisite for each transaction - a mechanism to connect demand and supply. This way, we introduce a novel way to substitute traditional market institutions and intermediaries by transferring the guidance and governance of human interactions to formalized rule sets implemented by algorithms [7] borne by the blockchain's distributed network.

2.2   Significance to Practice

From a practical perspective, we provide the design and implementation of a blockchain-based market mechanism that entails the core functionality to trade stocks and constitutes a low-cost and resilient decentralized market platform. In combination with the ability of smart contracts to represent highly customizable financial assets, our prototype illustrates a new way to resolve inefficiencies, such as high search and bargaining costs, in low-volume over-the-counter (OTC) markets [3]. Furthermore, token-based equity issuances provide an alternative mechanism for entrepreneurs to raise venture capital, by lowering regulatory barriers and simultaneously increasing the investors' control [6].

3   Artifact Design

3.1   Design Science Approach

To guide the creation, evaluation, and presentation of our IT-artifact, we follow the guidelines proposed by Hevner et al. [5] and search for a solution to the problems stated in Sect. 2. To evaluate the identified solution and to demonstrate our prototype's utility, quality, and efficacy, we apply various structural and functional testing procedures (Sect. 4). In addition, we ensure our research's rigor by utilizing well established frameworks [5, 8] as well as blockchain-specific approaches [10] that guide the creation of our IT-artifact. Overall, we build on existing knowledge [8] in the field of blockchain-based economic systems and iteratively adapt the instantiations of our prototype throughout the development process. Eventually, to maximize impact and to present our results to both, technology-oriented as well as management-oriented audiences, we provide the underlying economic principles (Sect. 2) as well as a detailed description of the software architecture and the artifact's features (Sect. 3.2).

3.2   Artifact Features

Within the Ethereum framework [2,9], digital assets such as currencies or stocks can be realized in the form of standardized smart contracts called tokens. From a technical perspective a token comprises a database, that enables data transactions in a distributed setup and allows the definition of arbitrary asset characteristics. Eventually the token contract is stored on the blockchain and the Ethereum virtual machine executes the code fragments, while the token logic provides an immutable set of rules governing the actions of the issuers and holders of tokens without the requirement of a centralized third party. In the context of a stock exchange, a token represents the shares of one specific firm and implements storage and transfer functionalities. In addition, we allow convenience features, such as elections on annual general meetings or the distribution of dividends. In the case of venture capital investments, the total amount of funded capital could be locked into the contract and released piecewise subject to milestones in the business plan or the collective will of the investors promoting investor protection. Overall, we implement the decentralized exchange as a combination of two smart contracts, in which the exchange contract utilizes the token contract's functions to trade shares on the users' behalf. Figure 1 shows the full software structure of our prototype including its contracts and storage structures; the corresponding source code is available under https://goo.gl/NpVmuJ. In the first step, a newly created token contract (`TokenStandard`) needs to be registered with the exchange contract (`DSX`) by passing the token's address to the `registerToken()` function. Upon the reception of the information, the `DSX` creates a `Market` containing the order book for the associated token. In order to make his or her shares tradeable, the token owner furthermore needs to grant the `DSX` control over some tokens, and thus determine the number of shares in the initial public offering (IPO) (`deposit()`). Now the `DSX` is able to credit tokens to the accounts of investors and keeps track of stock ownership. To actually raise capital, companies need to sell their tokens (`sell()`). Figure 2 illustrates the steps of the funding process in greater detail. In addition, https://goo.gl/v6axZo provides a brief demonstration and showcases our HTML interface. After the IPO, `sell()` and `buy()` allow investors to place market or limit orders to trade shares and implicitly performs clearing by ensuring that the seller has enough stocks and the buyer has enough money. All information associated with an order, such as `volume`, `price`, `marketId`, or the `blockNumber`, is saved in the `Order`. Following their submission, we use the orders' unique `OrderIds` to collect all orders for a share and create a globally distributed limit order book for each token within the `Market`. Everytime a new order is submitted, the `DSX` triggers a continuous double auction, that facilitates order execution based on best price matching (`match()`). Eventually, shares and funds get transferred directly between the users as matching, clearing, and settlement is unified in one joint step, and recorded by the blockchain's immutable transaction log. This log provides a history of all transactions, facilitating transparency and preventing fraud.

4   Artifact Evaluation

To evaluate the formal correctness and the accurate functioning of the prototype, we choose a laboratory-based test setting and apply structural and

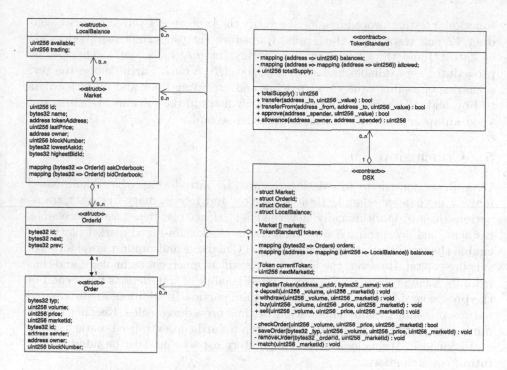

Fig. 1. Software architecture of the decentralized market framework

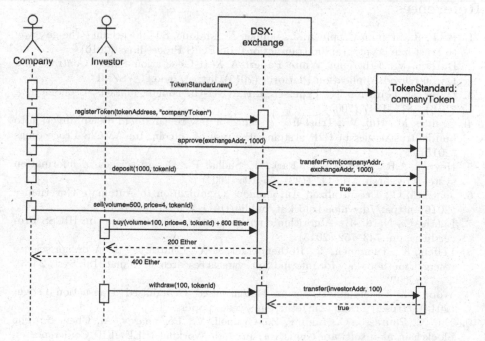

Fig. 2. Sequence diagram: a blockchain-based IPO

functional testing procedures [5]. To verify the prototype's correctness, we conduct 12 unit tests using the Truffle framework (https://truffle.readthedocs.io/en/latest/) and the Chai Assertian Library (http://chaijs.com/). The specific procedures are available under https://goo.gl/NpVmuJ. Furthermore, the test scenarios of issuing equity and placing and executing limit and market orders to buy and sell shares, enable us to identify flaws in the software structure and yield an upper limit of two transactions per second.

5   Conclusion

Overall, we contribute to existing research by introducing a blockchain-based market mechanism, that facilitates low-cost and intermediary-free asset transactions in an algorithmically governed and thus trust-free, easily accessible, resilient, and decentralized way. As a result, blockchain-based market platforms enable the resolution of inefficiencies in OTC markets and support novel forms of venture capital. However, the blockchain is still an emergent technology, and thus exhibits some problems, such as a limited number of transactions per second or the provision of information by trusted third parties. In addition, its distributed nature prevents the implementation of time precedence rules. Keeping this in mind, our prototype is only an initial step towards decentralized market setups and economic, technological, and regulatory aspects need to be addressed in future research efforts.

References

1. Beck, R., Stenum Czepluch, J., Lollike, N., Malone, S.: Blockchain - the gateway to trust-free cryptographic transactions. In: ECIS Proceedings (2016)
2. Buterin, V.: Ethereum White Paper: A Next-Generation Smart Contract and Decentralized Application Platform (2013). https://goo.gl/VSZs4I
3. Duffie, D., Gârleanu, N., Pedersen, L.H.: Over-the-counter markets. Econometrica 73(6), 1815–1847 (2005)
4. Greiner, M., Hui, W.: Trust-free systems - a new research and design direction to handle trust-issues in P2P systems: the case of bitcoin. In: AMCIS Proceedings (2015)
5. Hevner, A.R., March, S.T., Park, J., Sudha, R.: Design science in information systems research. MIS Q. 1(28), 75–105 (2004)
6. Jentzsch, C.: Decentralized Autonomous Organization to Automate Governance (2016). https://download.slock.it/public/DAO/WhitePaper.pdf
7. Lustig, C., Nardi, B.: Algorithmic authority: the case of bitcoin. In: HICSS Proceedings, pp. 743–752 (2015)
8. Peffers, K., Tuunanen, T., Rothenberger, M.A., Chatterjee, S.: A design science research methodology for information systems research. J. Manag. Inf. Syst. 24(3), 45–77 (2007)
9. Wood, G.: Ethereum: A Secure Decentralised Generalised Transaction Ledger (2014). https://github.com/ethereum/yellowpaper
10. Xu, X., Pautasso, C., Liming, Z., Gramoli, V., Ponomarev, A., Chen, S.: The blockchain as a software connector. In: 13th Working IEEE/IFIP Conference on Software Architecture (WICSA) (2016)

Designing Live Biofeedback for Groups to Support Emotion Management in Digital Collaboration

Michael T. Knierim[(✉)], Dominik Jung, Verena Dorner,
and Christof Weinhardt

Institute for Information Systems and Marketing (IISM),
Karlsruhe Institute of Technology (KIT),
Fritz-Erler-Straße 23, 76133 Karlsruhe, Germany
{michael.knierim,d.jung,verena.dorner,
christof.weinhardt}@kit.edu

Abstract. Digital collaboration of individuals has increased in diverse areas such as gaming, learning and product innovation. Across scenarios, adequate intra- and interpersonal emotion management is increasingly acknowledged to be beneficial to cognitive and affective interaction outcomes. Unfortunately, individuals differ notably in their emotion management abilities. Additionally, many types of computer mediated collaboration lack the richness of affective cues traditionally found in face-to-face interaction. We envision psychophysiology-based emotion feedback as an automated tool to improve emotion management, and therefore group performance and satisfaction. The presented prototype presents a first iteration of this idea, centered around information on emotional arousal derived from peripheral nervous system measures.

Keywords: Digital collaboration · Emotion management · Live biofeedback · Group feedback

1 Introduction

Over the past two decades, possibilities for digital collaborations have skyrocketed, not only in the workplace, but also in leisure activities such as multiplayer gaming [1] or product co-creation [2]. Digital collaboration activities are defined by a common goal that contributors work towards interdependently. Hence, group performance and performance goals play a central role in such collaborations. While group performance research has traditionally focused on task- and context-specific performance determinants, researchers increasingly acknowledge that adequate management of emotions plays an important part in performance across scenarios [3, 4]. Similar findings point to the importance of emotion management to improve affective collaboration outcomes, like the satisfaction with an interaction [5, 6]. Unfortunately, individuals vary in their emotion management abilities. Furthermore, many types of computer-mediated collaboration lack a richness of affective cues traditionally found in face-to-face interaction, complicating adequate emotion management [7]. It has therefore been proposed

A. Maedche et al. (Eds.): DESRIST 2017, LNCS 10243, pp. 479–484, 2017.
DOI: 10.1007/978-3-319-59144-5_35

that re-introduction or amplification of affective cues could significantly improve cognitive and affective collaboration outcomes [4]. The main purpose of this work is to investigate the technical feasibility and practical utility of a psychophysiology-based system to support emotion management in digital collaborations.

2   Design of the Artifact

2.1   Design Principles and Related Work

Building on ability models of emotional intelligence [5], also referred to as emotional competence models [8], we consider the management of individuals' own emotions, and the management of other group members' emotions to be of importance to collaborative endeavors. Furthermore, we consider them as mediators of the influence of emotion biofeedback on group performance and interaction satisfaction outcomes. Biofeedback on their own emotional state can help individuals to more effectively recognize and regulate own emotional experiences [9]. Biofeedback on other individuals' emotional states can be utilized to support emotion management in dyadic interaction [10]. These effects have been proposed to similarly extend to small group settings [11]. In this prototype instantiation, we focus on the display of emotional arousal to investigate how this somewhat abstract information can support emotion management in groups.

2.2   System Overview

The system for live emotion biofeedback for groups is based on our open source platform brownie [12]. Brownie is a Java-based platform for client-server interactions, and a NeuroIS tool for economic experiments.

System Description: Physiological data collection and processing is performed on the level of the individual group member's client computer. Data from each member is collected using applied sensors, and transmitted continuously to each client through a signal hub[1]. Client data is streamed to the aggregation server, where different client inputs, the re-distribution of collected group biofeedback data, as well as the flow of the interaction are managed. The data flow is illustrated in Fig. 1.

Physiological Measurement: In order to detect emotional arousal states, cardiac activity is derived from electrocardiographic (ECG) signals measurements. ECG patterns reflect parasympathetic and sympathetic activity of the autonomous nervous system and can thus be used to infer emotional arousal [13]. In this instance, gelled chest electrodes were used for data collection. Arousal computation occurs as the relation of a five-second average of cardiac activity to a baseline value.

Feedback-Design: In the first iteration of our design science approach, we implemented isolated bar graphs which show each members' individual arousal state. Bars

---

[1] Biosignalsplux by Plux Wireless Biosignals S.A.: http://biosignalsplux.com/index.php/en/.

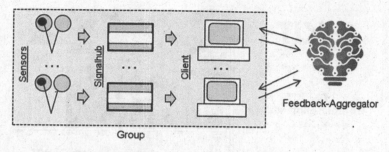

Fig. 1. Architecture of the live bio-feedback artifact in a group setting with a third party.

take on three different colors to facilitate recognition of arousal levels. Guiding principles were to provide a familiar thermometer-like visualization, indicating cold (blue – low arousal), beneficial (green - moderate arousal), and hot (red - high arousal) states. This format was found in pre-tests to be more intuitive in comparison to for example radial gauges. Furthermore, a crucial factor was to keep all group member information in a central space, to facilitate orientation and reference. Lastly, we tried to keep the information complexity and amount to a minimum to facilitate comprehension as concurrent task processing could complicate complex feedback processing.

3   Evaluation of the Artifact

To evaluate the prototype, we performed two exploratory pilot tests with 6 participants each (12 in total) in the KD2lab[2]. Groups were given a diverse set of digital tasks based on the collective intelligence task battery [3, 4]. In the first test, a collaborative computer game[3] was utilized in addition. In the second test, instead of the game, groups additionally worked on the 'Desert Survival Task' [14]. Alongside the tasks, group members received live biofeedback in an adjacent display window (illustrated in Fig. 2). All participants engaged in short initial practice sessions, to ensure a minimum level of familiarity and interaction with each other and with the artifact. Subjects participated in these tests on a voluntary basis. Questionnaires revealed that some participants liked to use the artifact to monitor their own arousal state with the aim of not getting too emotional during task performance. One participant remarked that she used it to engage more with the contributions of a fellow team member. In a few tasks, participants stated that they were unable to use the artifact because too much visual attention was required elsewhere (e.g. one task requires re-typing text under time pressure). Also, some participants felt the feedback did not reflect their emotional state with sufficient accuracy, which points to the role of additional subjective evaluation of algorithms used to derive emotion information, that should be addressed in future work. Future work should also quantify psychological and behavioral changes using

---

[2] The DFG-funded Karlsruhe Decision & Design Lab (KD2Lab) is one of the largest computer-based experimental laboratories world-wide: http://www.kd2lab.kit.edu.

[3] Rocket League by developer Psyonix: https://rocketleaguegame.com.

Fig. 2. Screenshots of the biofeedback element (left), and the system in a collaborative gaming task (top right), and a group brainstorming interaction (bottom right). (Color figure online)

comparison between treatment and control conditions. Also, objective metrics like eye-tracking should be employed. Furthermore, future work should integrate comparison of different feedback visualizations (e.g. more granular arousal levels or integration of phasic and tonic changes in bullet chart form).

4 Significance of the Artifact

The test findings have theoretical implications for research in small group collaboration, especially for the design of emotion management support systems. This IT-artifact provides a technical basis to investigate the effects of emotion phenomena, and emotion feedback in group settings. Many application scenarios for daily work situations in teams are also conceivable. Consider the case of a distributed, collaborating product innovation or software development team [15]. The feedback-aggregator could gather physiological states of the group members through video-monitoring (e.g. rPPG) and re-distribute the information on a window integrated with a conferencing system. This has been demonstrated for the case of communication behavior support through a Google Hangout plugin [16]. Beyond the group members, a moderator or mediator could use the feedback information to estimate mental states of the group and intervene appropriately, as has previously been demonstrated in the setting of trader team support [17]. Overall, the system could readily tie in with more ubiquitous ambient information system that support daily collaboration activity [18].

5   Demonstration of the Artifact

The artifact is built on our open source platform brownie [12], which was designed for conducting IS experiments with or without neurophysiological measurements (e.g. recordings of ECG, EDA, or EEG). Researchers and practitioners can use brownie in a wide range of computerized experiments in the laboratory. The artifact is available from the authors upon request and will be integrated in future releases of brownie.

References

1. Cole, H., Griffiths, M.D.: Social interactions in massively multiplayer online role-playing gamers. Cyberpsychol. Behav. **10**, 575–583 (2007)
2. Zwass, V.: Co-creation: toward a taxonomy and an integrated research perspective. Int. J. Electron. Commer. **15**, 11–48 (2010)
3. Engel, D., Woolley, A.W., Jing, L.X., Chabris, C.F., Malone, T.W.: Reading the mind in the eyes or reading between the lines? Theory of mind predicts collective intelligence equally well online and face-to-face. PLoS ONE **9**, 1–16 (2014)
4. Woolley, A.W., Chabris, C.F., Pentland, A., Hashmi, N., Malone, T.W.: Evidence for a collective intelligence factor in the performance of human groups. Science **330**(6004), 686–688 (2010). http://science.sciencemag.org/content/330/6004/686
5. Mayer, J.D., Roberts, R.D., Barsade, S.G.: Human abilities: emotional intelligence. Annu. Rev. Psychol. **59**, 507–536 (2008)
6. Menges, J.I., Kilduff, M.: Group emotions: cutting the gordian knots concerning terms, levels of analysis, and processes. Acad. Manag. Ann. **9**, 845–928 (2015)
7. Derks, D., Fischer, A.H., Bos, A.E.R.: The role of emotion in computer-mediated communication: a review. Comput. Hum. Behav. **24**, 766–785 (2008)
8. Mikolajczak, M.: Going beyond the ability-trait debate: the three-level model of emotional intelligence. Electron. J. Appl. Psychol. **5**, 25–31 (2009)
9. Peira, N., Fredrikson, M., Pourtois, G.: Controlling the emotional heart: heart rate biofeedback improves cardiac control during emotional reactions. Int. J. Psychophysiol. **91**, 225–231 (2014)
10. Snyder, J., Matthews, M., Chien, J., Chang, P.F., Sun, E., Abdullah, S., Gay, G.: MoodLight : exploring personal and social implications of ambient display of biosensor data. In: CSCW 2015, pp. 143–153 (2015)
11. Chanel, G., Mühl, C.: Connecting brains and bodies: applying physiological computing to support social interaction. Interact. Comput. **27**, 534–550 (2015)
12. Hariharan, A., Adam, M.T.P., Dorner, V., Lux, E., Müller, M.B., Pfeiffer, J., Weinhardt, C.: Brownie: a platform for conducting NeuroIS experiments, SSRN 2639047. (2016)
13. Berntson, G.G., Quigley, K.S., Lozano, D.: Cardiovascular psychophysiology. In: Cacioppo, J.T., Tassinary, L.G., Berntson, G.G. (eds.) Handbook of Psychophysiology, pp. 182–210. Cambridge University Press, Cambridge (2007)
14. Lafferty, J.C., Pond, A.W.: Desert Survival Situation. Human Synergistics International, Plymouth (1987)
15. Guzman, E., Bruegge, B.: Towards emotional awareness in software development teams. In: Proceedings of the 9th Joint Meeting on Foundations of Software Engineering, pp. 671–674 (2013)

16. Calacci, D., Lederman, O., Shrier, D., Pentland, A.: Breakout: an open measurement and intervention tool for distributed peer learning groups, pp. 1–6. arXiv Preprint. arXiv:1607.01443 (2016)
17. Fernández, J.M., Augusto, J.C., Trombino, G., Seepold, R., Madrid, N.M.: Self-aware trader: a new approach to safer trading. J. Univ. Comput. Sci. **19**, 2292–2319 (2013)
18. Pousman, Z., Stasko, J.: A taxonomy of ambient information systems: four patterns of design. In: Proceedings of the Working Conference on Advanced Visual Interfaces, pp. 67–74 (2006)

Design and Evaluation of a Mobile Chat App for the Open Source Behavioral Health Intervention Platform MobileCoach

Tobias Kowatsch[1]([⊠]), Dirk Volland[2], Iris Shih[2], Dominik Rüegger[2],
Florian Künzler[2], Filipe Barata[2], Andreas Filler[1,3], Dirk Büchter[4],
Björn Brogle[4], Katrin Heldt[4], Pauline Gindrat[5],
Nathalie Farpour-Lambert[6], and Dagmar l'Allemand[4]

[1] Institute of Technology Management,
University of St. Gallen, St. Gallen, Switzerland
tobias.kowatsch@unisg.ch
[2] Department of Management, Technology and Economics,
ETH Zurich, Zurich, Switzerland
[3] Energy Efficient Systems Group, University of Bamberg, Bamberg, Germany
[4] Children's Hospital of Eastern Switzerland, St. Gallen, Switzerland
[5] Fondation SportSmile, Nyon, Switzerland
[6] Department of Community Medicine, Primary Care and Emergency,
University Hospital of Geneva/University of Geneva, Geneva, Switzerland

Abstract. The open source platform MobileCoach (mobile-coach.eu) has been used for various behavioral health interventions in the public health context. However, so far, MobileCoach is limited to text message-based interactions. That is, participants use error-prone and laborious text-input fields and have to bear the SMS costs. Moreover, MobileCoach does not provide a dedicated chat channel for individual requests beyond the processing capabilities of its chatbot. Intervention designers are also limited to text-based self-report data. In this paper, we thus present a mobile chat app with pre-defined answer options, a dedicated chat channel for patients and health professionals and sensor data integration for the MobileCoach platform. Results of a pretest ($N = 11$) and preliminary findings of a randomized controlled clinical trial ($N = 14$) with young patients, who participate in an intervention for the treatment of obesity, are promising with respect to the utility of the chat app.

Keywords: Health intervention · Digital coaching · Chat-based interaction

1 Introduction

Non communicable diseases (NCDs) such as heart diseases, asthma, obesity, diabetes or chronic kidney disease impose the greatest burden on global health [14]. According to WHO's NCD global monitoring framework, many of these diseases are consequences of adverse health behaviors, for example, harmful use of alcohol and tobacco or physical inactivity [15]. However, health personnel is strongly limited [2]. Consequently, scalable behavioral health interventions are required.

© Springer International Publishing AG 2017
A. Maedche et al. (Eds.): DESRIST 2017, LNCS 10243, pp. 485–489, 2017.
DOI: 10.1007/978-3-319-59144-5_36

Innovative digital health interventions (DHIs) have not only the potential to improve the efficacy of preventive or therapeutic behavioral health interventions but also to reduce their costs [1]. With the goal to provide an open source platform that allows health professionals to design scalable, low-cost and evidence-based DHIs, MobileCoach (mobile-coach.eu) was developed [5] and evaluated [9].

However, it uses the short message service (SMS) for delivering behavioral health interventions, and thus comes with various shortcomings as outlined in the next section. We therefore present in this paper the first mobile chat app for the Mobile-Coach platform that addresses these shortcomings and thus, complements existing communication such as personal exchange, SMS-based, phone-based or video-based interactions.

The remainder of this paper is structured as follows. Next, we describe the design of the chat app. Then, the app's significance to research and practice is outlined. Finally, we present results from an empirical study with 11 obese children who assessed the new chat app as the first target group.

2   Design of the Chat App

Hands-on experience with several MobileCoach-based interventions [7–9] has revealed four major shortcomings related to its text messaging approach. First, participants have to bear the SMS costs which may be an entry barrier if the caregiver does not provide a monetary compensation. Second, participants are always requested to manually type in text to answer even Likert-scale type questions. These answers are then parsed by the MobileCoach, which is error-prone in case the answer does not perfectly fit to the question. Processing these answers is a time-consuming process for the caregiver, too. Third, participant-initiated requests usually require an individual answer from a caregiver instead of a scripted answer by a chatbot. A rule-based chatbot does therefore not always fit to the communication needs of the participants. Fourth, text-messaging is limited to self-report data, i.e. health professionals cannot use objective sensor data from a smartphone (e.g., accelerometer data used to measure physical activity) or sensor data from devices connected to that smartphone (e.g., Bluetooth-enabled blood glucose or peak flow meters) for the design of their DHIs.

Regarding these shortcomings and against the background of smartphone pervasiveness [4], the following requirements have been defined: (R1) The app must not rely on the short message service for communication purposes; (R2) the app must implement pre-defined answer sets for efficient and error-free chat interaction; (R3) the app must implement a chat channel for individual communication needs that complements the scalable chatbot channel; (R4) the app must be able to access sensor data from the smartphone or smartphone-connected devices.

By considering these four requirements, we built a first mock-up of a mobile app and evaluated it with six behavioural health experts. As a result of that assessment, a generic dashboard view was designed. Its purpose is to summarize key statistics of the envisioned behavioural health interventions for self-monitoring purposes (e.g. steps achieved per day, intervention progress or goals achieved). Based on this generic mock-up, we implemented a native chat app for Android smartphones for the Mobi-leCoach platform. Figures 1, 2 and 3 show the graphical user interface of the chat app.

Fig. 1. Dashboard view, individual caregiver chat channel PathMate and channel with chatbot Anna

Fig. 2. Chatbot Anna, predefined answer options and sensor integration; steps are tracked and used in the chat

Fig. 3. Chat channel with the caregiver; the PathMate study team of the children's hospital

3 Significance to Research and Practice

The mobile chat app presented in this paper allows behavioral scientists and health professionals to enrich self-report data with objective sensor data in the everyday life of their clients. This paves the way for a better understanding of whether psychological/ self-report data and physiological/objective data are rather complement or alternative measures, a recent research question in the field of NeuroIS [13].

Moreover, it is by far not clear how to design and frame chatbots for DHIs (e.g., as an expert or a "patient like me") and its interplay with a "physical" caregiver such that they have a positive effect on the bond between caregiver and their clients and thus, also on therapeutic outcomes [6]. In contrast to general purpose chat agents such as Siri (Apple), Alexa (Amazon) or Cortana (Microsoft) and agents with a health focus such as Florence (getflorence.co.uk), Molly (sense.ly) or Lark (lark.com), our chat app allows full control of personal health data and a generic framework to manipulate the design and communication style of chatbots in lab and field settings.

Finally and consistent with the MobileCoach platform, the chat app will be made open source under the Apache 2.0 license to enable a community-driven design such that research teams and (business) organizations interested in chat-based digital coaching approaches do not have to start from scratch but can re-use, revise and improve the existing code together with the MobileCoach platform.

4   Evaluation of the Artifact

Based on prior work demonstrating the acceptance of chat apps by adolescents [11], the first test of the novel chat app was conducted in a children's hospital in December 2016 with 11 patients (age$_{Mean}$ = 12.6 years, SD = 2.4; 8 girls), who participated in an intervention for the treatment of obesity. The goal of this test was (1) to assess enjoyment, ease of use, usefulness and the intention to use the app [10], and (2) to identify and address major usability problems with the app [12] prior to a randomized controlled trial (RCT), in which the efficacy of a chat-based six-month DHI for the treatment of childhood obesity will be compared to a control group.

First, a chat-based DHI was collaboratively designed by computer scientists, physicians, a psychotherapist, diet and sport experts. The patients were then asked to select a chatbot of their liking, i.e. they could choose between a female and male chatbot (Anna or Lukas). Then, they interacted with the bot for 10 min including various chat-based photo, physical activity and quiz interactions. The patients were observed during these interactions by a computer scientist and physician. Afterwards, patients were asked to fill out a questionnaire to assess the app and to provide qualitative feedback on their experience with the app. Similar to prior work [10], we assessed technology perceptions and behavioral intentions with seven-point Likert scales anchored from strongly disagree (1) to strongly agree (7). As young patients deserve special consideration, we used single-item measures to reduce the burden of evaluation [3].

The descriptive statistics of the evaluation are shown in Table 1. Results indicate that the chat app was perceived positive regarding all four constructs. A sign test against the neutral Likert-scale median of 4 supports this observation. Finally, we found no major usability problems based on the observations and the qualitative feedback.

Table 1. Descriptive statistics and results of a sign test against the neutral value 4 on a 7-point Likert-scale (N = 11). Note: Perceived ease of use (PEU), Perceived enjoyment (PEN), Perceived usefulness (PU) and Intention to use (IU); Significance */**/*** $p < .05$ /.01 /.001

#	Item	Mean	Median	SD	p-value
PEU	I found the chat easy to use	6.7	7.0	0.7	***
PEN	I enjoyed chatting	6.2	7.0	1.5	**
PU	Chatting with Lukas/Anna could motivate me to accomplish my intervention tasks	5.9	6.0	1.1	*
IU	I could imagine chatting daily that way	5.6	6.0	1.4	*

First findings of the aforementioned RCT show that new young patients assigned to the chat-based DHI (N = 14) completed successfully approx. 61% of the daily intervention tasks over the first two months. The efficacy of this DHI will be finally measured by the Body Mass Index after the six-month RCT. We hypothesize that the chat-based DHI is more effective as the chatbot can provide everyday support on therapy goals and tasks, thus increasing therapy adherence compared to patients of the treatment-as-usual control group without everyday support.

In our future work, we will test chat-based DHIs with older patient populations and different therapies to assess the degree to which our findings can be generalized.

Acknowledgements. We would like to thank the CSS Insurance and the Swiss National Science Foundation for their support through grants 159289 and 162724.

References

1. Agarwal, R., Gao, G., DesRoches, C., et al.: The digital transformation of healthcare: current status and the road ahead. Inf. Syst. Res. **21**, 796–809 (2010)
2. Aluttis, C., Bishaw, T., Frank, M.W.: The workforce for health in a globalized context – global shortages and international migration. Glob. Health Action **7** (2014). https://www.ncbi.nlm.nih.gov/pmc/articles/PMC3926986/
3. Bergkvist, L., Rossiter, J.R.: The predictive validity of multiple-item versus single-item measures of the same constructs. J. Mark. Res. **44**, 175–184 (2007)
4. Chaffey, D.: Mobile Marketing Statistics compilation (2016). http://www.smartinsights.com/ . Accessed Feb 2017
5. Filler, A., Kowatsch, T., Haug, S., et al.: MobileCoach: a novel open source platform for the design of evidence-based, scalable and low-cost behavioral health interventions. In: 14th Annual Wireless Telecommunications Symposium (WTS 2015), New York (2015)
6. Flückiger, C., Del Re, A.C., Wampold, B.E., et al.: How central is the alliance in psychotherapy? A multilevel longitudinal meta-analysis. J. Couns. Psychol. **59**, 10–17 (2012)
7. Haug, S., Kowatsch, T., Paz Castro, R., et al.: Efficacy of a web- and text messaging-based intervention to reduce problem drinking in young people: study protocol of a cluster-randomised controlled trial. BMC Public Health **14**, 1–8 (2014)
8. Haug, S., Paz Castro, R., Filler, A., et al.: Efficacy of an internet and SMS-based integrated smoking cessation and alcohol intervention for smoking cessation in young people: study protocol of a two-arm cluster randomised controlled trial. BMC Public Health **14**, 1140 (2014)
9. Haug, S., Paz, R., Kowatsch, T., et al.: Efficacy of a web- and text messaging-based intervention to reduce problem drinking in adolescents: Results of a cluster-randomised controlled trial. J. Consult. Clin. Psychol. **85**, 147–159 (2017)
10. Kamis, A., Koufaris, M., Stern, T.: Using an attribute-based decision support system for user-customized products online: an experimental investigation. MIS Q. **32**, 159–177 (2008)
11. Lilian, S., Gregor, W., Sarah, G., et al.: MIKE - Medien, Interaktion, Kinder, Eltern. Zürcher Hochschule für Angewandte Wissenschaften, Zürich (2015)
12. Nielsen, J., Landauer, T.K.: A mathematical model of the finding of usability problems. In: CHI 1993 Proceedings of the INTERACT 1993 and CHI 1993 Conference on Human Factors in Computing Systems, pp. 206–213. ACM, Amsterdam (1993)
13. Tams, S., Hill, K., de Guinea, A.O., et al.: NeuroIS - alternative or complement to existing methods? Illustrating the holistic effects of neuroscience and self-reported data in the context of technostress research. J. Assoc. Inf. Syst. **15**, Article 1 (2014)
14. WHO: Global Health and Aging. World Health Organization, Genéve, Switzerland (2011)
15. WHO: Draft comprehensive global monitoring framework and targets for the prevention and control of noncommunicable diseases. World Health Organization, Genéve, Switzerland (2013)

Author Index

Printed in the United States
By Bookmasters